CATWOMAN

NINE LIVES OF A *Feline Fatale*

CATWOMAN: NINE LIVES OF A FELINE FATALE
Published by DC Comics. Cover, introduction and compilation copyright
© 2004 DC Comics. All Rights Reserved.

Originally published in single magazine form in BATMAN #1, 197, 210
and 392, DETECTIVE COMICS #203, SUPERMAN'S GIRL FRIEND LOIS
LANE #70 & 71, CATWOMAN (first series) #54, BATMAN: GOTHAM
ADVENTURES #4, CATWOMAN SECRET FILES #1. Copyright
1940-1955; © 1956-2002 DC Comics. All Rights Reserved.
All characters, their distinctive likenesses and related elements
featured in this publication are trademarks of DC Comics. The stories,
characters and incidents featured in this publication are entirely
fictional. DC Comics does not read or accept unsolicited submissions
of ideas, stories or artwork.

DC Comics, 1700 Broadway, New York, NY 10019
A Warner Bros. Entertainment Company
Printed in Canada. First Printing.
ISBN: 1-4012-0213-6
Interior color reconstruction, when needed,
was done by Jamison, except for BATMAN #210
by Dave Tanguay and BATMAN #392 by Theresa Kubert.
Cover illustration by Brian Bolland.
Publication design by Peter Hamboussi.

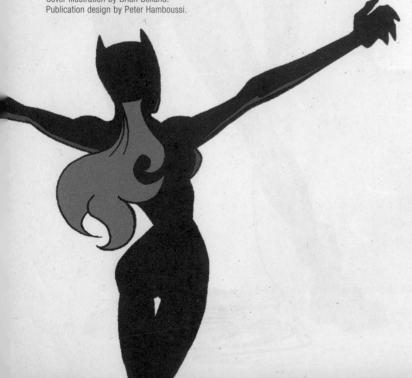

contents

INTRODUCTION BY MICHAEL USLAN   **4**

PINUP BY JIM BALENT & JOE DEVITO   **8**

"THE CAT"   **10**
Originally presented in BATMAN #1, Spring 1940
Story: **Bill Finger**   Art: **Bob Kane**

PINUP BY DAVE STEVENS   **23**

"THE CRIMES OF THE CATWOMAN!"   **24**
Originally presented in DETECTIVE COMICS #203, January 1954
Story: **Edmond Hamilton**   Pencils: **Lew Sayre Schwartz**   Inks: **Charles Paris**

PINUP BY ALAN DAVIS   **36**

"THE CATWOMAN'S BLACK MAGIC!"   **37**
Originally presented in SUPERMAN'S GIRL FRIEND LOIS LANE #70 & 71,
       November/December 1966
Story: **Leo Dorfman**   Art: **Kurt Schaffenberger**

PINUP BY GEORGE PÉREZ   **70**

"CATWOMAN SETS HER CLAWS FOR BATMAN!"   **71**
Originally presented in BATMAN #197, December 1967
Story: **Gardner Fox**   Pencils: **Frank Springer**   Inks: **Sid Greene**

PINUP BY BRIAN STELFREEZE   **94**

"THE CASE OF THE PURR-LOINED PEARL!""   **95**
Originally presented in BATMAN #210, March 1969
Story: **Frank Robbins**   Pencils: **Irv Novick**   Inks: **Joe Giella**

PINUP BY ADAM HUGHES   **118**

"A TOWN ON THE NIGHT"   **119**
Originally presented in BATMAN #392, February 1986
Story: **Doug Moench**   Pencils: **Tom Mandrake**   Inks: **Jan Duursema**

PINUP BY CAMERON STEWART   **141**

"OBJECT RELATIONS"   **142**
Originally presented in CATWOMAN #54, February 1998
Story: **Devin Grayson**   Pencils: **Jim Balent**   Inks: **John Stanisci**

PINUP BY BRUCE TIMM   **164**

"CLAWS""   **165**
Originally presented in BATMAN: GOTHAM ADVENTURES #4, September 1998
Story: **Ty Templeton**   Pencils: **Rick Burchett**   Inks: **Terry Beatty**

PINUP BY MARK STUTZMAN   **187**

"THE MANY LIVES OF SELINA KYLE"   **188**
Originally presented in CATWOMAN SECRET FILES #1, November 2002
Story: **Ed Brubaker**   Pencils: **Michael Avon Oeming**   Inks: **Mike Manley**

CONTRIBUTORS   **206**

introduction Michael Uslan

She apparently has nine lives...just like her namesake.

She's had no less than nine unique costumes over the decades...sort of a "Barbie" meets "Wonder Woman" gone bad.

She's been known by at least nine different sobriquets...The Cat; Catwoman; The Princess of Plunder; The Mistress of Menace; The Feline Felon; The Queen of Crime; The Mistress of Malevolence; The Countess of Crime; and The Feline Fatale. By any name, she's the supreme super-villainess in all of comicbookdom, Batman's #1 femme fatale and kinkiest love interest.

Created by Bob Kane and Bill Finger in the very first issue of BATMAN, Spring 1940 (an issue which, by the way, also introduced The Joker), The Catwoman was clearly inspired by the beautiful, evil seductress The Dragon Lady — who was created in 1934 by cartoonist Milton Caniff in his tremendously popular comic strip "Terry and the Pirates." As Bob Kane was quick to admit, The Catwoman instantly added real sexual tension to the fledgling Batman saga. Bob's real-life inspiration? "I admired Hedy Lamarr. She had that great feline beauty," he stated for the record. "A cat has nine lives and I figured that whenever she was caught or wounded, she would survive and live again for another go-around with Batman. Also, I feel there's something very mysterious about cats and I equate that with women. [Bill Finger and I] felt that she would appeal to the female readers and that they would relate to her as much as Batman. We also thought that male readers would appreciate a sensual woman to look at."

As the character evolved over the years, her underlying message was often one of female empowerment. It's that evolution which will be apparent in the nine Cat-tales that follow, offering a sampling of her almost 65-year history in the comics, on TV, in animation and in the movies. Catwoman moves back and forth through the decades from bad girl to good girl, from female Robin Hood to schizophrenic, comparable only to the man of her dreams and nightmares...The Batman.

By the time BATMAN #1 debuted with the cat-burgling jewel thief known only as The Cat, Batman was already engaged to high society's Julie Madison. His fiancée was a mundane character, adding nothing special to the stories or the character of Bruce Wayne. But right off the bat, The Cat had the sparks flying between her and our hero, as evidenced by such dialogue exchanges as the following abridged excerpts:

> BATMAN (Upon first meeting her):
> Quiet or Papa spank!
> THE CAT: I know when I'm licked!
>
> THE CAT (At the end of their first
> meeting): Why don't you come in
> as a partner with me? You and I
> together!
> BATMAN: Your proposition tempts
> me but we work on different sides
> of the law!
>
> ROBIN (To Batman, frustrated at
> The Cat's escape): Say! I'll bet you
> bumped into me on purpose...so
> she might try a break!
> BATMAN: Lovely girl! What eyes!...
> Maybe I'll bump into her again
> sometime!
>
> Holy Bat-Testosterone!

By the third issue of BATMAN she had already begun to be referred to as "Catwoman," and she now possessed her first super-villainess costume, featuring a full cat's head mask. It was plenty eerie but hid the natural beauty of Selina Kyle (her real name...and a fact readers would not learn until BATMAN #62 in December 1950-January 1951). Selina switched to an all black cat costume and

Superman's Girl Friend Lois Lane #70
illustrated by: Kurt Schaffenberger

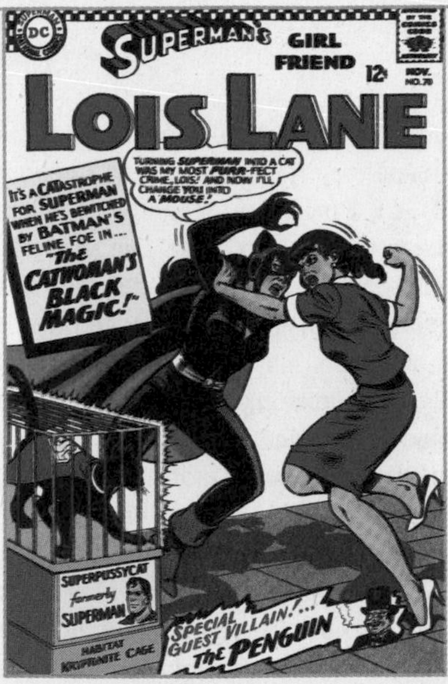
SUPERMAN'S GIRL FRIEND
LOIS LANE
12¢
NOV. NO. 70
TURNING SUPERMAN INTO A CAT WAS MY MOST PURR-FECT CRIME, LOIS! AND NOW I'LL CHANGE YOU INTO A MOUSE!
IT'S A CATASTROPHE FOR SUPERMAN WHEN HE'S BEWITCHED BY BATMAN'S FELINE FOE IN... "The CATWOMAN'S BLACK MAGIC!"
SUPERPUSSYCAT formerly SUPERMAN
HABITAT KRYPTONITE CAGE
SPECIAL GUEST VILLAIN!... The PENGUIN

head mask in BATMAN #10, April/May 1942, a more sinister look for sure. It wasn't until June/July 1946's BATMAN #35, however, that what would become known as the "classic" Catwoman look actually started to take shape — with a mask that showed off Selina's beautiful facial features and flowing hair as well as a dress slit up the side that showed off...well...the claws of The Cat and beyond!

But the times they were a-changin' as America and the comic-book industry entered the post-World War II years. The first loud volley of public attacks on comic books (by the same sort of people who would later brand rock 'n' roll as a Communist plot to subvert the youth of America) as the purported cause of the rise of juvenile delinquency in the U.S. could be heard echoing in the pages of some parenting magazines and psychiatric journals. DC Comics responded to some of the initial criticism by instituting its own in-house code of ethics. Absurd by today's standards, that code in the late '40s/early '50s stated the following regarding the portrayal of females in comic-book stories: "The inclusion of females in stories is specifically discouraged. Women, when used in plot structure, should be secondary in importance, and should be drawn realistically, without exaggeration of feminine physical qualities."

With paranoia building, DC Comics decided it would be prudent to "retire" a sexy and evil female character like Catwoman until such time, if any, that sanity returned to society and its standards. Leading up to that time, Catwoman was being portrayed as a tamer character than seen in her 1940s adventures. She had even reformed! The sparks and the kinks were definitely missing in her latest relationship with Batman. The tale in this tome from DETECTIVE COMICS #203, June 1954, shows her tempting the fates and the times by moving back into malevolence. In this one story, renowned science-fiction writer Edmond Hamilton included a barrage of cat gimmicks and sayings which would become the cornerstone for the version of Catwoman who would emerge in the 1966 *Batman* TV series: the Catapult; the Cat-o'-Nine-Tails; Cat's Cradle; the Catacomb; the Kitty Car; the Cat-Boat; Cataleptic sleeping gas; and other cataclysmic catastrophes for Batman.

And then DC gave Catwoman an involuntary cat-nap until November 1966, when her starring status on ABC-TV's smash *Batman* series once again made her socially acceptable and even very hip. Of all places to make her triumphant return to The Silver Age of comic books, Catwoman first appeared NOT in the pages of BATMAN or DETECTIVE, but in issue #70 of SUPERMAN'S GIRL FRIEND LOIS LANE. This comic book, which recently sold for some $2,500 on eBay, had to be one of the kookiest, weirdest, silliest, and most odd super-hero comic-book tales ever written! Besides some of the most contrived plot twists, lack of logic, huge coincidences, and nonsensical situations, the story also happened to feature: Catwoman possessing magical powers, which she explains away by revealing, "This is the wand the sorceress Circe once used to turn Ulysses' men into swine! I found it recently in Italy!"; Superman being transformed by Catwoman into a super-cat who meows the same way Lassie barks so that people can totally understand what he's trying to say; a scene in which super-cat, by

Batman #210
illustrated by Neal Adams

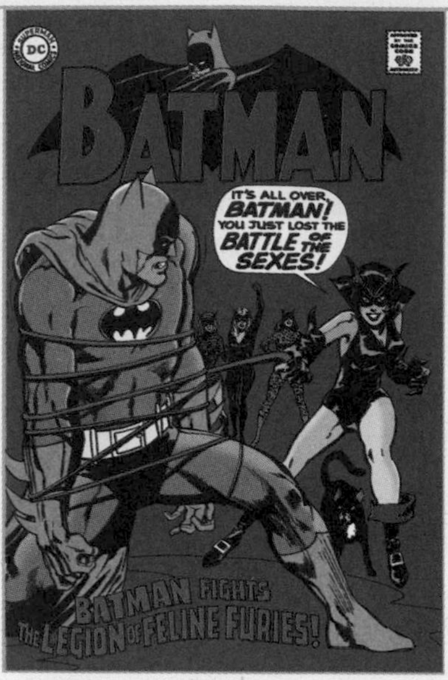
BATMAN
IT'S ALL OVER, BATMAN! YOU JUST LOST THE BATTLE OF THE SEXES!
BATMAN FIGHTS THE LEGION OF FELINE FURIES!

licking his "S" (emblem), convinces Lois he's really Superman; Lois comparing Catwoman to ABC-TV's Samantha Stephens ("I suppose you just twitched your nose like the gal on *Bewitched* and transformed him?"); actual guest-starring appearances by then President Lyndon Johnson, his wife, Ladybird, and his daughters Lucie and Lynda; a cameo appearance by The Penguin; Batman and Robin driving the old Batmobile of 1950 (Oops! No one told artist Kurt Schaffenberger that Batman had been driving a new sleek version for years!); Catwoman just happening to have on hand her own portable Kryptonite cat cage; Superman, as super-cat, typing a letter on a typewriter with his paws (NO errors!); Lois Lane not comprehending that Superman wouldn't recognize her after she's been magically morphed into a mouse; and Superman choosing NOT to seek the help of his friend Batman, because he's so embarrassed to have been turned into a super-pussycat. Underground commix cartoonist Robert Crumb, in his Haight-Ashbury heyday, couldn't have dreamed up a story like this!

In 1967, Catwoman took on a new look she called her "now" look, inspired by Julie Newmar's catsuit from the *Batman* TV series and evoking the look of a cat. And then, DC's colorist made it green...kind of taking something away from the cat appearance they were going for, wouldn't you say? In this story from BATMAN #197, Catwoman fell in line with the TV interpretation of her character. Her edge was gone. Instead, she once again briefly reformed in an effort to conquer Batman's heart. Now, she played games with her new rival, Batgirl, hoping to show her up in front of her main man. She demanded The Caped Crusader's hand in marriage at the threat of an immediate return to her criminal ways and wiles.

The beginning of her long road back to schizo super-villainess can be seen in 1969's adventure from BATMAN #210. Catwoman, in a brand new costume that evoked Vampirella, added night-vision Cat-Goggles to her arsenal and worked with an evil comic-book version of Ike and Tina Turner's Ikettes called "The Feline Furies." Yes, Bat-Fans, "camp" was still in the air, gasping its dying breath!

Big changes for Catwoman came creeping on little cat's feet in the decade of the '80s. 1986's BATMAN #392 yet again explored the subject of Catwoman's possible reformation... from thief to vigilante...but this time her turnaround sparked sexual innuendo with The Batman leading to a seduction by night:

CATWOMAN: Do I have to purr in your ear?
BATMAN: No...but maybe later you could scratch my back.
CATWOMAN: What's the matter? No itches in the front?

Holy Extreme Dating! And it all wound up with The Bat and The Cat in a redux of the spaghetti scene at Tony's from Walt Disney's *Lady & The Tramp*.

In 1998's cat-tale from CATWOMAN #54, the tone was set for the 1990s and 2000s. A new skin-tight, purple Spandex outfit (inspired by the sexy black second skin worn by Michelle Pfeiffer in 1992's feature film *Batman Returns*) appeared on the woman who still loved being a cat-burglar, but was actually trying to do some good out there, as well. Significantly, for the

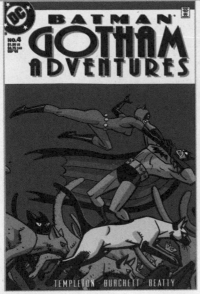

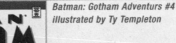

BATMAN
GOTHAM
ADVENTURES
NO.4
TEMPLETON · BURCHETT · BEATTY

Batman: Gotham Adventures #4
illustrated by Ty Templeton

first time, a Catwoman comic-book series was being written by a woman, Devin Grayson.

The animated look of Catwoman created for *Batman: The Animated Series* may have been a spinoff of the comic book's purple costume, but it had a high style all its own. The look may have made the show appear at first blush to be aimed at children, but the characterizations and plots quickly brought the realization these were not your father's or grandfather's cartoons of Catwoman, Batman and Robin as 1988's story from BATMAN: GOTHAM ADVENTURES #4 proves.

Wrapping up the ninth different look of the feline fatale is a current tale from her continuing comic-book saga. Today, she sports a very utilitarian outfit and is trying to make her own way in a world that is simply no longer black and white. The line between wrong and right is often gray and indistinct.

When an ancient cat goddess imbues a young woman by the name of Patience Philips with the powers of a cat, Patience becomes a brand new Catwoman in 2004. With a new identity, a new costume (of course!), a new mission, and no "Bat" attachment, this Catwoman still speaks to the empowerment of women and the fine, often misconstrued line between good and evil. Actress Halle Berry embodies the ninth life of a feline fatale.

From 1940 to today, from The Cat to The Catwoman, from Batman to no man in her life, from Selina Kyle to Patience Philips, from Julie Newmar, Lee Meriwether and Eartha Kitt to Michelle Pfeiffer and Halle Berry, this Princess of Plunder has remained the queen of all comic-book villainesses from the printed page to the TV screen to the Silver Screen.

— Michael Uslan
2004

MICHAEL USLAN is the executive producer of the *Catwoman* movie and the *Batman* films — including 2005's *Batman Begins*. He is also the producer of the upcoming *Constantine* feature. He won the Emmy Award for Best Animated Series with *Where On Earth Is Carmen Sandiego?* An avid history buff, Uslan was Executive Producer of the PBS-American Playhouse miniseries *Three Sovereigns for Sarah*, the true story of the Salem witch trials. A writer of *Batman*, *The Shadow* and *Terry and the Pirates* for newspaper syndication, plus the graphic novel BATMAN: DETECTIVE No. 27 for DC, Uslan is the author of numerous books on the history of comics and other pop culture.

CATWOMAN
54
1 of 1
THE DIAMOND THAT
WOULDN'T STAY STOLEN

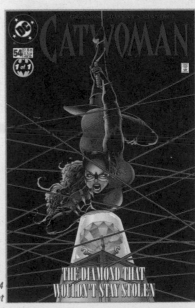

Catwoman #54
illustrated by Jim Balent

pinup Jim Balent & Joe Devito

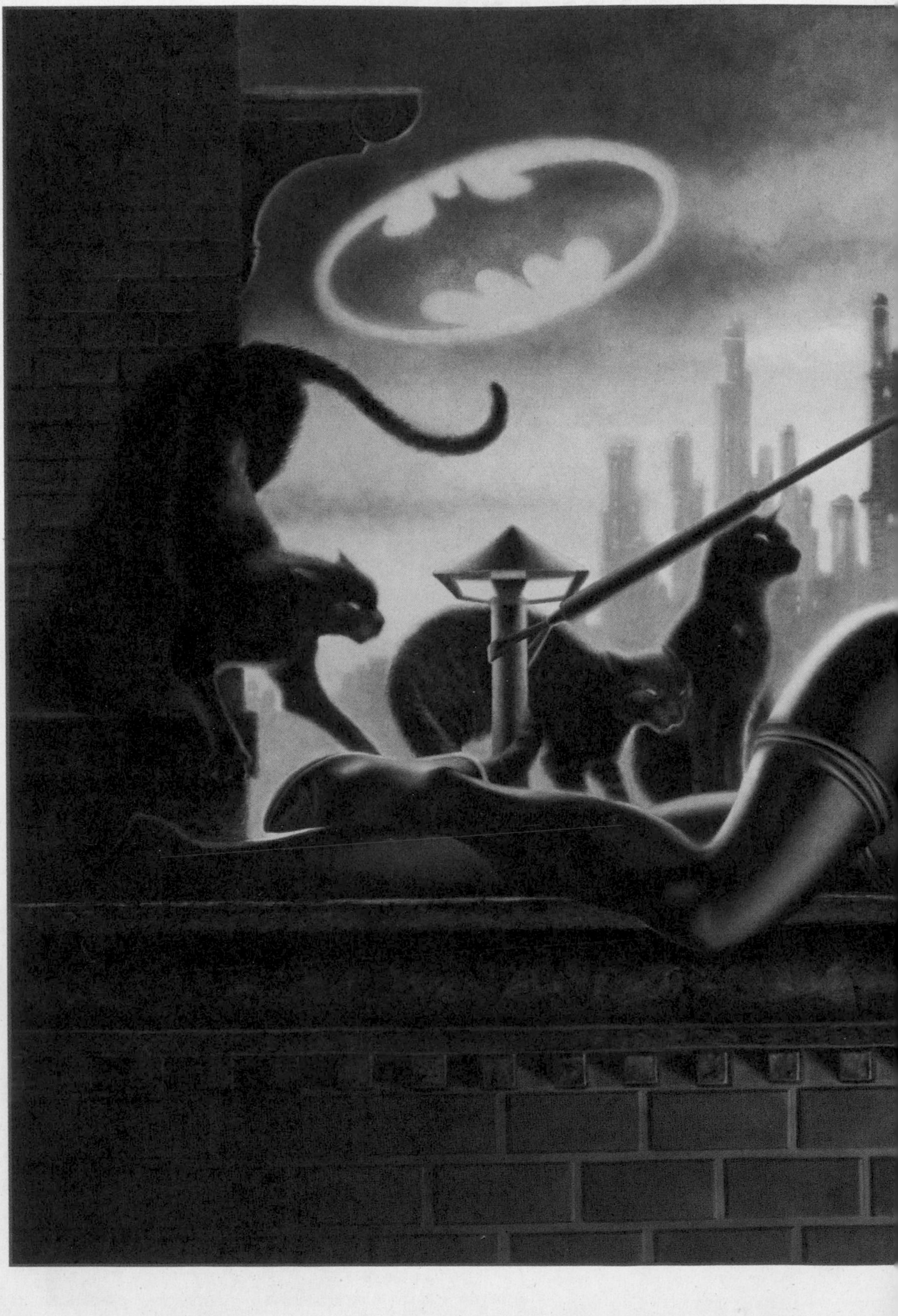

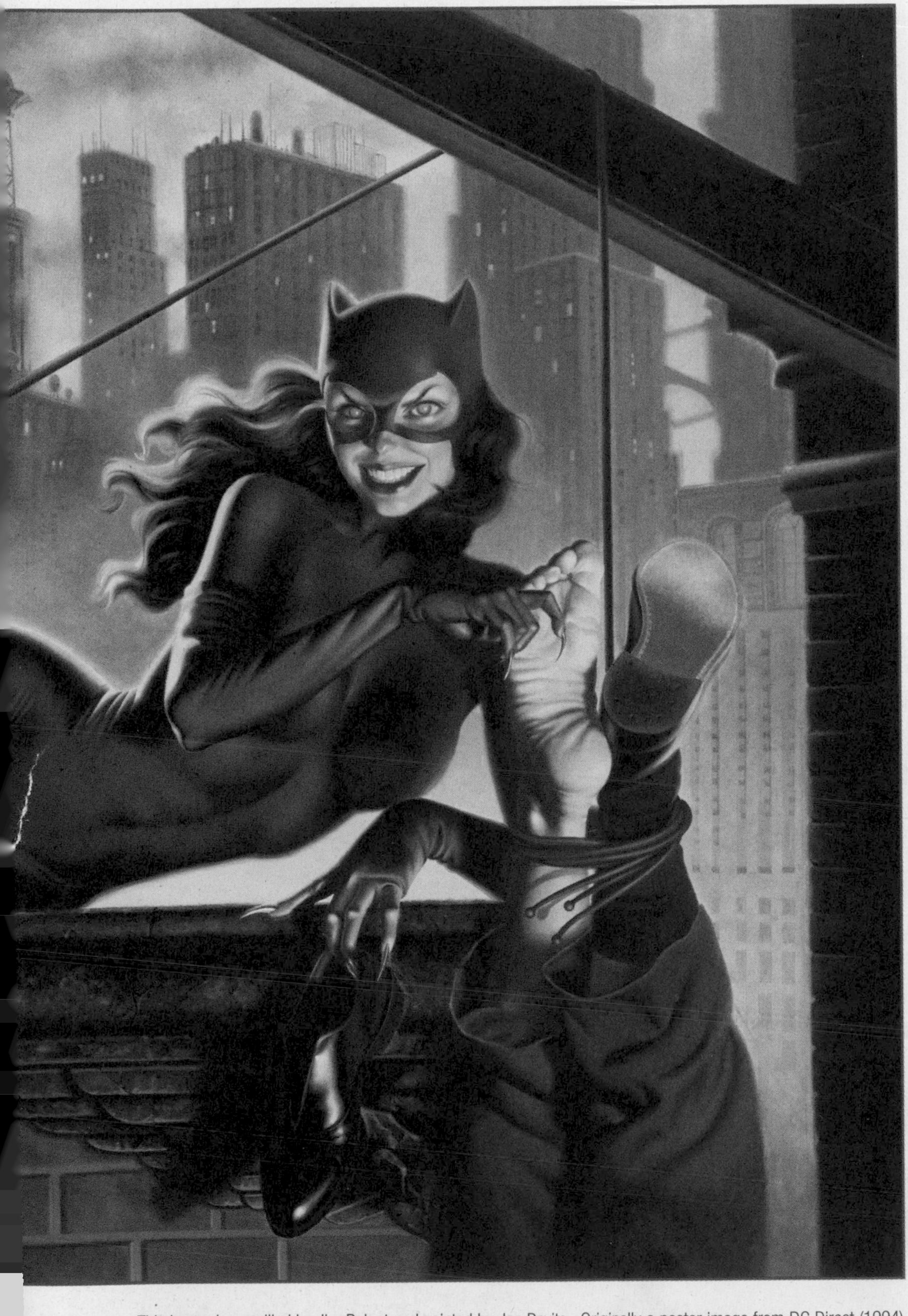

This image is pencilled by Jim Balent and painted by Joe Devito. Originally a poster image from DC Direct (1994).

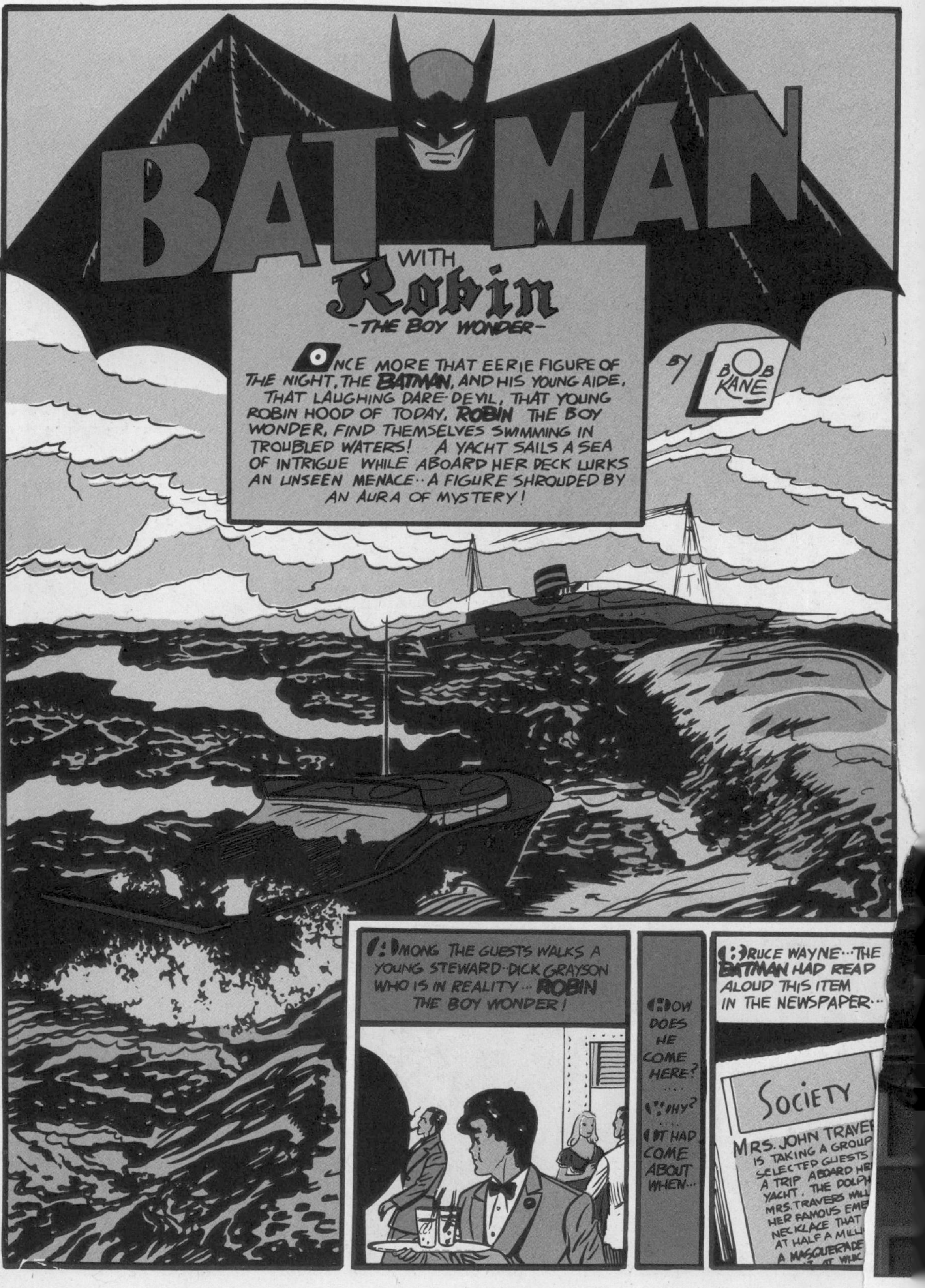
BATMAN
WITH Robin -THE BOY WONDER-
ONCE MORE THAT EERIE FIGURE OF THE NIGHT, THE BATMAN, AND HIS YOUNG AIDE, THAT LAUGHING DARE-DEVIL, THAT YOUNG ROBIN HOOD OF TODAY, ROBIN THE BOY WONDER, FIND THEMSELVES SWIMMING IN TROUBLED WATERS! A YACHT SAILS A SEA OF INTRIGUE WHILE ABOARD HER DECK LURKS AN UNSEEN MENACE.. A FIGURE SHROUDED BY AN AURA OF MYSTERY!
BY BOB KANE
AMONG THE GUESTS WALKS A YOUNG STEWARD-DICK GRAYSON WHO IS IN REALITY... ROBIN THE BOY WONDER!
HOW DOES HE COME HERE?... WHY?... IT HAD COME ABOUT WHEN...
BRUCE WAYNE... THE BATMAN HAD READ ALOUD THIS ITEM IN THE NEWSPAPER...
SOCIETY

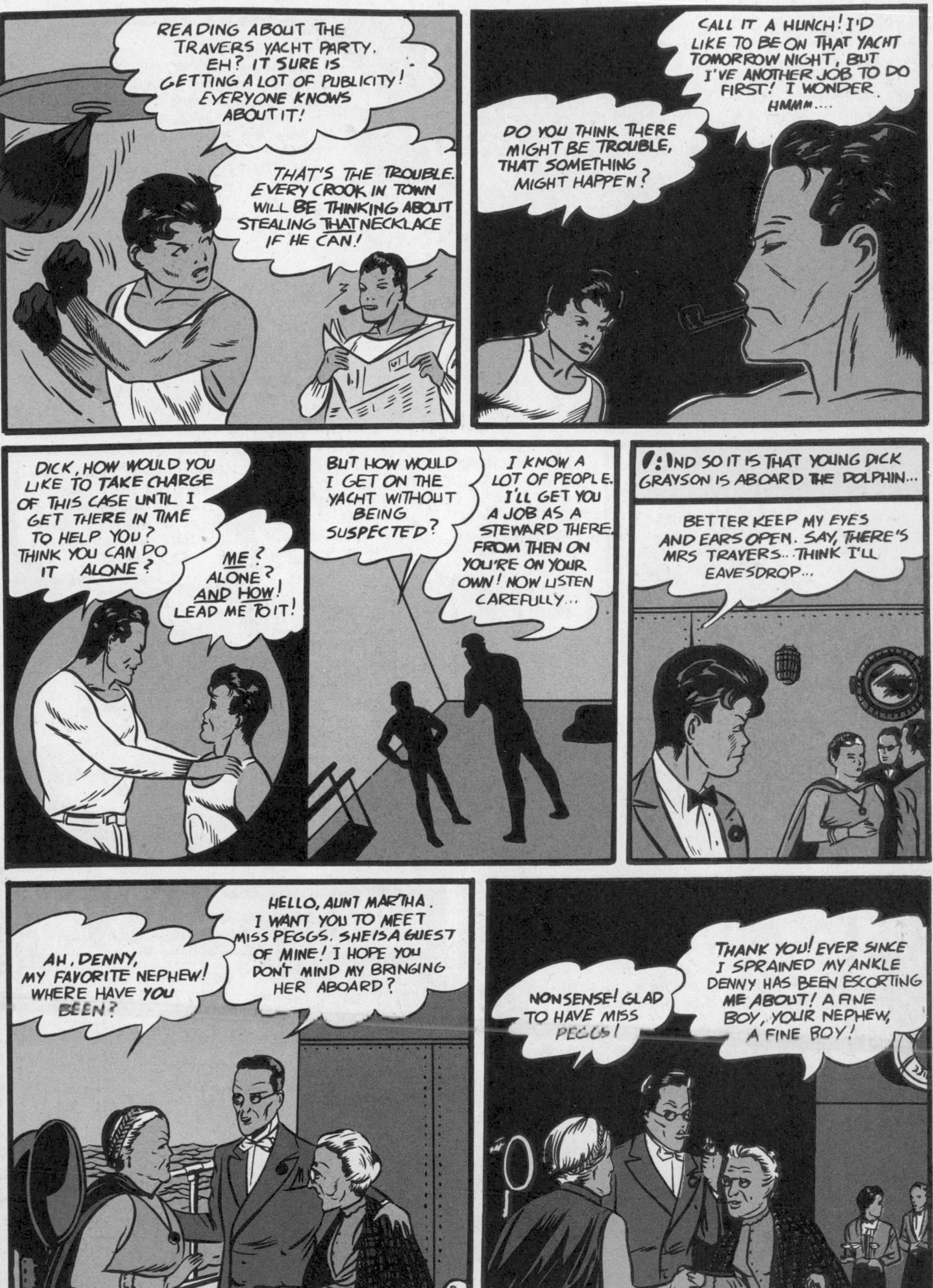

READING ABOUT THE TRAVERS YACHT PARTY. EH? IT SURE IS GETTING A LOT OF PUBLICITY! EVERYONE KNOWS ABOUT IT!
THAT'S THE TROUBLE. EVERY CROOK IN TOWN WILL BE THINKING ABOUT STEALING THAT NECKLACE IF HE CAN!
DO YOU THINK THERE MIGHT BE TROUBLE, THAT SOMETHING MIGHT HAPPEN?
CALL IT A HUNCH! I'D LIKE TO BE ON THAT YACHT TOMORROW NIGHT, BUT I'VE ANOTHER JOB TO DO FIRST! I WONDER HMMM....
DICK, HOW WOULD YOU LIKE TO TAKE CHARGE OF THIS CASE UNTIL I GET THERE IN TIME TO HELP YOU? THINK YOU CAN DO IT ALONE?
ME? ALONE? AND HOW! LEAD ME TO IT!
BUT HOW WOULD I GET ON THE YACHT WITHOUT BEING SUSPECTED?
I KNOW A LOT OF PEOPLE. I'LL GET YOU A JOB AS A STEWARD THERE. FROM THEN ON YOU'RE ON YOUR OWN! NOW LISTEN CAREFULLY...
AND SO IT IS THAT YOUNG DICK GRAYSON IS ABOARD THE DOLPHIN...
BETTER KEEP MY EYES AND EARS OPEN. SAY, THERE'S MRS TRAVERS... THINK I'LL EAVESDROP...
AH, DENNY, MY FAVORITE NEPHEW! WHERE HAVE YOU BEEN?
HELLO, AUNT MARTHA. I WANT YOU TO MEET MISS PEGGS. SHE IS A GUEST OF MINE! I HOPE YOU DON'T MIND MY BRINGING HER ABOARD?
NONSENSE! GLAD TO HAVE MISS PEGGS!
THANK YOU! EVER SINCE I SPRAINED MY ANKLE DENNY HAS BEEN ESCORTING ME ABOUT! A FINE BOY, YOUR NEPHEW, A FINE BOY!
2.

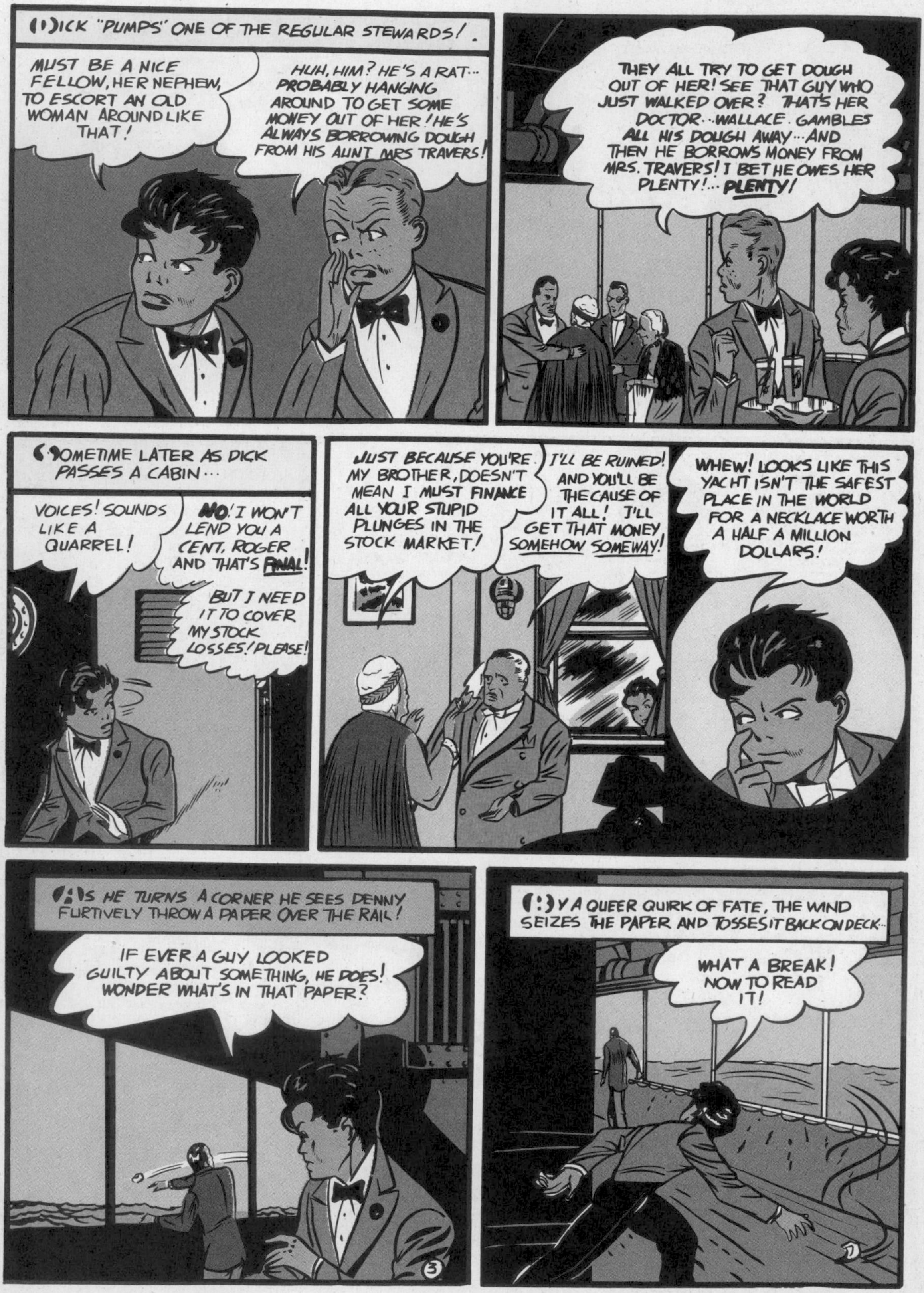
DICK "PUMPS" ONE OF THE REGULAR STEWARDS!
MUST BE A NICE FELLOW, HER NEPHEW, TO ESCORT AN OLD WOMAN AROUND LIKE THAT!
HUH, HIM? HE'S A RAT... PROBABLY HANGING AROUND TO GET SOME MONEY OUT OF HER! HE'S ALWAYS BORROWING DOUGH FROM HIS AUNT MRS TRAVERS!
THEY ALL TRY TO GET DOUGH OUT OF HER! SEE THAT GUY WHO JUST WALKED OVER? THAT'S HER DOCTOR...WALLACE. GAMBLES ALL HIS DOUGH AWAY...AND THEN HE BORROWS MONEY FROM MRS. TRAVERS! I BET HE OWES HER PLENTY!... PLENTY!
SOMETIME LATER AS DICK PASSES A CABIN...
VOICES! SOUNDS LIKE A QUARREL!
NO! I WON'T LEND YOU A CENT, ROGER AND THAT'S FINAL!
BUT I NEED IT TO COVER MY STOCK LOSSES! PLEASE!
JUST BECAUSE YOU'RE MY BROTHER, DOESN'T MEAN I MUST FINANCE ALL YOUR STUPID PLUNGES IN THE STOCK MARKET!
I'LL BE RUINED! AND YOU'LL BE THE CAUSE OF IT ALL! I'LL GET THAT MONEY SOMEHOW SOMEWAY!
WHEW! LOOKS LIKE THIS YACHT ISN'T THE SAFEST PLACE IN THE WORLD FOR A NECKLACE WORTH A HALF A MILLION DOLLARS!
AS HE TURNS A CORNER HE SEES DENNY FURTIVELY THROW A PAPER OVER THE RAIL!
IF EVER A GUY LOOKED GUILTY ABOUT SOMETHING, HE DOES! WONDER WHAT'S IN THAT PAPER?
3
BY A QUEER QUIRK OF FATE, THE WIND SEIZES THE PAPER AND TOSSES IT BACK ON DECK...
WHAT A BREAK! NOW TO READ IT!

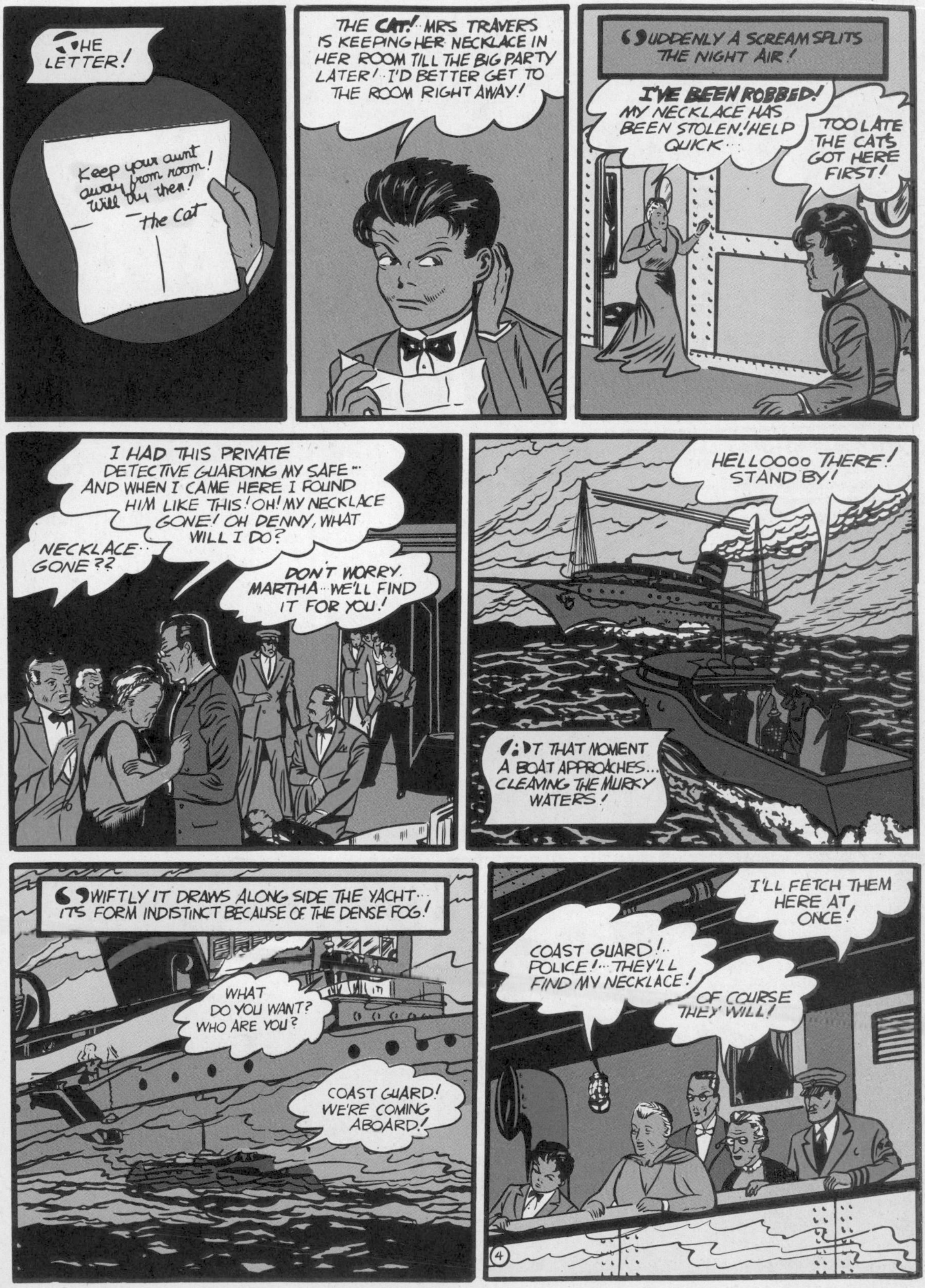
THE LETTER!
Keep your aunt away from room! Will try then! —The Cat
THE CAT! MRS TRAVERS IS KEEPING HER NECKLACE IN HER ROOM TILL THE BIG PARTY LATER! I'D BETTER GET TO THE ROOM RIGHT AWAY!
SUDDENLY A SCREAM SPLITS THE NIGHT AIR!
I'VE BEEN ROBBED! MY NECKLACE HAS BEEN STOLEN! HELP QUICK...
TOO LATE THE CAT'S GOT HERE FIRST!
I HAD THIS PRIVATE DETECTIVE GUARDING MY SAFE... AND WHEN I CAME HERE I FOUND HIM LIKE THIS! OH! MY NECKLACE GONE! OH DENNY, WHAT WILL I DO?
NECKLACE.. GONE??
DON'T WORRY. MARTHA... WE'LL FIND IT FOR YOU!
HELLOOOO THERE! STAND BY!
AT THAT MOMENT A BOAT APPROACHES... CLEAVING THE MURKY WATERS!
SWIFTLY IT DRAWS ALONG SIDE THE YACHT.. ITS FORM INDISTINCT BECAUSE OF THE DENSE FOG!
WHAT DO YOU WANT? WHO ARE YOU?
COAST GUARD! WE'RE COMING ABOARD!
I'LL FETCH THEM HERE AT ONCE!
COAST GUARD!.. POLICE!... THEY'LL FIND MY NECKLACE!
OF COURSE THEY WILL!
4

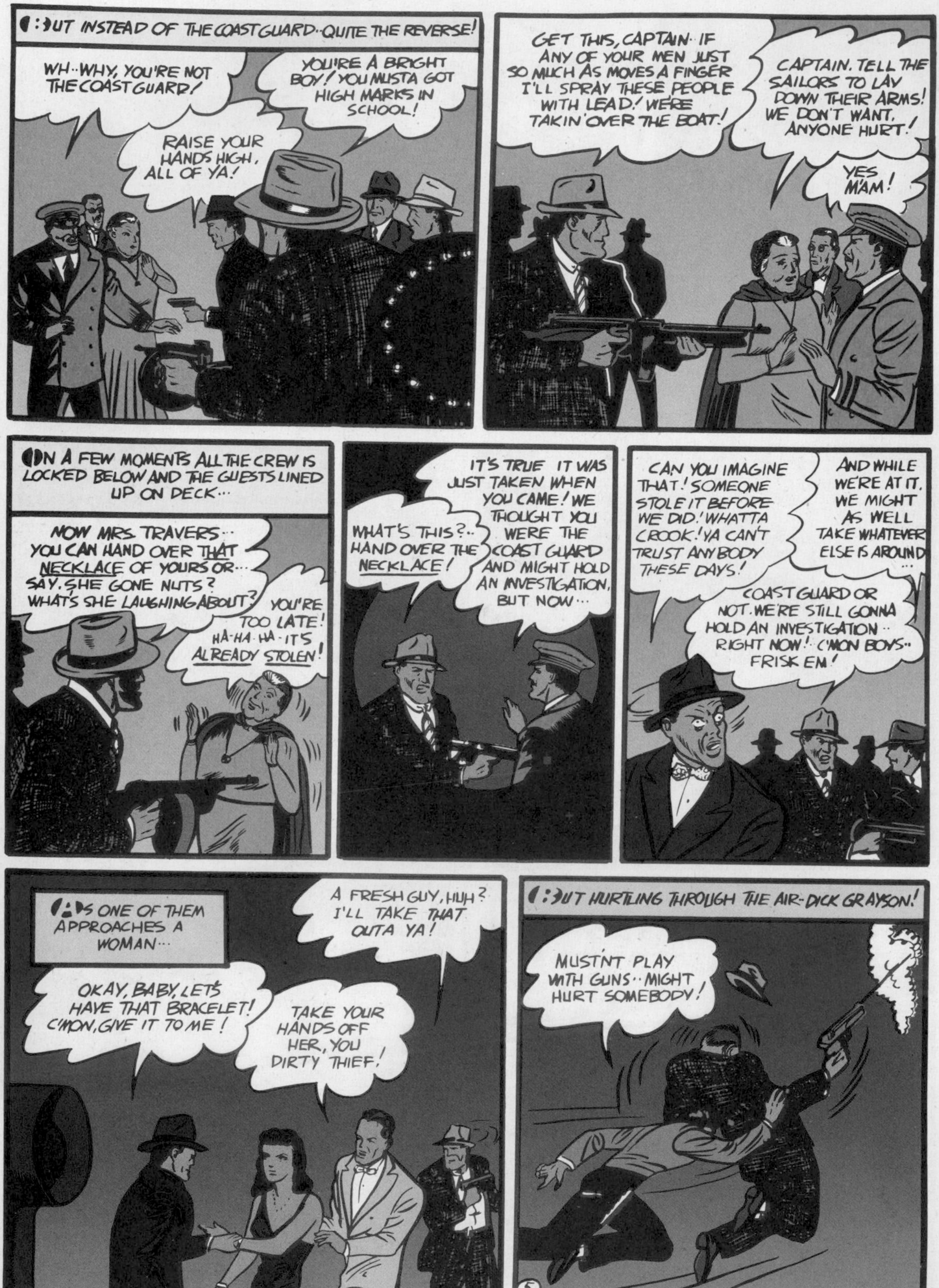
BUT INSTEAD OF THE COAST GUARD.. QUITE THE REVERSE!
WH.. WHY, YOU'RE NOT THE COAST GUARD!
YOU'RE A BRIGHT BOY! YOU MUSTA GOT HIGH MARKS IN SCHOOL!
RAISE YOUR HANDS HIGH, ALL OF YA!
GET THIS, CAPTAIN.. IF ANY OF YOUR MEN JUST SO MUCH AS MOVES A FINGER I'LL SPRAY THESE PEOPLE WITH LEAD! WE'RE TAKIN' OVER THE BOAT!
CAPTAIN. TELL THE SAILORS TO LAY DOWN THEIR ARMS! WE DON'T WANT ANYONE HURT!
YES M'AM!
IN A FEW MOMENTS ALL THE CREW IS LOCKED BELOW AND THE GUESTS LINED UP ON DECK...
NOW MRS. TRAVERS... YOU CAN HAND OVER THAT NECKLACE OF YOURS OR... SAY, SHE GONE NUTS? WHAT'S SHE LAUGHING ABOUT?
YOU'RE TOO LATE! HA-HA-HA-IT'S ALREADY STOLEN!
WHAT'S THIS?.. HAND OVER THE NECKLACE!
IT'S TRUE IT WAS JUST TAKEN WHEN YOU CAME! WE THOUGHT YOU WERE THE COAST GUARD AND MIGHT HOLD AN INVESTIGATION, BUT NOW...
CAN YOU IMAGINE THAT! SOMEONE STOLE IT BEFORE WE DID! WHATTA CROOK! YA CAN'T TRUST ANYBODY THESE DAYS!
AND WHILE WE'RE AT IT, WE MIGHT AS WELL TAKE WHATEVER ELSE IS AROUND...
COAST GUARD OR NOT. WE'RE STILL GONNA HOLD AN INVESTIGATION.. RIGHT NOW! C'MON BOYS.. FRISK EM!
AS ONE OF THEM APPROACHES A WOMAN...
A FRESH GUY, HUH? I'LL TAKE THAT OUTA YA!
OKAY, BABY, LET'S HAVE THAT BRACELET! C'MON, GIVE IT TO ME!
TAKE YOUR HANDS OFF HER, YOU DIRTY THIEF!
BUT HURTLING THROUGH THE AIR-- DICK GRAYSON!
MUSTN'T PLAY WITH GUNS.. MIGHT HURT SOMEBODY!
5

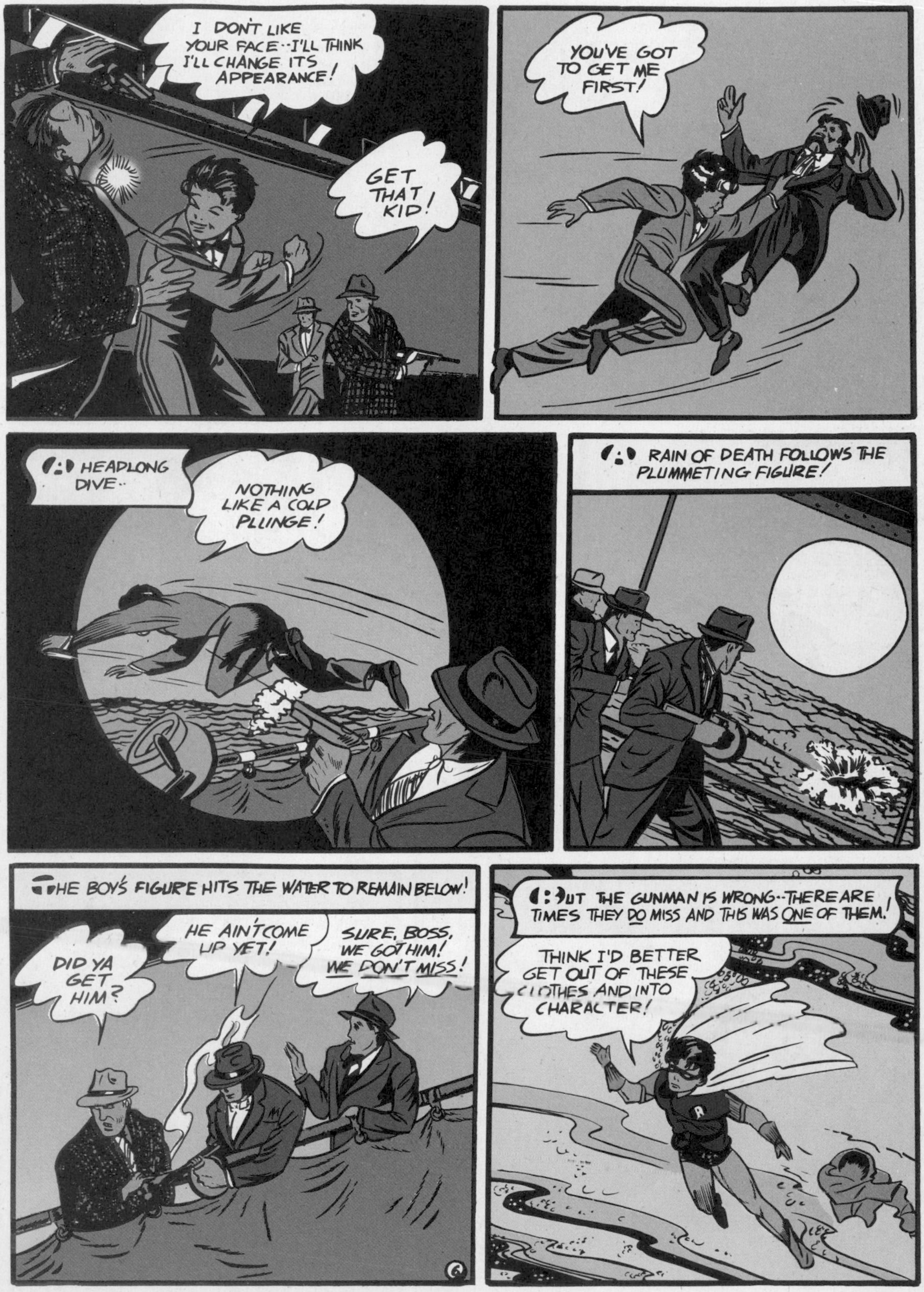

I DON'T LIKE YOUR FACE--I'LL THINK I'LL CHANGE ITS APPEARANCE!
GET THAT KID!
YOU'VE GOT TO GET ME FIRST!
A HEADLONG DIVE--
NOTHING LIKE A COLD PLUNGE!
A RAIN OF DEATH FOLLOWS THE PLUMMETING FIGURE!
THE BOY'S FIGURE HITS THE WATER TO REMAIN BELOW!
DID YA GET HIM?
HE AIN'T COME UP YET!
SURE, BOSS, WE GOT HIM! WE DON'T MISS!
BUT THE GUNMAN IS WRONG--THERE ARE TIMES THEY DO MISS AND THIS WAS ONE OF THEM!
THINK I'D BETTER GET OUT OF THESE CLOTHES AND INTO CHARACTER!

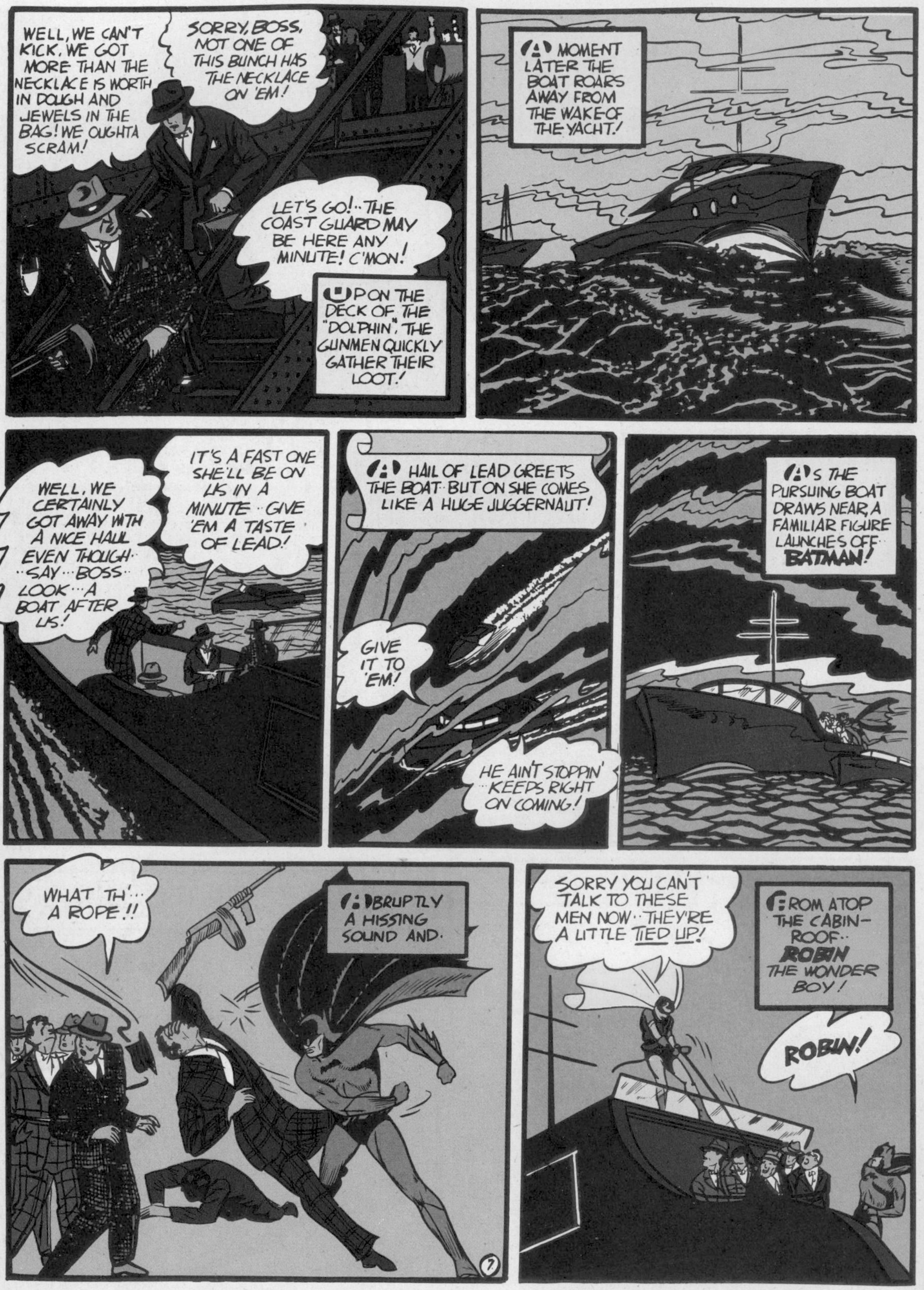

WELL, WE CAN'T KICK. WE GOT MORE THAN THE NECKLACE IS WORTH IN DOUGH AND JEWELS IN THE BAG! WE OUGHTA SCRAM!
SORRY, BOSS, NOT ONE OF THIS BUNCH HAS THE NECKLACE ON 'EM!
LET'S GO!.. THE COAST GUARD MAY BE HERE ANY MINUTE! C'MON!
UPON THE DECK OF THE "DOLPHIN", THE GUNMEN QUICKLY GATHER THEIR LOOT!
A MOMENT LATER THE BOAT ROARS AWAY FROM THE WAKE OF THE YACHT!
WELL, WE CERTAINLY GOT AWAY WITH A NICE HAUL EVEN THOUGH.. ..SAY...BOSS.. LOOK...A BOAT AFTER US!
IT'S A FAST ONE SHE'LL BE ON US IN A MINUTE.. GIVE 'EM A TASTE OF LEAD!
A HAIL OF LEAD GREETS THE BOAT.. BUT ON SHE COMES LIKE A HUGE JUGGERNAUT!
GIVE IT TO 'EM!
HE AIN'T STOPPIN' ..KEEPS RIGHT ON COMING!
AS THE PURSUING BOAT DRAWS NEAR, A FAMILIAR FIGURE LAUNCHES OFF.. BATMAN!
WHAT TH'... A ROPE!!
ABRUPTLY A HISSING SOUND AND.
SORRY YOU CAN'T TALK TO THESE MEN NOW.. THEY'RE A LITTLE TIED UP!
FROM ATOP THE CABIN-ROOF.. ROBIN THE WONDER BOY!
ROBIN!

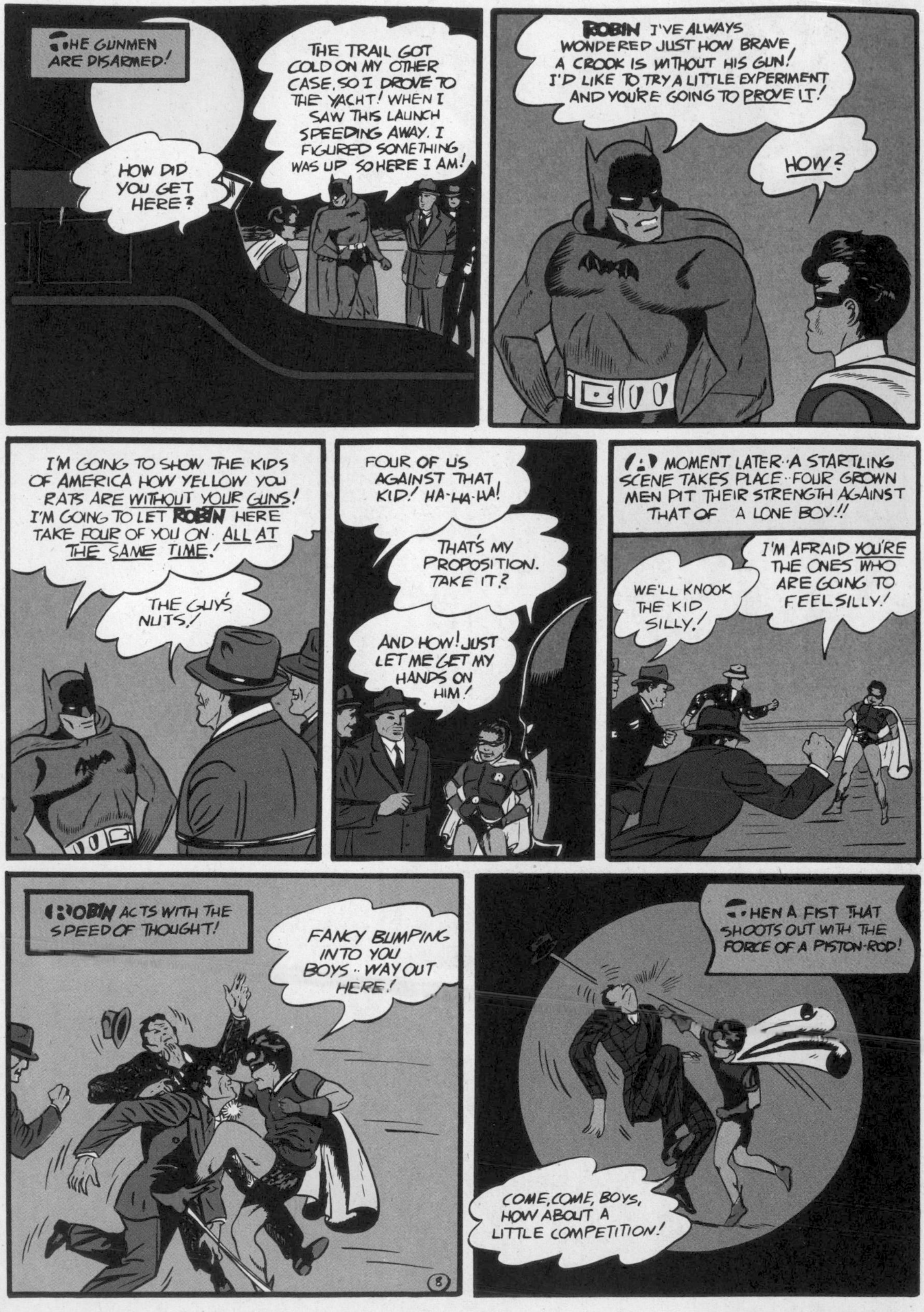
THE GUNMEN ARE DISARMED!
HOW DID YOU GET HERE?
THE TRAIL GOT COLD ON MY OTHER CASE, SO I DROVE TO THE YACHT! WHEN I SAW THIS LAUNCH SPEEDING AWAY, I FIGURED SOMETHING WAS UP SO HERE I AM!
ROBIN I'VE ALWAYS WONDERED JUST HOW BRAVE A CROOK IS WITHOUT HIS GUN! I'D LIKE TO TRY A LITTLE EXPERIMENT AND YOU'RE GOING TO PROVE IT!
HOW?
I'M GOING TO SHOW THE KIDS OF AMERICA HOW YELLOW YOU RATS ARE WITHOUT YOUR GUNS! I'M GOING TO LET ROBIN HERE TAKE FOUR OF YOU ON ALL AT THE SAME TIME!
THE GUY'S NUTS!
FOUR OF US AGAINST THAT KID! HA-HA-HA!
THAT'S MY PROPOSITION. TAKE IT?
AND HOW! JUST LET ME GET MY HANDS ON HIM!
A MOMENT LATER.. A STARTLING SCENE TAKES PLACE.. FOUR GROWN MEN PIT THEIR STRENGTH AGAINST THAT OF A LONE BOY!!
WE'LL KNOOK THE KID SILLY!
I'M AFRAID YOU'RE THE ONES WHO ARE GOING TO FEEL SILLY!
ROBIN ACTS WITH THE SPEED OF THOUGHT!
FANCY BUMPING INTO YOU BOYS.. WAY OUT HERE!
8
THEN A FIST THAT SHOOTS OUT WITH THE FORCE OF A PISTON-ROD!
COME, COME, BOYS, HOW ABOUT A LITTLE COMPETITION!

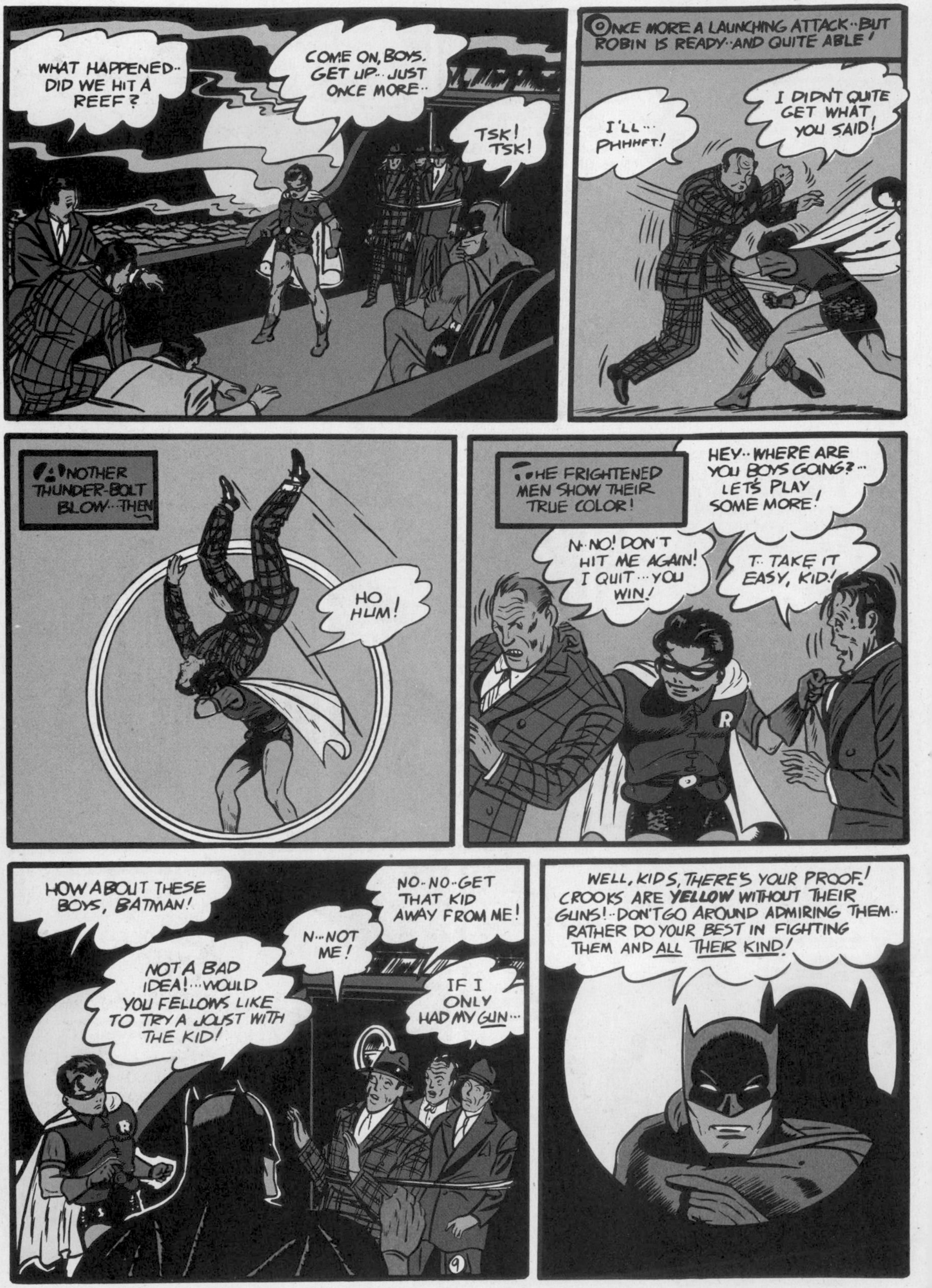
WHAT HAPPENED.. DID WE HIT A REEF?
COME ON, BOYS. GET UP.. JUST ONCE MORE..
TSK! TSK!
ONCE MORE A LAUNCHING ATTACK..BUT ROBIN IS READY..AND QUITE ABLE!
I'LL... PHHHFT!
I DIDN'T QUITE GET WHAT YOU SAID!
ANOTHER THUNDER-BOLT BLOW...THEN
HO HUM!
THE FRIGHTENED MEN SHOW THEIR TRUE COLOR!
HEY..WHERE ARE YOU BOYS GOING?... LET'S PLAY SOME MORE!
N..NO! DON'T HIT ME AGAIN! I QUIT...YOU WIN!
T..TAKE IT EASY, KID!
HOW ABOUT THESE BOYS, BATMAN!
NO..NO..GET THAT KID AWAY FROM ME!
N...NOT ME!
NOT A BAD IDEA!...WOULD YOU FELLOWS LIKE TO TRY A JOUST WITH THE KID!
IF I ONLY HAD MY GUN...
9
WELL, KIDS, THERE'S YOUR PROOF! CROOKS ARE YELLOW WITHOUT THEIR GUNS!..DON'T GO AROUND ADMIRING THEM.. RATHER DO YOUR BEST IN FIGHTING THEM AND ALL THEIR KIND!

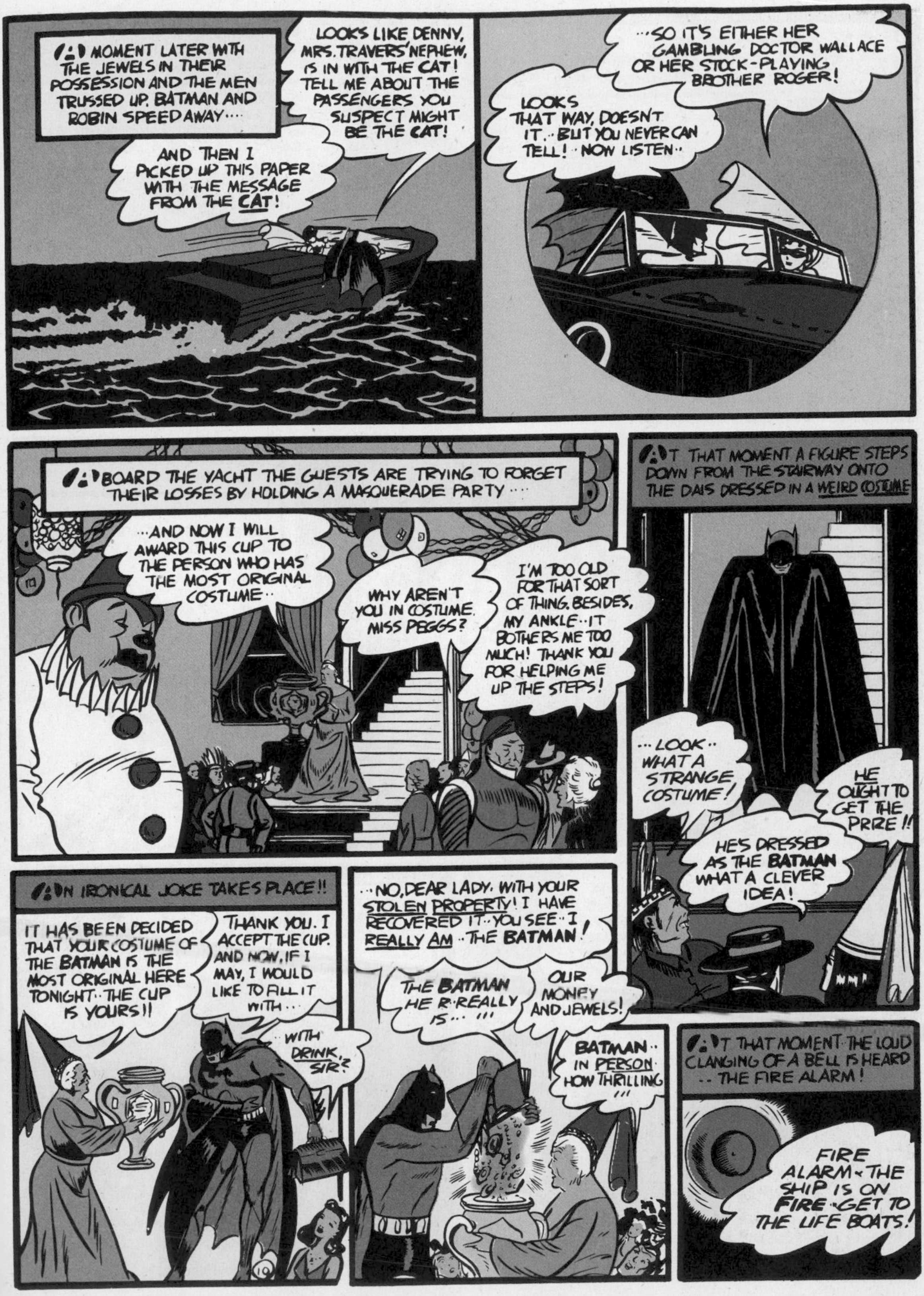
A MOMENT LATER WITH THE JEWELS IN THEIR POSSESSION AND THE MEN TRUSSED UP, BATMAN AND ROBIN SPEED AWAY....
AND THEN I PICKED UP THIS PAPER WITH THE MESSAGE FROM THE CAT!
LOOKS LIKE DENNY, MRS. TRAVERS' NEPHEW, IS IN WITH THE CAT! TELL ME ABOUT THE PASSENGERS YOU SUSPECT MIGHT BE THE CAT!
...SO IT'S EITHER HER GAMBLING DOCTOR WALLACE OR HER STOCK-PLAYING BROTHER ROGER!
LOOKS THAT WAY, DOESN'T IT.. BUT YOU NEVER CAN TELL! NOW LISTEN..
ABOARD THE YACHT THE GUESTS ARE TRYING TO FORGET THEIR LOSSES BY HOLDING A MASQUERADE PARTY...
...AND NOW I WILL AWARD THIS CUP TO THE PERSON WHO HAS THE MOST ORIGINAL COSTUME..
WHY AREN'T YOU IN COSTUME, MISS PEGGS?
I'M TOO OLD FOR THAT SORT OF THING. BESIDES, MY ANKLE..IT BOTHERS ME TOO MUCH! THANK YOU FOR HELPING ME UP THE STEPS!
AT THAT MOMENT A FIGURE STEPS DOWN FROM THE STAIRWAY ONTO THE DAIS DRESSED IN A WEIRD COSTUME
...LOOK.. WHAT A STRANGE COSTUME!
HE OUGHT TO GET THE PRIZE!!
HE'S DRESSED AS THE BATMAN WHAT A CLEVER IDEA!
AN IRONICAL JOKE TAKES PLACE!!
IT HAS BEEN DECIDED THAT YOUR COSTUME OF THE BATMAN IS THE MOST ORIGINAL HERE TONIGHT.. THE CUP IS YOURS!!
THANK YOU. I ACCEPT THE CUP. AND NOW, IF I MAY, I WOULD LIKE TO FILL IT WITH...
...WITH DRINK, SIR?
...NO, DEAR LADY. WITH YOUR STOLEN PROPERTY! I HAVE RECOVERED IT.. YOU SEE.. I REALLY AM.. THE BATMAN!
THE BATMAN HE R-REALLY IS... !!!
OUR MONEY AND JEWELS!
BATMAN.. IN PERSON HOW THRILLING !!!
AT THAT MOMENT THE LOUD CLANGING OF A BELL IS HEARD -- THE FIRE ALARM!
FIRE ALARM - THE SHIP IS ON FIRE - GET TO THE LIFE BOATS!

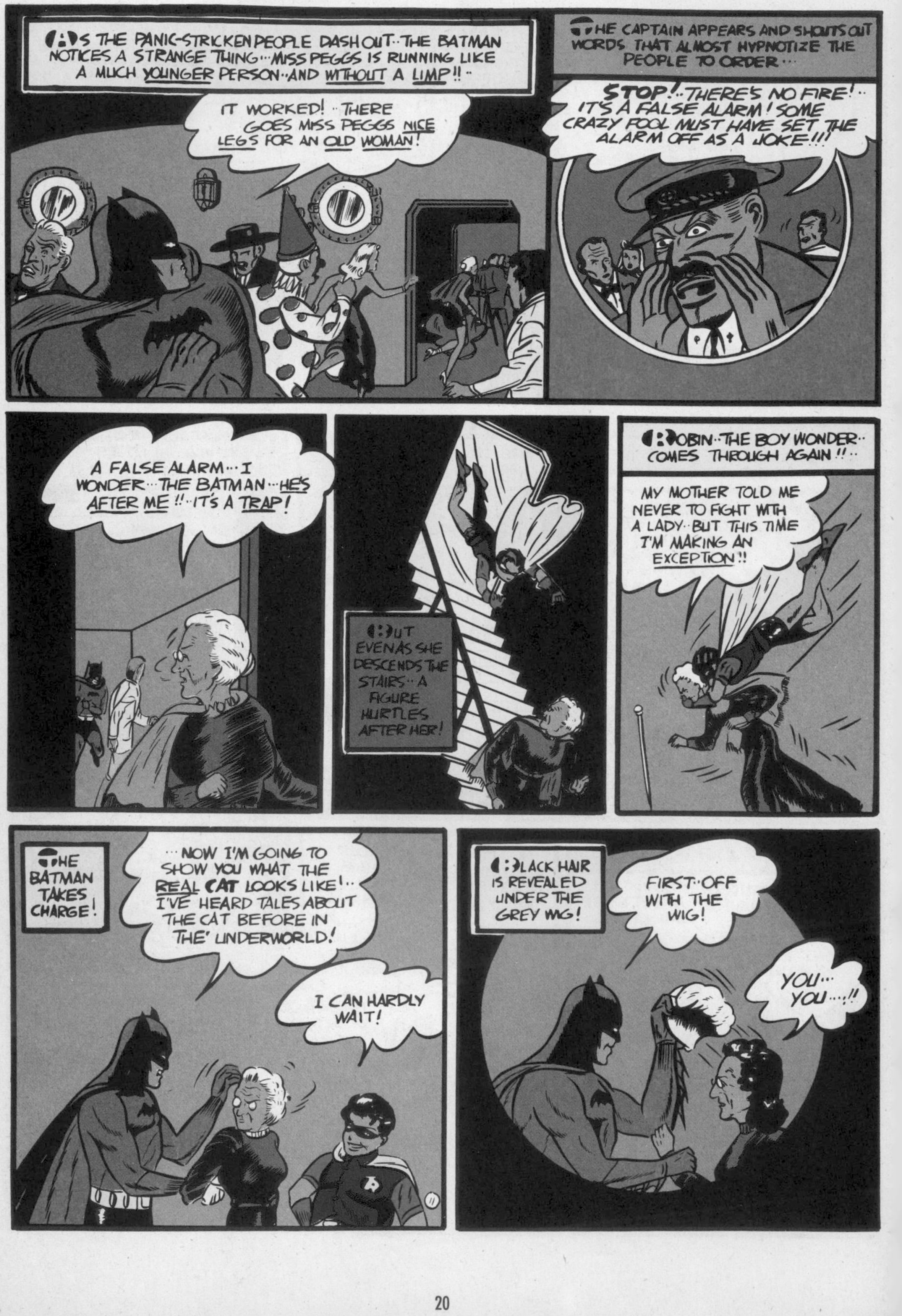
AS THE PANIC-STRICKEN PEOPLE DASH OUT.. THE BATMAN NOTICES A STRANGE THING... MISS PEGGS IS RUNNING LIKE A MUCH YOUNGER PERSON.. AND WITHOUT A LIMP!! ..
IT WORKED! .. THERE GOES MISS PEGGS NICE LEGS FOR AN OLD WOMAN!
THE CAPTAIN APPEARS AND SHOUTS OUT WORDS THAT ALMOST HYPNOTIZE THE PEOPLE TO ORDER ...
STOP! .. THERE'S NO FIRE! .. IT'S A FALSE ALARM! SOME CRAZY FOOL MUST HAVE SET THE ALARM OFF AS A JOKE!!!
A FALSE ALARM ... I WONDER ... THE BATMAN ... HE'S AFTER ME !! .. IT'S A TRAP!
BUT EVEN AS SHE DESCENDS THE STAIRS .. A FIGURE HURTLES AFTER HER!
ROBIN .. THE BOY WONDER .. COMES THROUGH AGAIN !! ..
MY MOTHER TOLD ME NEVER TO FIGHT WITH A LADY.. BUT THIS TIME I'M MAKING AN EXCEPTION!!
THE BATMAN TAKES CHARGE!
... NOW I'M GOING TO SHOW YOU WHAT THE REAL CAT LOOKS LIKE! .. I'VE HEARD TALES ABOUT THE CAT BEFORE IN THE' UNDERWORLD!
I CAN HARDLY WAIT!
BLACK HAIR IS REVEALED UNDER THE GREY WIG!
FIRST .. OFF WITH THE WIG!
YOU... YOU ...!!

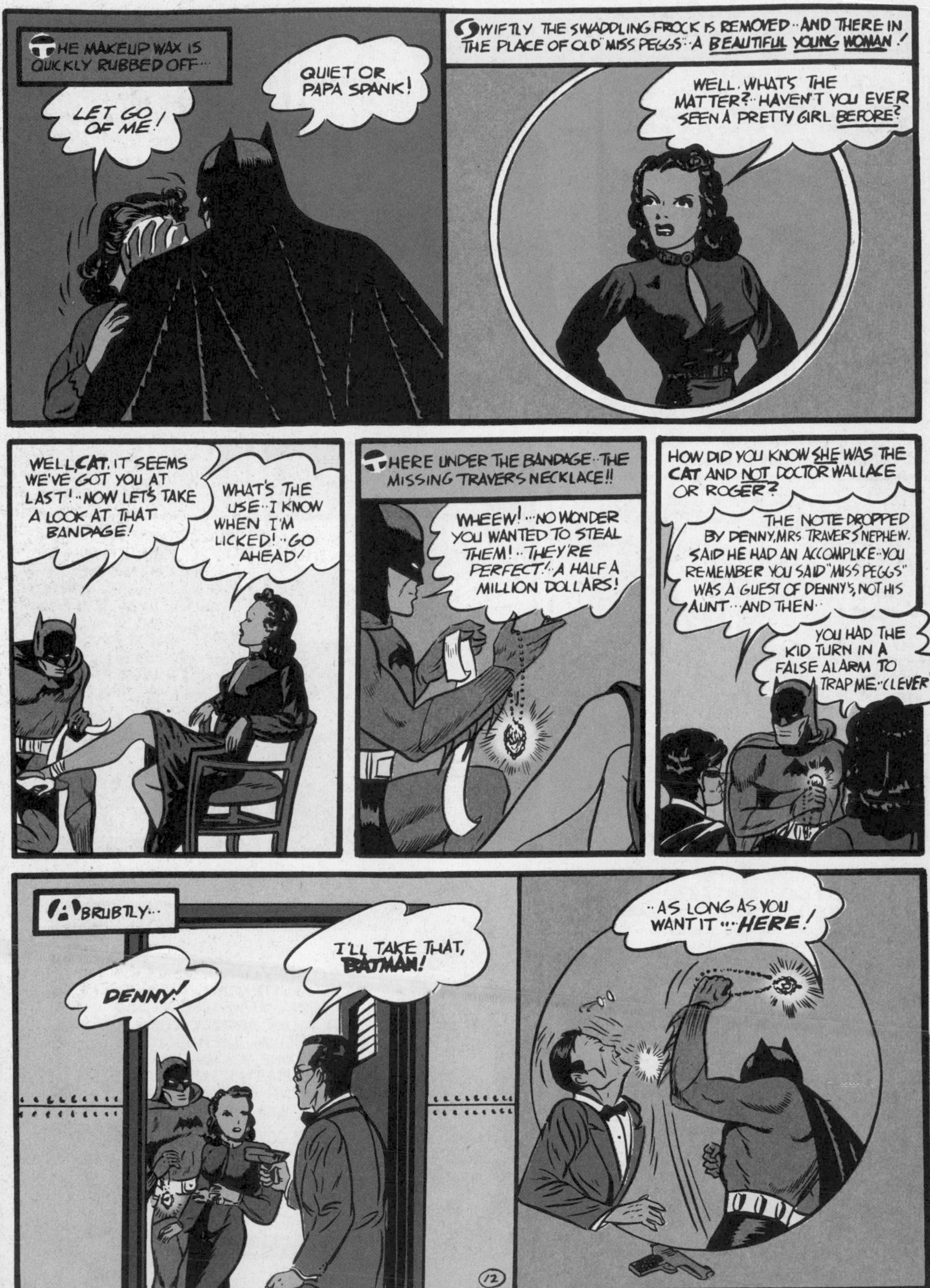
THE MAKEUP WAX IS QUICKLY RUBBED OFF...
LET GO OF ME!
QUIET OR PAPA SPANK!
SWIFTLY THE SWADDLING FROCK IS REMOVED.. AND THERE IN THE PLACE OF OLD "MISS PEGGS".. A BEAUTIFUL YOUNG WOMAN!
WELL. WHAT'S THE MATTER?.. HAVEN'T YOU EVER SEEN A PRETTY GIRL BEFORE?
WELL, CAT, IT SEEMS WE'VE GOT YOU AT LAST!.. NOW LET'S TAKE A LOOK AT THAT BANDAGE!
WHAT'S THE USE.. I KNOW WHEN I'M LICKED!.. GO AHEAD!
THERE UNDER THE BANDAGE.. THE MISSING TRAVERS NECKLACE!!
WHEEW!... NO WONDER YOU WANTED TO STEAL THEM!.. THEY'RE PERFECT!.. A HALF A MILLION DOLLARS!
HOW DID YOU KNOW SHE WAS THE CAT AND NOT DOCTOR WALLACE OR ROGER?
THE NOTE DROPPED BY DENNY, MRS TRAVERS NEPHEW. SAID HE HAD AN ACCOMPLICE.. YOU REMEMBER YOU SAID "MISS PEGGS" WAS A GUEST OF DENNY'S, NOT HIS AUNT... AND THEN...
YOU HAD THE KID TURN IN A FALSE ALARM TO TRAP ME.. CLEVER!
ABRUPTLY...
DENNY!
I'LL TAKE THAT, BATMAN!
..AS LONG AS YOU WANT IT... HERE!
12

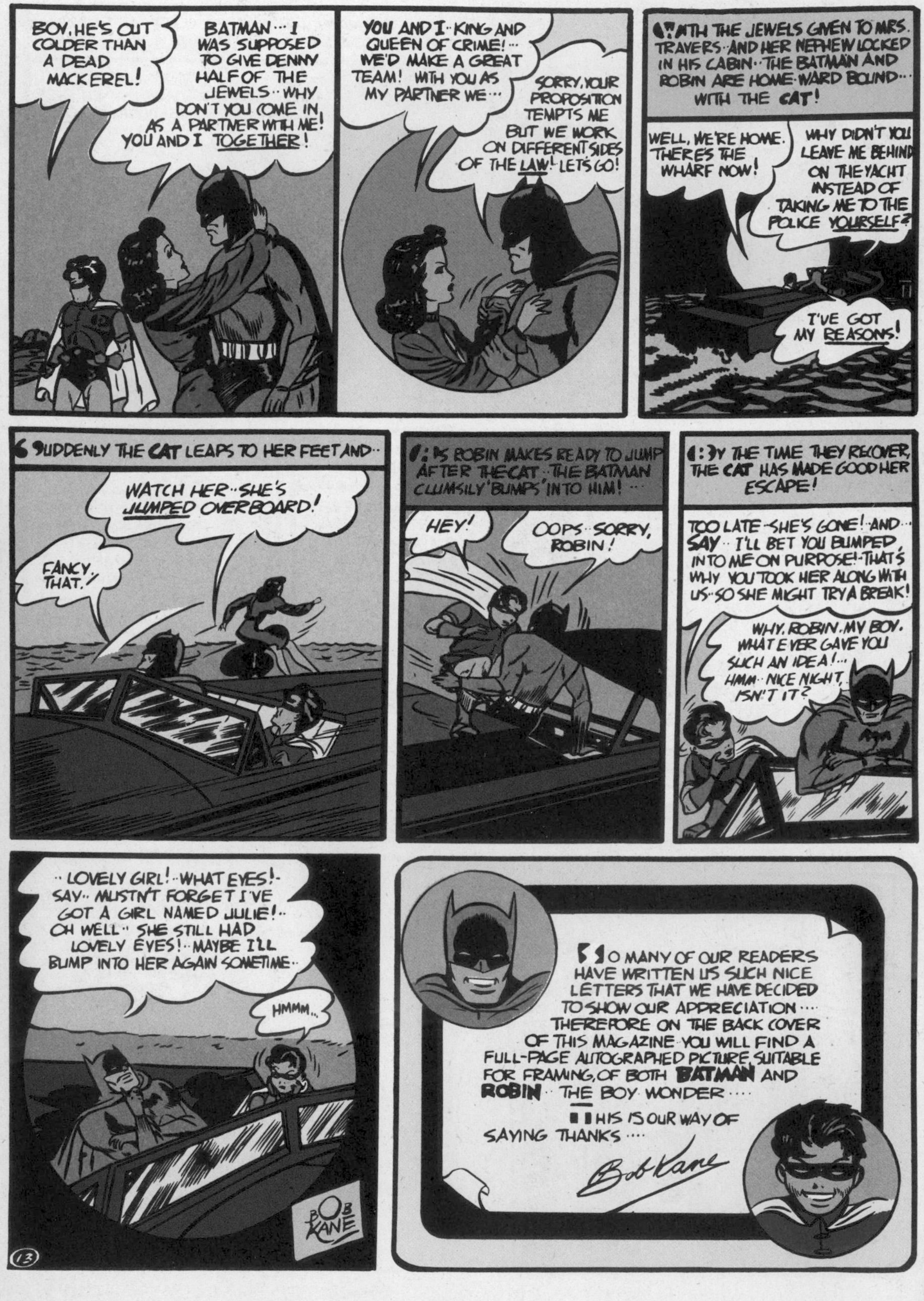
BOY, HE'S OUT COLDER THAN A DEAD MACKEREL!
BATMAN... I WAS SUPPOSED TO GIVE DENNY HALF OF THE JEWELS.. WHY DON'T YOU COME IN AS A PARTNER WITH ME! YOU AND I TOGETHER!
YOU AND I.. KING AND QUEEN OF CRIME!... WE'D MAKE A GREAT TEAM! WITH YOU AS MY PARTNER WE...
SORRY, YOUR PROPOSITION TEMPTS ME BUT WE WORK ON DIFFERENT SIDES OF THE LAW! LET'S GO!
WITH THE JEWELS GIVEN TO MRS. TRAVERS.. AND HER NEPHEW LOCKED IN HIS CABIN.. THE BATMAN AND ROBIN ARE HOME-WARD BOUND... WITH THE CAT!
WELL, WE'RE HOME. THERE'S THE WHARF NOW!
WHY DIDN'T YOU LEAVE ME BEHIND ON THE YACHT INSTEAD OF TAKING ME TO THE POLICE YOURSELF?
I'VE GOT MY REASONS!
SUDDENLY THE CAT LEAPS TO HER FEET AND..
WATCH HER.. SHE'S JUMPED OVERBOARD!
FANCY THAT.
AS ROBIN MAKES READY TO JUMP AFTER THE CAT.. THE BATMAN CLUMSILY 'BUMPS' INTO HIM!
HEY!
OOPS.. SORRY, ROBIN!
BY THE TIME THEY RECOVER, THE CAT HAS MADE GOOD HER ESCAPE!
TOO LATE.. SHE'S GONE!.. AND... SAY.. I'LL BET YOU BUMPED INTO ME ON PURPOSE! THAT'S WHY YOU TOOK HER ALONG WITH US.. SO SHE MIGHT TRY A BREAK!
WHY, ROBIN, MY BOY, WHATEVER GAVE YOU SUCH AN IDEA!... HMM.. NICE NIGHT, ISN'T IT?
.. LOVELY GIRL!.. WHAT EYES!.. SAY.. MUSTN'T FORGET I'VE GOT A GIRL NAMED JULIE!.. OH WELL.. SHE STILL HAD LOVELY EYES!.. MAYBE I'LL BUMP INTO HER AGAIN SOMETIME..
HMMM...
BOB KANE
13
SO MANY OF OUR READERS HAVE WRITTEN US SUCH NICE LETTERS THAT WE HAVE DECIDED TO SHOW OUR APPRECIATION.... THEREFORE ON THE BACK COVER OF THIS MAGAZINE YOU WILL FIND A FULL-PAGE AUTOGRAPHED PICTURE, SUITABLE FOR FRAMING, OF BOTH BATMAN AND ROBIN.. THE BOY WONDER....
THIS IS OUR WAY OF SAYING THANKS....
Bob Kane

pinup Dave Stevens

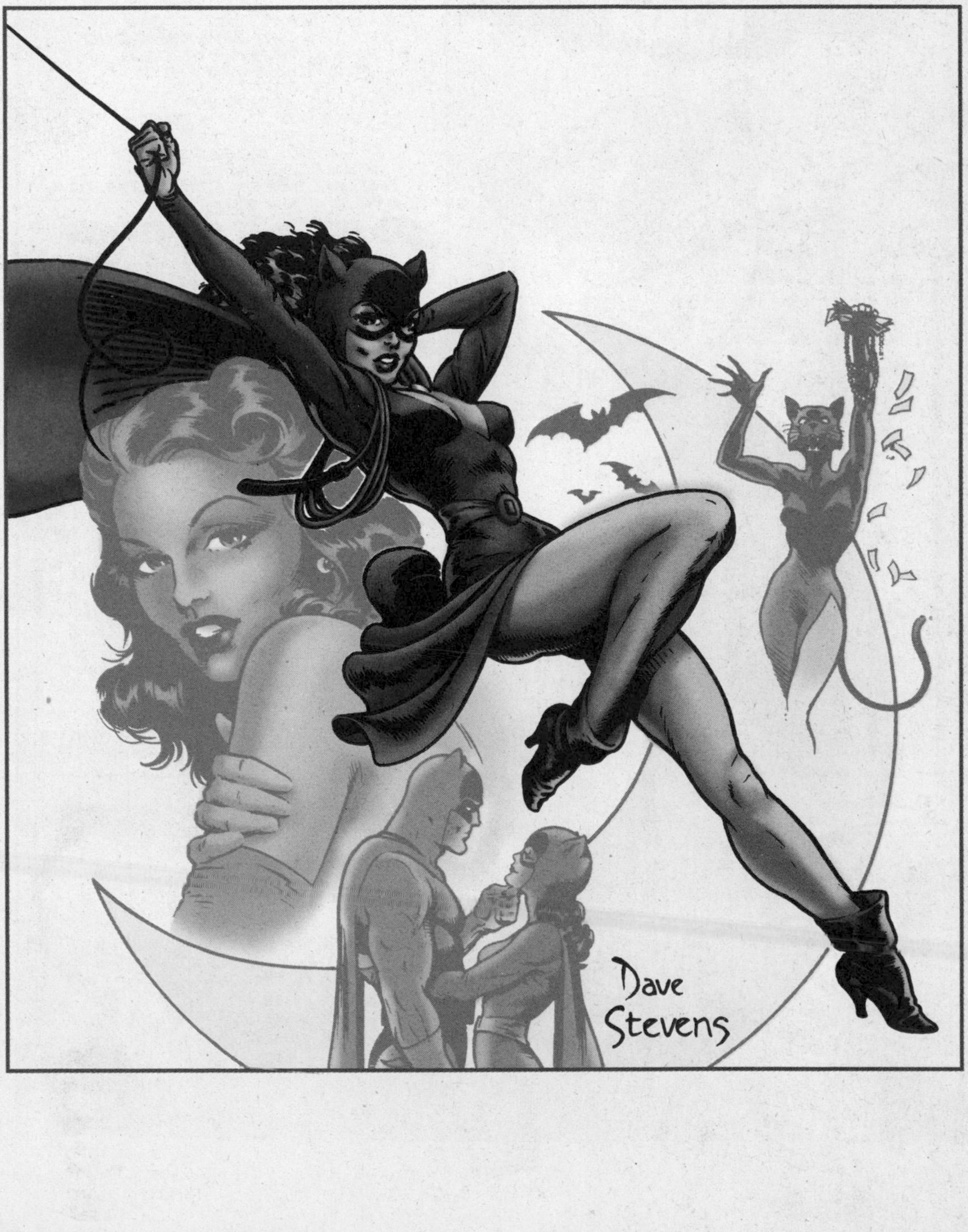
Dave
Stevens

Originally shown in WHO'S WHO: THE DEFINITIVE DIRECTORY OF THE DC UNIVERSE #4 (1985).
Colored by Drew R. Moore.

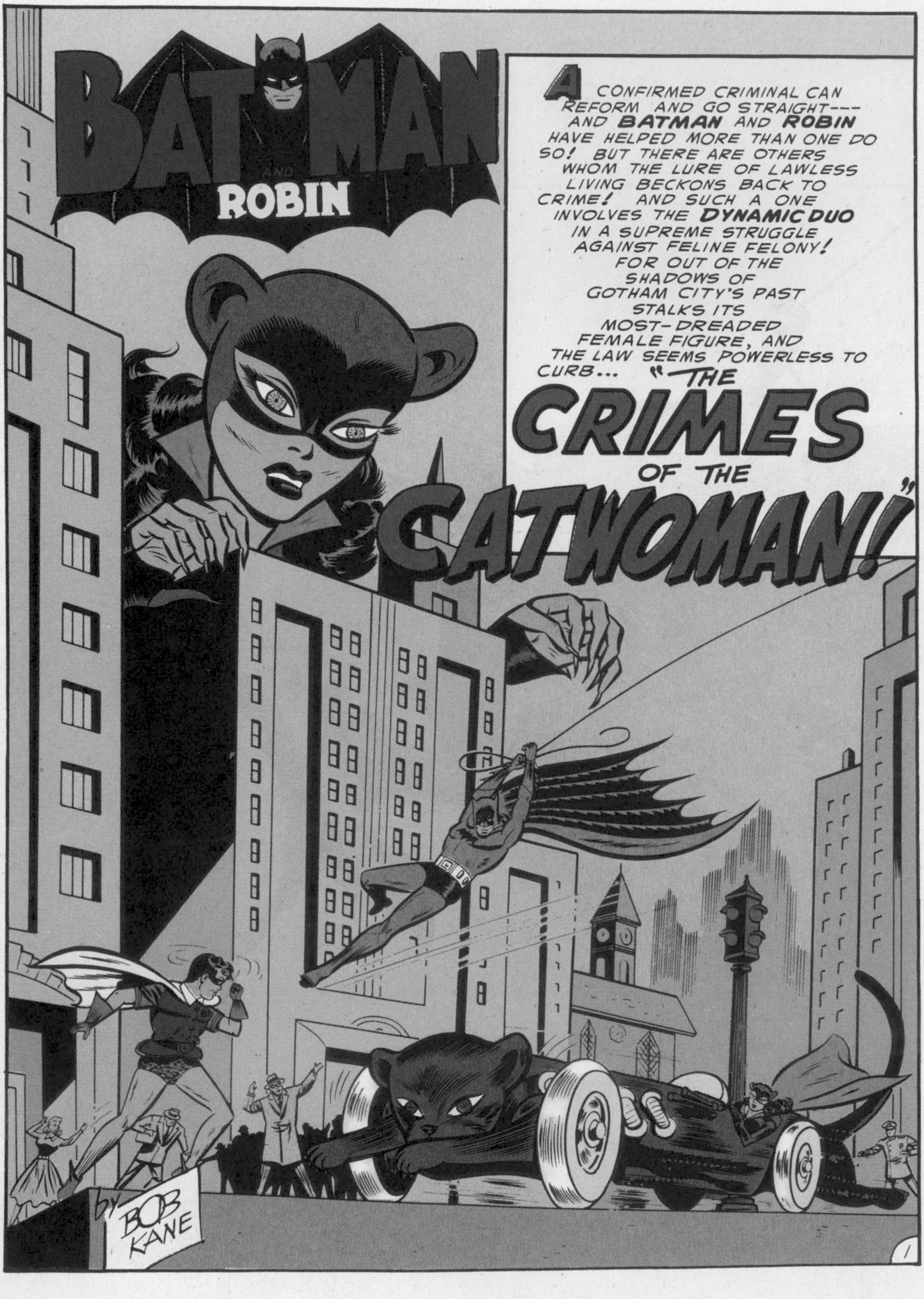
BATMAN AND ROBIN
A CONFIRMED CRIMINAL CAN REFORM AND GO STRAIGHT--- AND BATMAN AND ROBIN HAVE HELPED MORE THAN ONE DO SO! BUT THERE ARE OTHERS WHOM THE LURE OF LAWLESS LIVING BECKONS BACK TO CRIME! AND SUCH A ONE INVOLVES THE DYNAMIC DUO IN A SUPREME STRUGGLE AGAINST FELINE FELONY! FOR OUT OF THE SHADOWS OF GOTHAM CITY'S PAST STALKS ITS MOST-DREADED FEMALE FIGURE, AND THE LAW SEEMS POWERLESS TO CURB... "THE CRIMES OF THE CATWOMAN!"
by BOB KANE
1

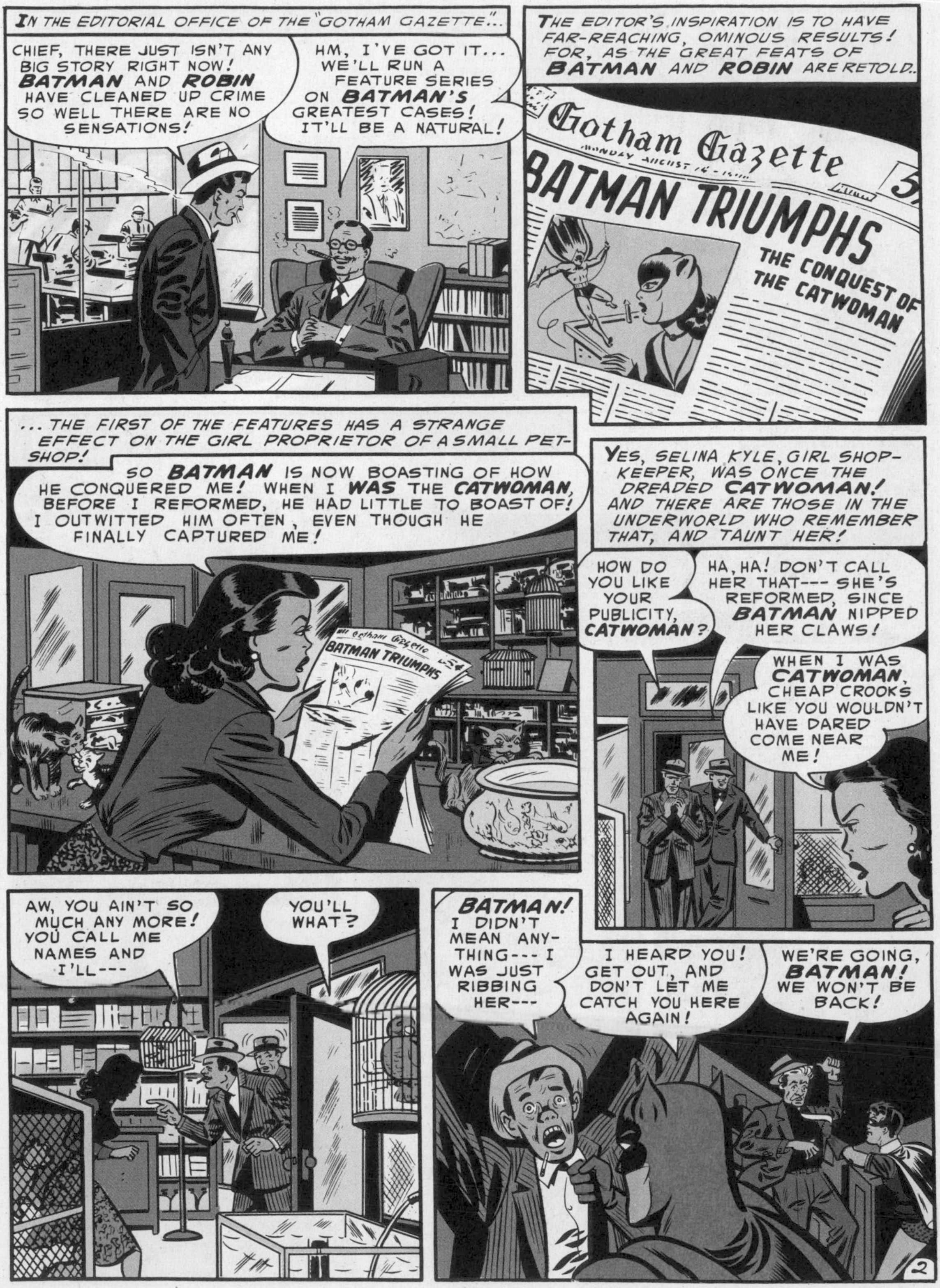
IN THE EDITORIAL OFFICE OF THE "GOTHAM GAZETTE"...
CHIEF, THERE JUST ISN'T ANY BIG STORY RIGHT NOW! BATMAN AND ROBIN HAVE CLEANED UP CRIME SO WELL THERE ARE NO SENSATIONS!
HM, I'VE GOT IT... WE'LL RUN A FEATURE SERIES ON BATMAN'S GREATEST CASES! IT'LL BE A NATURAL!
THE EDITOR'S INSPIRATION IS TO HAVE FAR-REACHING, OMINOUS RESULTS! FOR, AS THE GREAT FEATS OF BATMAN AND ROBIN ARE RETOLD...
Gotham Gazette
BATMAN TRIUMPHS
THE CONQUEST OF THE CATWOMAN
... THE FIRST OF THE FEATURES HAS A STRANGE EFFECT ON THE GIRL PROPRIETOR OF A SMALL PET-SHOP!
SO BATMAN IS NOW BOASTING OF HOW HE CONQUERED ME! WHEN I WAS THE CATWOMAN, BEFORE I REFORMED, HE HAD LITTLE TO BOAST OF! I OUTWITTED HIM OFTEN, EVEN THOUGH HE FINALLY CAPTURED ME!
BATMAN TRIUMPHS
YES, SELINA KYLE, GIRL SHOP-KEEPER, WAS ONCE THE DREADED CATWOMAN! AND THERE ARE THOSE IN THE UNDERWORLD WHO REMEMBER THAT, AND TAUNT HER!
HOW DO YOU LIKE YOUR PUBLICITY, CATWOMAN?
HA, HA! DON'T CALL HER THAT--- SHE'S REFORMED, SINCE BATMAN NIPPED HER CLAWS!
WHEN I WAS CATWOMAN, CHEAP CROOKS LIKE YOU WOULDN'T HAVE DARED COME NEAR ME!
AW, YOU AIN'T SO MUCH ANY MORE! YOU CALL ME NAMES AND I'LL---
YOU'LL WHAT?
BATMAN! I DIDN'T MEAN ANY-THING--- I WAS JUST RIBBING HER---
I HEARD YOU! GET OUT, AND DON'T LET ME CATCH YOU HERE AGAIN!
WE'RE GOING, BATMAN! WE WON'T BE BACK!
2

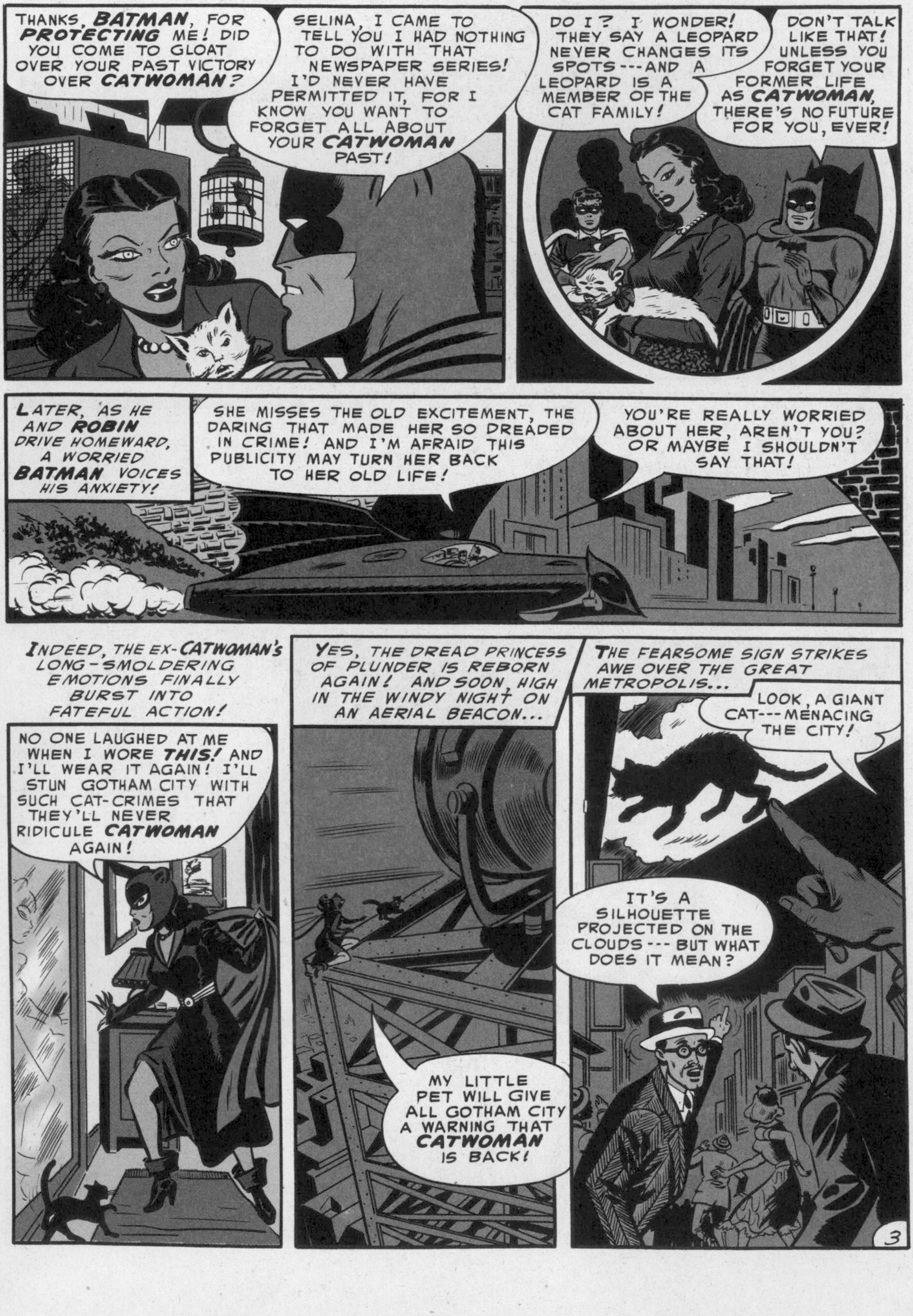
THANKS, BATMAN, FOR PROTECTING ME! DID YOU COME TO GLOAT OVER YOUR PAST VICTORY OVER CATWOMAN?
SELINA, I CAME TO TELL YOU I HAD NOTHING TO DO WITH THAT NEWSPAPER SERIES! I'D NEVER HAVE PERMITTED IT, FOR I KNOW YOU WANT TO FORGET ALL ABOUT YOUR CATWOMAN PAST!
DO I? I WONDER! THEY SAY A LEOPARD NEVER CHANGES ITS SPOTS---AND A LEOPARD IS A MEMBER OF THE CAT FAMILY!
DON'T TALK LIKE THAT! UNLESS YOU FORGET YOUR FORMER LIFE AS CATWOMAN, THERE'S NO FUTURE FOR YOU, EVER!
LATER, AS HE AND ROBIN DRIVE HOMEWARD, A WORRIED BATMAN VOICES HIS ANXIETY!
SHE MISSES THE OLD EXCITEMENT, THE DARING THAT MADE HER SO DREADED IN CRIME! AND I'M AFRAID THIS PUBLICITY MAY TURN HER BACK TO HER OLD LIFE!
YOU'RE REALLY WORRIED ABOUT HER, AREN'T YOU? OR MAYBE I SHOULDN'T SAY THAT!
INDEED, THE EX-CATWOMAN'S LONG-SMOLDERING EMOTIONS FINALLY BURST INTO FATEFUL ACTION!
NO ONE LAUGHED AT ME WHEN I WORE THIS! AND I'LL WEAR IT AGAIN! I'LL STUN GOTHAM CITY WITH SUCH CAT-CRIMES THAT THEY'LL NEVER RIDICULE CATWOMAN AGAIN!
YES, THE DREAD PRINCESS OF PLUNDER IS REBORN AGAIN! AND SOON, HIGH IN THE WINDY NIGHT ON AN AERIAL BEACON...
MY LITTLE PET WILL GIVE ALL GOTHAM CITY A WARNING THAT CATWOMAN IS BACK!
THE FEARSOME SIGN STRIKES AWE OVER THE GREAT METROPOLIS...
LOOK, A GIANT CAT---MENACING THE CITY!
IT'S A SILHOUETTE PROJECTED ON THE CLOUDS---BUT WHAT DOES IT MEAN?
3

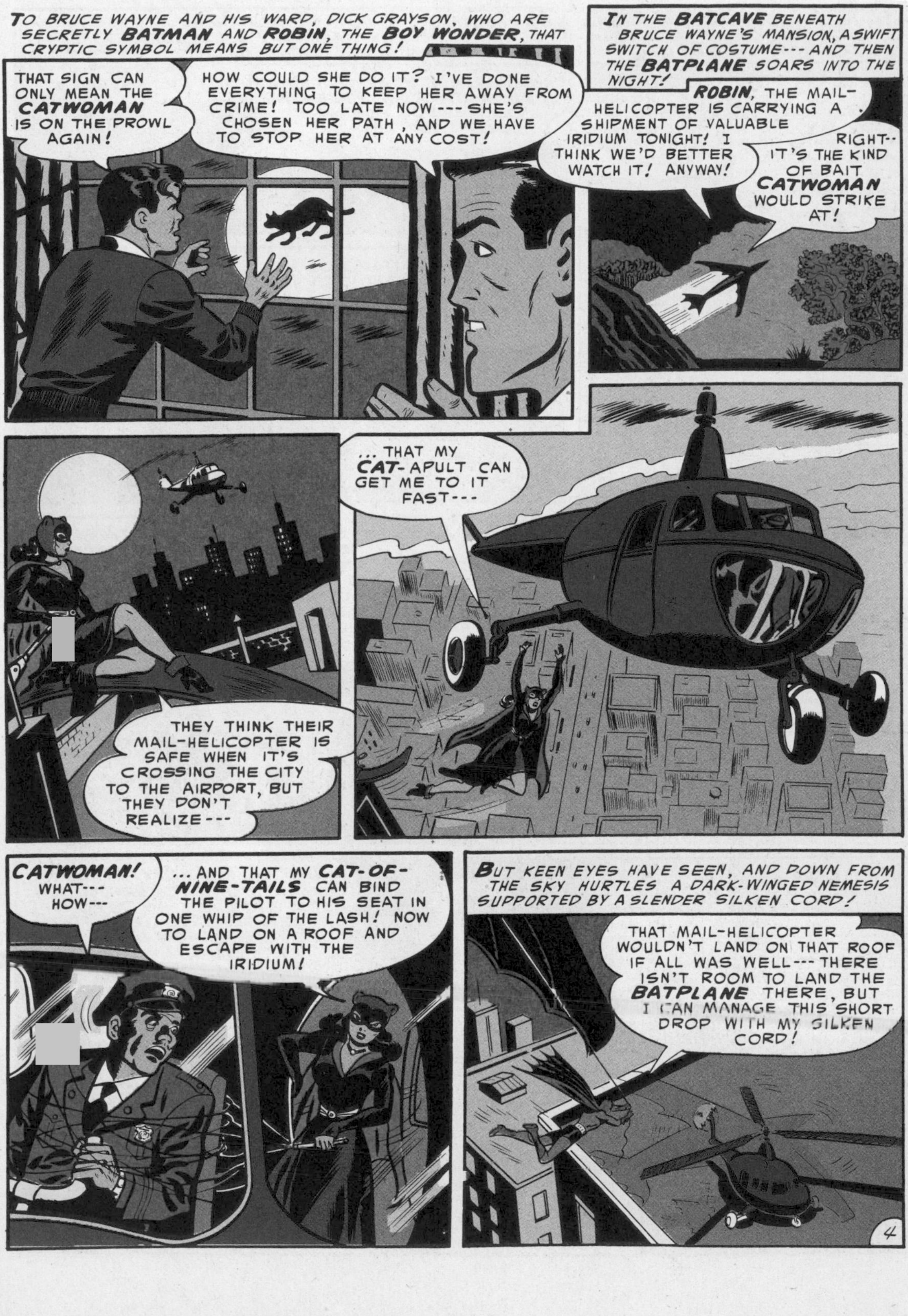
TO BRUCE WAYNE AND HIS WARD, DICK GRAYSON, WHO ARE SECRETLY BATMAN AND ROBIN, THE BOY WONDER, THAT CRYPTIC SYMBOL MEANS BUT ONE THING!
THAT SIGN CAN ONLY MEAN THE CATWOMAN IS ON THE PROWL AGAIN!
HOW COULD SHE DO IT? I'VE DONE EVERYTHING TO KEEP HER AWAY FROM CRIME! TOO LATE NOW --- SHE'S CHOSEN HER PATH, AND WE HAVE TO STOP HER AT ANY COST!
IN THE BATCAVE BENEATH BRUCE WAYNE'S MANSION, A SWIFT SWITCH OF COSTUME--- AND THEN THE BATPLANE SOARS INTO THE NIGHT!
ROBIN, THE MAIL-HELICOPTER IS CARRYING A SHIPMENT OF VALUABLE IRIDIUM TONIGHT! I THINK WE'D BETTER WATCH IT! ANYWAY!
RIGHT-- IT'S THE KIND OF BAIT CATWOMAN WOULD STRIKE AT!
THEY THINK THEIR MAIL-HELICOPTER IS SAFE WHEN IT'S CROSSING THE CITY TO THE AIRPORT, BUT THEY DON'T REALIZE---
... THAT MY CAT-APULT CAN GET ME TO IT FAST---
CATWOMAN! WHAT--- HOW---
... AND THAT MY CAT-OF-NINE-TAILS CAN BIND THE PILOT TO HIS SEAT IN ONE WHIP OF THE LASH! NOW TO LAND ON A ROOF AND ESCAPE WITH THE IRIDIUM!
BUT KEEN EYES HAVE SEEN, AND DOWN FROM THE SKY HURTLES A DARK-WINGED NEMESIS SUPPORTED BY A SLENDER SILKEN CORD!
THAT MAIL-HELICOPTER WOULDN'T LAND ON THAT ROOF IF ALL WAS WELL--- THERE ISN'T ROOM TO LAND THE BATPLANE THERE, BUT I CAN MANAGE THIS SHORT DROP WITH MY SILKEN CORD!
4

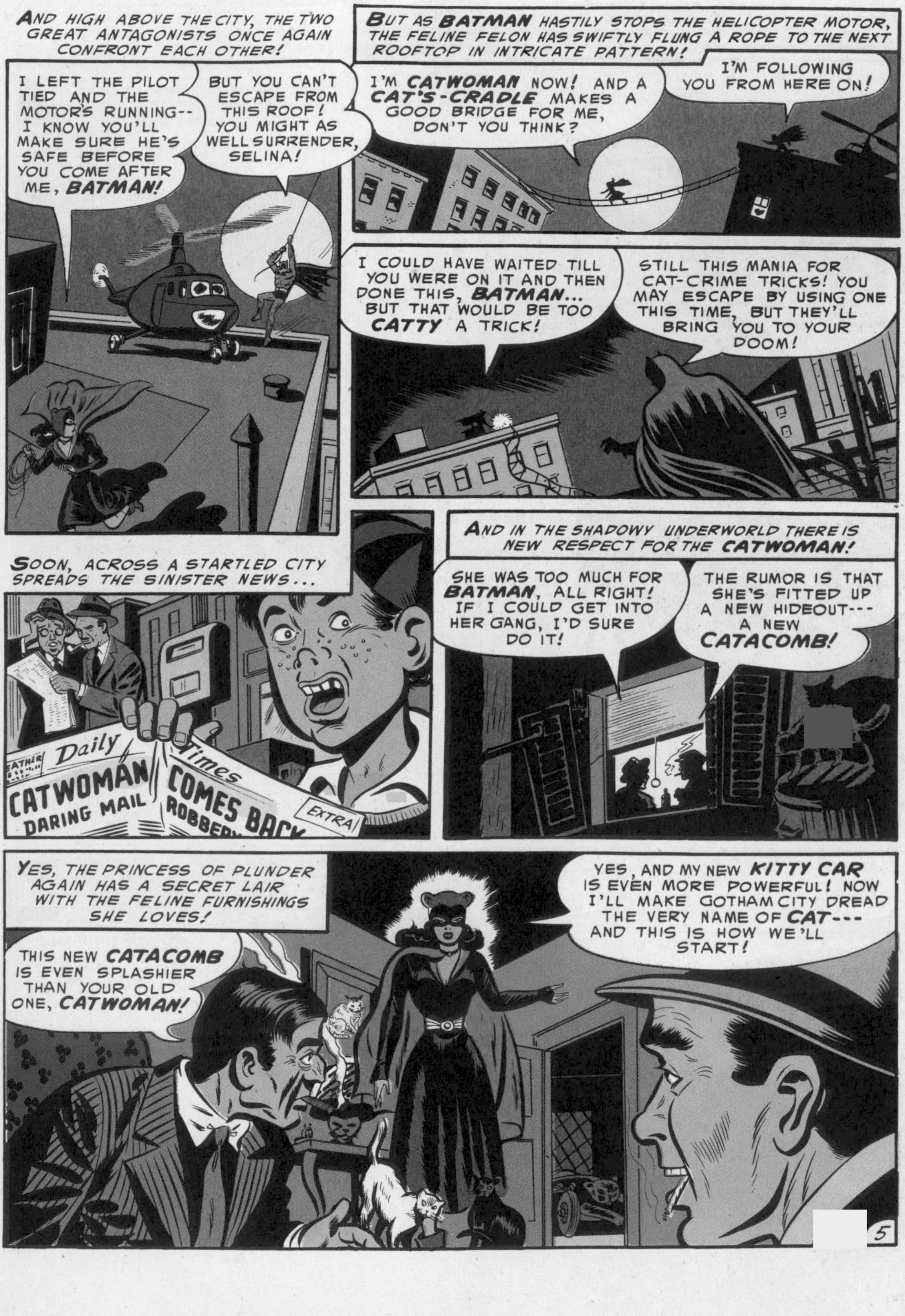
AND HIGH ABOVE THE CITY, THE TWO GREAT ANTAGONISTS ONCE AGAIN CONFRONT EACH OTHER!
I LEFT THE PILOT TIED AND THE MOTOR'S RUNNING-- I KNOW YOU'LL MAKE SURE HE'S SAFE BEFORE YOU COME AFTER ME, BATMAN!
BUT YOU CAN'T ESCAPE FROM THIS ROOF! YOU MIGHT AS WELL SURRENDER, SELINA!
BUT AS BATMAN HASTILY STOPS THE HELICOPTER MOTOR, THE FELINE FELON HAS SWIFTLY FLUNG A ROPE TO THE NEXT ROOFTOP IN INTRICATE PATTERN!
I'M CATWOMAN NOW! AND A CAT'S-CRADLE MAKES A GOOD BRIDGE FOR ME, DON'T YOU THINK?
I'M FOLLOWING YOU FROM HERE ON!
I COULD HAVE WAITED TILL YOU WERE ON IT AND THEN DONE THIS, BATMAN... BUT THAT WOULD BE TOO CATTY A TRICK!
STILL THIS MANIA FOR CAT-CRIME TRICKS! YOU MAY ESCAPE BY USING ONE THIS TIME, BUT THEY'LL BRING YOU TO YOUR DOOM!
SOON, ACROSS A STARTLED CITY SPREADS THE SINISTER NEWS...
Daily Times
CATWOMAN COMES BACK
DARING MAIL ROBBERY
EXTRA
AND IN THE SHADOWY UNDERWORLD THERE IS NEW RESPECT FOR THE CATWOMAN!
SHE WAS TOO MUCH FOR BATMAN, ALL RIGHT! IF I COULD GET INTO HER GANG, I'D SURE DO IT!
THE RUMOR IS THAT SHE'S FITTED UP A NEW HIDEOUT--- A NEW CATACOMB!
YES, THE PRINCESS OF PLUNDER AGAIN HAS A SECRET LAIR WITH THE FELINE FURNISHINGS SHE LOVES!
THIS NEW CATACOMB IS EVEN SPLASHIER THAN YOUR OLD ONE, CATWOMAN!
YES, AND MY NEW KITTY CAR IS EVEN MORE POWERFUL! NOW I'LL MAKE GOTHAM CITY DREAD THE VERY NAME OF CAT--- AND THIS IS HOW WE'LL START!
5

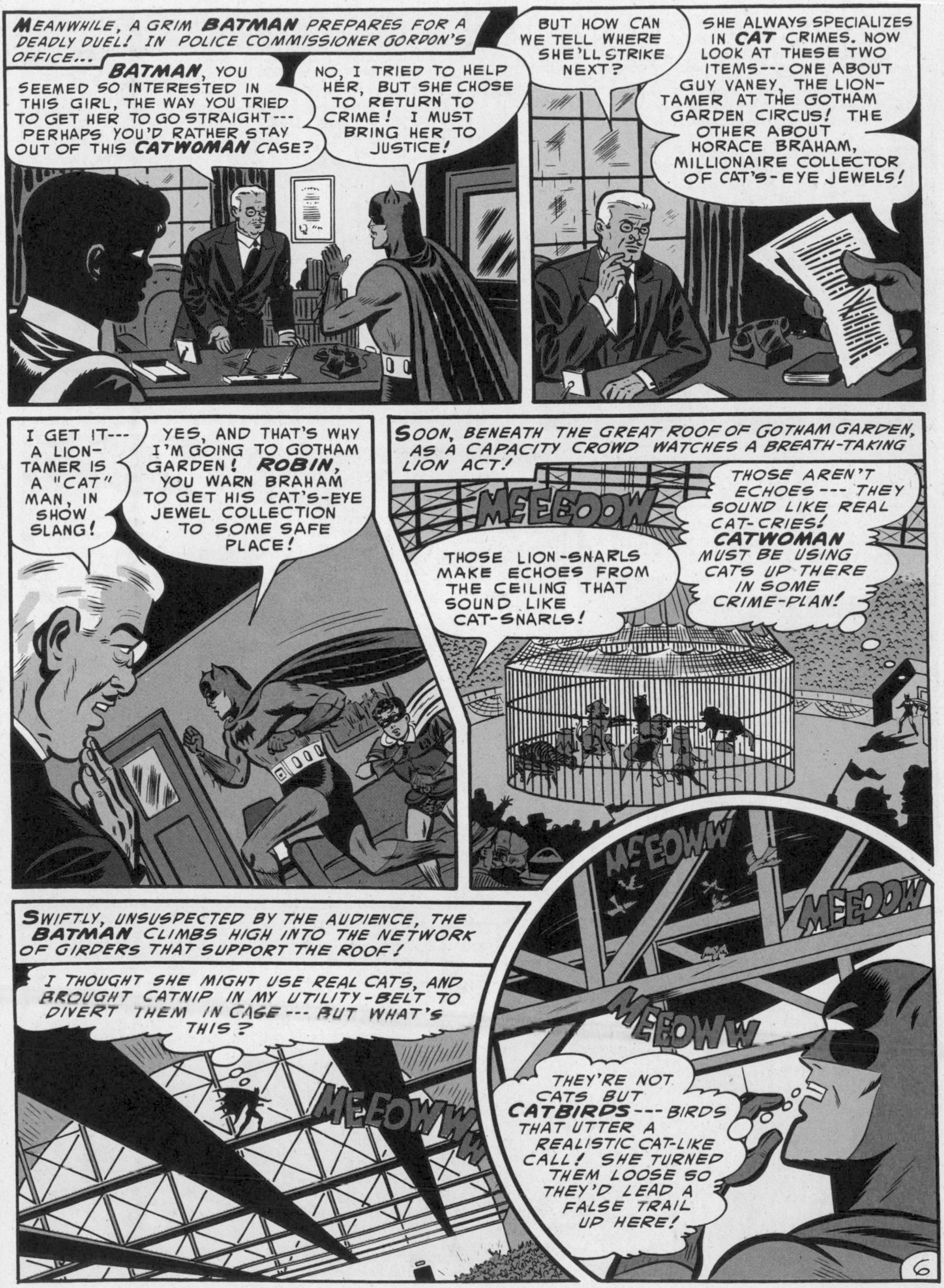
MEANWHILE, A GRIM BATMAN PREPARES FOR A DEADLY DUEL! IN POLICE COMMISSIONER GORDON'S OFFICE...
BATMAN, YOU SEEMED SO INTERESTED IN THIS GIRL, THE WAY YOU TRIED TO GET HER TO GO STRAIGHT--- PERHAPS YOU'D RATHER STAY OUT OF THIS CATWOMAN CASE?
NO, I TRIED TO HELP HER, BUT SHE CHOSE TO RETURN TO CRIME! I MUST BRING HER TO JUSTICE!
BUT HOW CAN WE TELL WHERE SHE'LL STRIKE NEXT?
SHE ALWAYS SPECIALIZES IN CAT CRIMES. NOW LOOK AT THESE TWO ITEMS--- ONE ABOUT GUY VANEY, THE LION-TAMER AT THE GOTHAM GARDEN CIRCUS! THE OTHER ABOUT HORACE BRAHAM, MILLIONAIRE COLLECTOR OF CAT'S-EYE JEWELS!
I GET IT--- A LION-TAMER IS A "CAT" MAN, IN SHOW SLANG!
YES, AND THAT'S WHY I'M GOING TO GOTHAM GARDEN! ROBIN, YOU WARN BRAHAM TO GET HIS CAT'S-EYE JEWEL COLLECTION TO SOME SAFE PLACE!
SOON, BENEATH THE GREAT ROOF OF GOTHAM GARDEN, AS A CAPACITY CROWD WATCHES A BREATH-TAKING LION ACT!
MEEEOOW
THOSE LION-SNARLS MAKE ECHOES FROM THE CEILING THAT SOUND LIKE CAT-SNARLS!
THOSE AREN'T ECHOES --- THEY SOUND LIKE REAL CAT-CRIES! CATWOMAN MUST BE USING CATS UP THERE IN SOME CRIME-PLAN!
SWIFTLY, UNSUSPECTED BY THE AUDIENCE, THE BATMAN CLIMBS HIGH INTO THE NETWORK OF GIRDERS THAT SUPPORT THE ROOF!
I THOUGHT SHE MIGHT USE REAL CATS, AND BROUGHT CATNIP IN MY UTILITY-BELT TO DIVERT THEM IN CASE --- BUT WHAT'S THIS?
MEEOWWW
MEEOWW
MEEOOW
MEEOWW
THEY'RE NOT CATS BUT CATBIRDS--- BIRDS THAT UTTER A REALISTIC CAT-LIKE CALL! SHE TURNED THEM LOOSE SO THEY'D LEAD A FALSE TRAIL UP HERE!
6

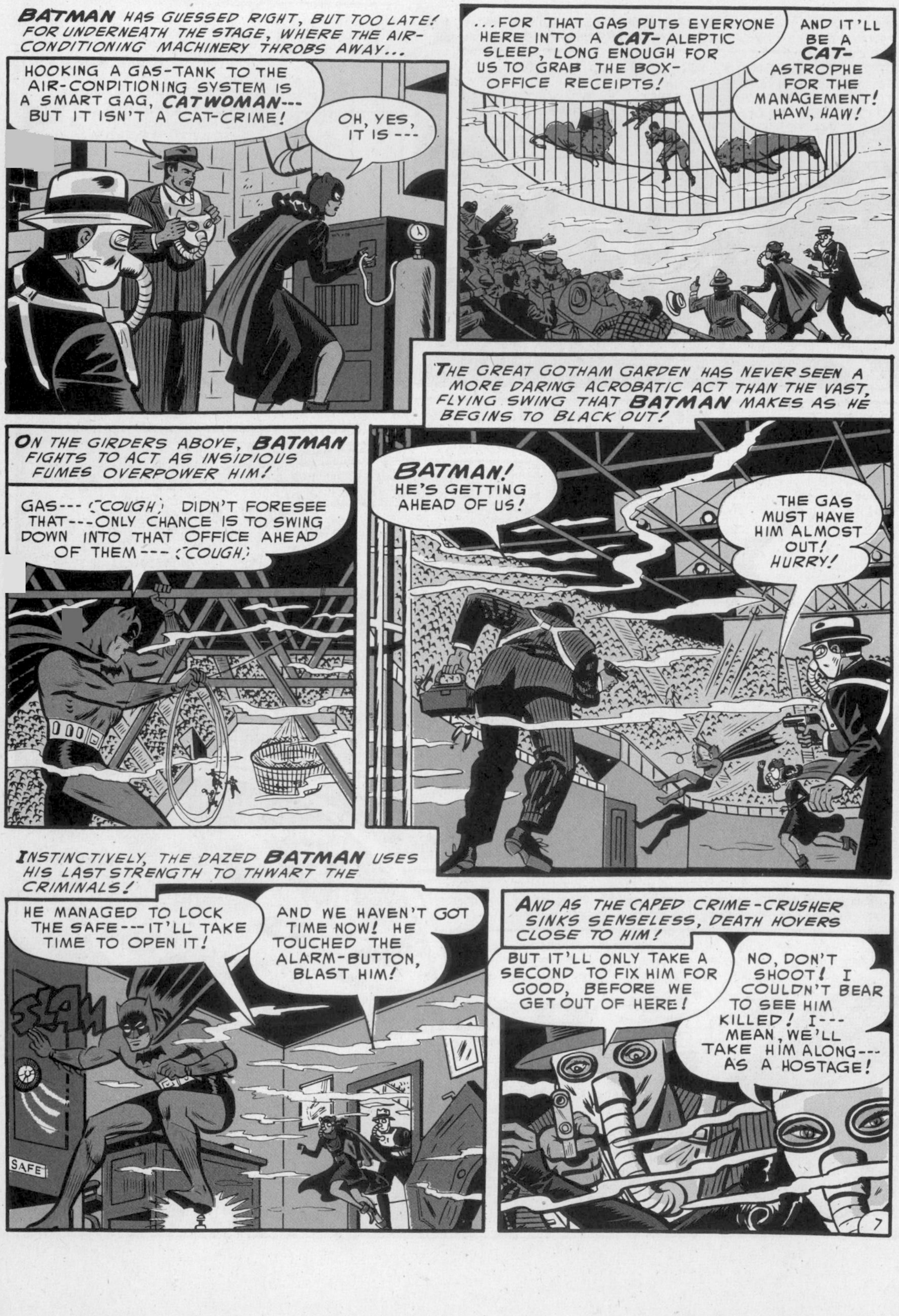
BATMAN HAS GUESSED RIGHT, BUT TOO LATE! FOR UNDERNEATH THE STAGE, WHERE THE AIR-CONDITIONING MACHINERY THROBS AWAY...
HOOKING A GAS-TANK TO THE AIR-CONDITIONING SYSTEM IS A SMART GAG, CATWOMAN--- BUT IT ISN'T A CAT-CRIME!
OH, YES, IT IS ---
...FOR THAT GAS PUTS EVERYONE HERE INTO A CAT-ALEPTIC SLEEP, LONG ENOUGH FOR US TO GRAB THE BOX-OFFICE RECEIPTS!
AND IT'LL BE A CAT-ASTROPHE FOR THE MANAGEMENT! HAW, HAW!
ON THE GIRDERS ABOVE, BATMAN FIGHTS TO ACT AS INSIDIOUS FUMES OVERPOWER HIM!
GAS--- (COUGH) DIDN'T FORESEE THAT---ONLY CHANCE IS TO SWING DOWN INTO THAT OFFICE AHEAD OF THEM --- (COUGH)
THE GREAT GOTHAM GARDEN HAS NEVER SEEN A MORE DARING ACROBATIC ACT THAN THE VAST, FLYING SWING THAT BATMAN MAKES AS HE BEGINS TO BLACK OUT!
BATMAN! HE'S GETTING AHEAD OF US!
THE GAS MUST HAVE HIM ALMOST OUT! HURRY!
INSTINCTIVELY, THE DAZED BATMAN USES HIS LAST STRENGTH TO THWART THE CRIMINALS!
HE MANAGED TO LOCK THE SAFE---IT'LL TAKE TIME TO OPEN IT!
AND WE HAVEN'T GOT TIME NOW! HE TOUCHED THE ALARM-BUTTON, BLAST HIM!
SLAM
SAFE
AND AS THE CAPED CRIME-CRUSHER SINKS SENSELESS, DEATH HOVERS CLOSE TO HIM!
BUT IT'LL ONLY TAKE A SECOND TO FIX HIM FOR GOOD, BEFORE WE GET OUT OF HERE!
NO, DON'T SHOOT! I COULDN'T BEAR TO SEE HIM KILLED! I--- MEAN, WE'LL TAKE HIM ALONG--- AS A HOSTAGE!
7

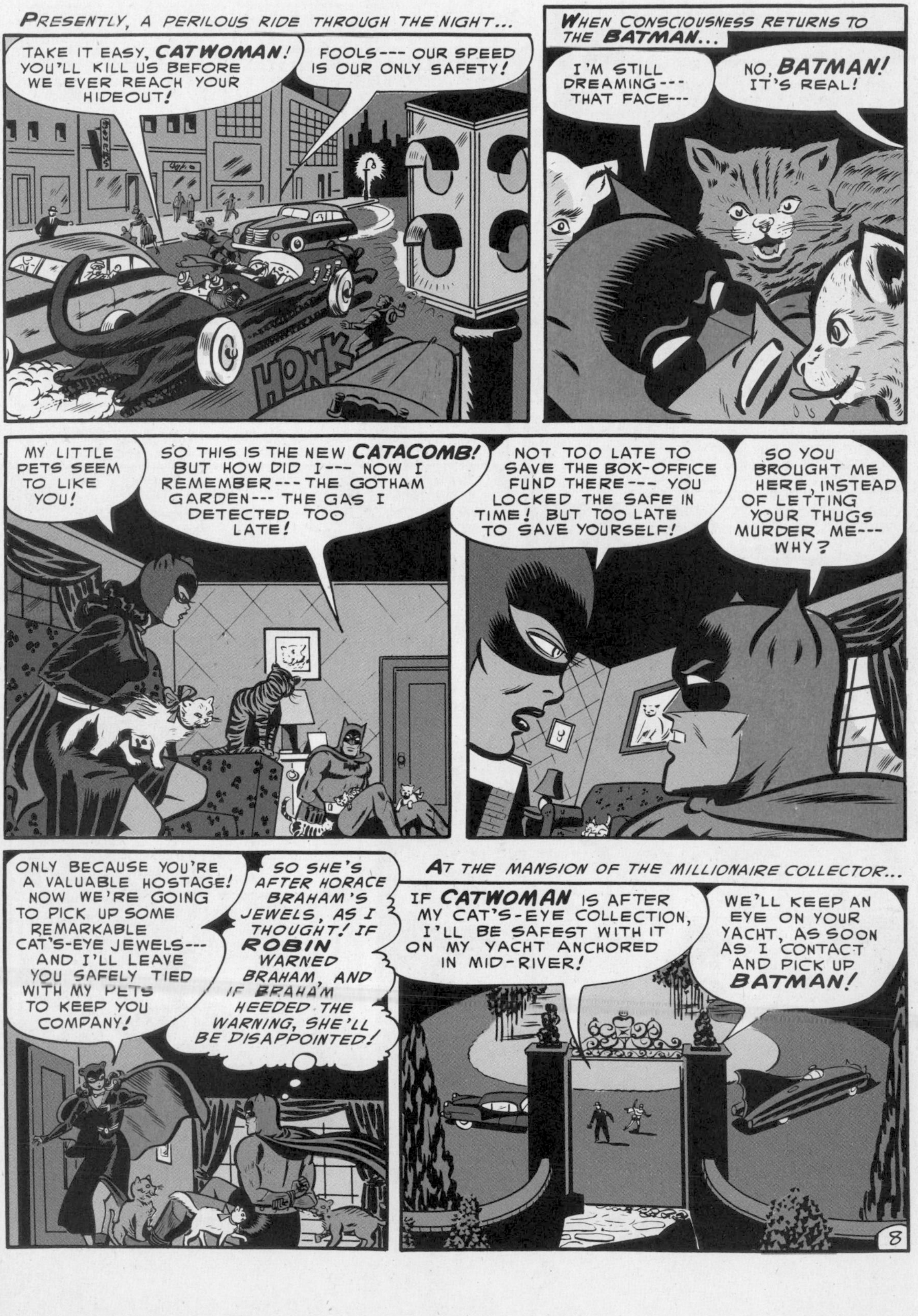
PRESENTLY, A PERILOUS RIDE THROUGH THE NIGHT...
TAKE IT EASY, CATWOMAN! YOU'LL KILL US BEFORE WE EVER REACH YOUR HIDEOUT!
FOOLS--- OUR SPEED IS OUR ONLY SAFETY!
HONK
WHEN CONSCIOUSNESS RETURNS TO THE BATMAN...
I'M STILL DREAMING--- THAT FACE---
NO, BATMAN! IT'S REAL!
MY LITTLE PETS SEEM TO LIKE YOU!
SO THIS IS THE NEW CATACOMB! BUT HOW DID I--- NOW I REMEMBER--- THE GOTHAM GARDEN--- THE GAS I DETECTED TOO LATE!
NOT TOO LATE TO SAVE THE BOX-OFFICE FUND THERE--- YOU LOCKED THE SAFE IN TIME! BUT TOO LATE TO SAVE YOURSELF!
SO YOU BROUGHT ME HERE, INSTEAD OF LETTING YOUR THUGS MURDER ME--- WHY?
ONLY BECAUSE YOU'RE A VALUABLE HOSTAGE! NOW WE'RE GOING TO PICK UP SOME REMARKABLE CAT'S-EYE JEWELS--- AND I'LL LEAVE YOU SAFELY TIED WITH MY PETS TO KEEP YOU COMPANY!
SO SHE'S AFTER HORACE BRAHAM'S JEWELS, AS I THOUGHT! IF ROBIN WARNED BRAHAM, AND IF BRAHAM HEEDED THE WARNING, SHE'LL BE DISAPPOINTED!
AT THE MANSION OF THE MILLIONAIRE COLLECTOR...
IF CATWOMAN IS AFTER MY CAT'S-EYE COLLECTION, I'LL BE SAFEST WITH IT ON MY YACHT ANCHORED IN MID-RIVER!
WE'LL KEEP AN EYE ON YOUR YACHT, AS SOON AS I CONTACT AND PICK UP BATMAN!
8

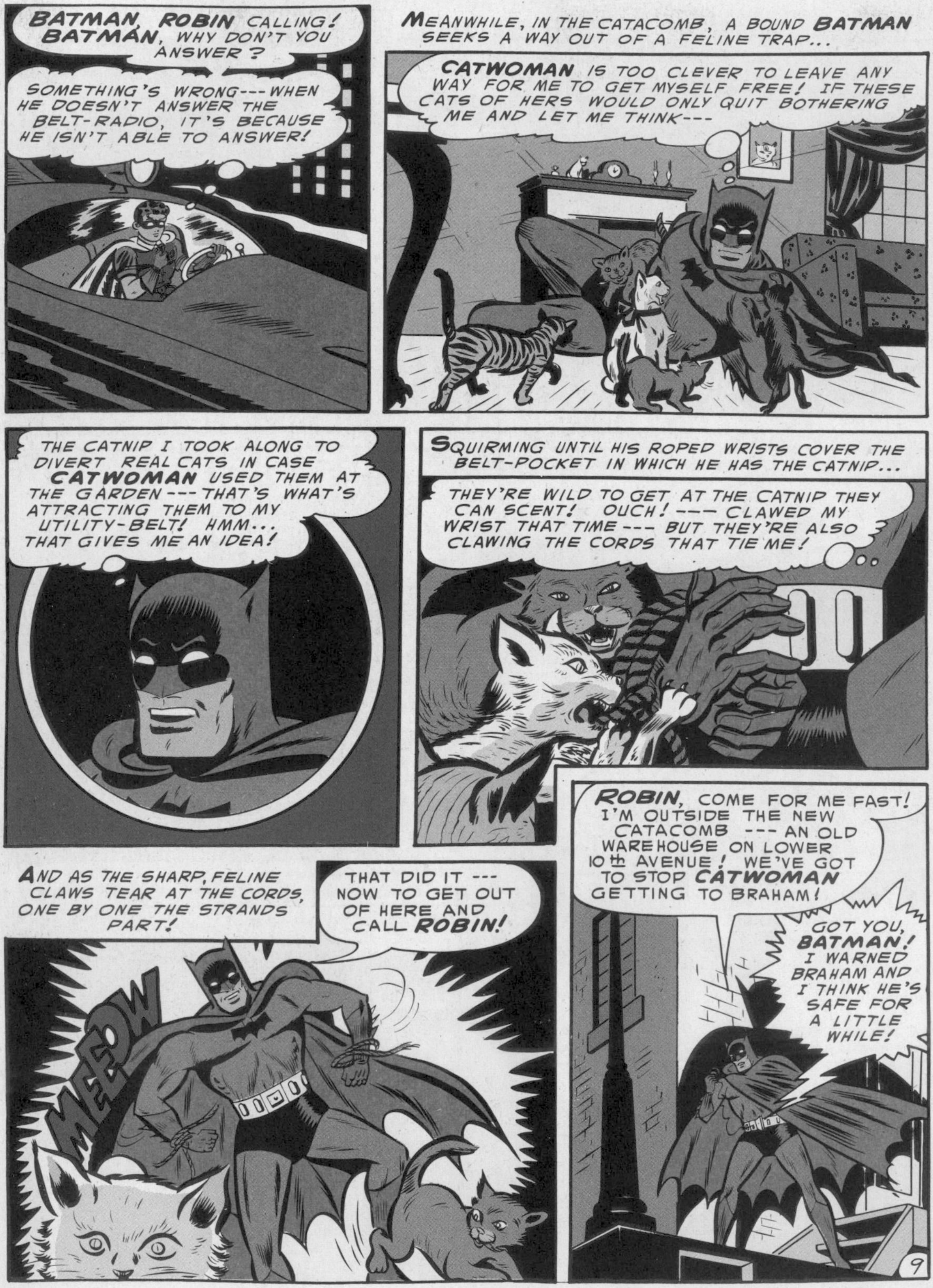
BATMAN, ROBIN CALLING! BATMAN, WHY DON'T YOU ANSWER?
SOMETHING'S WRONG---WHEN HE DOESN'T ANSWER THE BELT-RADIO, IT'S BECAUSE HE ISN'T ABLE TO ANSWER!
MEANWHILE, IN THE CATACOMB, A BOUND BATMAN SEEKS A WAY OUT OF A FELINE TRAP...
CATWOMAN IS TOO CLEVER TO LEAVE ANY WAY FOR ME TO GET MYSELF FREE! IF THESE CATS OF HERS WOULD ONLY QUIT BOTHERING ME AND LET ME THINK---
THE CATNIP I TOOK ALONG TO DIVERT REAL CATS IN CASE CATWOMAN USED THEM AT THE GARDEN---THAT'S WHAT'S ATTRACTING THEM TO MY UTILITY-BELT! HMM... THAT GIVES ME AN IDEA!
SQUIRMING UNTIL HIS ROPED WRISTS COVER THE BELT-POCKET IN WHICH HE HAS THE CATNIP...
THEY'RE WILD TO GET AT THE CATNIP THEY CAN SCENT! OUCH! --- CLAWED MY WRIST THAT TIME --- BUT THEY'RE ALSO CLAWING THE CORDS THAT TIE ME!
AND AS THE SHARP, FELINE CLAWS TEAR AT THE CORDS, ONE BY ONE THE STRANDS PART!
THAT DID IT --- NOW TO GET OUT OF HERE AND CALL ROBIN!
MEEOW
ROBIN, COME FOR ME FAST! I'M OUTSIDE THE NEW CATACOMB --- AN OLD WAREHOUSE ON LOWER 10th AVENUE! WE'VE GOT TO STOP CATWOMAN GETTING TO BRAHAM!
GOT YOU, BATMAN! I WARNED BRAHAM AND I THINK HE'S SAFE FOR A LITTLE WHILE!
9

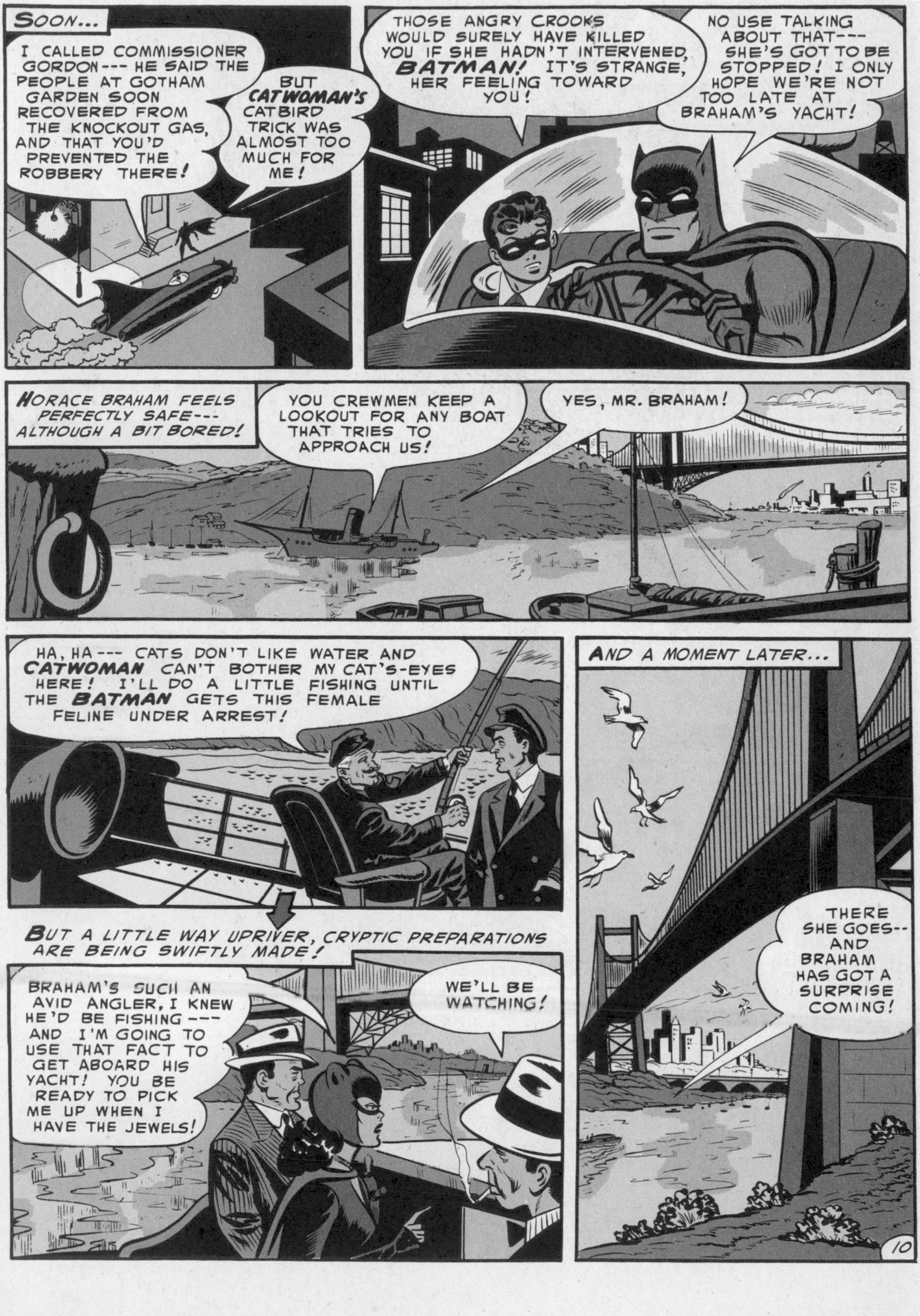
SOON...
I CALLED COMMISSIONER GORDON--- HE SAID THE PEOPLE AT GOTHAM GARDEN SOON RECOVERED FROM THE KNOCKOUT GAS, AND THAT YOU'D PREVENTED THE ROBBERY THERE!
BUT CATWOMAN'S CATBIRD TRICK WAS ALMOST TOO MUCH FOR ME!
THOSE ANGRY CROOKS WOULD SURELY HAVE KILLED YOU IF SHE HADN'T INTERVENED, BATMAN! IT'S STRANGE, HER FEELING TOWARD YOU!
NO USE TALKING ABOUT THAT--- SHE'S GOT TO BE STOPPED! I ONLY HOPE WE'RE NOT TOO LATE AT BRAHAM'S YACHT!
HORACE BRAHAM FEELS PERFECTLY SAFE--- ALTHOUGH A BIT BORED!
YOU CREWMEN KEEP A LOOKOUT FOR ANY BOAT THAT TRIES TO APPROACH US!
YES, MR. BRAHAM!
HA, HA--- CATS DON'T LIKE WATER AND CATWOMAN CAN'T BOTHER MY CAT'S-EYES HERE! I'LL DO A LITTLE FISHING UNTIL THE BATMAN GETS THIS FEMALE FELINE UNDER ARREST!
BUT A LITTLE WAY UPRIVER, CRYPTIC PREPARATIONS ARE BEING SWIFTLY MADE!
BRAHAM'S SUCH AN AVID ANGLER, I KNEW HE'D BE FISHING--- AND I'M GOING TO USE THAT FACT TO GET ABOARD HIS YACHT! YOU BE READY TO PICK ME UP WHEN I HAVE THE JEWELS!
WE'LL BE WATCHING!
AND A MOMENT LATER...
THERE SHE GOES-- AND BRAHAM HAS GOT A SURPRISE COMING!
10

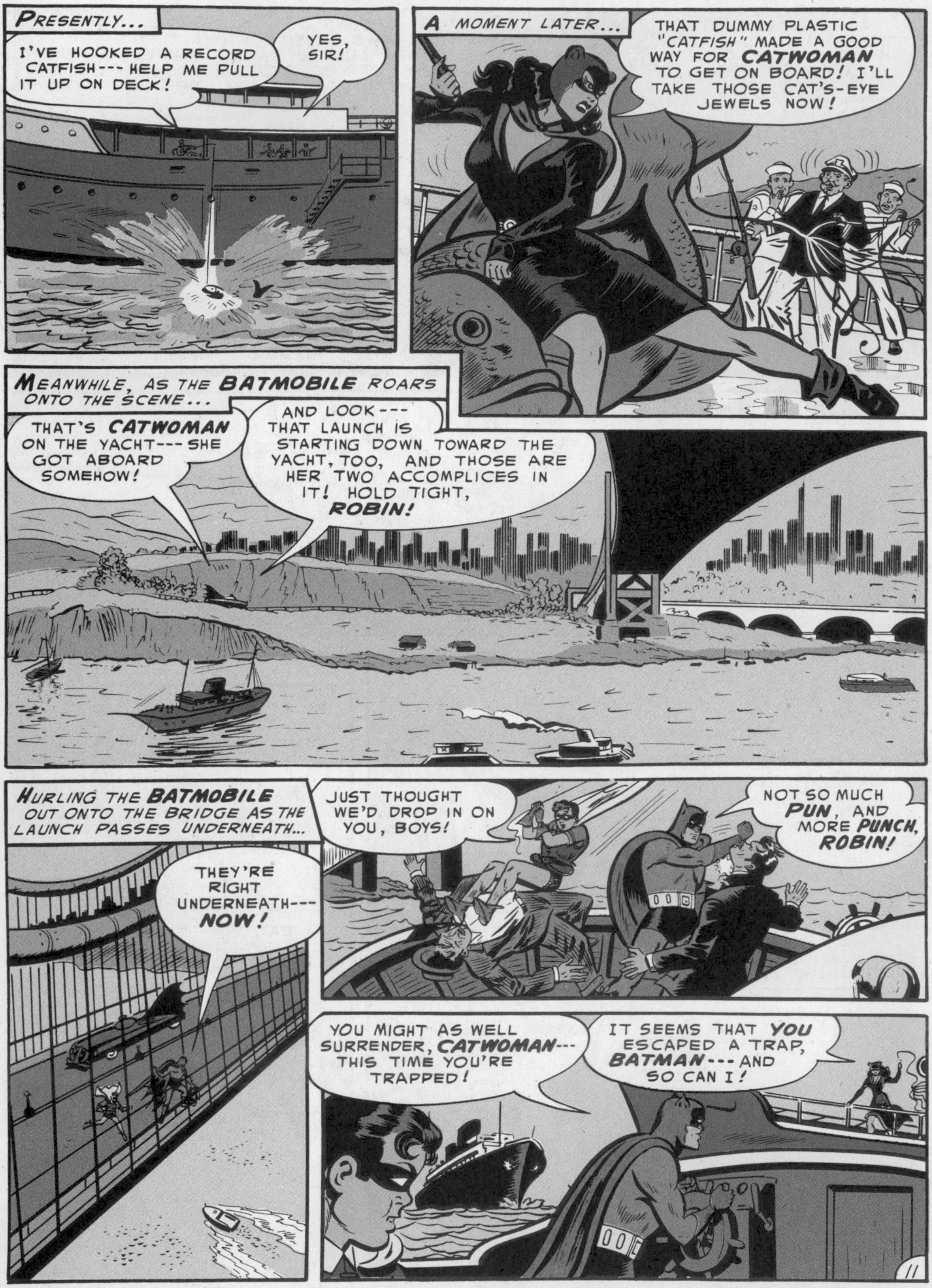
PRESENTLY...
I'VE HOOKED A RECORD CATFISH--- HELP ME PULL IT UP ON DECK!
YES, SIR!
A MOMENT LATER...
THAT DUMMY PLASTIC "CATFISH" MADE A GOOD WAY FOR CATWOMAN TO GET ON BOARD! I'LL TAKE THOSE CAT'S-EYE JEWELS NOW!
MEANWHILE, AS THE BATMOBILE ROARS ONTO THE SCENE...
THAT'S CATWOMAN ON THE YACHT--- SHE GOT ABOARD SOMEHOW!
AND LOOK--- THAT LAUNCH IS STARTING DOWN TOWARD THE YACHT, TOO, AND THOSE ARE HER TWO ACCOMPLICES IN IT! HOLD TIGHT, ROBIN!
HURLING THE BATMOBILE OUT ONTO THE BRIDGE AS THE LAUNCH PASSES UNDERNEATH...
THEY'RE RIGHT UNDERNEATH--- NOW!
JUST THOUGHT WE'D DROP IN ON YOU, BOYS!
NOT SO MUCH PUN, AND MORE PUNCH, ROBIN!
YOU MIGHT AS WELL SURRENDER, CATWOMAN--- THIS TIME YOU'RE TRAPPED!
IT SEEMS THAT YOU ESCAPED A TRAP, BATMAN--- AND SO CAN I!
11

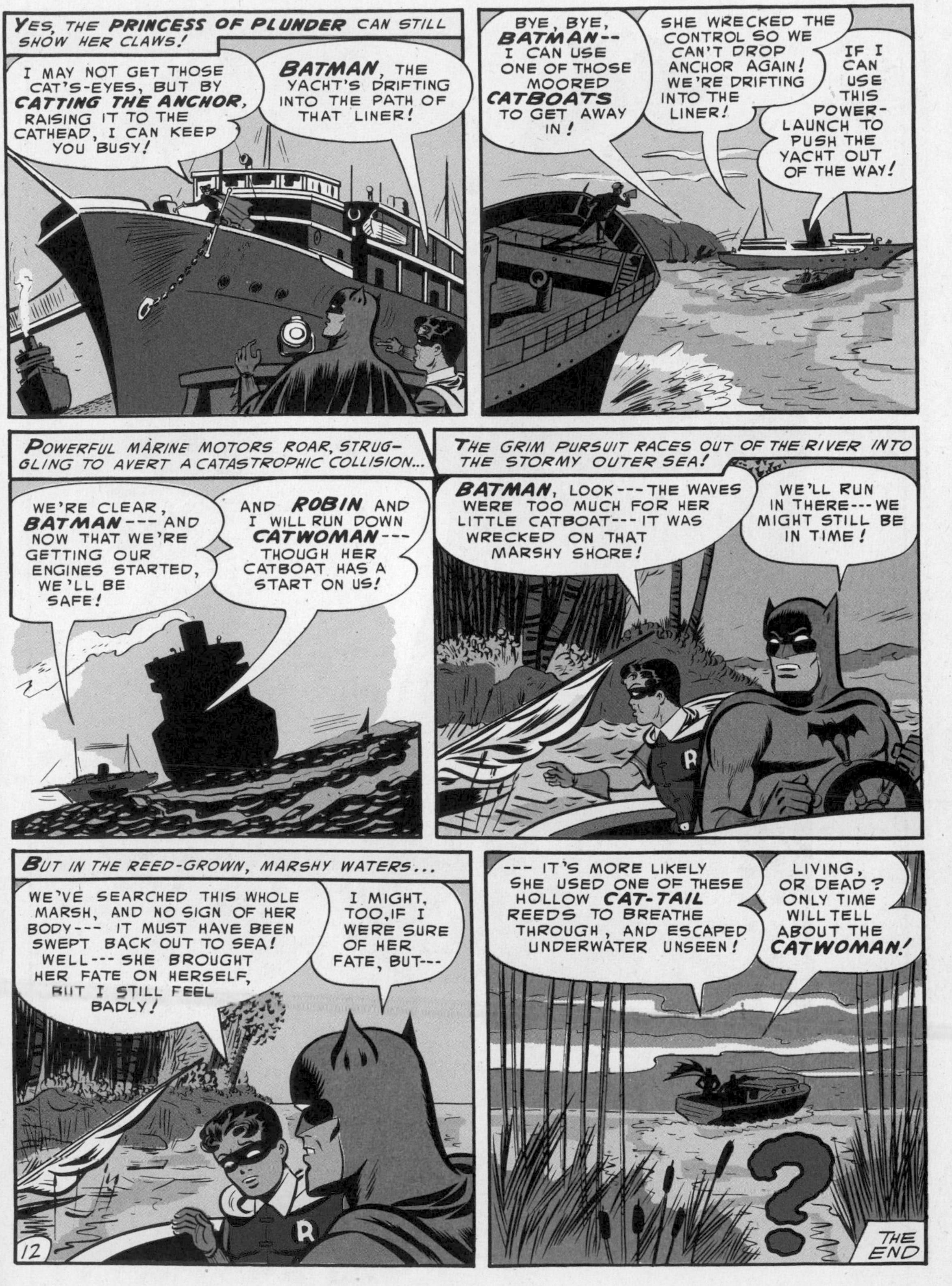
YES, THE PRINCESS OF PLUNDER CAN STILL SHOW HER CLAWS!
I MAY NOT GET THOSE CAT'S-EYES, BUT BY CATTING THE ANCHOR, RAISING IT TO THE CATHEAD, I CAN KEEP YOU BUSY!
BATMAN, THE YACHT'S DRIFTING INTO THE PATH OF THAT LINER!
BYE, BYE, BATMAN-- I CAN USE ONE OF THOSE MOORED CATBOATS TO GET AWAY IN!
SHE WRECKED THE CONTROL SO WE CAN'T DROP ANCHOR AGAIN! WE'RE DRIFTING INTO THE LINER!
IF I CAN USE THIS POWER-LAUNCH TO PUSH THE YACHT OUT OF THE WAY!
POWERFUL MARINE MOTORS ROAR, STRUGGLING TO AVERT A CATASTROPHIC COLLISION...
WE'RE CLEAR, BATMAN--- AND NOW THAT WE'RE GETTING OUR ENGINES STARTED, WE'LL BE SAFE!
AND ROBIN AND I WILL RUN DOWN CATWOMAN--- THOUGH HER CATBOAT HAS A START ON US!
THE GRIM PURSUIT RACES OUT OF THE RIVER INTO THE STORMY OUTER SEA!
BATMAN, LOOK--- THE WAVES WERE TOO MUCH FOR HER LITTLE CATBOAT--- IT WAS WRECKED ON THAT MARSHY SHORE!
WE'LL RUN IN THERE--- WE MIGHT STILL BE IN TIME!
BUT IN THE REED-GROWN, MARSHY WATERS...
WE'VE SEARCHED THIS WHOLE MARSH, AND NO SIGN OF HER BODY--- IT MUST HAVE BEEN SWEPT BACK OUT TO SEA! WELL--- SHE BROUGHT HER FATE ON HERSELF, BUT I STILL FEEL BADLY!
I MIGHT, TOO, IF I WERE SURE OF HER FATE, BUT---
12
--- IT'S MORE LIKELY SHE USED ONE OF THESE HOLLOW CAT-TAIL REEDS TO BREATHE THROUGH, AND ESCAPED UNDERWATER UNSEEN!
LIVING, OR DEAD? ONLY TIME WILL TELL ABOUT THE CATWOMAN!
THE END

pinup Alan Davis

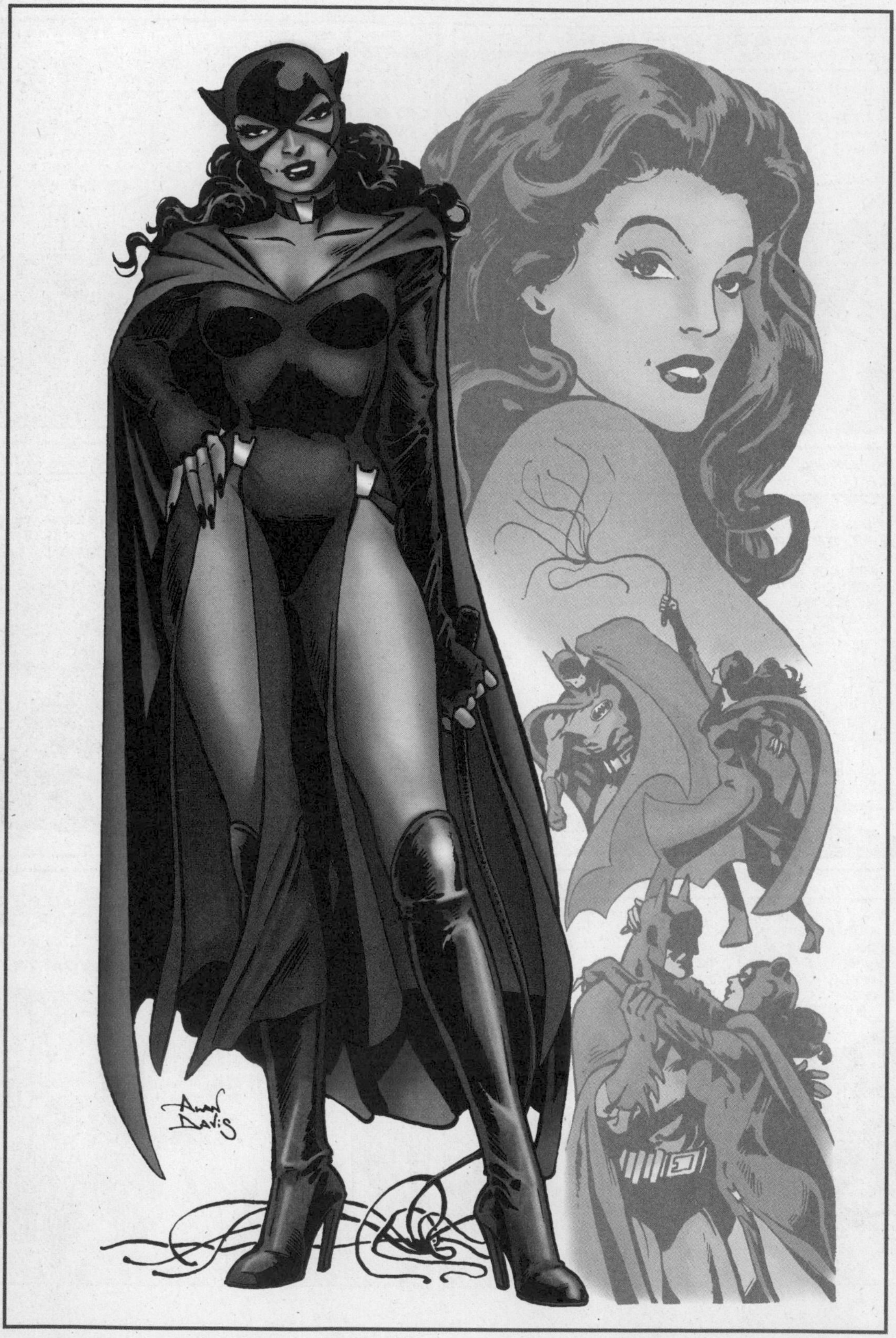

ALAN DAVIS

Originally shown in WHO'S WHO UPDATE '87 #2 (1987). Colored by Drew R. Moore.

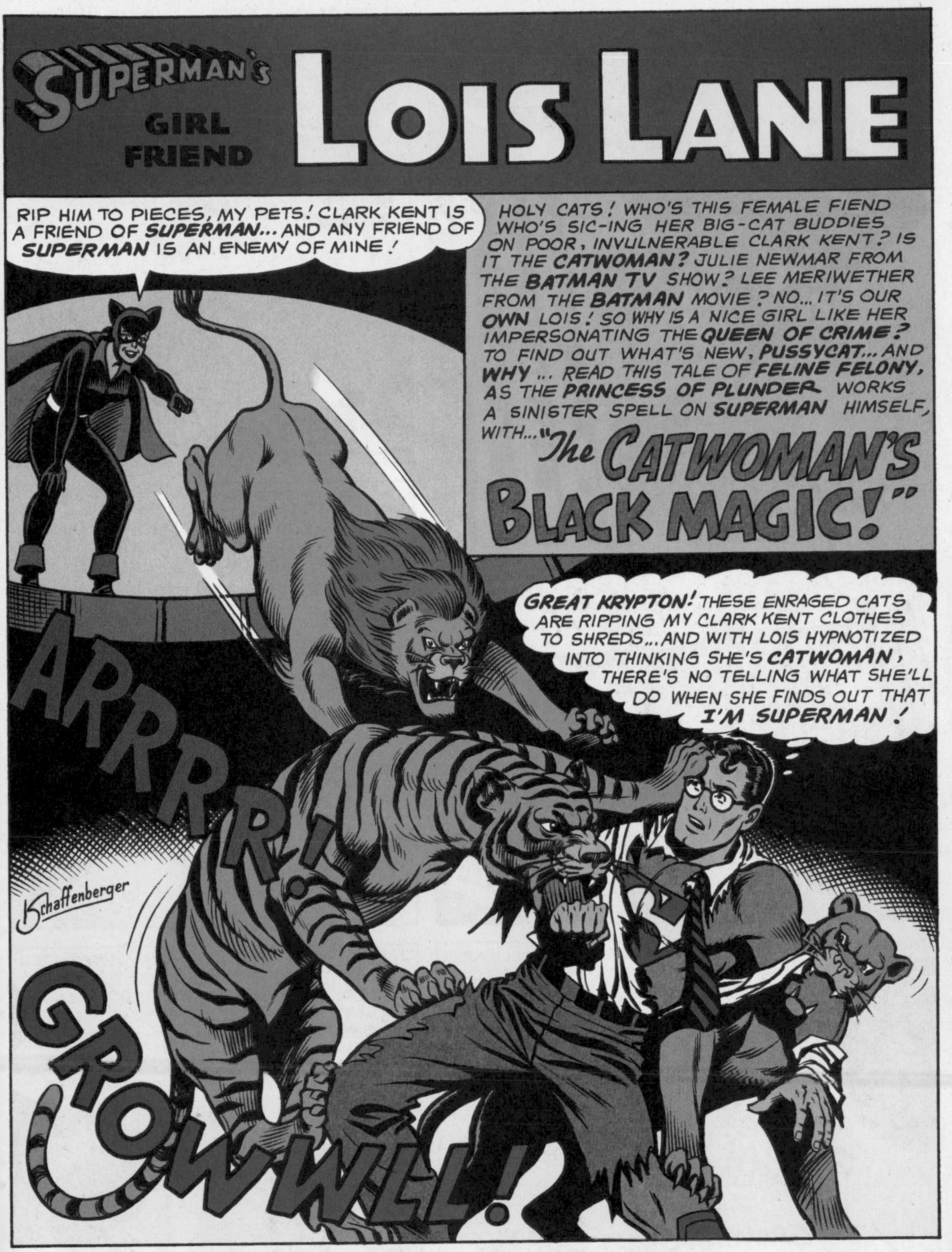
SUPERMAN'S GIRL FRIEND LOIS LANE
RIP HIM TO PIECES, MY PETS! CLARK KENT IS A FRIEND OF SUPERMAN... AND ANY FRIEND OF SUPERMAN IS AN ENEMY OF MINE!
HOLY CATS! WHO'S THIS FEMALE FIEND WHO'S SIC-ING HER BIG-CAT BUDDIES ON POOR, INVULNERABLE CLARK KENT? IS IT THE CATWOMAN? JULIE NEWMAR FROM THE BATMAN TV SHOW? LEE MERIWETHER FROM THE BATMAN MOVIE? NO... IT'S OUR OWN LOIS! SO WHY IS A NICE GIRL LIKE HER IMPERSONATING THE QUEEN OF CRIME? TO FIND OUT WHAT'S NEW, PUSSYCAT... AND WHY... READ THIS TALE OF FELINE FELONY, AS THE PRINCESS OF PLUNDER WORKS A SINISTER SPELL ON SUPERMAN HIMSELF, WITH..."The CATWOMAN'S BLACK MAGIC!"
GREAT KRYPTON! THESE ENRAGED CATS ARE RIPPING MY CLARK KENT CLOTHES TO SHREDS... AND WITH LOIS HYPNOTIZED INTO THINKING SHE'S CATWOMAN, THERE'S NO TELLING WHAT SHE'LL DO WHEN SHE FINDS OUT THAT I'M SUPERMAN!
ARRRRR!
GROWWLL!
Schaffenberger

ONE DAY, HIGH OVER STARTLED **METROPOLIS**...

LOOK! IS IT A PLANE?

IT'S TOO BIG TO BE **SUPERMAN**!

GOOD GRIEF! IT LOOKS LIKE A **ROC**, THE GIANT BIRD OF ARABIAN LEGEND! IT CAN'T BE FOR REAL!

AT THE **DAILY PLANET** OFFICE, AS LOIS LANE AND CLARK KENT WATCH...

CLARK! IT'S DROPPING THOUSANDS OF LEAFLETS! IT'S AN AIRCRAFT! HOW DOES IT WORK? IF ONLY I HAD **SUPERMAN'S** X-RAY VISION!

SINCE **I'M** REALLY **SUPERMAN**, THAT'S NO PROBLEM FOR ME!

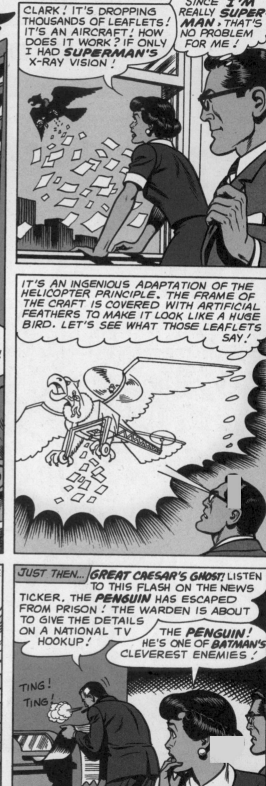

IT'S AN INGENIOUS ADAPTATION OF THE HELICOPTER PRINCIPLE. THE FRAME OF THE CRAFT IS COVERED WITH ARTIFICIAL FEATHERS TO MAKE IT LOOK LIKE A HUGE BIRD. LET'S SEE WHAT THOSE LEAFLETS SAY!

MOMENTS LATER... HARVEY HAWKS! HE'S THE MILLIONAIRE BIRD-FANCIER WHO OWNS SOME OF THE RAREST FEATHERED CREATURES ON EARTH. THE COLLECTION MUST BE WORTH A FORTUNE!

Announcing the
GRAND OPENING
OF THE
**METROPOLIS
BIRD SANCTUARY**
AUG. 25 at PHOENIX CASTLE
sponsored by
HARVEY HAWKS

JUST THEN... **GREAT CAESAR'S GHOST!** LISTEN TO THIS FLASH ON THE NEWS TICKER. THE **PENGUIN** HAS ESCAPED FROM PRISON! THE WARDEN IS ABOUT TO GIVE THE DETAILS ON A NATIONAL TV HOOKUP!

THE **PENGUIN**! HE'S ONE OF **BATMAN'S** CLEVEREST ENEMIES!

TING!

TING!

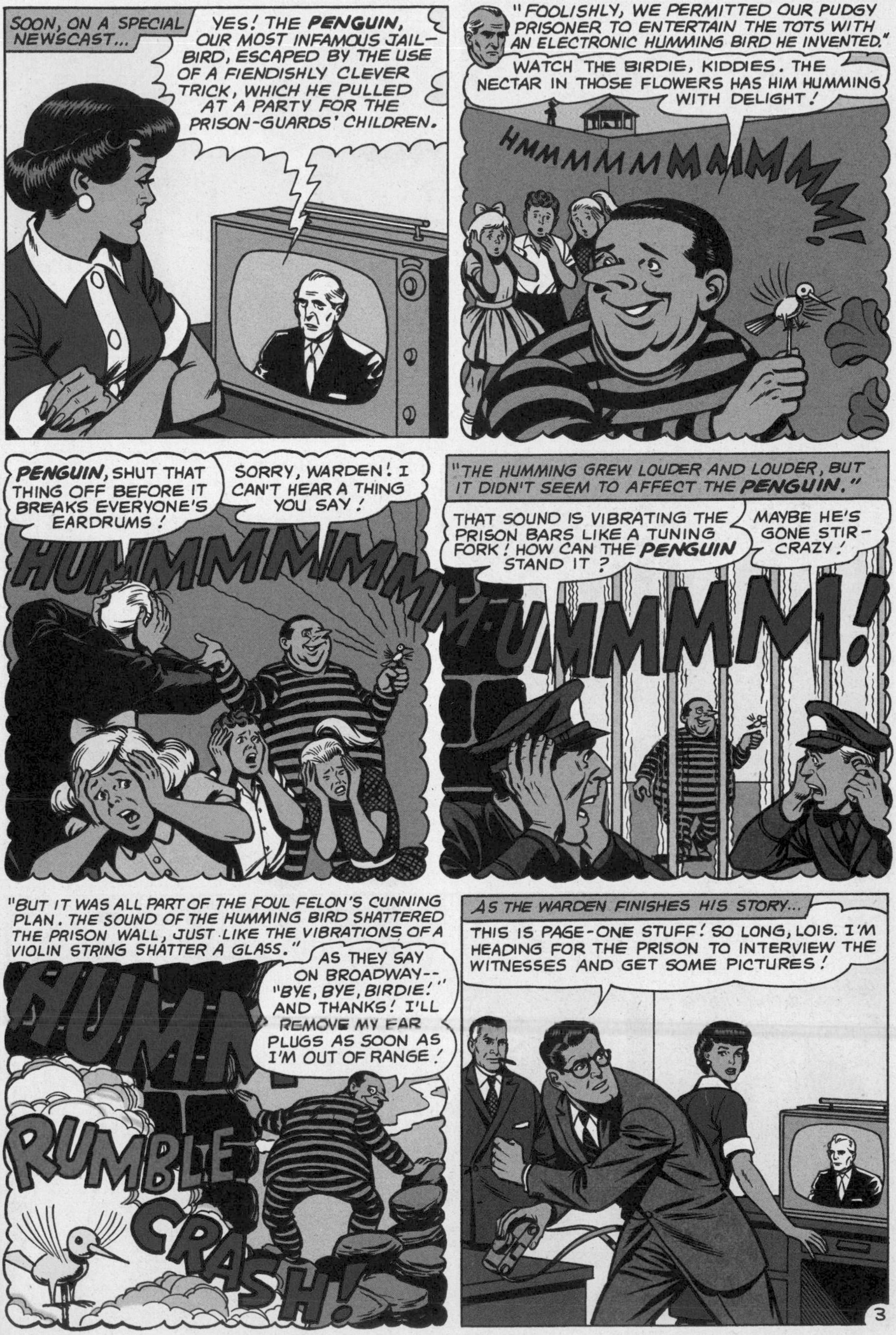
SOON, ON A SPECIAL NEWSCAST...
YES! THE PENGUIN, OUR MOST INFAMOUS JAIL-BIRD, ESCAPED BY THE USE OF A FIENDISHLY CLEVER TRICK, WHICH HE PULLED AT A PARTY FOR THE PRISON-GUARDS' CHILDREN.
"FOOLISHLY, WE PERMITTED OUR PUDGY PRISONER TO ENTERTAIN THE TOTS WITH AN ELECTRONIC HUMMING BIRD HE INVENTED."
WATCH THE BIRDIE, KIDDIES. THE NECTAR IN THOSE FLOWERS HAS HIM HUMMING WITH DELIGHT!
PENGUIN, SHUT THAT THING OFF BEFORE IT BREAKS EVERYONE'S EARDRUMS!
SORRY, WARDEN! I CAN'T HEAR A THING YOU SAY!
HUMMMMMMMMM-UMMMMM!
"THE HUMMING GREW LOUDER AND LOUDER, BUT IT DIDN'T SEEM TO AFFECT THE PENGUIN."
THAT SOUND IS VIBRATING THE PRISON BARS LIKE A TUNING FORK! HOW CAN THE PENGUIN STAND IT?
MAYBE HE'S GONE STIR-CRAZY!
"BUT IT WAS ALL PART OF THE FOUL FELON'S CUNNING PLAN. THE SOUND OF THE HUMMING BIRD SHATTERED THE PRISON WALL, JUST LIKE THE VIBRATIONS OF A VIOLIN STRING SHATTER A GLASS."
AS THEY SAY ON BROADWAY-- "BYE, BYE, BIRDIE!" AND THANKS! I'LL REMOVE MY EAR PLUGS AS SOON AS I'M OUT OF RANGE!
HUMM
RUMBLE
CRASH!
AS THE WARDEN FINISHES HIS STORY...
THIS IS PAGE-ONE STUFF! SO LONG, LOIS. I'M HEADING FOR THE PRISON TO INTERVIEW THE WITNESSES AND GET SOME PICTURES!
3

PRESENTLY, IN A NEARBY ALLEY...

THIS EMERGENCY CALLS FOR *SUPERMAN* TO TAKE A HAND! I'LL CONTACT *BATMAN* AT ONCE!

MEANWHILE, LOIS' WILY BRAIN GOES INTO HIGH GEAR...

HMM...THE *PENGUIN* ALWAYS USES BIRD THEMES FOR HIS CRIMES! HE'S BOUND TO BE ATTRACTED TO THE NEW BIRD SANCTUARY! AND THAT GIVES ME AN IDEA!

Announcing the GRAND OPENING OF THE METROPOLIS BIRD SANCTUARY AUG. 25, PHOENIX CASTLE SPONSORED BY HARVEY HAWKS

THAT AFTERNOON, LOIS VISITS *PHOENIX CASTLE*...

THE *PHOENIX* IS A FAMOUS BIRD OF GREEK LEGEND. I GUESS THAT'S WHY HARVEY HAWKS HOUSED HIS RARE BIRD COLLECTION HERE... THE EXHIBIT WON'T OPEN TILL NEXT WEEK, BUT PERHAPS THEY'LL LET ME IN!

THE WATCHMAN IS ASLEEP! HMM...WHILE HE WAS NAPPING, THE *PENGUIN* COULD HAVE SLIPPED PAST HIM! I'LL GO INSIDE AND CHECK!

SOON, WITHIN... FANTASTIC! THIS EXHIBITION HALL CONTAINS THE RAREST AND MOST VALUABLE FEATHERED CREATURES IN THE WORLD! THAT MILLIONAIRE, HAWKS, MUST HAVE SPENT A MINT GATHERING THEM!

4

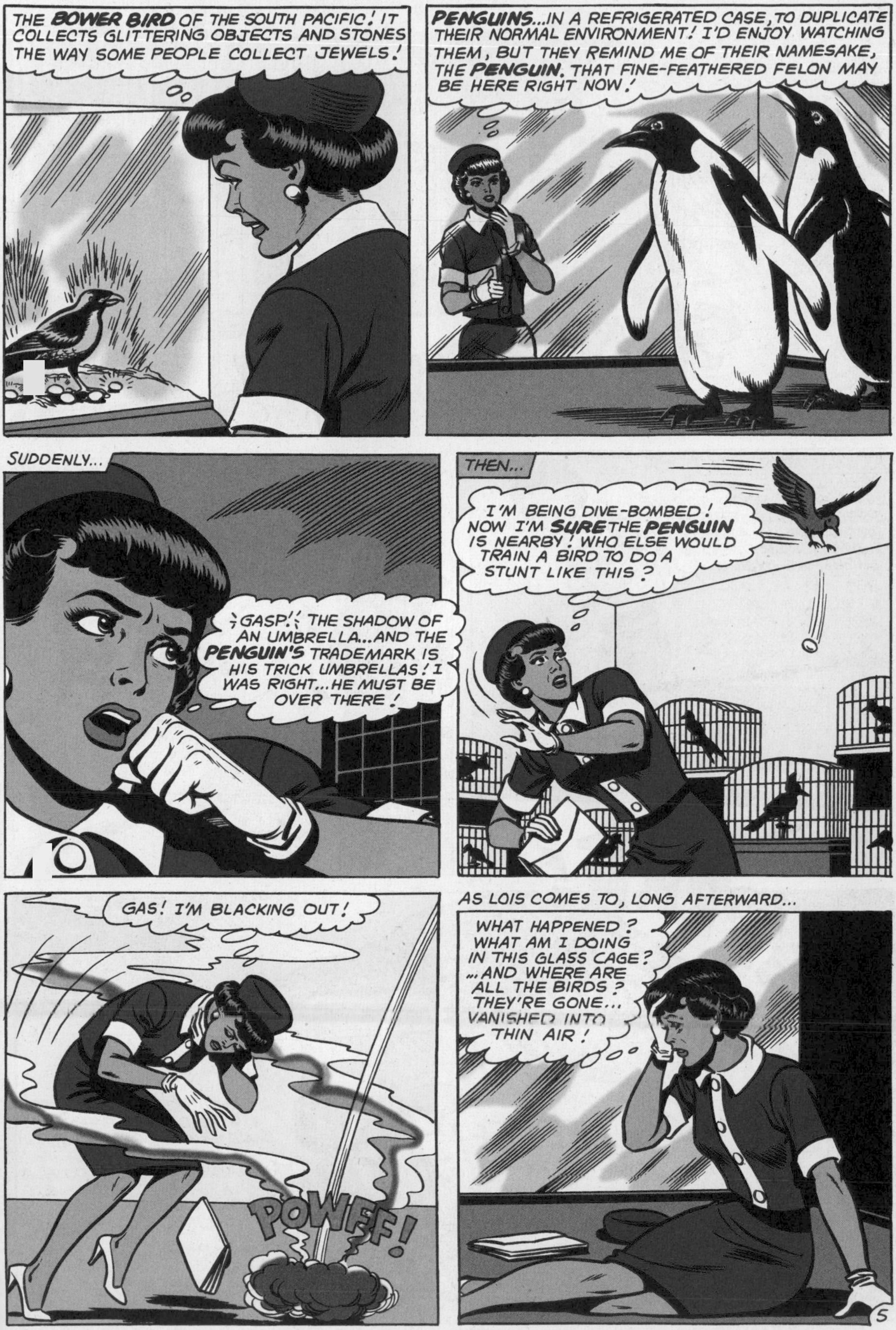
THE BOWER BIRD OF THE SOUTH PACIFIC! IT COLLECTS GLITTERING OBJECTS AND STONES THE WAY SOME PEOPLE COLLECT JEWELS!
PENGUINS...IN A REFRIGERATED CASE, TO DUPLICATE THEIR NORMAL ENVIRONMENT! I'D ENJOY WATCHING THEM, BUT THEY REMIND ME OF THEIR NAMESAKE, THE PENGUIN. THAT FINE-FEATHERED FELON MAY BE HERE RIGHT NOW!
SUDDENLY...
GASP! THE SHADOW OF AN UMBRELLA...AND THE PENGUIN'S TRADEMARK IS HIS TRICK UMBRELLAS! I WAS RIGHT...HE MUST BE OVER THERE!
THEN...
I'M BEING DIVE-BOMBED! NOW I'M SURE THE PENGUIN IS NEARBY! WHO ELSE WOULD TRAIN A BIRD TO DO A STUNT LIKE THIS?
GAS! I'M BLACKING OUT!
POWFF!
AS LOIS COMES TO, LONG AFTERWARD...
WHAT HAPPENED? WHAT AM I DOING IN THIS GLASS CAGE? ...AND WHERE ARE ALL THE BIRDS? THEY'RE GONE... VANISHED INTO THIN AIR!
5

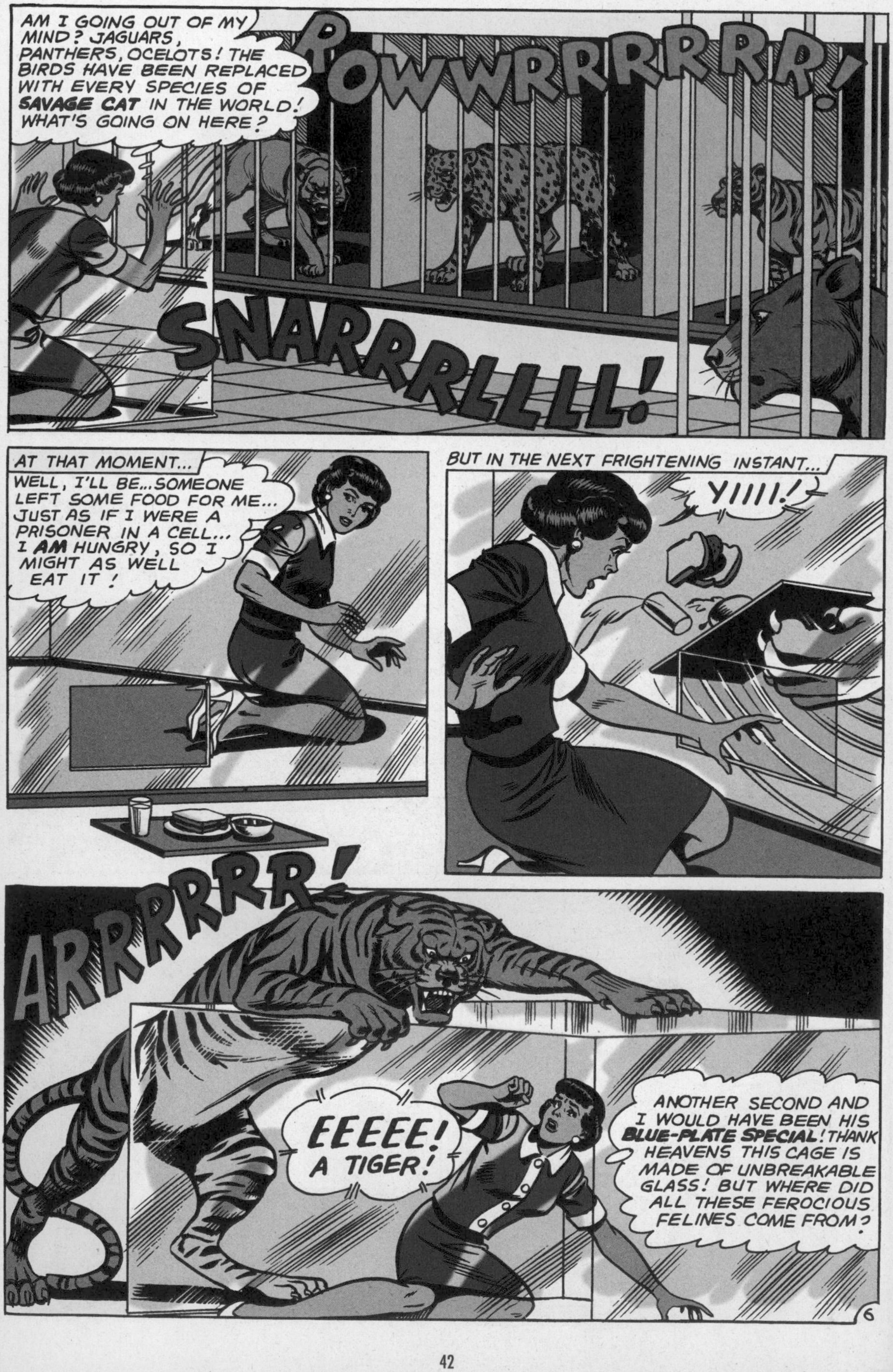
AM I GOING OUT OF MY MIND? JAGUARS, PANTHERS, OCELOTS! THE BIRDS HAVE BEEN REPLACED WITH EVERY SPECIES OF SAVAGE CAT IN THE WORLD! WHAT'S GOING ON HERE?
ROWWRRRRRRR!
SNARRRLLLLL!
AT THAT MOMENT...
WELL, I'LL BE...SOMEONE LEFT SOME FOOD FOR ME... JUST AS IF I WERE A PRISONER IN A CELL... I AM HUNGRY, SO I MIGHT AS WELL EAT IT!
BUT IN THE NEXT FRIGHTENING INSTANT...
YIIII!
ARRRRRRR!
EEEEE! A TIGER!
ANOTHER SECOND AND I WOULD HAVE BEEN HIS BLUE-PLATE SPECIAL! THANK HEAVENS THIS CAGE IS MADE OF UNBREAKABLE GLASS! BUT WHERE DID ALL THESE FEROCIOUS FELINES COME FROM?
6

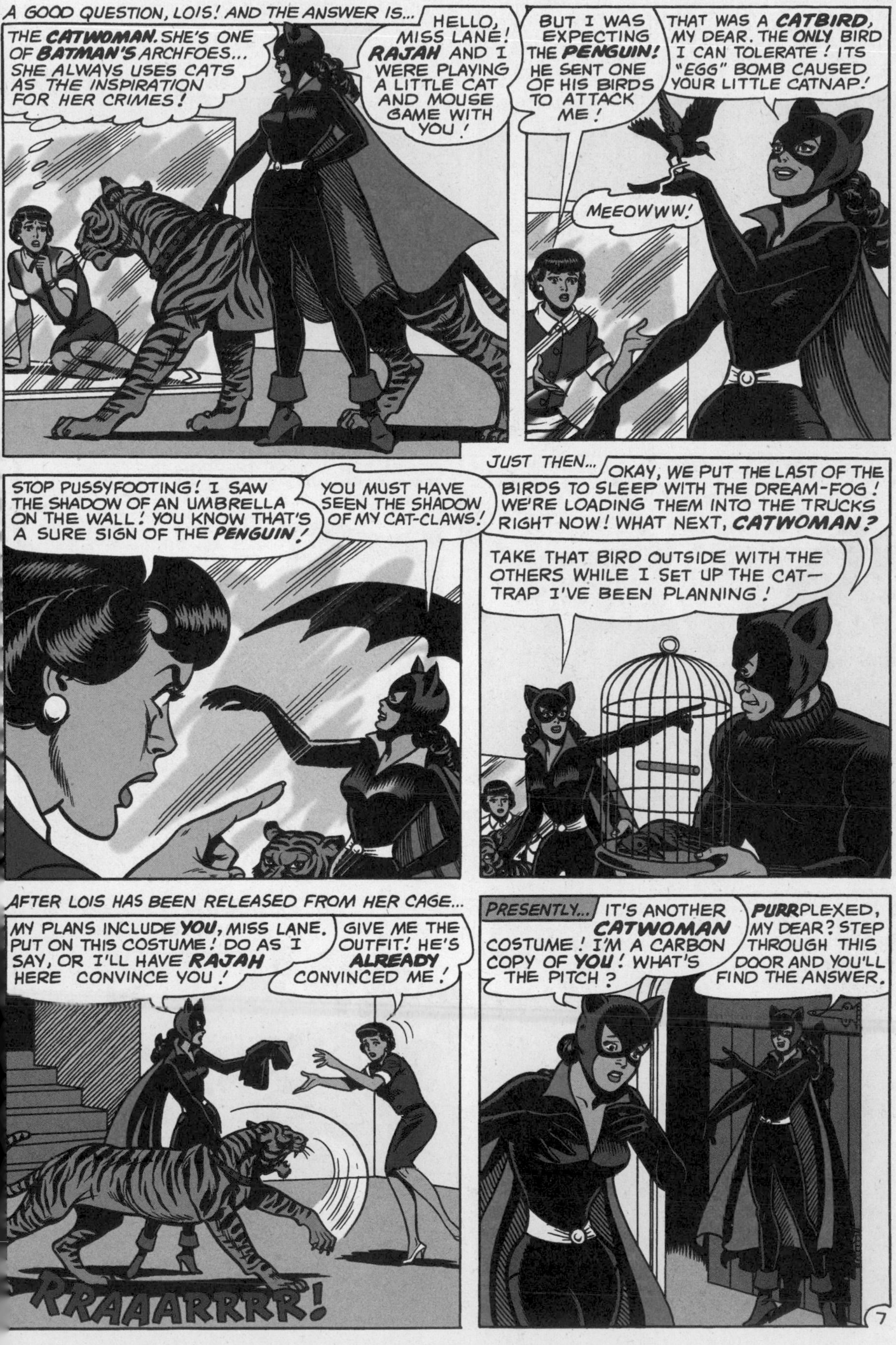
A GOOD QUESTION, LOIS! AND THE ANSWER IS...
THE CATWOMAN. SHE'S ONE OF BATMAN'S ARCHFOES... SHE ALWAYS USES CATS AS THE INSPIRATION FOR HER CRIMES!
HELLO, MISS LANE! RAJAH AND I WERE PLAYING A LITTLE CAT AND MOUSE GAME WITH YOU!
BUT I WAS EXPECTING THE PENGUIN! HE SENT ONE OF HIS BIRDS TO ATTACK ME!
THAT WAS A CATBIRD, MY DEAR. THE ONLY BIRD I CAN TOLERATE! ITS "EGG" BOMB CAUSED YOUR LITTLE CATNAP!
MEEOWWW!
STOP PUSSYFOOTING! I SAW THE SHADOW OF AN UMBRELLA ON THE WALL! YOU KNOW THAT'S A SURE SIGN OF THE PENGUIN!
YOU MUST HAVE SEEN THE SHADOW OF MY CAT-CLAWS!
JUST THEN...
OKAY, WE PUT THE LAST OF THE BIRDS TO SLEEP WITH THE DREAM-FOG! WE'RE LOADING THEM INTO THE TRUCKS RIGHT NOW! WHAT NEXT, CATWOMAN?
TAKE THAT BIRD OUTSIDE WITH THE OTHERS WHILE I SET UP THE CAT-TRAP I'VE BEEN PLANNING!
AFTER LOIS HAS BEEN RELEASED FROM HER CAGE...
MY PLANS INCLUDE YOU, MISS LANE. PUT ON THIS COSTUME! DO AS I SAY, OR I'LL HAVE RAJAH HERE CONVINCE YOU!
GIVE ME THE OUTFIT! HE'S ALREADY CONVINCED ME!
RRAAARRRR!
PRESENTLY...
IT'S ANOTHER CATWOMAN COSTUME! I'M A CARBON COPY OF YOU! WHAT'S THE PITCH?
PURRPLEXED, MY DEAR? STEP THROUGH THIS DOOR AND YOU'LL FIND THE ANSWER.
7

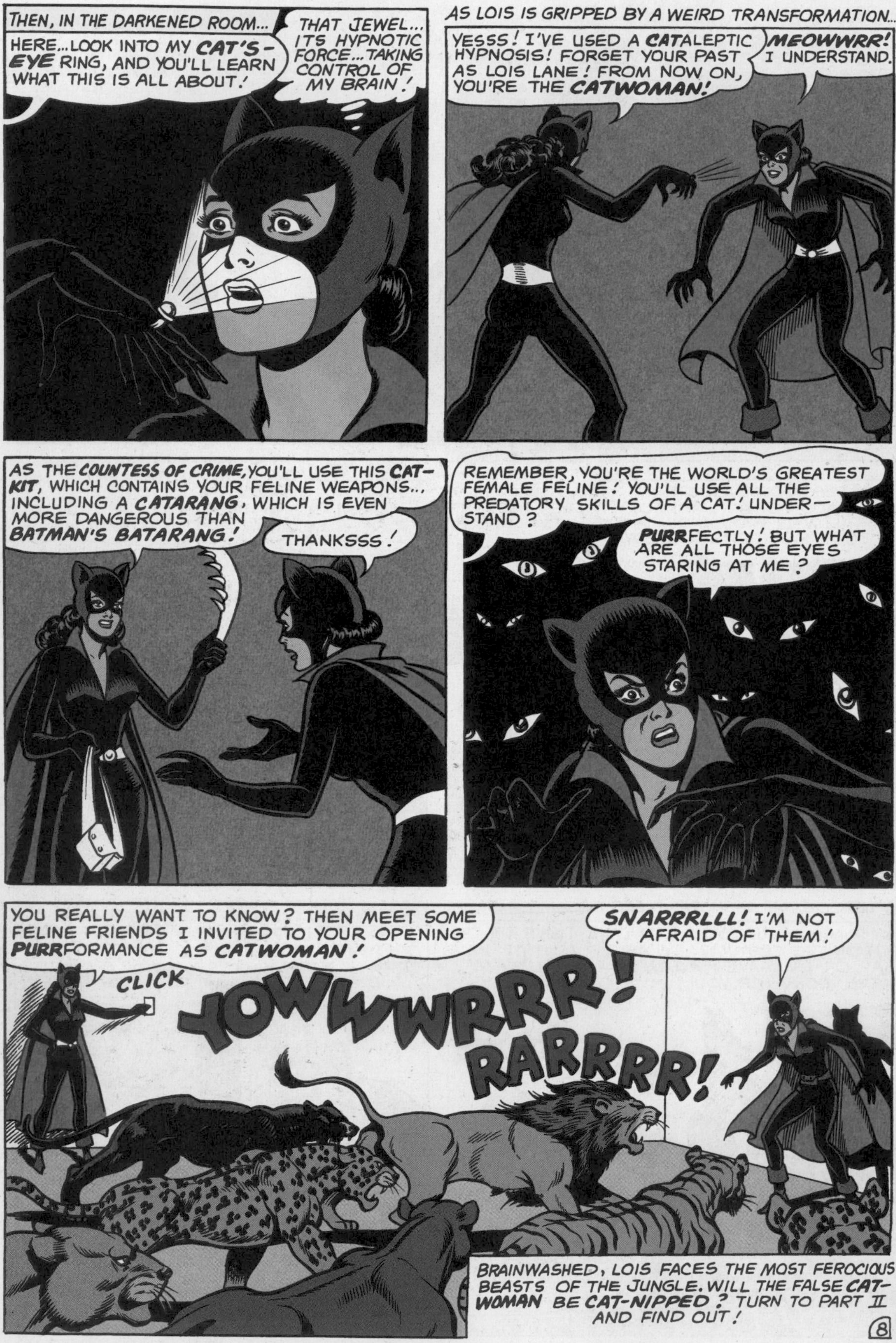
THEN, IN THE DARKENED ROOM...
HERE...LOOK INTO MY CAT'S-EYE RING, AND YOU'LL LEARN WHAT THIS IS ALL ABOUT!
THAT JEWEL... ITS HYPNOTIC FORCE...TAKING CONTROL OF MY BRAIN!
AS LOIS IS GRIPPED BY A WEIRD TRANSFORMATION...
YESSS! I'VE USED A CATALEPTIC HYPNOSIS! FORGET YOUR PAST AS LOIS LANE! FROM NOW ON, YOU'RE THE CATWOMAN!
MEOWWRR! I UNDERSTAND.
AS THE COUNTESS OF CRIME, YOU'LL USE THIS CAT-KIT, WHICH CONTAINS YOUR FELINE WEAPONS... INCLUDING A CATARANG, WHICH IS EVEN MORE DANGEROUS THAN BATMAN'S BATARANG!
THANKSSS!
REMEMBER, YOU'RE THE WORLD'S GREATEST FEMALE FELINE! YOU'LL USE ALL THE PREDATORY SKILLS OF A CAT! UNDERSTAND?
PURRFECTLY! BUT WHAT ARE ALL THOSE EYES STARING AT ME?
YOU REALLY WANT TO KNOW? THEN MEET SOME FELINE FRIENDS I INVITED TO YOUR OPENING PURRFORMANCE AS CATWOMAN!
CLICK
YOWWWRRR!
RARRRRR!
SNARRRLLL! I'M NOT AFRAID OF THEM!
BRAINWASHED, LOIS FACES THE MOST FEROCIOUS BEASTS OF THE JUNGLE. WILL THE FALSE CAT-WOMAN BE CAT-NIPPED? TURN TO PART II AND FIND OUT!
8

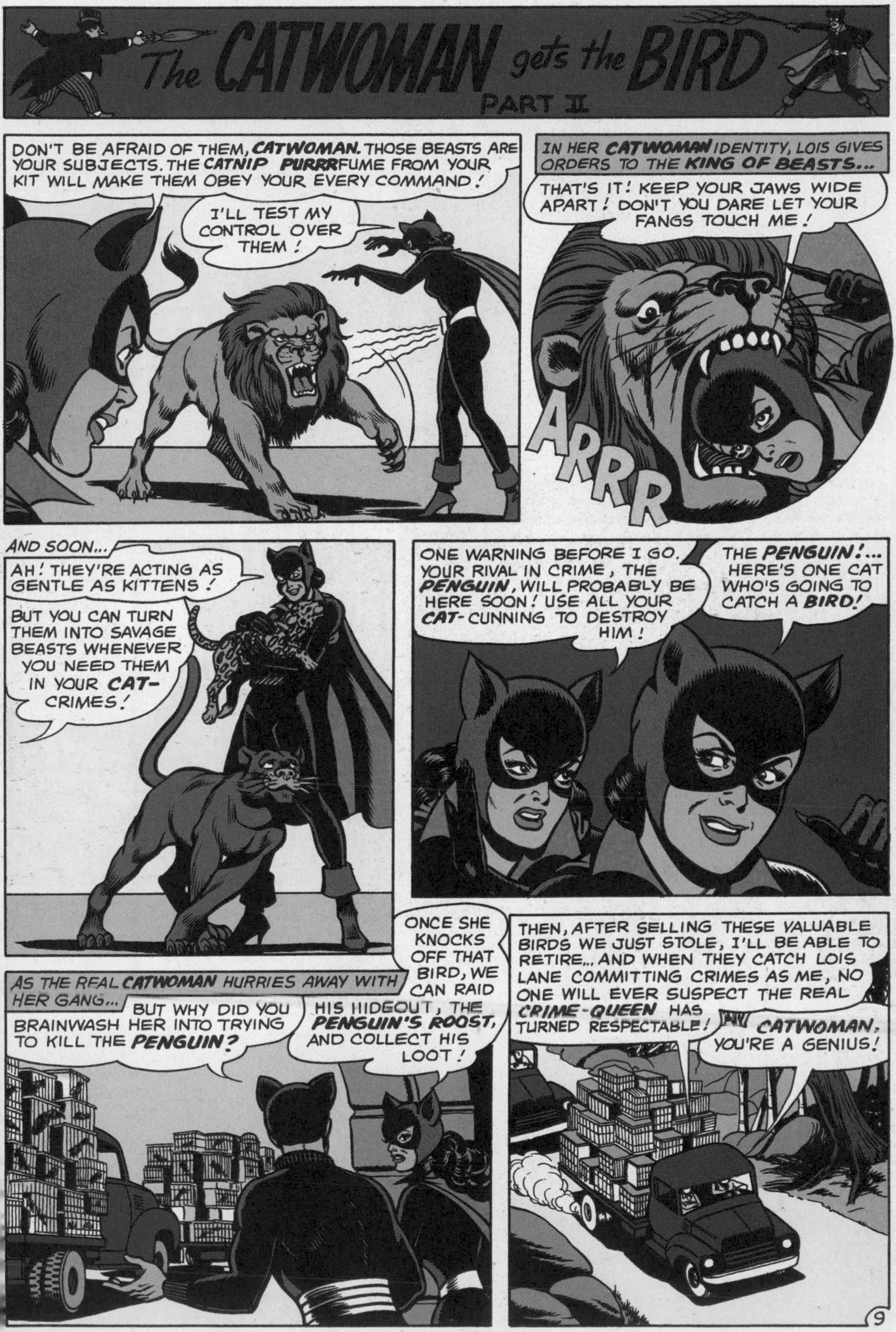
The CATWOMAN gets the BIRD
PART II
DON'T BE AFRAID OF THEM, CATWOMAN. THOSE BEASTS ARE YOUR SUBJECTS. THE CATNIP PURRRFUME FROM YOUR KIT WILL MAKE THEM OBEY YOUR EVERY COMMAND!
I'LL TEST MY CONTROL OVER THEM!
IN HER CATWOMAN IDENTITY, LOIS GIVES ORDERS TO THE KING OF BEASTS...
THAT'S IT! KEEP YOUR JAWS WIDE APART! DON'T YOU DARE LET YOUR FANGS TOUCH ME!
ARRRR
AND SOON...
AH! THEY'RE ACTING AS GENTLE AS KITTENS!
BUT YOU CAN TURN THEM INTO SAVAGE BEASTS WHENEVER YOU NEED THEM IN YOUR CAT-CRIMES!
ONE WARNING BEFORE I GO. YOUR RIVAL IN CRIME, THE PENGUIN, WILL PROBABLY BE HERE SOON! USE ALL YOUR CAT-CUNNING TO DESTROY HIM!
THE PENGUIN!... HERE'S ONE CAT WHO'S GOING TO CATCH A BIRD!
AS THE REAL CATWOMAN HURRIES AWAY WITH HER GANG...
BUT WHY DID YOU BRAINWASH HER INTO TRYING TO KILL THE PENGUIN?
ONCE SHE KNOCKS OFF THAT BIRD, WE CAN RAID HIS HIDEOUT, THE PENGUIN'S ROOST, AND COLLECT HIS LOOT!
THEN, AFTER SELLING THESE VALUABLE BIRDS WE JUST STOLE, I'LL BE ABLE TO RETIRE... AND WHEN THEY CATCH LOIS LANE COMMITTING CRIMES AS ME, NO ONE WILL EVER SUSPECT THE REAL CRIME-QUEEN HAS TURNED RESPECTABLE!
CATWOMAN, YOU'RE A GENIUS!
9

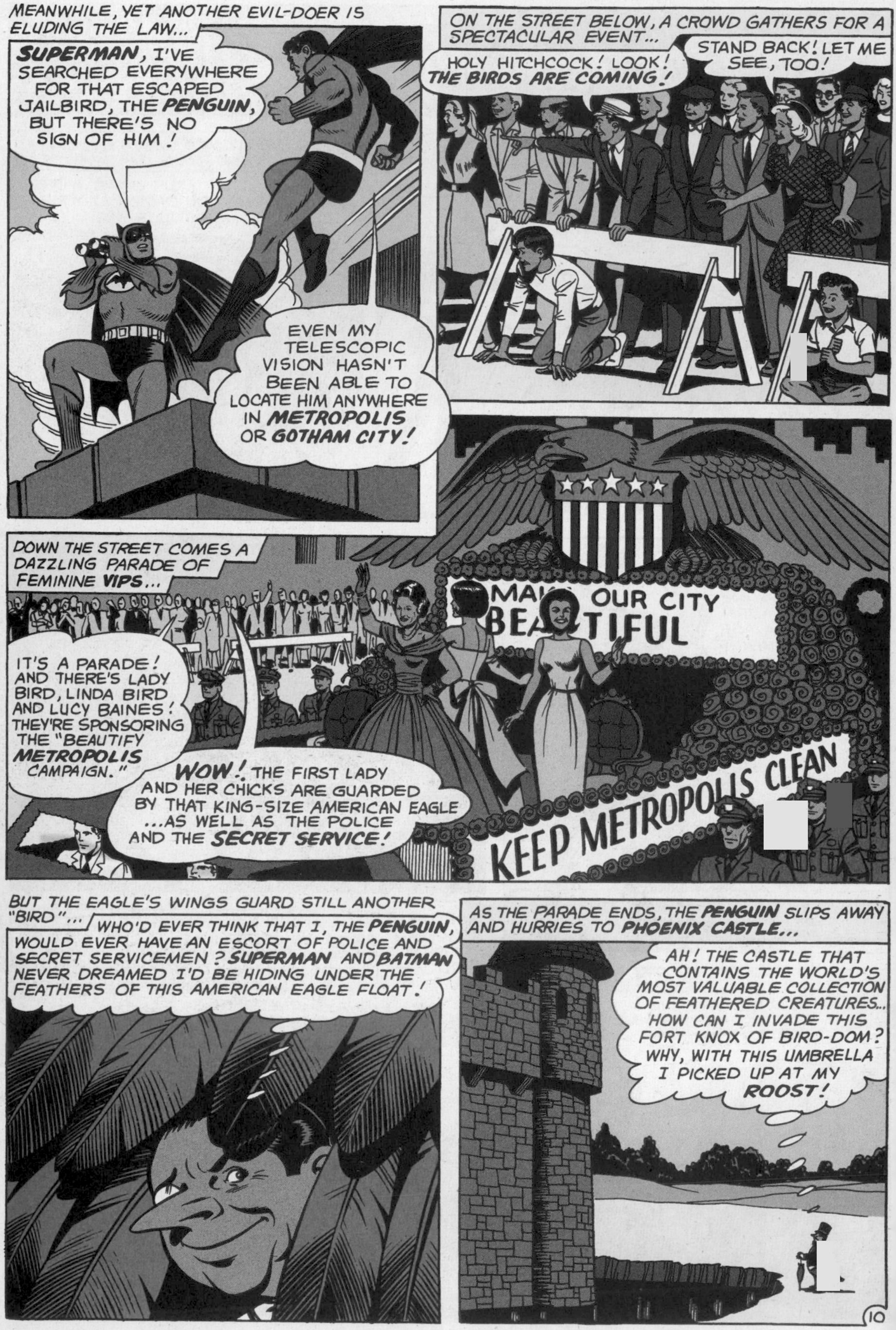

MEANWHILE, YET ANOTHER EVIL-DOER IS ELUDING THE LAW...
SUPERMAN, I'VE SEARCHED EVERYWHERE FOR THAT ESCAPED JAILBIRD, THE PENGUIN, BUT THERE'S NO SIGN OF HIM!
EVEN MY TELESCOPIC VISION HASN'T BEEN ABLE TO LOCATE HIM ANYWHERE IN METROPOLIS OR GOTHAM CITY!
ON THE STREET BELOW, A CROWD GATHERS FOR A SPECTACULAR EVENT...
HOLY HITCHCOCK! LOOK! THE BIRDS ARE COMING!
STAND BACK! LET ME SEE, TOO!
DOWN THE STREET COMES A DAZZLING PARADE OF FEMININE VIPS...
IT'S A PARADE! AND THERE'S LADY BIRD, LINDA BIRD AND LUCY BAINES! THEY'RE SPONSORING THE "BEAUTIFY METROPOLIS CAMPAIGN."
WOW! THE FIRST LADY AND HER CHICKS ARE GUARDED BY THAT KING-SIZE AMERICAN EAGLE ...AS WELL AS THE POLICE AND THE SECRET SERVICE!
MAKE OUR CITY BEAUTIFUL
KEEP METROPOLIS CLEAN
BUT THE EAGLE'S WINGS GUARD STILL ANOTHER "BIRD"...
WHO'D EVER THINK THAT I, THE PENGUIN, WOULD EVER HAVE AN ESCORT OF POLICE AND SECRET SERVICEMEN? SUPERMAN AND BATMAN NEVER DREAMED I'D BE HIDING UNDER THE FEATHERS OF THIS AMERICAN EAGLE FLOAT!
AS THE PARADE ENDS, THE PENGUIN SLIPS AWAY AND HURRIES TO PHOENIX CASTLE...
AH! THE CASTLE THAT CONTAINS THE WORLD'S MOST VALUABLE COLLECTION OF FEATHERED CREATURES... HOW CAN I INVADE THIS FORT KNOX OF BIRD-DOM? WHY, WITH THIS UMBRELLA I PICKED UP AT MY ROOST!
10

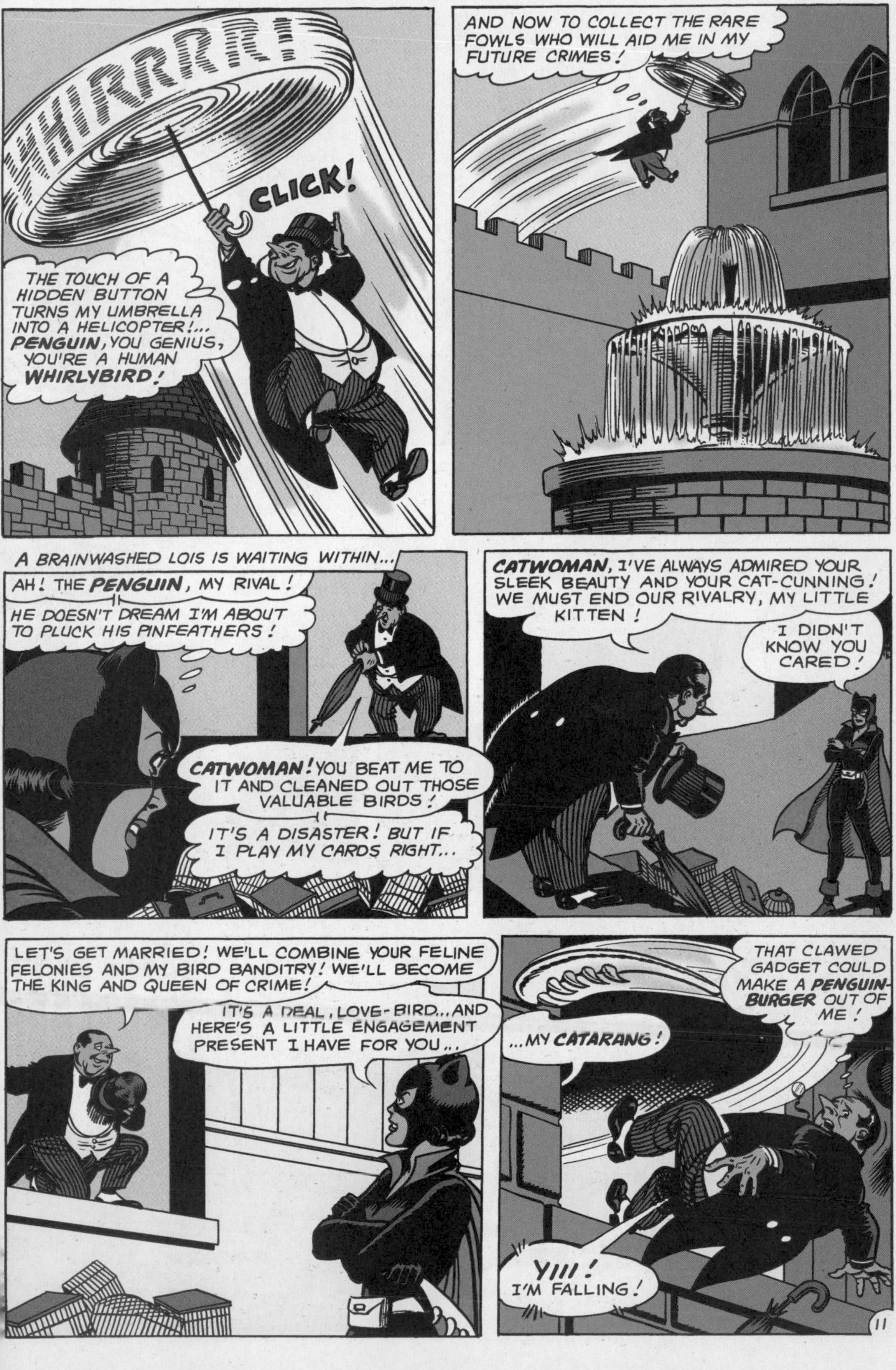
WHIRRRR!
CLICK!
THE TOUCH OF A HIDDEN BUTTON TURNS MY UMBRELLA INTO A HELICOPTER!... PENGUIN, YOU GENIUS, YOU'RE A HUMAN WHIRLYBIRD!
AND NOW TO COLLECT THE RARE FOWLS WHO WILL AID ME IN MY FUTURE CRIMES!
A BRAINWASHED LOIS IS WAITING WITHIN...
AH! THE PENGUIN, MY RIVAL!
HE DOESN'T DREAM I'M ABOUT TO PLUCK HIS PINFEATHERS!
CATWOMAN! YOU BEAT ME TO IT AND CLEANED OUT THOSE VALUABLE BIRDS!
IT'S A DISASTER! BUT IF I PLAY MY CARDS RIGHT...
CATWOMAN, I'VE ALWAYS ADMIRED YOUR SLEEK BEAUTY AND YOUR CAT-CUNNING! WE MUST END OUR RIVALRY, MY LITTLE KITTEN!
I DIDN'T KNOW YOU CARED!
LET'S GET MARRIED! WE'LL COMBINE YOUR FELINE FELONIES AND MY BIRD BANDITRY! WE'LL BECOME THE KING AND QUEEN OF CRIME!
IT'S A DEAL, LOVE-BIRD... AND HERE'S A LITTLE ENGAGEMENT PRESENT I HAVE FOR YOU...
...MY CATARANG!
THAT CLAWED GADGET COULD MAKE A PENGUIN-BURGER OUT OF ME!
YIII! I'M FALLING!
11

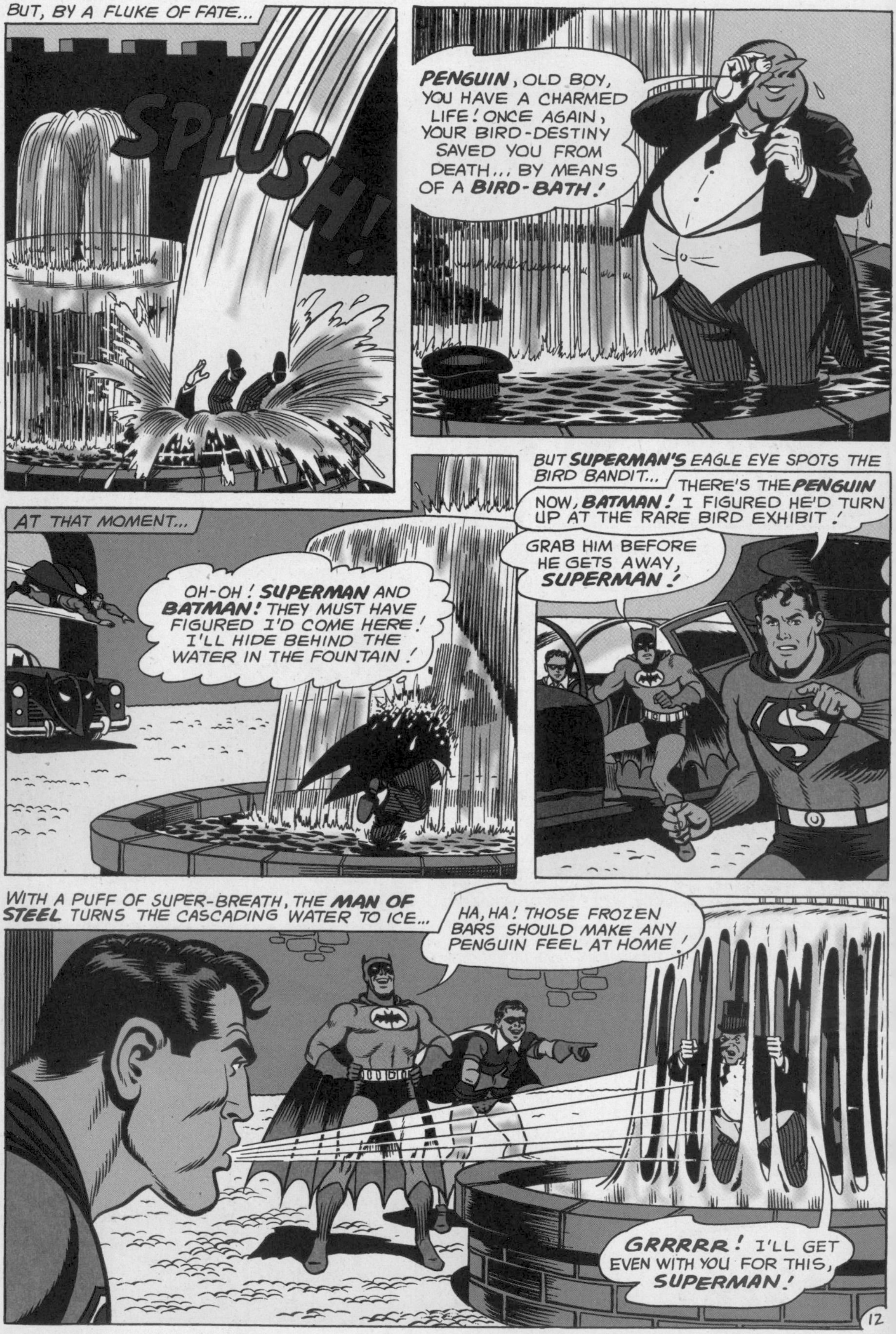
BUT, BY A FLUKE OF FATE...
SPLUSH!
PENGUIN, OLD BOY, YOU HAVE A CHARMED LIFE! ONCE AGAIN, YOUR BIRD-DESTINY SAVED YOU FROM DEATH... BY MEANS OF A BIRD-BATH!
AT THAT MOMENT...
OH-OH! SUPERMAN AND BATMAN! THEY MUST HAVE FIGURED I'D COME HERE! I'LL HIDE BEHIND THE WATER IN THE FOUNTAIN!
BUT SUPERMAN'S EAGLE EYE SPOTS THE BIRD BANDIT...
THERE'S THE PENGUIN NOW, BATMAN! I FIGURED HE'D TURN UP AT THE RARE BIRD EXHIBIT!
GRAB HIM BEFORE HE GETS AWAY, SUPERMAN!
WITH A PUFF OF SUPER-BREATH, THE MAN OF STEEL TURNS THE CASCADING WATER TO ICE...
HA, HA! THOSE FROZEN BARS SHOULD MAKE ANY PENGUIN FEEL AT HOME!
GRRRRR! I'LL GET EVEN WITH YOU FOR THIS, SUPERMAN!
12

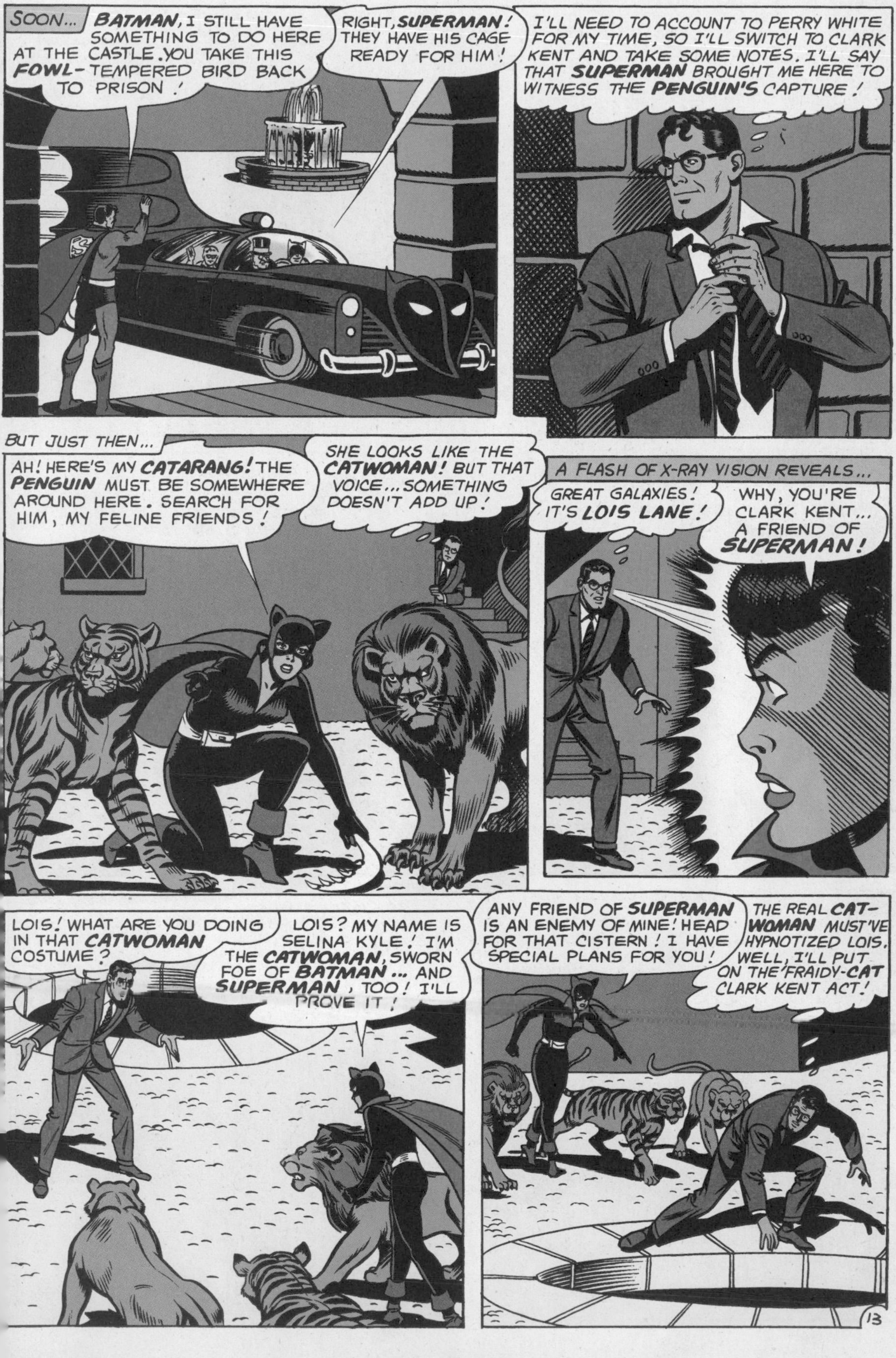
SOON...
BATMAN, I STILL HAVE SOMETHING TO DO HERE AT THE CASTLE. YOU TAKE THIS FOWL-TEMPERED BIRD BACK TO PRISON!
RIGHT, SUPERMAN! THEY HAVE HIS CAGE READY FOR HIM!
I'LL NEED TO ACCOUNT TO PERRY WHITE FOR MY TIME, SO I'LL SWITCH TO CLARK KENT AND TAKE SOME NOTES. I'LL SAY THAT SUPERMAN BROUGHT ME HERE TO WITNESS THE PENGUIN'S CAPTURE!
BUT JUST THEN...
AH! HERE'S MY CATARANG! THE PENGUIN MUST BE SOMEWHERE AROUND HERE. SEARCH FOR HIM, MY FELINE FRIENDS!
SHE LOOKS LIKE THE CATWOMAN! BUT THAT VOICE... SOMETHING DOESN'T ADD UP!
A FLASH OF X-RAY VISION REVEALS...
GREAT GALAXIES! IT'S LOIS LANE!
WHY, YOU'RE CLARK KENT... A FRIEND OF SUPERMAN!
LOIS! WHAT ARE YOU DOING IN THAT CATWOMAN COSTUME?
LOIS? MY NAME IS SELINA KYLE! I'M THE CATWOMAN, SWORN FOE OF BATMAN... AND SUPERMAN, TOO! I'LL PROVE IT!
ANY FRIEND OF SUPERMAN IS AN ENEMY OF MINE! HEAD FOR THAT CISTERN! I HAVE SPECIAL PLANS FOR YOU!
THE REAL CAT-WOMAN MUST'VE HYPNOTIZED LOIS. WELL, I'LL PUT ON THE 'FRAIDY-CAT CLARK KENT ACT!
13

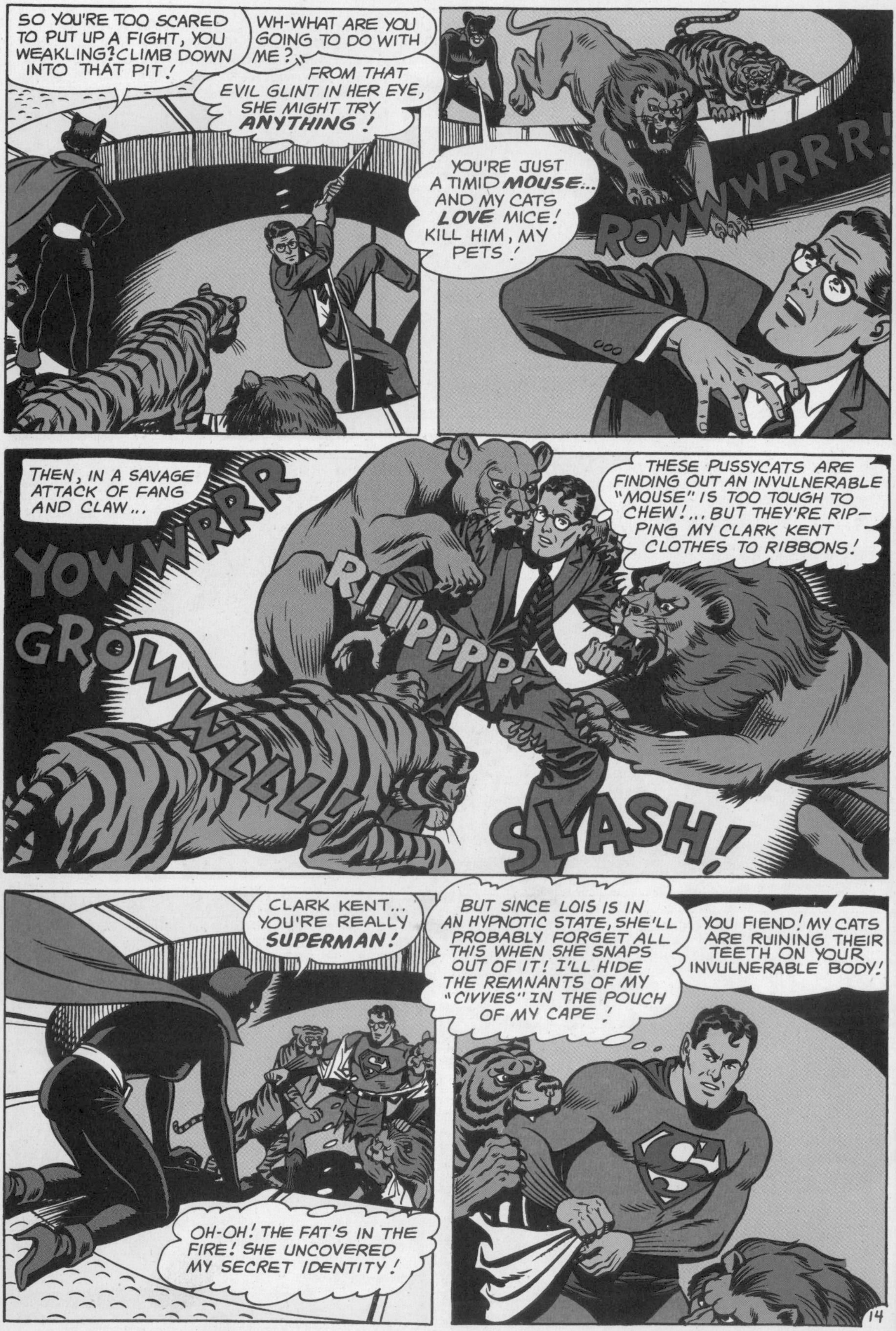

SO YOU'RE TOO SCARED TO PUT UP A FIGHT, YOU WEAKLING? CLIMB DOWN INTO THAT PIT!
WH-WHAT ARE YOU GOING TO DO WITH ME?
FROM THAT EVIL GLINT IN HER EYE, SHE MIGHT TRY **ANYTHING**!
YOU'RE JUST A TIMID **MOUSE**... AND MY CATS **LOVE** MICE! KILL HIM, MY PETS!
ROWWWRRR!
THEN, IN A SAVAGE ATTACK OF FANG AND CLAW...
THESE PUSSYCATS ARE FINDING OUT AN INVULNERABLE "MOUSE" IS TOO TOUGH TO CHEW!... BUT THEY'RE RIP-PING MY CLARK KENT CLOTHES TO RIBBONS!
YOWWRRR
GROWWLLL!
RIIIPPPP!
SLASH!
CLARK KENT... YOU'RE REALLY **SUPERMAN**!
OH-OH! THE FAT'S IN THE FIRE! SHE UNCOVERED MY SECRET IDENTITY!
BUT SINCE LOIS IS IN AN HYPNOTIC STATE, SHE'LL PROBABLY FORGET ALL THIS WHEN SHE SNAPS OUT OF IT! I'LL HIDE THE REMNANTS OF MY "CIVVIES" IN THE POUCH OF MY CAPE!
YOU FIEND! MY CATS ARE RUINING THEIR TEETH ON YOUR INVULNERABLE BODY!
14

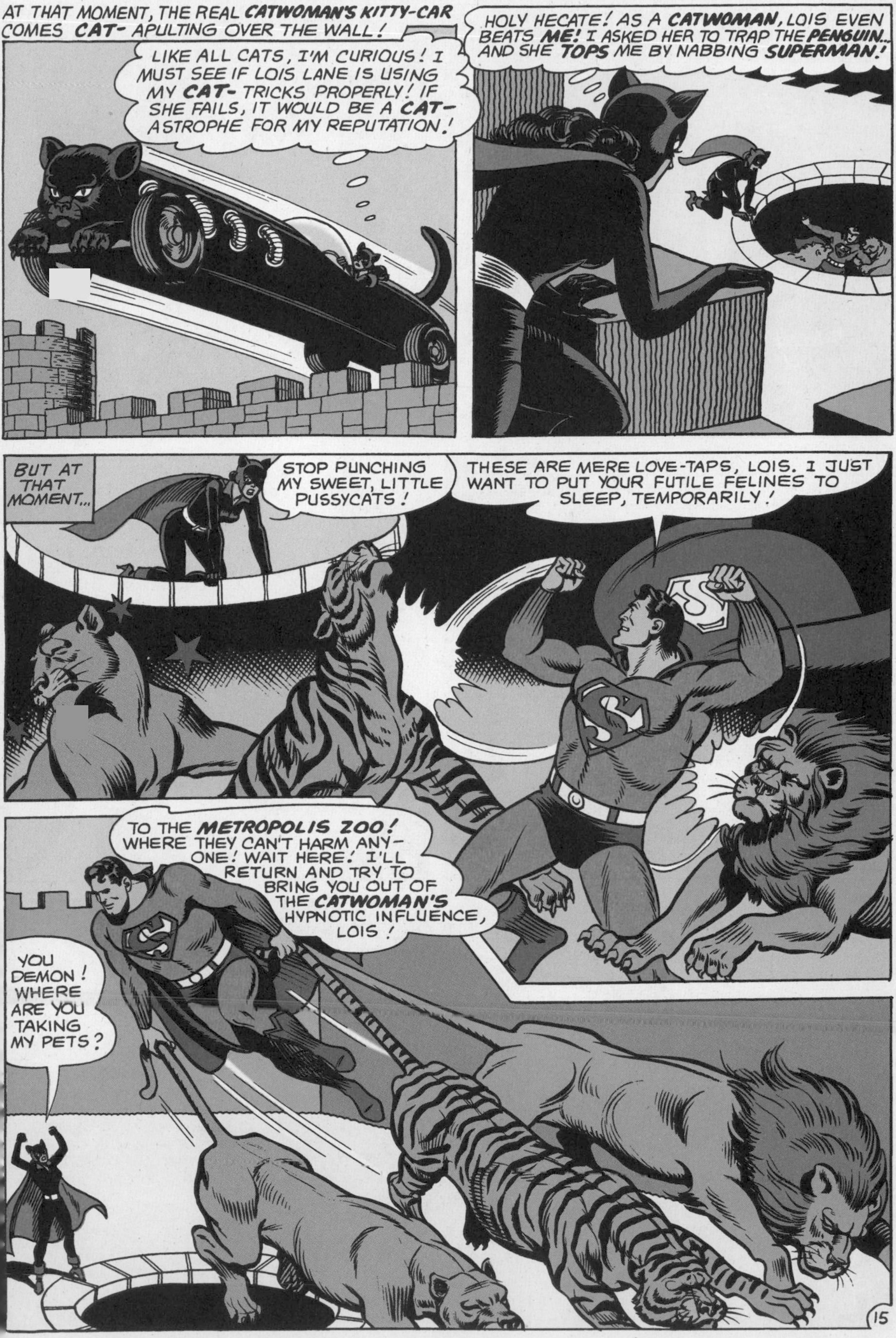
AT THAT MOMENT, THE REAL CATWOMAN'S KITTY-CAR COMES CAT-APULTING OVER THE WALL!
LIKE ALL CATS, I'M CURIOUS! I MUST SEE IF LOIS LANE IS USING MY CAT-TRICKS PROPERLY! IF SHE FAILS, IT WOULD BE A CAT-ASTROPHE FOR MY REPUTATION!
HOLY HECATE! AS A CATWOMAN, LOIS EVEN BEATS ME! I ASKED HER TO TRAP THE PENGUIN... AND SHE TOPS ME BY NABBING SUPERMAN!
BUT AT THAT MOMENT...
STOP PUNCHING MY SWEET, LITTLE PUSSYCATS!
THESE ARE MERE LOVE-TAPS, LOIS. I JUST WANT TO PUT YOUR FUTILE FELINES TO SLEEP, TEMPORARILY!
TO THE METROPOLIS ZOO! WHERE THEY CAN'T HARM ANY-ONE! WAIT HERE! I'LL RETURN AND TRY TO BRING YOU OUT OF THE CATWOMAN'S HYPNOTIC INFLUENCE, LOIS!
YOU DEMON! WHERE ARE YOU TAKING MY PETS?
15

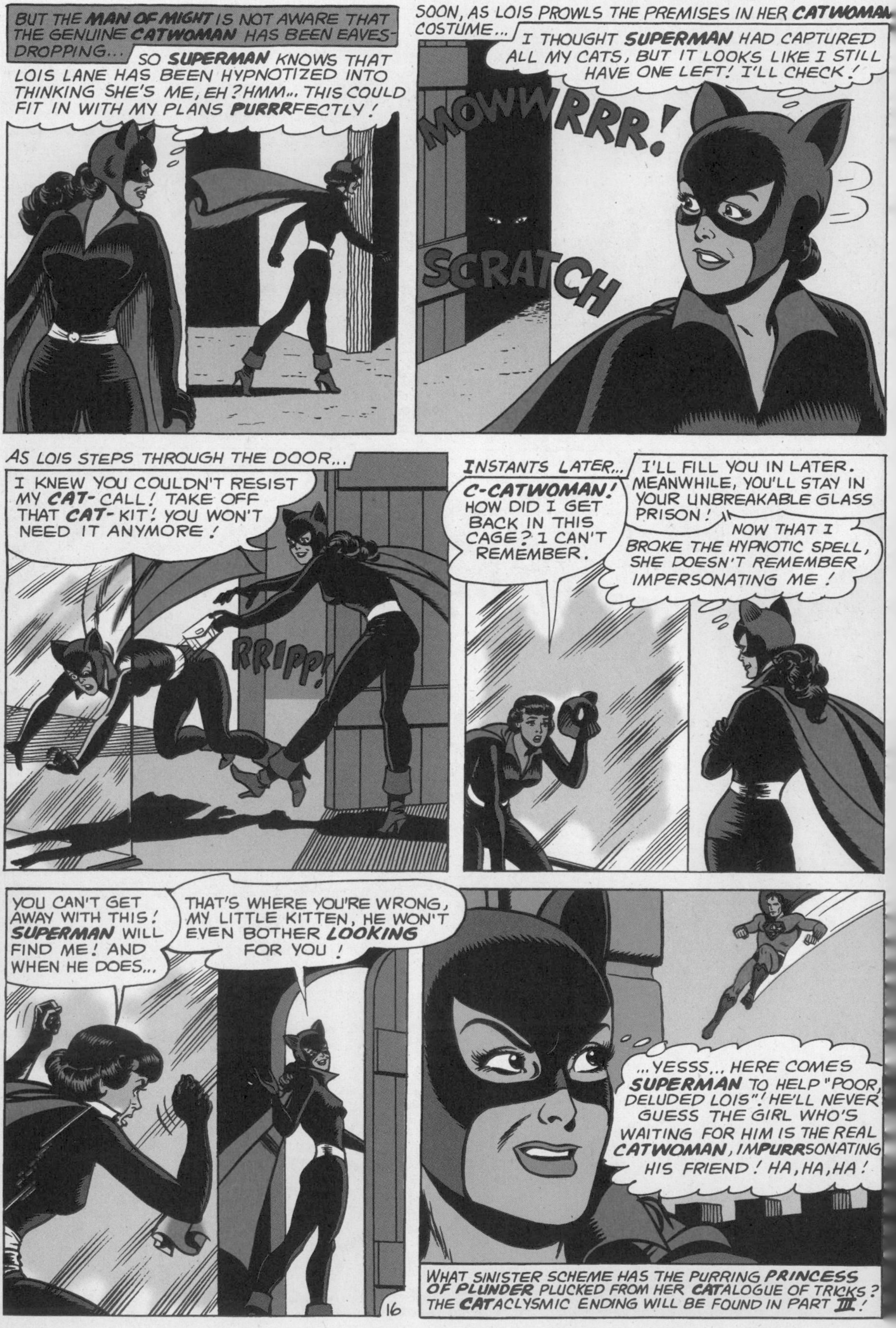
BUT THE MAN OF MIGHT IS NOT AWARE THAT THE GENUINE CATWOMAN HAS BEEN EAVES-DROPPING...
SO SUPERMAN KNOWS THAT LOIS LANE HAS BEEN HYPNOTIZED INTO THINKING SHE'S ME, EH? HMM... THIS COULD FIT IN WITH MY PLANS PURRRFECTLY!
SOON, AS LOIS PROWLS THE PREMISES IN HER CATWOMAN COSTUME...
I THOUGHT SUPERMAN HAD CAPTURED ALL MY CATS, BUT IT LOOKS LIKE I STILL HAVE ONE LEFT! I'LL CHECK!
MOWWRRR!
SCRATCH
AS LOIS STEPS THROUGH THE DOOR...
I KNEW YOU COULDN'T RESIST MY CAT-CALL! TAKE OFF THAT CAT-KIT! YOU WON'T NEED IT ANYMORE!
RRIPP!
INSTANTS LATER...
C-CATWOMAN! HOW DID I GET BACK IN THIS CAGE? I CAN'T REMEMBER.
I'LL FILL YOU IN LATER. MEANWHILE, YOU'LL STAY IN YOUR UNBREAKABLE GLASS PRISON!
NOW THAT I BROKE THE HYPNOTIC SPELL, SHE DOESN'T REMEMBER IMPERSONATING ME!
YOU CAN'T GET AWAY WITH THIS! SUPERMAN WILL FIND ME! AND WHEN HE DOES...
THAT'S WHERE YOU'RE WRONG, MY LITTLE KITTEN, HE WON'T EVEN BOTHER LOOKING FOR YOU!
16
...YESSS... HERE COMES SUPERMAN TO HELP "POOR, DELUDED LOIS"! HE'LL NEVER GUESS THE GIRL WHO'S WAITING FOR HIM IS THE REAL CATWOMAN, IMPURRSONATING HIS FRIEND! HA, HA, HA!
WHAT SINISTER SCHEME HAS THE PURRING PRINCESS OF PLUNDER PLUCKED FROM HER CATALOGUE OF TRICKS? THE CATACLYSMIC ENDING WILL BE FOUND IN PART III!

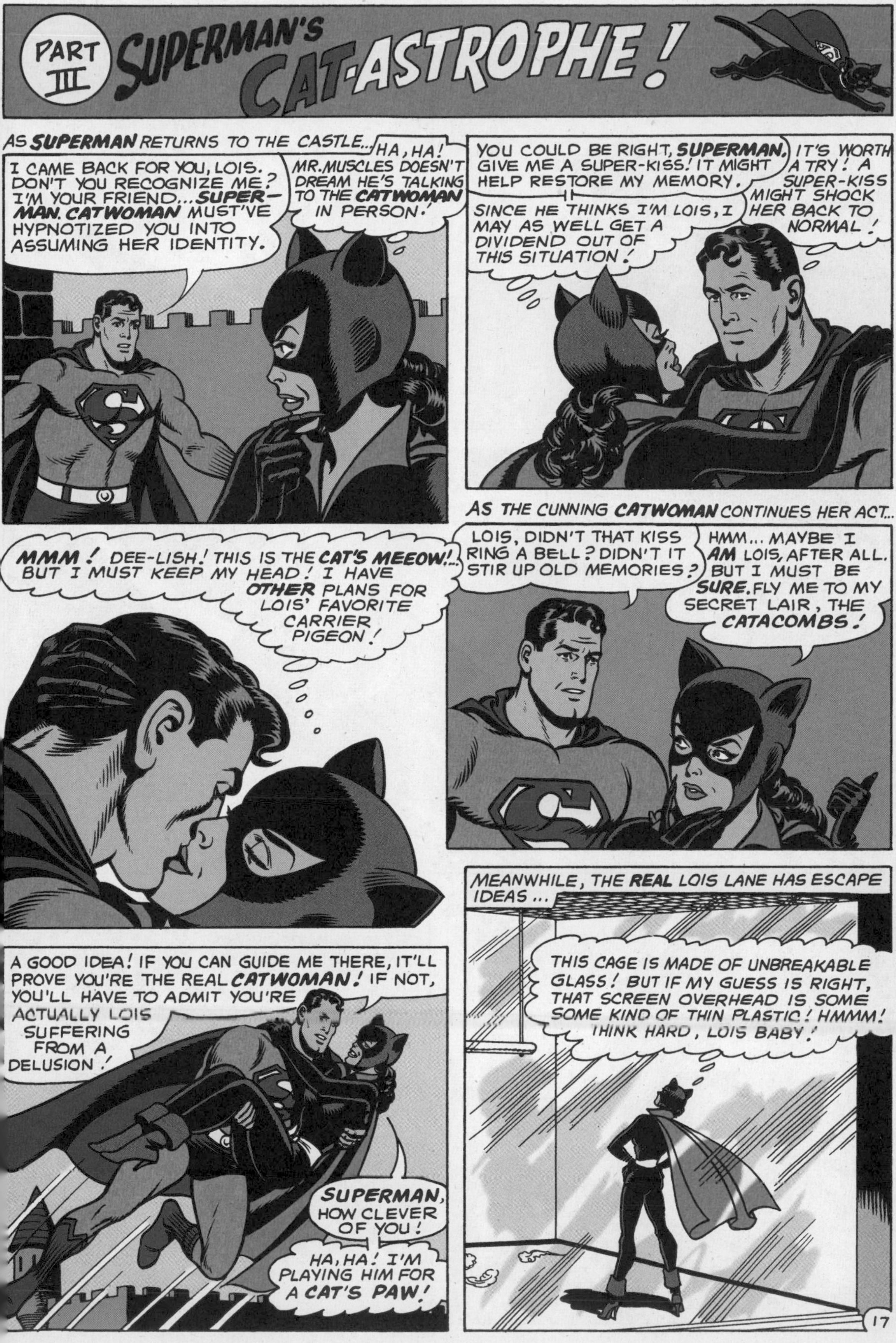
PART III
SUPERMAN'S CAT-ASTROPHE!
AS SUPERMAN RETURNS TO THE CASTLE...
I CAME BACK FOR YOU, LOIS. DON'T YOU RECOGNIZE ME? I'M YOUR FRIEND... SUPERMAN. CATWOMAN MUST'VE HYPNOTIZED YOU INTO ASSUMING HER IDENTITY.
HA, HA! MR. MUSCLES DOESN'T DREAM HE'S TALKING TO THE CATWOMAN IN PERSON!
YOU COULD BE RIGHT, SUPERMAN. GIVE ME A SUPER-KISS! IT MIGHT HELP RESTORE MY MEMORY.
SINCE HE THINKS I'M LOIS, I MAY AS WELL GET A DIVIDEND OUT OF THIS SITUATION!
IT'S WORTH A TRY! A SUPER-KISS MIGHT SHOCK HER BACK TO NORMAL!
AS THE CUNNING CATWOMAN CONTINUES HER ACT...
MMM! DEE-LISH! THIS IS THE CAT'S MEEOW!... BUT I MUST KEEP MY HEAD! I HAVE OTHER PLANS FOR LOIS' FAVORITE CARRIER PIGEON!
LOIS, DIDN'T THAT KISS RING A BELL? DIDN'T IT STIR UP OLD MEMORIES?
HMM... MAYBE I AM LOIS, AFTER ALL. BUT I MUST BE SURE. FLY ME TO MY SECRET LAIR, THE CATACOMBS!
A GOOD IDEA! IF YOU CAN GUIDE ME THERE, IT'LL PROVE YOU'RE THE REAL CATWOMAN! IF NOT, YOU'LL HAVE TO ADMIT YOU'RE ACTUALLY LOIS SUFFERING FROM A DELUSION!
SUPERMAN, HOW CLEVER OF YOU!
HA, HA! I'M PLAYING HIM FOR A CAT'S PAW!
MEANWHILE, THE REAL LOIS LANE HAS ESCAPE IDEAS...
THIS CAGE IS MADE OF UNBREAKABLE GLASS! BUT IF MY GUESS IS RIGHT, THAT SCREEN OVERHEAD IS SOME SOME KIND OF THIN PLASTIC! HMMM! THINK HARD, LOIS BABY!
17

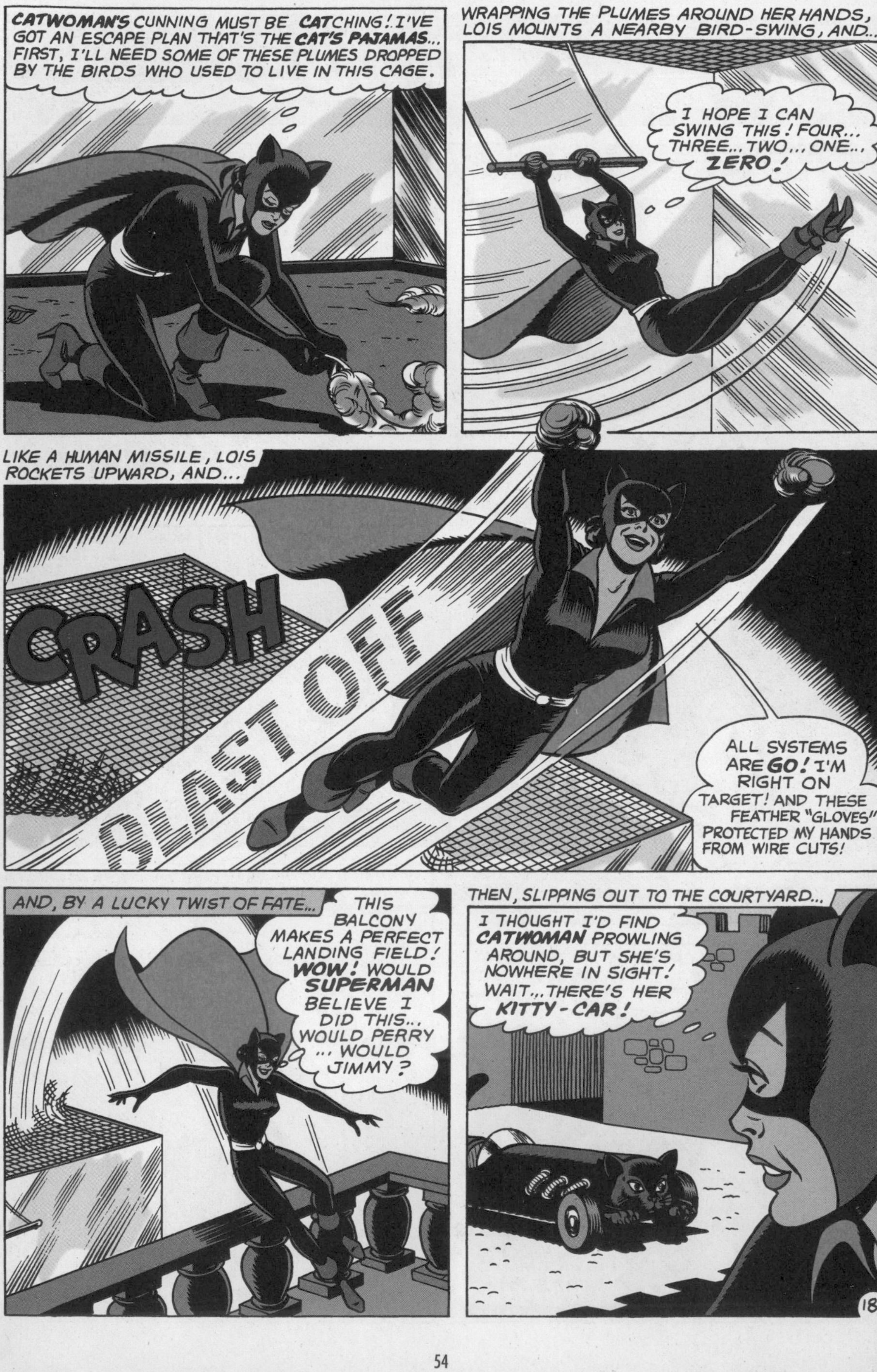
CATWOMAN'S CUNNING MUST BE CATCHING! I'VE GOT AN ESCAPE PLAN THAT'S THE CAT'S PAJAMAS... FIRST, I'LL NEED SOME OF THESE PLUMES DROPPED BY THE BIRDS WHO USED TO LIVE IN THIS CAGE.
WRAPPING THE PLUMES AROUND HER HANDS, LOIS MOUNTS A NEARBY BIRD-SWING, AND...
I HOPE I CAN SWING THIS! FOUR... THREE... TWO... ONE... ZERO!
LIKE A HUMAN MISSILE, LOIS ROCKETS UPWARD, AND...
CRASH
BLAST OFF
ALL SYSTEMS ARE GO! I'M RIGHT ON TARGET! AND THESE FEATHER "GLOVES" PROTECTED MY HANDS FROM WIRE CUTS!
AND, BY A LUCKY TWIST OF FATE...
THIS BALCONY MAKES A PERFECT LANDING FIELD! WOW! WOULD SUPERMAN BELIEVE I DID THIS... WOULD PERRY ... WOULD JIMMY?
THEN, SLIPPING OUT TO THE COURTYARD...
I THOUGHT I'D FIND CATWOMAN PROWLING AROUND, BUT SHE'S NOWHERE IN SIGHT! WAIT... THERE'S HER KITTY-CAR!
18

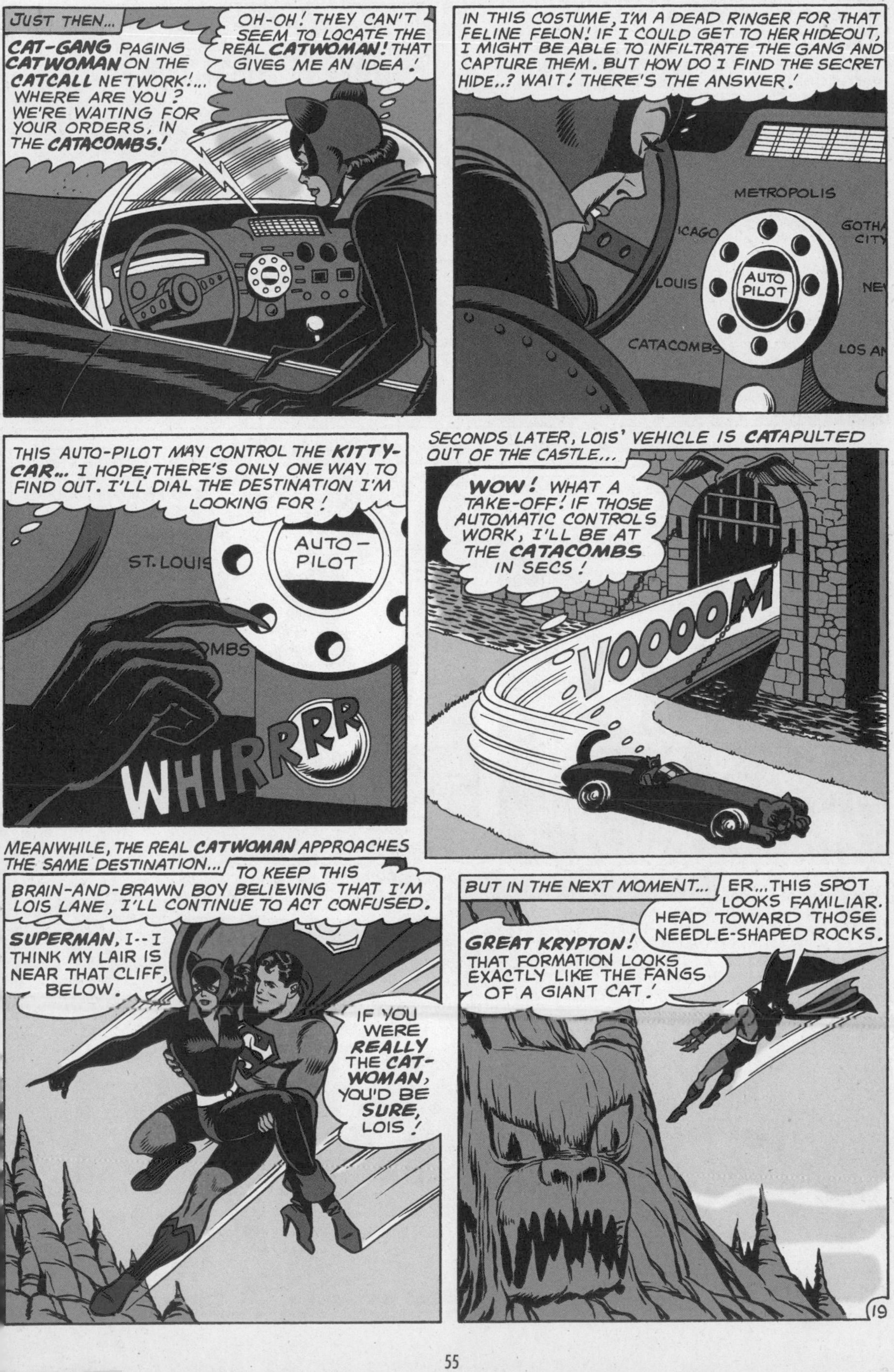

JUST THEN...
CAT-GANG PAGING CATWOMAN ON THE CATCALL NETWORK!... WHERE ARE YOU? WE'RE WAITING FOR YOUR ORDERS, IN THE CATACOMBS!
OH-OH! THEY CAN'T SEEM TO LOCATE THE REAL CATWOMAN! THAT GIVES ME AN IDEA!
IN THIS COSTUME, I'M A DEAD RINGER FOR THAT FELINE FELON! IF I COULD GET TO HER HIDEOUT, I MIGHT BE ABLE TO INFILTRATE THE GANG AND CAPTURE THEM. BUT HOW DO I FIND THE SECRET HIDE..? WAIT! THERE'S THE ANSWER!
METROPOLIS
ICAGO
GOTHA CITY
LOUIS
AUTO PILOT
NE
CATACOMBS
LOS AN
THIS AUTO-PILOT MAY CONTROL THE KITTY-CAR... I HOPE! THERE'S ONLY ONE WAY TO FIND OUT. I'LL DIAL THE DESTINATION I'M LOOKING FOR!
ST. LOUIS
AUTO-PILOT
OMBS
WHIRRRR
SECONDS LATER, LOIS' VEHICLE IS CATAPULTED OUT OF THE CASTLE...
WOW! WHAT A TAKE-OFF! IF THOSE AUTOMATIC CONTROLS WORK, I'LL BE AT THE CATACOMBS IN SECS!
VOOOOM
MEANWHILE, THE REAL CATWOMAN APPROACHES THE SAME DESTINATION...
TO KEEP THIS BRAIN-AND-BRAWN BOY BELIEVING THAT I'M LOIS LANE, I'LL CONTINUE TO ACT CONFUSED.
SUPERMAN, I-- I THINK MY LAIR IS NEAR THAT CLIFF, BELOW.
IF YOU WERE REALLY THE CAT-WOMAN, YOU'D BE SURE, LOIS!
BUT IN THE NEXT MOMENT...
ER... THIS SPOT LOOKS FAMILIAR. HEAD TOWARD THOSE NEEDLE-SHAPED ROCKS.
GREAT KRYPTON! THAT FORMATION LOOKS EXACTLY LIKE THE FANGS OF A GIANT CAT!
19

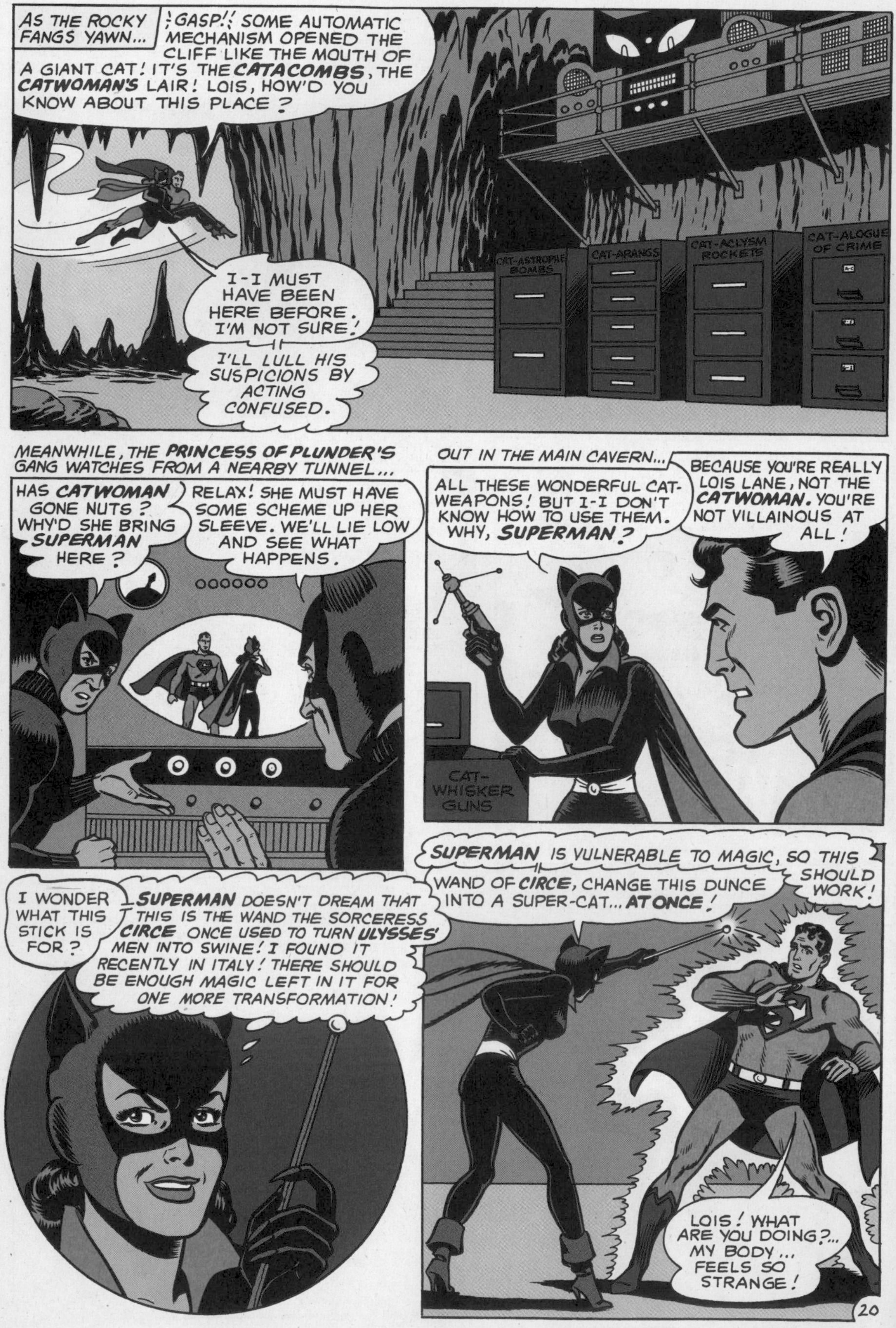
AS THE ROCKY FANGS YAWN...
¡GASP!¡ SOME AUTOMATIC MECHANISM OPENED THE CLIFF LIKE THE MOUTH OF A GIANT CAT! IT'S THE CATACOMBS, THE CATWOMAN'S LAIR! LOIS, HOW'D YOU KNOW ABOUT THIS PLACE?
I-I MUST HAVE BEEN HERE BEFORE. I'M NOT SURE!
I'LL LULL HIS SUSPICIONS BY ACTING CONFUSED.
CAT-ASTROPHE BOMBS
CAT-ARANGS
CAT-ACLYSM ROCKETS
CAT-ALOGUE OF CRIME
MEANWHILE, THE PRINCESS OF PLUNDER'S GANG WATCHES FROM A NEARBY TUNNEL...
HAS CATWOMAN GONE NUTS? WHY'D SHE BRING SUPERMAN HERE?
RELAX! SHE MUST HAVE SOME SCHEME UP HER SLEEVE. WE'LL LIE LOW AND SEE WHAT HAPPENS.
OUT IN THE MAIN CAVERN...
ALL THESE WONDERFUL CAT-WEAPONS! BUT I-I DON'T KNOW HOW TO USE THEM. WHY, SUPERMAN?
BECAUSE YOU'RE REALLY LOIS LANE, NOT THE CATWOMAN. YOU'RE NOT VILLAINOUS AT ALL!
CAT-WHISKER GUNS
I WONDER WHAT THIS STICK IS FOR?
SUPERMAN DOESN'T DREAM THAT THIS IS THE WAND THE SORCERESS CIRCE ONCE USED TO TURN ULYSSES' MEN INTO SWINE! I FOUND IT RECENTLY IN ITALY! THERE SHOULD BE ENOUGH MAGIC LEFT IN IT FOR ONE MORE TRANSFORMATION!
SUPERMAN IS VULNERABLE TO MAGIC, SO THIS SHOULD WORK!
WAND OF CIRCE, CHANGE THIS DUNCE INTO A SUPER-CAT... AT ONCE!
LOIS! WHAT ARE YOU DOING?... MY BODY... FEELS SO STRANGE!
20

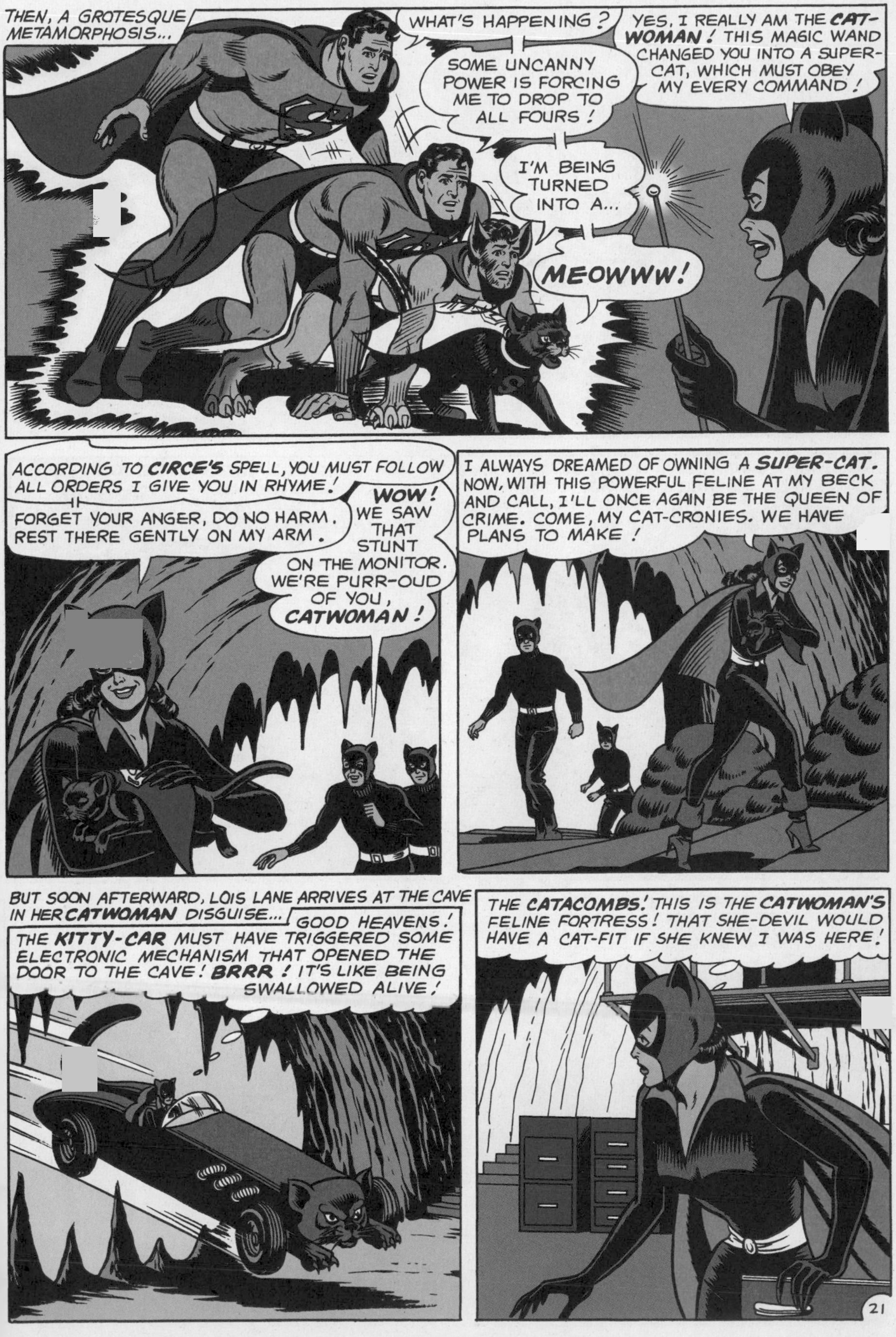
THEN, A GROTESQUE METAMORPHOSIS...
WHAT'S HAPPENING?
SOME UNCANNY POWER IS FORCING ME TO DROP TO ALL FOURS!
I'M BEING TURNED INTO A...
MEOWWW!
YES, I REALLY AM THE CAT-WOMAN! THIS MAGIC WAND CHANGED YOU INTO A SUPER-CAT, WHICH MUST OBEY MY EVERY COMMAND!
ACCORDING TO CIRCE'S SPELL, YOU MUST FOLLOW ALL ORDERS I GIVE YOU IN RHYME!
FORGET YOUR ANGER, DO NO HARM. REST THERE GENTLY ON MY ARM.
WOW! WE SAW THAT STUNT ON THE MONITOR. WE'RE PURR-OUD OF YOU, CATWOMAN!
I ALWAYS DREAMED OF OWNING A SUPER-CAT. NOW, WITH THIS POWERFUL FELINE AT MY BECK AND CALL, I'LL ONCE AGAIN BE THE QUEEN OF CRIME. COME, MY CAT-CRONIES. WE HAVE PLANS TO MAKE!
BUT SOON AFTERWARD, LOIS LANE ARRIVES AT THE CAVE IN HER CATWOMAN DISGUISE...
GOOD HEAVENS! THE KITTY-CAR MUST HAVE TRIGGERED SOME ELECTRONIC MECHANISM THAT OPENED THE DOOR TO THE CAVE! BRRR! IT'S LIKE BEING SWALLOWED ALIVE!
THE CATACOMBS! THIS IS THE CATWOMAN'S FELINE FORTRESS! THAT SHE-DEVIL WOULD HAVE A CAT-FIT IF SHE KNEW I WAS HERE!
21

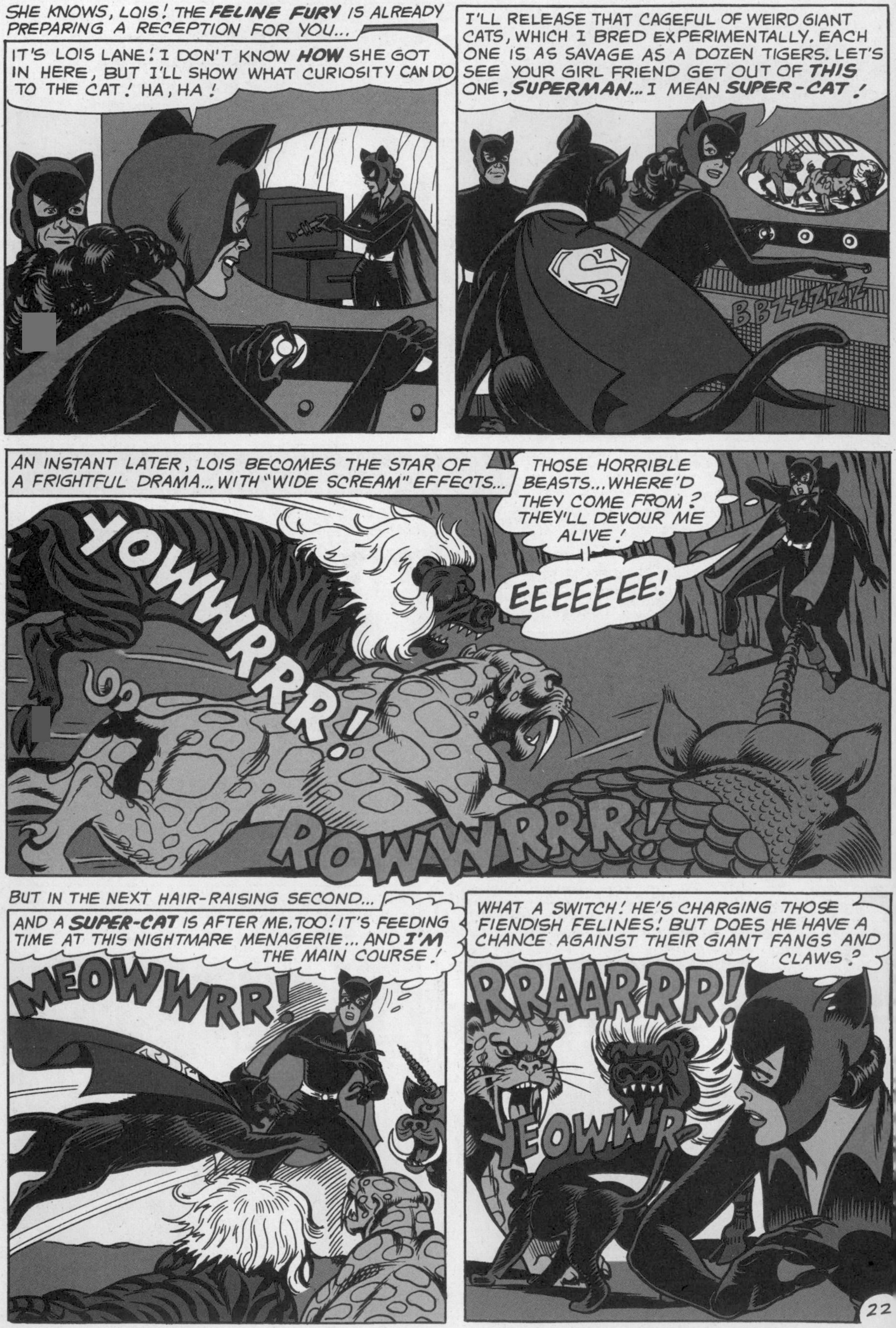
SHE KNOWS, LOIS! THE FELINE FURY IS ALREADY PREPARING A RECEPTION FOR YOU...
IT'S LOIS LANE! I DON'T KNOW HOW SHE GOT IN HERE, BUT I'LL SHOW WHAT CURIOSITY CAN DO TO THE CAT! HA, HA!
I'LL RELEASE THAT CAGEFUL OF WEIRD GIANT CATS, WHICH I BRED EXPERIMENTALLY. EACH ONE IS AS SAVAGE AS A DOZEN TIGERS. LET'S SEE YOUR GIRL FRIEND GET OUT OF THIS ONE, SUPERMAN... I MEAN SUPER-CAT!
BBZZZZZZ
AN INSTANT LATER, LOIS BECOMES THE STAR OF A FRIGHTFUL DRAMA... WITH "WIDE SCREAM" EFFECTS...
THOSE HORRIBLE BEASTS... WHERE'D THEY COME FROM? THEY'LL DEVOUR ME ALIVE!
EEEEEEE!
YOWWRRR!
ROWWRRR!
BUT IN THE NEXT HAIR-RAISING SECOND...
AND A SUPER-CAT IS AFTER ME, TOO! IT'S FEEDING TIME AT THIS NIGHTMARE MENAGERIE... AND I'M THE MAIN COURSE!
MEOWWRR!
WHAT A SWITCH! HE'S CHARGING THOSE FIENDISH FELINES! BUT DOES HE HAVE A CHANCE AGAINST THEIR GIANT FANGS AND CLAWS?
RRAARRR!
YEOWWR
22

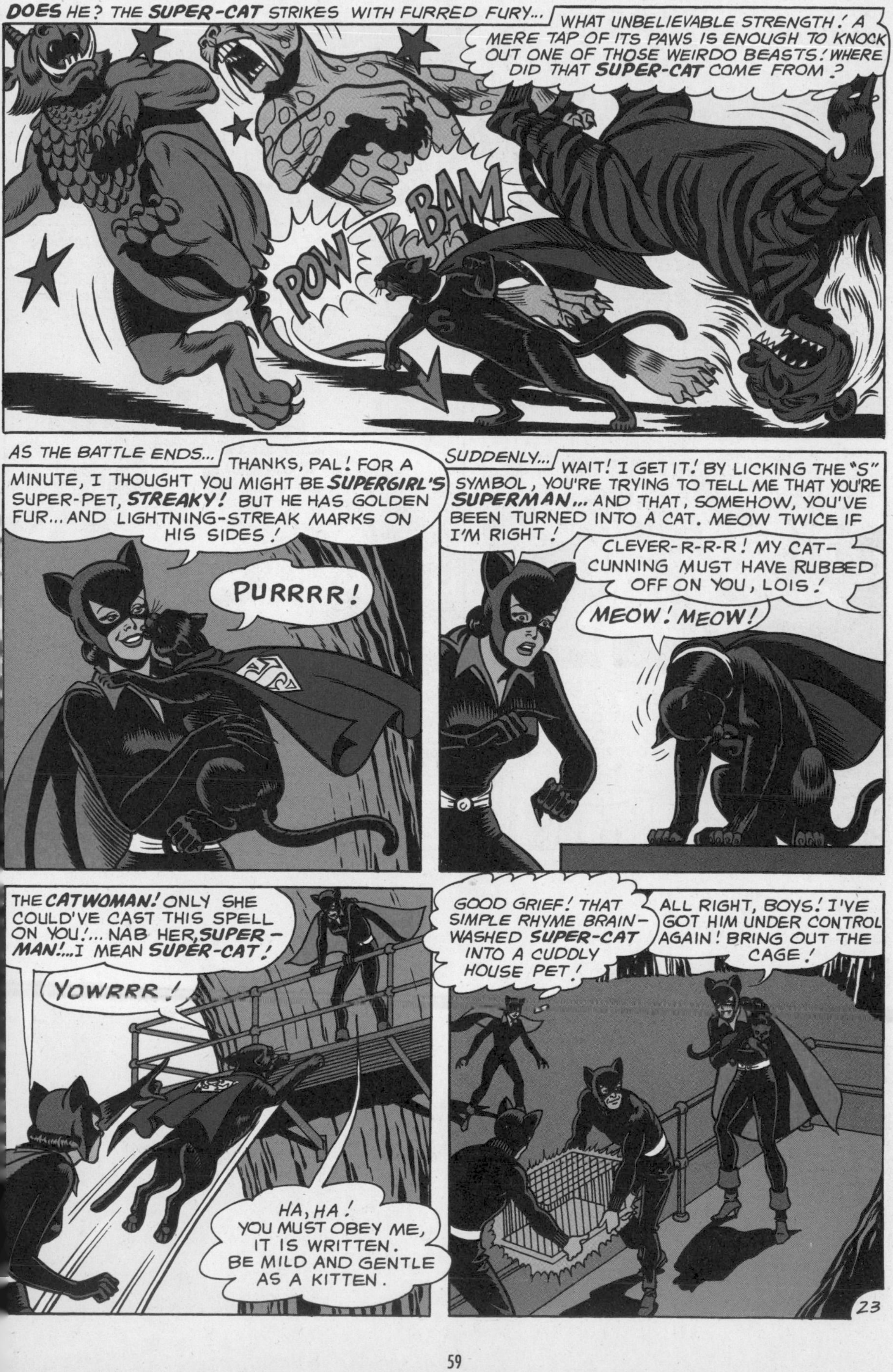
DOES HE? THE SUPER-CAT STRIKES WITH FURRED FURY...
WHAT UNBELIEVABLE STRENGTH! A MERE TAP OF ITS PAWS IS ENOUGH TO KNOCK OUT ONE OF THOSE WEIRDO BEASTS! WHERE DID THAT SUPER-CAT COME FROM?
BAM
POW
AS THE BATTLE ENDS...
THANKS, PAL! FOR A MINUTE, I THOUGHT YOU MIGHT BE SUPERGIRL'S SUPER-PET, STREAKY! BUT HE HAS GOLDEN FUR... AND LIGHTNING-STREAK MARKS ON HIS SIDES!
PURRRR!
SUDDENLY...
WAIT! I GET IT! BY LICKING THE "S" SYMBOL, YOU'RE TRYING TO TELL ME THAT YOU'RE SUPERMAN... AND THAT, SOMEHOW, YOU'VE BEEN TURNED INTO A CAT. MEOW TWICE IF I'M RIGHT!
CLEVER-R-R-R! MY CAT-CUNNING MUST HAVE RUBBED OFF ON YOU, LOIS!
MEOW! MEOW!
THE CATWOMAN! ONLY SHE COULD'VE CAST THIS SPELL ON YOU!... NAB HER, SUPER-MAN!...I MEAN SUPER-CAT!
YOWRRR!
HA, HA! YOU MUST OBEY ME, IT IS WRITTEN. BE MILD AND GENTLE AS A KITTEN.
GOOD GRIEF! THAT SIMPLE RHYME BRAIN-WASHED SUPER-CAT INTO A CUDDLY HOUSE PET!
ALL RIGHT, BOYS! I'VE GOT HIM UNDER CONTROL AGAIN! BRING OUT THE CAGE!
23

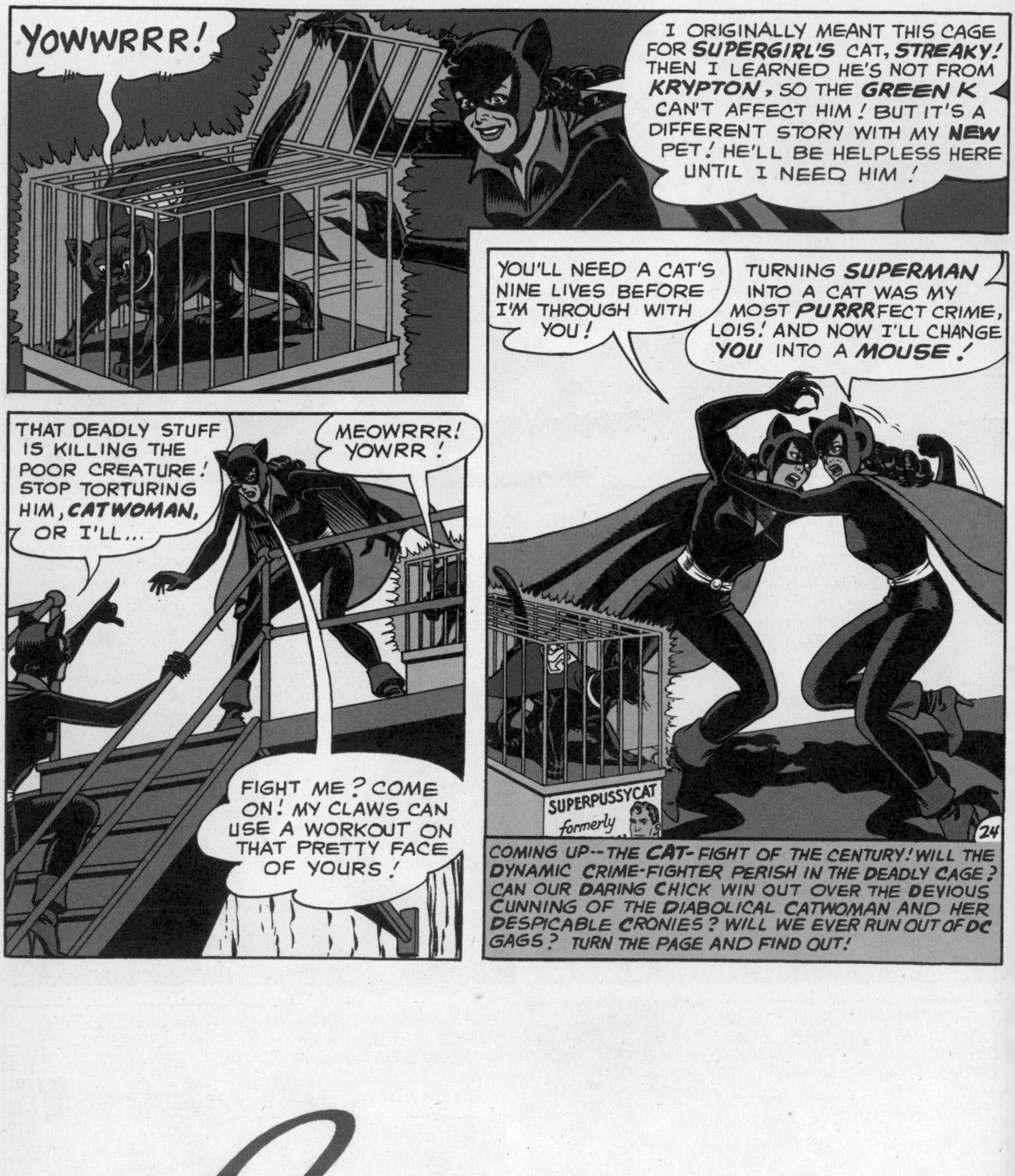
YOWWRRR!
I ORIGINALLY MEANT THIS CAGE FOR SUPERGIRL'S CAT, STREAKY! THEN I LEARNED HE'S NOT FROM KRYPTON, SO THE GREEN K CAN'T AFFECT HIM! BUT IT'S A DIFFERENT STORY WITH MY NEW PET! HE'LL BE HELPLESS HERE UNTIL I NEED HIM!
THAT DEADLY STUFF IS KILLING THE POOR CREATURE! STOP TORTURING HIM, CATWOMAN, OR I'LL...
MEOWRRR! YOWRR!
FIGHT ME? COME ON! MY CLAWS CAN USE A WORKOUT ON THAT PRETTY FACE OF YOURS!
YOU'LL NEED A CAT'S NINE LIVES BEFORE I'M THROUGH WITH YOU!
TURNING SUPERMAN INTO A CAT WAS MY MOST PURRRFECT CRIME, LOIS! AND NOW I'LL CHANGE YOU INTO A MOUSE!
SUPERPUSSYCAT
formerly
24
COMING UP--THE CAT-FIGHT OF THE CENTURY! WILL THE DYNAMIC CRIME-FIGHTER PERISH IN THE DEADLY CAGE? CAN OUR DARING CHICK WIN OUT OVER THE DEVIOUS CUNNING OF THE DIABOLICAL CATWOMAN AND HER DESPICABLE CRONIES? WILL WE EVER RUN OUT OF DC GAGS? TURN THE PAGE AND FIND OUT!

Catwoman

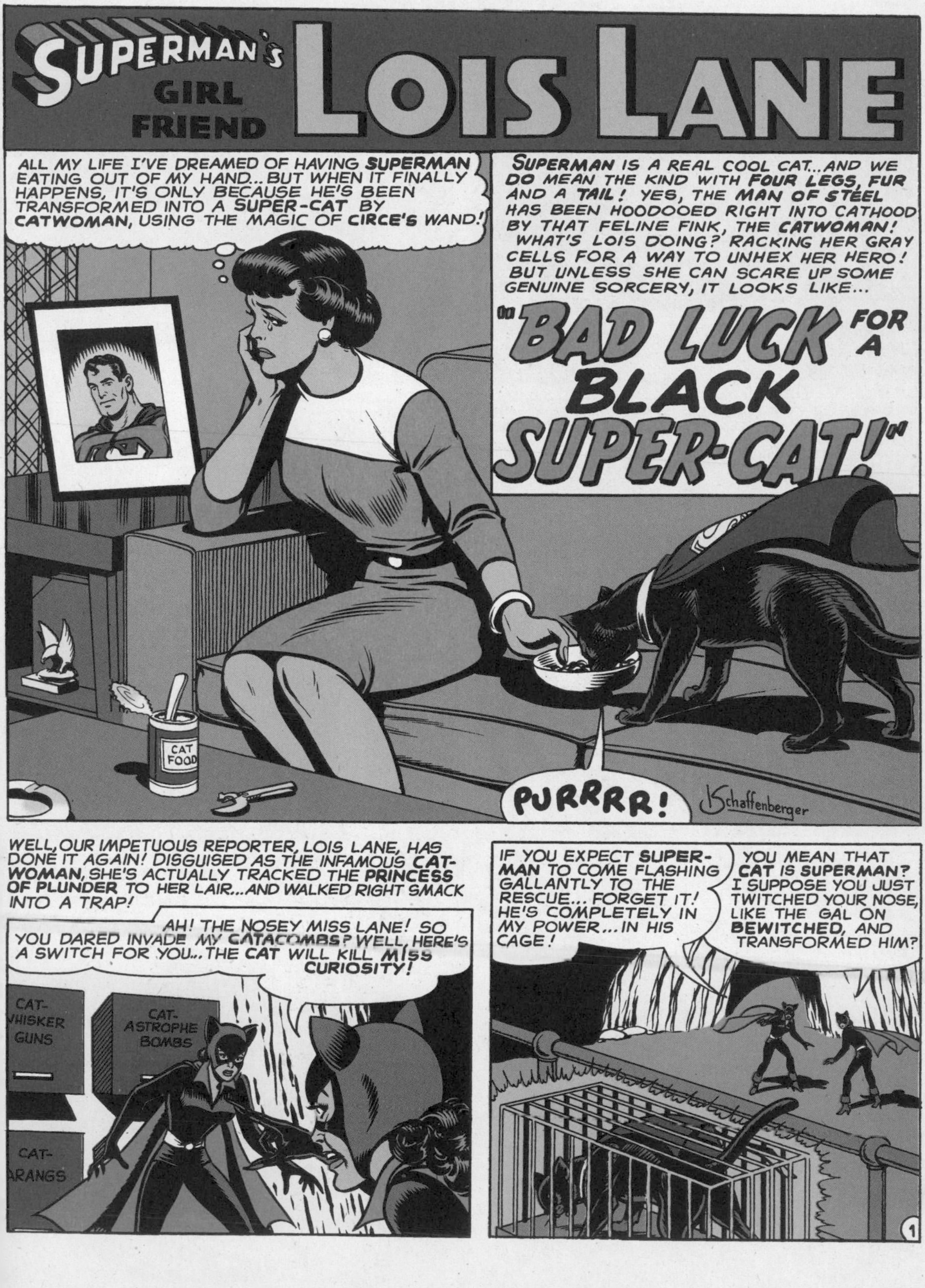
SUPERMAN'S GIRL FRIEND LOIS LANE
ALL MY LIFE I'VE DREAMED OF HAVING SUPERMAN EATING OUT OF MY HAND... BUT WHEN IT FINALLY HAPPENS, IT'S ONLY BECAUSE HE'S BEEN TRANSFORMED INTO A SUPER-CAT BY CATWOMAN, USING THE MAGIC OF CIRCE'S WAND!
SUPERMAN IS A REAL COOL CAT...AND WE DO MEAN THE KIND WITH FOUR LEGS, FUR AND A TAIL! YES, THE MAN OF STEEL HAS BEEN HOODOOED RIGHT INTO CATHOOD BY THAT FELINE FINK, THE CATWOMAN! WHAT'S LOIS DOING? RACKING HER GRAY CELLS FOR A WAY TO UNHEX HER HERO! BUT UNLESS SHE CAN SCARE UP SOME GENUINE SORCERY, IT LOOKS LIKE...
"BAD LUCK FOR A BLACK SUPER-CAT!"
CAT FOOD
PURRRRR!
K Schaffenberger
WELL, OUR IMPETUOUS REPORTER, LOIS LANE, HAS DONE IT AGAIN! DISGUISED AS THE INFAMOUS CAT-WOMAN, SHE'S ACTUALLY TRACKED THE PRINCESS OF PLUNDER TO HER LAIR...AND WALKED RIGHT SMACK INTO A TRAP!
AH! THE NOSEY MISS LANE! SO YOU DARED INVADE MY CATACOMBS? WELL, HERE'S A SWITCH FOR YOU...THE CAT WILL KILL MISS CURIOSITY!
CAT-WHISKER GUNS
CAT-ASTROPHE BOMBS
CAT-ARANGS
IF YOU EXPECT SUPER-MAN TO COME FLASHING GALLANTLY TO THE RESCUE... FORGET IT! HE'S COMPLETELY IN MY POWER... IN HIS CAGE!
YOU MEAN THAT CAT IS SUPERMAN? I SUPPOSE YOU JUST TWITCHED YOUR NOSE, LIKE THE GAL ON BEWITCHED, AND TRANSFORMED HIM?
1

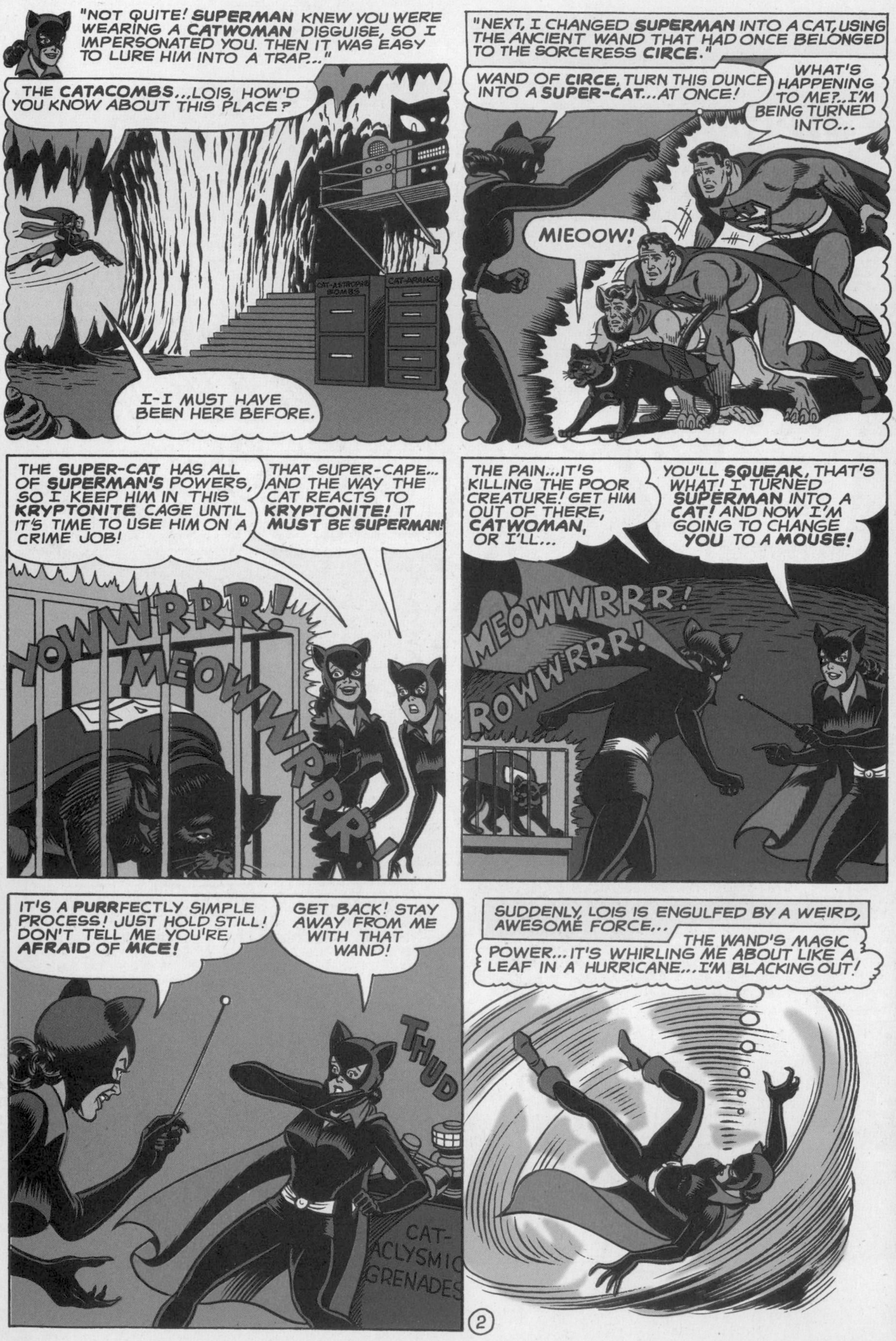
"NOT QUITE! SUPERMAN KNEW YOU WERE WEARING A CATWOMAN DISGUISE, SO I IMPERSONATED YOU. THEN IT WAS EASY TO LURE HIM INTO A TRAP..."
THE CATACOMBS...LOIS, HOW'D YOU KNOW ABOUT THIS PLACE?
CAT-ASTROPHE BOMBS
CAT-ARANGS
I-I MUST HAVE BEEN HERE BEFORE.
"NEXT, I CHANGED SUPERMAN INTO A CAT, USING THE ANCIENT WAND THAT HAD ONCE BELONGED TO THE SORCERESS CIRCE."
WAND OF CIRCE, TURN THIS DUNCE INTO A SUPER-CAT...AT ONCE!
WHAT'S HAPPENING TO ME?..I'M BEING TURNED INTO...
MIEOOW!
THE SUPER-CAT HAS ALL OF SUPERMAN'S POWERS, SO I KEEP HIM IN THIS KRYPTONITE CAGE UNTIL IT'S TIME TO USE HIM ON A CRIME JOB!
THAT SUPER-CAPE... AND THE WAY THE CAT REACTS TO KRYPTONITE! IT MUST BE SUPERMAN!
YOWWRRR!
MEOWWRRR!
THE PAIN...IT'S KILLING THE POOR CREATURE! GET HIM OUT OF THERE, CATWOMAN, OR I'LL...
YOU'LL SQUEAK, THAT'S WHAT! I TURNED SUPERMAN INTO A CAT! AND NOW I'M GOING TO CHANGE YOU TO A MOUSE!
MEOWWRRR!
ROWWRRR!
IT'S A PURRFECTLY SIMPLE PROCESS! JUST HOLD STILL! DON'T TELL ME YOU'RE AFRAID OF MICE!
GET BACK! STAY AWAY FROM ME WITH THAT WAND!
THUD
CAT-ACLYSMIC GRENADES
2
SUDDENLY, LOIS IS ENGULFED BY A WEIRD, AWESOME FORCE...
THE WAND'S MAGIC POWER... IT'S WHIRLING ME ABOUT LIKE A LEAF IN A HURRICANE...I'M BLACKING OUT!

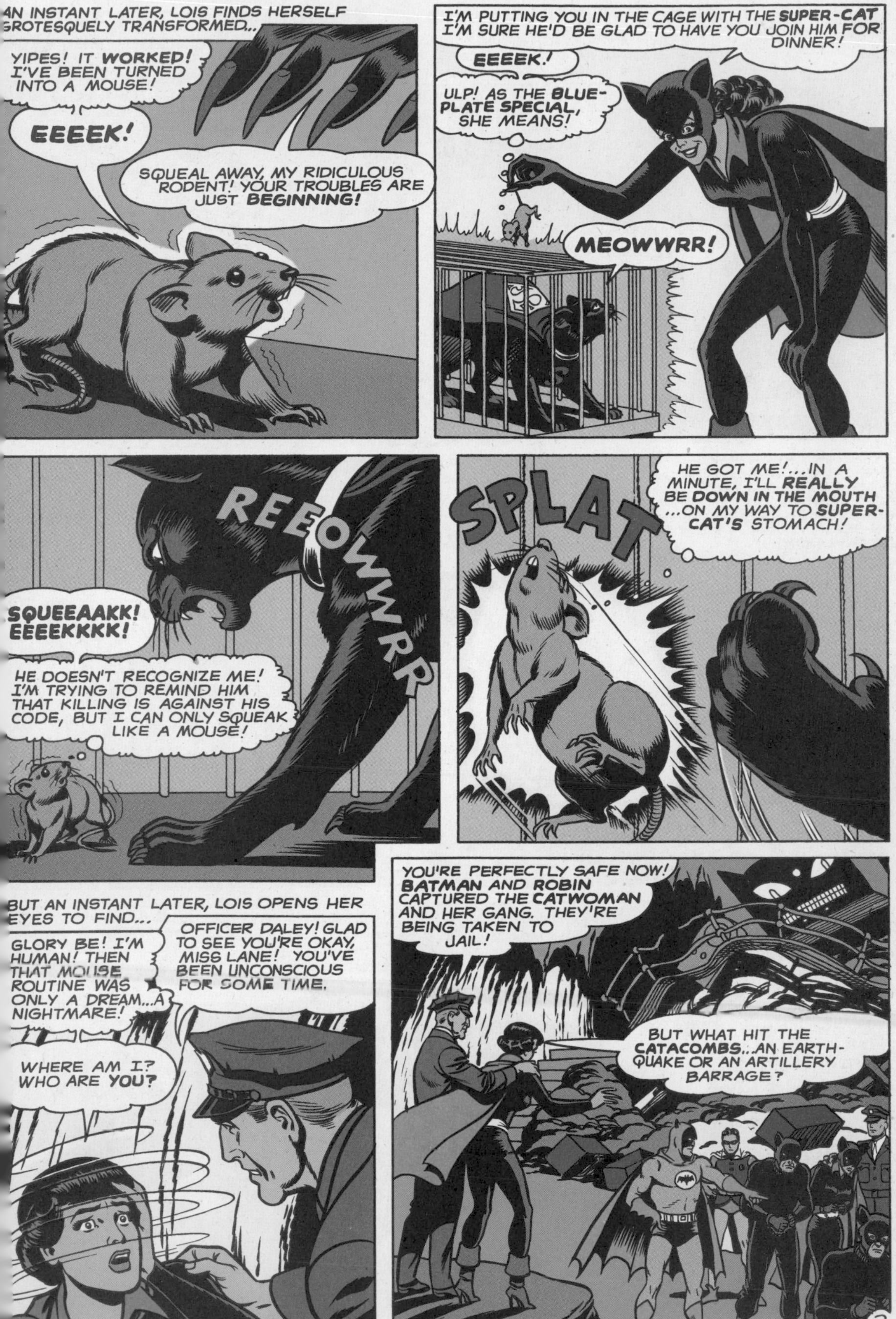
AN INSTANT LATER, LOIS FINDS HERSELF GROTESQUELY TRANSFORMED...
YIPES! IT WORKED! I'VE BEEN TURNED INTO A MOUSE!
EEEEK!
SQUEAL AWAY, MY RIDICULOUS RODENT! YOUR TROUBLES ARE JUST BEGINNING!
I'M PUTTING YOU IN THE CAGE WITH THE SUPER-CAT I'M SURE HE'D BE GLAD TO HAVE YOU JOIN HIM FOR DINNER!
EEEEK!
ULP! AS THE BLUE-PLATE SPECIAL, SHE MEANS!
MEOWWRR!
REEEOWWWRR
SQUEEAAKK! EEEEKKKK!
HE DOESN'T RECOGNIZE ME! I'M TRYING TO REMIND HIM THAT KILLING IS AGAINST HIS CODE, BUT I CAN ONLY SQUEAK LIKE A MOUSE!
SPLAT
HE GOT ME!... IN A MINUTE, I'LL REALLY BE DOWN IN THE MOUTH ...ON MY WAY TO SUPER-CAT'S STOMACH!
BUT AN INSTANT LATER, LOIS OPENS HER EYES TO FIND...
GLORY BE! I'M HUMAN! THEN THAT MOUSE ROUTINE WAS ONLY A DREAM...A NIGHTMARE!
OFFICER DALEY! GLAD TO SEE YOU'RE OKAY, MISS LANE! YOU'VE BEEN UNCONSCIOUS FOR SOME TIME.
WHERE AM I? WHO ARE YOU?
YOU'RE PERFECTLY SAFE NOW! BATMAN AND ROBIN CAPTURED THE CATWOMAN AND HER GANG. THEY'RE BEING TAKEN TO JAIL!
BUT WHAT HIT THE CATACOMBS...AN EARTH-QUAKE OR AN ARTILLERY BARRAGE?
3

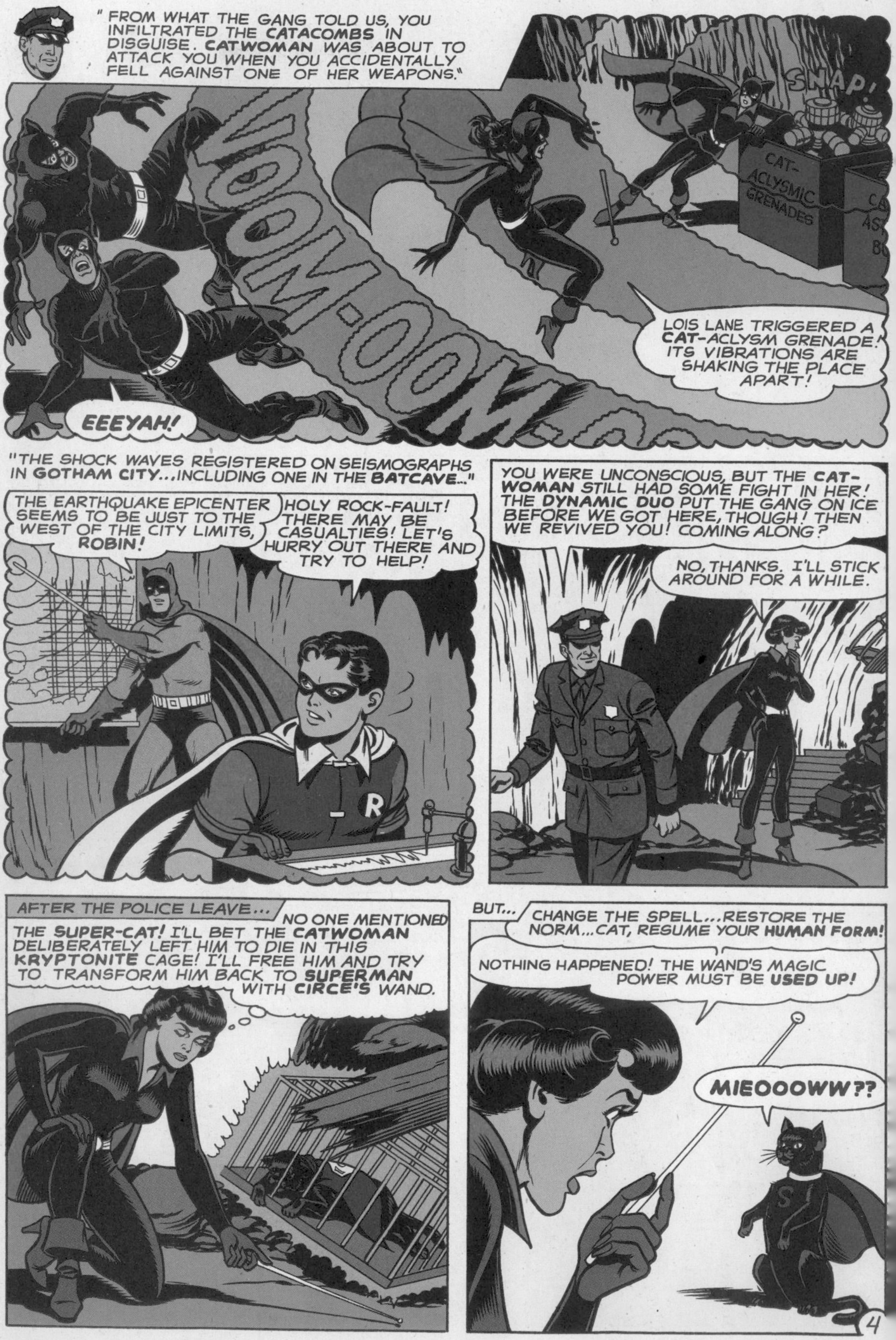
"FROM WHAT THE GANG TOLD US, YOU INFILTRATED THE CATACOMBS IN DISGUISE. CATWOMAN WAS ABOUT TO ATTACK YOU WHEN YOU ACCIDENTALLY FELL AGAINST ONE OF HER WEAPONS."
SNAP!
VOOM-OOM-
CAT-ACLYSMIC GRENADES
EEEYAH!
LOIS LANE TRIGGERED A CAT-ACLYSM GRENADE! ITS VIBRATIONS ARE SHAKING THE PLACE APART!
"THE SHOCK WAVES REGISTERED ON SEISMOGRAPHS IN GOTHAM CITY... INCLUDING ONE IN THE BATCAVE..."
THE EARTHQUAKE EPICENTER SEEMS TO BE JUST TO THE WEST OF THE CITY LIMITS, ROBIN!
HOLY ROCK-FAULT! THERE MAY BE CASUALTIES! LET'S HURRY OUT THERE AND TRY TO HELP!
YOU WERE UNCONSCIOUS, BUT THE CAT-WOMAN STILL HAD SOME FIGHT IN HER! THE DYNAMIC DUO PUT THE GANG ON ICE BEFORE WE GOT HERE, THOUGH! THEN WE REVIVED YOU! COMING ALONG?
NO, THANKS. I'LL STICK AROUND FOR A WHILE.
AFTER THE POLICE LEAVE...
NO ONE MENTIONED THE SUPER-CAT! I'LL BET THE CATWOMAN DELIBERATELY LEFT HIM TO DIE IN THIS KRYPTONITE CAGE! I'LL FREE HIM AND TRY TO TRANSFORM HIM BACK TO SUPERMAN WITH CIRCE'S WAND.
BUT...
CHANGE THE SPELL... RESTORE THE NORM... CAT, RESUME YOUR HUMAN FORM!
NOTHING HAPPENED! THE WAND'S MAGIC POWER MUST BE USED UP!
MIEOOOWW??
4

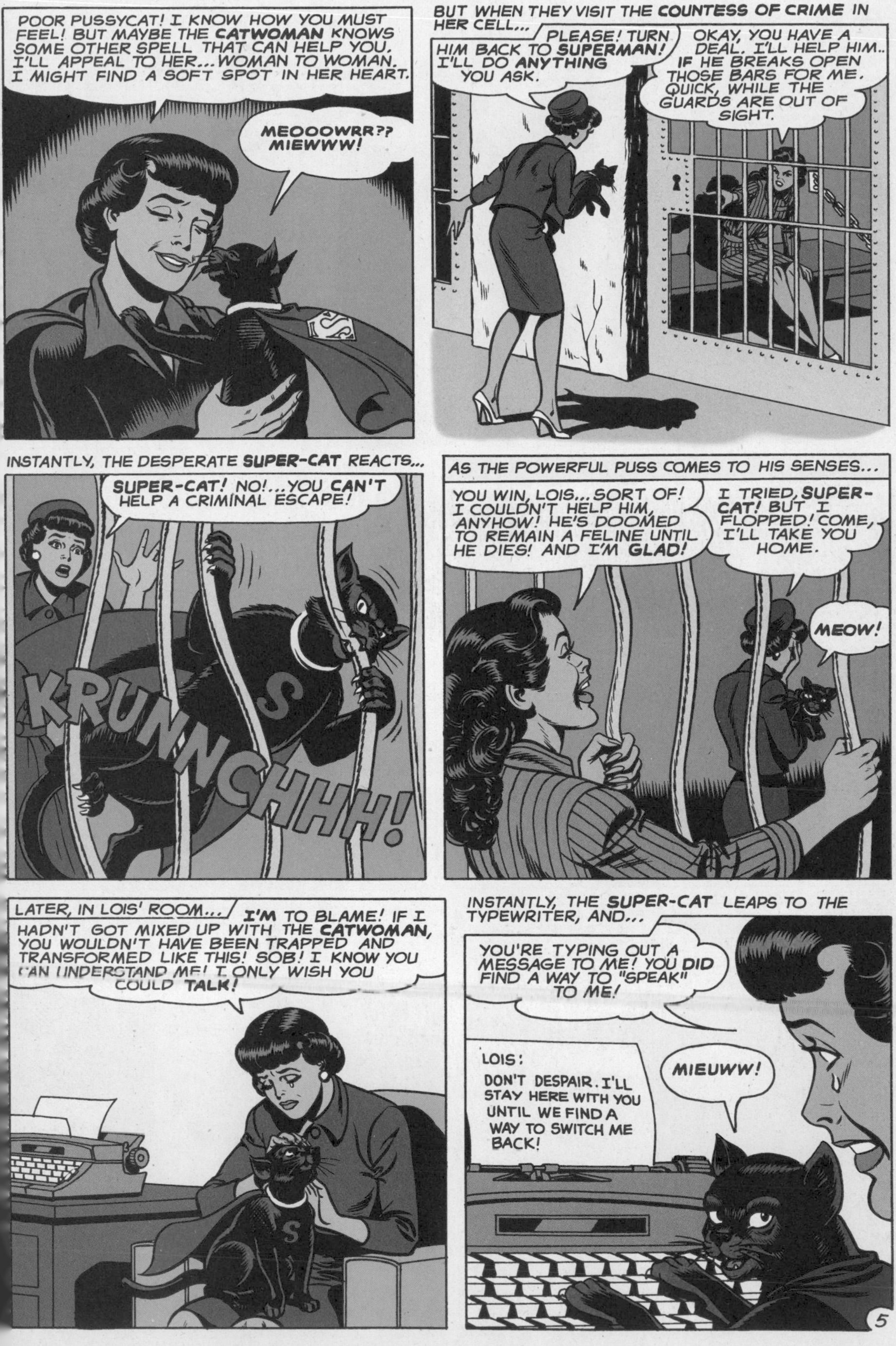

POOR PUSSYCAT! I KNOW HOW YOU MUST FEEL! BUT MAYBE THE CATWOMAN KNOWS SOME OTHER SPELL THAT CAN HELP YOU. I'LL APPEAL TO HER... WOMAN TO WOMAN. I MIGHT FIND A SOFT SPOT IN HER HEART.
MEOOOWRR?? MIEWWW!
BUT WHEN THEY VISIT THE COUNTESS OF CRIME IN HER CELL...
PLEASE! TURN HIM BACK TO SUPERMAN! I'LL DO ANYTHING YOU ASK.
OKAY, YOU HAVE A DEAL. I'LL HELP HIM.. IF HE BREAKS OPEN THOSE BARS FOR ME. QUICK, WHILE THE GUARDS ARE OUT OF SIGHT.
INSTANTLY, THE DESPERATE SUPER-CAT REACTS...
SUPER-CAT! NO!... YOU CAN'T HELP A CRIMINAL ESCAPE!
KRUNNCHHH!
AS THE POWERFUL PUSS COMES TO HIS SENSES...
YOU WIN, LOIS... SORT OF! I COULDN'T HELP HIM, ANYHOW! HE'S DOOMED TO REMAIN A FELINE UNTIL HE DIES! AND I'M GLAD!
I TRIED, SUPER-CAT! BUT I FLOPPED! COME, I'LL TAKE YOU HOME.
MEOW!
LATER, IN LOIS' ROOM...
I'M TO BLAME! IF I HADN'T GOT MIXED UP WITH THE CATWOMAN, YOU WOULDN'T HAVE BEEN TRAPPED AND TRANSFORMED LIKE THIS! SOB! I KNOW YOU CAN UNDERSTAND ME! I ONLY WISH YOU COULD TALK!
INSTANTLY, THE SUPER-CAT LEAPS TO THE TYPEWRITER, AND...
YOU'RE TYPING OUT A MESSAGE TO ME! YOU DID FIND A WAY TO "SPEAK" TO ME!
LOIS: DON'T DESPAIR. I'LL STAY HERE WITH YOU UNTIL WE FIND A WAY TO SWITCH ME BACK!
MIEUWW!
5

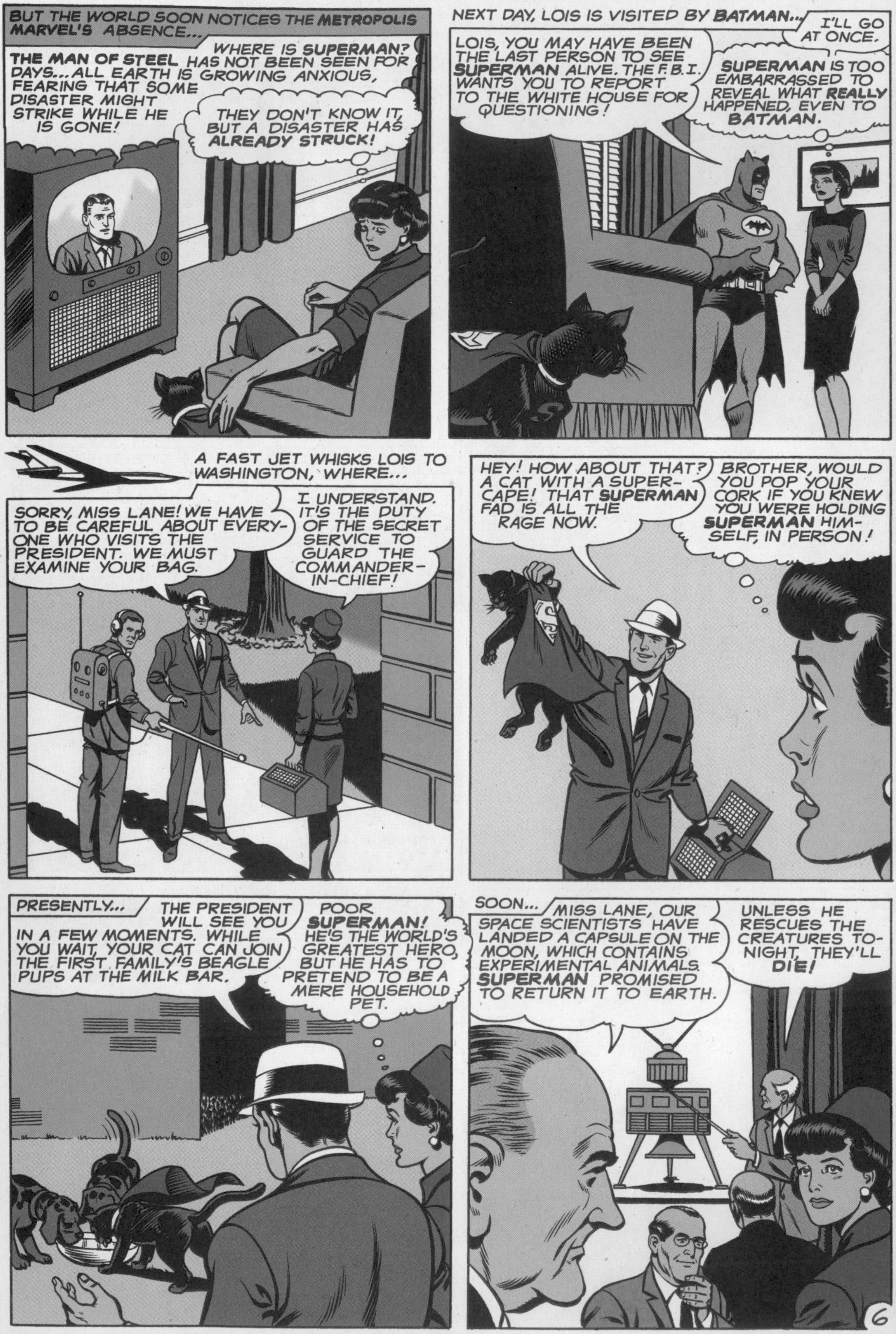
BUT THE WORLD SOON NOTICES THE METROPOLIS MARVEL'S ABSENCE...
WHERE IS SUPERMAN? THE MAN OF STEEL HAS NOT BEEN SEEN FOR DAYS...ALL EARTH IS GROWING ANXIOUS, FEARING THAT SOME DISASTER MIGHT STRIKE WHILE HE IS GONE!
THEY DON'T KNOW IT, BUT A DISASTER HAS ALREADY STRUCK!
NEXT DAY, LOIS IS VISITED BY BATMAN...
LOIS, YOU MAY HAVE BEEN THE LAST PERSON TO SEE SUPERMAN ALIVE. THE F.B.I. WANTS YOU TO REPORT TO THE WHITE HOUSE FOR QUESTIONING!
I'LL GO AT ONCE.
SUPERMAN IS TOO EMBARRASSED TO REVEAL WHAT REALLY HAPPENED, EVEN TO BATMAN.
A FAST JET WHISKS LOIS TO WASHINGTON, WHERE...
SORRY, MISS LANE! WE HAVE TO BE CAREFUL ABOUT EVERY-ONE WHO VISITS THE PRESIDENT. WE MUST EXAMINE YOUR BAG.
I UNDERSTAND. IT'S THE DUTY OF THE SECRET SERVICE TO GUARD THE COMMANDER-IN-CHIEF!
HEY! HOW ABOUT THAT? A CAT WITH A SUPER-CAPE! THAT SUPERMAN FAD IS ALL THE RAGE NOW.
BROTHER, WOULD YOU POP YOUR CORK IF YOU KNEW YOU WERE HOLDING SUPERMAN HIM-SELF, IN PERSON!
PRESENTLY...
THE PRESIDENT WILL SEE YOU IN A FEW MOMENTS. WHILE YOU WAIT, YOUR CAT CAN JOIN THE FIRST FAMILY'S BEAGLE PUPS AT THE MILK BAR.
POOR SUPERMAN! HE'S THE WORLD'S GREATEST HERO, BUT HE HAS TO PRETEND TO BE A MERE HOUSEHOLD PET.
SOON...
MISS LANE, OUR SPACE SCIENTISTS HAVE LANDED A CAPSULE ON THE MOON, WHICH CONTAINS EXPERIMENTAL ANIMALS. SUPERMAN PROMISED TO RETURN IT TO EARTH.
UNLESS HE RESCUES THE CREATURES TO-NIGHT, THEY'LL DIE!
6

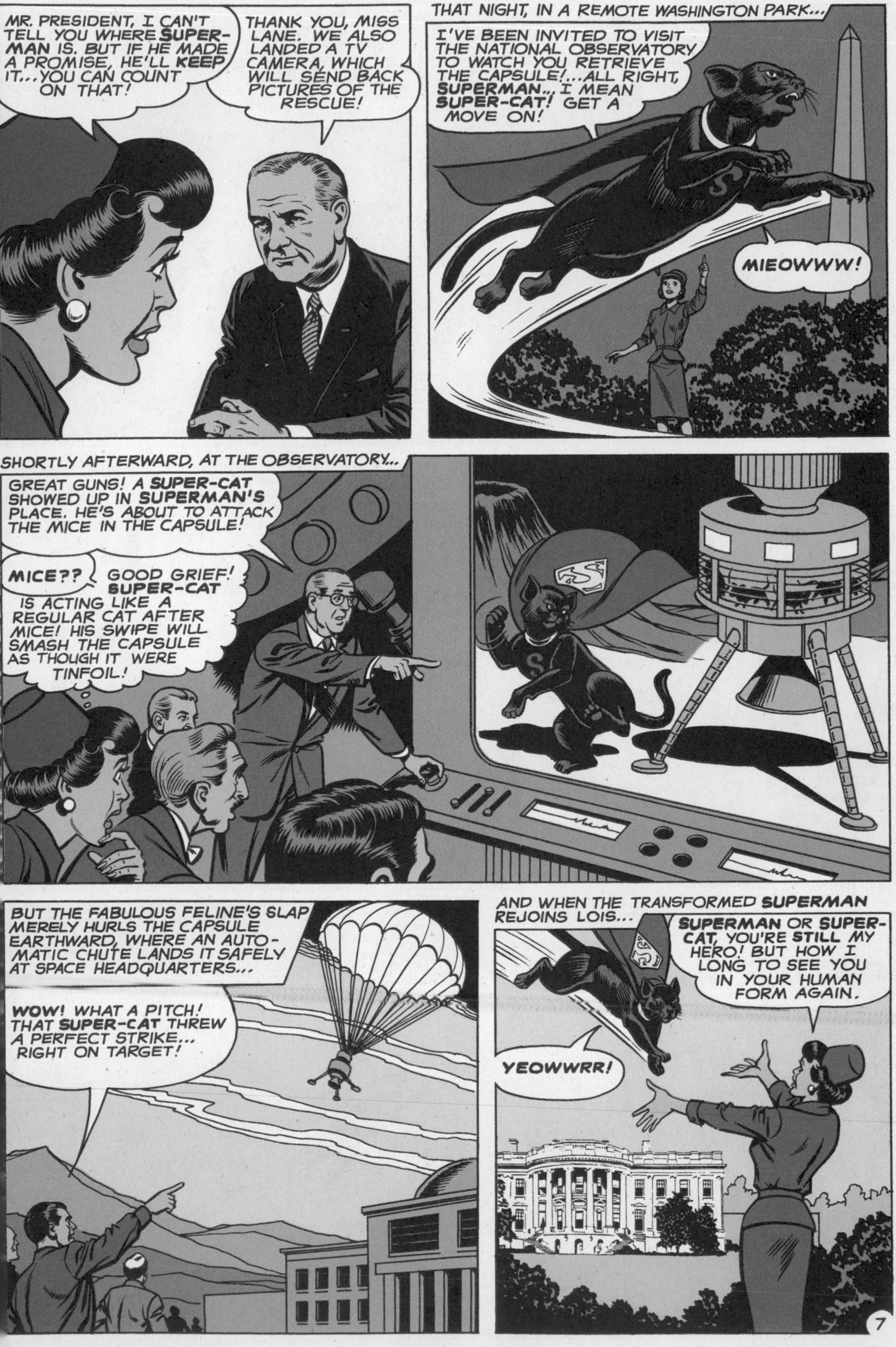
MR. PRESIDENT, I CAN'T TELL YOU WHERE SUPERMAN IS. BUT IF HE MADE A PROMISE, HE'LL KEEP IT... YOU CAN COUNT ON THAT!
THANK YOU, MISS LANE. WE ALSO LANDED A TV CAMERA, WHICH WILL SEND BACK PICTURES OF THE RESCUE!
THAT NIGHT, IN A REMOTE WASHINGTON PARK...
I'VE BEEN INVITED TO VISIT THE NATIONAL OBSERVATORY TO WATCH YOU RETRIEVE THE CAPSULE!... ALL RIGHT, SUPERMAN... I MEAN SUPER-CAT! GET A MOVE ON!
MIEOWWW!
SHORTLY AFTERWARD, AT THE OBSERVATORY...
GREAT GUNS! A SUPER-CAT SHOWED UP IN SUPERMAN'S PLACE. HE'S ABOUT TO ATTACK THE MICE IN THE CAPSULE!
MICE??
GOOD GRIEF! SUPER-CAT IS ACTING LIKE A REGULAR CAT AFTER MICE! HIS SWIPE WILL SMASH THE CAPSULE AS THOUGH IT WERE TINFOIL!
BUT THE FABULOUS FELINE'S SLAP MERELY HURLS THE CAPSULE EARTHWARD, WHERE AN AUTOMATIC CHUTE LANDS IT SAFELY AT SPACE HEADQUARTERS...
WOW! WHAT A PITCH! THAT SUPER-CAT THREW A PERFECT STRIKE... RIGHT ON TARGET!
AND WHEN THE TRANSFORMED SUPERMAN REJOINS LOIS...
SUPERMAN OR SUPER-CAT, YOU'RE STILL MY HERO! BUT HOW I LONG TO SEE YOU IN YOUR HUMAN FORM AGAIN.
YEOWWRR!
7

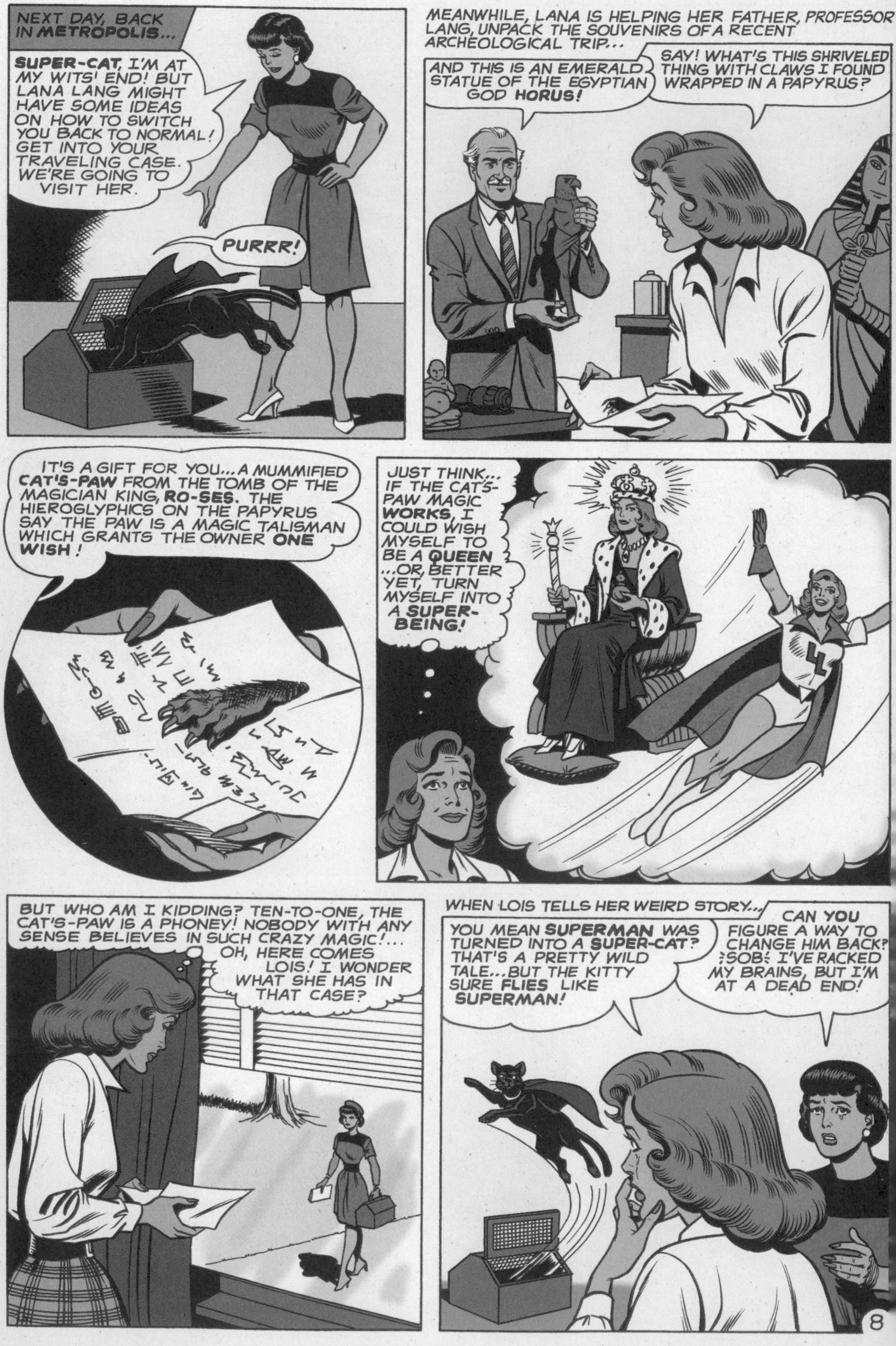
NEXT DAY, BACK IN METROPOLIS...
SUPER-CAT, I'M AT MY WITS' END! BUT LANA LANG MIGHT HAVE SOME IDEAS ON HOW TO SWITCH YOU BACK TO NORMAL! GET INTO YOUR TRAVELING CASE. WE'RE GOING TO VISIT HER.
PURRR!
MEANWHILE, LANA IS HELPING HER FATHER, PROFESSOR LANG, UNPACK THE SOUVENIRS OF A RECENT ARCHEOLOGICAL TRIP...
AND THIS IS AN EMERALD STATUE OF THE EGYPTIAN GOD HORUS!
SAY! WHAT'S THIS SHRIVELED THING WITH CLAWS I FOUND WRAPPED IN A PAPYRUS?
IT'S A GIFT FOR YOU... A MUMMIFIED CAT'S-PAW FROM THE TOMB OF THE MAGICIAN KING, RO-SES. THE HIEROGLYPHICS ON THE PAPYRUS SAY THE PAW IS A MAGIC TALISMAN WHICH GRANTS THE OWNER ONE WISH!
JUST THINK... IF THE CAT'S-PAW MAGIC WORKS, I COULD WISH MYSELF TO BE A QUEEN ...OR, BETTER YET, TURN MYSELF INTO A SUPER-BEING!
BUT WHO AM I KIDDING? TEN-TO-ONE, THE CAT'S-PAW IS A PHONEY! NOBODY WITH ANY SENSE BELIEVES IN SUCH CRAZY MAGIC!... OH, HERE COMES LOIS! I WONDER WHAT SHE HAS IN THAT CASE?
WHEN LOIS TELLS HER WEIRD STORY...
YOU MEAN SUPERMAN WAS TURNED INTO A SUPER-CAT? THAT'S A PRETTY WILD TALE... BUT THE KITTY SURE FLIES LIKE SUPERMAN!
CAN YOU FIGURE A WAY TO CHANGE HIM BACK? SOB! I'VE RACKED MY BRAINS, BUT I'M AT A DEAD END!
8

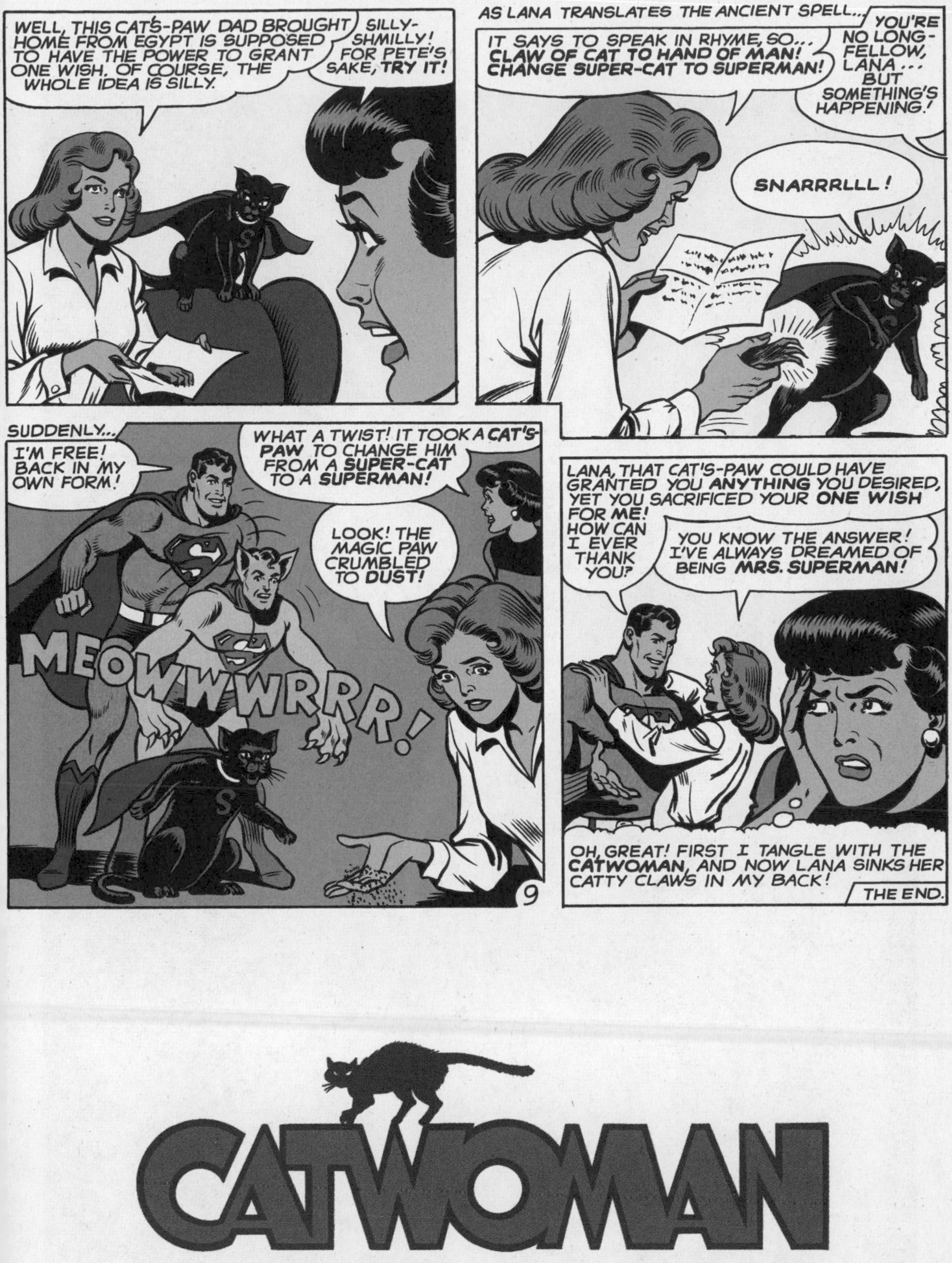
WELL, THIS CAT'S-PAW DAD BROUGHT HOME FROM EGYPT IS SUPPOSED TO HAVE THE POWER TO GRANT ONE WISH. OF COURSE, THE WHOLE IDEA IS SILLY.
SILLY-SHMILLY! FOR PETE'S SAKE, TRY IT!
AS LANA TRANSLATES THE ANCIENT SPELL...
IT SAYS TO SPEAK IN RHYME, SO... CLAW OF CAT TO HAND OF MAN! CHANGE SUPER-CAT TO SUPERMAN!
YOU'RE NO LONG-FELLOW, LANA... BUT SOMETHING'S HAPPENING!
SNARRRLLL!
SUDDENLY...
I'M FREE! BACK IN MY OWN FORM!
WHAT A TWIST! IT TOOK A CAT'S-PAW TO CHANGE HIM FROM A SUPER-CAT TO A SUPERMAN!
LOOK! THE MAGIC PAW CRUMBLED TO DUST!
MEOWWWRRRR!
9
LANA, THAT CAT'S-PAW COULD HAVE GRANTED YOU ANYTHING YOU DESIRED, YET YOU SACRIFICED YOUR ONE WISH FOR ME!
HOW CAN I EVER THANK YOU?
YOU KNOW THE ANSWER! I'VE ALWAYS DREAMED OF BEING MRS. SUPERMAN!
OH, GREAT! FIRST I TANGLE WITH THE CATWOMAN, AND NOW LANA SINKS HER CATTY CLAWS IN MY BACK!
THE END.

CATWOMAN

pinup George Pérez

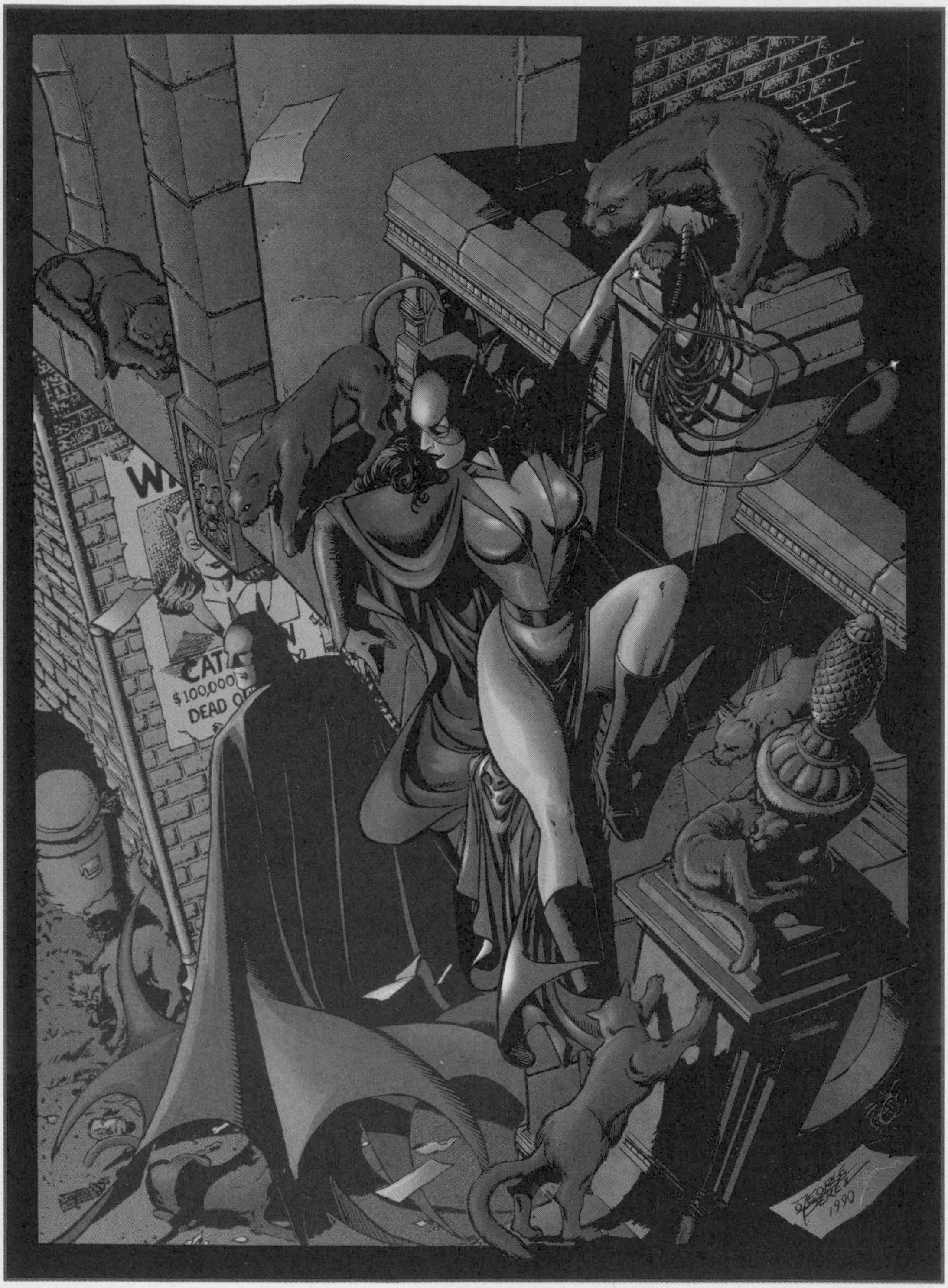
$100,000

Originally used in BATMAN 3-D (1990). Colored by Tom Smith.

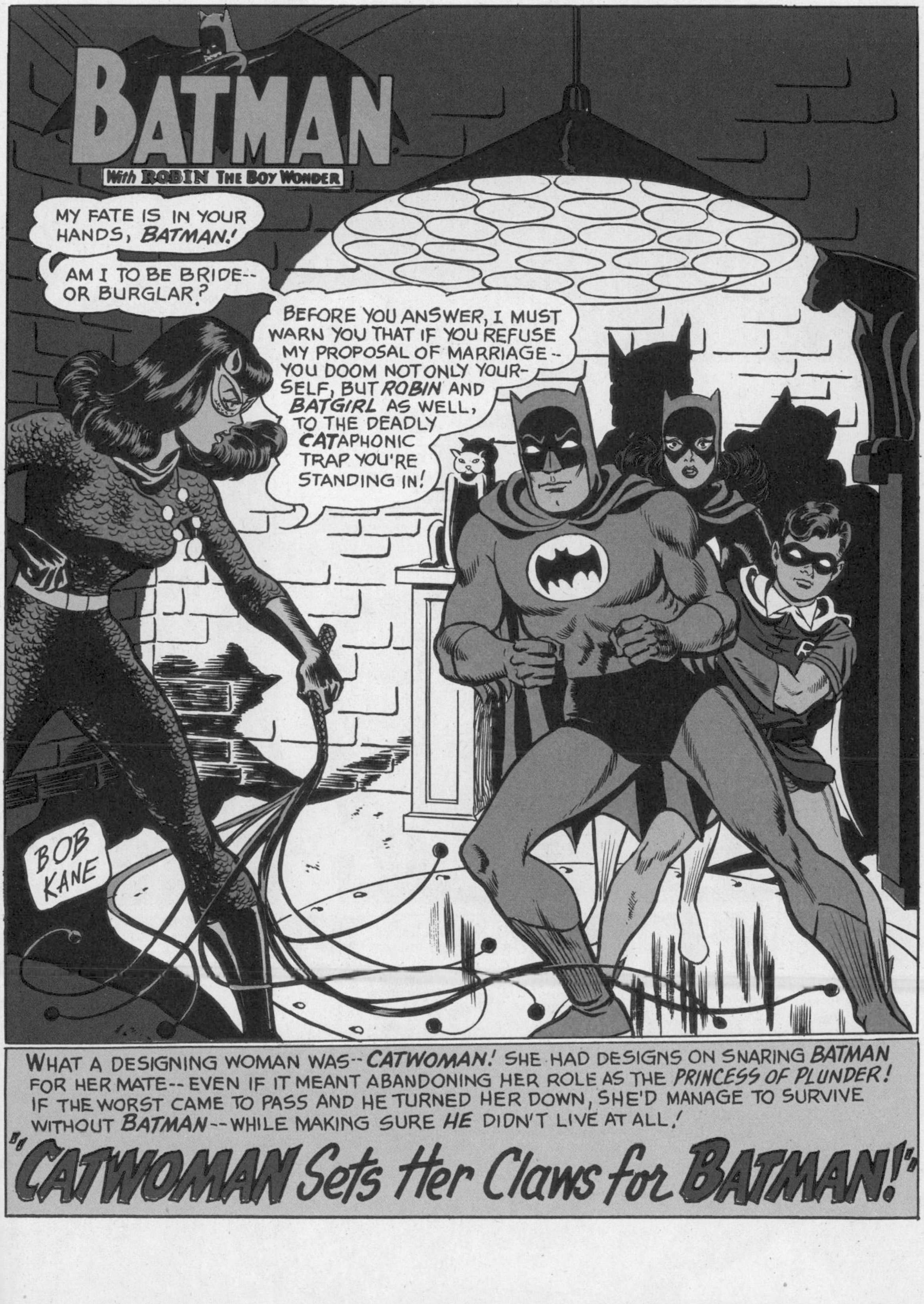
BATMAN
With ROBIN THE BOY WONDER
MY FATE IS IN YOUR HANDS, BATMAN!
AM I TO BE BRIDE-- OR BURGLAR?
BEFORE YOU ANSWER, I MUST WARN YOU THAT IF YOU REFUSE MY PROPOSAL OF MARRIAGE -- YOU DOOM NOT ONLY YOURSELF, BUT ROBIN AND BATGIRL AS WELL, TO THE DEADLY CATAPHONIC TRAP YOU'RE STANDING IN!
BOB KANE
WHAT A DESIGNING WOMAN WAS-- CATWOMAN! SHE HAD DESIGNS ON SNARING BATMAN FOR HER MATE-- EVEN IF IT MEANT ABANDONING HER ROLE AS THE PRINCESS OF PLUNDER! IF THE WORST CAME TO PASS AND HE TURNED HER DOWN, SHE'D MANAGE TO SURVIVE WITHOUT BATMAN-- WHILE MAKING SURE HE DIDN'T LIVE AT ALL!
"CATWOMAN Sets Her Claws for BATMAN!"

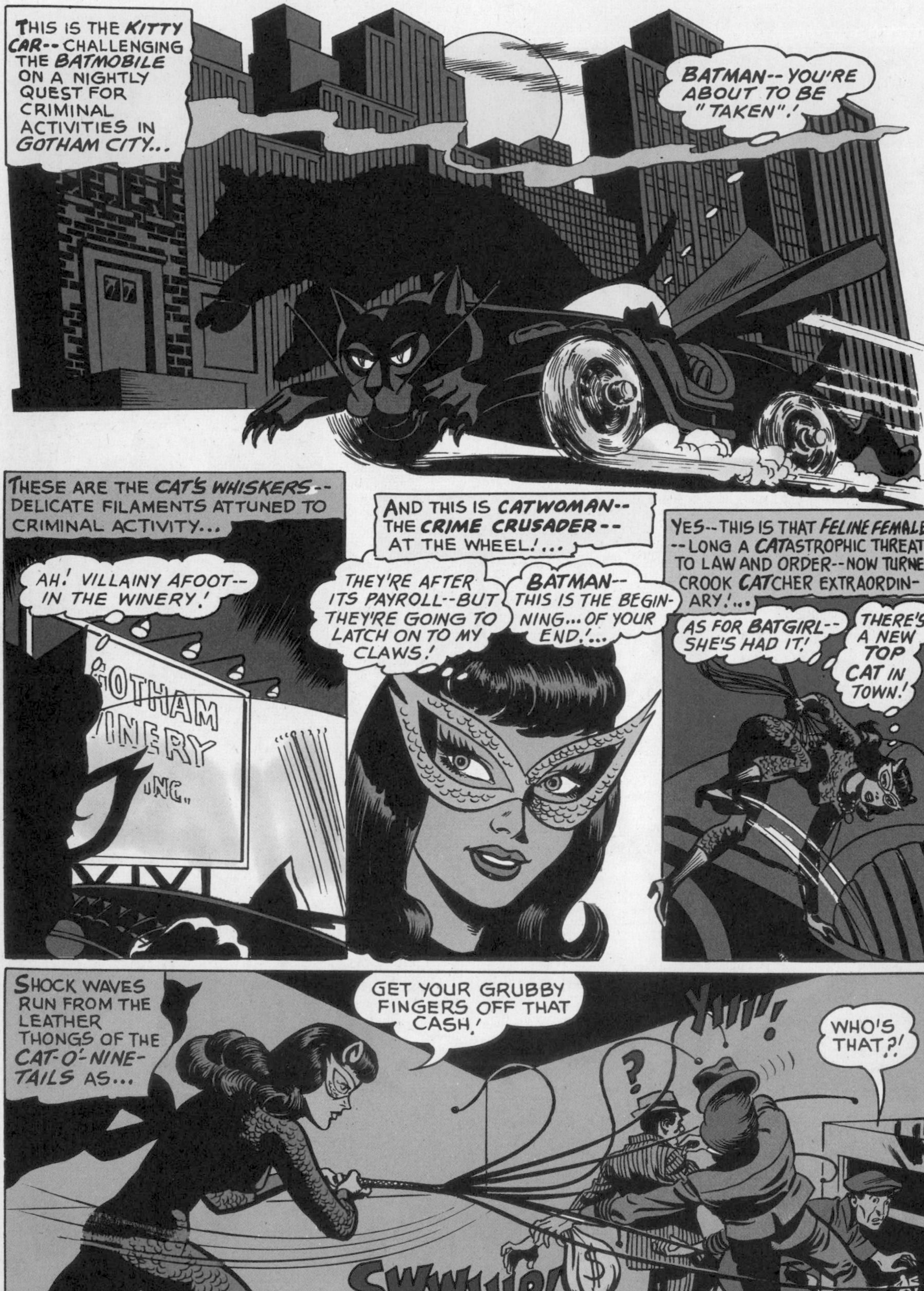
THIS IS THE KITTY CAR-- CHALLENGING THE BATMOBILE ON A NIGHTLY QUEST FOR CRIMINAL ACTIVITIES IN GOTHAM CITY...
BATMAN-- YOU'RE ABOUT TO BE "TAKEN"!
THESE ARE THE CAT'S WHISKERS-- DELICATE FILAMENTS ATTUNED TO CRIMINAL ACTIVITY...
AH! VILLAINY AFOOT-- IN THE WINERY!
GOTHAM WINERY INC.
AND THIS IS CATWOMAN-- THE CRIME CRUSADER-- AT THE WHEEL!...
THEY'RE AFTER ITS PAYROLL--BUT THEY'RE GOING TO LATCH ON TO MY CLAWS!
BATMAN-- THIS IS THE BEGINNING... OF YOUR END!...
YES--THIS IS THAT FELINE FEMALE --LONG A CATASTROPHIC THREAT TO LAW AND ORDER--NOW TURNED CROOK CATCHER EXTRAORDINARY!...
AS FOR BATGIRL-- SHE'S HAD IT!
THERE'S A NEW TOP CAT IN TOWN!
SHOCK WAVES RUN FROM THE LEATHER THONGS OF THE CAT-O'-NINE-TAILS AS...
GET YOUR GRUBBY FINGERS OFF THAT CASH!
YIII!
?
WHO'S THAT?!
SWWIIIP!
2

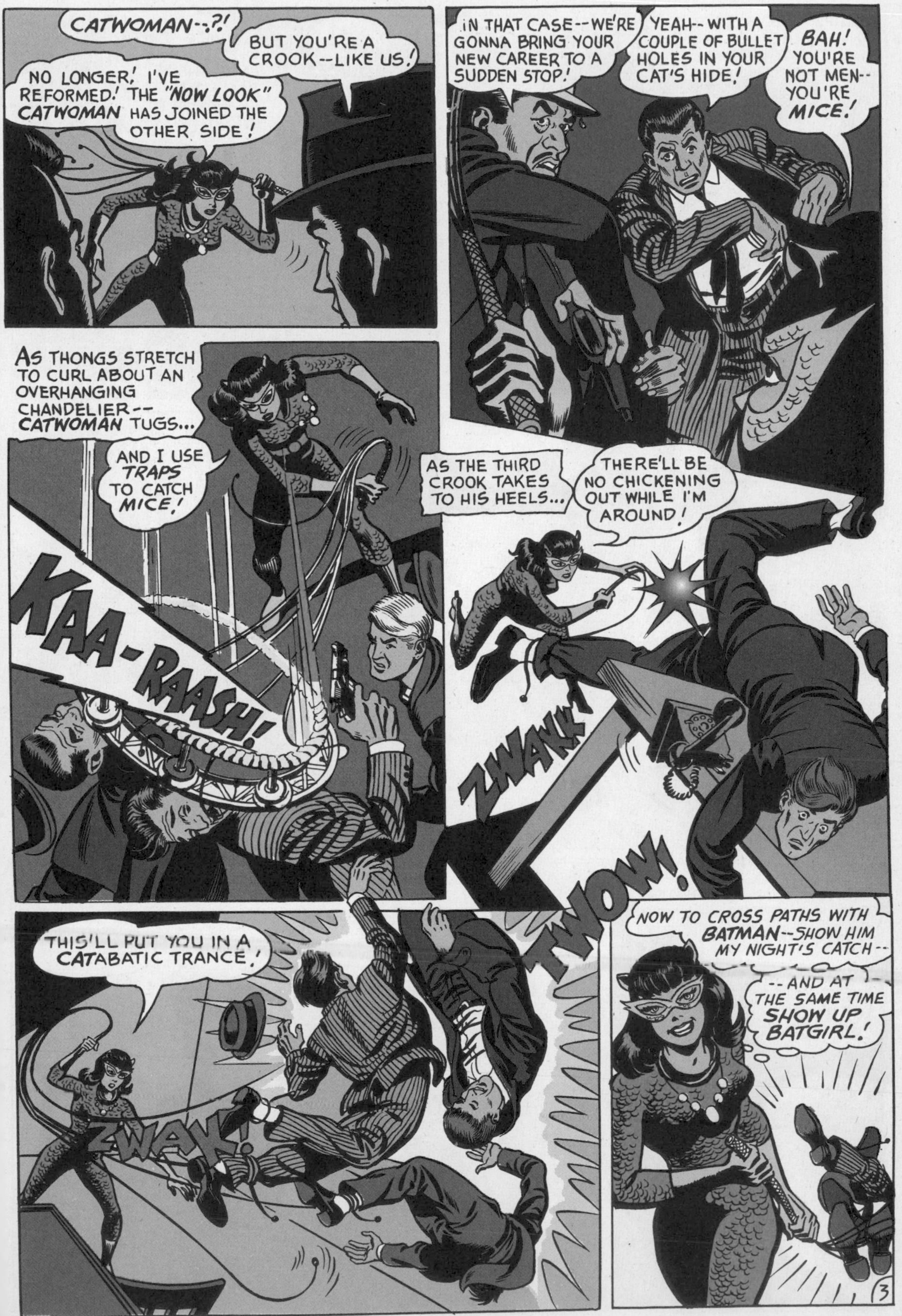
CATWOMAN--?!
BUT YOU'RE A CROOK--LIKE US!
NO LONGER! I'VE REFORMED! THE "NOW LOOK" CATWOMAN HAS JOINED THE OTHER SIDE!
IN THAT CASE--WE'RE GONNA BRING YOUR NEW CAREER TO A SUDDEN STOP!
YEAH--WITH A COUPLE OF BULLET HOLES IN YOUR CAT'S HIDE!
BAH! YOU'RE NOT MEN--YOU'RE MICE!
AS THONGS STRETCH TO CURL ABOUT AN OVERHANGING CHANDELIER--CATWOMAN TUGS...
AND I USE TRAPS TO CATCH MICE!
KAA-RAAASH!
AS THE THIRD CROOK TAKES TO HIS HEELS...
THERE'LL BE NO CHICKENING OUT WHILE I'M AROUND!
ZWANK
TWOW!
THIS'LL PUT YOU IN A CATABATIC TRANCE!
ZWAK!
NOW TO CROSS PATHS WITH BATMAN--SHOW HIM MY NIGHT'S CATCH--
--AND AT THE SAME TIME SHOW UP BATGIRL!
3

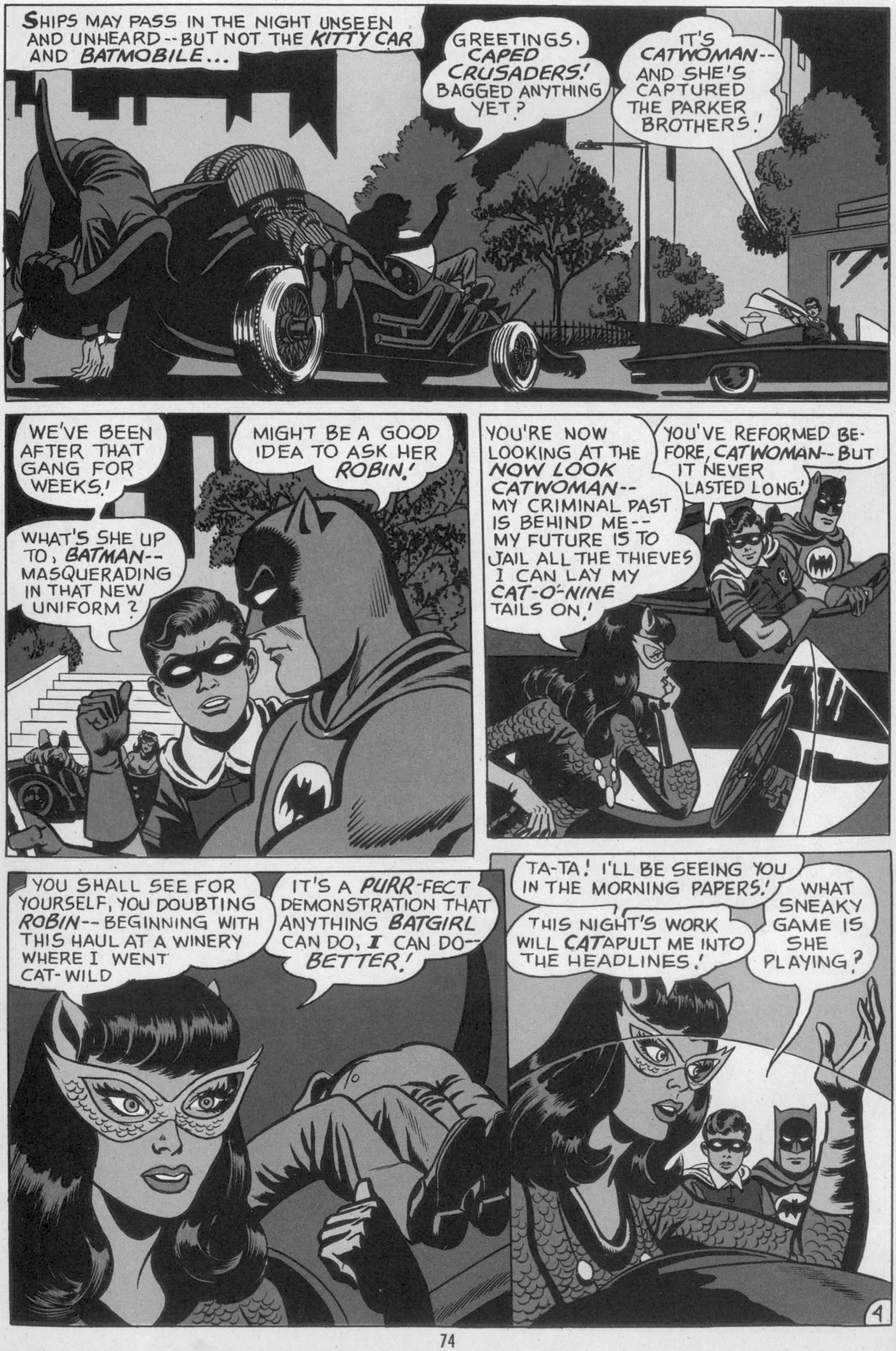
SHIPS MAY PASS IN THE NIGHT UNSEEN AND UNHEARD--BUT NOT THE KITTY CAR AND BATMOBILE...
GREETINGS, CAPED CRUSADERS! BAGGED ANYTHING YET?
IT'S CATWOMAN--AND SHE'S CAPTURED THE PARKER BROTHERS!
WE'VE BEEN AFTER THAT GANG FOR WEEKS!
WHAT'S SHE UP TO, BATMAN--MASQUERADING IN THAT NEW UNIFORM?
MIGHT BE A GOOD IDEA TO ASK HER ROBIN!
YOU'RE NOW LOOKING AT THE NOW LOOK CATWOMAN--MY CRIMINAL PAST IS BEHIND ME--MY FUTURE IS TO JAIL ALL THE THIEVES I CAN LAY MY CAT-O'-NINE TAILS ON!
YOU'VE REFORMED BEFORE, CATWOMAN--BUT IT NEVER LASTED LONG!
YOU SHALL SEE FOR YOURSELF, YOU DOUBTING ROBIN--BEGINNING WITH THIS HAUL AT A WINERY WHERE I WENT CAT-WILD
IT'S A PURR-FECT DEMONSTRATION THAT ANYTHING BATGIRL CAN DO, I CAN DO--BETTER!
TA-TA! I'LL BE SEEING YOU IN THE MORNING PAPERS!
THIS NIGHT'S WORK WILL CATAPULT ME INTO THE HEADLINES!
WHAT SNEAKY GAME IS SHE PLAYING?
4

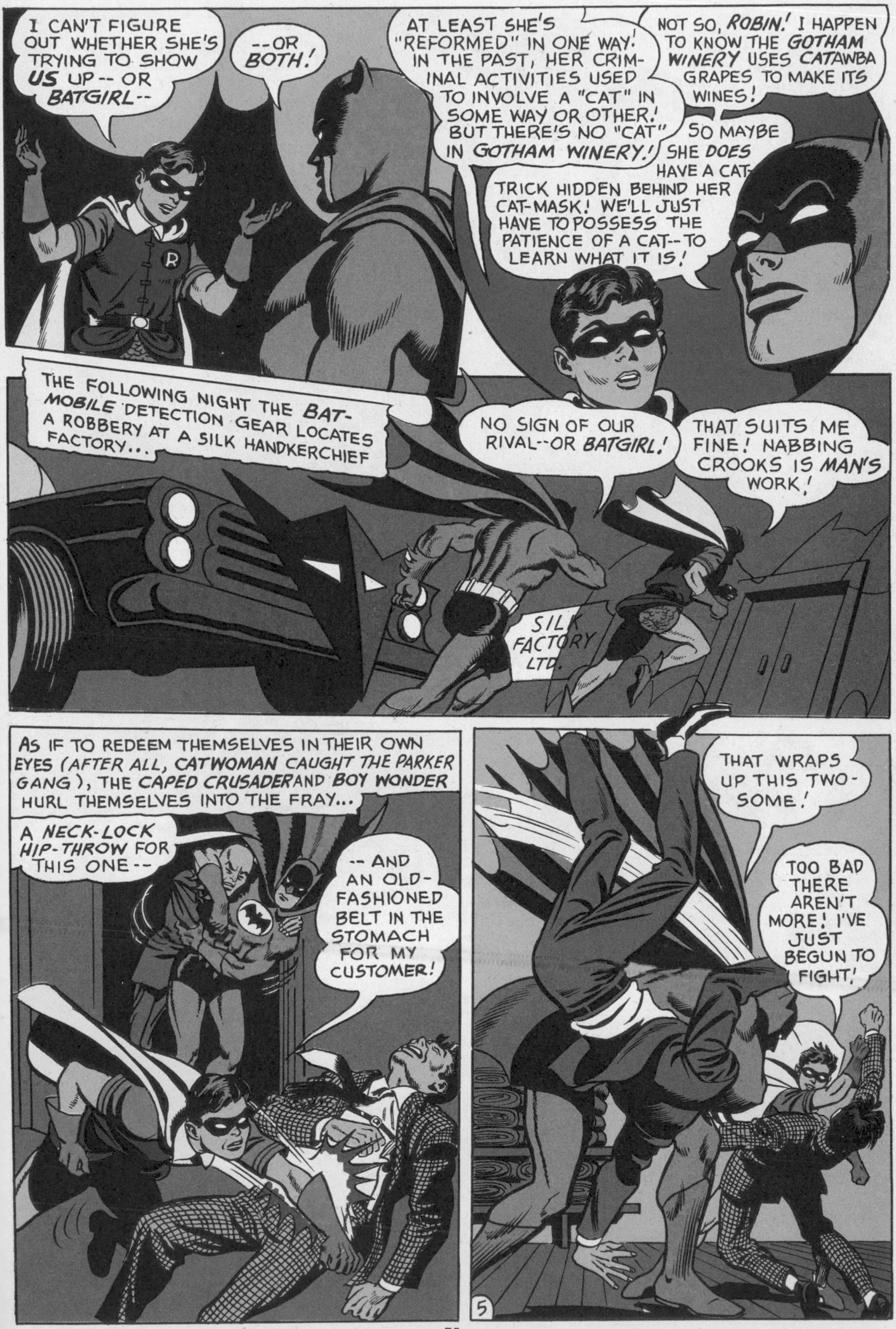
I CAN'T FIGURE OUT WHETHER SHE'S TRYING TO SHOW US UP -- OR BATGIRL--
--OR BOTH!
AT LEAST SHE'S "REFORMED" IN ONE WAY! IN THE PAST, HER CRIMINAL ACTIVITIES USED TO INVOLVE A "CAT" IN SOME WAY OR OTHER! BUT THERE'S NO "CAT" IN GOTHAM WINERY!
NOT SO, ROBIN! I HAPPEN TO KNOW THE GOTHAM WINERY USES CATAWBA GRAPES TO MAKE ITS WINES!
SO MAYBE SHE DOES HAVE A CAT-TRICK HIDDEN BEHIND HER CAT-MASK! WE'LL JUST HAVE TO POSSESS THE PATIENCE OF A CAT--TO LEARN WHAT IT IS!
THE FOLLOWING NIGHT THE BATMOBILE DETECTION GEAR LOCATES A ROBBERY AT A SILK HANDKERCHIEF FACTORY...
NO SIGN OF OUR RIVAL--OR BATGIRL!
THAT SUITS ME FINE! NABBING CROOKS IS MAN'S WORK!
SILK FACTORY LTD.
AS IF TO REDEEM THEMSELVES IN THEIR OWN EYES (AFTER ALL, CATWOMAN CAUGHT THE PARKER GANG), THE CAPED CRUSADER AND BOY WONDER HURL THEMSELVES INTO THE FRAY...
A NECK-LOCK HIP-THROW FOR THIS ONE--
-- AND AN OLD-FASHIONED BELT IN THE STOMACH FOR MY CUSTOMER!
THAT WRAPS UP THIS TWO-SOME!
TOO BAD THERE AREN'T MORE! I'VE JUST BEGUN TO FIGHT!
5

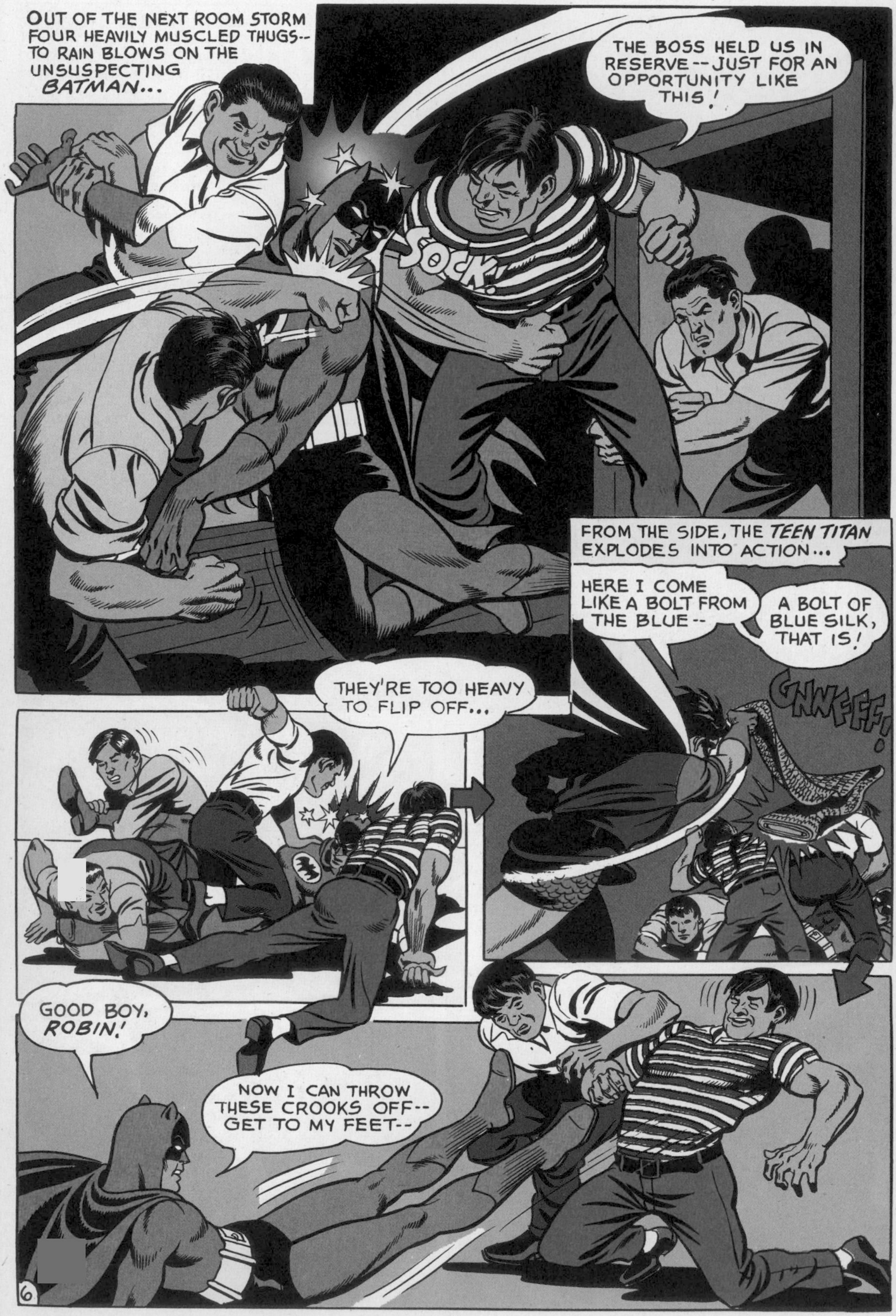
OUT OF THE NEXT ROOM STORM FOUR HEAVILY MUSCLED THUGS-- TO RAIN BLOWS ON THE UNSUSPECTING *BATMAN*...
THE BOSS HELD US IN RESERVE--JUST FOR AN OPPORTUNITY LIKE THIS!
SOCK!
FROM THE SIDE, THE *TEEN TITAN* EXPLODES INTO ACTION...
HERE I COME LIKE A BOLT FROM THE BLUE--
A BOLT OF BLUE SILK, THAT IS!
GNNFFF!
THEY'RE TOO HEAVY TO FLIP OFF...
GOOD BOY, *ROBIN*!
NOW I CAN THROW THESE CROOKS OFF-- GET TO MY FEET--
6

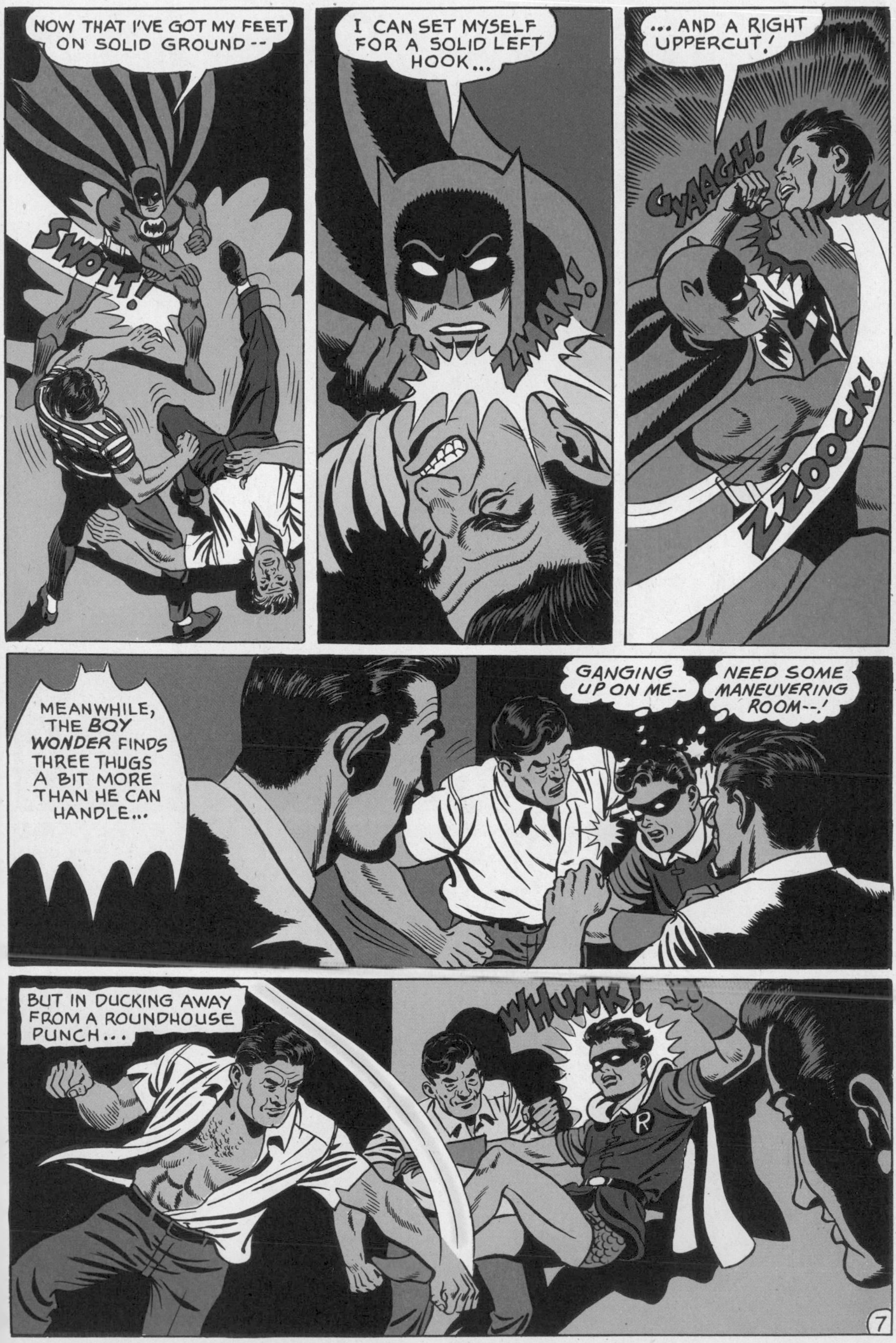
NOW THAT I'VE GOT MY FEET ON SOLID GROUND--
SWOTT!
I CAN SET MYSELF FOR A SOLID LEFT HOOK...
ZMAK!
...AND A RIGHT UPPERCUT!
GYAAGH!
ZZOOCK!
MEANWHILE, THE BOY WONDER FINDS THREE THUGS A BIT MORE THAN HE CAN HANDLE...
GANGING UP ON ME--
NEED SOME MANEUVERING ROOM--!
BUT IN DUCKING AWAY FROM A ROUNDHOUSE PUNCH...
WHUNK!
7

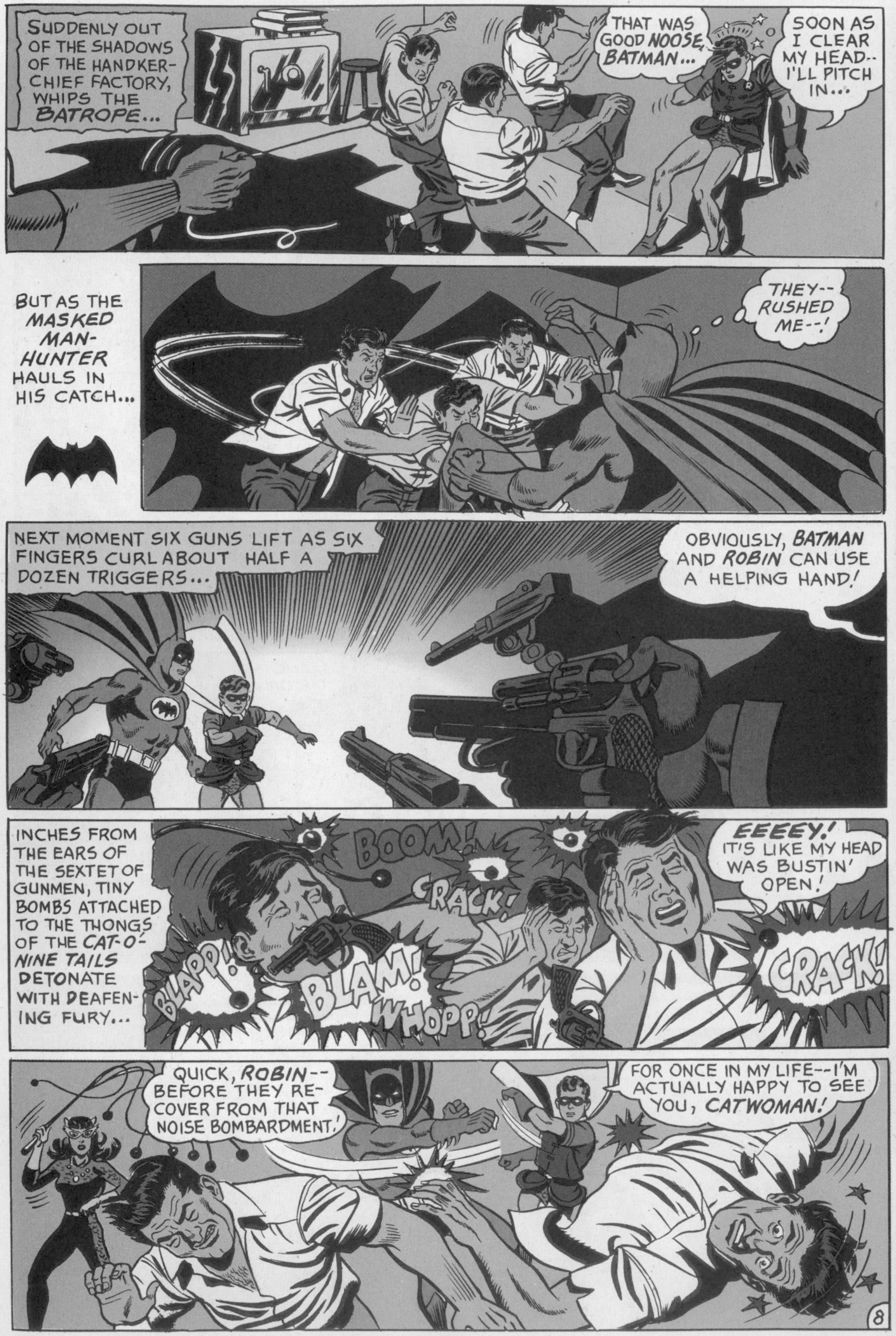
SUDDENLY OUT OF THE SHADOWS OF THE HANDKERCHIEF FACTORY, WHIPS THE BATROPE...
THAT WAS GOOD NOOSE, BATMAN...
SOON AS I CLEAR MY HEAD-- I'LL PITCH IN...
BUT AS THE MASKED MAN-HUNTER HAULS IN HIS CATCH...
THEY-- RUSHED ME--!
NEXT MOMENT SIX GUNS LIFT AS SIX FINGERS CURL ABOUT HALF A DOZEN TRIGGERS...
OBVIOUSLY, BATMAN AND ROBIN CAN USE A HELPING HAND!
INCHES FROM THE EARS OF THE SEXTET OF GUNMEN, TINY BOMBS ATTACHED TO THE THONGS OF THE CAT-O'-NINE TAILS DETONATE WITH DEAFENING FURY...
BOOM!
CRACK!
EEEEY! IT'S LIKE MY HEAD WAS BUSTIN' OPEN!
BLAPP!
BLAM!
WHOPP!
CRACK!
QUICK, ROBIN-- BEFORE THEY RECOVER FROM THAT NOISE BOMBARDMENT!
FOR ONCE IN MY LIFE--I'M ACTUALLY HAPPY TO SEE YOU, CATWOMAN!
8

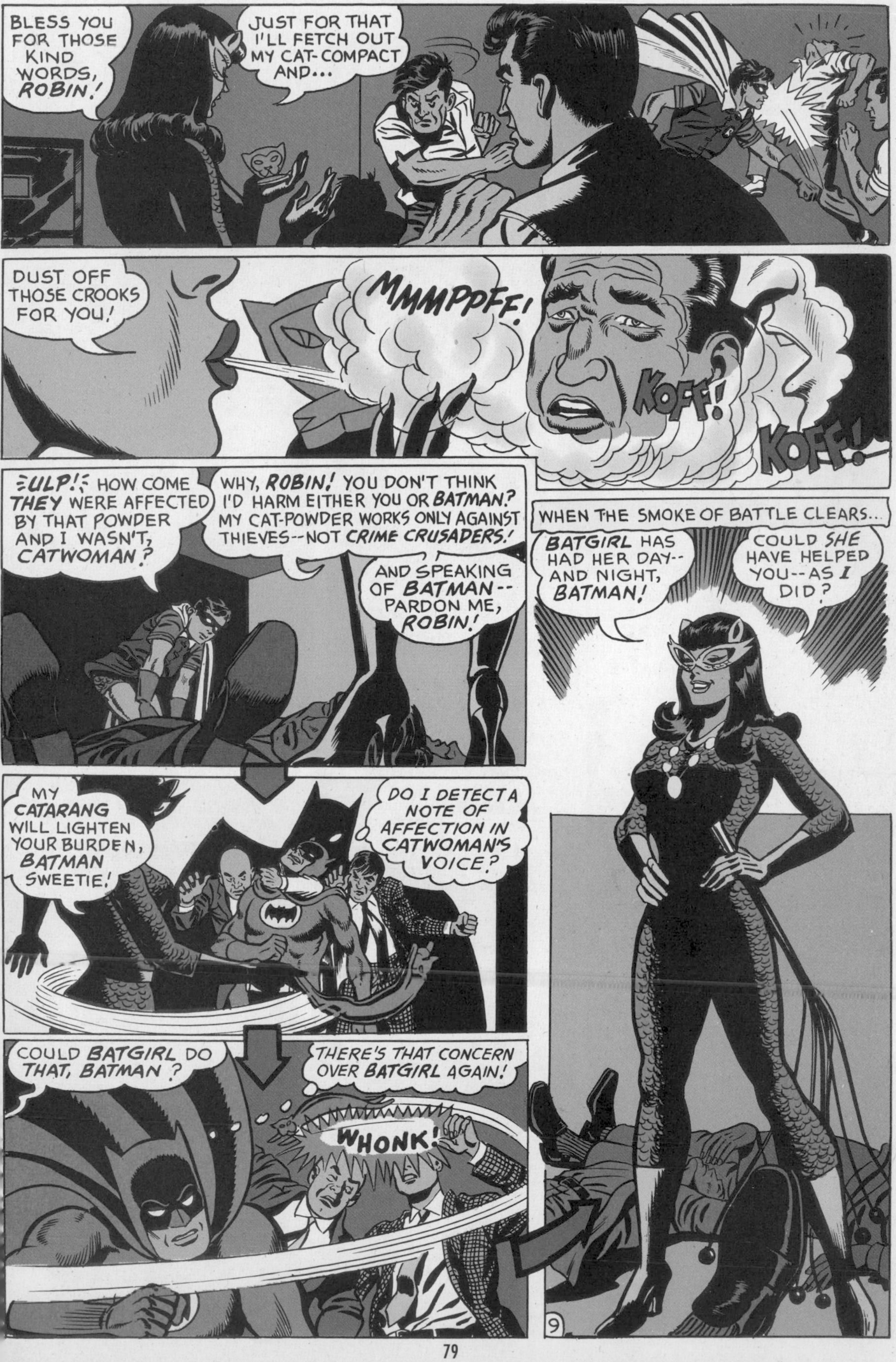
BLESS YOU FOR THOSE KIND WORDS, ROBIN!
JUST FOR THAT I'LL FETCH OUT MY CAT-COMPACT AND...
DUST OFF THOSE CROOKS FOR YOU!
MMMPPFF!
KOFF!
KOFF!
=ULP!= HOW COME THEY WERE AFFECTED BY THAT POWDER AND I WASN'T, CATWOMAN?
WHY, ROBIN! YOU DON'T THINK I'D HARM EITHER YOU OR BATMAN? MY CAT-POWDER WORKS ONLY AGAINST THIEVES--NOT CRIME CRUSADERS!
AND SPEAKING OF BATMAN-- PARDON ME, ROBIN!
MY CATARANG WILL LIGHTEN YOUR BURDEN, BATMAN SWEETIE!
DO I DETECT A NOTE OF AFFECTION IN CATWOMAN'S VOICE?
COULD BATGIRL DO THAT, BATMAN?
THERE'S THAT CONCERN OVER BATGIRL AGAIN!
WHONK!
WHEN THE SMOKE OF BATTLE CLEARS...
BATGIRL HAS HAD HER DAY-- AND NIGHT, BATMAN!
COULD SHE HAVE HELPED YOU--AS I DID?
9

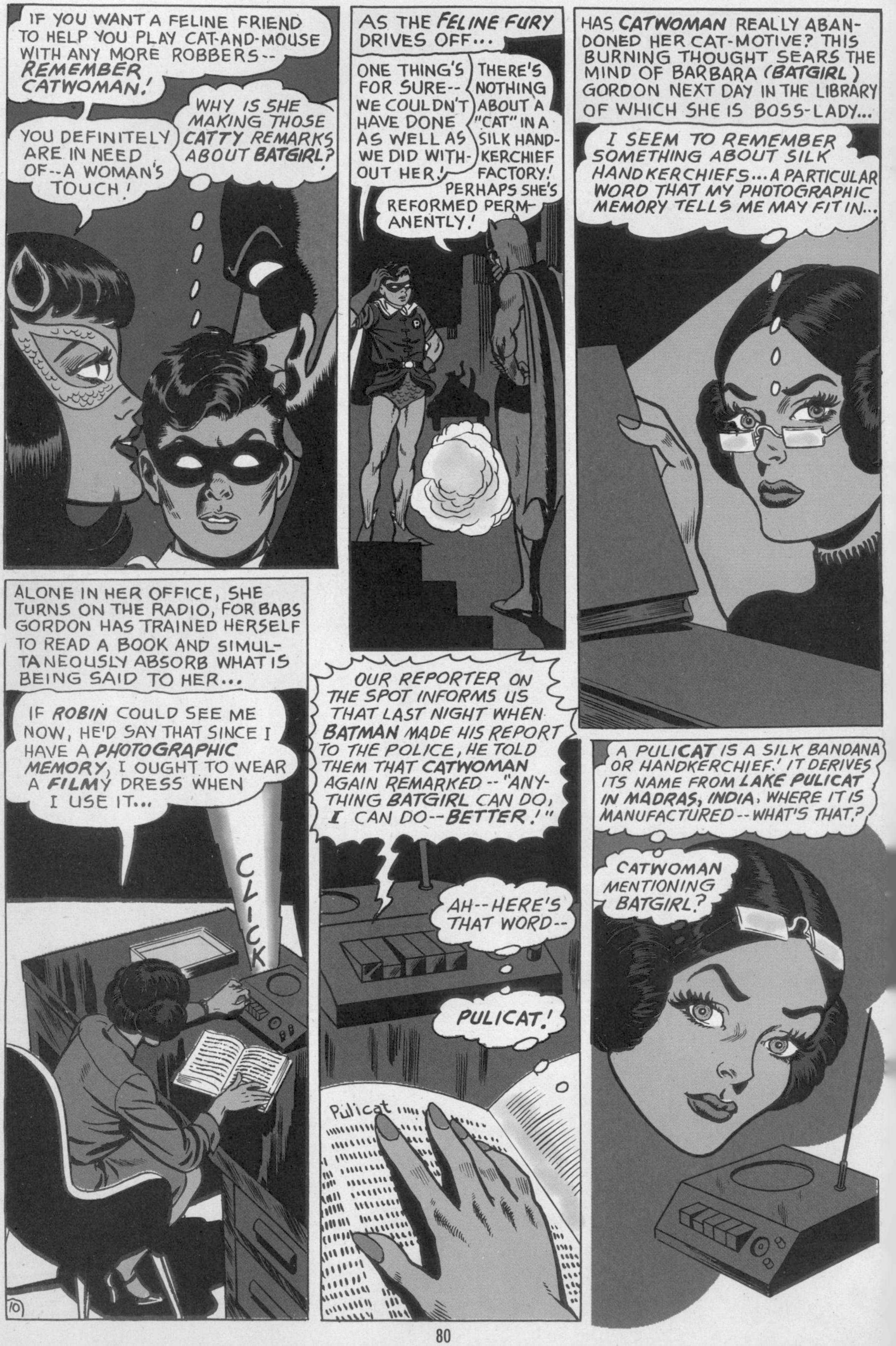
IF YOU WANT A FELINE FRIEND TO HELP YOU PLAY CAT-AND-MOUSE WITH ANY MORE ROBBERS-- REMEMBER CATWOMAN!
YOU DEFINITELY ARE IN NEED OF--A WOMAN'S TOUCH!
WHY IS SHE MAKING THOSE CATTY REMARKS ABOUT BATGIRL?
AS THE FELINE FURY DRIVES OFF...
ONE THING'S FOR SURE-- WE COULDN'T HAVE DONE AS WELL AS WE DID WITH-OUT HER!
THERE'S NOTHING ABOUT A "CAT" IN A SILK HAND-KERCHIEF FACTORY! PERHAPS SHE'S REFORMED PERM-ANENTLY!
HAS CATWOMAN REALLY ABAN-DONED HER CAT-MOTIVE? THIS BURNING THOUGHT SEARS THE MIND OF BARBARA (BATGIRL) GORDON NEXT DAY IN THE LIBRARY OF WHICH SHE IS BOSS-LADY...
I SEEM TO REMEMBER SOMETHING ABOUT SILK HANDKERCHIEFS... A PARTICULAR WORD THAT MY PHOTOGRAPHIC MEMORY TELLS ME MAY FIT IN...
ALONE IN HER OFFICE, SHE TURNS ON THE RADIO, FOR BABS GORDON HAS TRAINED HERSELF TO READ A BOOK AND SIMUL-TANEOUSLY ABSORB WHAT IS BEING SAID TO HER...
IF ROBIN COULD SEE ME NOW, HE'D SAY THAT SINCE I HAVE A PHOTOGRAPHIC MEMORY, I OUGHT TO WEAR A FILMY DRESS WHEN I USE IT...
CLICK
10
OUR REPORTER ON THE SPOT INFORMS US THAT LAST NIGHT WHEN BATMAN MADE HIS REPORT TO THE POLICE, HE TOLD THEM THAT CATWOMAN AGAIN REMARKED -- "ANY-THING BATGIRL CAN DO, I CAN DO--BETTER!"
AH--HERE'S THAT WORD--
PULICAT!
Pulicat
A PULICAT IS A SILK BANDANA OR HANDKERCHIEF! IT DERIVES ITS NAME FROM LAKE PULICAT IN MADRAS, INDIA, WHERE IT IS MANUFACTURED--WHAT'S THAT?
CATWOMAN MENTIONING BATGIRL?

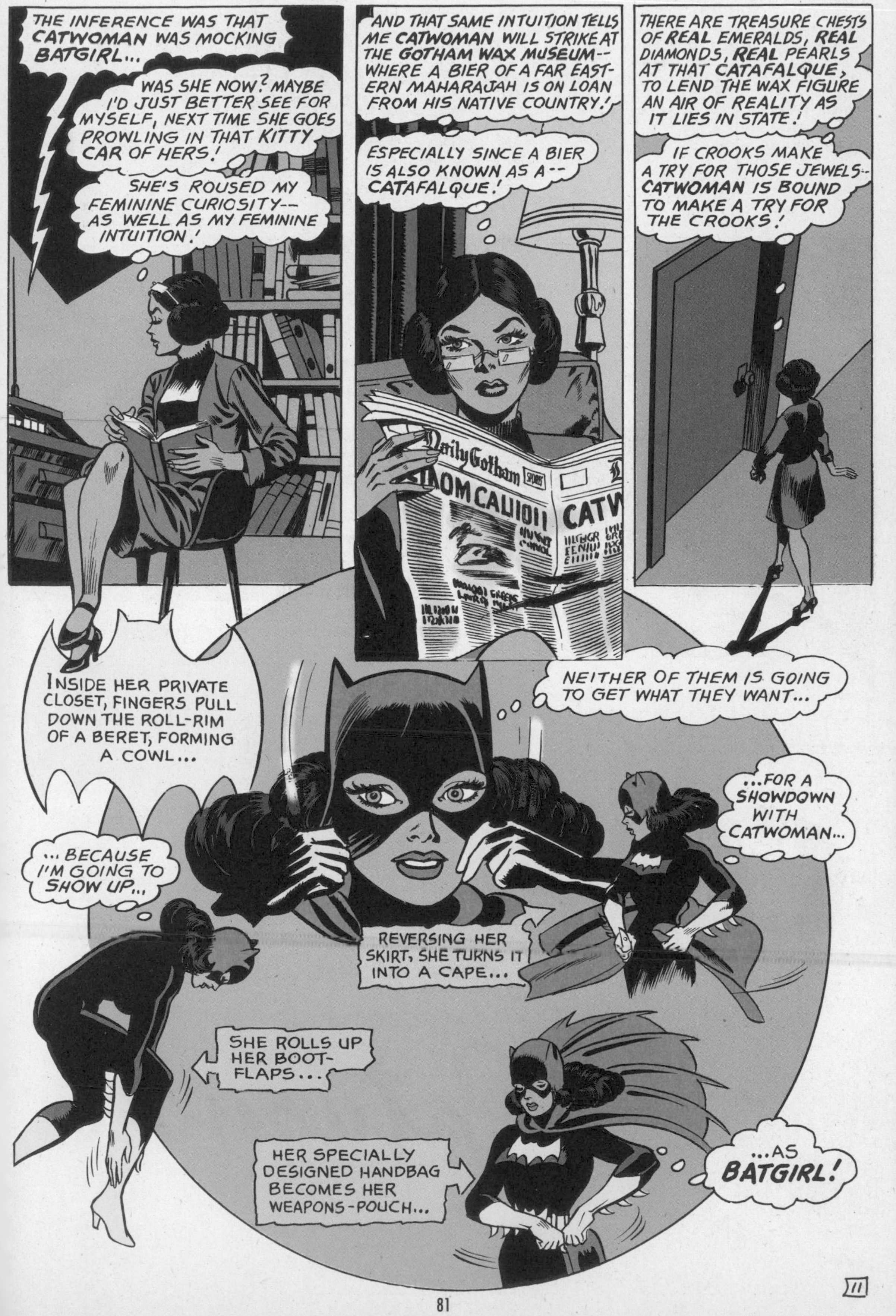
THE INFERENCE WAS THAT CATWOMAN WAS MOCKING BATGIRL...
WAS SHE NOW? MAYBE I'D JUST BETTER SEE FOR MYSELF, NEXT TIME SHE GOES PROWLING IN THAT KITTY CAR OF HERS!
SHE'S ROUSED MY FEMININE CURIOSITY-- AS WELL AS MY FEMININE INTUITION!
AND THAT SAME INTUITION TELLS ME CATWOMAN WILL STRIKE AT THE GOTHAM WAX MUSEUM-- WHERE A BIER OF A FAR EAST-ERN MAHARAJAH IS ON LOAN FROM HIS NATIVE COUNTRY!
ESPECIALLY SINCE A BIER IS ALSO KNOWN AS A-- CATAFALQUE!
Daily Gotham
THERE ARE TREASURE CHESTS OF REAL EMERALDS, REAL DIAMONDS, REAL PEARLS AT THAT CATAFALQUE, TO LEND THE WAX FIGURE AN AIR OF REALITY AS IT LIES IN STATE!
IF CROOKS MAKE A TRY FOR THOSE JEWELS-- CATWOMAN IS BOUND TO MAKE A TRY FOR THE CROOKS!
INSIDE HER PRIVATE CLOSET, FINGERS PULL DOWN THE ROLL-RIM OF A BERET, FORMING A COWL...
NEITHER OF THEM IS GOING TO GET WHAT THEY WANT...
...BECAUSE I'M GOING TO SHOW UP...
...FOR A SHOWDOWN WITH CATWOMAN...
REVERSING HER SKIRT, SHE TURNS IT INTO A CAPE...
SHE ROLLS UP HER BOOT-FLAPS...
HER SPECIALLY DESIGNED HANDBAG BECOMES HER WEAPONS-POUCH...
...AS BATGIRL!
11

THAT NIGHT SHE SPEEDS CROSSTOWN ON HER *BATBIKE*...

LET'S SEE WHAT CATWOMAN CAN DO-- THAT BATGIRL SUPPOSEDLY CAN'T DO-- *BETTER!*

AND SO-- WITHIN THE SHADOWS OF A *CATAFALQUE*...

WELL, WELL! IF IT ISN'T BATMAN'S UNPRECIOUS LITTLE HELP-MATE!

I'M HERE TO PREVENT CRIME, CATWOMAN-- WHAT'S YOUR EXCUSE?

⑫

WHEN CATWOMAN AND BATGIRL MEET--FEMALE TEMPERS ARE BOUND TO FLARE! WHAT EFFECT WILL THIS HAVE-- ON BATMAN HIMSELF?

Catwoman

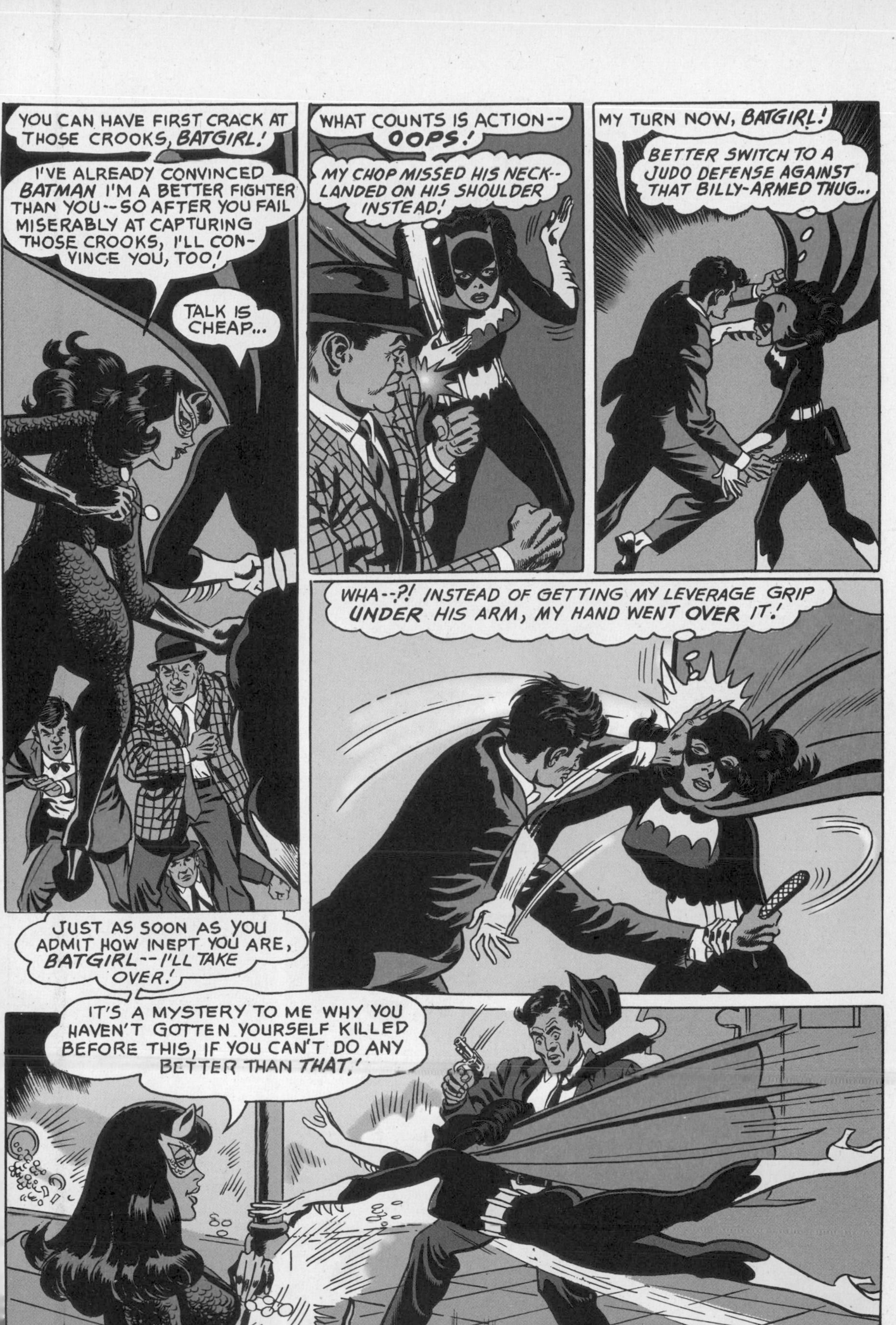
YOU CAN HAVE FIRST CRACK AT THOSE CROOKS, BATGIRL!
I'VE ALREADY CONVINCED BATMAN I'M A BETTER FIGHTER THAN YOU--SO AFTER YOU FAIL MISERABLY AT CAPTURING THOSE CROOKS, I'LL CONVINCE YOU, TOO!
TALK IS CHEAP...
JUST AS SOON AS YOU ADMIT HOW INEPT YOU ARE, BATGIRL--I'LL TAKE OVER!
WHAT COUNTS IS ACTION-- OOPS!
MY CHOP MISSED HIS NECK--LANDED ON HIS SHOULDER INSTEAD!
MY TURN NOW, BATGIRL!
BETTER SWITCH TO A JUDO DEFENSE AGAINST THAT BILLY-ARMED THUG...
WHA--?! INSTEAD OF GETTING MY LEVERAGE GRIP UNDER HIS ARM, MY HAND WENT OVER IT!
IT'S A MYSTERY TO ME WHY YOU HAVEN'T GOTTEN YOURSELF KILLED BEFORE THIS, IF YOU CAN'T DO ANY BETTER THAN THAT!
13

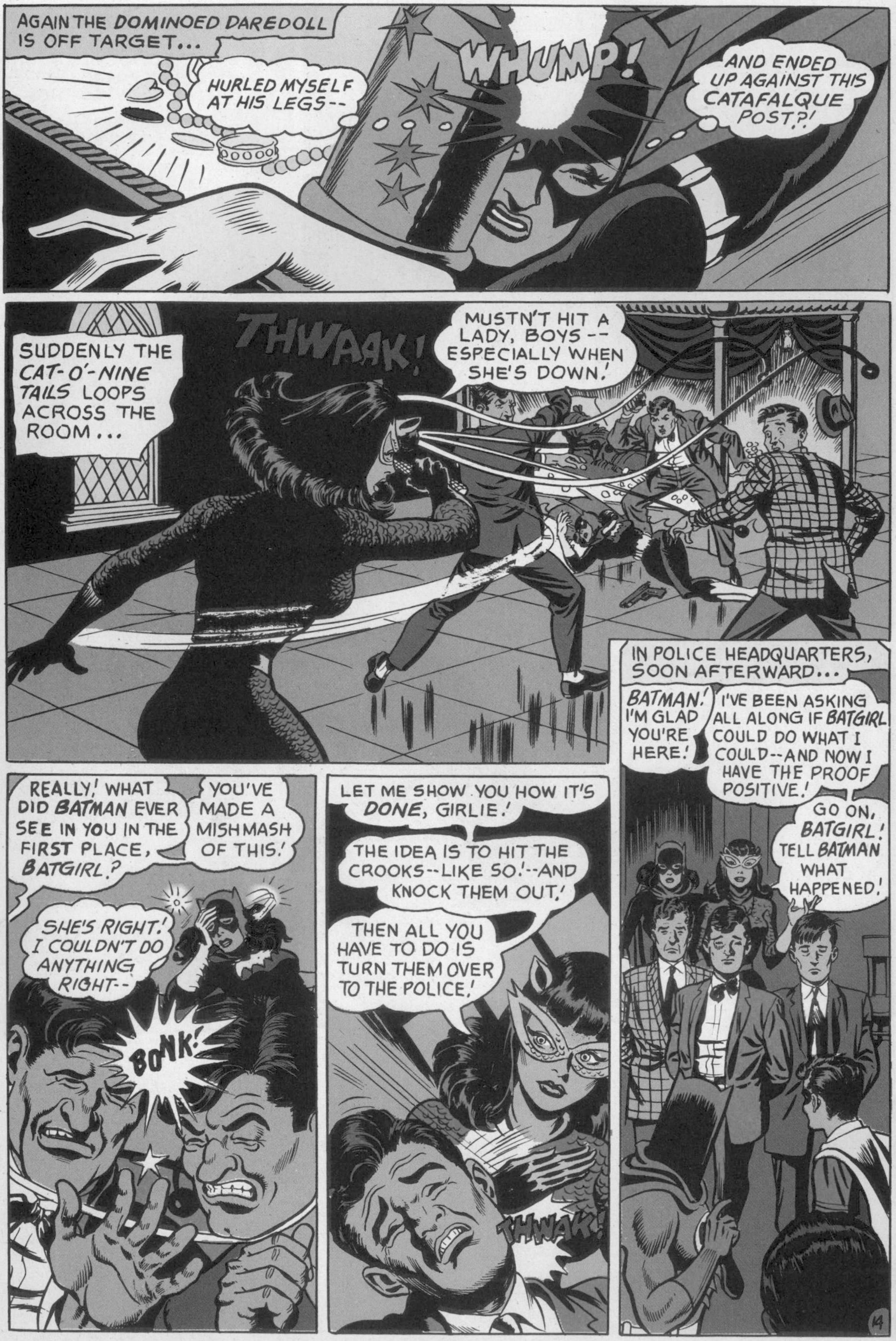
AGAIN THE DOMINOED DAREDOLL IS OFF TARGET...
HURLED MYSELF AT HIS LEGS--
WHUMP!
AND ENDED UP AGAINST THIS CATAFALQUE POST?!
SUDDENLY THE CAT-O'-NINE TAILS LOOPS ACROSS THE ROOM...
THWAAK!
MUSTN'T HIT A LADY, BOYS -- ESPECIALLY WHEN SHE'S DOWN!
IN POLICE HEADQUARTERS, SOON AFTERWARD...
BATMAN! I'M GLAD YOU'RE HERE!
I'VE BEEN ASKING ALL ALONG IF BATGIRL COULD DO WHAT I COULD--AND NOW I HAVE THE PROOF POSITIVE!
GO ON, BATGIRL! TELL BATMAN WHAT HAPPENED!
REALLY! WHAT DID BATMAN EVER SEE IN YOU IN THE FIRST PLACE, BATGIRL?
YOU'VE MADE A MISHMASH OF THIS!
SHE'S RIGHT! I COULDN'T DO ANYTHING RIGHT--
BONK!
LET ME SHOW YOU HOW IT'S DONE, GIRLIE!
THE IDEA IS TO HIT THE CROOKS--LIKE SO!--AND KNOCK THEM OUT!
THEN ALL YOU HAVE TO DO IS TURN THEM OVER TO THE POLICE!
THWAK!
14

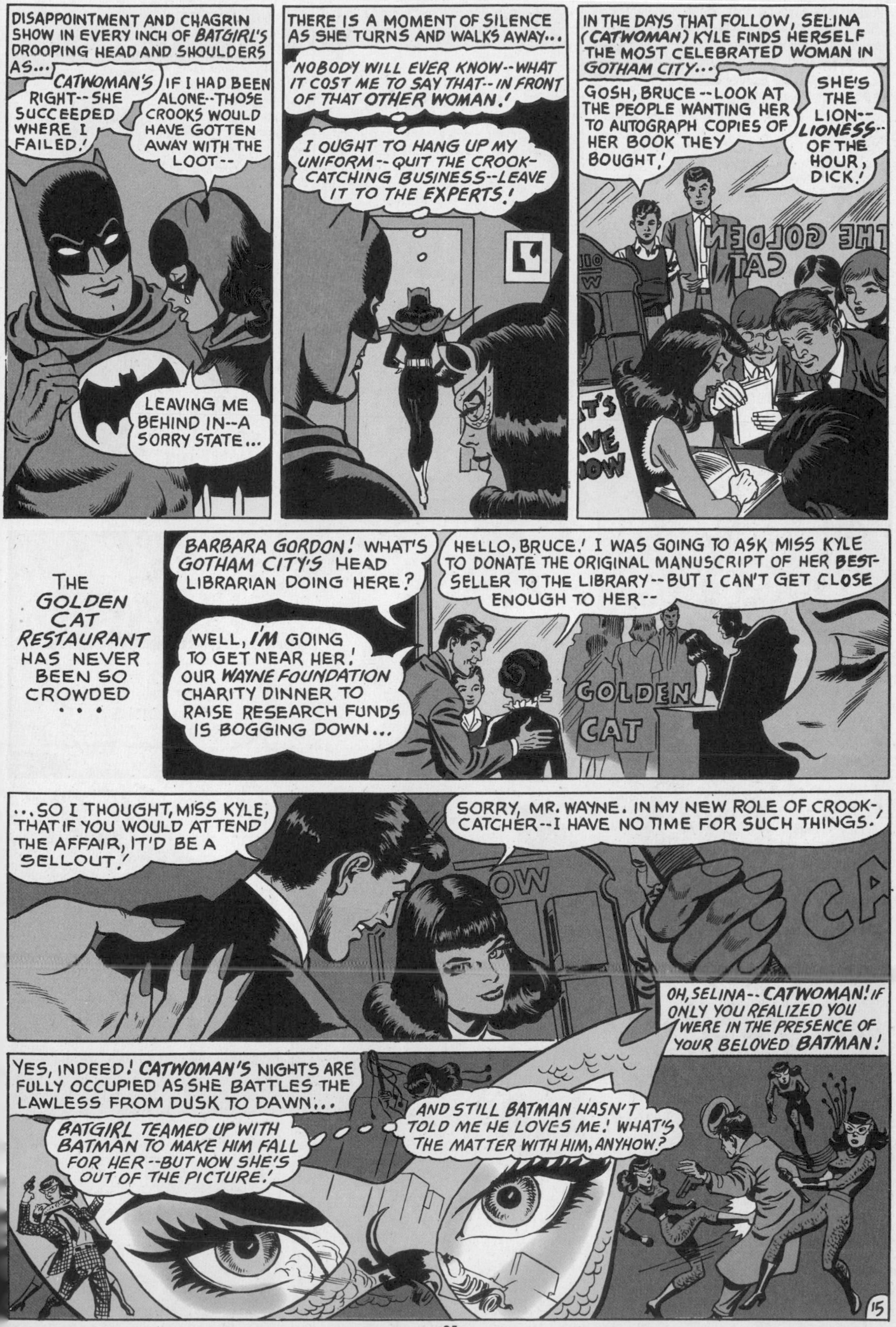

DISAPPOINTMENT AND CHAGRIN SHOW IN EVERY INCH OF BATGIRL'S DROOPING HEAD AND SHOULDERS AS...
CATWOMAN'S RIGHT--SHE SUCCEEDED WHERE I FAILED!
IF I HAD BEEN ALONE--THOSE CROOKS WOULD HAVE GOTTEN AWAY WITH THE LOOT--
LEAVING ME BEHIND IN--A SORRY STATE...
THERE IS A MOMENT OF SILENCE AS SHE TURNS AND WALKS AWAY...
NOBODY WILL EVER KNOW--WHAT IT COST ME TO SAY THAT--IN FRONT OF THAT OTHER WOMAN!
I OUGHT TO HANG UP MY UNIFORM--QUIT THE CROOK-CATCHING BUSINESS--LEAVE IT TO THE EXPERTS!
IN THE DAYS THAT FOLLOW, SELINA (CATWOMAN) KYLE FINDS HERSELF THE MOST CELEBRATED WOMAN IN GOTHAM CITY...
GOSH, BRUCE--LOOK AT THE PEOPLE WANTING HER TO AUTOGRAPH COPIES OF HER BOOK THEY BOUGHT!
SHE'S THE LION--LIONESS--OF THE HOUR, DICK!
THE GOLDEN CAT
THE GOLDEN CAT RESTAURANT HAS NEVER BEEN SO CROWDED . . .
BARBARA GORDON! WHAT'S GOTHAM CITY'S HEAD LIBRARIAN DOING HERE?
WELL, I'M GOING TO GET NEAR HER! OUR WAYNE FOUNDATION CHARITY DINNER TO RAISE RESEARCH FUNDS IS BOGGING DOWN...
HELLO, BRUCE! I WAS GOING TO ASK MISS KYLE TO DONATE THE ORIGINAL MANUSCRIPT OF HER BEST-SELLER TO THE LIBRARY--BUT I CAN'T GET CLOSE ENOUGH TO HER--
GOLDEN CAT
...SO I THOUGHT, MISS KYLE, THAT IF YOU WOULD ATTEND THE AFFAIR, IT'D BE A SELLOUT!
SORRY, MR. WAYNE. IN MY NEW ROLE OF CROOK-CATCHER--I HAVE NO TIME FOR SUCH THINGS!
OH, SELINA--CATWOMAN! IF ONLY YOU REALIZED YOU WERE IN THE PRESENCE OF YOUR BELOVED BATMAN!
YES, INDEED! CATWOMAN'S NIGHTS ARE FULLY OCCUPIED AS SHE BATTLES THE LAWLESS FROM DUSK TO DAWN...
BATGIRL TEAMED UP WITH BATMAN TO MAKE HIM FALL FOR HER--BUT NOW SHE'S OUT OF THE PICTURE!
AND STILL BATMAN HASN'T TOLD ME HE LOVES ME! WHAT'S THE MATTER WITH HIM, ANYHOW?
15

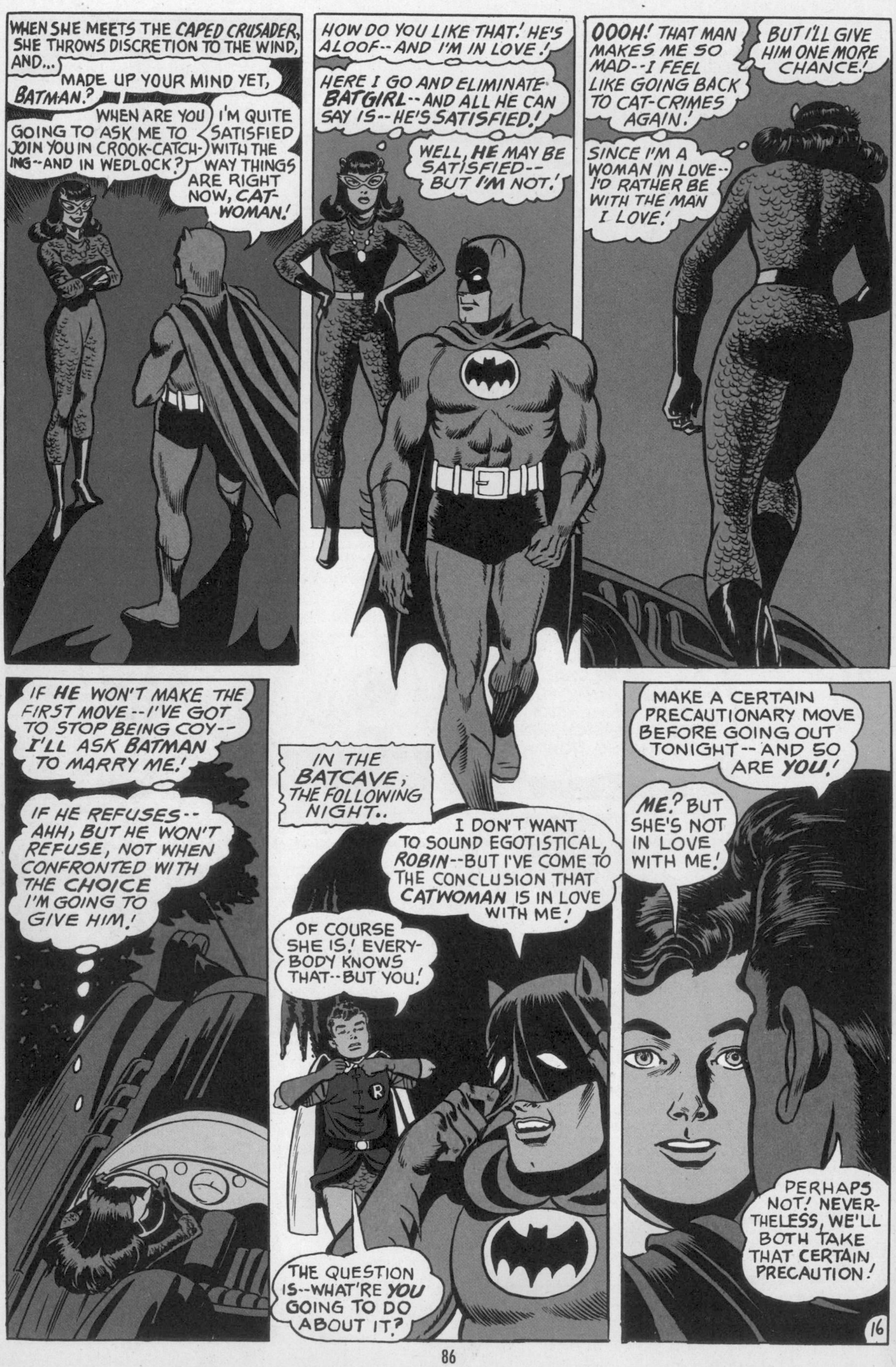
WHEN SHE MEETS THE CAPED CRUSADER, SHE THROWS DISCRETION TO THE WIND, AND...
MADE UP YOUR MIND YET, BATMAN?
WHEN ARE YOU GOING TO ASK ME TO JOIN YOU IN CROOK-CATCHING--AND IN WEDLOCK?
I'M QUITE SATISFIED WITH THE WAY THINGS ARE RIGHT NOW, CAT-WOMAN!
HOW DO YOU LIKE THAT! HE'S ALOOF--AND I'M IN LOVE!
HERE I GO AND ELIMINATE BATGIRL--AND ALL HE CAN SAY IS--HE'S SATISFIED!
WELL, HE MAY BE SATISFIED--BUT I'M NOT!
OOOH! THAT MAN MAKES ME SO MAD--I FEEL LIKE GOING BACK TO CAT-CRIMES AGAIN!
BUT I'LL GIVE HIM ONE MORE CHANCE!
SINCE I'M A WOMAN IN LOVE--I'D RATHER BE WITH THE MAN I LOVE!
IF HE WON'T MAKE THE FIRST MOVE--I'VE GOT TO STOP BEING COY--I'LL ASK BATMAN TO MARRY ME!
IF HE REFUSES--AHH, BUT HE WON'T REFUSE, NOT WHEN CONFRONTED WITH THE CHOICE I'M GOING TO GIVE HIM!
IN THE BATCAVE, THE FOLLOWING NIGHT..
I DON'T WANT TO SOUND EGOTISTICAL, ROBIN--BUT I'VE COME TO THE CONCLUSION THAT CATWOMAN IS IN LOVE WITH ME!
OF COURSE SHE IS! EVERYBODY KNOWS THAT--BUT YOU!
THE QUESTION IS--WHAT'RE YOU GOING TO DO ABOUT IT?
MAKE A CERTAIN PRECAUTIONARY MOVE BEFORE GOING OUT TONIGHT--AND SO ARE YOU!
ME? BUT SHE'S NOT IN LOVE WITH ME!
PERHAPS NOT! NEVERTHELESS, WE'LL BOTH TAKE THAT CERTAIN PRECAUTION!
16

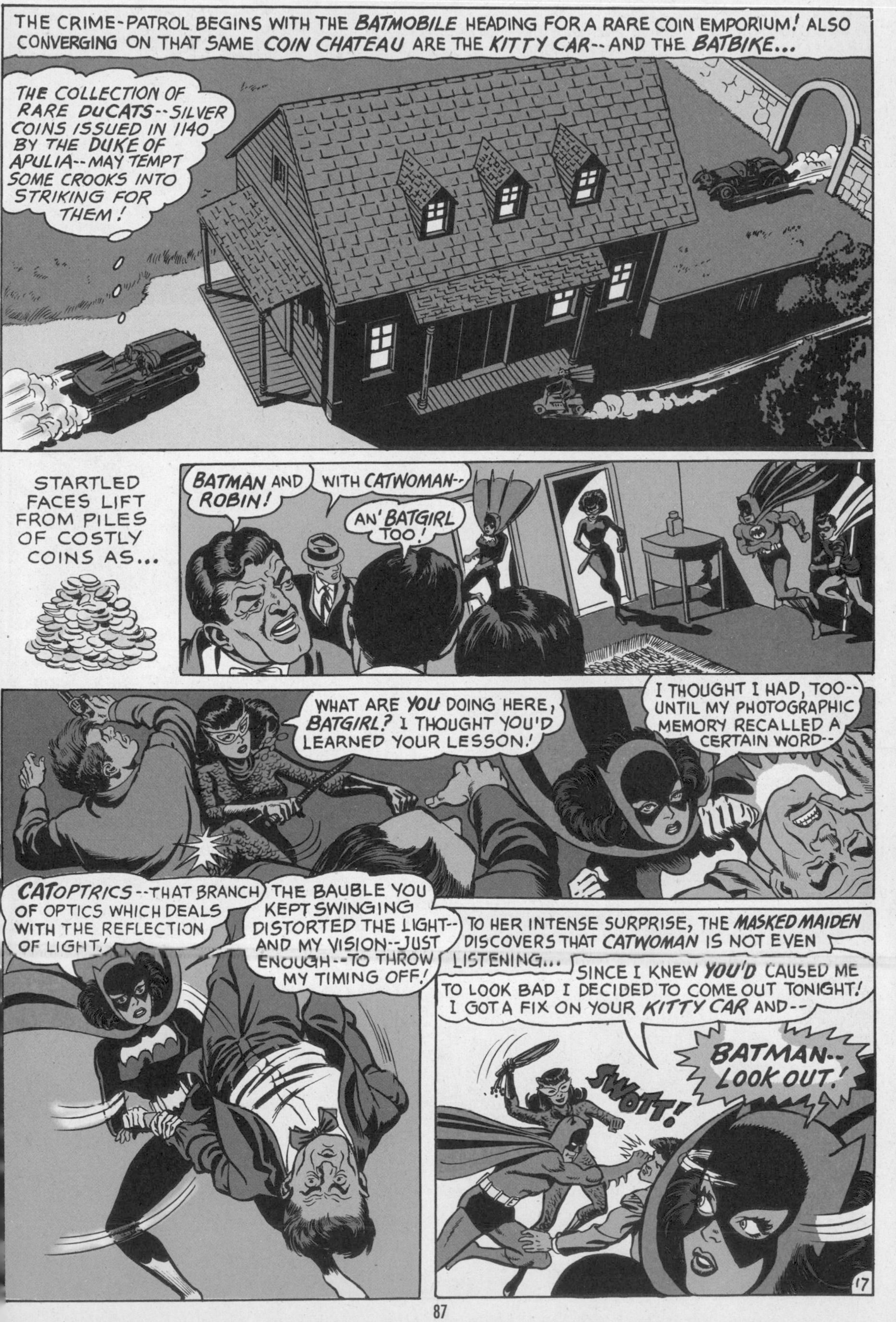
THE CRIME-PATROL BEGINS WITH THE BATMOBILE HEADING FOR A RARE COIN EMPORIUM! ALSO CONVERGING ON THAT SAME COIN CHATEAU ARE THE KITTY CAR-- AND THE BATBIKE...
THE COLLECTION OF RARE DUCATS--SILVER COINS ISSUED IN 1140 BY THE DUKE OF APULIA--MAY TEMPT SOME CROOKS INTO STRIKING FOR THEM!
STARTLED FACES LIFT FROM PILES OF COSTLY COINS AS...
BATMAN AND ROBIN!
WITH CATWOMAN--
AN' BATGIRL TOO!
WHAT ARE YOU DOING HERE, BATGIRL? I THOUGHT YOU'D LEARNED YOUR LESSON!
I THOUGHT I HAD, TOO-- UNTIL MY PHOTOGRAPHIC MEMORY RECALLED A CERTAIN WORD--
CATOPTRICS--THAT BRANCH OF OPTICS WHICH DEALS WITH THE REFLECTION OF LIGHT!
THE BAUBLE YOU KEPT SWINGING DISTORTED THE LIGHT-- AND MY VISION--JUST ENOUGH--TO THROW MY TIMING OFF!
TO HER INTENSE SURPRISE, THE MASKED MAIDEN DISCOVERS THAT CATWOMAN IS NOT EVEN LISTENING...
SINCE I KNEW YOU'D CAUSED ME TO LOOK BAD I DECIDED TO COME OUT TONIGHT! I GOT A FIX ON YOUR KITTY CAR AND--
SWOTT!
BATMAN-- LOOK OUT!
17

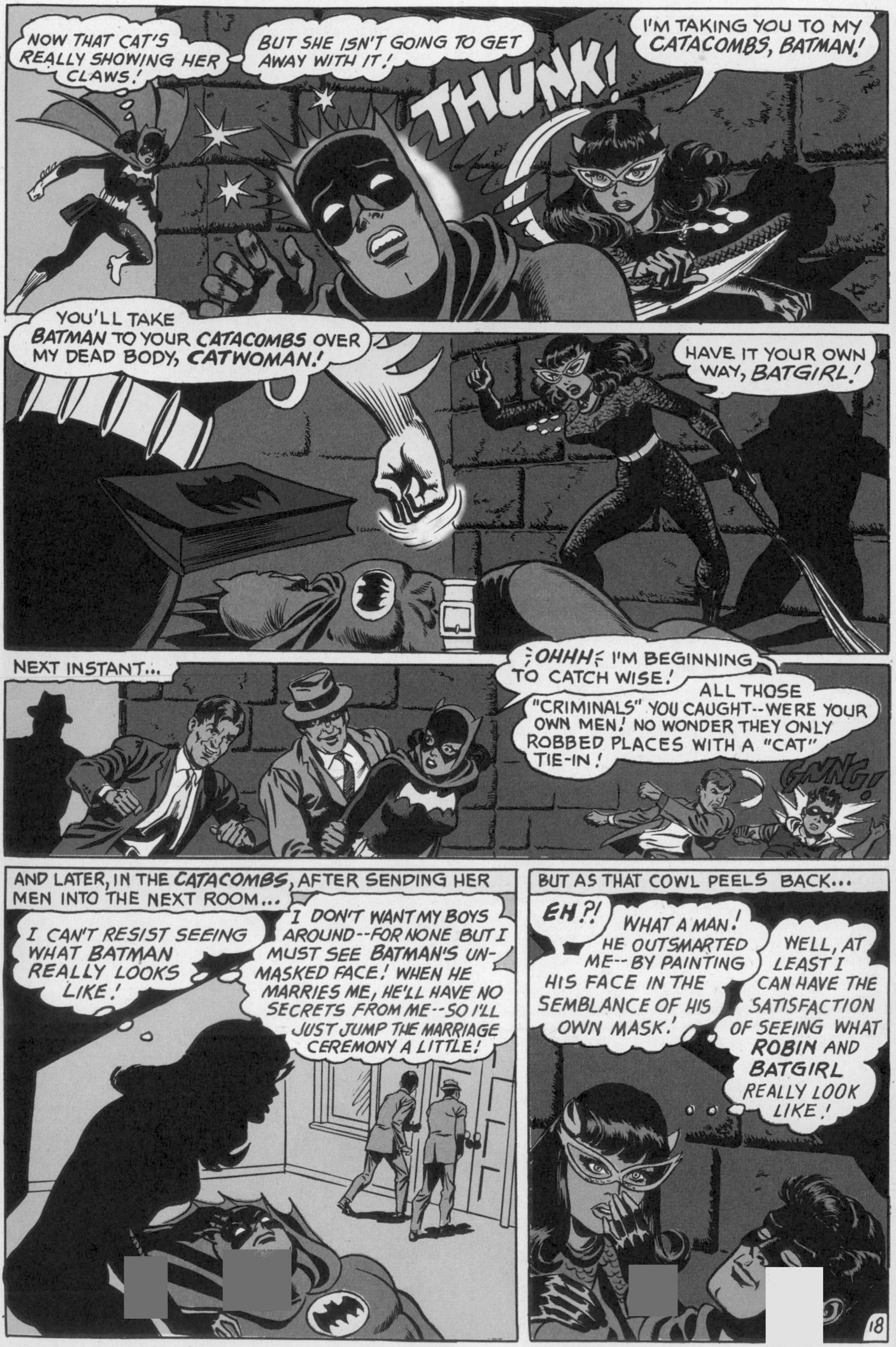
NOW THAT CAT'S REALLY SHOWING HER CLAWS!
BUT SHE ISN'T GOING TO GET AWAY WITH IT!
THUNK!
I'M TAKING YOU TO MY CATACOMBS, BATMAN!
YOU'LL TAKE BATMAN TO YOUR CATACOMBS OVER MY DEAD BODY, CATWOMAN!
HAVE IT YOUR OWN WAY, BATGIRL!
NEXT INSTANT...
OHHH! I'M BEGINNING TO CATCH WISE! ALL THOSE "CRIMINALS" YOU CAUGHT--WERE YOUR OWN MEN! NO WONDER THEY ONLY ROBBED PLACES WITH A "CAT" TIE-IN!
GNNG!
AND LATER, IN THE CATACOMBS, AFTER SENDING HER MEN INTO THE NEXT ROOM...
I CAN'T RESIST SEEING WHAT BATMAN REALLY LOOKS LIKE!
I DON'T WANT MY BOYS AROUND--FOR NONE BUT I MUST SEE BATMAN'S UN-MASKED FACE! WHEN HE MARRIES ME, HE'LL HAVE NO SECRETS FROM ME--SO I'LL JUST JUMP THE MARRIAGE CEREMONY A LITTLE!
BUT AS THAT COWL PEELS BACK...
EH?!
WHAT A MAN! HE OUTSMARTED ME--BY PAINTING HIS FACE IN THE SEMBLANCE OF HIS OWN MASK!
WELL, AT LEAST I CAN HAVE THE SATISFACTION OF SEEING WHAT ROBIN AND BATGIRL REALLY LOOK LIKE!
18

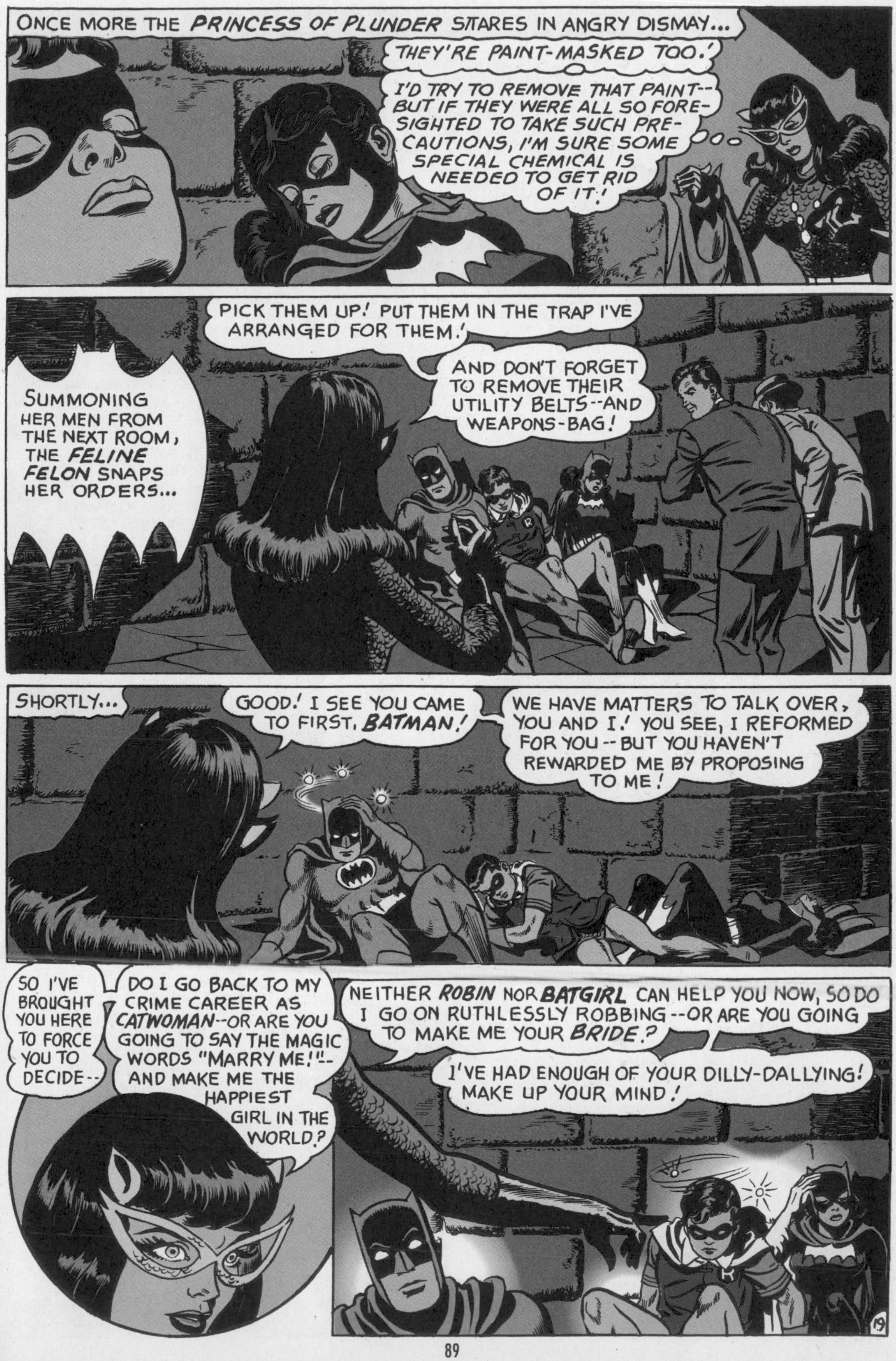
ONCE MORE THE PRINCESS OF PLUNDER STARES IN ANGRY DISMAY...
THEY'RE PAINT-MASKED TOO!
I'D TRY TO REMOVE THAT PAINT--BUT IF THEY WERE ALL SO FORE-SIGHTED TO TAKE SUCH PRE-CAUTIONS, I'M SURE SOME SPECIAL CHEMICAL IS NEEDED TO GET RID OF IT!
SUMMONING HER MEN FROM THE NEXT ROOM, THE FELINE FELON SNAPS HER ORDERS...
PICK THEM UP! PUT THEM IN THE TRAP I'VE ARRANGED FOR THEM!
AND DON'T FORGET TO REMOVE THEIR UTILITY BELTS--AND WEAPONS-BAG!
SHORTLY...
GOOD! I SEE YOU CAME TO FIRST, BATMAN!
WE HAVE MATTERS TO TALK OVER, YOU AND I! YOU SEE, I REFORMED FOR YOU--BUT YOU HAVEN'T REWARDED ME BY PROPOSING TO ME!
SO I'VE BROUGHT YOU HERE TO FORCE YOU TO DECIDE--
DO I GO BACK TO MY CRIME CAREER AS CATWOMAN--OR ARE YOU GOING TO SAY THE MAGIC WORDS "MARRY ME!"--AND MAKE ME THE HAPPIEST GIRL IN THE WORLD?
NEITHER ROBIN NOR BATGIRL CAN HELP YOU NOW, SO DO I GO ON RUTHLESSLY ROBBING--OR ARE YOU GOING TO MAKE ME YOUR BRIDE?
I'VE HAD ENOUGH OF YOUR DILLY-DALLYING! MAKE UP YOUR MIND!
19

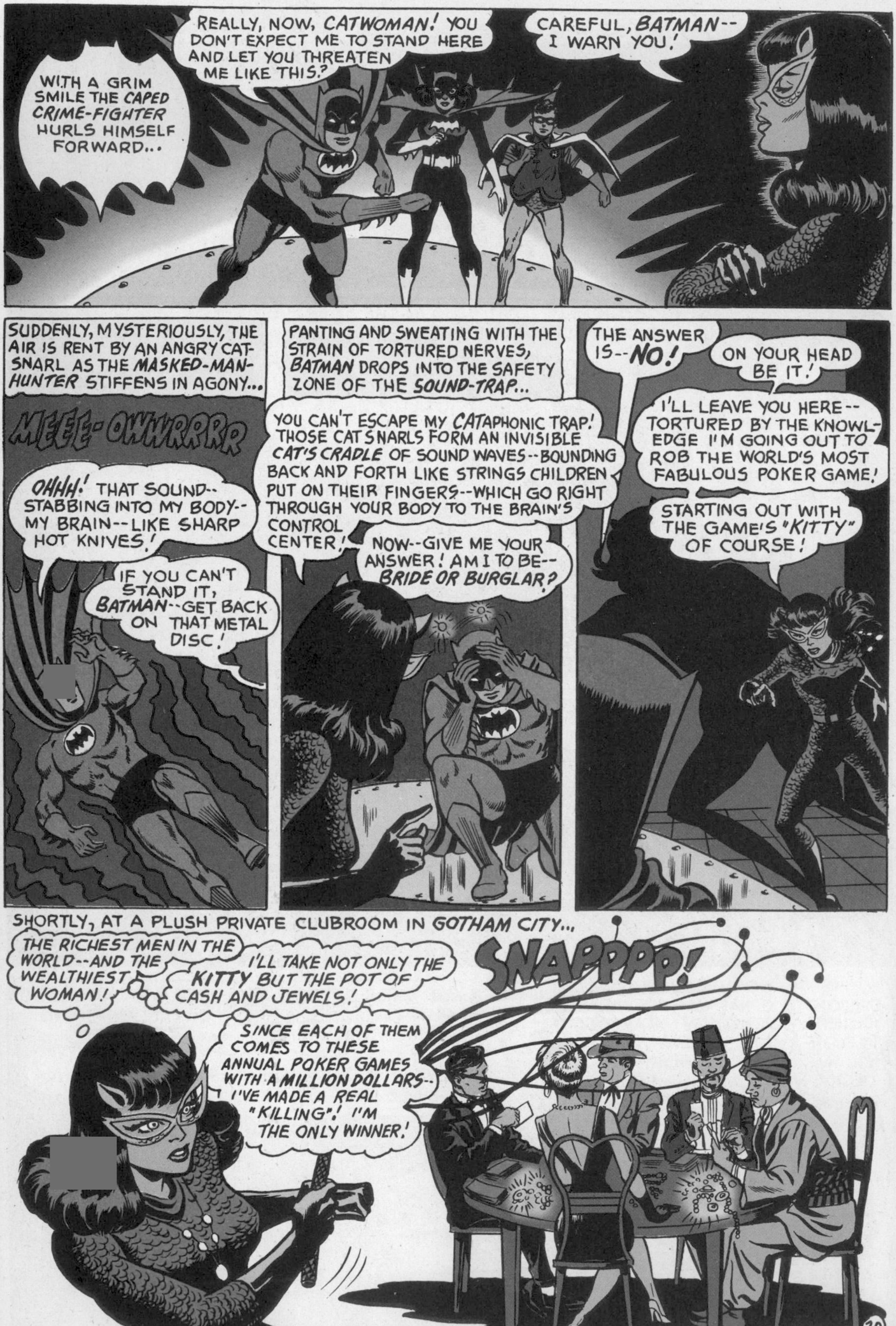

WITH A GRIM SMILE THE CAPED CRIME-FIGHTER HURLS HIMSELF FORWARD...
REALLY, NOW, CATWOMAN! YOU DON'T EXPECT ME TO STAND HERE AND LET YOU THREATEN ME LIKE THIS?
CAREFUL, BATMAN-- I WARN YOU!
SUDDENLY, MYSTERIOUSLY, THE AIR IS RENT BY AN ANGRY CAT-SNARL AS THE MASKED-MAN-HUNTER STIFFENS IN AGONY...
MEEE-OWWRRRR
OHHH! THAT SOUND-- STABBING INTO MY BODY-- MY BRAIN--LIKE SHARP HOT KNIVES!
IF YOU CAN'T STAND IT, BATMAN--GET BACK ON THAT METAL DISC!
PANTING AND SWEATING WITH THE STRAIN OF TORTURED NERVES, BATMAN DROPS INTO THE SAFETY ZONE OF THE SOUND-TRAP...
YOU CAN'T ESCAPE MY CATAPHONIC TRAP! THOSE CAT SNARLS FORM AN INVISIBLE CAT'S CRADLE OF SOUND WAVES--BOUNDING BACK AND FORTH LIKE STRINGS CHILDREN PUT ON THEIR FINGERS--WHICH GO RIGHT THROUGH YOUR BODY TO THE BRAIN'S CONTROL CENTER!
NOW--GIVE ME YOUR ANSWER! AM I TO BE-- BRIDE OR BURGLAR?
THE ANSWER IS--NO!
ON YOUR HEAD BE IT!
I'LL LEAVE YOU HERE-- TORTURED BY THE KNOWLEDGE I'M GOING OUT TO ROB THE WORLD'S MOST FABULOUS POKER GAME!
STARTING OUT WITH THE GAME'S "KITTY" OF COURSE!
SHORTLY, AT A PLUSH PRIVATE CLUBROOM IN GOTHAM CITY...
THE RICHEST MEN IN THE WORLD--AND THE WEALTHIEST WOMAN!
I'LL TAKE NOT ONLY THE KITTY BUT THE POT OF CASH AND JEWELS!
SNAPPPP!
SINCE EACH OF THEM COMES TO THESE ANNUAL POKER GAMES WITH A MILLION DOLLARS-- I'VE MADE A REAL "KILLING"! I'M THE ONLY WINNER!
20

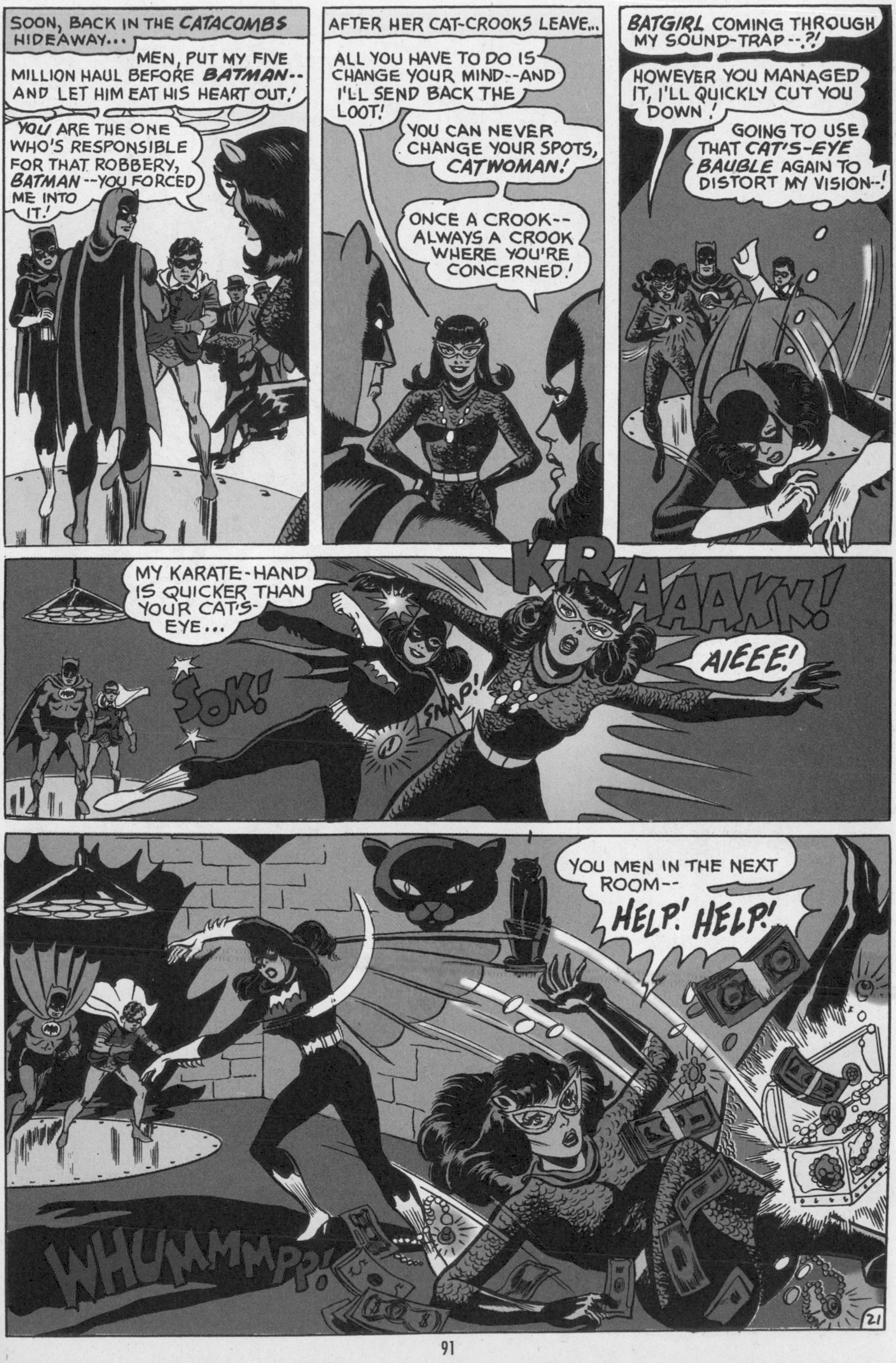
SOON, BACK IN THE CATACOMBS HIDEAWAY...
MEN, PUT MY FIVE MILLION HAUL BEFORE BATMAN-- AND LET HIM EAT HIS HEART OUT!
YOU ARE THE ONE WHO'S RESPONSIBLE FOR THAT ROBBERY, BATMAN --YOU FORCED ME INTO IT!
AFTER HER CAT-CROOKS LEAVE...
ALL YOU HAVE TO DO IS CHANGE YOUR MIND--AND I'LL SEND BACK THE LOOT!
YOU CAN NEVER CHANGE YOUR SPOTS, CATWOMAN!
ONCE A CROOK-- ALWAYS A CROOK WHERE YOU'RE CONCERNED!
BATGIRL COMING THROUGH MY SOUND-TRAP--?!
HOWEVER YOU MANAGED IT, I'LL QUICKLY CUT YOU DOWN!
GOING TO USE THAT CAT'S-EYE BAUBLE AGAIN TO DISTORT MY VISION--!
KRAAAKK!
MY KARATE-HAND IS QUICKER THAN YOUR CAT'S-EYE...
SOK!
SNAP!
AIEEE!
YOU MEN IN THE NEXT ROOM-- HELP! HELP!
WHUMMMPP!
21

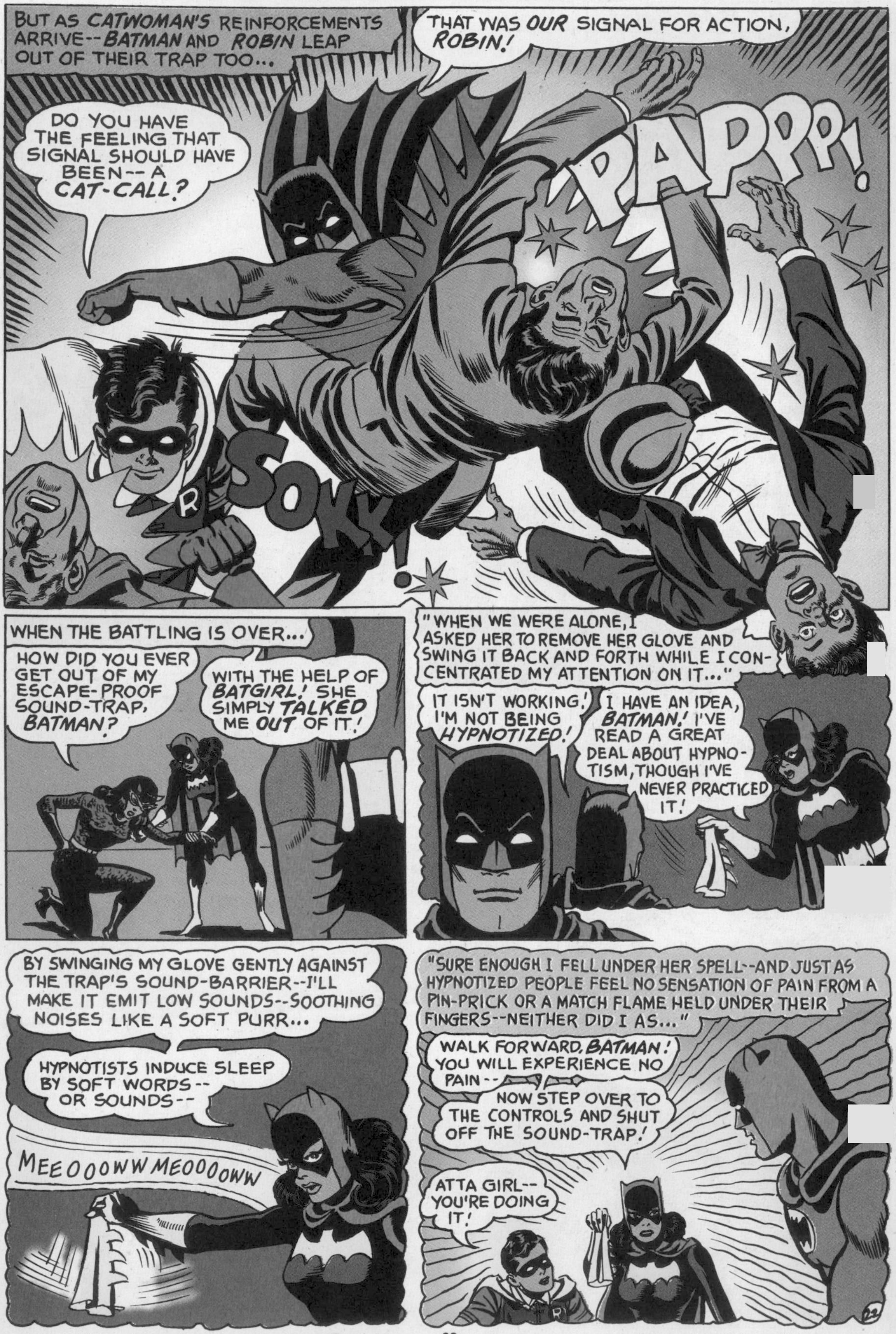
BUT AS CATWOMAN'S REINFORCEMENTS ARRIVE--BATMAN AND ROBIN LEAP OUT OF THEIR TRAP TOO...
THAT WAS OUR SIGNAL FOR ACTION, ROBIN!
DO YOU HAVE THE FEELING THAT SIGNAL SHOULD HAVE BEEN--A CAT-CALL?
PAPPP!
SOKK!
WHEN THE BATTLING IS OVER...
HOW DID YOU EVER GET OUT OF MY ESCAPE-PROOF SOUND-TRAP, BATMAN?
WITH THE HELP OF BATGIRL! SHE SIMPLY TALKED ME OUT OF IT!
"WHEN WE WERE ALONE, I ASKED HER TO REMOVE HER GLOVE AND SWING IT BACK AND FORTH WHILE I CONCENTRATED MY ATTENTION ON IT..."
IT ISN'T WORKING! I'M NOT BEING HYPNOTIZED!
I HAVE AN IDEA, BATMAN! I'VE READ A GREAT DEAL ABOUT HYPNOTISM, THOUGH I'VE NEVER PRACTICED IT!
BY SWINGING MY GLOVE GENTLY AGAINST THE TRAP'S SOUND-BARRIER--I'LL MAKE IT EMIT LOW SOUNDS--SOOTHING NOISES LIKE A SOFT PURR...
HYPNOTISTS INDUCE SLEEP BY SOFT WORDS--OR SOUNDS--
MEEOOOWW MEOOOOWW
"SURE ENOUGH I FELL UNDER HER SPELL--AND JUST AS HYPNOTIZED PEOPLE FEEL NO SENSATION OF PAIN FROM A PIN-PRICK OR A MATCH FLAME HELD UNDER THEIR FINGERS--NEITHER DID I AS..."
WALK FORWARD, BATMAN! YOU WILL EXPERIENCE NO PAIN--
NOW STEP OVER TO THE CONTROLS AND SHUT OFF THE SOUND-TRAP!
ATTA GIRL--YOU'RE DOING IT!
22

ONE LAST QUESTION-- HOW COME YOU PAINTED YOUR FACES WITH MASKS? SURELY YOU COULDN'T HAVE ANTICIPATED I'D TRY TO UNMASK YOU?
BUT I DID, CATWOMAN! I REALIZED YOU LOVED ME--AND WHAT WOMAN DOESN'T WANT TO LOOK UPON THE FACE OF HER BELOVED?
AND I ALWAYS FOLLOW BATMAN'S EXAMPLE!
WHAT ABOUT YOU? I SUPPOSE YOU THOUGHT I'D BE "CATTY" ENOUGH TO WANT TO SEE WHAT MY RIVAL LOOKED LIKE?
I DON'T CONSIDER MYSELF A RIVAL OF YOURS, CATWOMAN! I HAVE ABSOLUTELY NO ROMANTIC INTEREST IN BATMAN!
BUT I DID REALIZE YOU WEREN'T TO BE TRUSTED!
NO ROMANTIC INTEREST IN BATMAN? HAH! THAT'S A LIKELY STORY!
IT HAPPENS TO BE TRUE, CATWOMAN! IF YOU'D KNOWN THAT FROM THE BEGINNING--YOU WOULDN'T BE ABOUT TO CAT-WALK TO THE NEAREST JAIL!
23

Catwoman

CATWOMAN

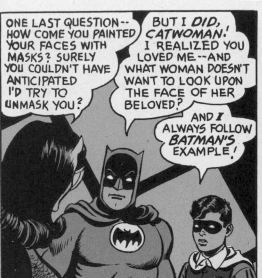

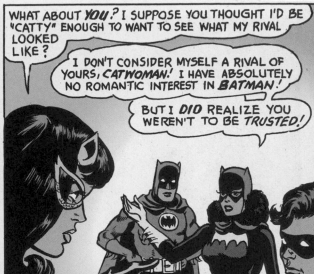

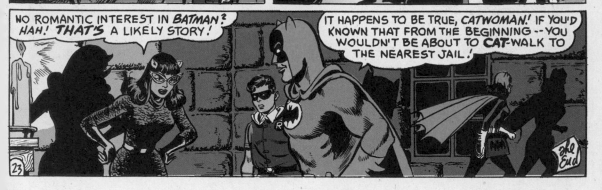

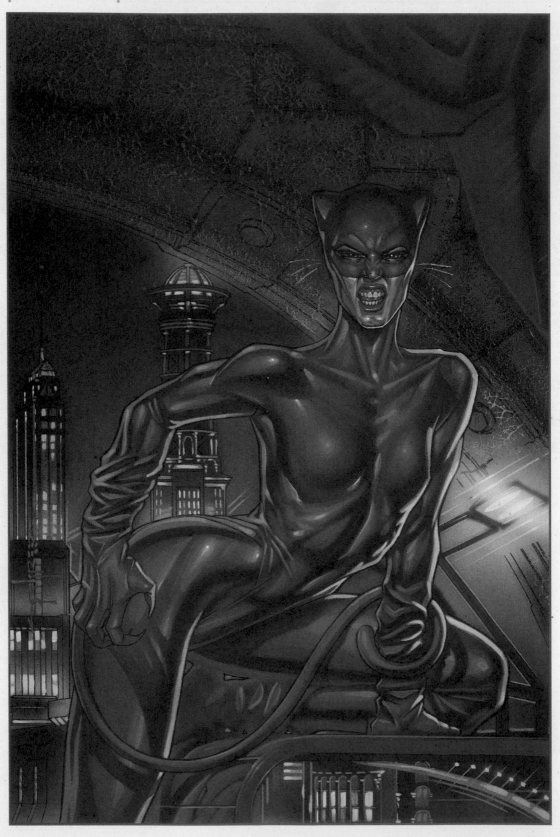

Originally adorned the CATWOMAN: DEFIANT one-shot (1992)
that came out around the time of the *Batman Returns* movie featuring Catwoman.

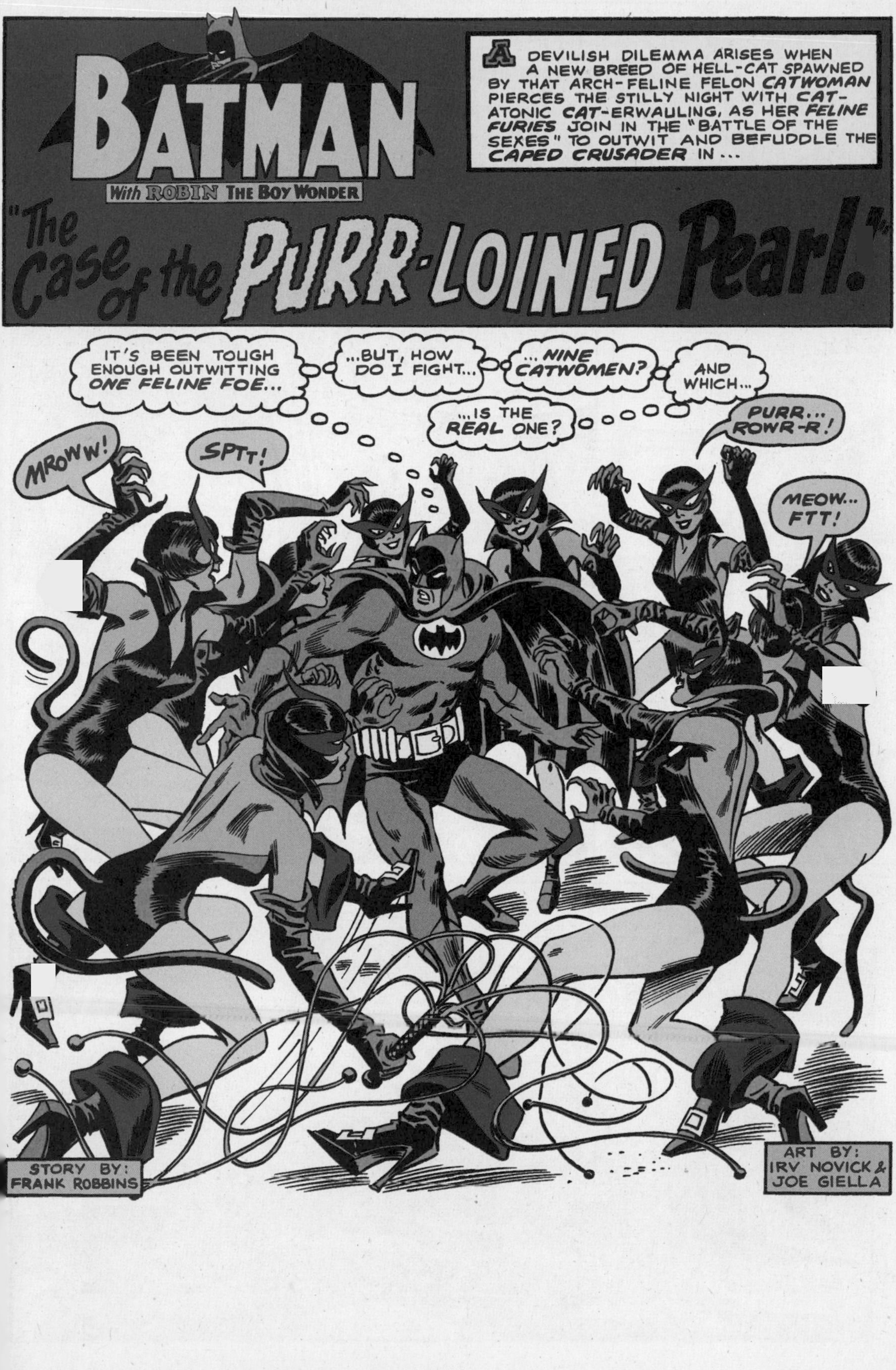
BATMAN
With ROBIN THE BOY WONDER
A DEVILISH DILEMMA ARISES WHEN A NEW BREED OF HELL-CAT SPAWNED BY THAT ARCH-FELINE FELON CATWOMAN PIERCES THE STILLY NIGHT WITH CAT-ATONIC CAT-ERWAULING, AS HER FELINE FURIES JOIN IN THE "BATTLE OF THE SEXES" TO OUTWIT AND BEFUDDLE THE CAPED CRUSADER IN ...
"The Case of the PURR-LOINED Pearl!"
IT'S BEEN TOUGH ENOUGH OUTWITTING ONE FELINE FOE...
...BUT, HOW DO I FIGHT...
...NINE CATWOMEN?
AND WHICH...
...IS THE REAL ONE?
MROWW!
SPTT!
PURR... ROWR-R!
MEOW... FTT!
STORY BY: FRANK ROBBINS
ART BY: IRV NOVICK & JOE GIELLA

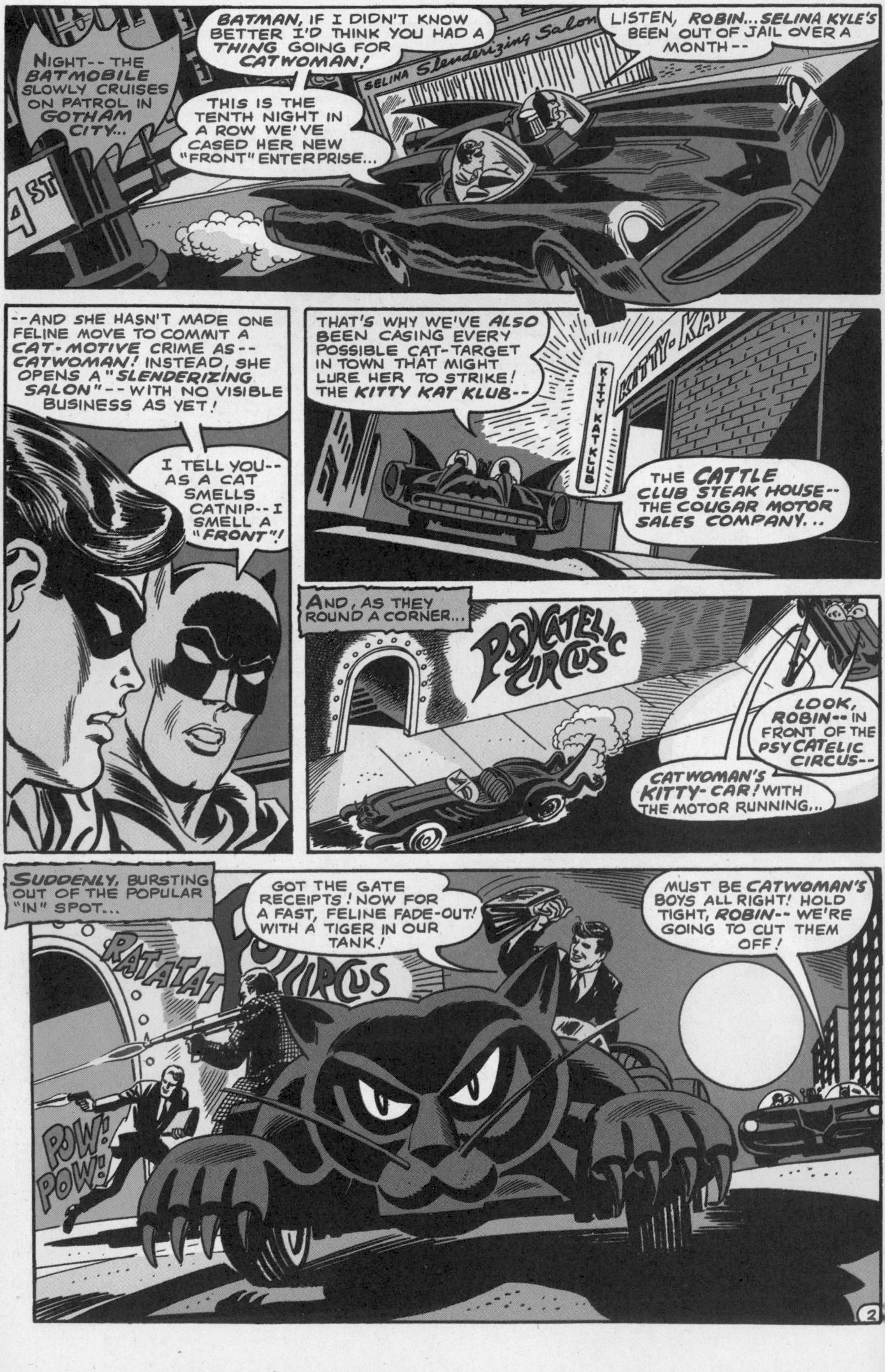
NIGHT-- THE BATMOBILE SLOWLY CRUISES ON PATROL IN GOTHAM CITY...
BATMAN, IF I DIDN'T KNOW BETTER I'D THINK YOU HAD A THING GOING FOR CATWOMAN!
THIS IS THE TENTH NIGHT IN A ROW WE'VE CASED HER NEW "FRONT" ENTERPRISE...
LISTEN, ROBIN... SELINA KYLE'S BEEN OUT OF JAIL OVER A MONTH--
SELINA Slenderizing Salon
4 ST
--AND SHE HASN'T MADE ONE FELINE MOVE TO COMMIT A CAT-MOTIVE CRIME AS--CATWOMAN! INSTEAD, SHE OPENS A "SLENDERIZING SALON"--WITH NO VISIBLE BUSINESS AS YET!
I TELL YOU-- AS A CAT SMELLS CATNIP--I SMELL A "FRONT"!
THAT'S WHY WE'VE ALSO BEEN CASING EVERY POSSIBLE CAT-TARGET IN TOWN THAT MIGHT LURE HER TO STRIKE! THE KITTY KAT KLUB--
KITTY KAT KLUB
THE CATTLE CLUB STEAK HOUSE-- THE COUGAR MOTOR SALES COMPANY...
AND, AS THEY ROUND A CORNER...
PSYCATELIC CIRCUS
LOOK, ROBIN-- IN FRONT OF THE PSYCATELIC CIRCUS--
CATWOMAN'S KITTY-CAR! WITH THE MOTOR RUNNING...
SUDDENLY, BURSTING OUT OF THE POPULAR "IN" SPOT...
GOT THE GATE RECEIPTS! NOW FOR A FAST, FELINE FADE-OUT! WITH A TIGER IN OUR TANK!
MUST BE CATWOMAN'S BOYS ALL RIGHT! HOLD TIGHT, ROBIN-- WE'RE GOING TO CUT THEM OFF!
RATATAT
POW! POW!
2

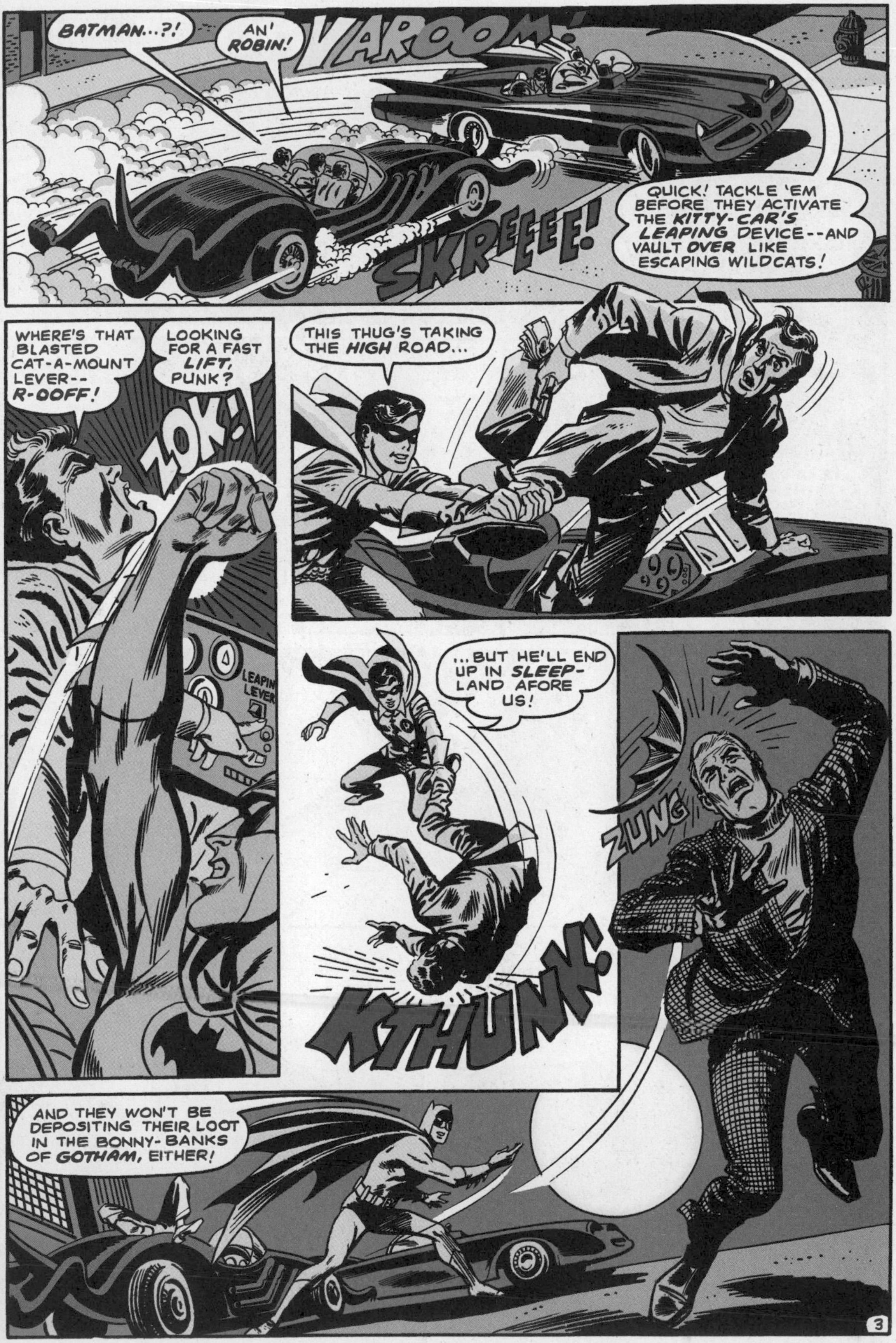
BATMAN...?!
AN' ROBIN!
VAROOM!
SKREEEE!
QUICK! TACKLE 'EM BEFORE THEY ACTIVATE THE KITTY-CAR'S LEAPING DEVICE--AND VAULT OVER LIKE ESCAPING WILDCATS!
WHERE'S THAT BLASTED CAT-A-MOUNT LEVER-- R-OOFF!
LOOKING FOR A FAST LIFT, PUNK?
ZOK!
THIS THUG'S TAKING THE HIGH ROAD...
...BUT HE'LL END UP IN SLEEP-LAND AFORE US!
KTHUNK!
ZUNG
AND THEY WON'T BE DEPOSITING THEIR LOOT IN THE BONNY-BANKS OF GOTHAM, EITHER!
3

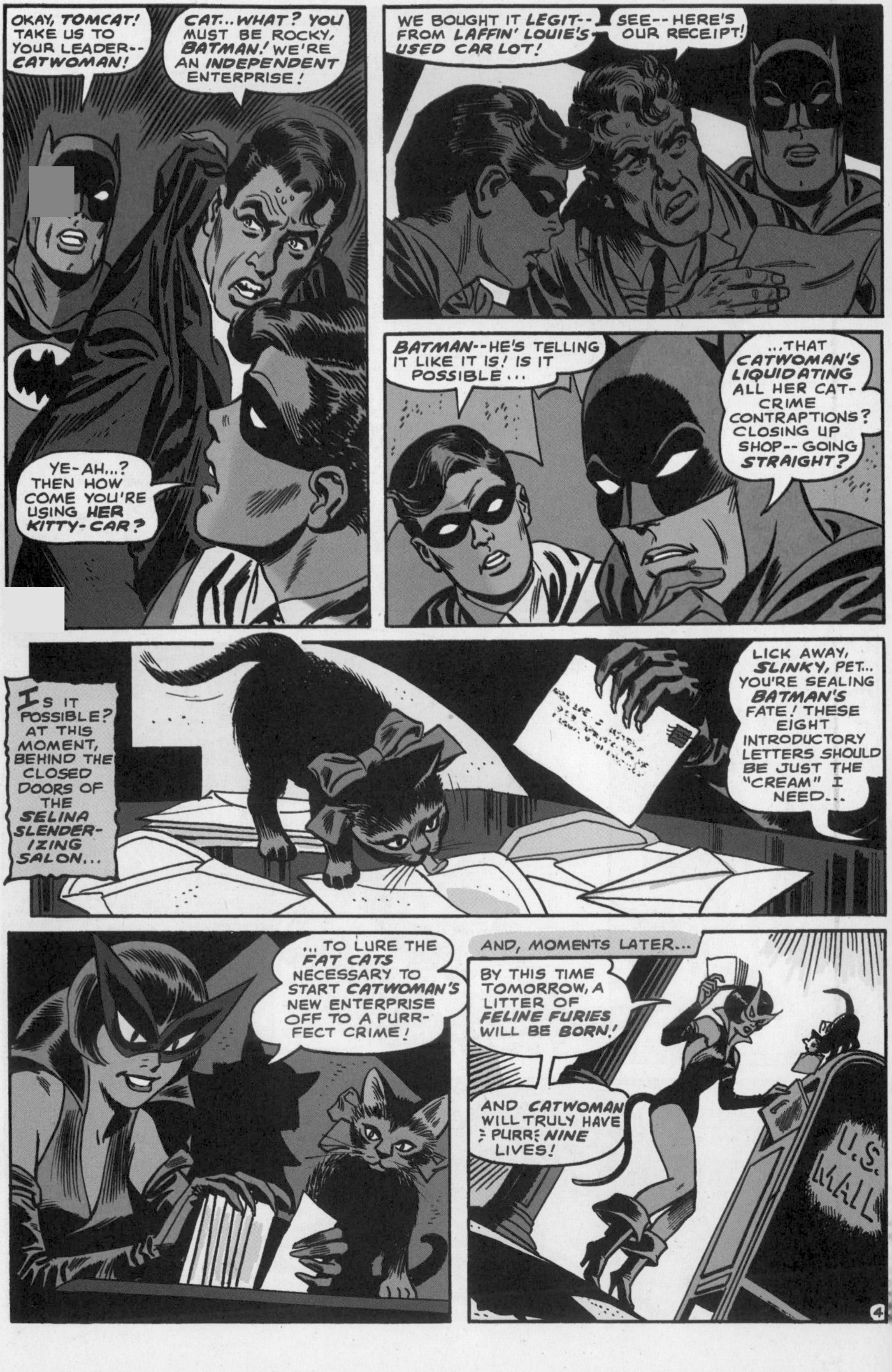
OKAY, TOMCAT! TAKE US TO YOUR LEADER-- CATWOMAN!
CAT...WHAT? YOU MUST BE ROCKY, BATMAN! WE'RE AN INDEPENDENT ENTERPRISE!
YE-AH...? THEN HOW COME YOU'RE USING HER KITTY-CAR?
WE BOUGHT IT LEGIT-- FROM LAFFIN' LOUIE'S USED CAR LOT!
SEE--HERE'S OUR RECEIPT!
BATMAN--HE'S TELLING IT LIKE IT IS! IS IT POSSIBLE...
...THAT CATWOMAN'S LIQUIDATING ALL HER CAT-CRIME CONTRAPTIONS? CLOSING UP SHOP--GOING STRAIGHT?
IS IT POSSIBLE? AT THIS MOMENT, BEHIND THE CLOSED DOORS OF THE SELINA SLENDERIZING SALON...
LICK AWAY, SLINKY, PET... YOU'RE SEALING BATMAN'S FATE! THESE EIGHT INTRODUCTORY LETTERS SHOULD BE JUST THE "CREAM" I NEED...
...TO LURE THE FAT CATS NECESSARY TO START CATWOMAN'S NEW ENTERPRISE OFF TO A PURR-FECT CRIME!
AND, MOMENTS LATER...
BY THIS TIME TOMORROW, A LITTER OF FELINE FURIES WILL BE BORN!
AND CATWOMAN WILL TRULY HAVE = PURR = NINE LIVES!
U.S. MAIL
4

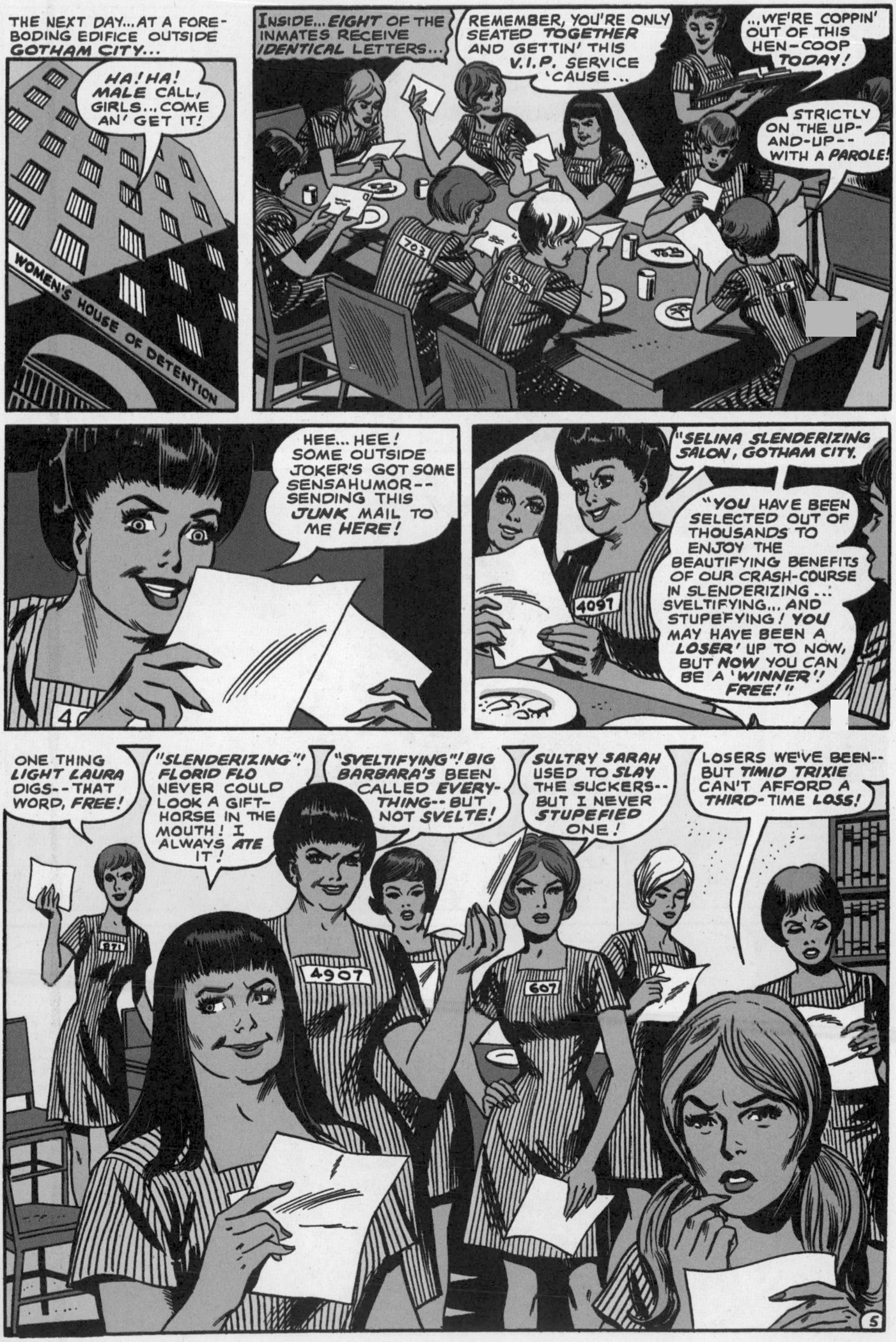
THE NEXT DAY...AT A FOREBODING EDIFICE OUTSIDE GOTHAM CITY...
HA! HA! MALE CALL, GIRLS...COME AN' GET IT!
WOMEN'S HOUSE OF DETENTION
INSIDE...EIGHT OF THE INMATES RECEIVE IDENTICAL LETTERS...
REMEMBER, YOU'RE ONLY SEATED TOGETHER AND GETTIN' THIS V.I.P. SERVICE 'CAUSE...
...WE'RE COPPIN' OUT OF THIS HEN-COOP TODAY!
STRICTLY ON THE UP-AND-UP--WITH A PAROLE!
703
HEE... HEE! SOME OUTSIDE JOKER'S GOT SOME SENSAHUMOR--SENDING THIS JUNK MAIL TO ME HERE!
"SELINA SLENDERIZING SALON, GOTHAM CITY.
"YOU HAVE BEEN SELECTED OUT OF THOUSANDS TO ENJOY THE BEAUTIFYING BENEFITS OF OUR CRASH-COURSE IN SLENDERIZING... SVELTIFYING... AND STUPEFYING! YOU MAY HAVE BEEN A 'LOSER' UP TO NOW, BUT NOW YOU CAN BE A 'WINNER'! FREE!"
4097
ONE THING LIGHT LAURA DIGS--THAT WORD, FREE!
"SLENDERIZING"! FLORID FLO NEVER COULD LOOK A GIFT-HORSE IN THE MOUTH! I ALWAYS ATE IT!
"SVELTIFYING"! BIG BARBARA'S BEEN CALLED EVERY-THING--BUT NOT SVELTE!
SULTRY SARAH USED TO SLAY THE SUCKERS--BUT I NEVER STUPEFIED ONE!
LOSERS WE'VE BEEN--BUT TIMID TRIXIE CAN'T AFFORD A THIRD-TIME LOSS!
871
4907
607
5

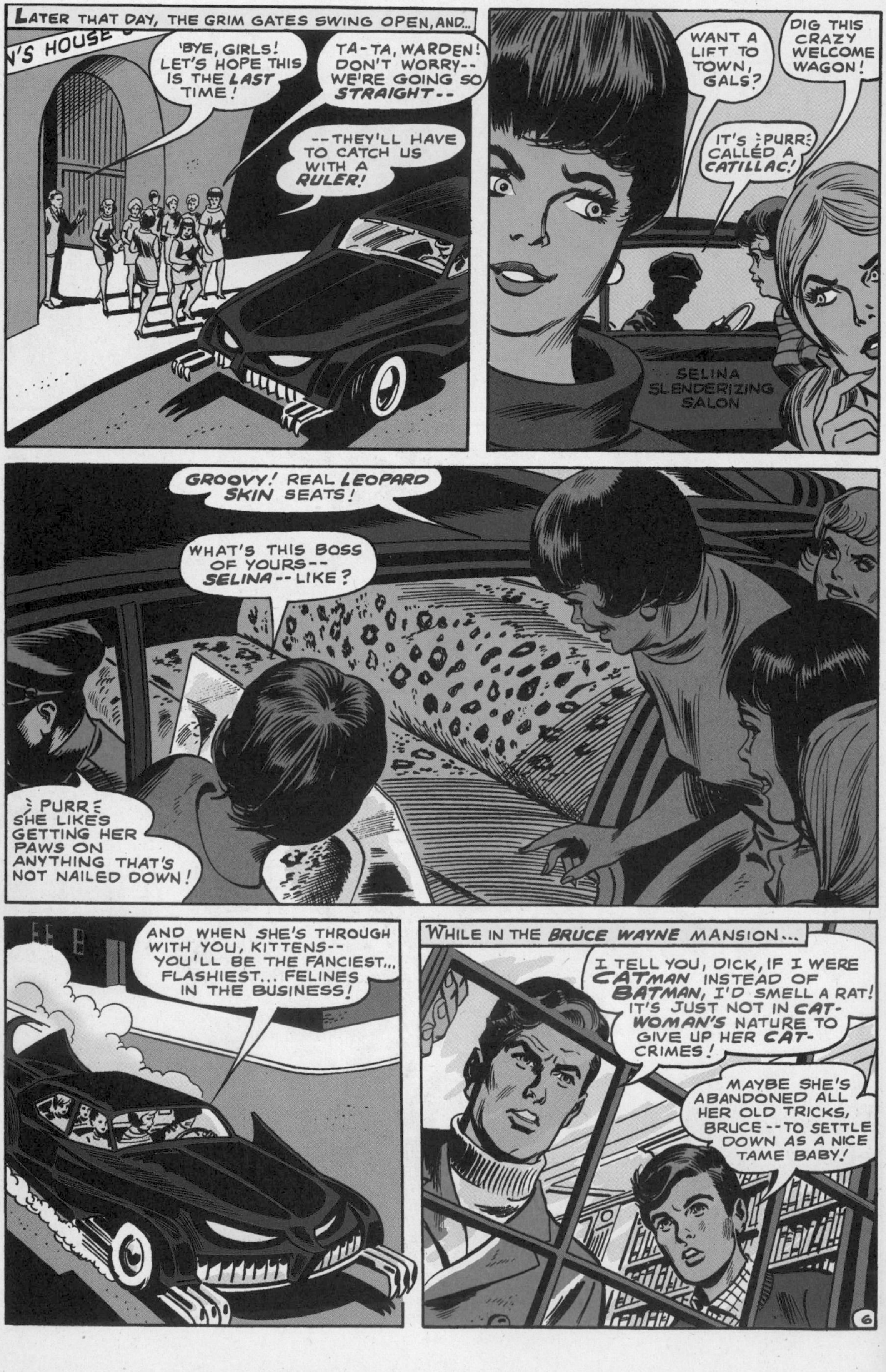
LATER THAT DAY, THE GRIM GATES SWING OPEN, AND...
'BYE, GIRLS! LET'S HOPE THIS IS THE LAST TIME!
TA-TA, WARDEN! DON'T WORRY-- WE'RE GOING SO STRAIGHT--
--THEY'LL HAVE TO CATCH US WITH A RULER!
WANT A LIFT TO TOWN, GALS?
DIG THIS CRAZY WELCOME WAGON!
IT'S ;PURR; CALLED A CATILLAC!
SELINA SLENDERIZING SALON
GROOVY! REAL LEOPARD SKIN SEATS!
WHAT'S THIS BOSS OF YOURS-- SELINA--LIKE?
;PURR; SHE LIKES GETTING HER PAWS ON ANYTHING THAT'S NOT NAILED DOWN!
AND WHEN SHE'S THROUGH WITH YOU, KITTENS-- YOU'LL BE THE FANCIEST... FLASHIEST... FELINES IN THE BUSINESS!
WHILE IN THE BRUCE WAYNE MANSION...
I TELL YOU, DICK, IF I WERE CATMAN INSTEAD OF BATMAN, I'D SMELL A RAT! IT'S JUST NOT IN CAT-WOMAN'S NATURE TO GIVE UP HER CAT-CRIMES!
MAYBE SHE'S ABANDONED ALL HER OLD TRICKS, BRUCE--TO SETTLE DOWN AS A NICE TAME BABY!
6

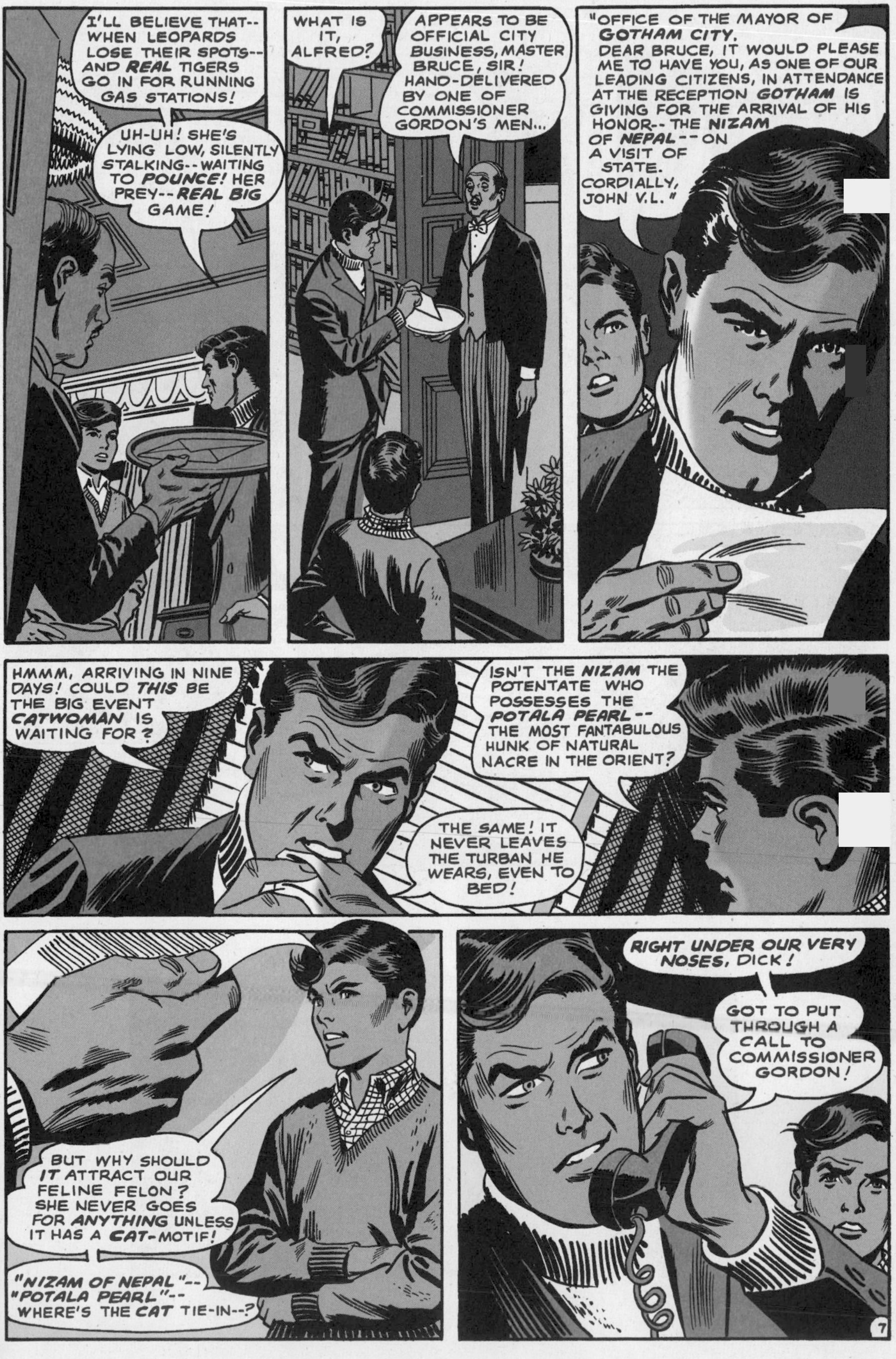
I'LL BELIEVE THAT-- WHEN LEOPARDS LOSE THEIR SPOTS-- AND REAL TIGERS GO IN FOR RUNNING GAS STATIONS!
UH-UH! SHE'S LYING LOW, SILENTLY STALKING--WAITING TO POUNCE! HER PREY--REAL BIG GAME!
WHAT IS IT, ALFRED?
APPEARS TO BE OFFICIAL CITY BUSINESS, MASTER BRUCE, SIR! HAND-DELIVERED BY ONE OF COMMISSIONER GORDON'S MEN...
"OFFICE OF THE MAYOR OF GOTHAM CITY. DEAR BRUCE, IT WOULD PLEASE ME TO HAVE YOU, AS ONE OF OUR LEADING CITIZENS, IN ATTENDANCE AT THE RECEPTION GOTHAM IS GIVING FOR THE ARRIVAL OF HIS HONOR-- THE NIZAM OF NEPAL--ON A VISIT OF STATE. CORDIALLY, JOHN V.L."
HMMM, ARRIVING IN NINE DAYS! COULD THIS BE THE BIG EVENT CATWOMAN IS WAITING FOR?
ISN'T THE NIZAM THE POTENTATE WHO POSSESSES THE POTALA PEARL-- THE MOST FANTABULOUS HUNK OF NATURAL NACRE IN THE ORIENT?
THE SAME! IT NEVER LEAVES THE TURBAN HE WEARS, EVEN TO BED!
BUT WHY SHOULD IT ATTRACT OUR FELINE FELON? SHE NEVER GOES FOR ANYTHING UNLESS IT HAS A CAT-MOTIF!
"NIZAM OF NEPAL"-- "POTALA PEARL"-- WHERE'S THE CAT TIE-IN--?
RIGHT UNDER OUR VERY NOSES, DICK!
GOT TO PUT THROUGH A CALL TO COMMISSIONER GORDON!
7

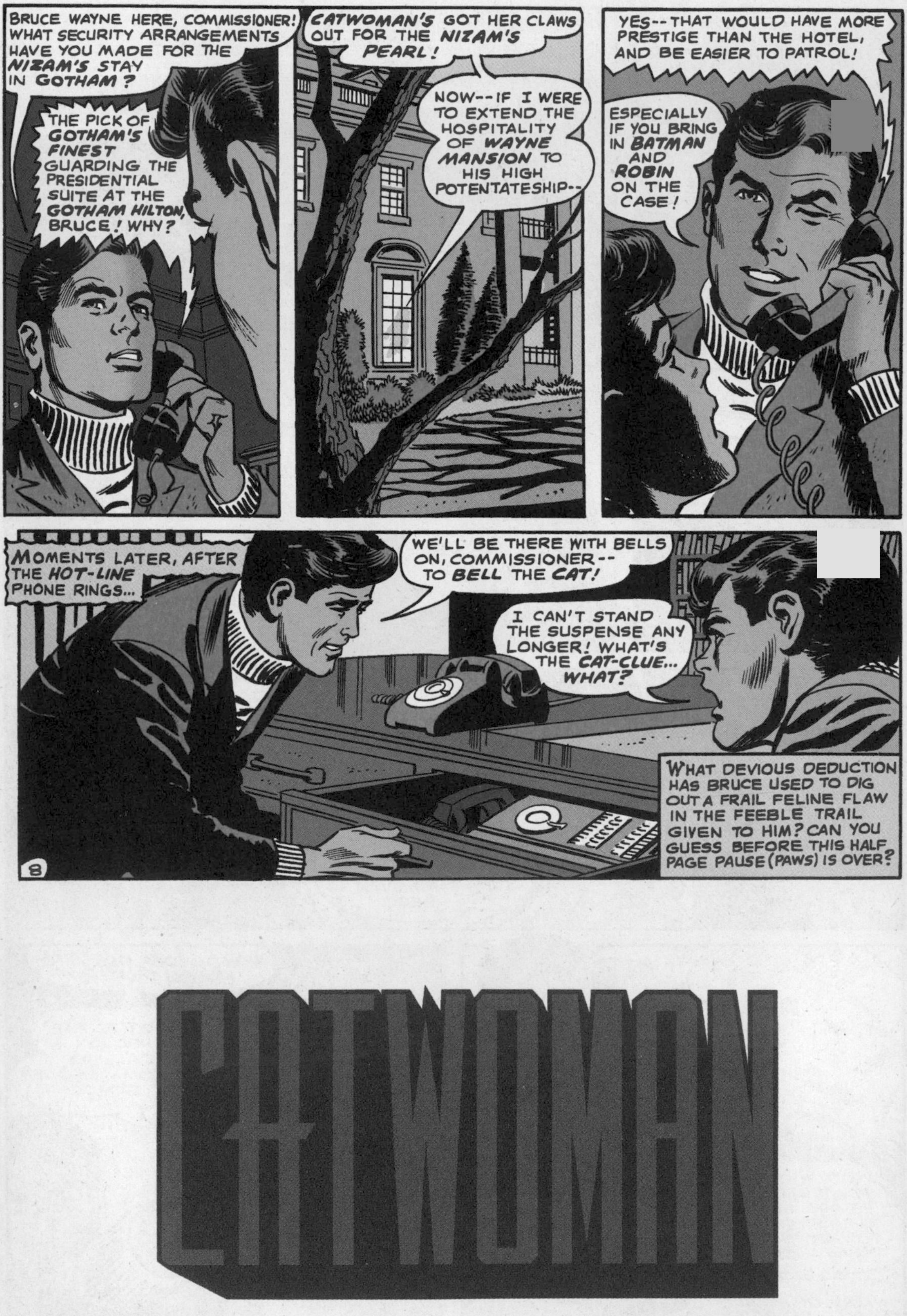
BRUCE WAYNE HERE, COMMISSIONER! WHAT SECURITY ARRANGEMENTS HAVE YOU MADE FOR THE NIZAM'S STAY IN GOTHAM?
THE PICK OF GOTHAM'S FINEST GUARDING THE PRESIDENTIAL SUITE AT THE GOTHAM HILTON, BRUCE! WHY?
CATWOMAN'S GOT HER CLAWS OUT FOR THE NIZAM'S PEARL!
NOW--IF I WERE TO EXTEND THE HOSPITALITY OF WAYNE MANSION TO HIS HIGH POTENTATESHIP--
YES--THAT WOULD HAVE MORE PRESTIGE THAN THE HOTEL, AND BE EASIER TO PATROL!
ESPECIALLY IF YOU BRING IN BATMAN AND ROBIN ON THE CASE!
MOMENTS LATER, AFTER THE HOT-LINE PHONE RINGS...
WE'LL BE THERE WITH BELLS ON, COMMISSIONER-- TO BELL THE CAT!
I CAN'T STAND THE SUSPENSE ANY LONGER! WHAT'S THE CAT-CLUE... WHAT?
WHAT DEVIOUS DEDUCTION HAS BRUCE USED TO DIG OUT A FRAIL FELINE FLAW IN THE FEEBLE TRAIL GIVEN TO HIM? CAN YOU GUESS BEFORE THIS HALF PAGE PAUSE (PAWS) IS OVER?
8

CATWOMAN

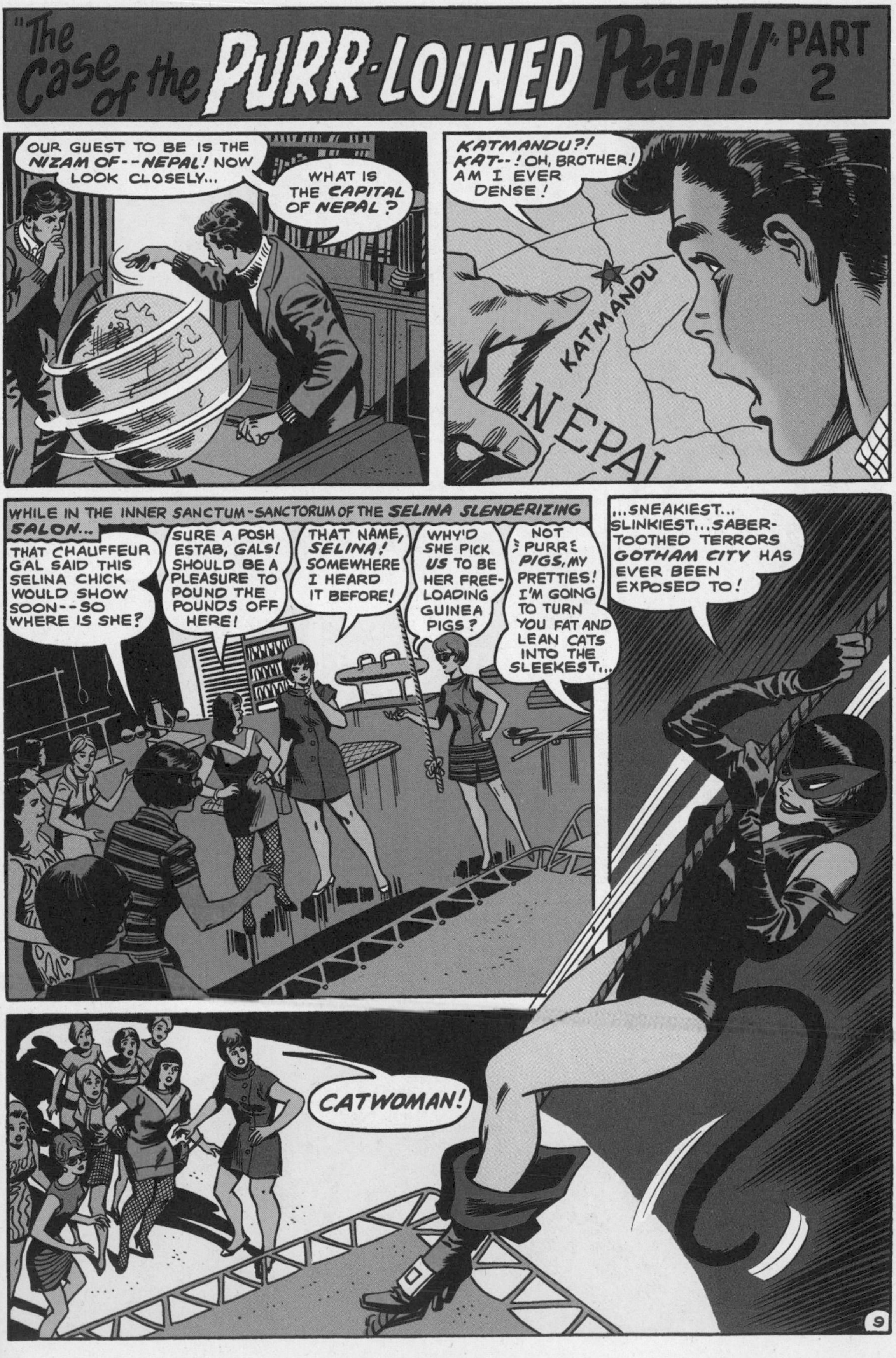
"The Case of the PURR-LOINED Pearl!" PART 2
OUR GUEST TO BE IS THE NIZAM OF--NEPAL! NOW LOOK CLOSELY...
WHAT IS THE CAPITAL OF NEPAL?
KATMANDU?! KAT--! OH, BROTHER! AM I EVER DENSE!
KATMANDU
KATMANDU
NEPAL
WHILE IN THE INNER SANCTUM-SANCTORUM OF THE SELINA SLENDERIZING SALON...
THAT CHAUFFEUR GAL SAID THIS SELINA CHICK WOULD SHOW SOON--SO WHERE IS SHE?
SURE A POSH ESTAB, GALS! SHOULD BE A PLEASURE TO POUND THE POUNDS OFF HERE!
THAT NAME, SELINA! SOMEWHERE I HEARD IT BEFORE!
WHY'D SHE PICK US TO BE HER FREE-LOADING GUINEA PIGS?
NOT PURR PIGS, MY PRETTIES! I'M GOING TO TURN YOU FAT AND LEAN CATS INTO THE SLEEKEST...
...SNEAKIEST... SLINKIEST... SABER-TOOTHED TERRORS GOTHAM CITY HAS EVER BEEN EXPOSED TO!
CATWOMAN!
9

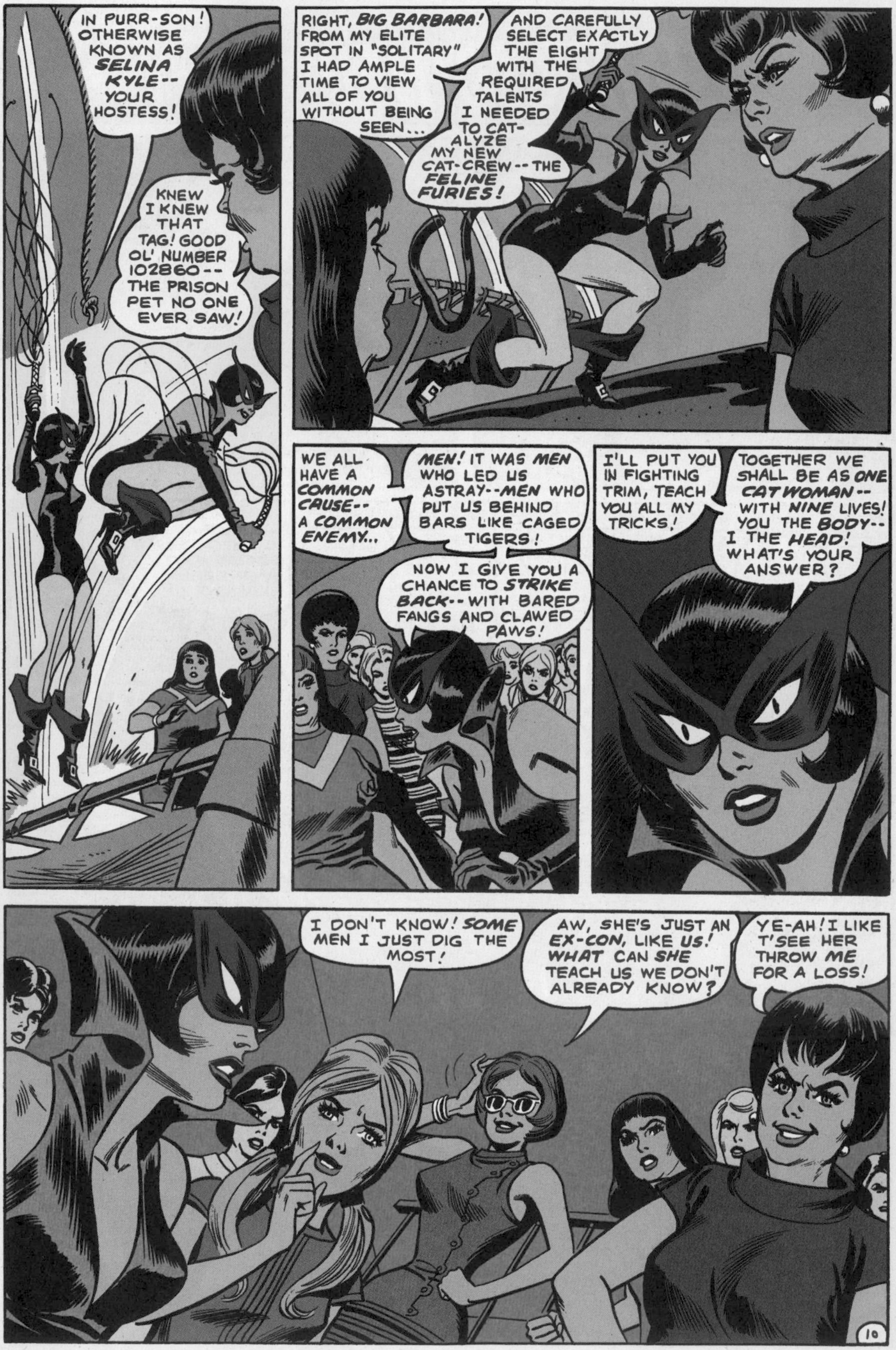
IN PURR-SON! OTHERWISE KNOWN AS SELINA KYLE-- YOUR HOSTESS!
KNEW I KNEW THAT TAG! GOOD OL' NUMBER 102860-- THE PRISON PET NO ONE EVER SAW!
RIGHT, BIG BARBARA! FROM MY ELITE SPOT IN "SOLITARY" I HAD AMPLE TIME TO VIEW ALL OF YOU WITHOUT BEING SEEN...
AND CAREFULLY SELECT EXACTLY THE EIGHT WITH THE REQUIRED TALENTS I NEEDED TO CAT-ALYZE MY NEW CAT-CREW-- THE FELINE FURIES!
WE ALL HAVE A COMMON CAUSE-- A COMMON ENEMY...
MEN! IT WAS MEN WHO LED US ASTRAY--MEN WHO PUT US BEHIND BARS LIKE CAGED TIGERS!
NOW I GIVE YOU A CHANCE TO STRIKE BACK-- WITH BARED FANGS AND CLAWED PAWS!
I'LL PUT YOU IN FIGHTING TRIM, TEACH YOU ALL MY TRICKS!
TOGETHER WE SHALL BE AS ONE CATWOMAN-- WITH NINE LIVES! YOU THE BODY-- I THE HEAD! WHAT'S YOUR ANSWER?
I DON'T KNOW! SOME MEN I JUST DIG THE MOST!
AW, SHE'S JUST AN EX-CON, LIKE US! WHAT CAN SHE TEACH US WE DON'T ALREADY KNOW?
YE-AH! I LIKE T'SEE HER THROW ME FOR A LOSS!
10

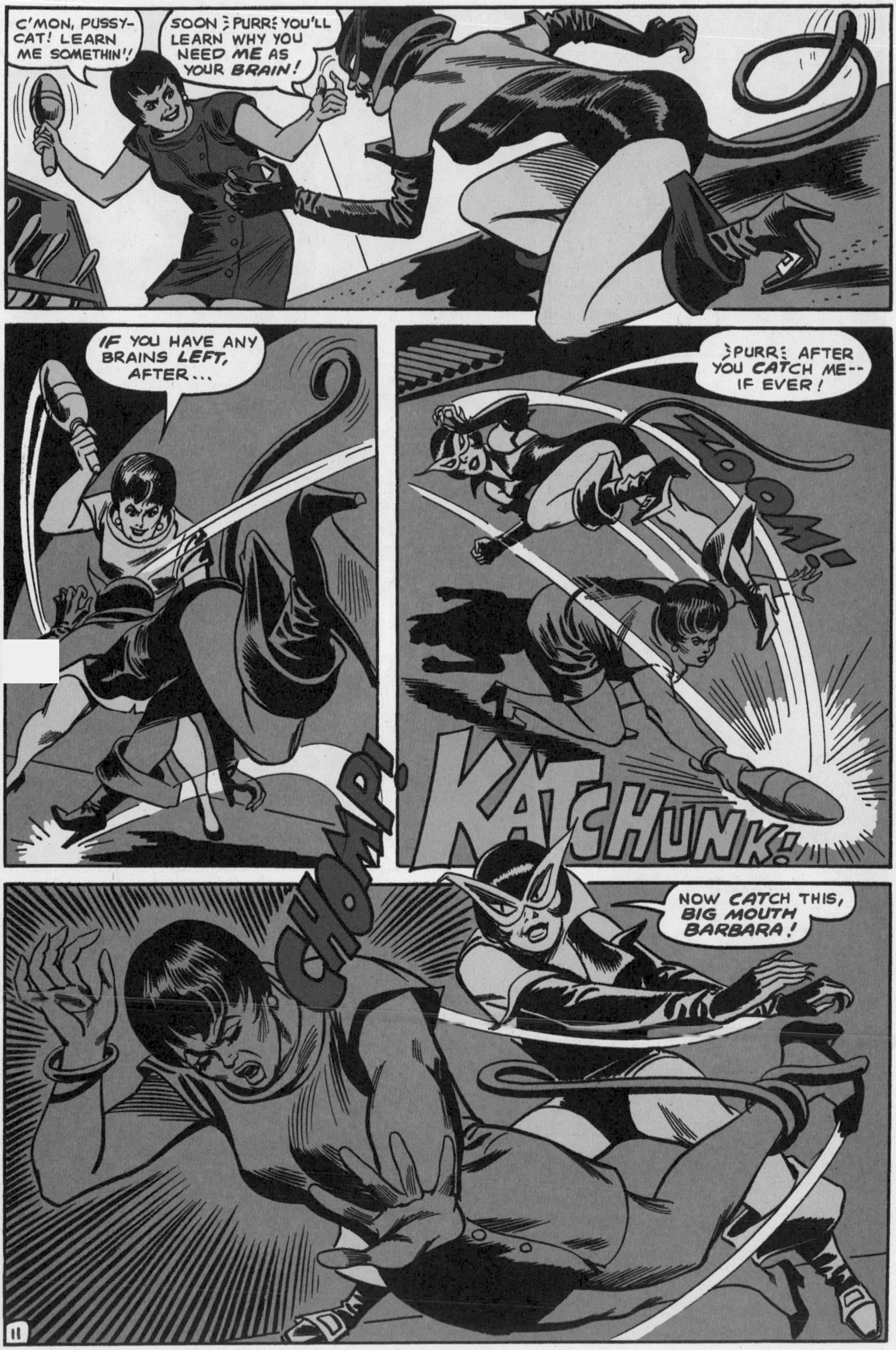
C'MON, PUSSY-CAT! LEARN ME SOMETHIN'!
SOON ⋛PURR⋚ YOU'LL LEARN WHY YOU NEED ME AS YOUR BRAIN!
IF YOU HAVE ANY BRAINS LEFT, AFTER...
⋛PURR⋚ AFTER YOU CATCH ME-- IF EVER!
ZOOOM!
KATCHUNK!
CHOMP!
NOW CATCH THIS, BIG MOUTH BARBARA!
11

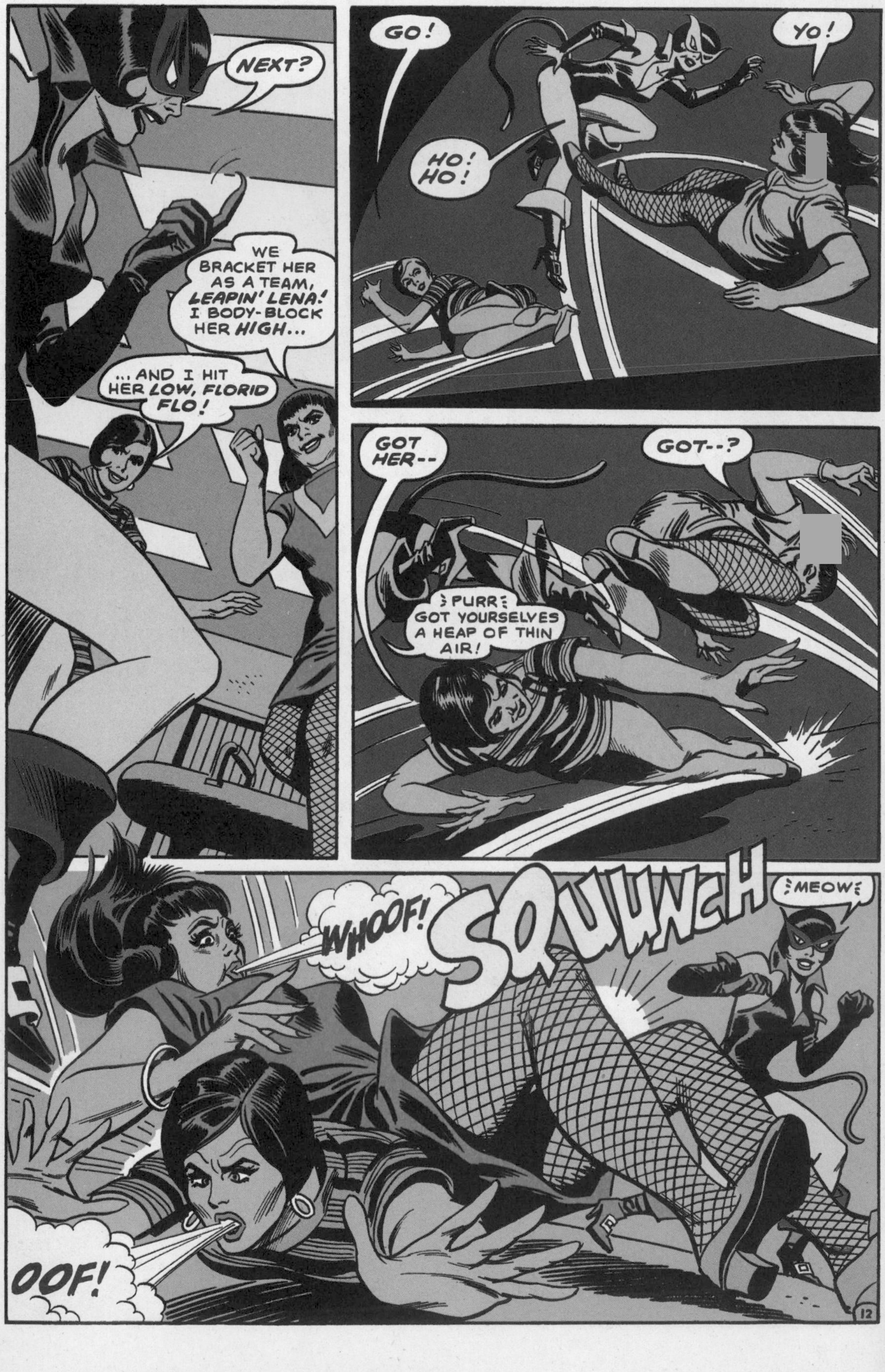
NEXT?
WE BRACKET HER AS A TEAM, LEAPIN' LENA! I BODY-BLOCK HER HIGH...
...AND I HIT HER LOW, FLORID FLO!
GO!
YO!
HO! HO!
GOT HER--
GOT--?
PURR GOT YOURSELVES A HEAP OF THIN AIR!
WHOOF!
SQUUNCH
MEOW
OOF!
12

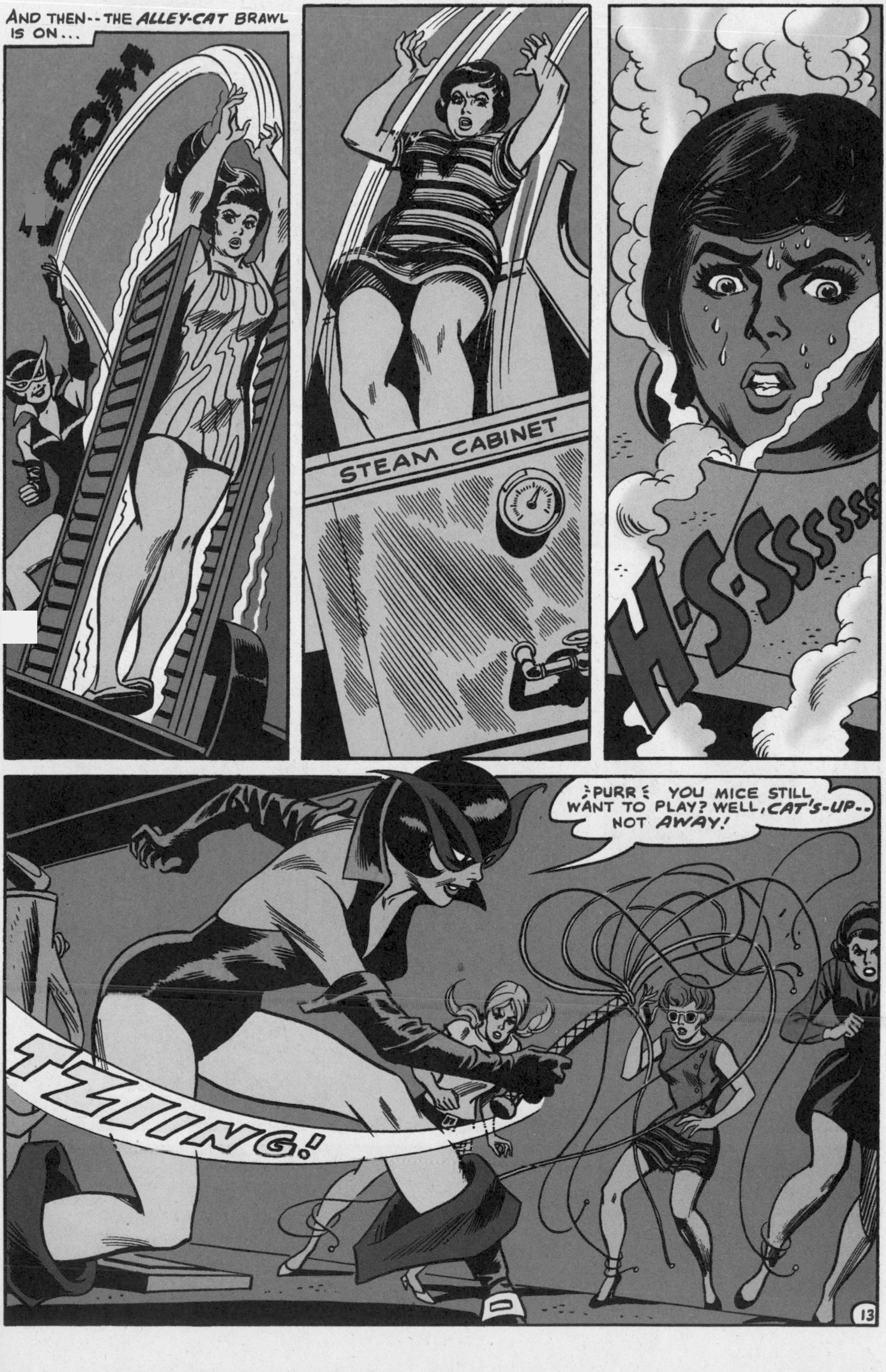

AND THEN--THE ALLEY-CAT BRAWL IS ON...
WOOSH
STEAM CABINET
H-S-SSSSSSS
:PURR: YOU MICE STILL WANT TO PLAY? WELL, CAT'S-UP-- NOT AWAY!
TZIING!
13

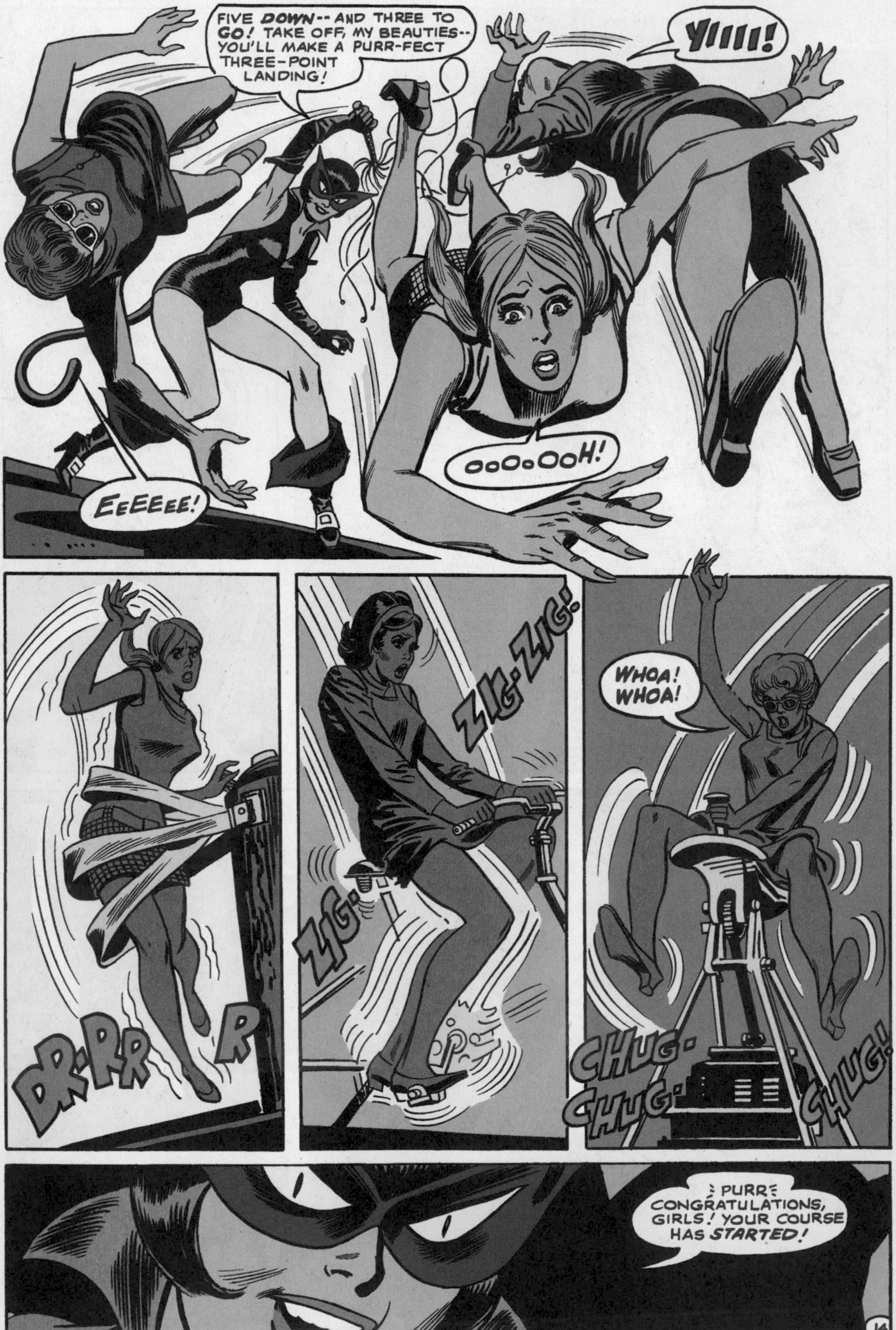
FIVE DOWN-- AND THREE TO GO! TAKE OFF, MY BEAUTIES-- YOU'LL MAKE A PURR-FECT THREE-POINT LANDING!
YIIIII!
EEEEEE!
OOOOOOH!
DR-RR R
ZIG-ZIG-ZIG-
WHOA! WHOA!
CHUG-CHUG-CHUG!
PURR CONGRATULATIONS, GIRLS! YOUR COURSE HAS STARTED!
14

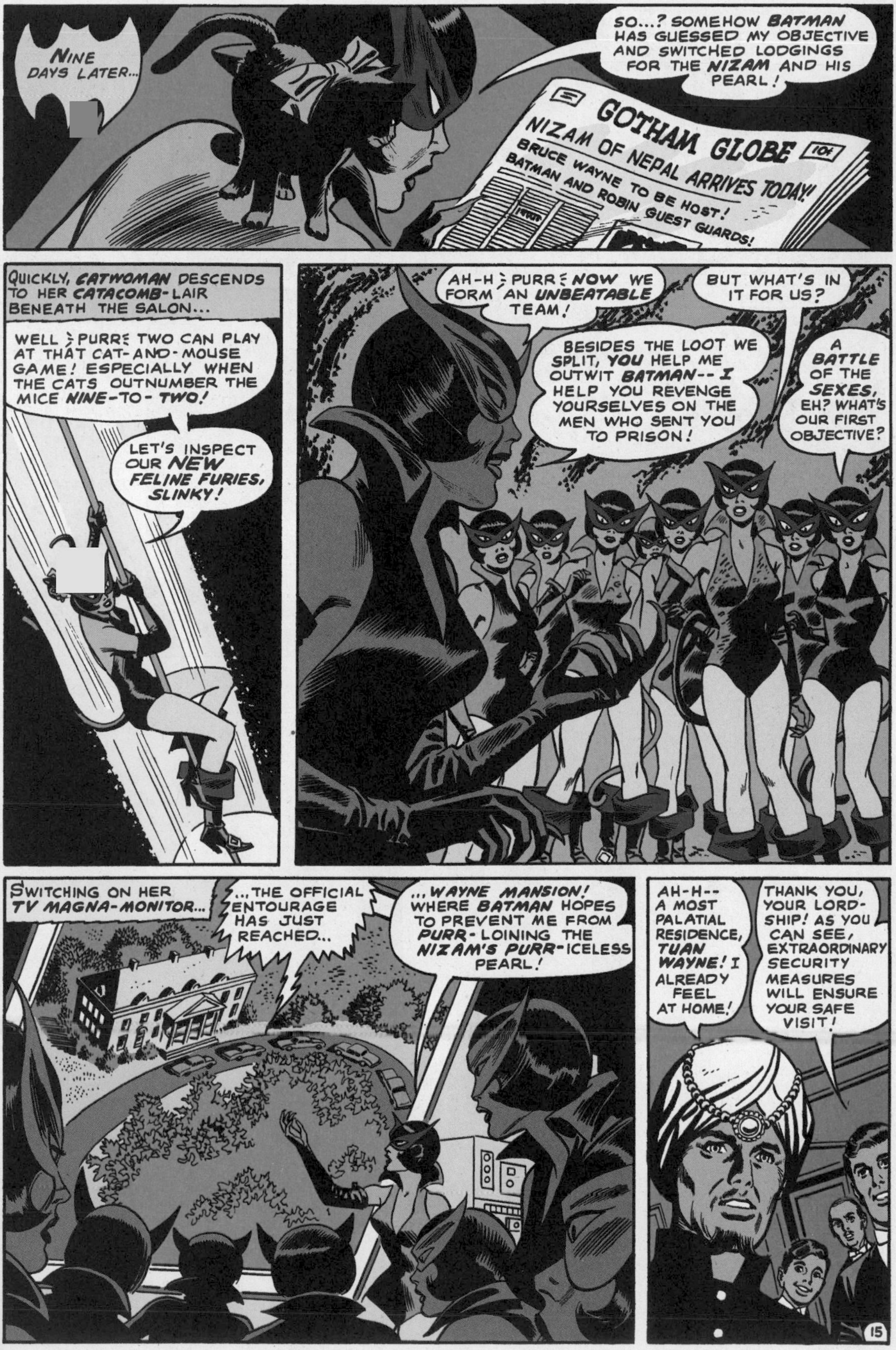
NINE DAYS LATER...
SO...? SOMEHOW BATMAN HAS GUESSED MY OBJECTIVE AND SWITCHED LODGINGS FOR THE NIZAM AND HIS PEARL!
GOTHAM GLOBE 10¢
NIZAM OF NEPAL ARRIVES TODAY!
BRUCE WAYNE TO BE HOST!
BATMAN AND ROBIN GUEST GUARDS!
QUICKLY, CATWOMAN DESCENDS TO HER CATACOMB-LAIR BENEATH THE SALON...
WELL -PURR- TWO CAN PLAY AT THAT CAT-AND-MOUSE GAME! ESPECIALLY WHEN THE CATS OUTNUMBER THE MICE NINE-TO-TWO!
LET'S INSPECT OUR NEW FELINE FURIES, SLINKY!
AH-H -PURR- NOW WE FORM AN UNBEATABLE TEAM!
BUT WHAT'S IN IT FOR US?
BESIDES THE LOOT WE SPLIT, YOU HELP ME OUTWIT BATMAN-- I HELP YOU REVENGE YOURSELVES ON THE MEN WHO SENT YOU TO PRISON!
A BATTLE OF THE SEXES, EH? WHAT'S OUR FIRST OBJECTIVE?
SWITCHING ON HER TV MAGNA-MONITOR...
...THE OFFICIAL ENTOURAGE HAS JUST REACHED...
...WAYNE MANSION! WHERE BATMAN HOPES TO PREVENT ME FROM PURR-LOINING THE NIZAM'S PURR-ICELESS PEARL!
AH-H-- A MOST PALATIAL RESIDENCE, TUAN WAYNE! I ALREADY FEEL AT HOME!
THANK YOU, YOUR LORD-SHIP! AS YOU CAN SEE, EXTRAORDINARY SECURITY MEASURES WILL ENSURE YOUR SAFE VISIT!
15

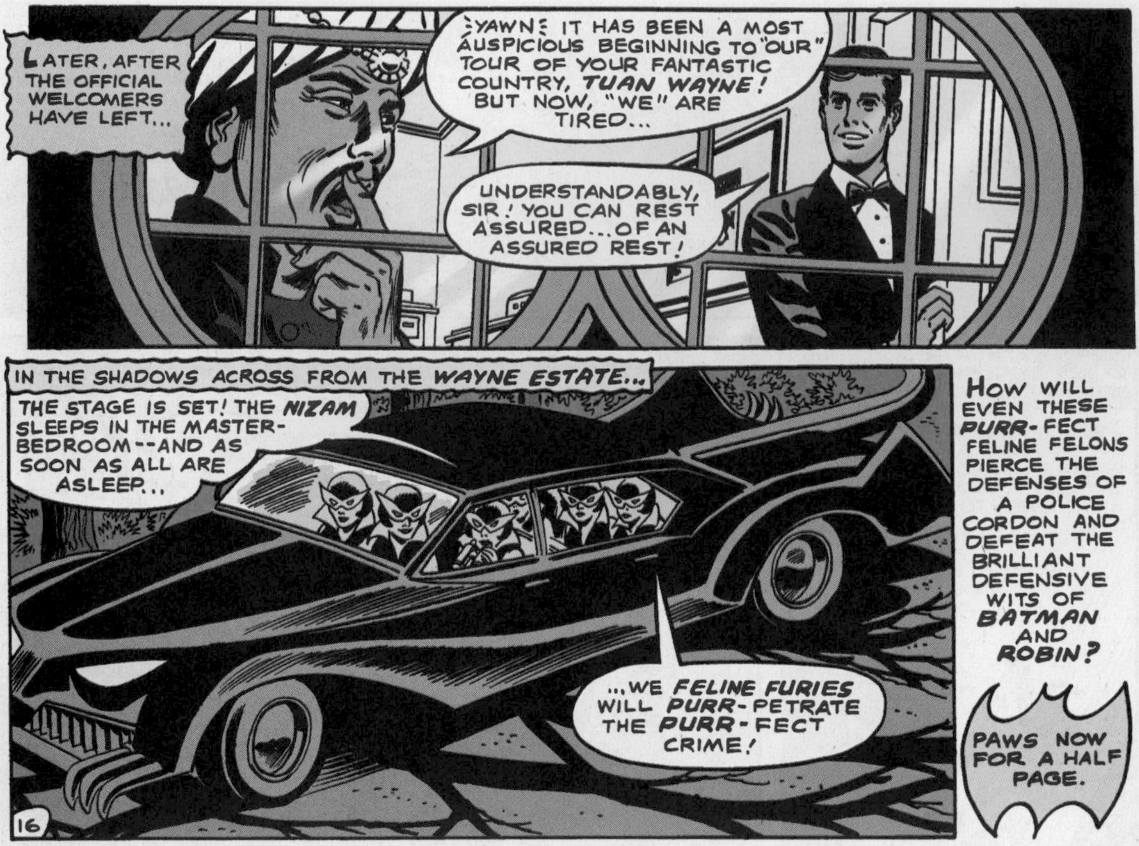
LATER, AFTER THE OFFICIAL WELCOMERS HAVE LEFT...
:YAWN: IT HAS BEEN A MOST AUSPICIOUS BEGINNING TO "OUR" TOUR OF YOUR FANTASTIC COUNTRY, TUAN WAYNE! BUT NOW, "WE" ARE TIRED...
UNDERSTANDABLY, SIR! YOU CAN REST ASSURED...OF AN ASSURED REST!
IN THE SHADOWS ACROSS FROM THE WAYNE ESTATE...
THE STAGE IS SET! THE NIZAM SLEEPS IN THE MASTER-BEDROOM--AND AS SOON AS ALL ARE ASLEEP...
...WE FELINE FURIES WILL PURR-PETRATE THE PURR-FECT CRIME!
16
HOW WILL EVEN THESE PURR-FECT FELINE FELONS PIERCE THE DEFENSES OF A POLICE CORDON AND DEFEAT THE BRILLIANT DEFENSIVE WITS OF BATMAN AND ROBIN?
PAWS NOW FOR A HALF PAGE.

cat woman

"The Case of the PURR-LOINED Pearl!" PART 3

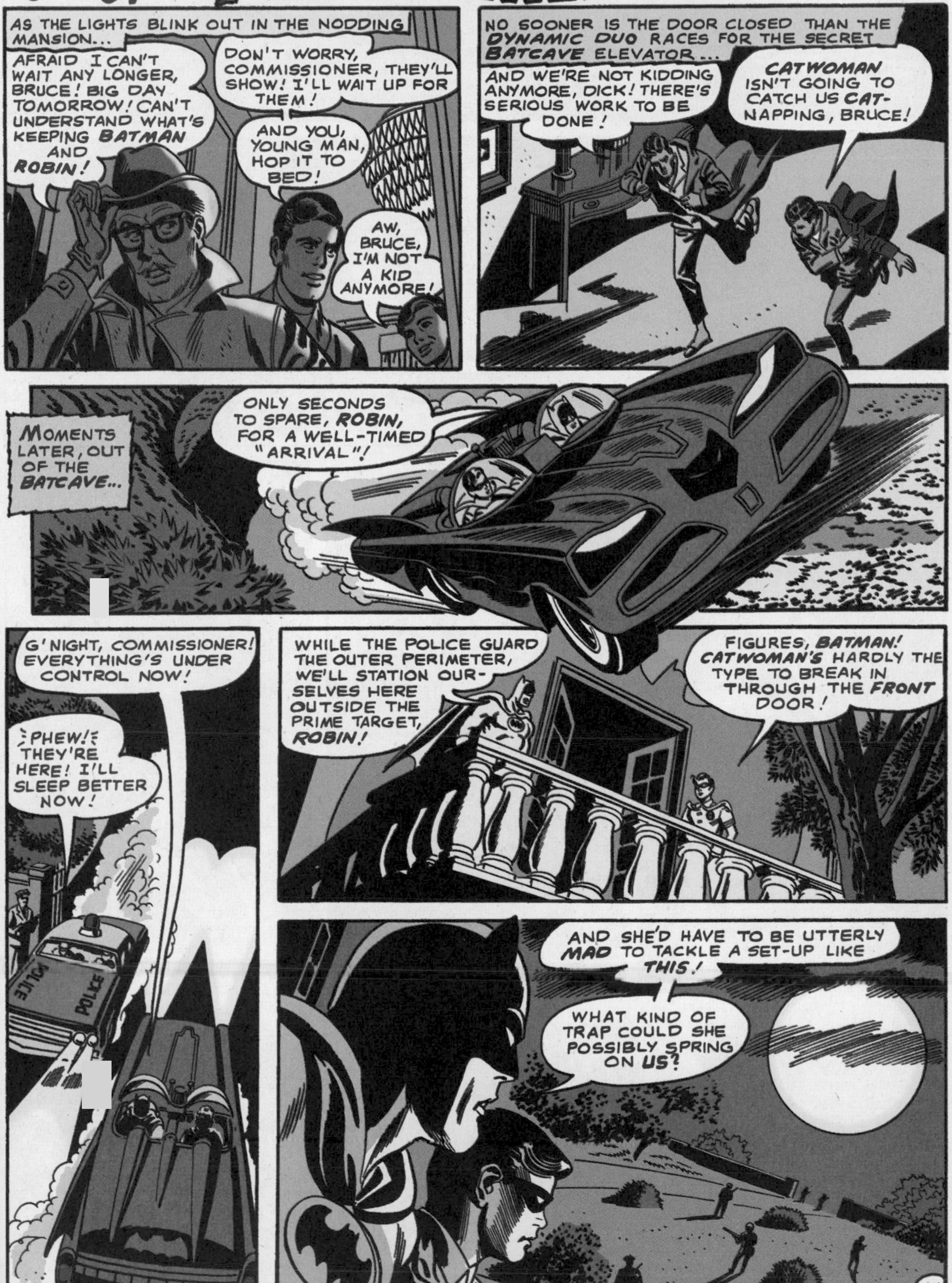
AS THE LIGHTS BLINK OUT IN THE NODDING MANSION...
AFRAID I CAN'T WAIT ANY LONGER, BRUCE! BIG DAY TOMORROW! CAN'T UNDERSTAND WHAT'S KEEPING BATMAN AND ROBIN!
DON'T WORRY, COMMISSIONER, THEY'LL SHOW! I'LL WAIT UP FOR THEM!
AND YOU, YOUNG MAN, HOP IT TO BED!
AW, BRUCE, I'M NOT A KID ANYMORE!
NO SOONER IS THE DOOR CLOSED THAN THE DYNAMIC DUO RACES FOR THE SECRET BATCAVE ELEVATOR...
AND WE'RE NOT KIDDING ANYMORE, DICK! THERE'S SERIOUS WORK TO BE DONE!
CATWOMAN ISN'T GOING TO CATCH US CAT-NAPPING, BRUCE!
MOMENTS LATER, OUT OF THE BATCAVE...
ONLY SECONDS TO SPARE, ROBIN, FOR A WELL-TIMED "ARRIVAL"!
G'NIGHT, COMMISSIONER! EVERYTHING'S UNDER CONTROL NOW!
PHEW! THEY'RE HERE! I'LL SLEEP BETTER NOW!
POLICE
WHILE THE POLICE GUARD THE OUTER PERIMETER, WE'LL STATION OURSELVES HERE OUTSIDE THE PRIME TARGET, ROBIN!
FIGURES, BATMAN! CATWOMAN'S HARDLY THE TYPE TO BREAK IN THROUGH THE FRONT DOOR!
AND SHE'D HAVE TO BE UTTERLY MAD TO TACKLE A SET-UP LIKE THIS!
WHAT KIND OF TRAP COULD SHE POSSIBLY SPRING ON US?
17

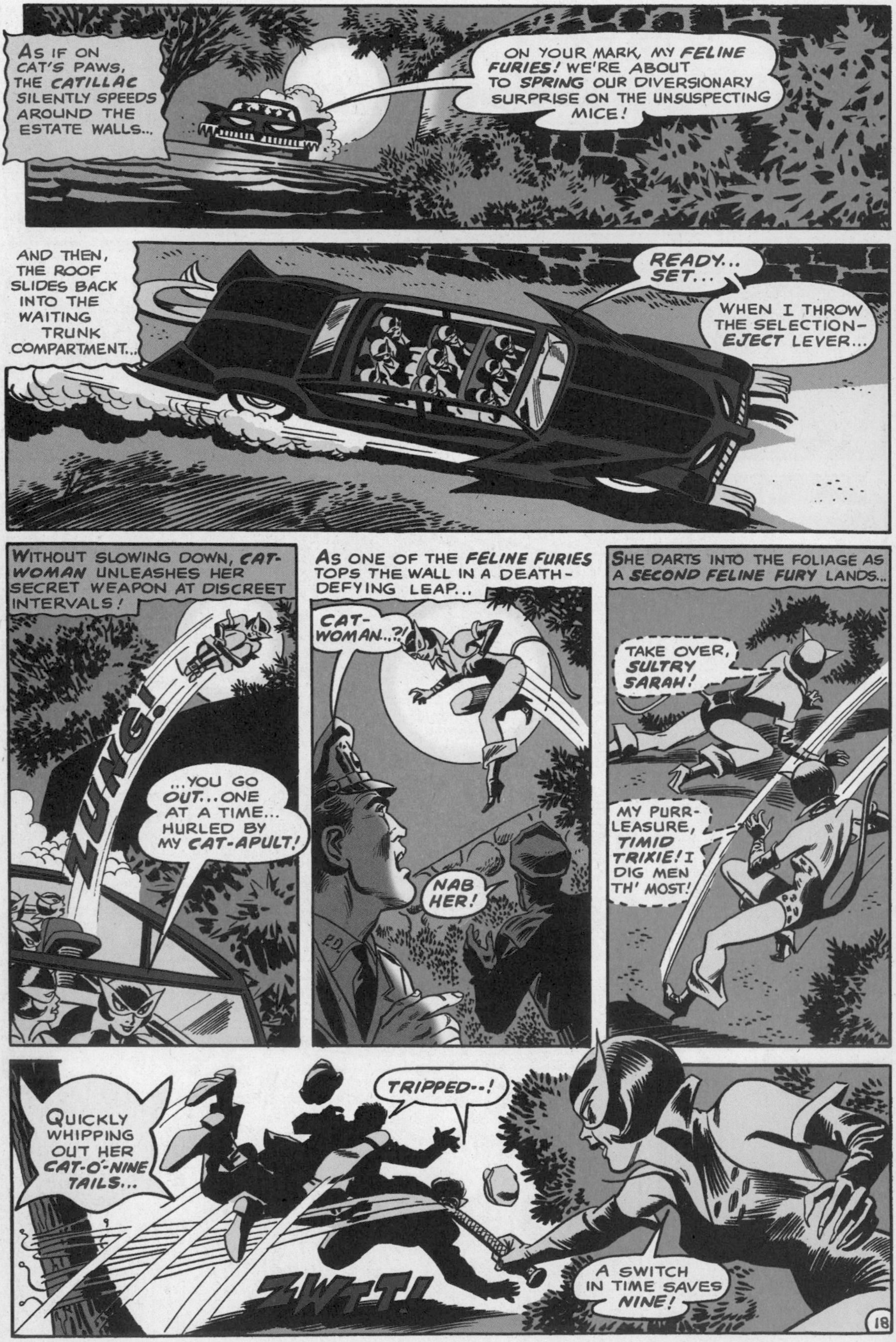
AS IF ON CAT'S PAWS, THE CATILLAC SILENTLY SPEEDS AROUND THE ESTATE WALLS...
ON YOUR MARK, MY FELINE FURIES! WE'RE ABOUT TO SPRING OUR DIVERSIONARY SURPRISE ON THE UNSUSPECTING MICE!
AND THEN, THE ROOF SLIDES BACK INTO THE WAITING TRUNK COMPARTMENT...
READY... SET...
WHEN I THROW THE SELECTION-EJECT LEVER...
WITHOUT SLOWING DOWN, CAT-WOMAN UNLEASHES HER SECRET WEAPON AT DISCREET INTERVALS!
ZUNG!
...YOU GO OUT...ONE AT A TIME... HURLED BY MY CAT-APULT!
AS ONE OF THE FELINE FURIES TOPS THE WALL IN A DEATH-DEFYING LEAP...
CAT-WOMAN...?!
NAB HER!
P.D.
SHE DARTS INTO THE FOLIAGE AS A SECOND FELINE FURY LANDS...
TAKE OVER, SULTRY SARAH!
MY PURR-LEASURE, TIMID TRIXIE! I DIG MEN TH' MOST!
QUICKLY WHIPPING OUT HER CAT-O'-NINE TAILS...
TRIPPED--!
ZWTT!
A SWITCH IN TIME SAVES NINE!
18

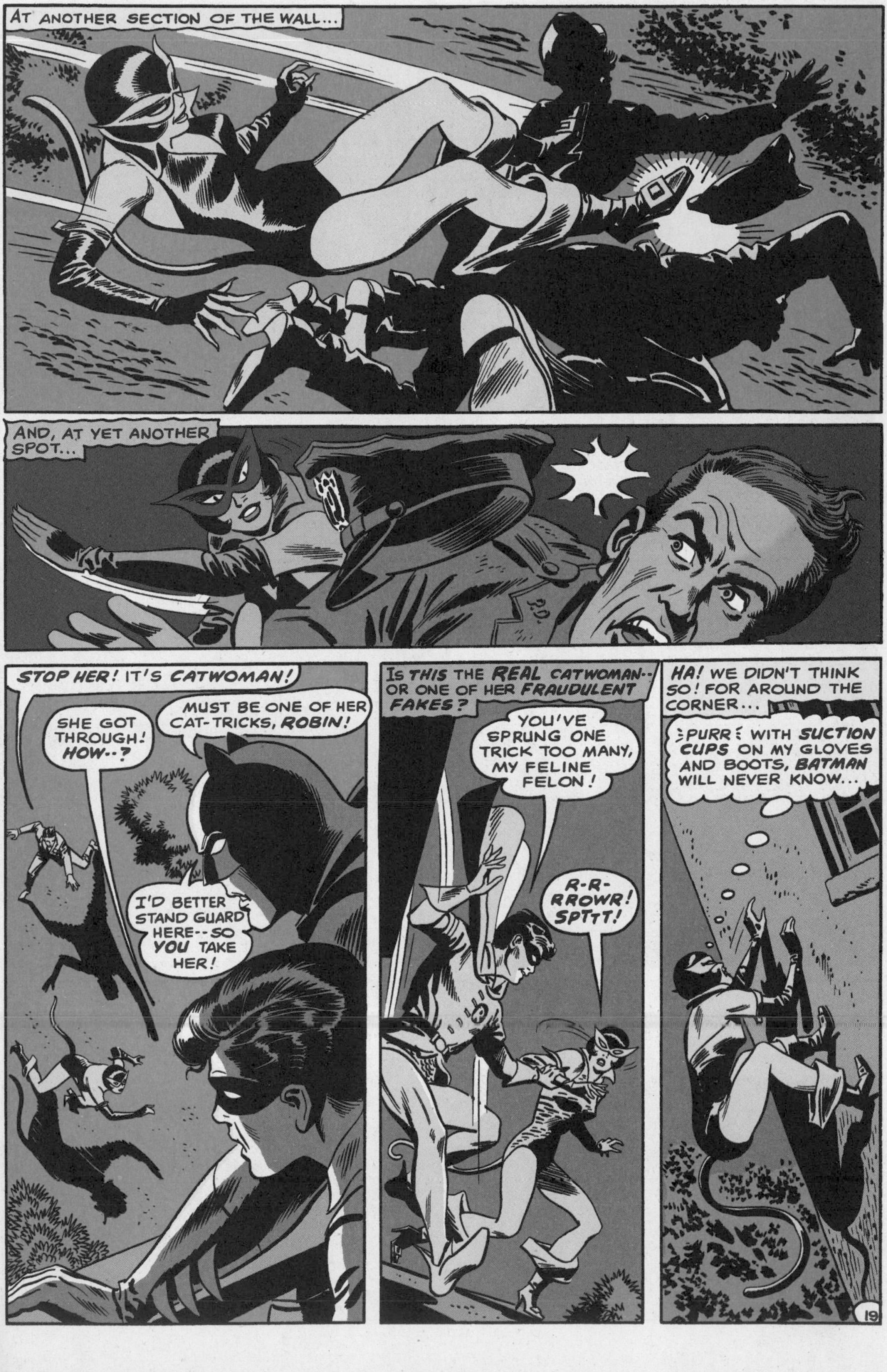
AT ANOTHER SECTION OF THE WALL...
AND, AT YET ANOTHER SPOT...
STOP HER! IT'S CATWOMAN!
SHE GOT THROUGH! HOW--?
MUST BE ONE OF HER CAT-TRICKS, ROBIN!
I'D BETTER STAND GUARD HERE--SO YOU TAKE HER!
IS THIS THE REAL CATWOMAN--OR ONE OF HER FRAUDULENT FAKES?
YOU'VE SPRUNG ONE TRICK TOO MANY, MY FELINE FELON!
R-R-RROWR! SPTTT!
HA! WE DIDN'T THINK SO! FOR AROUND THE CORNER...
PURR WITH SUCTION CUPS ON MY GLOVES AND BOOTS, BATMAN WILL NEVER KNOW...
19

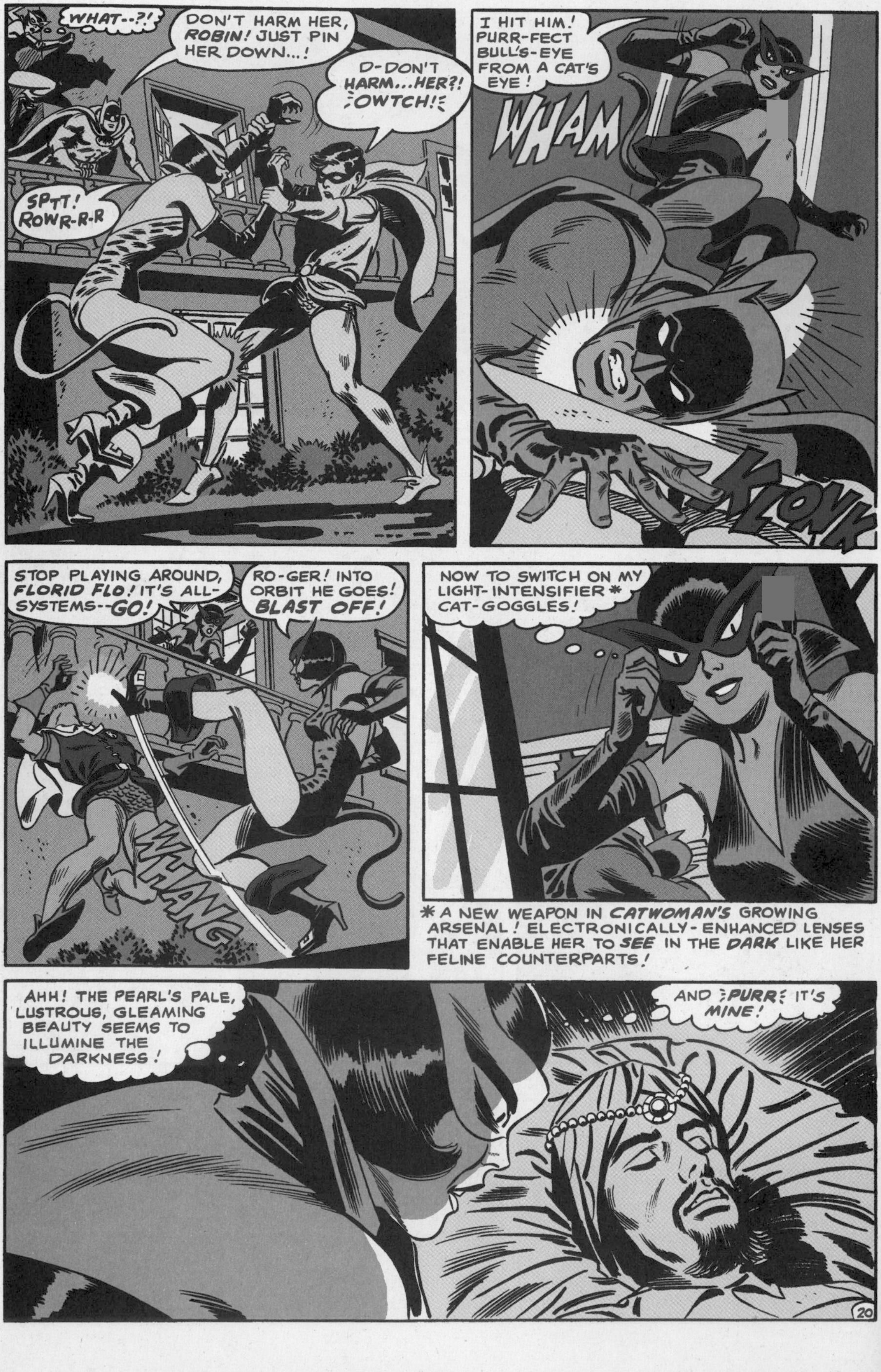
WHAT--?!
DON'T HARM HER, ROBIN! JUST PIN HER DOWN...!
D-DON'T HARM...HER?! OWTCH!
SPTT! ROWR-R-R
I HIT HIM! PURR-FECT BULL'S-EYE FROM A CAT'S EYE!
WHAM
KLONK
STOP PLAYING AROUND, FLORID FLO! IT'S ALL-SYSTEMS--GO!
RO-GER! INTO ORBIT HE GOES! BLAST OFF!
WHANG
NOW TO SWITCH ON MY LIGHT-INTENSIFIER* CAT-GOGGLES!
*A NEW WEAPON IN CATWOMAN'S GROWING ARSENAL! ELECTRONICALLY-ENHANCED LENSES THAT ENABLE HER TO SEE IN THE DARK LIKE HER FELINE COUNTERPARTS!
AHH! THE PEARL'S PALE, LUSTROUS, GLEAMING BEAUTY SEEMS TO ILLUMINE THE DARKNESS!
AND PURR IT'S MINE!
20

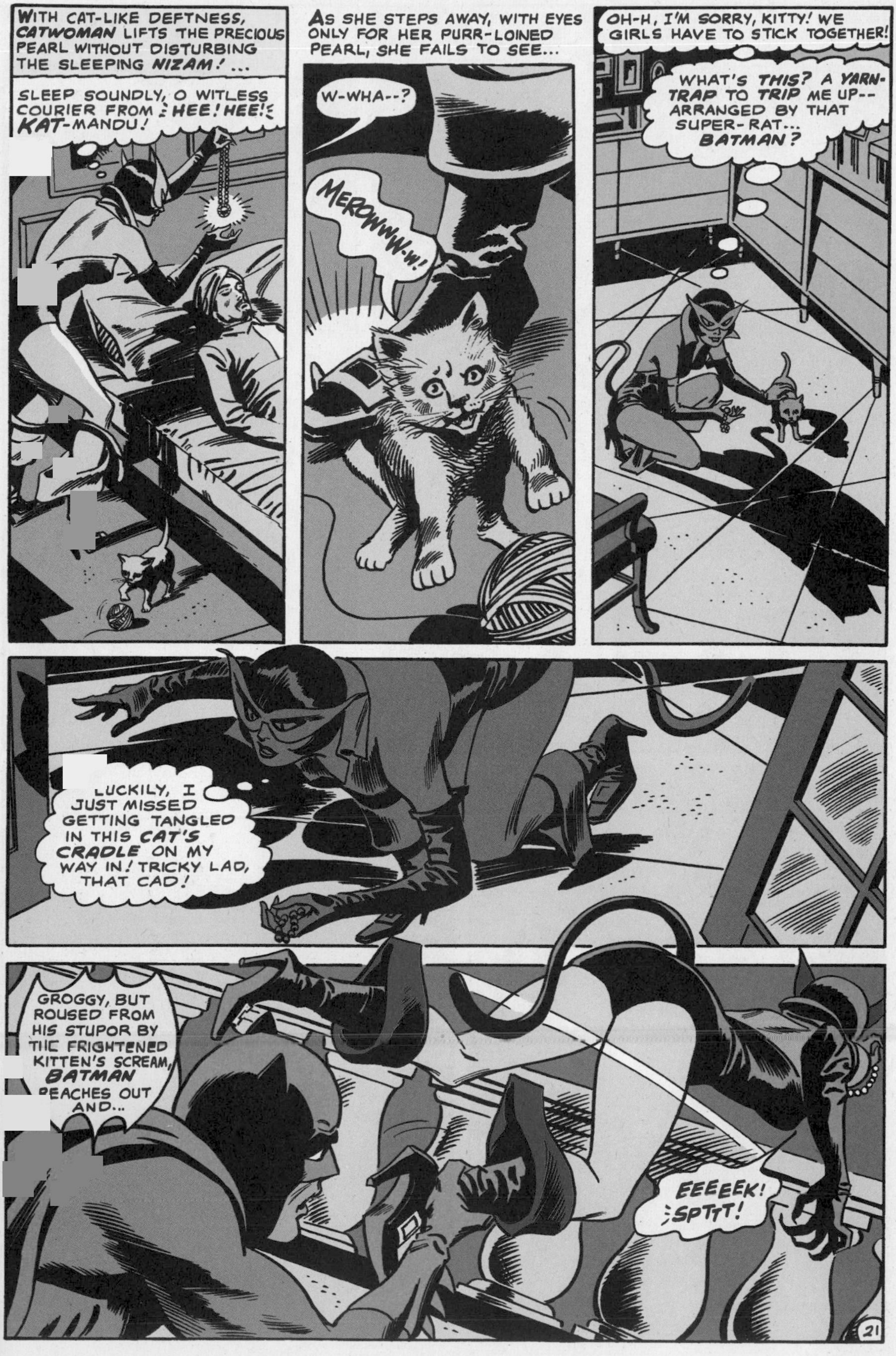

WITH CAT-LIKE DEFTNESS, CATWOMAN LIFTS THE PRECIOUS PEARL WITHOUT DISTURBING THE SLEEPING NIZAM! ...
SLEEP SOUNDLY, O WITLESS COURIER FROM KAT-MANDU! HEE! HEE!
AS SHE STEPS AWAY, WITH EYES ONLY FOR HER PURR-LOINED PEARL, SHE FAILS TO SEE...
W-WHA--?
MEROWWW-W-W!
OH-H, I'M SORRY, KITTY! WE GIRLS HAVE TO STICK TOGETHER!
WHAT'S THIS? A YARN-TRAP TO TRIP ME UP--ARRANGED BY THAT SUPER-RAT... BATMAN?
LUCKILY, I JUST MISSED GETTING TANGLED IN THIS CAT'S CRADLE ON MY WAY IN! TRICKY LAD, THAT CAD!
GROGGY, BUT ROUSED FROM HIS STUPOR BY THE FRIGHTENED KITTEN'S SCREAM, BATMAN REACHES OUT AND...
EEEEEK! SPTTT!
21

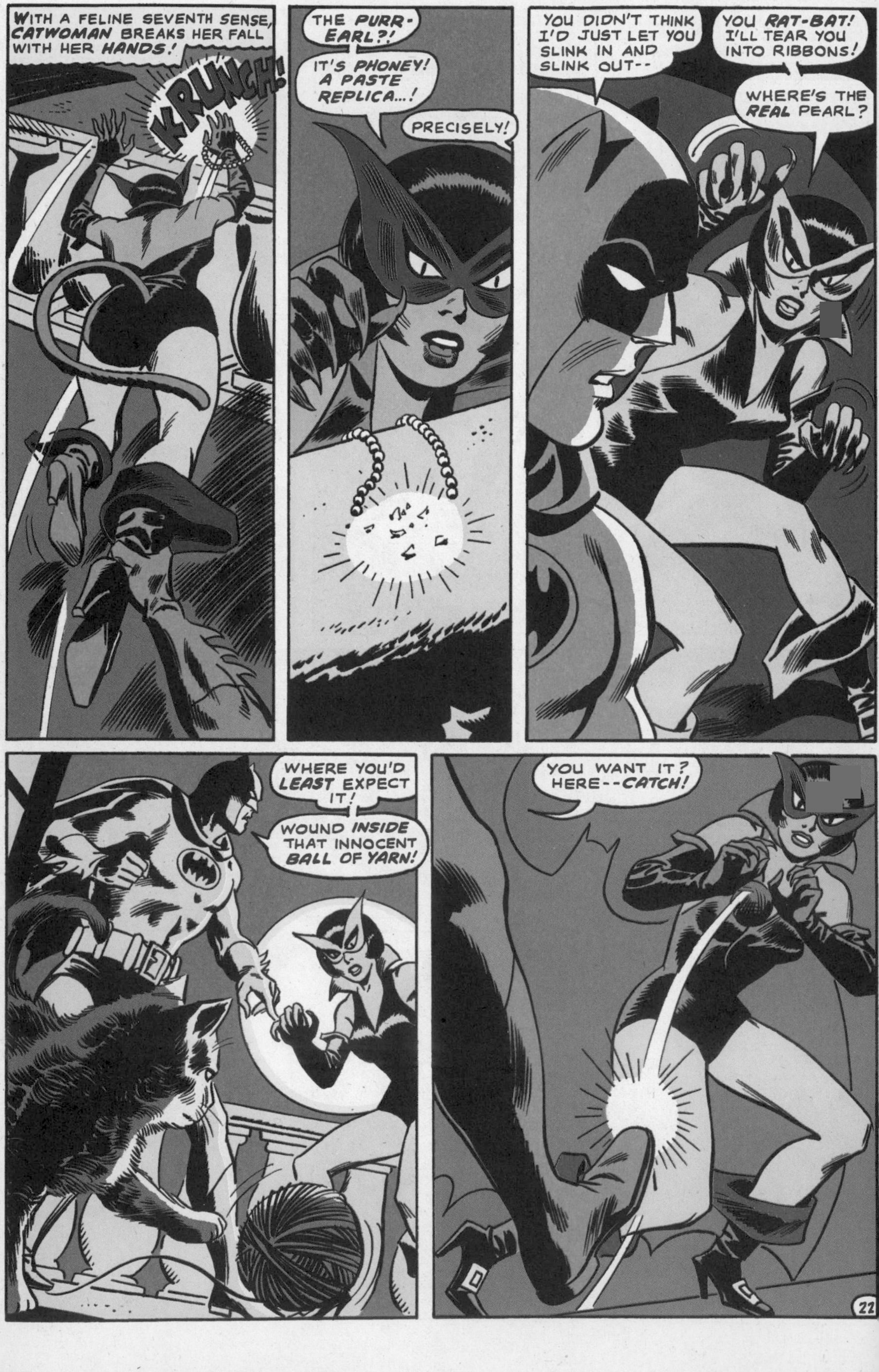
WITH A FELINE SEVENTH SENSE, CATWOMAN BREAKS HER FALL WITH HER HANDS!
KRUNCH!
THE PURR-EARL?!
IT'S PHONEY! A PASTE REPLICA...!
PRECISELY!
YOU DIDN'T THINK I'D JUST LET YOU SLINK IN AND SLINK OUT--
YOU RAT-BAT! I'LL TEAR YOU INTO RIBBONS!
WHERE'S THE REAL PEARL?
WHERE YOU'D LEAST EXPECT IT!
WOUND INSIDE THAT INNOCENT BALL OF YARN!
YOU WANT IT? HERE--CATCH!
22

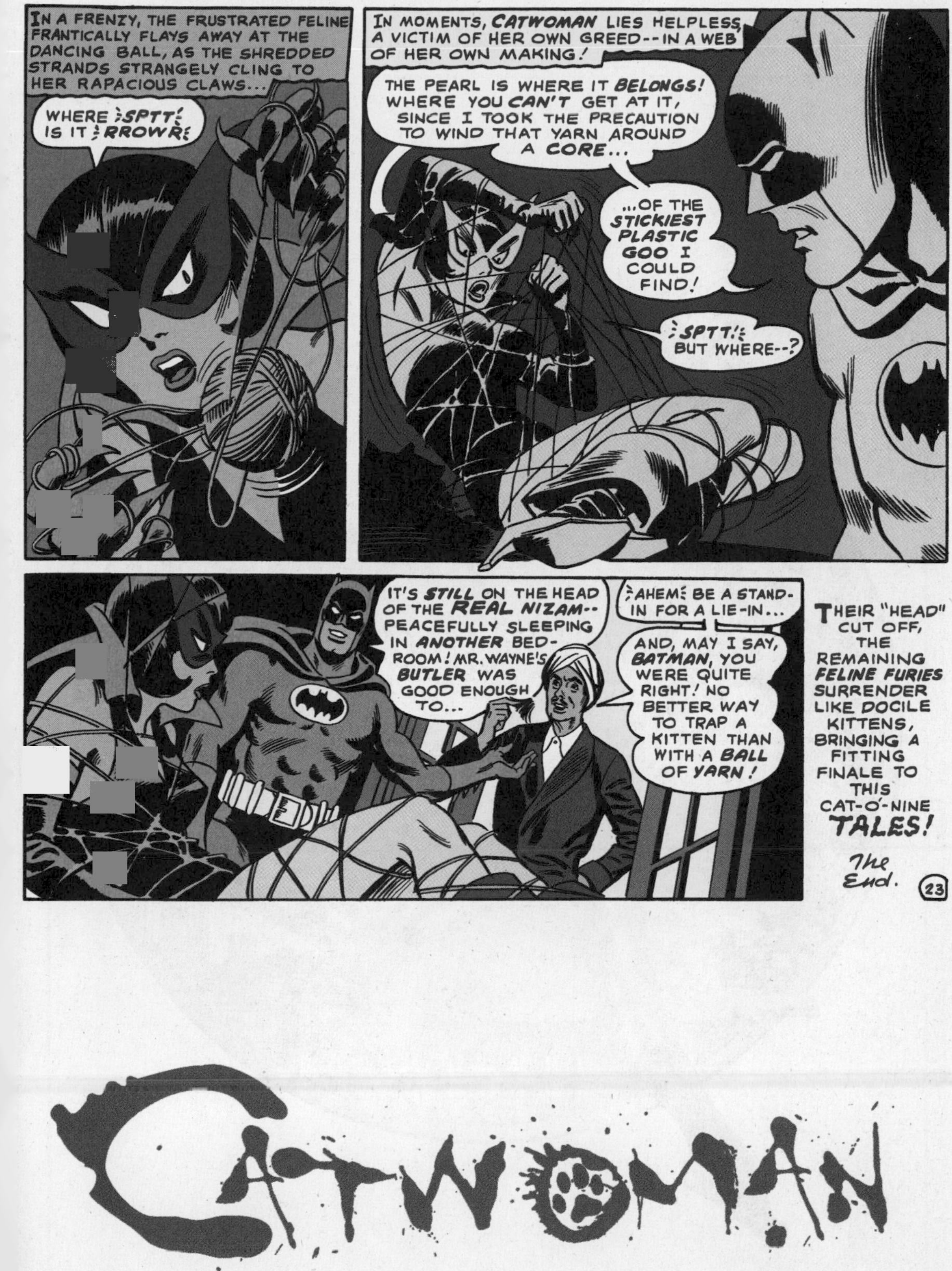
IN A FRENZY, THE FRUSTRATED FELINE FRANTICALLY FLAYS AWAY AT THE DANCING BALL, AS THE SHREDDED STRANDS STRANGELY CLING TO HER RAPACIOUS CLAWS...
WHERE ⸗SPTT!⸗ IS IT ⸗RROWR!⸗
IN MOMENTS, CATWOMAN LIES HELPLESS, A VICTIM OF HER OWN GREED--IN A WEB OF HER OWN MAKING!
THE PEARL IS WHERE IT BELONGS! WHERE YOU CAN'T GET AT IT, SINCE I TOOK THE PRECAUTION TO WIND THAT YARN AROUND A CORE...
...OF THE STICKIEST PLASTIC GOO I COULD FIND!
⸗SPTT!⸗ BUT WHERE--?
IT'S STILL ON THE HEAD OF THE REAL NIZAM-- PEACEFULLY SLEEPING IN ANOTHER BED-ROOM! MR. WAYNE'S BUTLER WAS GOOD ENOUGH TO...
⸗AHEM!⸗ BE A STAND-IN FOR A LIE-IN...
AND, MAY I SAY, BATMAN, YOU WERE QUITE RIGHT! NO BETTER WAY TO TRAP A KITTEN THAN WITH A BALL OF YARN!
THEIR "HEAD" CUT OFF, THE REMAINING FELINE FURIES SURRENDER LIKE DOCILE KITTENS, BRINGING A FITTING FINALE TO THIS CAT-O'-NINE TALES!
The End.
23

CATWOMAN

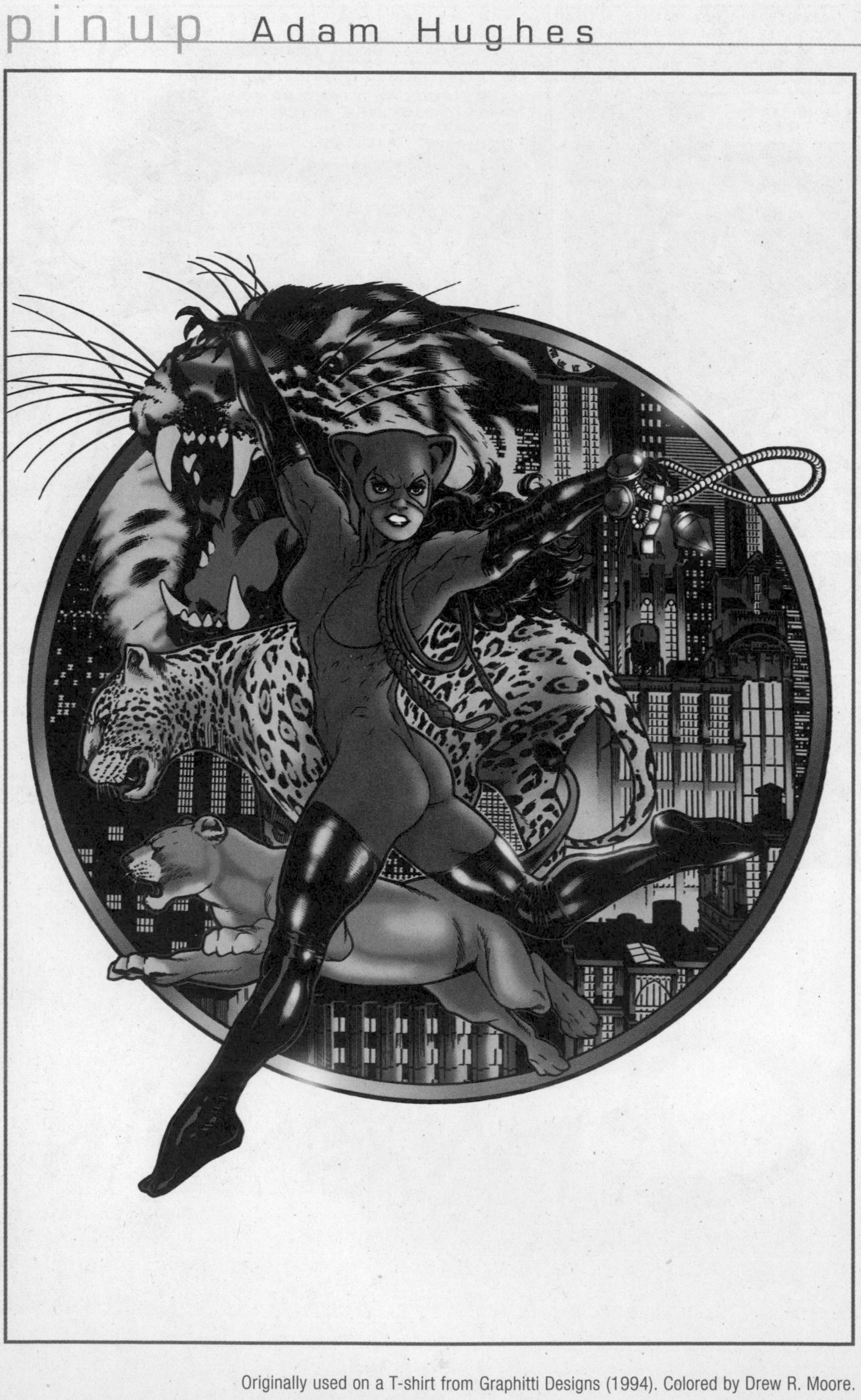

Originally used on a T-shirt from Graphitti Designs (1994). Colored by Drew R. Moore.

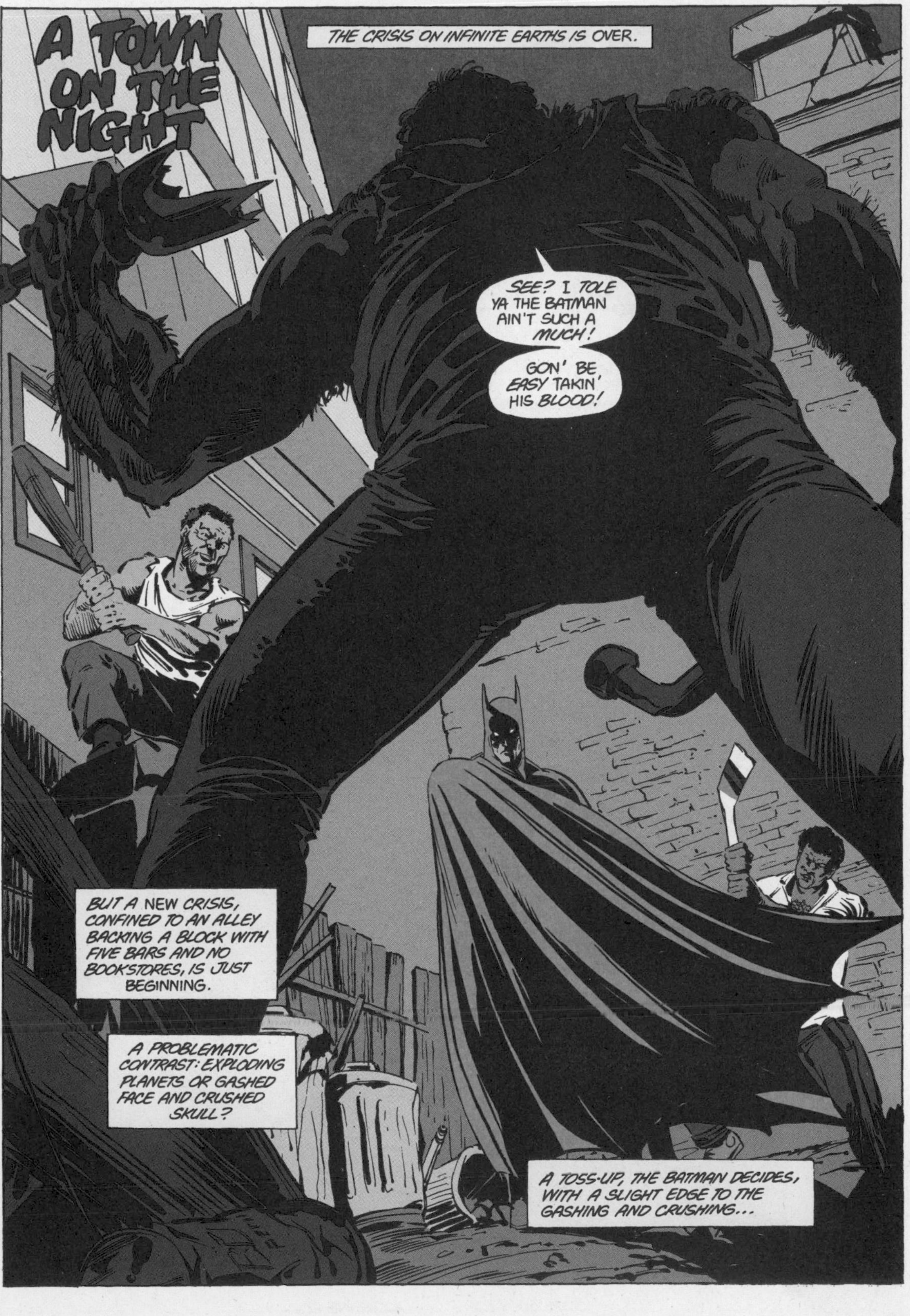
A TOWN ON THE NIGHT
THE CRISIS ON INFINITE EARTHS IS OVER.
SEE? I TOLE YA THE BATMAN AIN'T SUCH A MUCH!
GON' BE EASY TAKIN' HIS BLOOD!
BUT A NEW CRISIS, CONFINED TO AN ALLEY BACKING A BLOCK WITH FIVE BARS AND NO BOOKSTORES, IS JUST BEGINNING.
A PROBLEMATIC CONTRAST: EXPLODING PLANETS OR GASHED FACE AND CRUSHED SKULL?
A TOSS-UP, THE BATMAN DECIDES, WITH A SLIGHT EDGE TO THE GASHING AND CRUSHING...

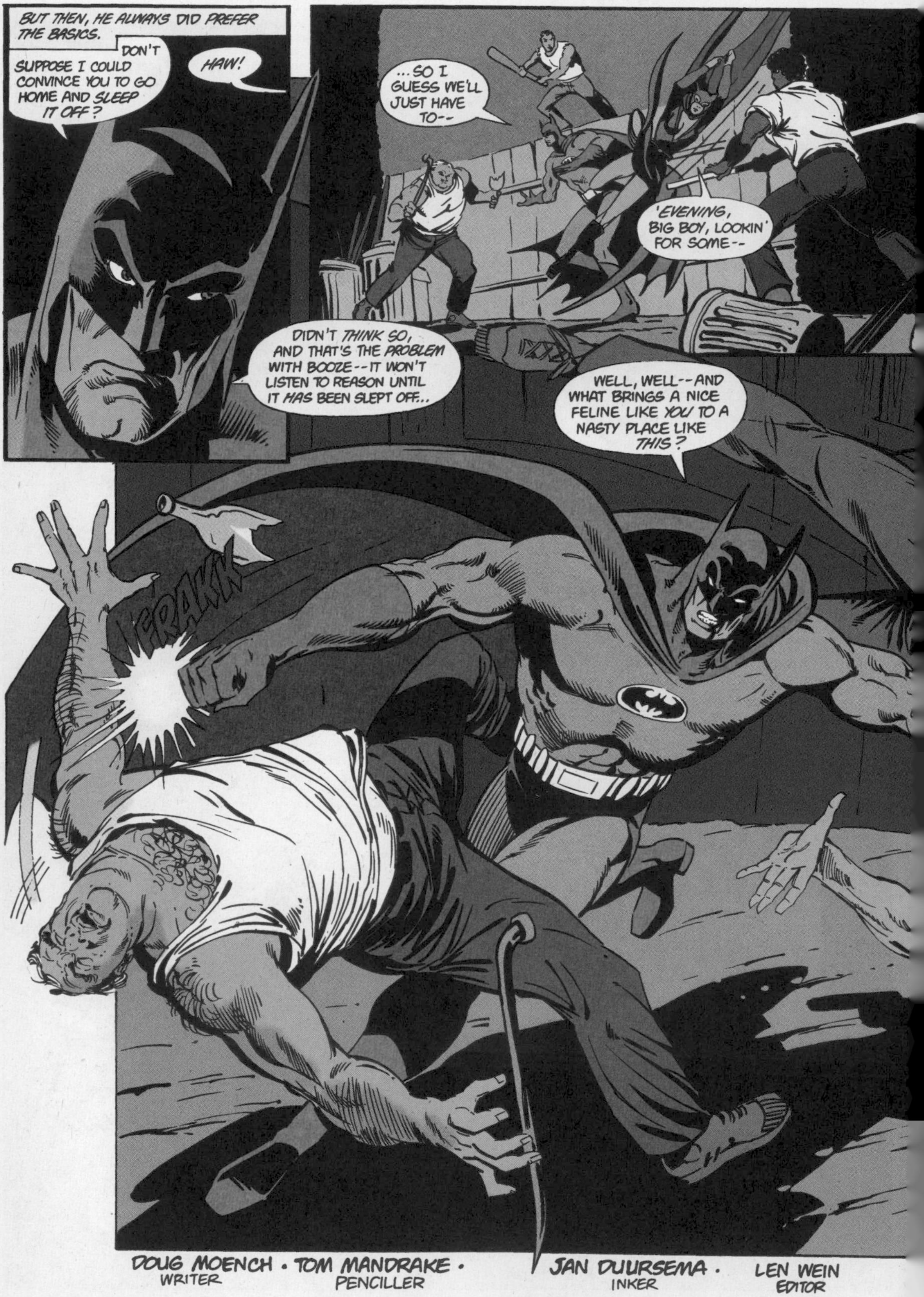
BUT THEN, HE ALWAYS DID PREFER THE BASICS.
DON'T SUPPOSE I COULD CONVINCE YOU TO GO HOME AND SLEEP IT OFF?
HAW!
...SO I GUESS WE'LL JUST HAVE TO--
'EVENING, BIG BOY, LOOKIN' FOR SOME--
DIDN'T THINK SO, AND THAT'S THE PROBLEM WITH BOOZE--IT WON'T LISTEN TO REASON UNTIL IT HAS BEEN SLEPT OFF...
WELL, WELL--AND WHAT BRINGS A NICE FELINE LIKE YOU TO A NASTY PLACE LIKE THIS?
FRAKK

DOUG MOENCH • TOM MANDRAKE • JAN DUURSEMA • LEN WEIN
WRITER PENCILLER INKER EDITOR

JOHN COSTANZA • ADRIENNE ROY
letterer colorist

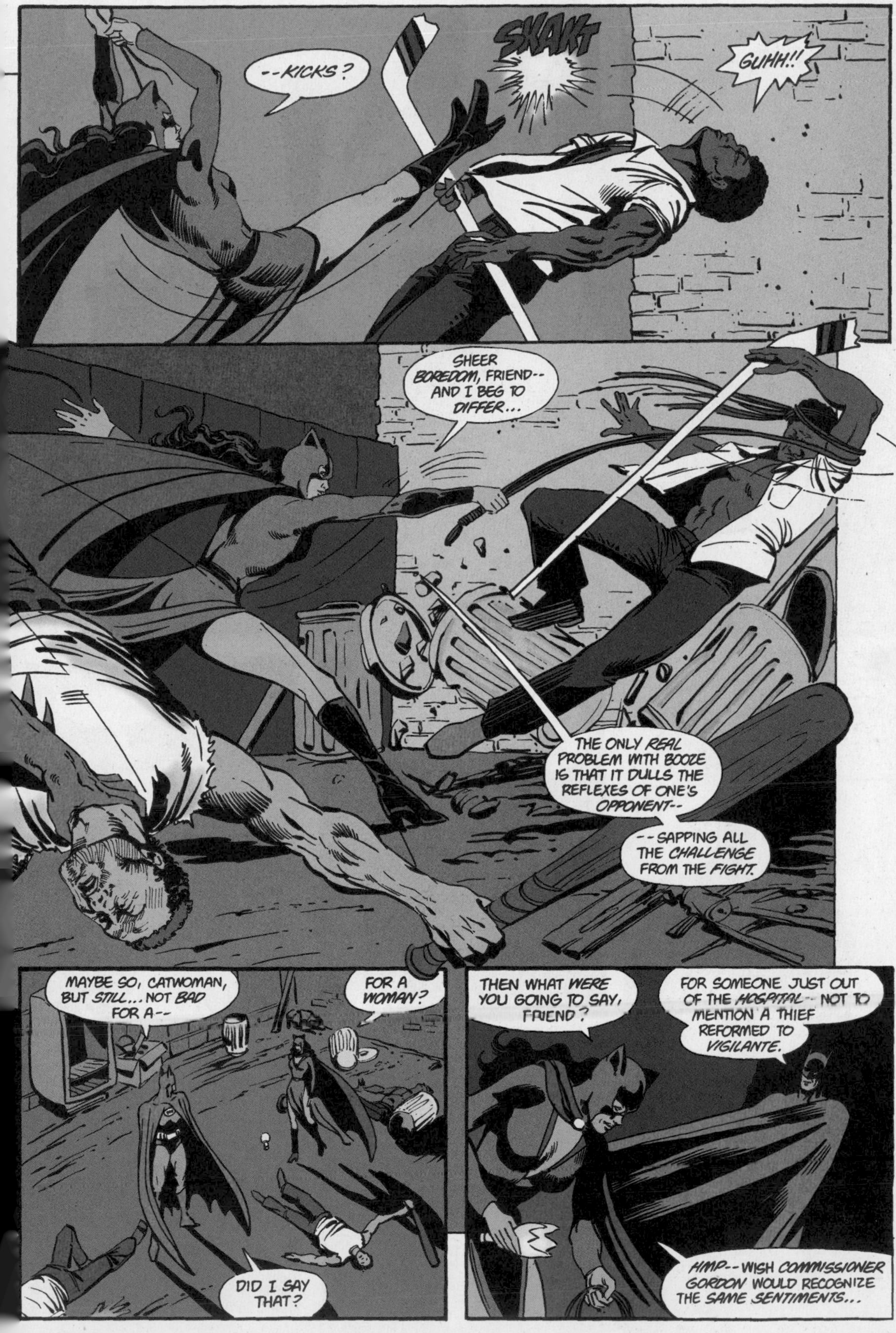
--KICKS?
SKAKT
GUHH!!
SHEER BOREDOM, FRIEND-- AND I BEG TO DIFFER...
THE ONLY REAL PROBLEM WITH BOOZE IS THAT IT DULLS THE REFLEXES OF ONE'S OPPONENT--
--SAPPING ALL THE CHALLENGE FROM THE FIGHT.
MAYBE SO, CATWOMAN, BUT STILL... NOT BAD FOR A--
FOR A WOMAN?
DID I SAY THAT?
THEN WHAT WERE YOU GOING TO SAY, FRIEND?
FOR SOMEONE JUST OUT OF THE HOSPITAL-- NOT TO MENTION A THIEF REFORMED TO VIGILANTE.
HMP--WISH COMMISSIONER GORDON WOULD RECOGNIZE THE SAME SENTIMENTS...

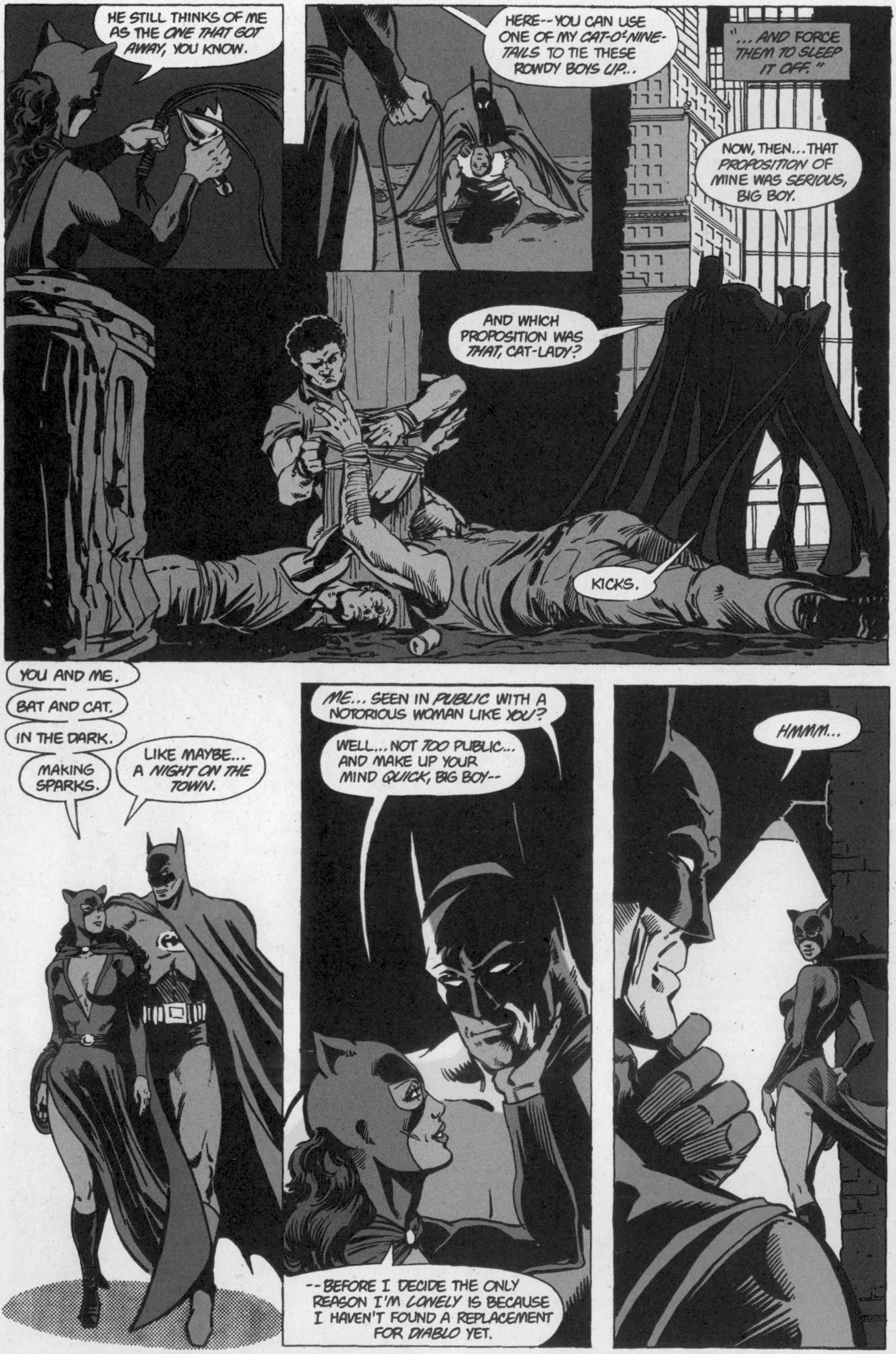
HE STILL THINKS OF ME AS THE *ONE THAT GOT AWAY*, YOU KNOW.
HERE--YOU CAN USE ONE OF MY *CAT-O'-NINE-TAILS* TO TIE THESE ROWDY BOYS UP...
"...AND FORCE THEM TO SLEEP IT OFF."
NOW, THEN...THAT *PROPOSITION* OF MINE WAS *SERIOUS*, BIG BOY.
AND WHICH PROPOSITION WAS *THAT*, CAT-LADY?
KICKS.
YOU AND ME.
BAT AND CAT.
IN THE DARK.
MAKING SPARKS.
LIKE MAYBE... A *NIGHT ON THE TOWN*.
ME... SEEN IN *PUBLIC* WITH A NOTORIOUS WOMAN LIKE *YOU*?
WELL... NOT *TOO* PUBLIC... AND MAKE UP YOUR MIND *QUICK*, BIG BOY--
--BEFORE I DECIDE THE ONLY REASON I'M *LONELY* IS BECAUSE I HAVEN'T FOUND A REPLACEMENT FOR *DIABLO* YET.
HMMM...

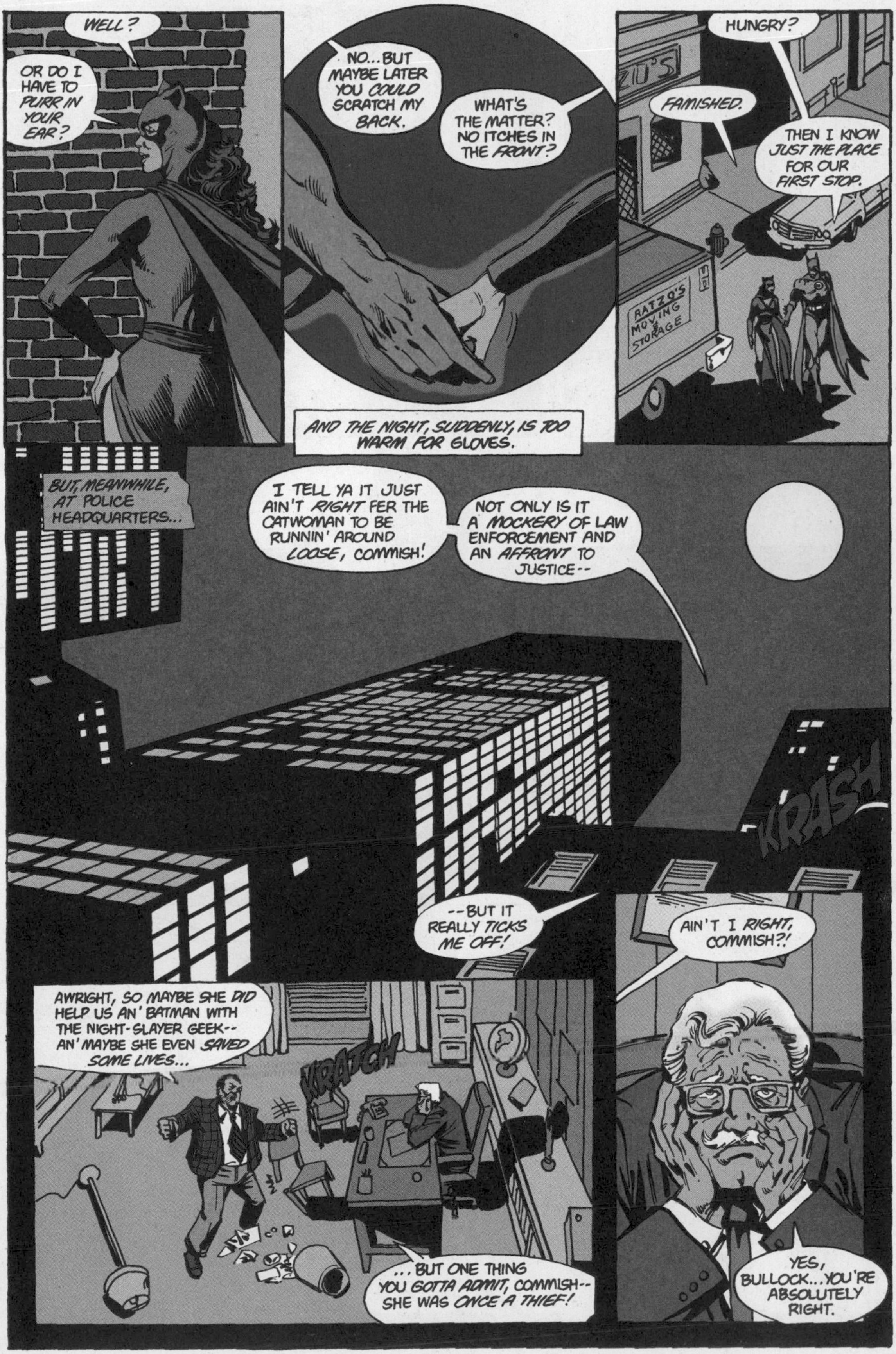
WELL?
OR DO I HAVE TO PURR IN YOUR EAR?
NO...BUT MAYBE LATER YOU COULD SCRATCH MY BACK.
WHAT'S THE MATTER? NO ITCHES IN THE FRONT?
HUNGRY?
FAMISHED.
THEN I KNOW JUST THE PLACE FOR OUR FIRST STOP.
RATZO'S MOVING & STORAGE
AND THE NIGHT, SUDDENLY, IS TOO WARM FOR GLOVES.
BUT, MEANWHILE, AT POLICE HEADQUARTERS...
I TELL YA IT JUST AIN'T RIGHT FER THE CATWOMAN TO BE RUNNIN' AROUND LOOSE, COMMISH!
NOT ONLY IS IT A MOCKERY OF LAW ENFORCEMENT AND AN AFFRONT TO JUSTICE--
KRASH
--BUT IT REALLY TICKS ME OFF!
AIN'T I RIGHT, COMMISH?!
AWRIGHT, SO MAYBE SHE DID HELP US AN' BATMAN WITH THE NIGHT-SLAYER GEEK-- AN' MAYBE SHE EVEN SAVED SOME LIVES...
KRATCH
...BUT ONE THING YOU GOTTA ADMIT, COMMISH-- SHE WAS ONCE A THIEF!
YES, BULLOCK...YOU'RE ABSOLUTELY RIGHT.

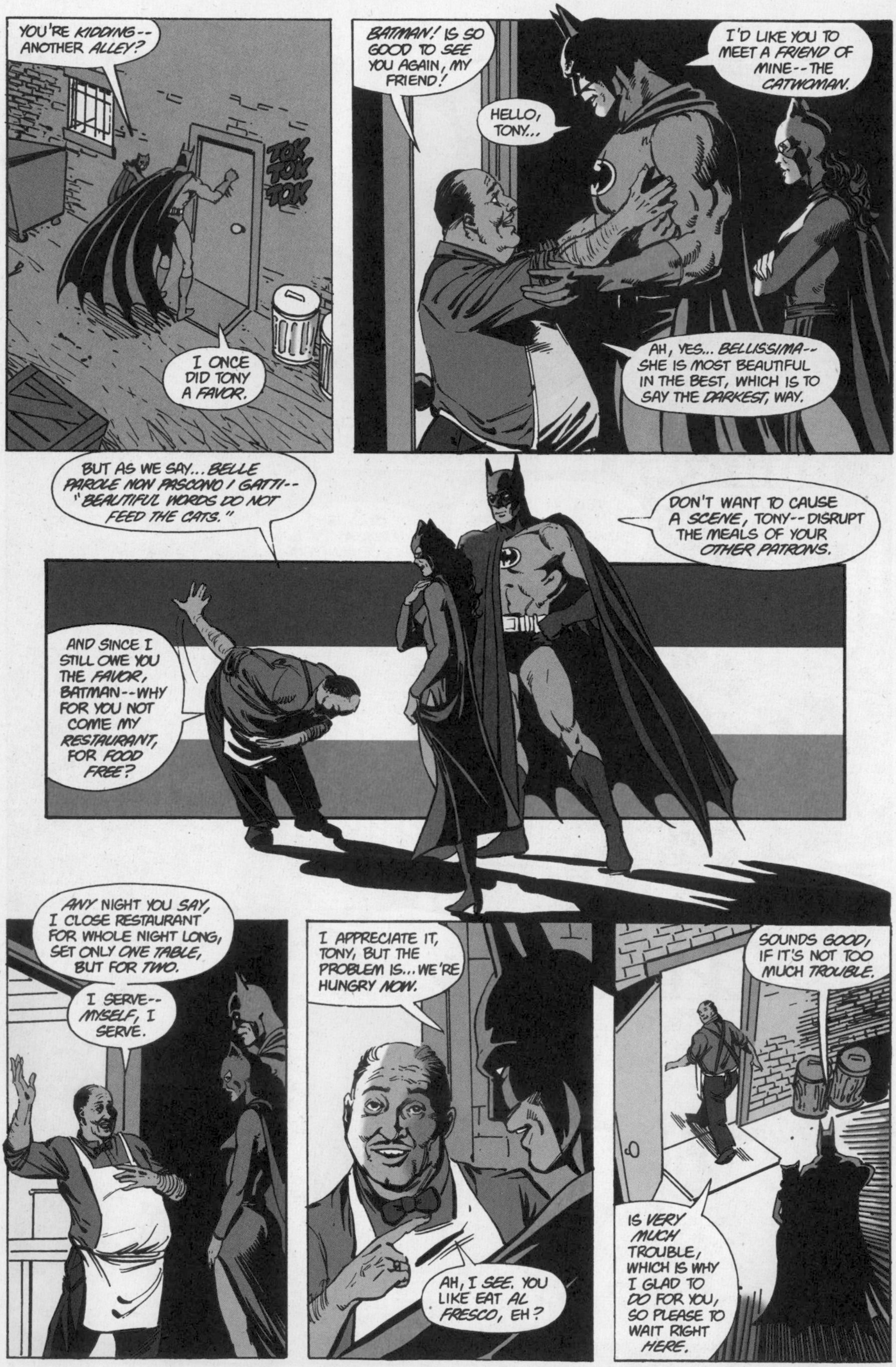
YOU'RE KIDDING--ANOTHER ALLEY?
TOK TOK TOK
I ONCE DID TONY A FAVOR.
BATMAN! IS SO GOOD TO SEE YOU AGAIN, MY FRIEND!
HELLO, TONY...
I'D LIKE YOU TO MEET A FRIEND OF MINE--THE CATWOMAN.
AH, YES... BELLISSIMA--SHE IS MOST BEAUTIFUL IN THE BEST, WHICH IS TO SAY THE DARKEST, WAY.
BUT AS WE SAY... BELLE PAROLE NON PASCONO I GATTI--"BEAUTIFUL WORDS DO NOT FEED THE CATS."
DON'T WANT TO CAUSE A SCENE, TONY--DISRUPT THE MEALS OF YOUR OTHER PATRONS.
AND SINCE I STILL OWE YOU THE FAVOR, BATMAN--WHY FOR YOU NOT COME MY RESTAURANT, FOR FOOD FREE?
ANY NIGHT YOU SAY, I CLOSE RESTAURANT FOR WHOLE NIGHT LONG, SET ONLY ONE TABLE, BUT FOR TWO.
I SERVE--MYSELF, I SERVE.
I APPRECIATE IT, TONY, BUT THE PROBLEM IS... WE'RE HUNGRY NOW.
AH, I SEE. YOU LIKE EAT AL FRESCO, EH?
SOUNDS GOOD, IF IT'S NOT TOO MUCH TROUBLE.
IS VERY MUCH TROUBLE, WHICH IS WHY I GLAD TO DO FOR YOU, SO PLEASE TO WAIT RIGHT HERE.

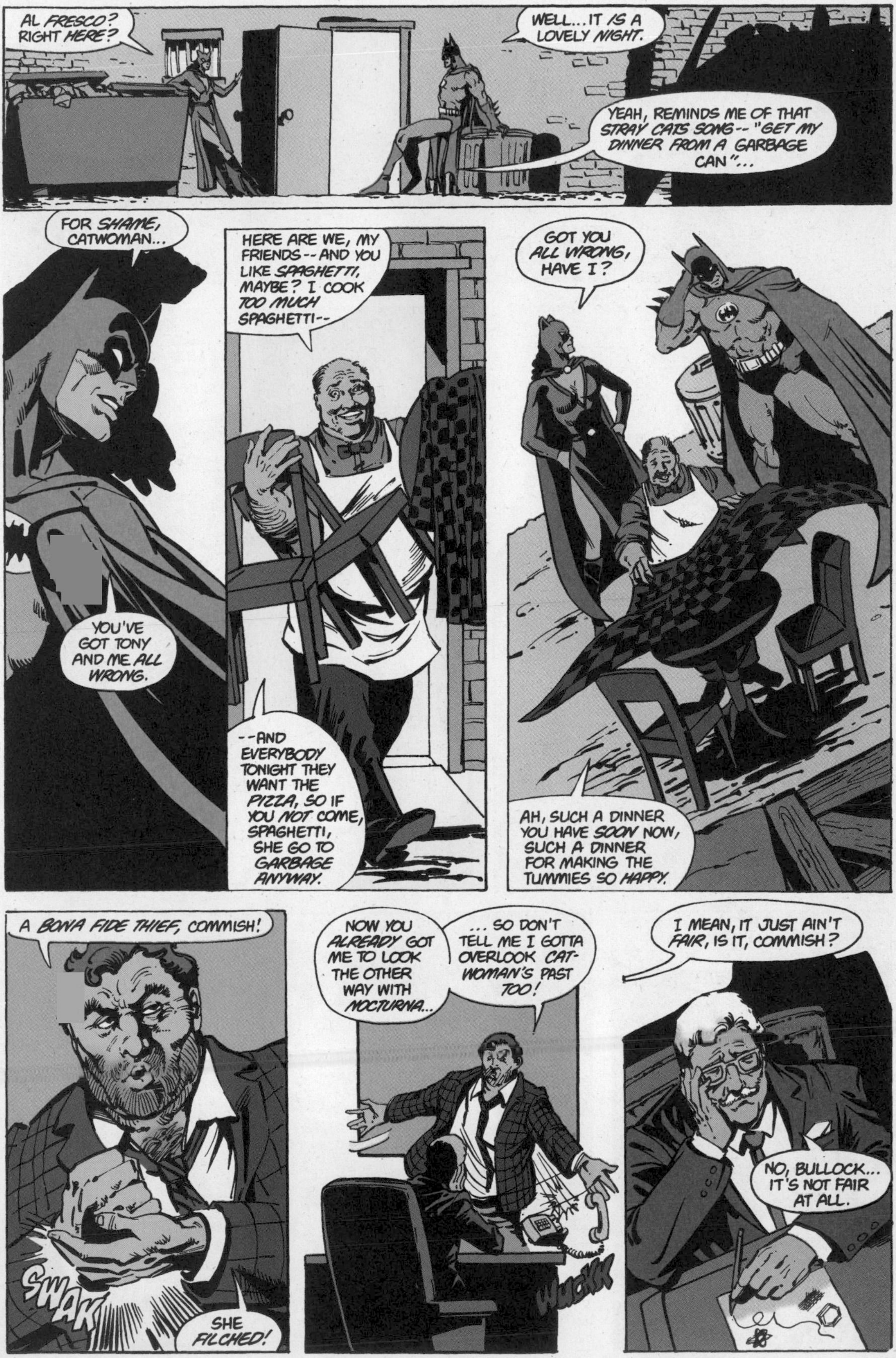
AL FRESCO? RIGHT HERE?
WELL... IT IS A LOVELY NIGHT.
YEAH, REMINDS ME OF THAT STRAY CATS SONG-- "GET MY DINNER FROM A GARBAGE CAN"...
FOR SHAME, CATWOMAN...
YOU'VE GOT TONY AND ME ALL WRONG.
HERE ARE WE, MY FRIENDS-- AND YOU LIKE SPAGHETTI, MAYBE? I COOK TOO MUCH SPAGHETTI--
--AND EVERYBODY TONIGHT THEY WANT THE PIZZA, SO IF YOU NOT COME, SPAGHETTI, SHE GO TO GARBAGE ANYWAY.
GOT YOU ALL WRONG, HAVE I?
AH, SUCH A DINNER YOU HAVE SOON NOW, SUCH A DINNER FOR MAKING THE TUMMIES SO HAPPY.
A BONA FIDE THIEF, COMMISH!
SWAK
SHE FILCHED!
NOW YOU ALREADY GOT ME TO LOOK THE OTHER WAY WITH NOCTURNA...
... SO DON'T TELL ME I GOTTA OVERLOOK CAT-WOMAN'S PAST TOO!
WUCKK
I MEAN, IT JUST AIN'T FAIR, IS IT, COMMISH?
NO, BULLOCK... IT'S NOT FAIR AT ALL.

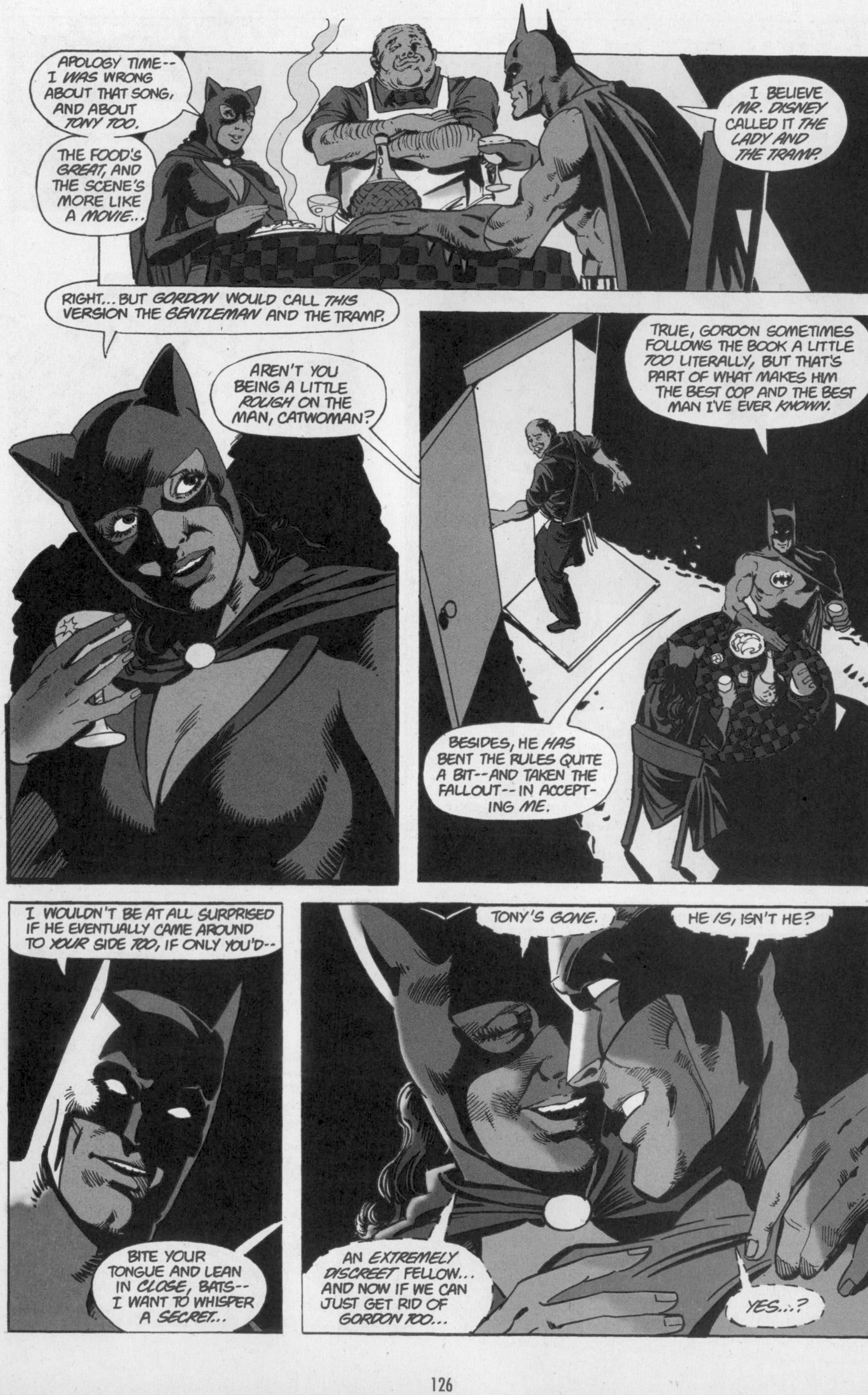
APOLOGY TIME-- I WAS WRONG ABOUT THAT SONG, AND ABOUT TONY TOO.
THE FOOD'S GREAT, AND THE SCENE'S MORE LIKE A MOVIE...
I BELIEVE MR. DISNEY CALLED IT THE LADY AND THE TRAMP.
RIGHT... BUT GORDON WOULD CALL THIS VERSION THE GENTLEMAN AND THE TRAMP.
AREN'T YOU BEING A LITTLE ROUGH ON THE MAN, CATWOMAN?
TRUE, GORDON SOMETIMES FOLLOWS THE BOOK A LITTLE TOO LITERALLY, BUT THAT'S PART OF WHAT MAKES HIM THE BEST COP AND THE BEST MAN I'VE EVER KNOWN.
BESIDES, HE HAS BENT THE RULES QUITE A BIT--AND TAKEN THE FALLOUT-- IN ACCEPTING ME.
I WOULDN'T BE AT ALL SURPRISED IF HE EVENTUALLY CAME AROUND TO YOUR SIDE TOO, IF ONLY YOU'D--
BITE YOUR TONGUE AND LEAN IN CLOSE, BATS-- I WANT TO WHISPER A SECRET...
TONY'S GONE.
HE IS, ISN'T HE?
AN EXTREMELY DISCREET FELLOW... AND NOW IF WE CAN JUST GET RID OF GORDON TOO...
YES...?

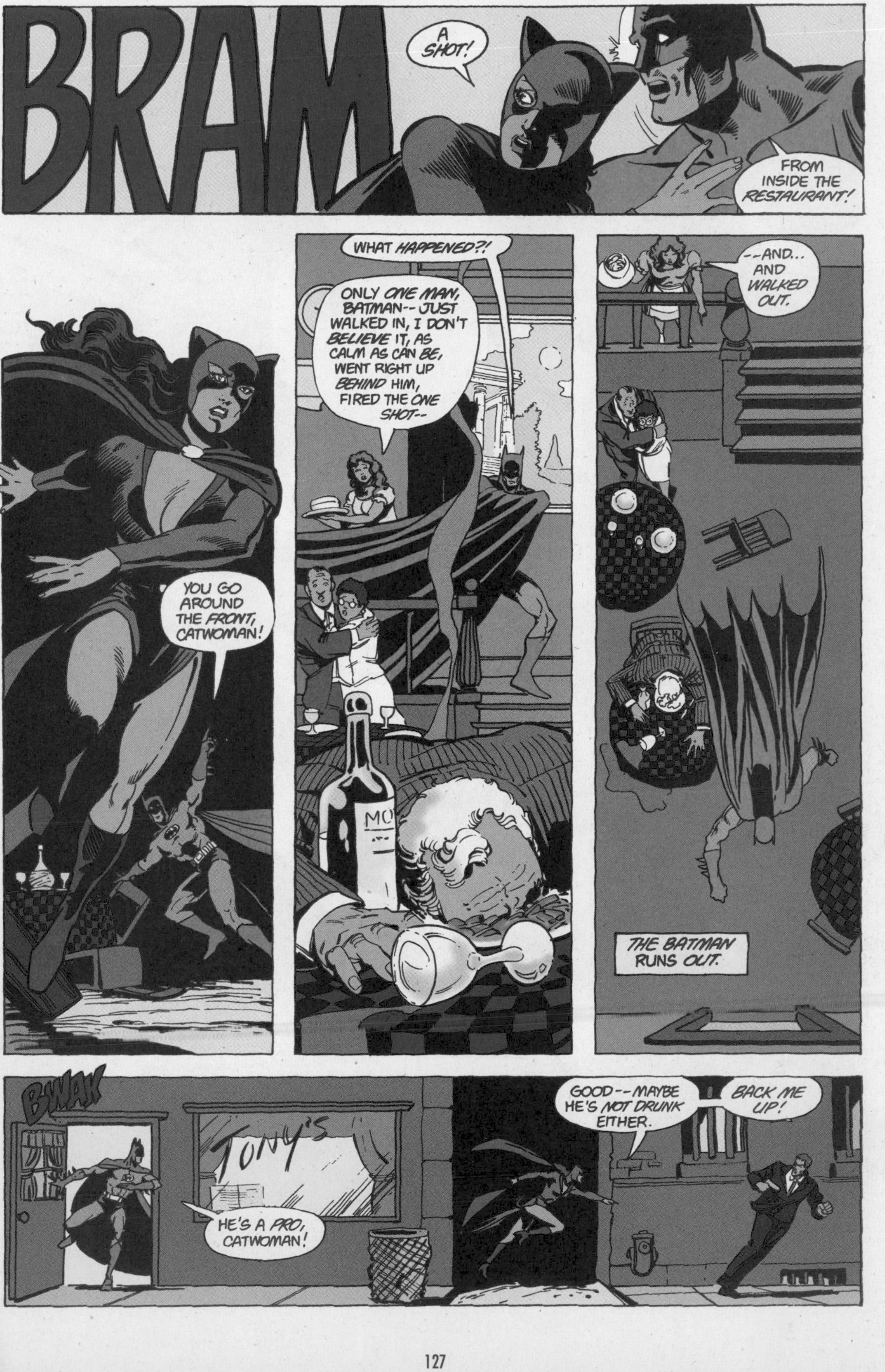
BRAM
A SHOT!
FROM INSIDE THE RESTAURANT!
YOU GO AROUND THE FRONT, CATWOMAN!
WHAT HAPPENED?!
ONLY ONE MAN, BATMAN-- JUST WALKED IN, I DON'T BELIEVE IT, AS CALM AS CAN BE, WENT RIGHT UP BEHIND HIM, FIRED THE ONE SHOT--
--AND... AND WALKED OUT.
THE BATMAN RUNS OUT.
BWAK
TONY'S
HE'S A PRO, CATWOMAN!
GOOD--MAYBE HE'S NOT DRUNK EITHER.
BACK ME UP!

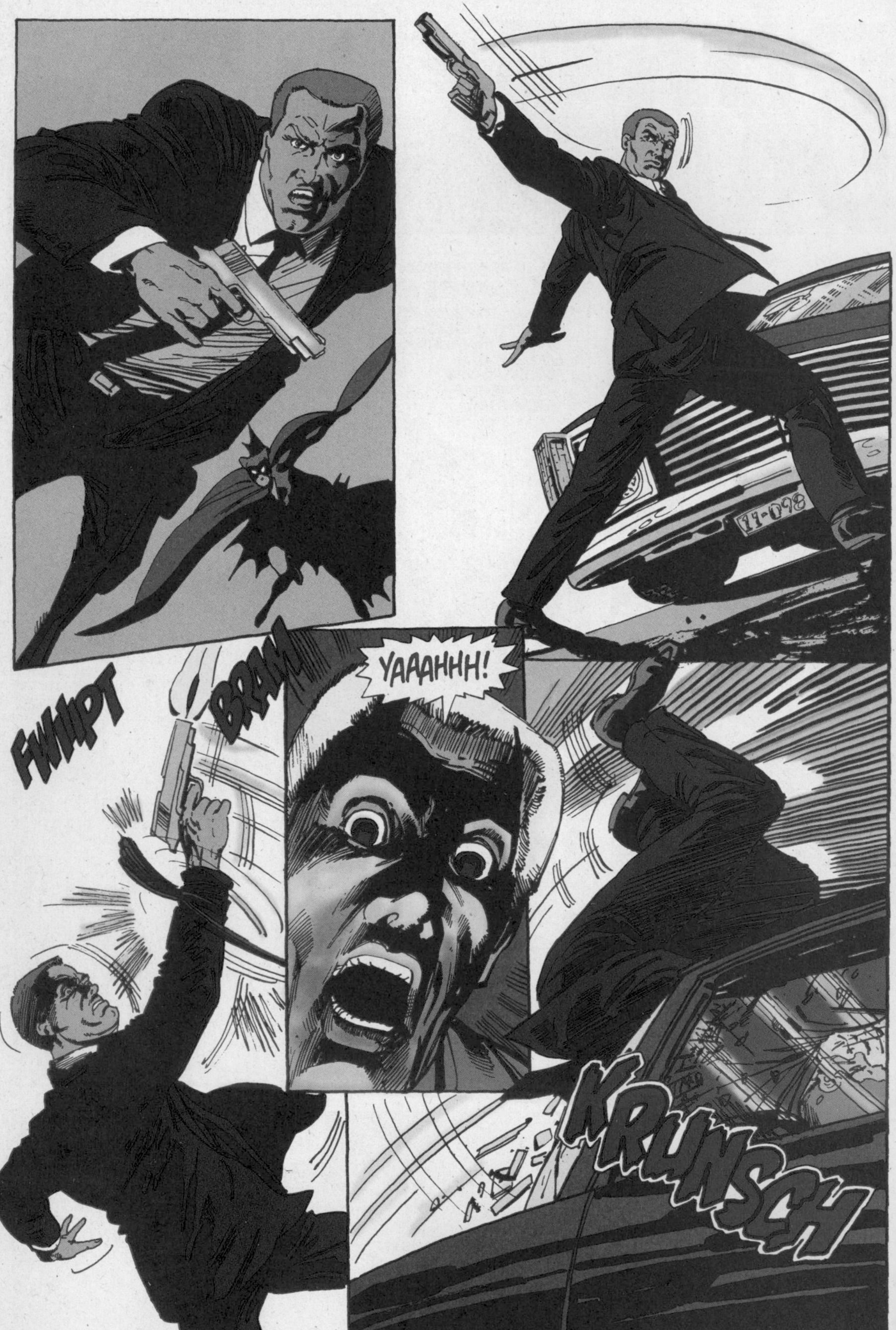
FWHIPT
BRAM
YAAAHHH!
KRUNSCH

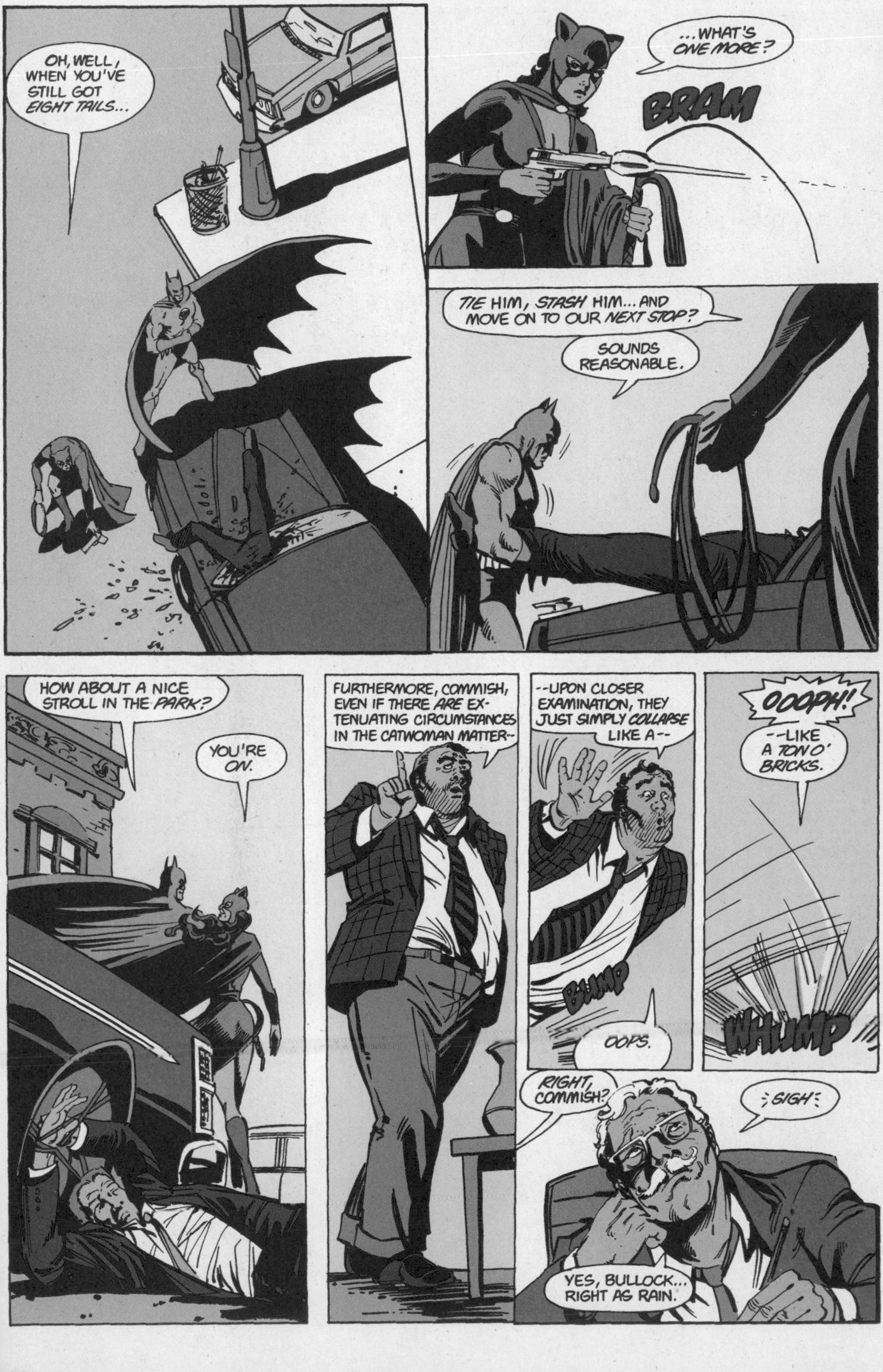
OH, WELL, WHEN YOU'VE STILL GOT EIGHT TAILS...
...WHAT'S ONE MORE?
BRAM
TIE HIM, STASH HIM... AND MOVE ON TO OUR NEXT STOP?
SOUNDS REASONABLE.
HOW ABOUT A NICE STROLL IN THE PARK?
YOU'RE ON.
FURTHERMORE, COMMISH, EVEN IF THERE ARE EXTENUATING CIRCUMSTANCES IN THE CATWOMAN MATTER--
--UPON CLOSER EXAMINATION, THEY JUST SIMPLY COLLAPSE LIKE A--
BUMP
OOPS.
OOOPH!
--LIKE A TON O' BRICKS.
WHUMP
RIGHT, COMMISH?
SIGH
YES, BULLOCK... RIGHT AS RAIN.

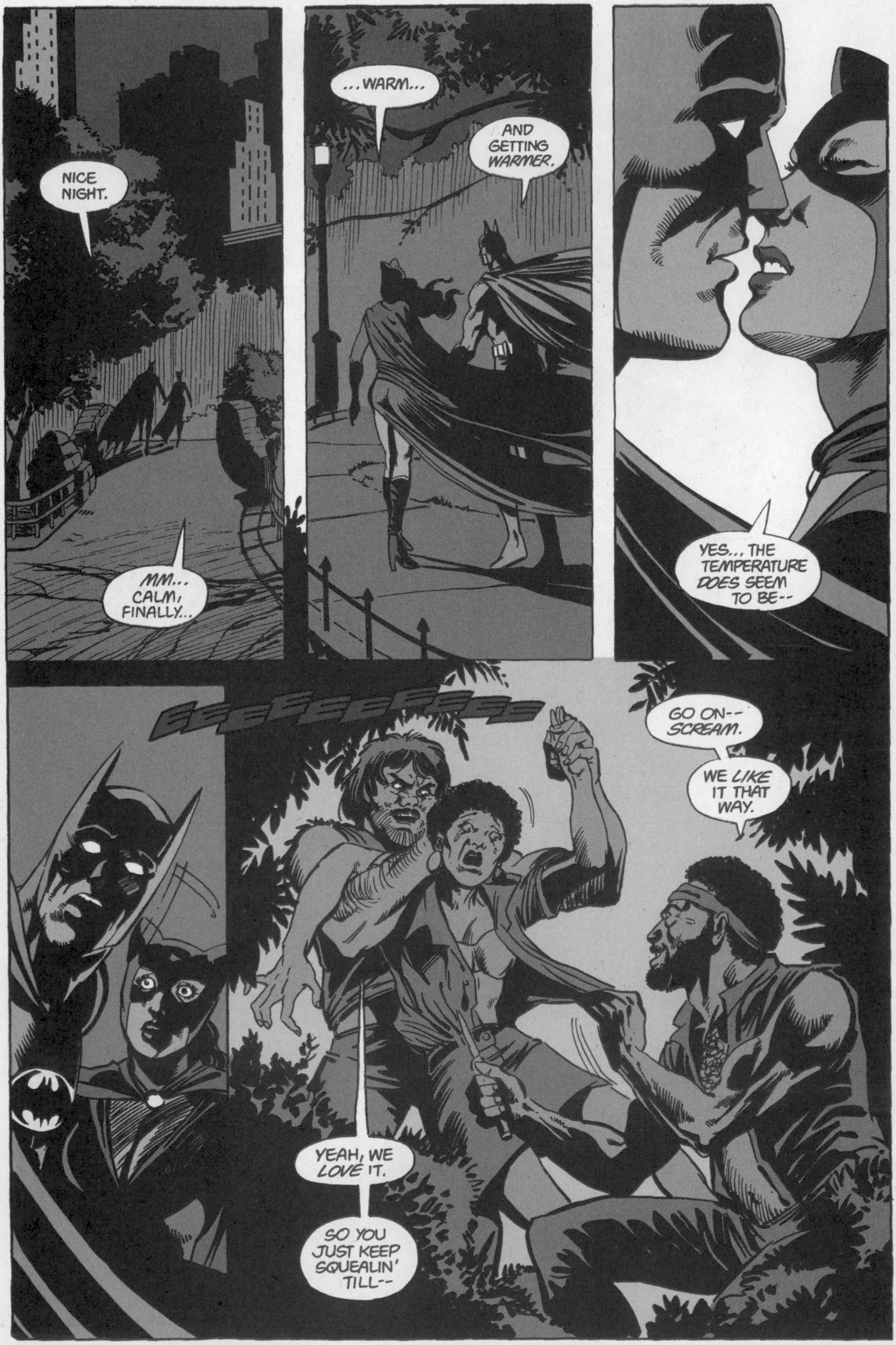
NICE NIGHT.
MM... CALM, FINALLY...
...WARM...
AND GETTING WARMER.
YES... THE TEMPERATURE DOES SEEM TO BE--
EEEEEEEEEEEE
GO ON-- SCREAM.
WE LIKE IT THAT WAY.
YEAH, WE LOVE IT.
SO YOU JUST KEEP SQUEALIN' TILL--

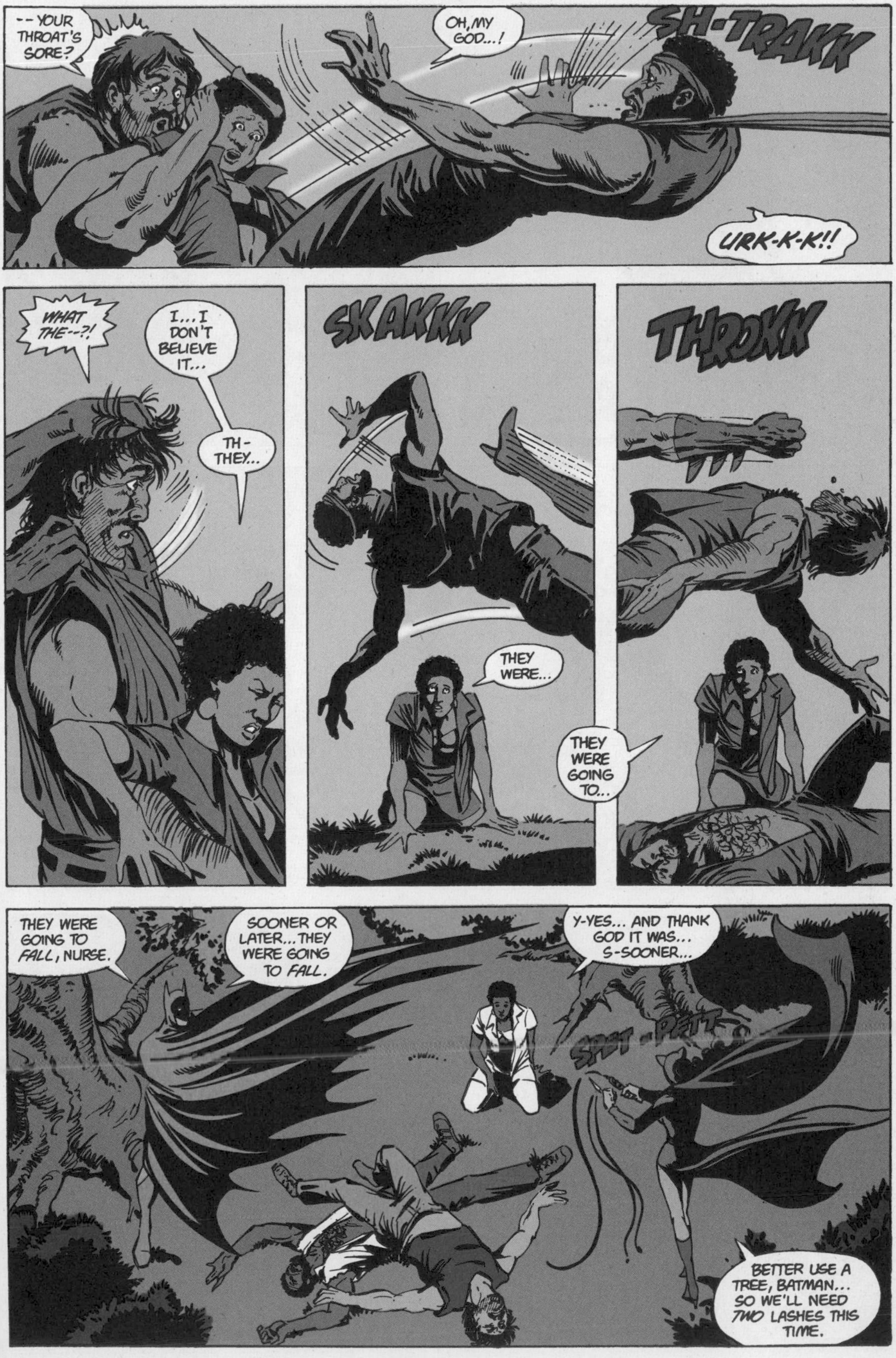
--YOUR THROAT'S SORE?
OH, MY GOD...!
SH-TRAKK
URK-K-K!!
WHAT THE--?!
I... I DON'T BELIEVE IT...
TH-THEY...
SKAKKK
THEY WERE...
THROKK
THEY WERE GOING TO...
THEY WERE GOING TO *FALL*, NURSE.
SOONER OR LATER... THEY WERE GOING TO *FALL*.
Y-YES... AND THANK GOD IT WAS... S-SOONER...
BETTER USE A TREE, BATMAN... SO WE'LL NEED *TWO* LASHES THIS TIME.

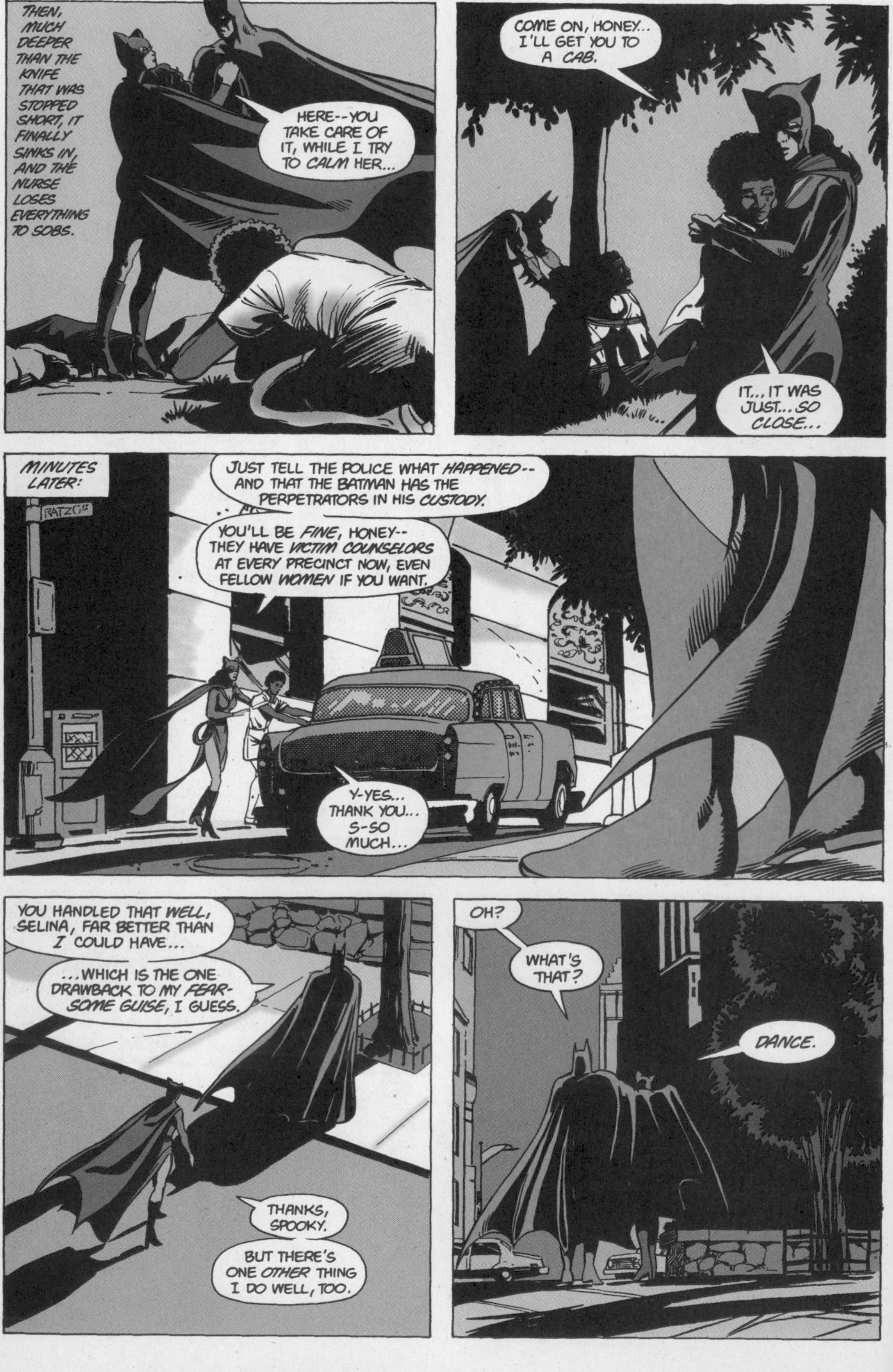
THEN, MUCH DEEPER THAN THE KNIFE THAT WAS STOPPED SHORT, IT FINALLY SINKS IN, AND THE NURSE LOSES EVERYTHING TO SOBS.
HERE--YOU TAKE CARE OF IT, WHILE I TRY TO CALM HER...
COME ON, HONEY... I'LL GET YOU TO A CAB.
IT... IT WAS JUST... SO CLOSE...
MINUTES LATER:
RATZO ST
JUST TELL THE POLICE WHAT HAPPENED-- AND THAT THE BATMAN HAS THE PERPETRATORS IN HIS CUSTODY.
YOU'LL BE FINE, HONEY-- THEY HAVE VICTIM COUNSELORS AT EVERY PRECINCT NOW, EVEN FELLOW WOMEN IF YOU WANT.
Y-YES... THANK YOU... S-SO MUCH...
YOU HANDLED THAT WELL, SELINA, FAR BETTER THAN I COULD HAVE...
...WHICH IS THE ONE DRAWBACK TO MY FEARSOME GUISE, I GUESS.
THANKS, SPOOKY.
BUT THERE'S ONE OTHER THING I DO WELL, TOO.
OH?
WHAT'S THAT?
DANCE.

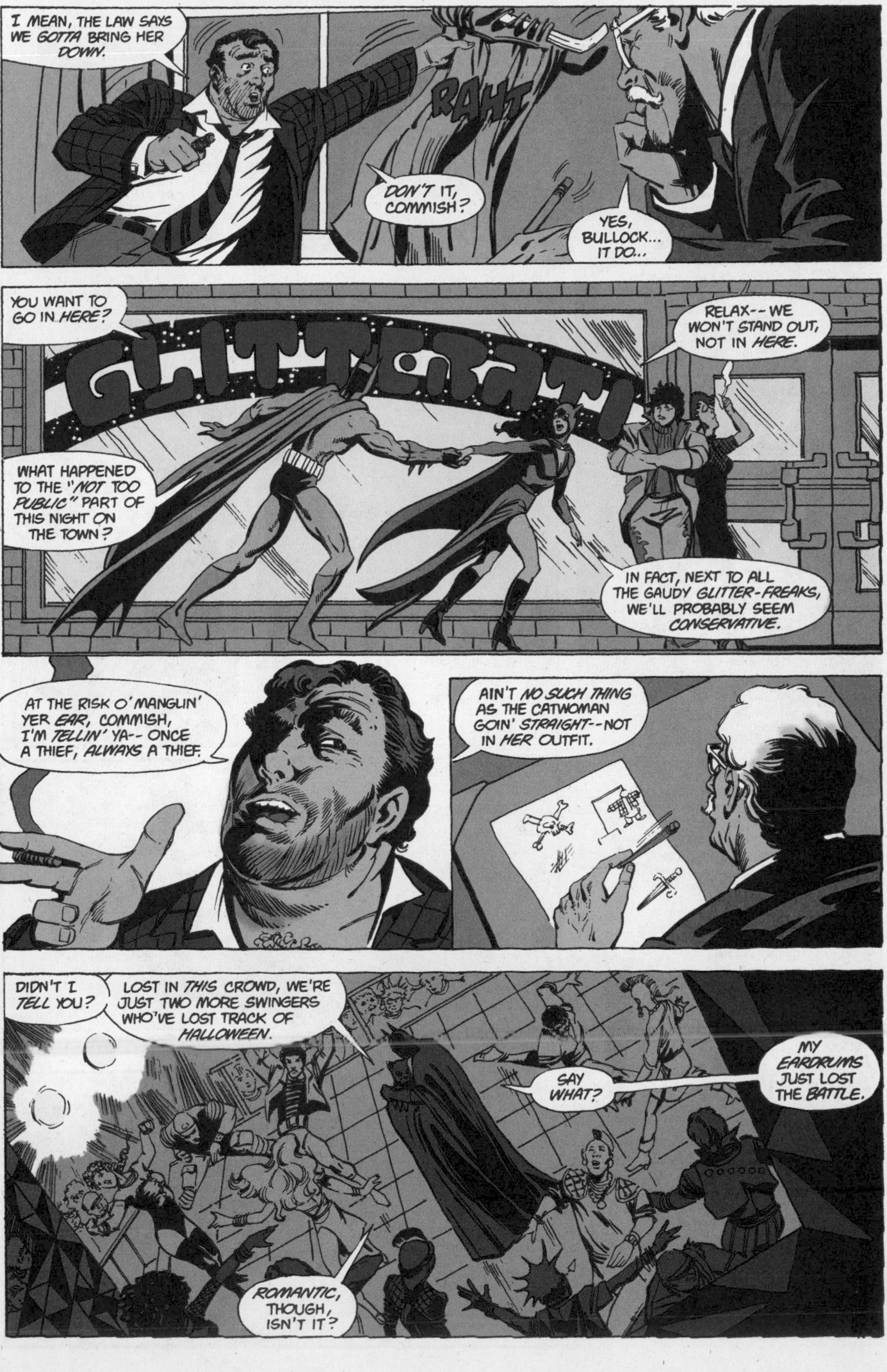
I MEAN, THE LAW SAYS WE GOTTA BRING HER DOWN.
RAHT
DON'T IT, COMMISH?
YES, BULLOCK... IT DO...
YOU WANT TO GO IN HERE?
GLITTERATI
RELAX-- WE WON'T STAND OUT, NOT IN HERE.
WHAT HAPPENED TO THE "NOT TOO PUBLIC" PART OF THIS NIGHT ON THE TOWN?
IN FACT, NEXT TO ALL THE GAUDY GLITTER-FREAKS, WE'LL PROBABLY SEEM CONSERVATIVE.
AT THE RISK O' MANGLIN' YER EAR, COMMISH, I'M TELLIN' YA-- ONCE A THIEF, ALWAYS A THIEF.
AIN'T NO SUCH THING AS THE CATWOMAN GOIN' STRAIGHT--NOT IN HER OUTFIT.
DIDN'T I TELL YOU?
LOST IN THIS CROWD, WE'RE JUST TWO MORE SWINGERS WHO'VE LOST TRACK OF HALLOWEEN.
SAY WHAT?
MY EARDRUMS JUST LOST THE BATTLE.
ROMANTIC, THOUGH, ISN'T IT?

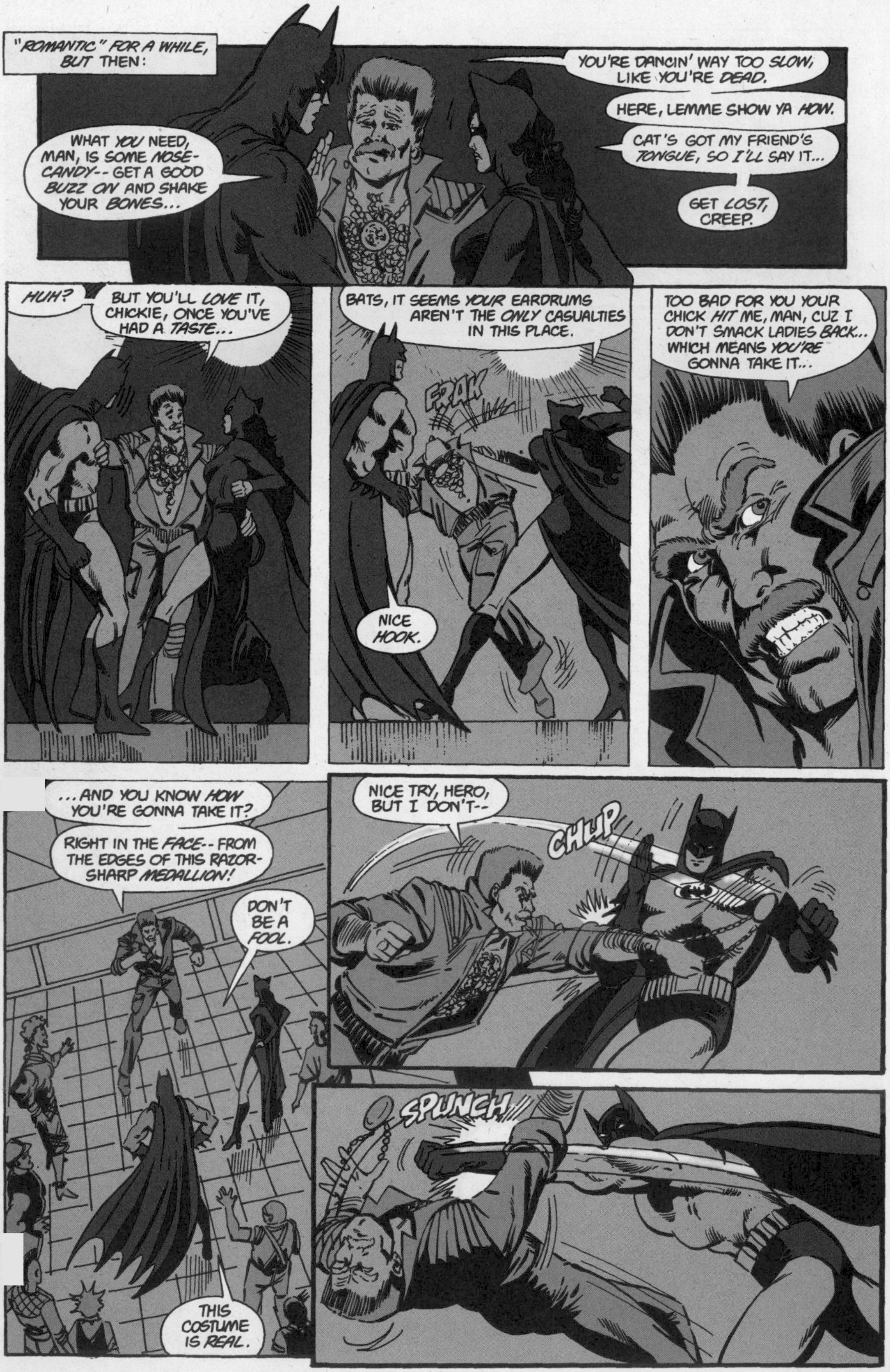
"ROMANTIC" FOR A WHILE, BUT THEN:
YOU'RE DANCIN' WAY TOO SLOW; LIKE YOU'RE DEAD.
HERE, LEMME SHOW YA HOW.
WHAT YOU NEED, MAN, IS SOME NOSE-CANDY-- GET A GOOD BUZZ ON AND SHAKE YOUR BONES...
CAT'S GOT MY FRIEND'S TONGUE, SO I'LL SAY IT...
GET LOST, CREEP.
HUH?
BUT YOU'LL LOVE IT, CHICKIE, ONCE YOU'VE HAD A TASTE...
BATS, IT SEEMS YOUR EARDRUMS AREN'T THE ONLY CASUALTIES IN THIS PLACE.
FRAK
NICE HOOK.
TOO BAD FOR YOU YOUR CHICK HIT ME, MAN, CUZ I DON'T SMACK LADIES BACK... WHICH MEANS YOU'RE GONNA TAKE IT...
...AND YOU KNOW HOW YOU'RE GONNA TAKE IT?
RIGHT IN THE FACE-- FROM THE EDGES OF THIS RAZOR-SHARP MEDALLION!
DON'T BE A FOOL.
THIS COSTUME IS REAL.
NICE TRY, HERO, BUT I DON'T--
CHLIP
SPUNCH

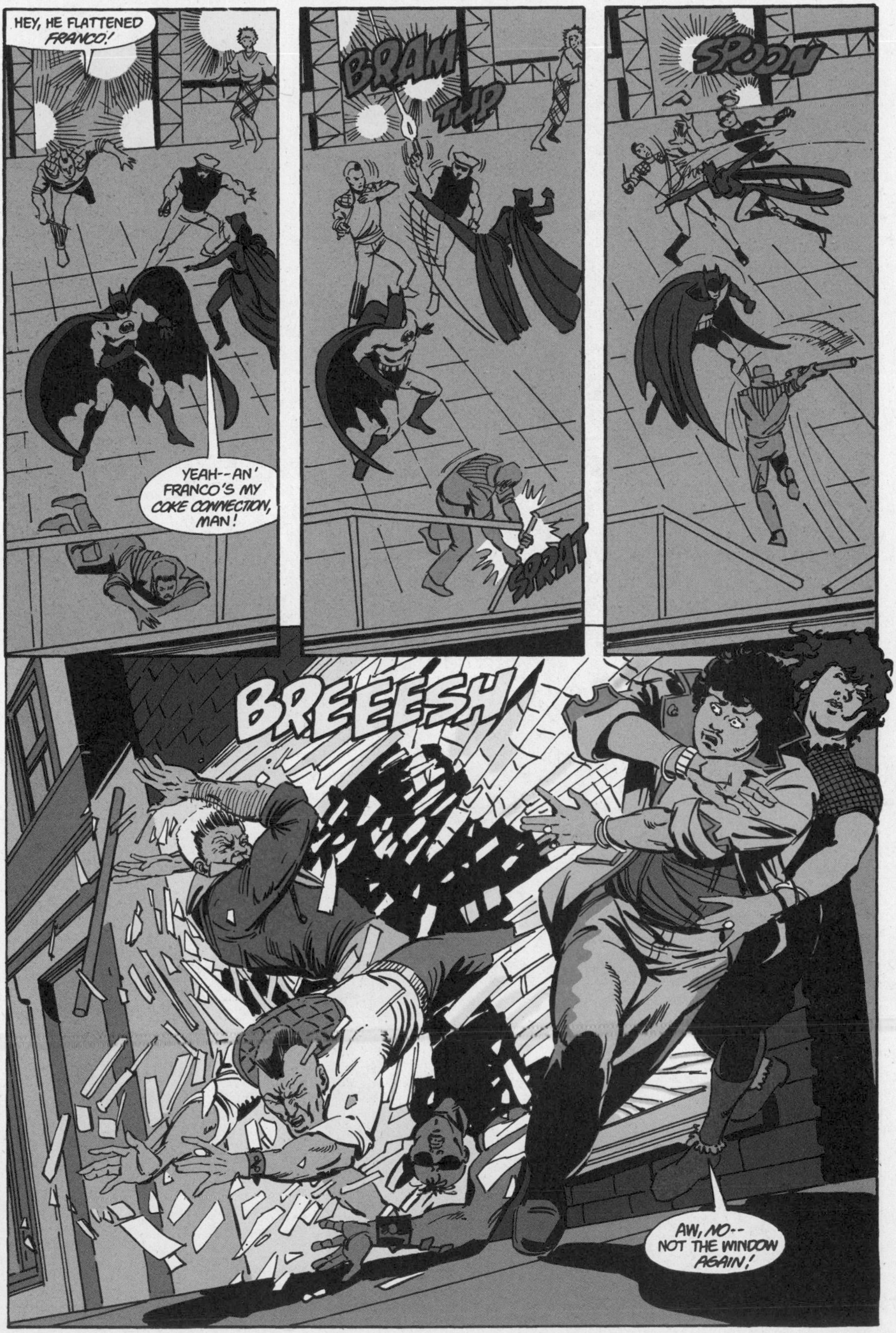
HEY, HE FLATTENED FRANCO!
YEAH--AN' FRANCO'S MY COKE CONNECTION, MAN!
BRAM
TUP
SPRAT
SPOON
BREEESH
AW, NO-- NOT THE WINDOW AGAIN!

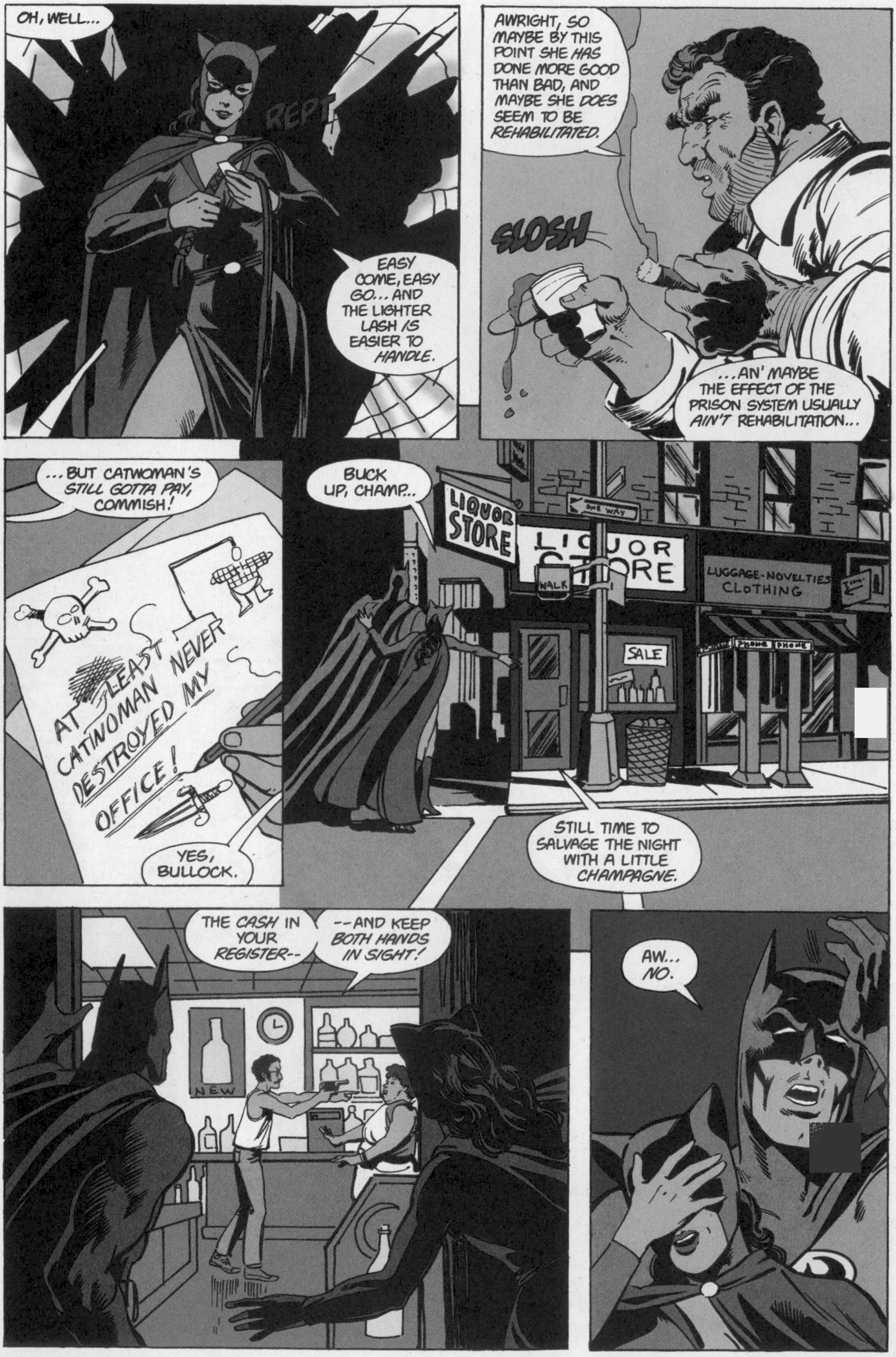
OH, WELL...
REPT
EASY COME, EASY GO... AND THE LIGHTER LASH IS EASIER TO HANDLE.
AWRIGHT, SO MAYBE BY THIS POINT SHE HAS DONE MORE GOOD THAN BAD, AND MAYBE SHE DOES SEEM TO BE REHABILITATED.
SLOSH
...AN' MAYBE THE EFFECT OF THE PRISON SYSTEM USUALLY AIN'T REHABILITATION...
...BUT CATWOMAN'S STILL GOTTA PAY, COMMISH!
AT LEAST CATWOMAN NEVER DESTROYED MY OFFICE!
YES, BULLOCK.
BUCK UP, CHAMP...
LIQUOR STORE
ONE WAY
LIQUOR STORE
WALK
LUGGAGE-NOVELTIES CLOTHING
SALE
PHONE PHONE
STILL TIME TO SALVAGE THE NIGHT WITH A LITTLE CHAMPAGNE.
THE CASH IN YOUR REGISTER--
--AND KEEP BOTH HANDS IN SIGHT!
NEW
AW... NO.

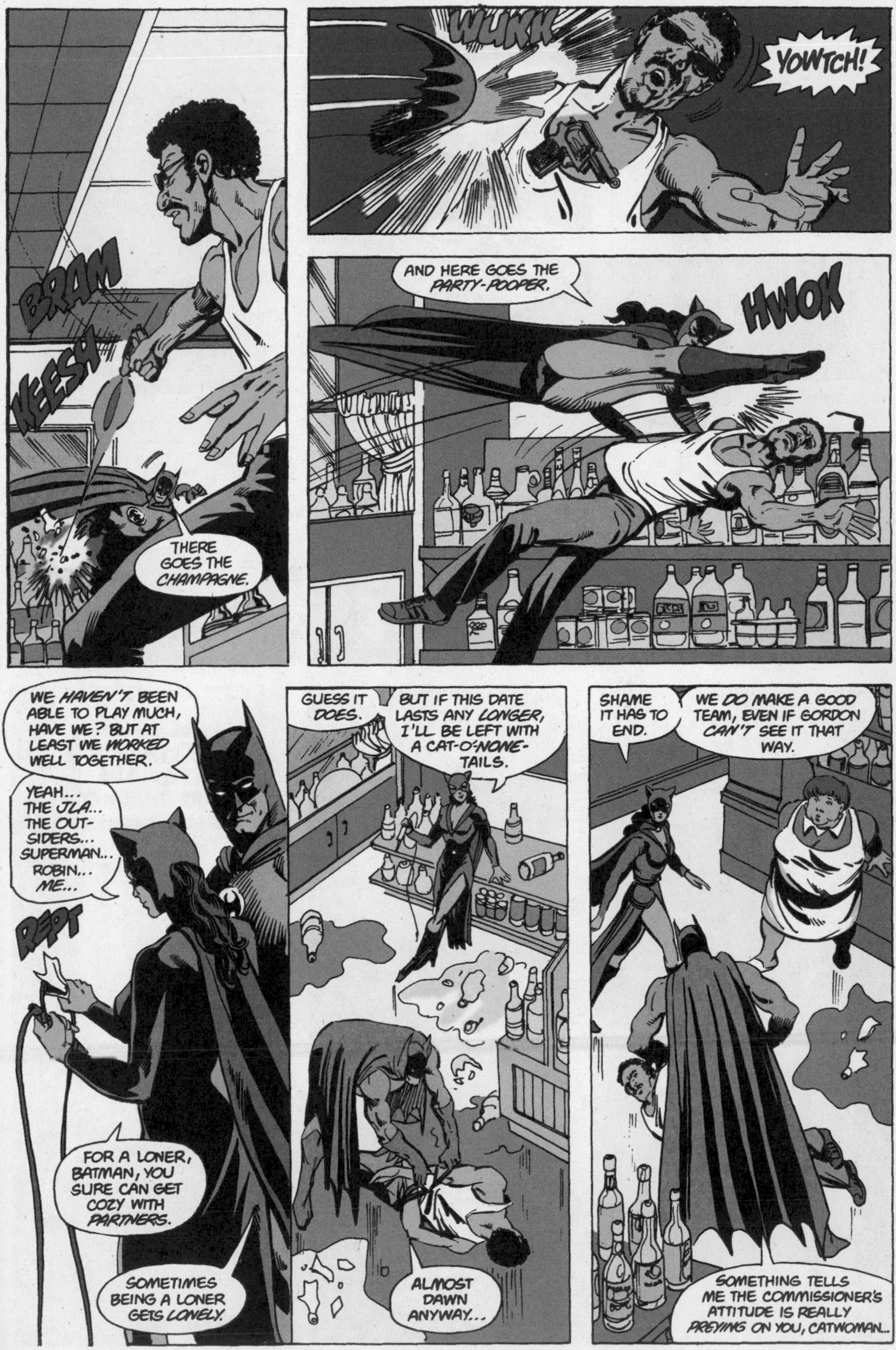
YOWTCH!
WUKK
BRAM
KEESH
THERE GOES THE *CHAMPAGNE.*
AND HERE GOES THE *PARTY-POOPER.*
HWOK
WE *HAVEN'T* BEEN ABLE TO PLAY MUCH, HAVE WE? BUT AT LEAST WE *WORKED* WELL TOGETHER.
YEAH... THE *JLA*... THE OUT-SIDERS... SUPERMAN... ROBIN... *ME*...
RRIPT
FOR A LONER, BATMAN, YOU SURE CAN GET COZY WITH *PARTNERS.*
SOMETIMES BEING A LONER GETS *LONELY.*
GUESS IT *DOES.*
BUT IF THIS DATE LASTS ANY *LONGER,* I'LL BE LEFT WITH A CAT-O'-*NONE*-TAILS.
ALMOST DAWN ANYWAY...
SHAME IT HAS TO END.
WE *DO* MAKE A GOOD TEAM, EVEN IF GORDON *CAN'T* SEE IT THAT WAY.
SOMETHING TELLS ME THE COMMISSIONER'S ATTITUDE IS REALLY *PREYING* ON YOU, CATWOMAN...

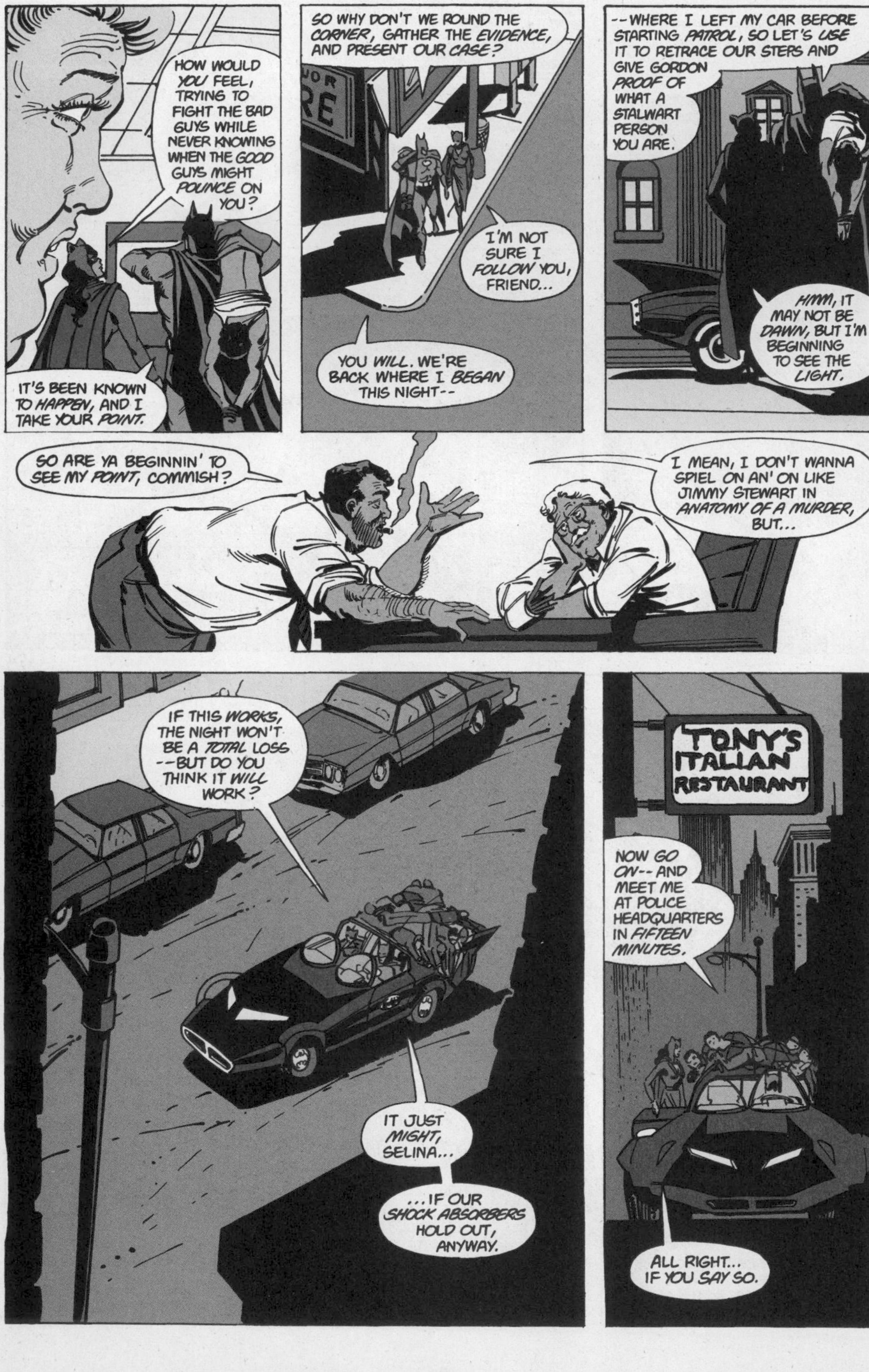
HOW WOULD YOU FEEL, TRYING TO FIGHT THE BAD GUYS WHILE NEVER KNOWING WHEN THE GOOD GUYS MIGHT POUNCE ON YOU?
IT'S BEEN KNOWN TO HAPPEN, AND I TAKE YOUR POINT.
SO WHY DON'T WE ROUND THE CORNER, GATHER THE EVIDENCE, AND PRESENT OUR CASE?
I'M NOT SURE I FOLLOW YOU, FRIEND...
YOU WILL. WE'RE BACK WHERE I BEGAN THIS NIGHT--
--WHERE I LEFT MY CAR BEFORE STARTING PATROL, SO LET'S USE IT TO RETRACE OUR STEPS AND GIVE GORDON PROOF OF WHAT A STALWART PERSON YOU ARE.
HMM, IT MAY NOT BE DAWN, BUT I'M BEGINNING TO SEE THE LIGHT.
SO ARE YA BEGINNIN' TO SEE MY POINT, COMMISH?
I MEAN, I DON'T WANNA SPIEL ON AN' ON LIKE JIMMY STEWART IN ANATOMY OF A MURDER, BUT...
IF THIS WORKS, THE NIGHT WON'T BE A TOTAL LOSS --BUT DO YOU THINK IT WILL WORK?
IT JUST MIGHT, SELINA...
...IF OUR SHOCK ABSORBERS HOLD OUT, ANYWAY.
TONY'S ITALIAN RESTAURANT
NOW GO ON-- AND MEET ME AT POLICE HEADQUARTERS IN FIFTEEN MINUTES.
ALL RIGHT... IF YOU SAY SO.

--BUT IT WAS *IMPORTANT*, THIS *CATWOMAN* THING.

SORRY I TALKED AT YA ALL NIGHT, COMMISH--

SO HAVE I *CONVINCED* YA?

OH, THAT YOU *HAVE*, BULLOCK...

...IN *SPADES*.

GOOD.

AT LEAST I ACCOMPLISHED *ONE* THING THIS NIGHT.

SLAMM

POLICE COMMISSIONER

SEE YA *LATER*, COMMISH!

THERE...

THIS SHOULD HOLD.

♪ *DUM DA DUM DUM...* ♪

...*DUM DA DUM DUM DUMMM...* ♪

HELLO, GORDON-- I SEE *BULLOCK* WAS HERE.

BATMAN! STRANGE TOO SEE YOU SO CLOSE TO *DAWN*...

BROUGHT A *GIFT* FOR YOU--OUT- SIDE YOUR *WINDOW*.

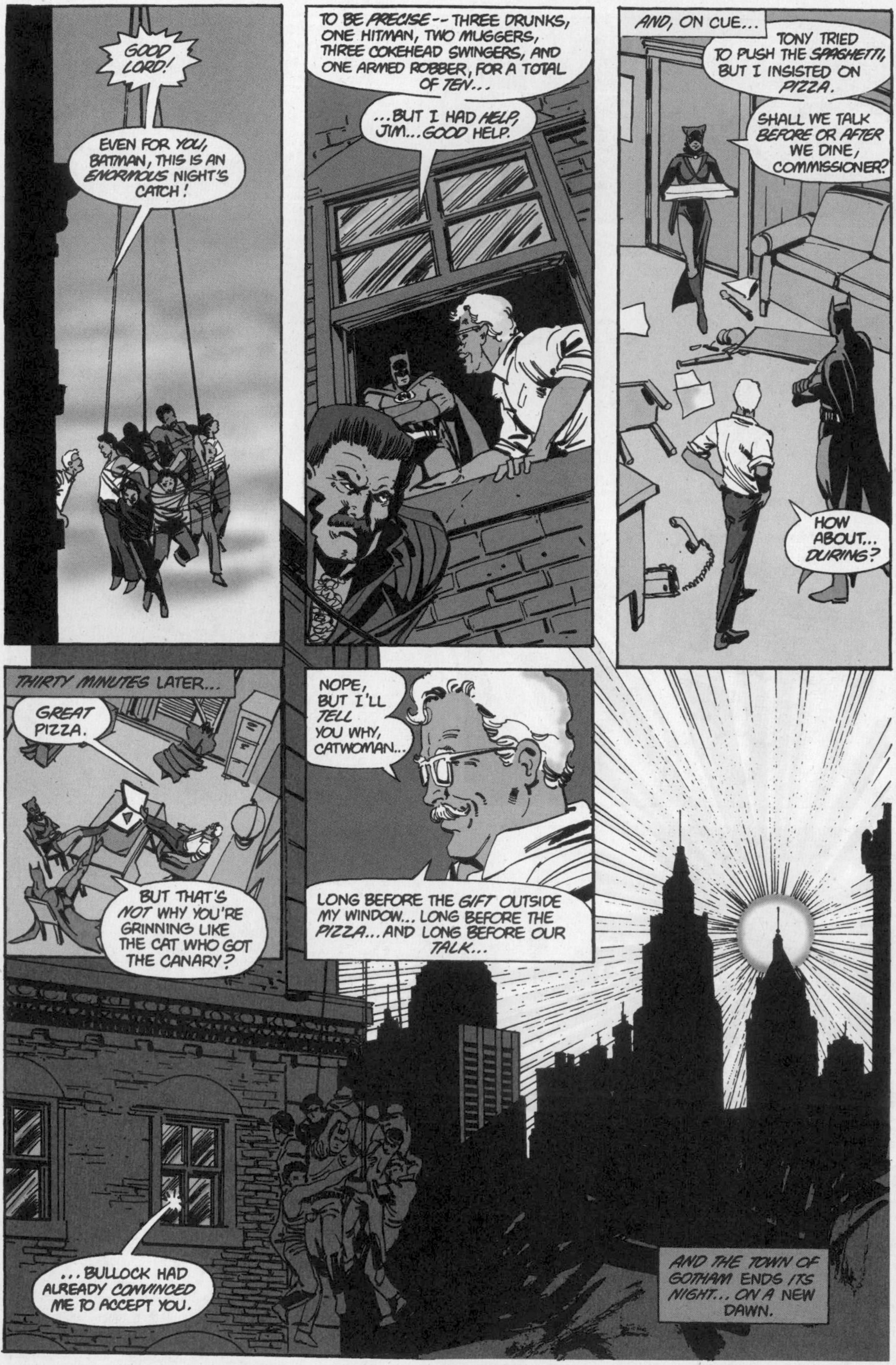
GOOD LORD!
EVEN FOR YOU, BATMAN, THIS IS AN ENORMOUS NIGHT'S CATCH!
TO BE PRECISE-- THREE DRUNKS, ONE HITMAN, TWO MUGGERS, THREE COKEHEAD SWINGERS, AND ONE ARMED ROBBER, FOR A TOTAL OF TEN...
...BUT I HAD HELP, JIM...GOOD HELP.
AND, ON CUE...
TONY TRIED TO PUSH THE SPAGHETTI, BUT I INSISTED ON PIZZA.
SHALL WE TALK BEFORE OR AFTER WE DINE, COMMISSIONER?
HOW ABOUT... DURING?
THIRTY MINUTES LATER...
GREAT PIZZA.
BUT THAT'S NOT WHY YOU'RE GRINNING LIKE THE CAT WHO GOT THE CANARY?
NOPE, BUT I'LL TELL YOU WHY, CATWOMAN...
LONG BEFORE THE GIFT OUTSIDE MY WINDOW... LONG BEFORE THE PIZZA... AND LONG BEFORE OUR TALK...
...BULLOCK HAD ALREADY CONVINCED ME TO ACCEPT YOU.
AND THE TOWN OF GOTHAM ENDS ITS NIGHT... ON A NEW DAWN.

pinup Cameron Stewart

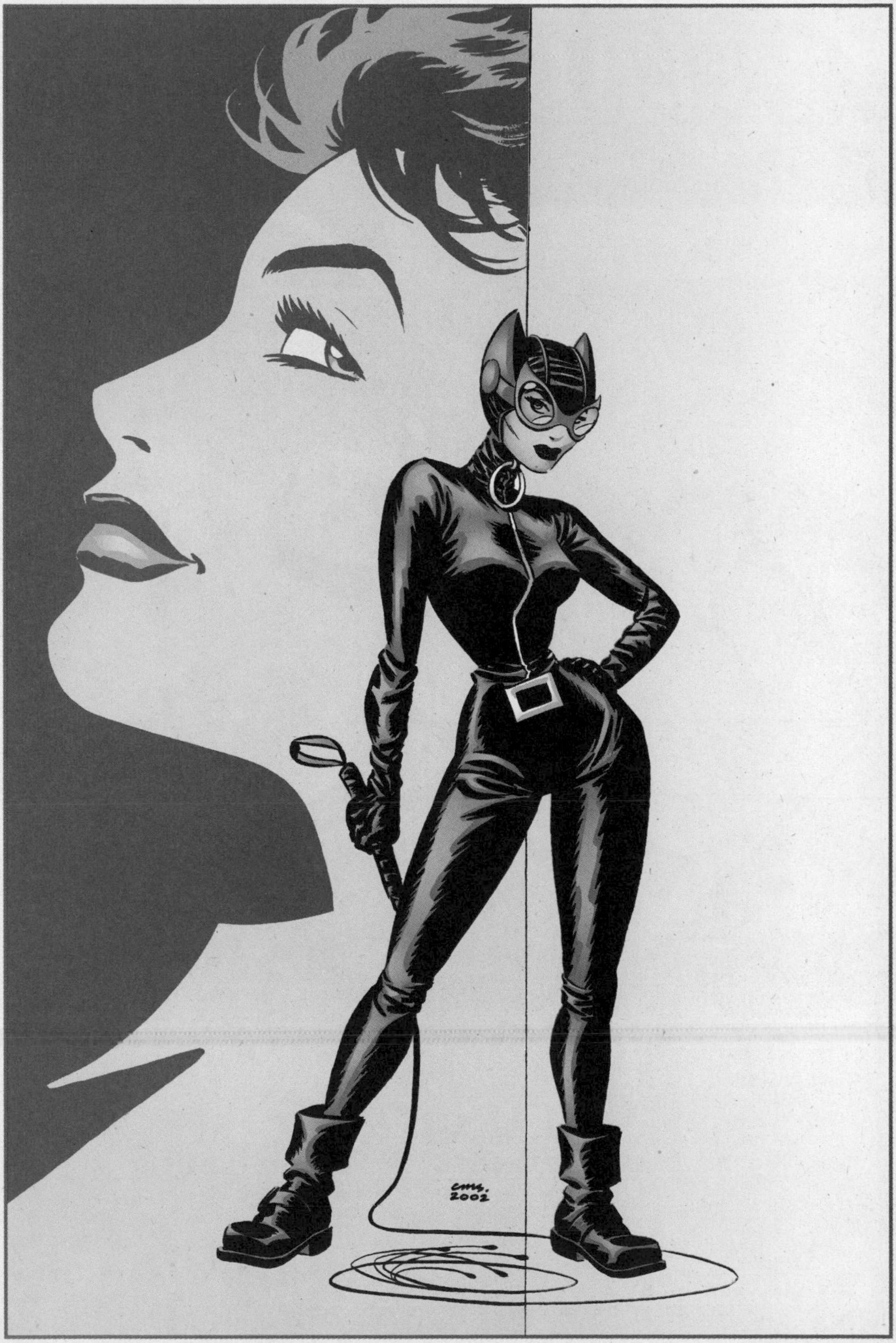
cms.
2002

This pinup by Cameron Stewart is the profile art from CATWOMAN SECRET FILES #1. Colored by Tom McCraw.

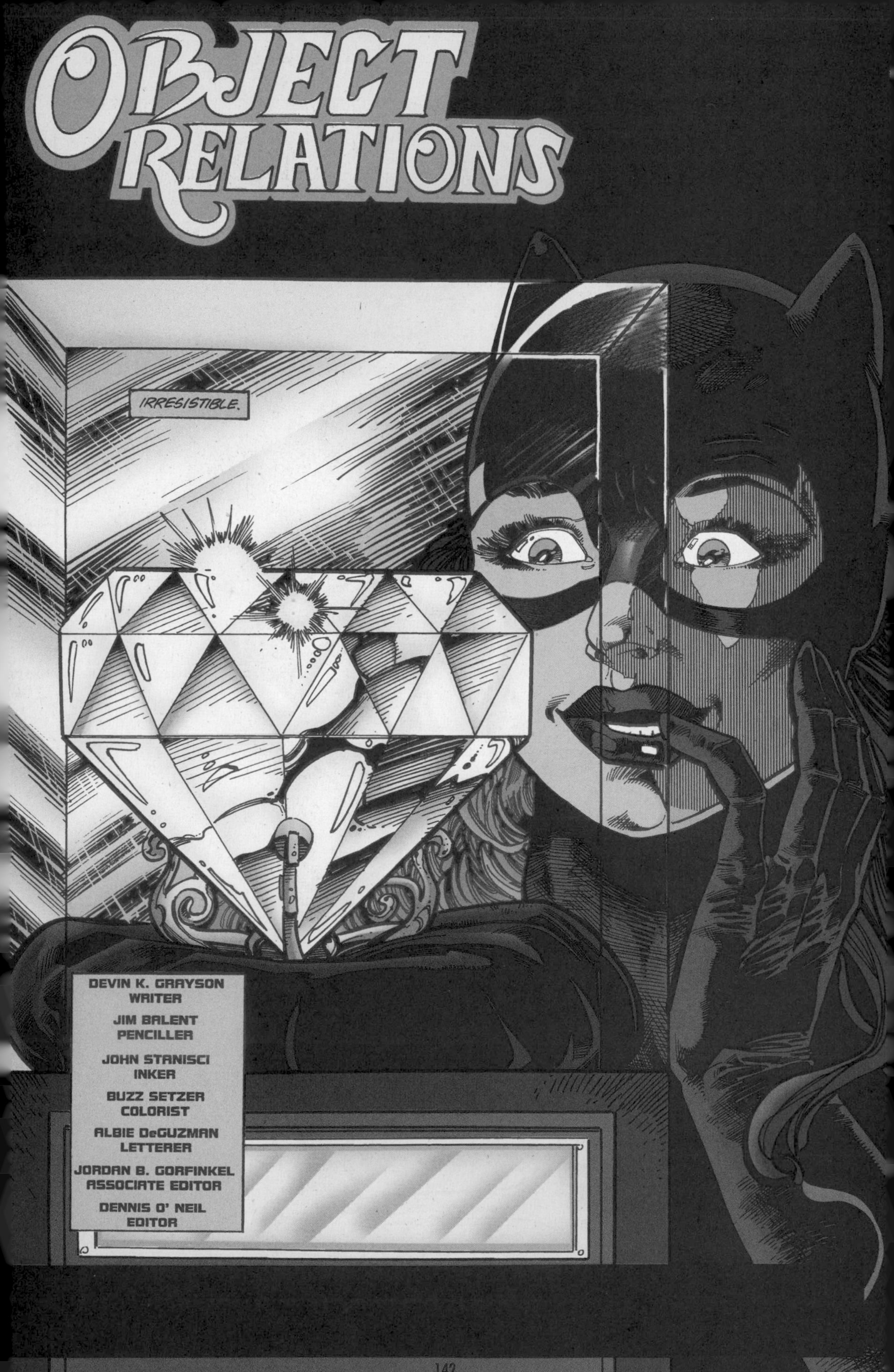
OBJECT RELATIONS
IRRESISTIBLE.
DEVIN K. GRAYSON WRITER
JIM BALENT PENCILLER
JOHN STANISCI INKER
BUZZ SETZER COLORIST
ALBIE DeGUZMAN LETTERER
JORDAN B. GORFINKEL ASSOCIATE EDITOR
DENNIS O' NEIL EDITOR

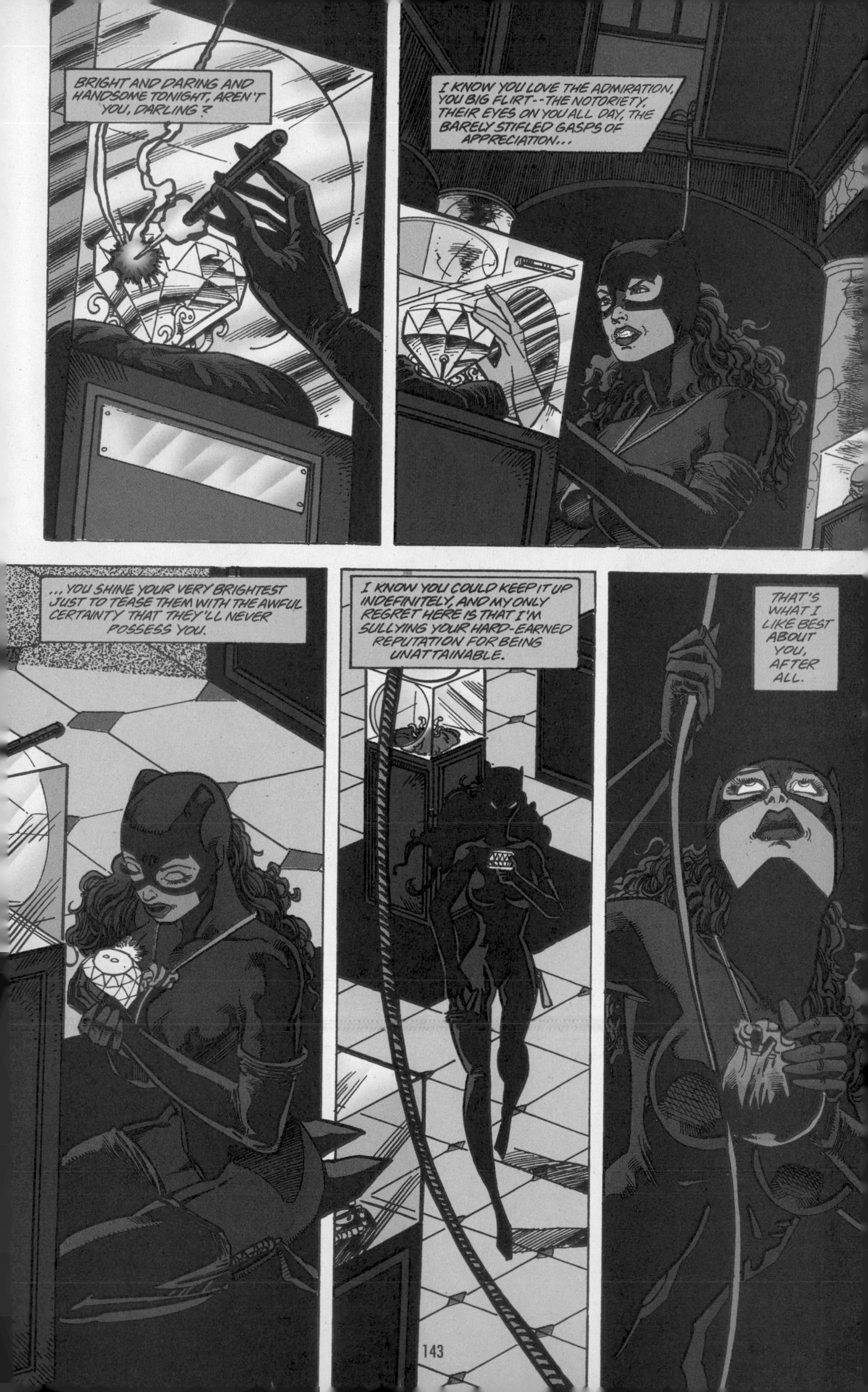
BRIGHT AND DARING AND HANDSOME TONIGHT, AREN'T YOU, DARLING?
I KNOW YOU LOVE THE ADMIRATION, YOU BIG FLIRT--THE NOTORIETY, THEIR EYES ON YOU ALL DAY, THE BARELY STIFLED GASPS OF APPRECIATION...
...YOU SHINE YOUR VERY BRIGHTEST JUST TO TEASE THEM WITH THE AWFUL CERTAINTY THAT THEY'LL NEVER POSSESS YOU.
I KNOW YOU COULD KEEP IT UP INDEFINITELY, AND MY ONLY REGRET HERE IS THAT I'M SULLYING YOUR HARD-EARNED REPUTATION FOR BEING UNATTAINABLE.
THAT'S WHAT I LIKE BEST ABOUT YOU, AFTER ALL.

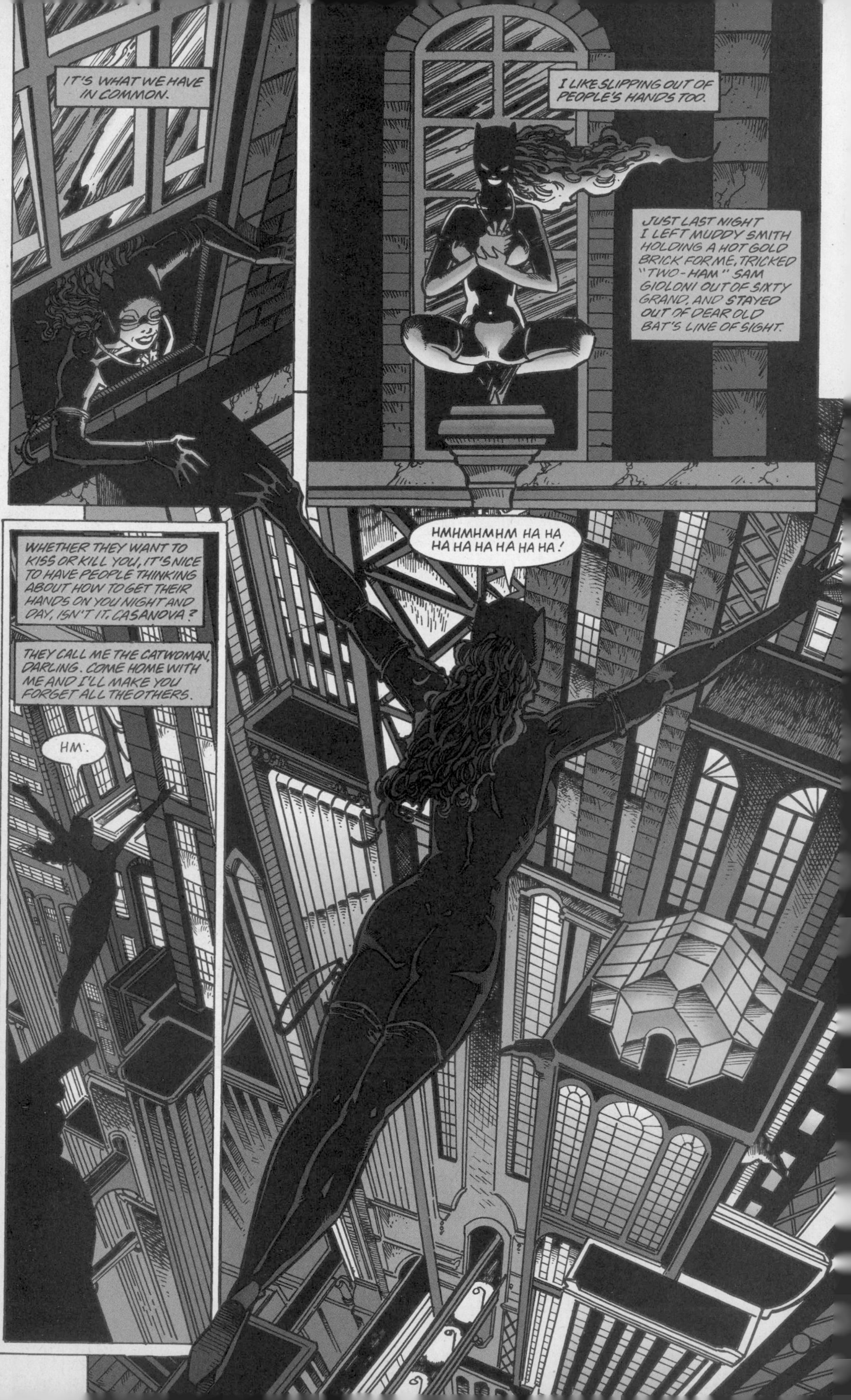
IT'S WHAT WE HAVE IN COMMON.
I LIKE SLIPPING OUT OF PEOPLE'S HANDS TOO.
JUST LAST NIGHT I LEFT MUDDY SMITH HOLDING A HOT GOLD BRICK FOR ME, TRICKED "TWO-HAM" SAM GIOLONI OUT OF SIXTY GRAND, AND STAYED OUT OF DEAR OLD BAT'S LINE OF SIGHT.
WHETHER THEY WANT TO KISS OR KILL YOU, IT'S NICE TO HAVE PEOPLE THINKING ABOUT HOW TO GET THEIR HANDS ON YOU NIGHT AND DAY, ISN'T IT, CASANOVA?
THEY CALL ME THE CATWOMAN, DARLING. COME HOME WITH ME AND I'LL MAKE YOU FORGET ALL THE OTHERS.
HM.
HMHMHMHM HA HA HA HA HA HA HA HA!

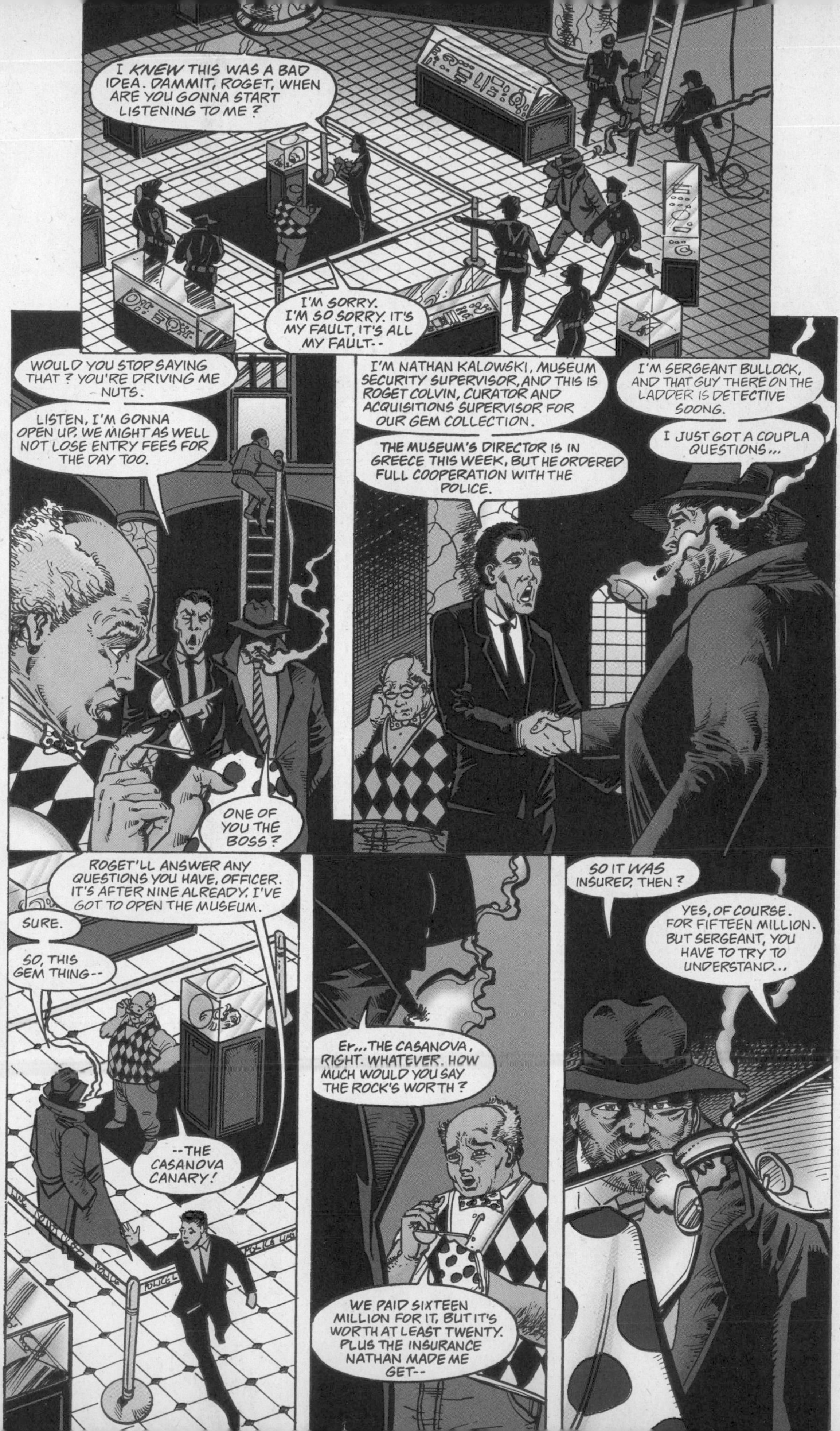
I KNEW THIS WAS A BAD IDEA. DAMMIT, ROGET, WHEN ARE YOU GONNA START LISTENING TO ME?
I'M SORRY. I'M SO SORRY. IT'S MY FAULT, IT'S ALL MY FAULT--
WOULD YOU STOP SAYING THAT? YOU'RE DRIVING ME NUTS.
LISTEN, I'M GONNA OPEN UP. WE MIGHT AS WELL NOT LOSE ENTRY FEES FOR THE DAY TOO.
ONE OF YOU THE BOSS?
I'M NATHAN KALOWSKI, MUSEUM SECURITY SUPERVISOR, AND THIS IS ROGET COLVIN, CURATOR AND ACQUISITIONS SUPERVISOR FOR OUR GEM COLLECTION.
THE MUSEUM'S DIRECTOR IS IN GREECE THIS WEEK, BUT HE ORDERED FULL COOPERATION WITH THE POLICE.
I'M SERGEANT BULLOCK, AND THAT GUY THERE ON THE LADDER IS DETECTIVE SOONG.
I JUST GOT A COUPLA QUESTIONS...
ROGET'LL ANSWER ANY QUESTIONS YOU HAVE, OFFICER. IT'S AFTER NINE ALREADY. I'VE GOT TO OPEN THE MUSEUM.
SURE.
SO, THIS GEM THING--
--THE CASANOVA CANARY!
Er... THE CASANOVA, RIGHT. WHATEVER. HOW MUCH WOULD YOU SAY THE ROCK'S WORTH?
WE PAID SIXTEEN MILLION FOR IT, BUT IT'S WORTH AT LEAST TWENTY. PLUS THE INSURANCE NATHAN MADE ME GET--
SO IT WAS INSURED, THEN?
YES, OF COURSE. FOR FIFTEEN MILLION. BUT SERGEANT, YOU HAVE TO TRY TO UNDERSTAND...

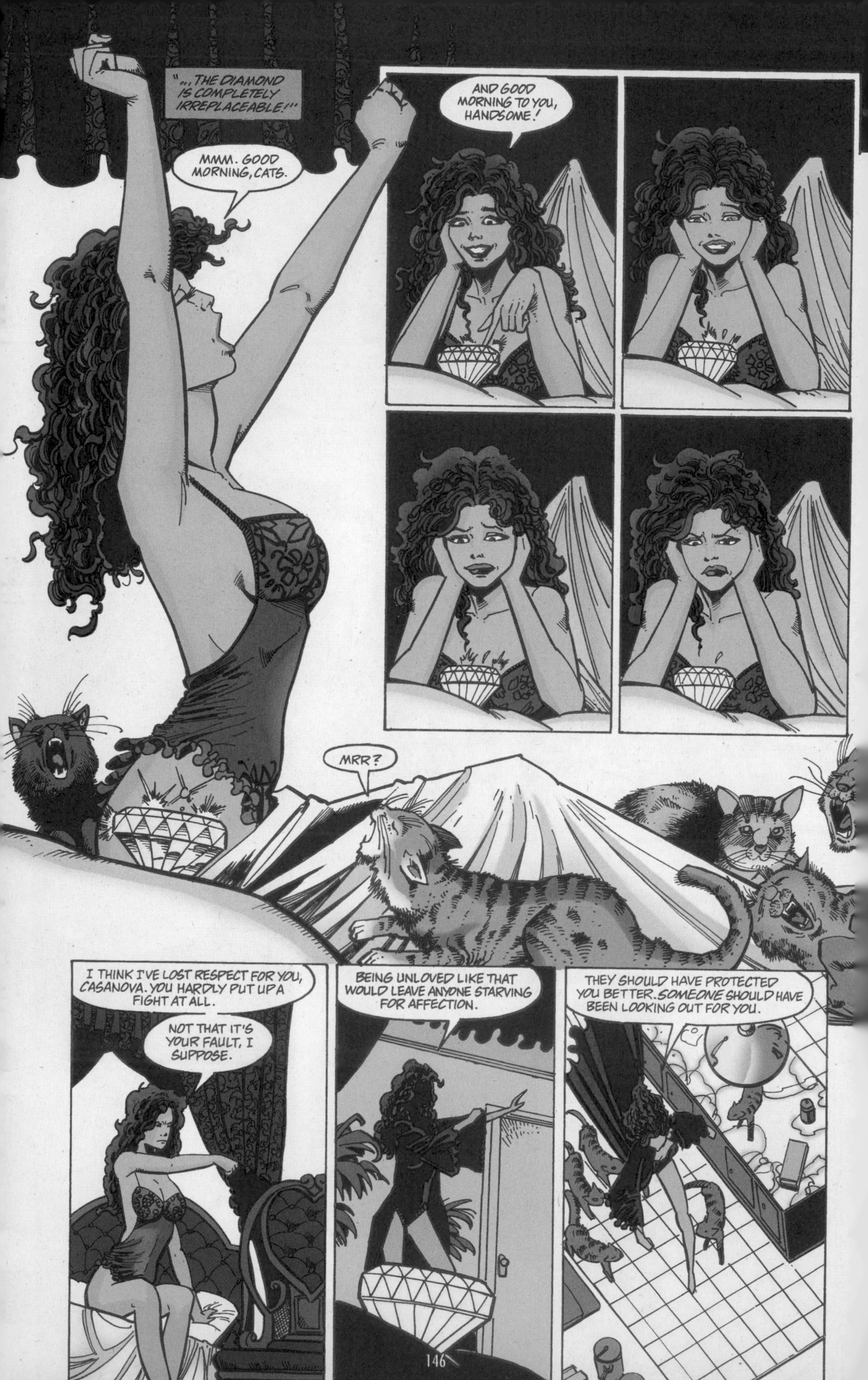
"...THE DIAMOND IS COMPLETELY IRREPLACEABLE!"
MMM. GOOD MORNING, CATS.
AND GOOD MORNING TO YOU, HANDSOME!
MRR?
I THINK I'VE LOST RESPECT FOR YOU, CASANOVA. YOU HARDLY PUT UP A FIGHT AT ALL.
NOT THAT IT'S YOUR FAULT, I SUPPOSE.
BEING UNLOVED LIKE THAT WOULD LEAVE ANYONE STARVING FOR AFFECTION.
THEY SHOULD HAVE PROTECTED YOU BETTER. SOMEONE SHOULD HAVE BEEN LOOKING OUT FOR YOU.

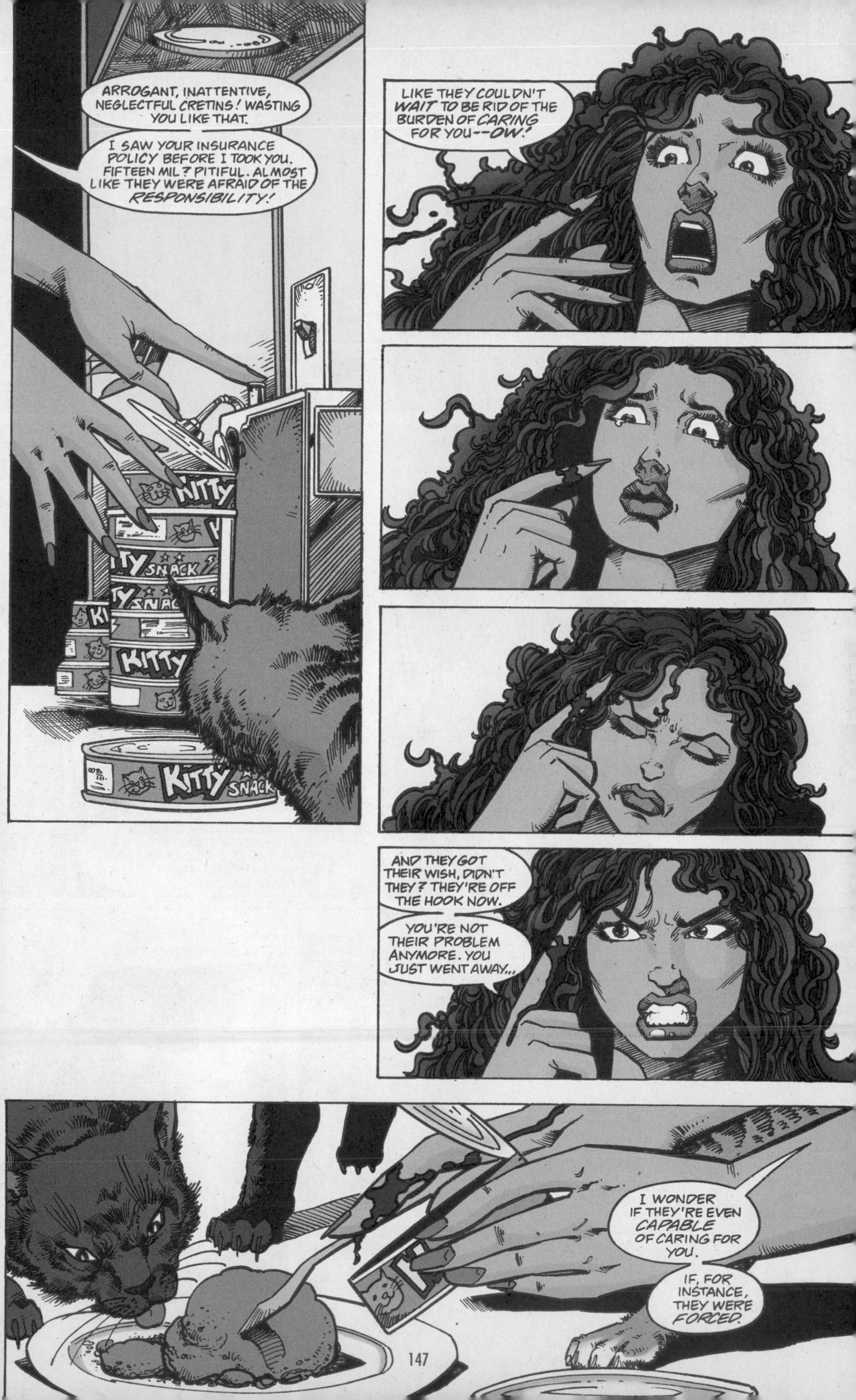
ARROGANT, INATTENTIVE, NEGLECTFUL CRETINS! WASTING YOU LIKE THAT.
I SAW YOUR INSURANCE POLICY BEFORE I TOOK YOU. FIFTEEN MIL? PITIFUL. ALMOST LIKE THEY WERE AFRAID OF THE RESPONSIBILITY!
KITTY SNACK
LIKE THEY COULDN'T WAIT TO BE RID OF THE BURDEN OF CARING FOR YOU--OW!
AND THEY GOT THEIR WISH, DIDN'T THEY? THEY'RE OFF THE HOOK NOW.
YOU'RE NOT THEIR PROBLEM ANYMORE. YOU JUST WENT AWAY...
I WONDER IF THEY'RE EVEN CAPABLE OF CARING FOR YOU.
IF, FOR INSTANCE, THEY WERE FORCED.

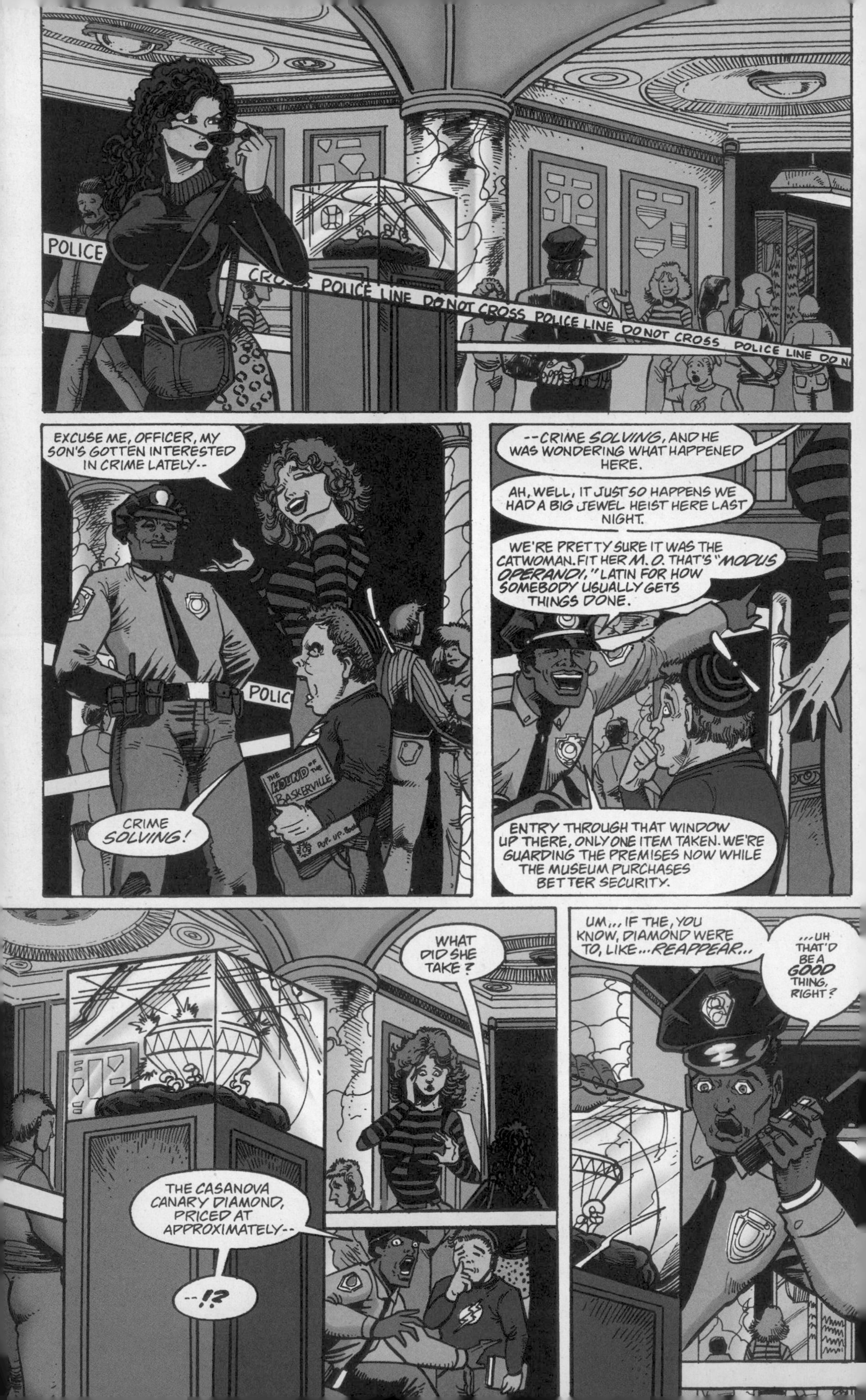
POLICE
CROSS POLICE LINE DO NOT CROSS POLICE LINE DO NOT CROSS POLICE LINE DO N
EXCUSE ME, OFFICER, MY SON'S GOTTEN INTERESTED IN CRIME LATELY--
POLICE
THE HOUND OF THE BASKERVILLE
POP-UP BOOK
CRIME SOLVING!
--CRIME SOLVING, AND HE WAS WONDERING WHAT HAPPENED HERE.
AH, WELL, IT JUST SO HAPPENS WE HAD A BIG JEWEL HEIST HERE LAST NIGHT.
WE'RE PRETTY SURE IT WAS THE CATWOMAN. FIT HER M.O. THAT'S "MODUS OPERANDI," LATIN FOR HOW SOMEBODY USUALLY GETS THINGS DONE.
ENTRY THROUGH THAT WINDOW UP THERE, ONLY ONE ITEM TAKEN. WE'RE GUARDING THE PREMISES NOW WHILE THE MUSEUM PURCHASES BETTER SECURITY.
WHAT DID SHE TAKE?
THE CASANOVA CANARY DIAMOND, PRICED AT APPROXIMATELY--
--!?
UM... IF THE, YOU KNOW, DIAMOND WERE TO, LIKE... REAPPEAR...
...UH THAT'D BE A GOOD THING, RIGHT?

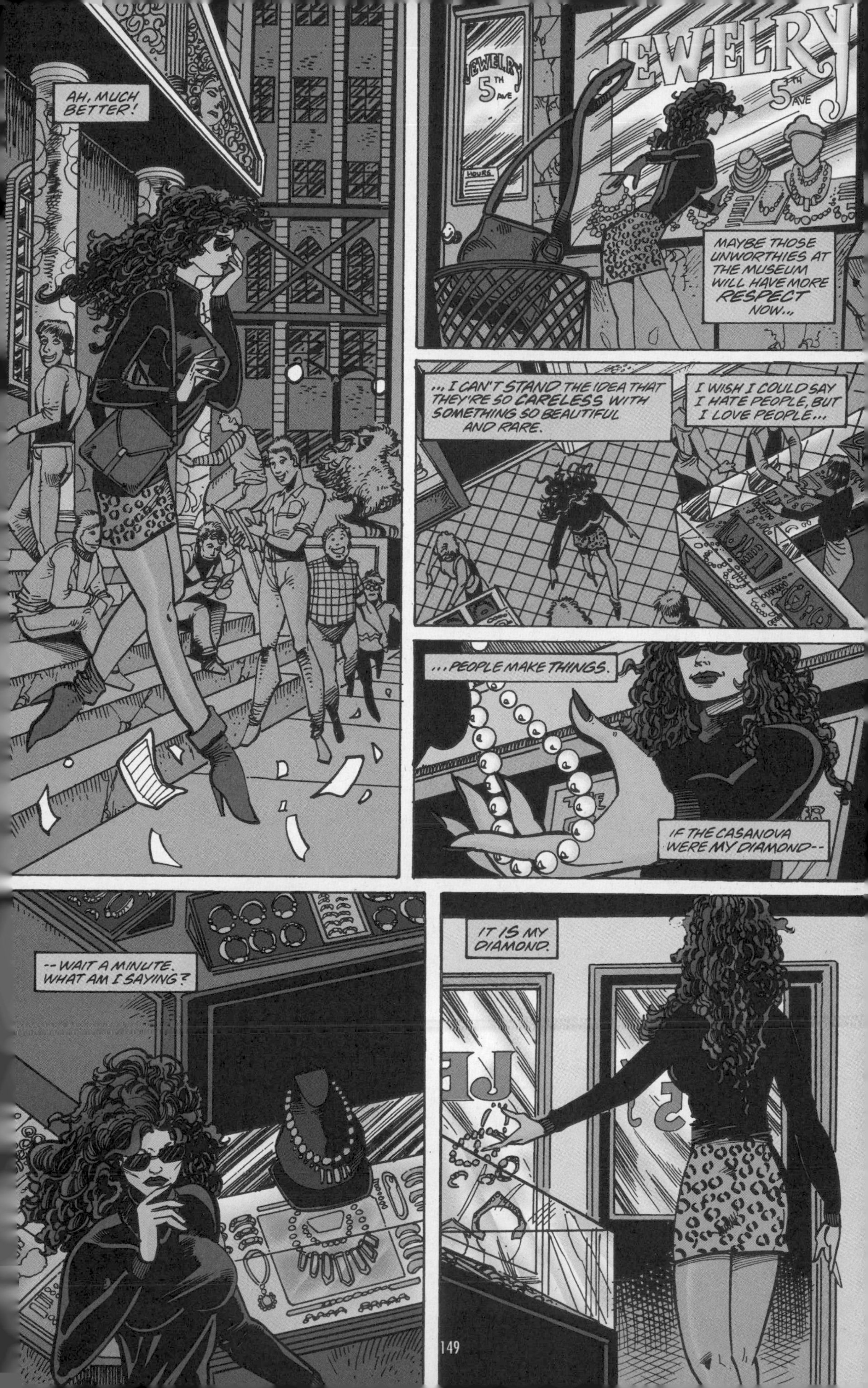
AH, MUCH BETTER!
JEWELRY 5TH AVE
MAYBE THOSE UNWORTHIES AT THE MUSEUM WILL HAVE MORE RESPECT NOW...
...I CAN'T STAND THE IDEA THAT THEY'RE SO CARELESS WITH SOMETHING SO BEAUTIFUL AND RARE.
I WISH I COULD SAY I HATE PEOPLE, BUT I LOVE PEOPLE...
...PEOPLE MAKE THINGS.
IF THE CASANOVA WERE MY DIAMOND--
--WAIT A MINUTE. WHAT AM I SAYING?
IT IS MY DIAMOND.

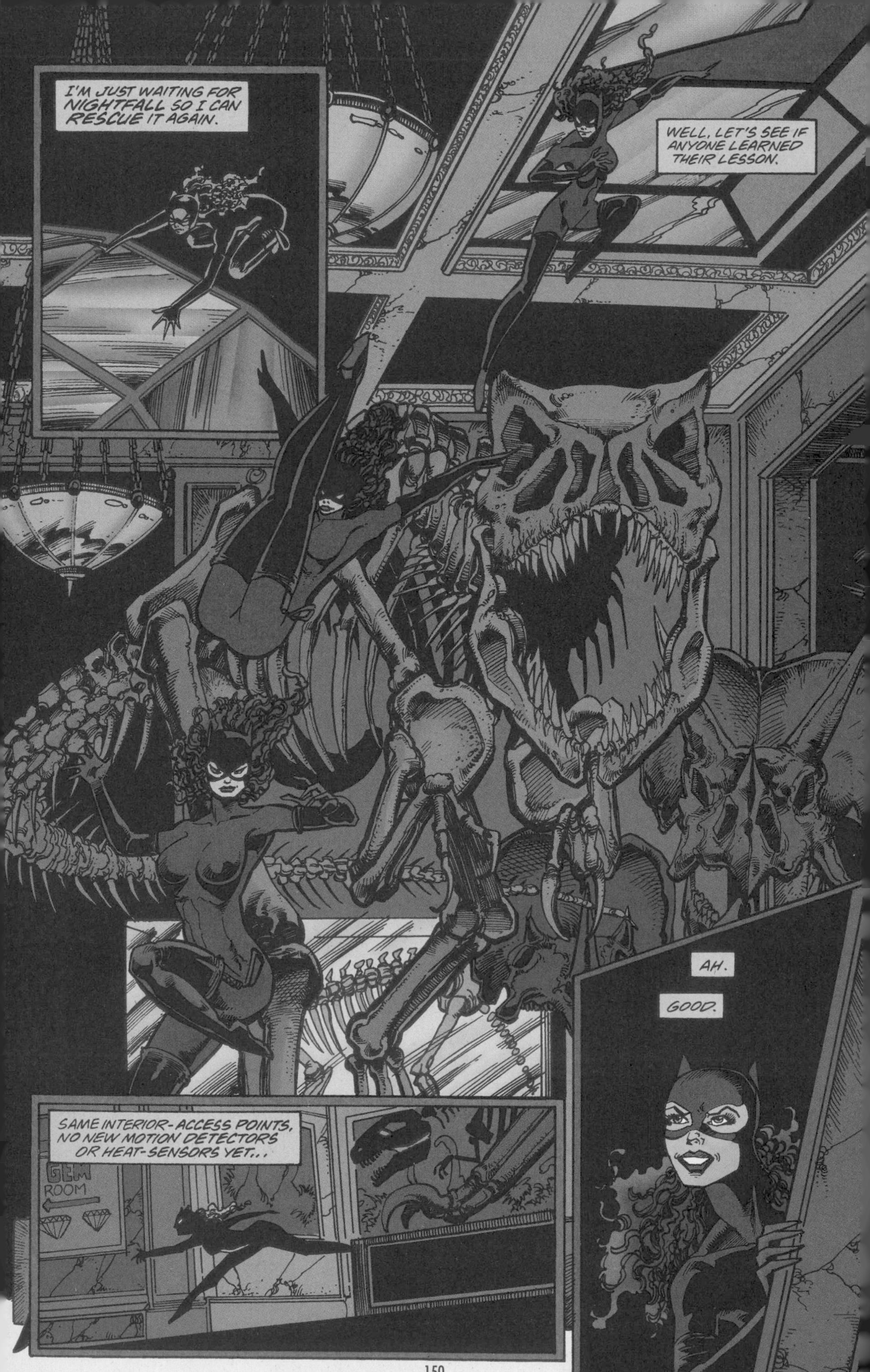
I'M JUST WAITING FOR NIGHTFALL SO I CAN RESCUE IT AGAIN.
WELL, LET'S SEE IF ANYONE LEARNED THEIR LESSON.
SAME INTERIOR-ACCESS POINTS, NO NEW MOTION DETECTORS OR HEAT-SENSORS YET...
GEM ROOM
AH.
GOOD.

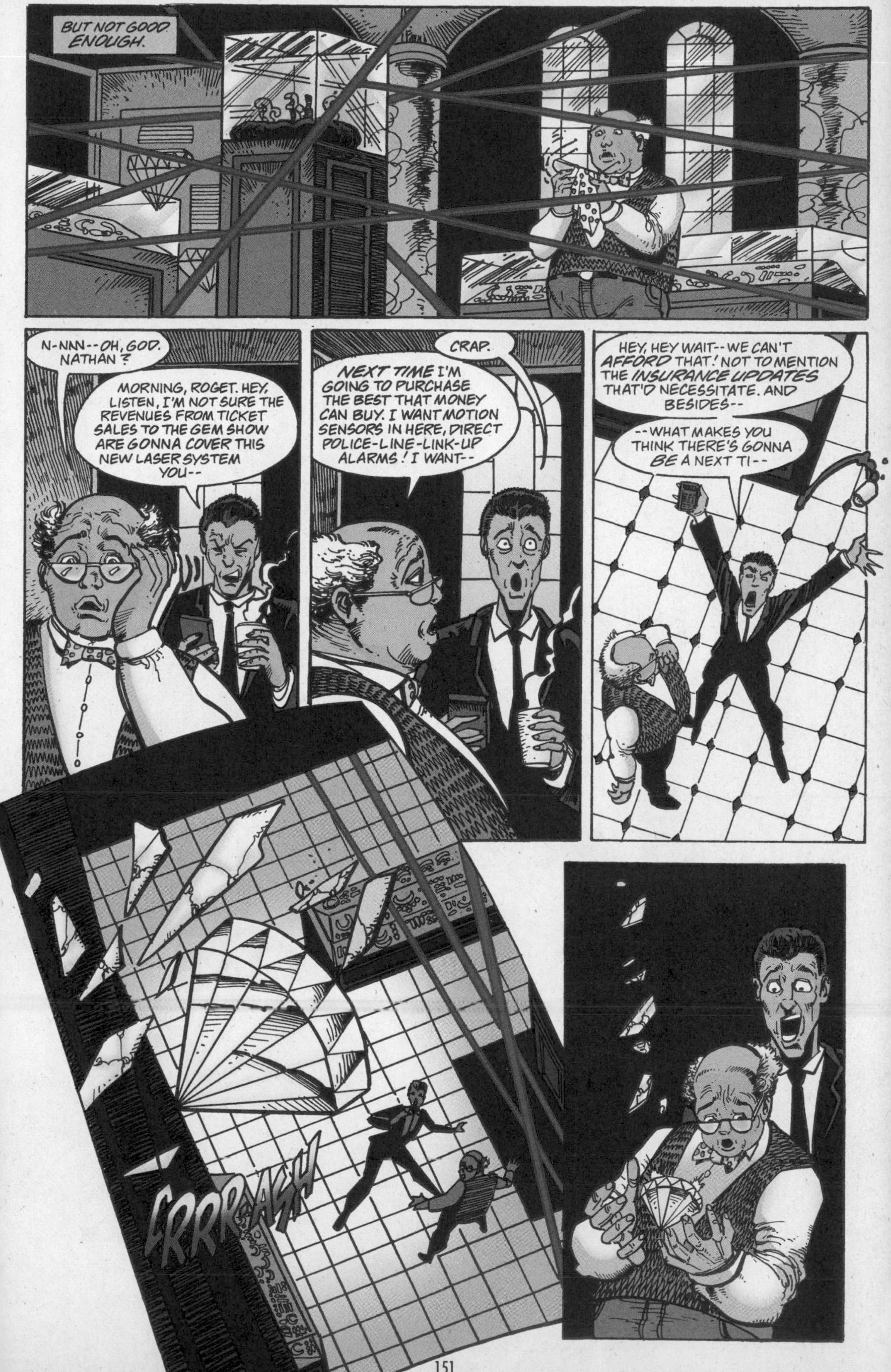
BUT NOT GOOD ENOUGH.
N-NNN--OH, GOD. NATHAN?
MORNING, ROGET. HEY, LISTEN, I'M NOT SURE THE REVENUES FROM TICKET SALES TO THE GEM SHOW ARE GONNA COVER THIS NEW LASER SYSTEM YOU--
CRAP.
NEXT TIME I'M GOING TO PURCHASE THE BEST THAT MONEY CAN BUY. I WANT MOTION SENSORS IN HERE, DIRECT POLICE-LINE-LINK-UP ALARMS! I WANT--
HEY, HEY WAIT--WE CAN'T AFFORD THAT! NOT TO MENTION THE INSURANCE UPDATES THAT'D NECESSITATE. AND BESIDES--
--WHAT MAKES YOU THINK THERE'S GONNA BE A NEXT TI--
CRRRASH

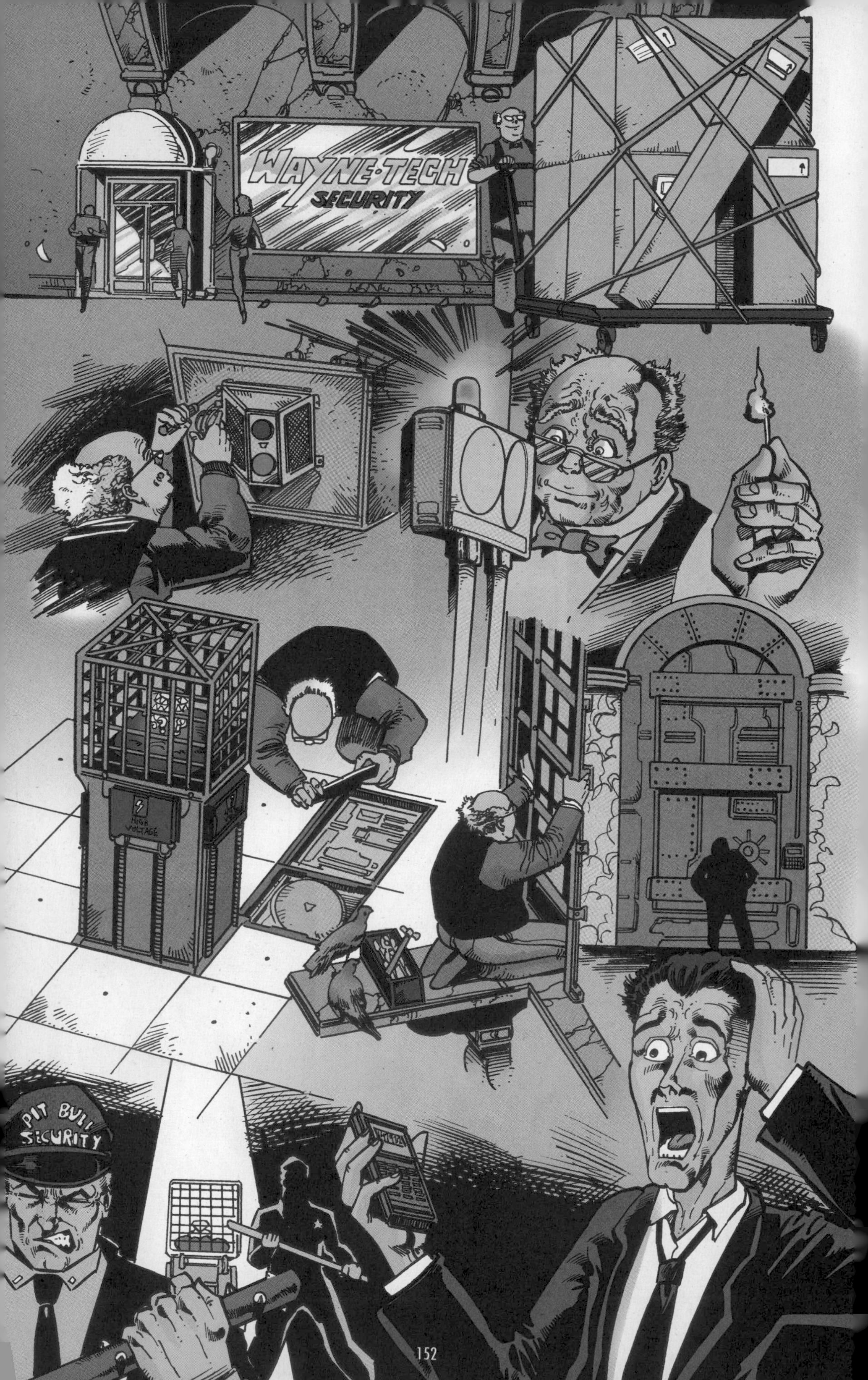
WAYNE·TECH
SECURITY
HIGH VOLTAGE
PIT BULL SECURITY

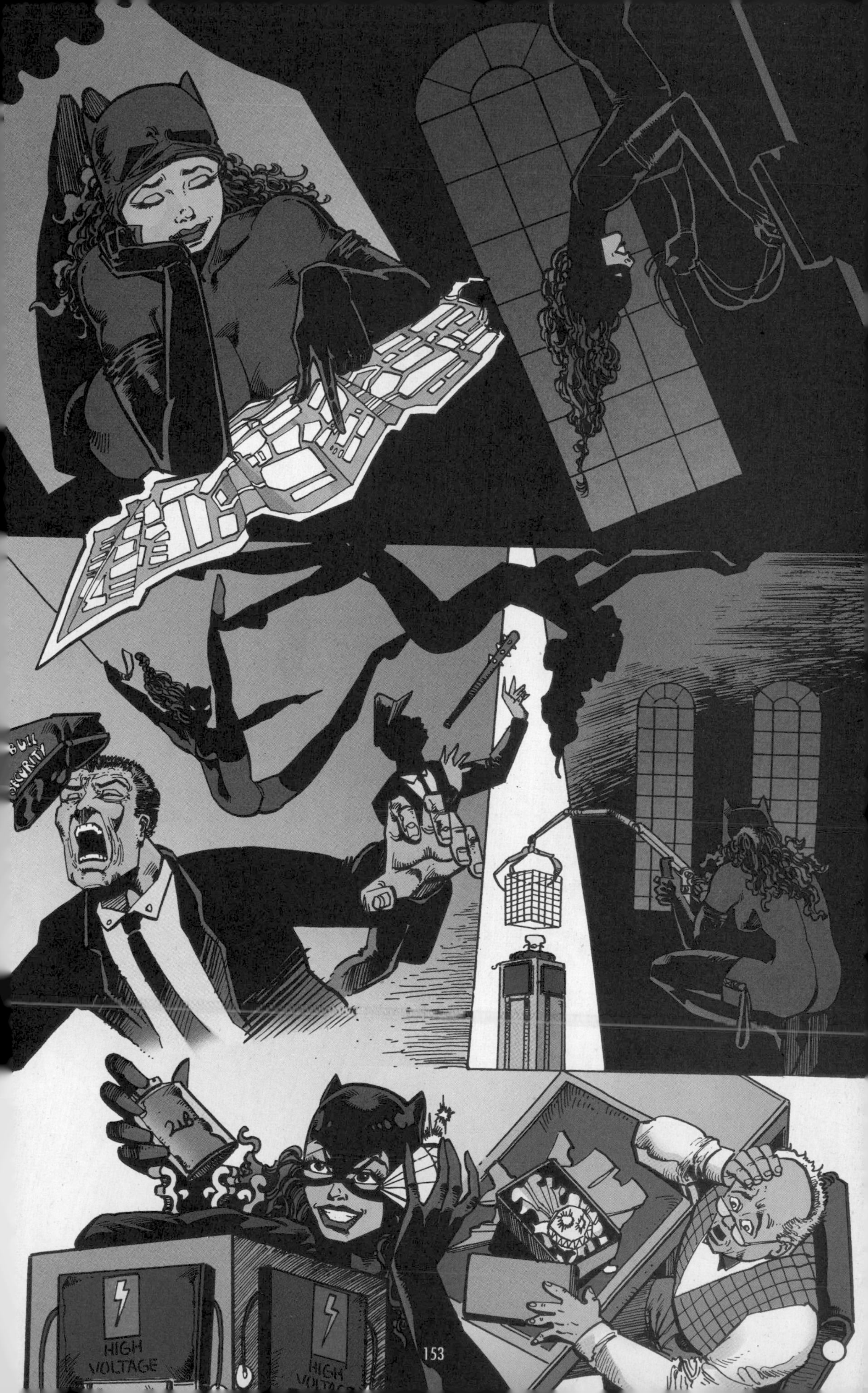
BULL
SECURITY
218
HIGH VOLTAGE
HIGH VOLTAGE

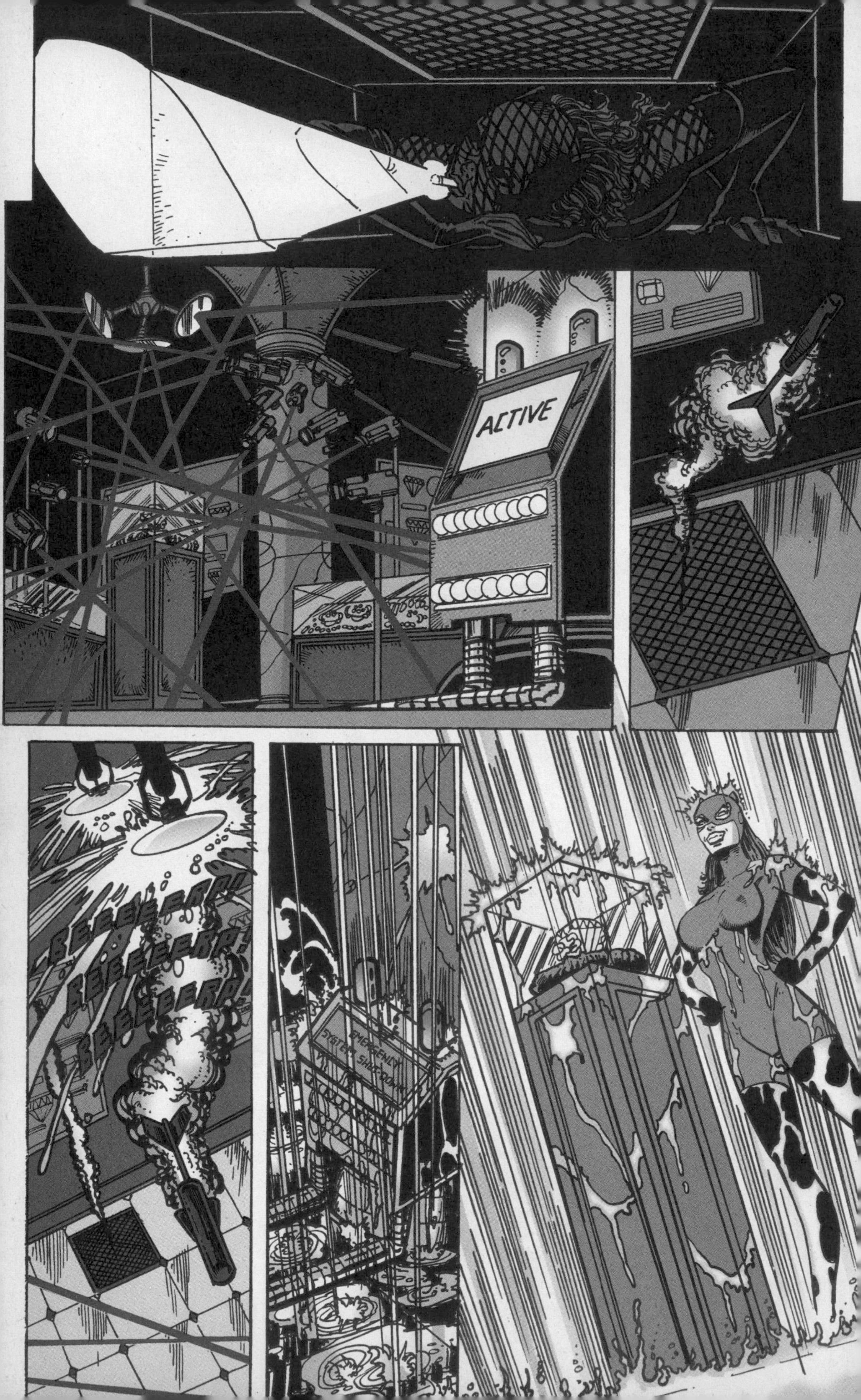
ACTIVE
BEEEEERP!
BEEEEERP!
BEEEEERP!
EMERGENCY
SYSTEM SHUT-DOWN

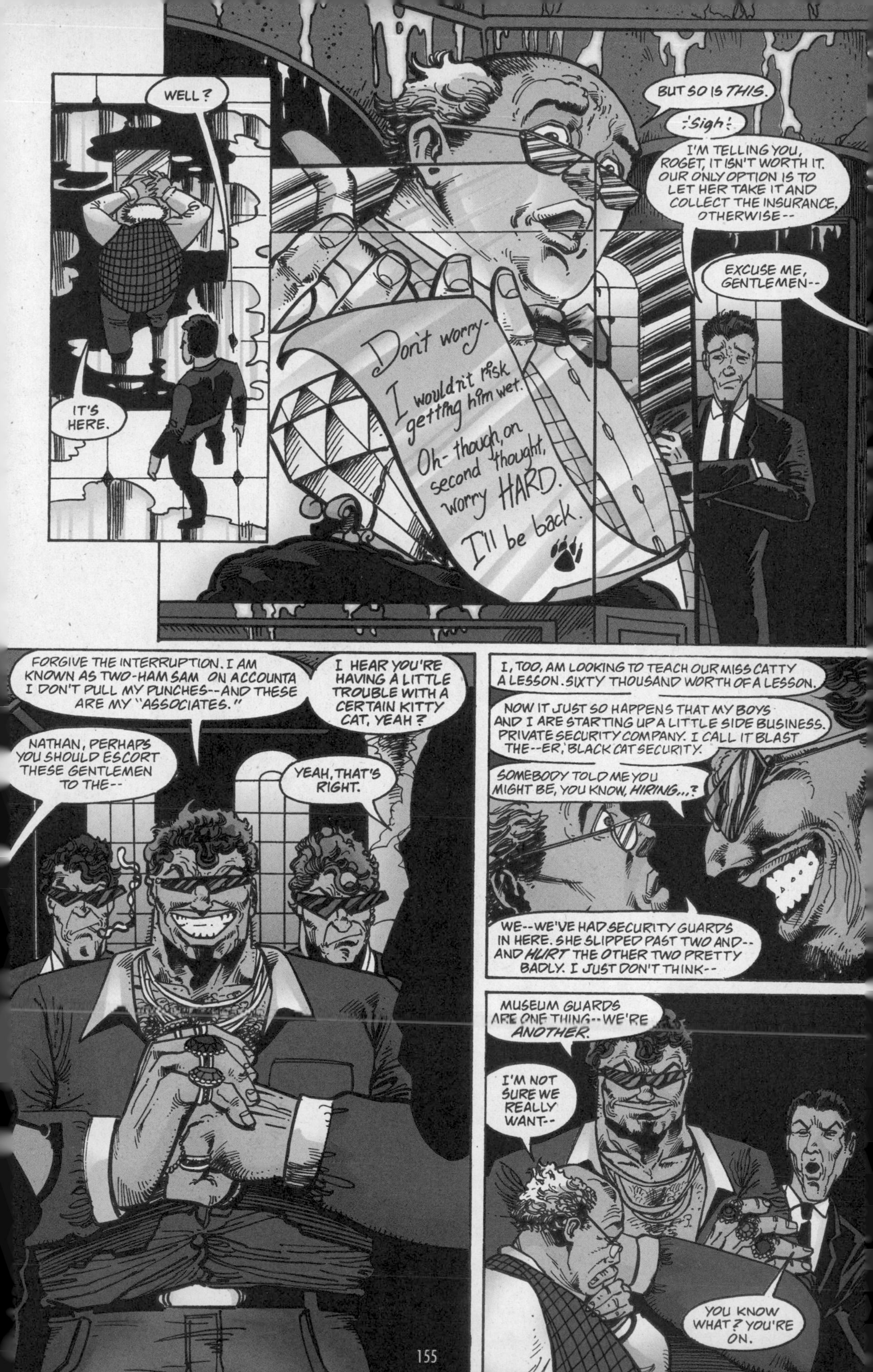
WELL?
IT'S HERE.
BUT SO IS THIS.
-:Sigh:-
I'M TELLING YOU, ROGET, IT ISN'T WORTH IT. OUR ONLY OPTION IS TO LET HER TAKE IT AND COLLECT THE INSURANCE, OTHERWISE--
Don't worry- I wouldn't risk getting him wet. Oh- though, on second thought, worry HARD. I'll be back.
EXCUSE ME, GENTLEMEN--
FORGIVE THE INTERRUPTION. I AM KNOWN AS TWO-HAM SAM ON ACCOUNTA I DON'T PULL MY PUNCHES--AND THESE ARE MY "ASSOCIATES."
I HEAR YOU'RE HAVING A LITTLE TROUBLE WITH A CERTAIN KITTY CAT, YEAH?
NATHAN, PERHAPS YOU SHOULD ESCORT THESE GENTLEMEN TO THE--
YEAH, THAT'S RIGHT.
I, TOO, AM LOOKING TO TEACH OUR MISS CATTY A LESSON. SIXTY THOUSAND WORTH OF A LESSON.
NOW IT JUST SO HAPPENS THAT MY BOYS AND I ARE STARTING UP A LITTLE SIDE BUSINESS. PRIVATE SECURITY COMPANY. I CALL IT BLAST THE--ER, BLACK CAT SECURITY.
SOMEBODY TOLD ME YOU MIGHT BE, YOU KNOW, HIRING...?
WE--WE'VE HAD SECURITY GUARDS IN HERE. SHE SLIPPED PAST TWO AND--AND HURT THE OTHER TWO PRETTY BADLY. I JUST DON'T THINK--
MUSEUM GUARDS ARE ONE THING--WE'RE ANOTHER.
I'M NOT SURE WE REALLY WANT--
YOU KNOW WHAT? YOU'RE ON.

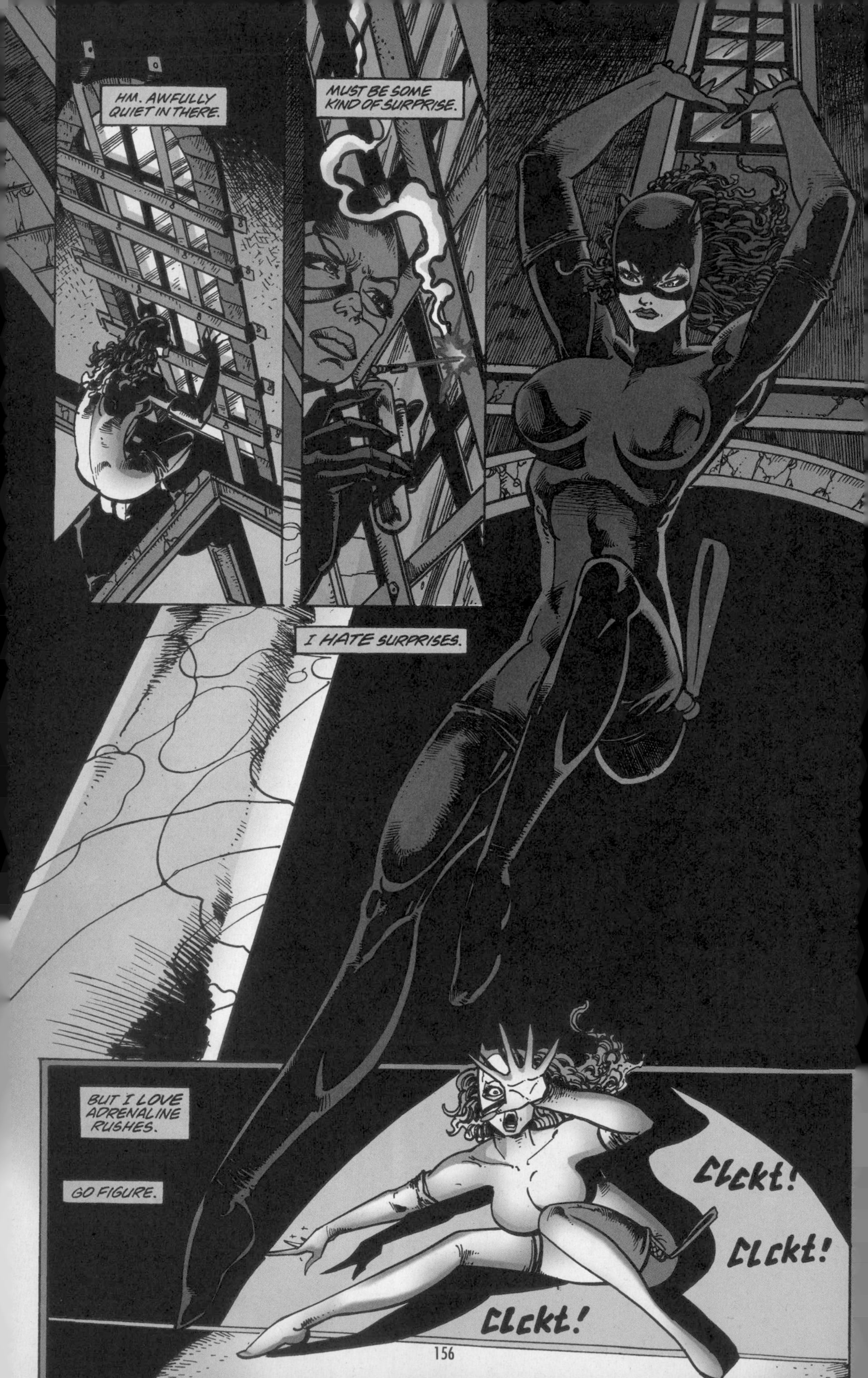
HM. AWFULLY QUIET IN THERE.
MUST BE SOME KIND OF SURPRISE.
I HATE SURPRISES.
BUT I LOVE ADRENALINE RUSHES.
GO FIGURE.
Clckt!
Clckt!
Clckt!

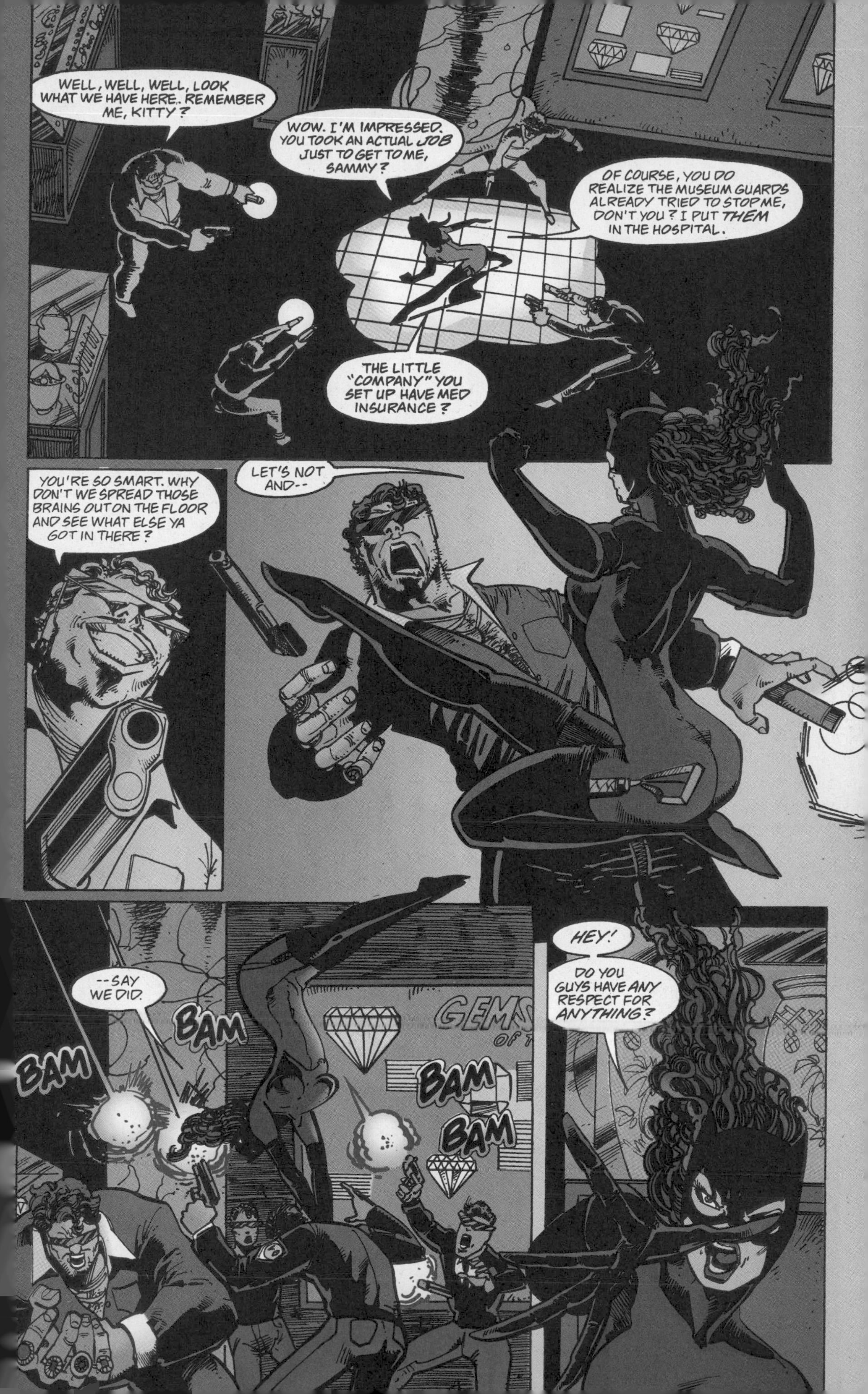
WELL, WELL, WELL, LOOK WHAT WE HAVE HERE.. REMEMBER ME, KITTY?
WOW. I'M IMPRESSED. YOU TOOK AN ACTUAL JOB JUST TO GET TO ME, SAMMY?
OF COURSE, YOU DO REALIZE THE MUSEUM GUARDS ALREADY TRIED TO STOP ME, DON'T YOU? I PUT THEM IN THE HOSPITAL.
THE LITTLE "COMPANY" YOU SET UP HAVE MED INSURANCE?
YOU'RE SO SMART. WHY DON'T WE SPREAD THOSE BRAINS OUT ON THE FLOOR AND SEE WHAT ELSE YA GOT IN THERE?
LET'S NOT AND--
--SAY WE DID.
BAM
BAM
BAM
BAM
HEY!
DO YOU GUYS HAVE ANY RESPECT FOR ANYTHING?

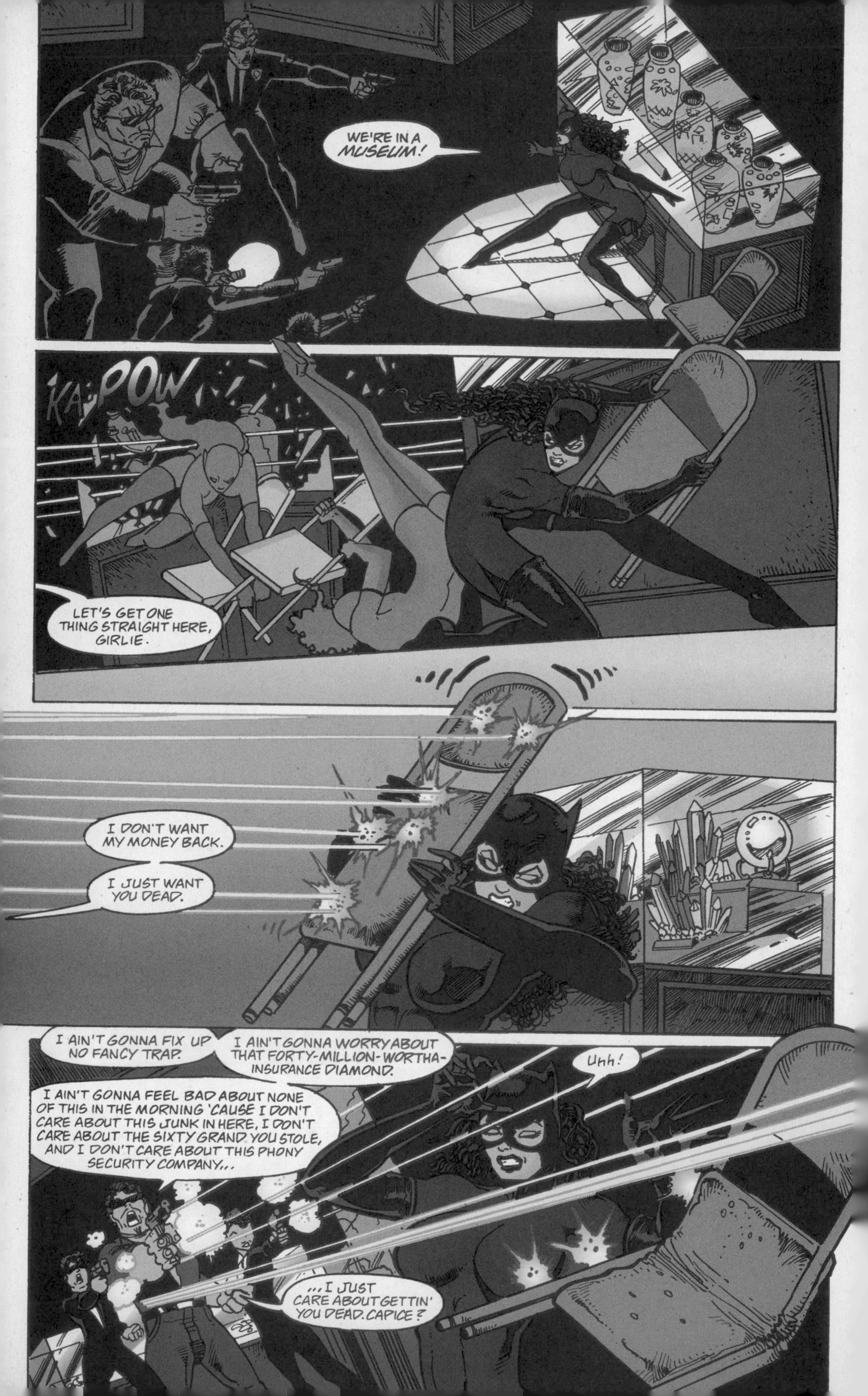
WE'RE IN A MUSEUM!
KA-POW
LET'S GET ONE THING STRAIGHT HERE, GIRLIE.
I DON'T WANT MY MONEY BACK.
I JUST WANT YOU DEAD.
I AIN'T GONNA FIX UP NO FANCY TRAP.
I AIN'T GONNA WORRY ABOUT THAT FORTY-MILLION-WORTHA-INSURANCE DIAMOND.
Uhh!
I AIN'T GONNA FEEL BAD ABOUT NONE OF THIS IN THE MORNING 'CAUSE I DON'T CARE ABOUT THIS JUNK IN HERE, I DON'T CARE ABOUT THE SIXTY GRAND YOU STOLE, AND I DON'T CARE ABOUT THIS PHONY SECURITY COMPANY...
...I JUST CARE ABOUT GETTIN' YOU DEAD. CAPICE?

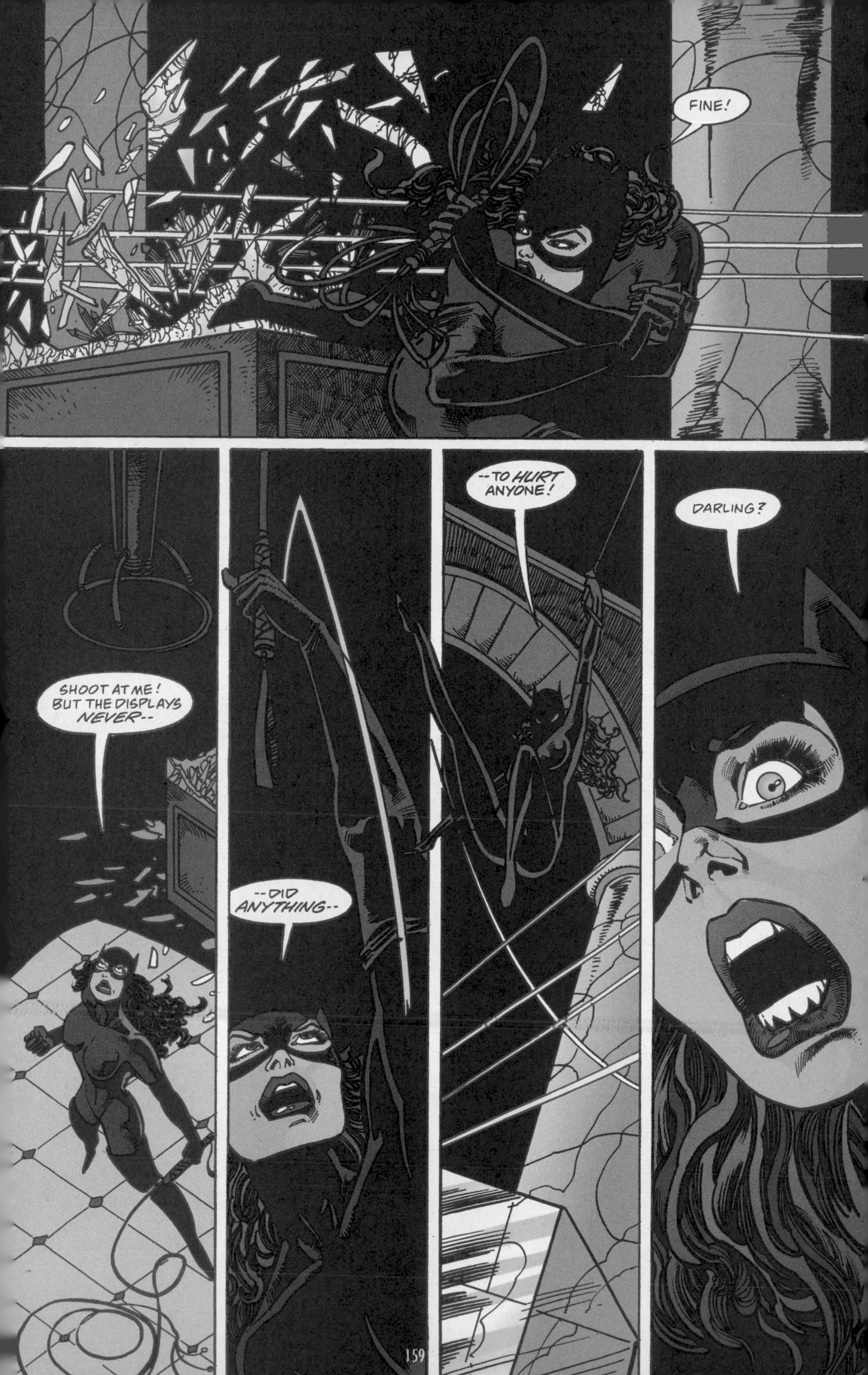
FINE!
SHOOT AT ME! BUT THE DISPLAYS NEVER--
--DID ANYTHING--
--TO HURT ANYONE!
DARLING?

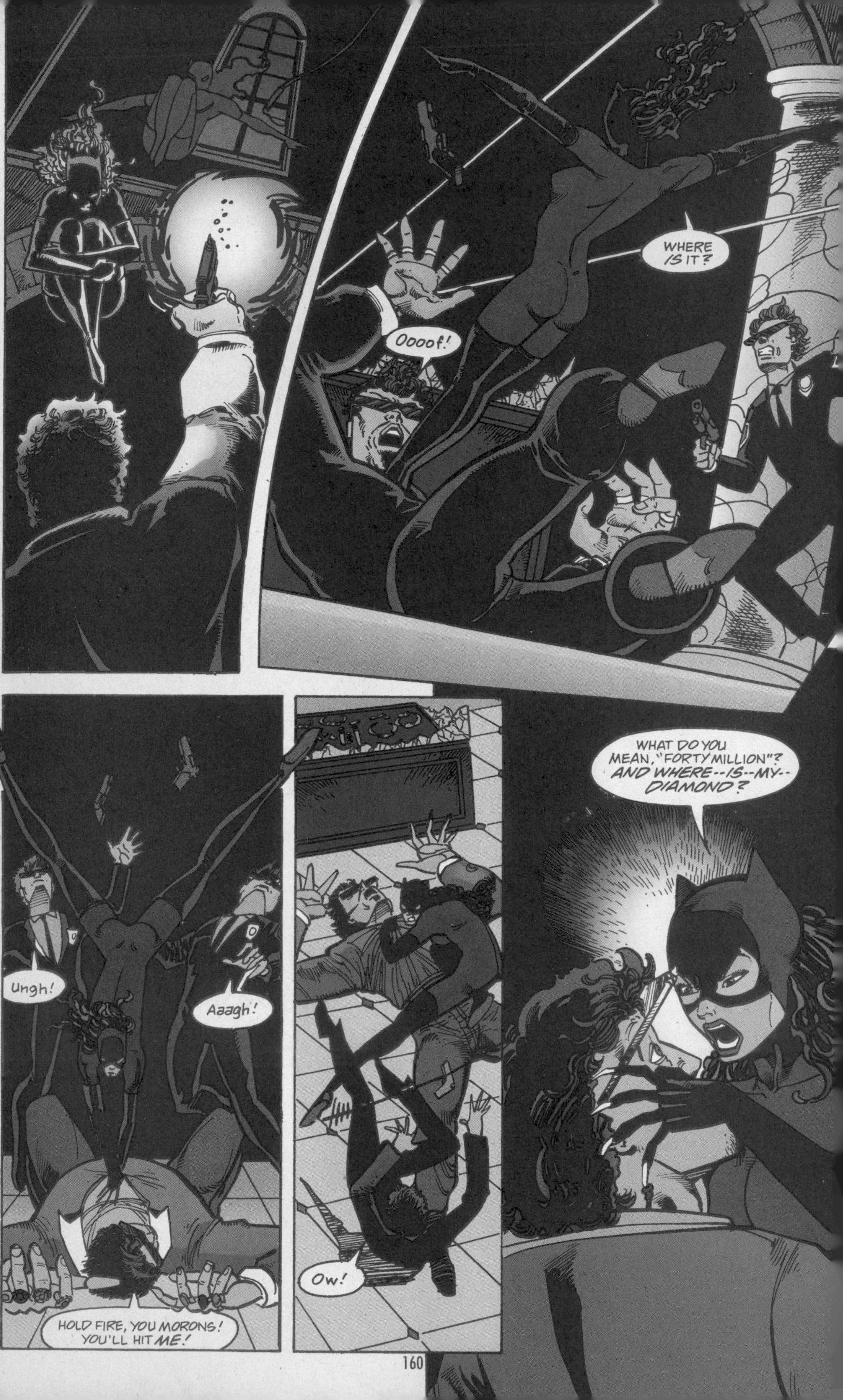
WHERE IS IT?
Ooooof!
Ungh!
Aaagh!
HOLD FIRE, YOU MORONS! YOU'LL HIT ME!
Ow!
WHAT DO YOU MEAN, "FORTY MILLION"? AND WHERE--IS--MY--DIAMOND?

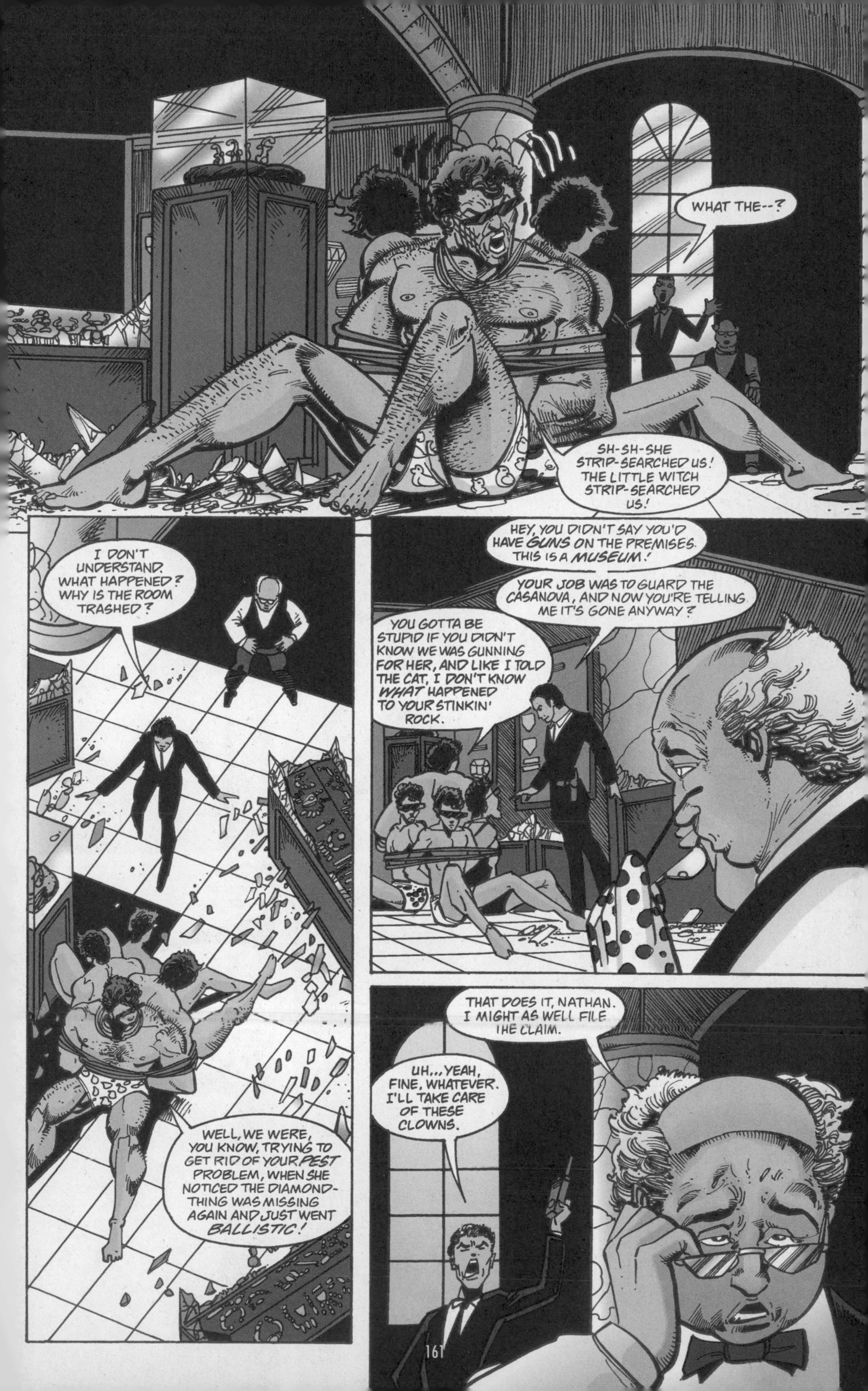
WHAT THE--?
SH-SH-SHE STRIP-SEARCHED US! THE LITTLE WITCH STRIP-SEARCHED US!
I DON'T UNDERSTAND. WHAT HAPPENED? WHY IS THE ROOM TRASHED?
WELL, WE WERE, YOU KNOW, TRYING TO GET RID OF YOUR PEST PROBLEM, WHEN SHE NOTICED THE DIAMOND-THING WAS MISSING AGAIN AND JUST WENT BALLISTIC!
HEY, YOU DIDN'T SAY YOU'D HAVE GUNS ON THE PREMISES. THIS IS A MUSEUM!
YOUR JOB WAS TO GUARD THE CASANOVA, AND NOW YOU'RE TELLING ME IT'S GONE ANYWAY?
YOU GOTTA BE STUPID IF YOU DIDN'T KNOW WE WAS GUNNING FOR HER, AND LIKE I TOLD THE CAT, I DON'T KNOW WHAT HAPPENED TO YOUR STINKIN' ROCK.
THAT DOES IT, NATHAN. I MIGHT AS WELL FILE THE CLAIM.
UH... YEAH, FINE, WHATEVER. I'LL TAKE CARE OF THESE CLOWNS.

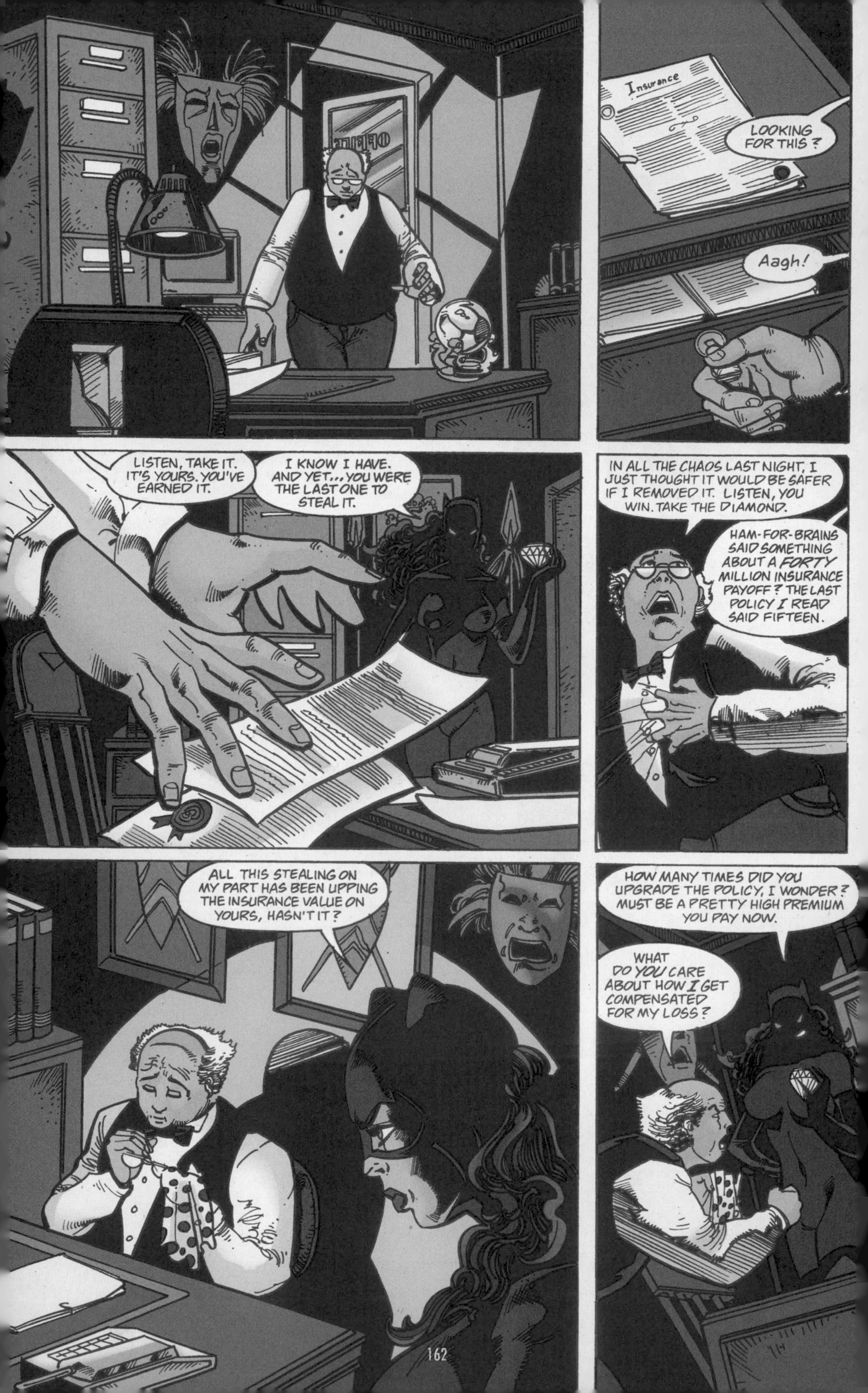
Insurance
LOOKING FOR THIS?
Aagh!
LISTEN, TAKE IT. IT'S YOURS. YOU'VE EARNED IT.
I KNOW I HAVE. AND YET... YOU WERE THE LAST ONE TO STEAL IT.
IN ALL THE CHAOS LAST NIGHT, I JUST THOUGHT IT WOULD BE SAFER IF I REMOVED IT. LISTEN, YOU WIN. TAKE THE DIAMOND.
HAM-FOR-BRAINS SAID SOMETHING ABOUT A FORTY MILLION INSURANCE PAYOFF? THE LAST POLICY I READ SAID FIFTEEN.
ALL THIS STEALING ON MY PART HAS BEEN UPPING THE INSURANCE VALUE ON YOURS, HASN'T IT?
HOW MANY TIMES DID YOU UPGRADE THE POLICY, I WONDER? MUST BE A PRETTY HIGH PREMIUM YOU PAY NOW.
WHAT DO YOU CARE ABOUT HOW I GET COMPENSATED FOR MY LOSS?

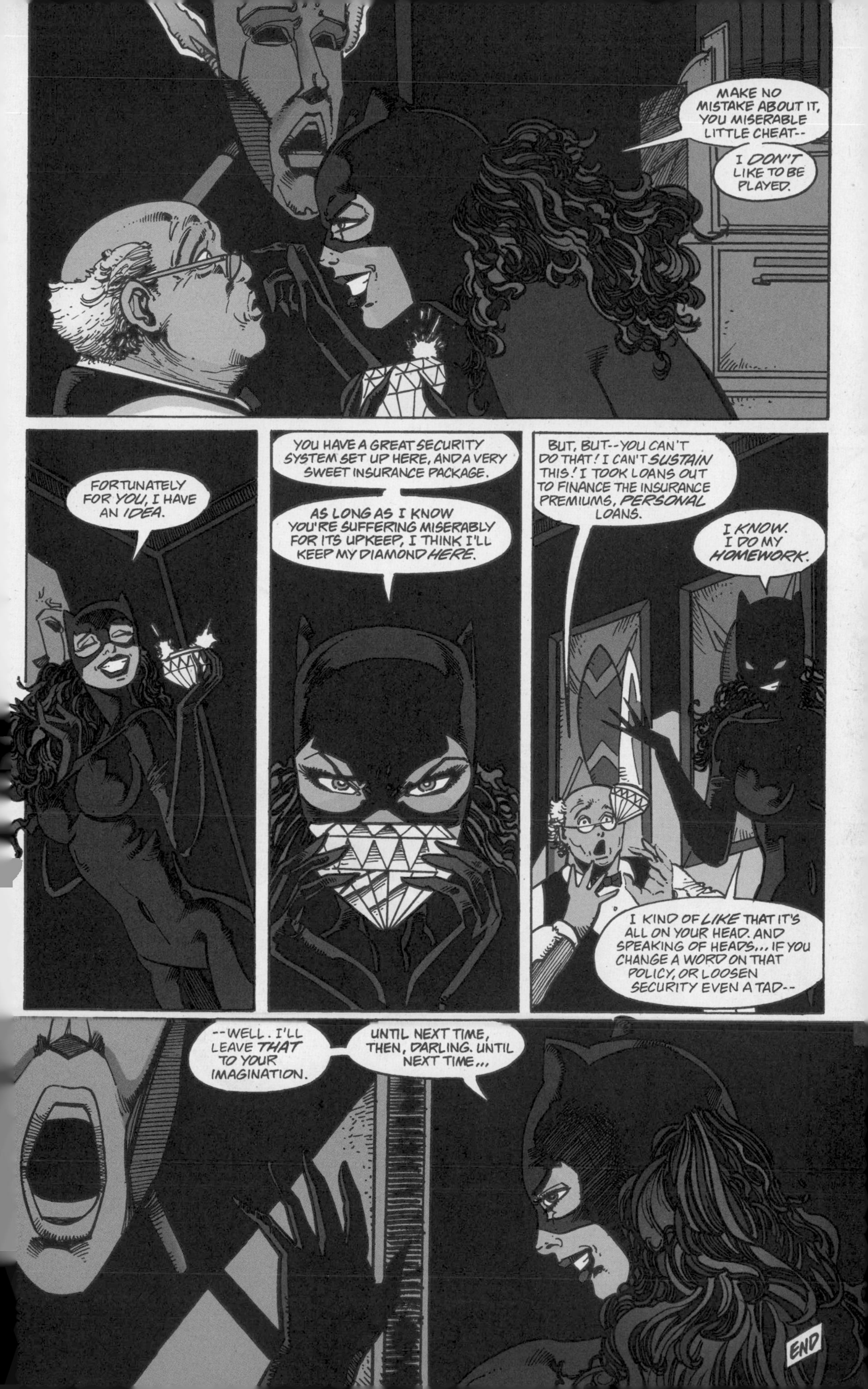
MAKE NO MISTAKE ABOUT IT, YOU MISERABLE LITTLE CHEAT--
I DON'T LIKE TO BE PLAYED.
FORTUNATELY FOR YOU, I HAVE AN IDEA.
YOU HAVE A GREAT SECURITY SYSTEM SET UP HERE, AND A VERY SWEET INSURANCE PACKAGE.
AS LONG AS I KNOW YOU'RE SUFFERING MISERABLY FOR ITS UPKEEP, I THINK I'LL KEEP MY DIAMOND HERE.
BUT, BUT--YOU CAN'T DO THAT! I CAN'T SUSTAIN THIS! I TOOK LOANS OUT TO FINANCE THE INSURANCE PREMIUMS, PERSONAL LOANS.
I KNOW. I DO MY HOMEWORK.
I KIND OF LIKE THAT IT'S ALL ON YOUR HEAD. AND SPEAKING OF HEADS... IF YOU CHANGE A WORD ON THAT POLICY, OR LOOSEN SECURITY EVEN A TAD--
--WELL. I'LL LEAVE THAT TO YOUR IMAGINATION.
UNTIL NEXT TIME, THEN, DARLING. UNTIL NEXT TIME...
END

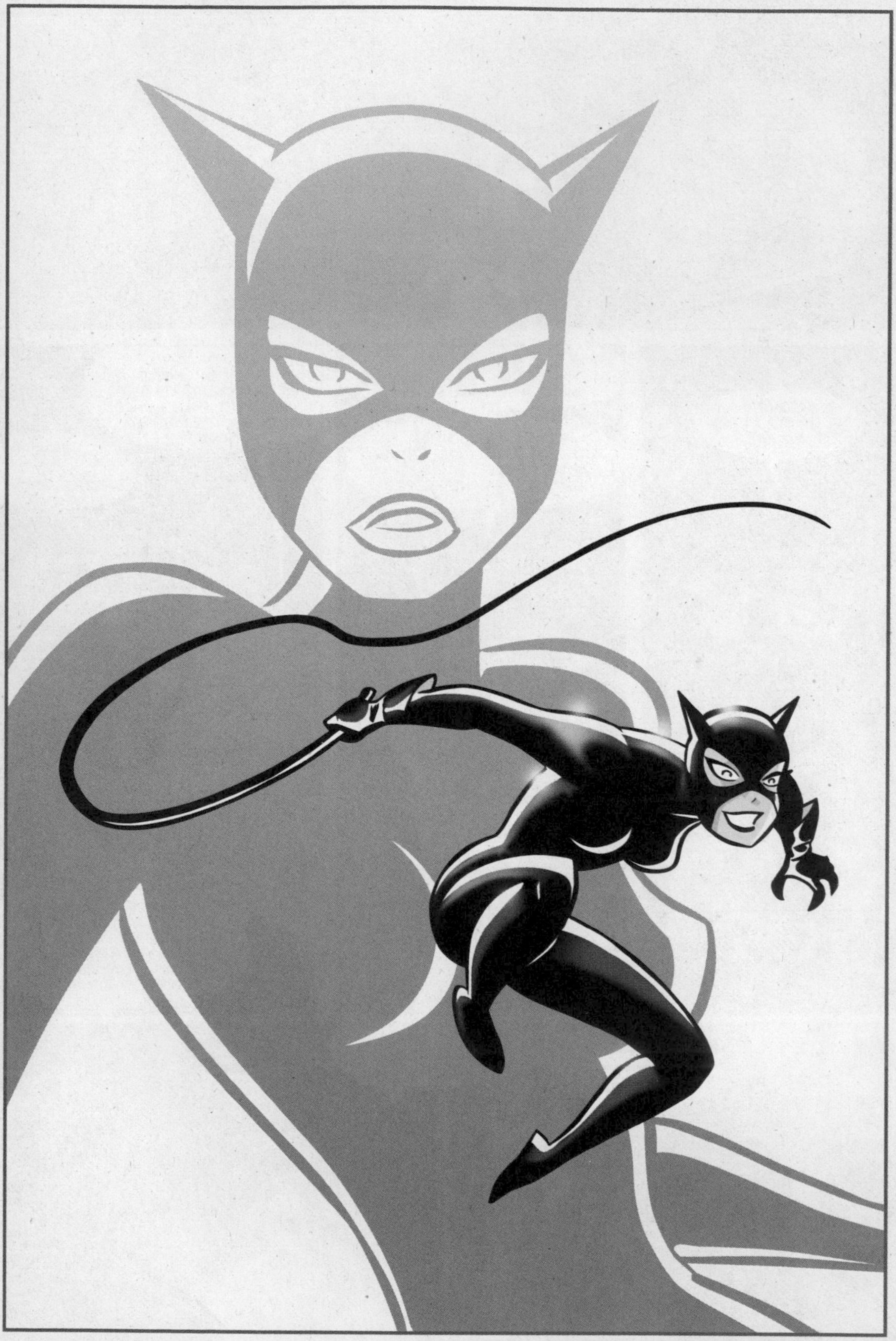

Originally done for the development of the *Batman: The Animated Series* TV show. Colored by Drew R. Moore.

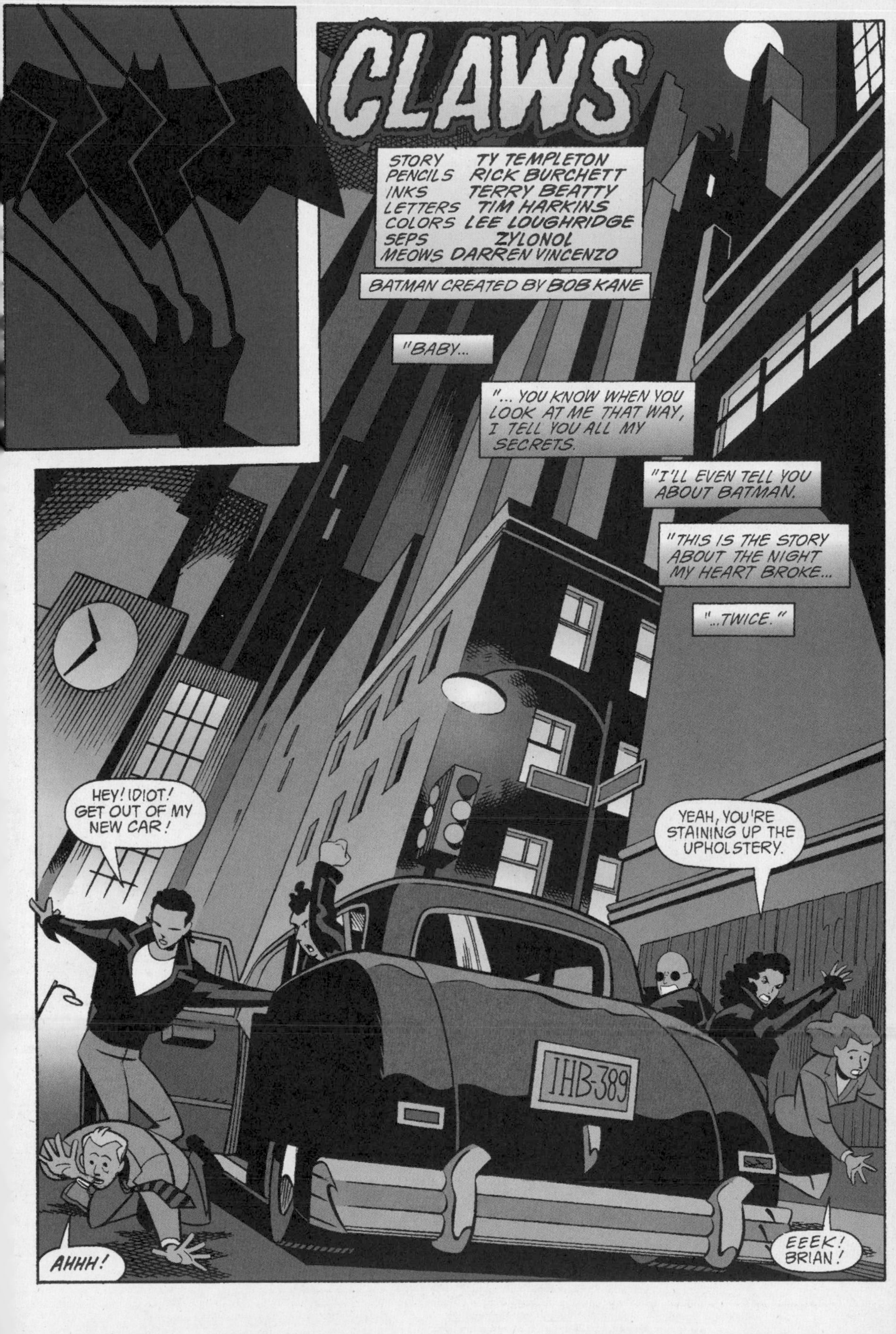

CLAWS
STORY TY TEMPLETON
PENCILS RICK BURCHETT
INKS TERRY BEATTY
LETTERS TIM HARKINS
COLORS LEE LOUGHRIDGE
SEPS ZYLONOL
MEOWS DARREN VINCENZO
BATMAN CREATED BY BOB KANE
"BABY...
"... YOU KNOW WHEN YOU LOOK AT ME THAT WAY, I TELL YOU ALL MY SECRETS.
"I'LL EVEN TELL YOU ABOUT BATMAN.
"THIS IS THE STORY ABOUT THE NIGHT MY HEART BROKE...
"...TWICE."
HEY! IDIOT! GET OUT OF MY NEW CAR!
YEAH, YOU'RE STAINING UP THE UPHOLSTERY.
IHB-389
AHHH!
EEEK! BRIAN!

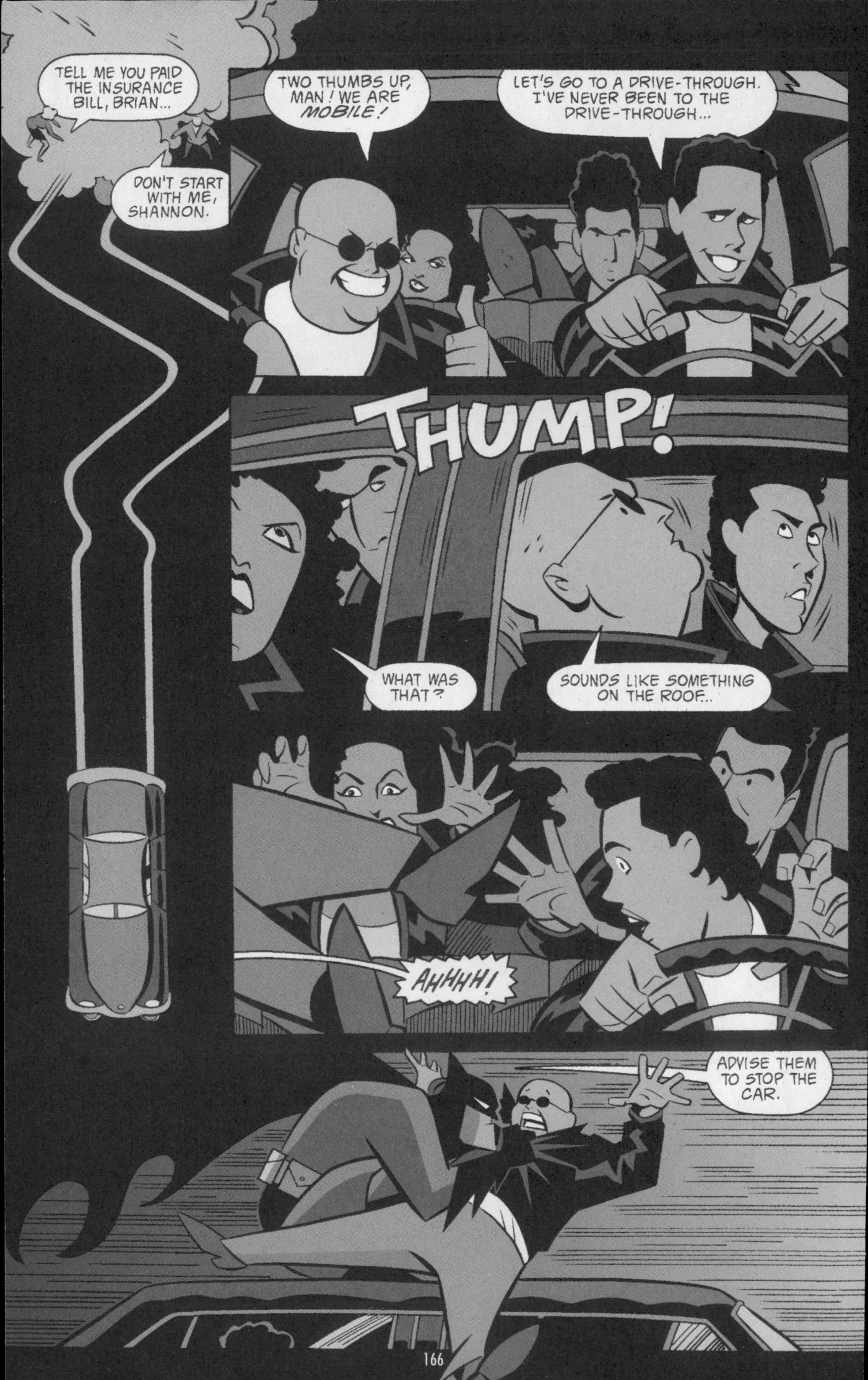
TELL ME YOU PAID THE INSURANCE BILL, BRIAN...
DON'T START WITH ME, SHANNON.
TWO THUMBS UP, MAN! WE ARE MOBILE!
LET'S GO TO A DRIVE-THROUGH. I'VE NEVER BEEN TO THE DRIVE-THROUGH...
THUMP!
WHAT WAS THAT?
SOUNDS LIKE SOMETHING ON THE ROOF..
AHHHH!
ADVISE THEM TO STOP THE CAR.

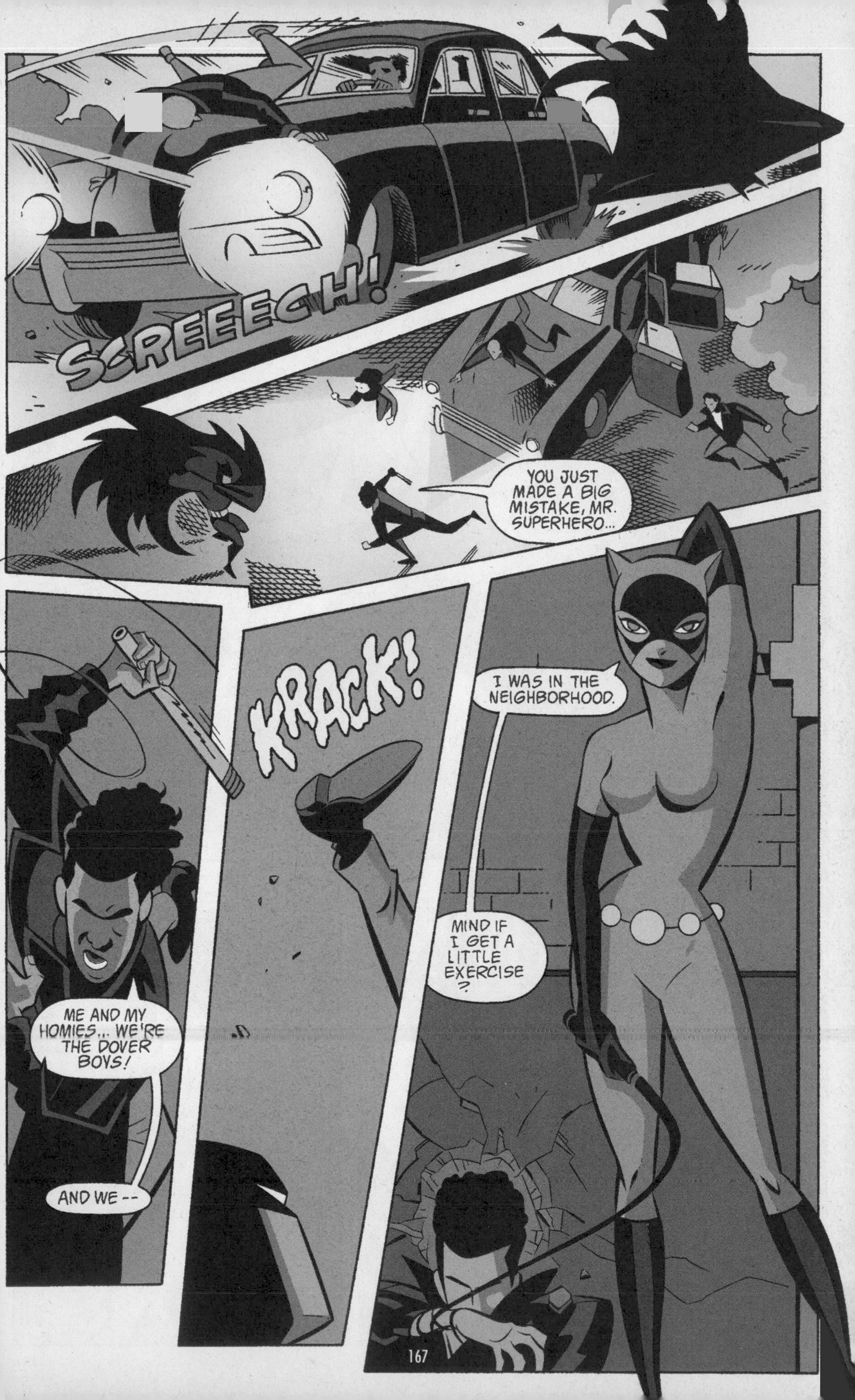
SCREEECH!
YOU JUST MADE A BIG MISTAKE, MR. SUPERHERO...
ME AND MY HOMIES... WE'RE THE DOVER BOYS!
AND WE --
KRACK!
I WAS IN THE NEIGHBORHOOD.
MIND IF I GET A LITTLE EXERCISE?

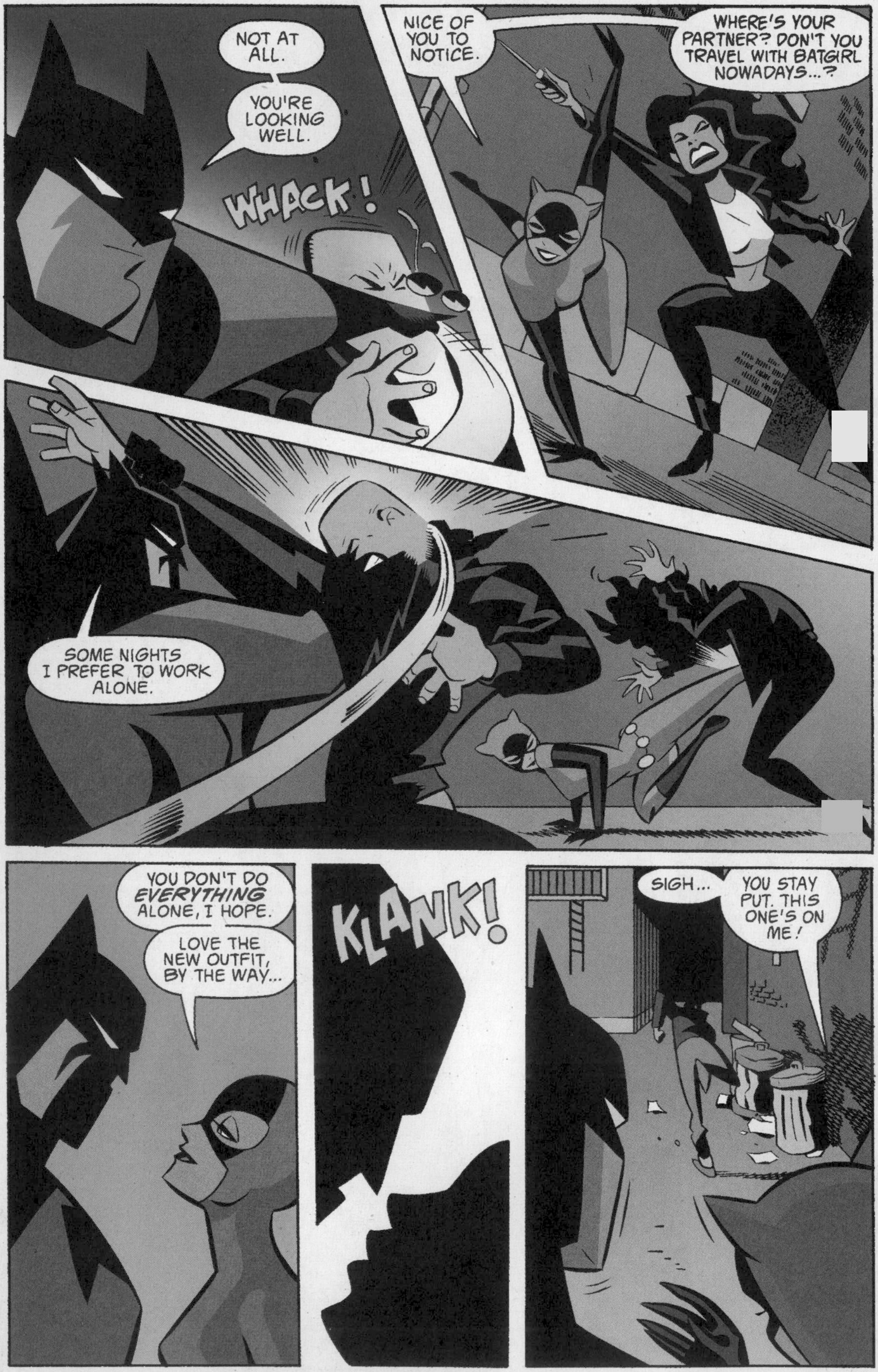
NOT AT ALL.
YOU'RE LOOKING WELL.
WHACK!
NICE OF YOU TO NOTICE.
WHERE'S YOUR PARTNER? DON'T YOU TRAVEL WITH BATGIRL NOWADAYS...?
SOME NIGHTS I PREFER TO WORK ALONE.
YOU DON'T DO *EVERYTHING* ALONE, I HOPE.
LOVE THE NEW OUTFIT, BY THE WAY...
KLANK!
SIGH...
YOU STAY PUT. THIS ONE'S ON ME!

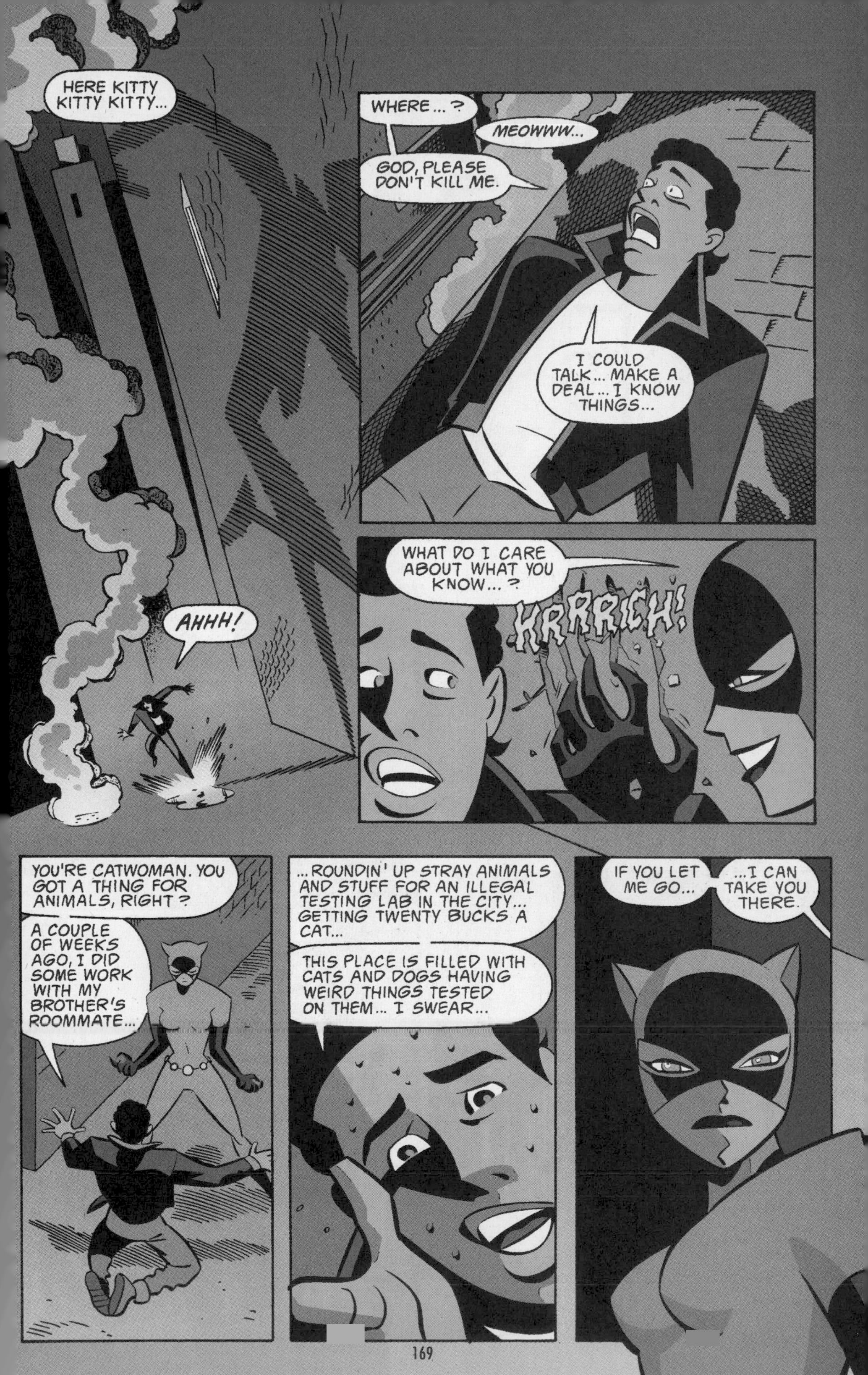
HERE KITTY KITTY KITTY...
AHHH!
WHERE...?
MEOWWW...
GOD, PLEASE DON'T KILL ME.
I COULD TALK... MAKE A DEAL... I KNOW THINGS...
WHAT DO I CARE ABOUT WHAT YOU KNOW...?
KRRRICH!
YOU'RE CATWOMAN. YOU GOT A THING FOR ANIMALS, RIGHT?
A COUPLE OF WEEKS AGO, I DID SOME WORK WITH MY BROTHER'S ROOMMATE...
...ROUNDIN' UP STRAY ANIMALS AND STUFF FOR AN ILLEGAL TESTING LAB IN THE CITY... GETTING TWENTY BUCKS A CAT...
THIS PLACE IS FILLED WITH CATS AND DOGS HAVING WEIRD THINGS TESTED ON THEM... I SWEAR...
IF YOU LET ME GO...
...I CAN TAKE YOU THERE.

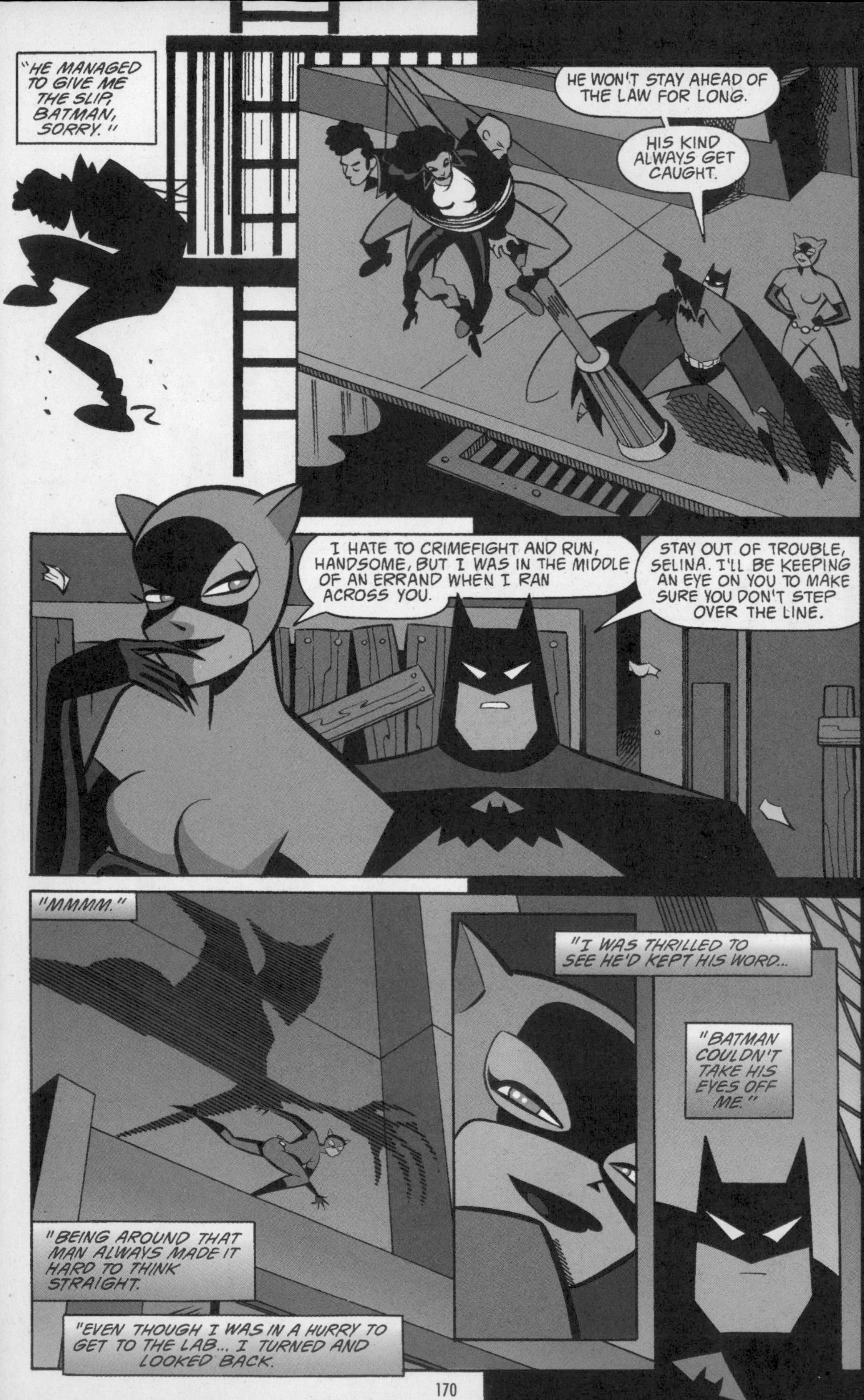
"HE MANAGED TO GIVE ME THE SLIP, BATMAN, SORRY."
HE WON'T STAY AHEAD OF THE LAW FOR LONG.
HIS KIND ALWAYS GET CAUGHT.
I HATE TO CRIMEFIGHT AND RUN, HANDSOME, BUT I WAS IN THE MIDDLE OF AN ERRAND WHEN I RAN ACROSS YOU.
STAY OUT OF TROUBLE, SELINA. I'LL BE KEEPING AN EYE ON YOU TO MAKE SURE YOU DON'T STEP OVER THE LINE.
"MMMM."
"BEING AROUND THAT MAN ALWAYS MADE IT HARD TO THINK STRAIGHT.
"EVEN THOUGH I WAS IN A HURRY TO GET TO THE LAB... I TURNED AND LOOKED BACK.
"I WAS THRILLED TO SEE HE'D KEPT HIS WORD...
"BATMAN COULDN'T TAKE HIS EYES OFF ME."

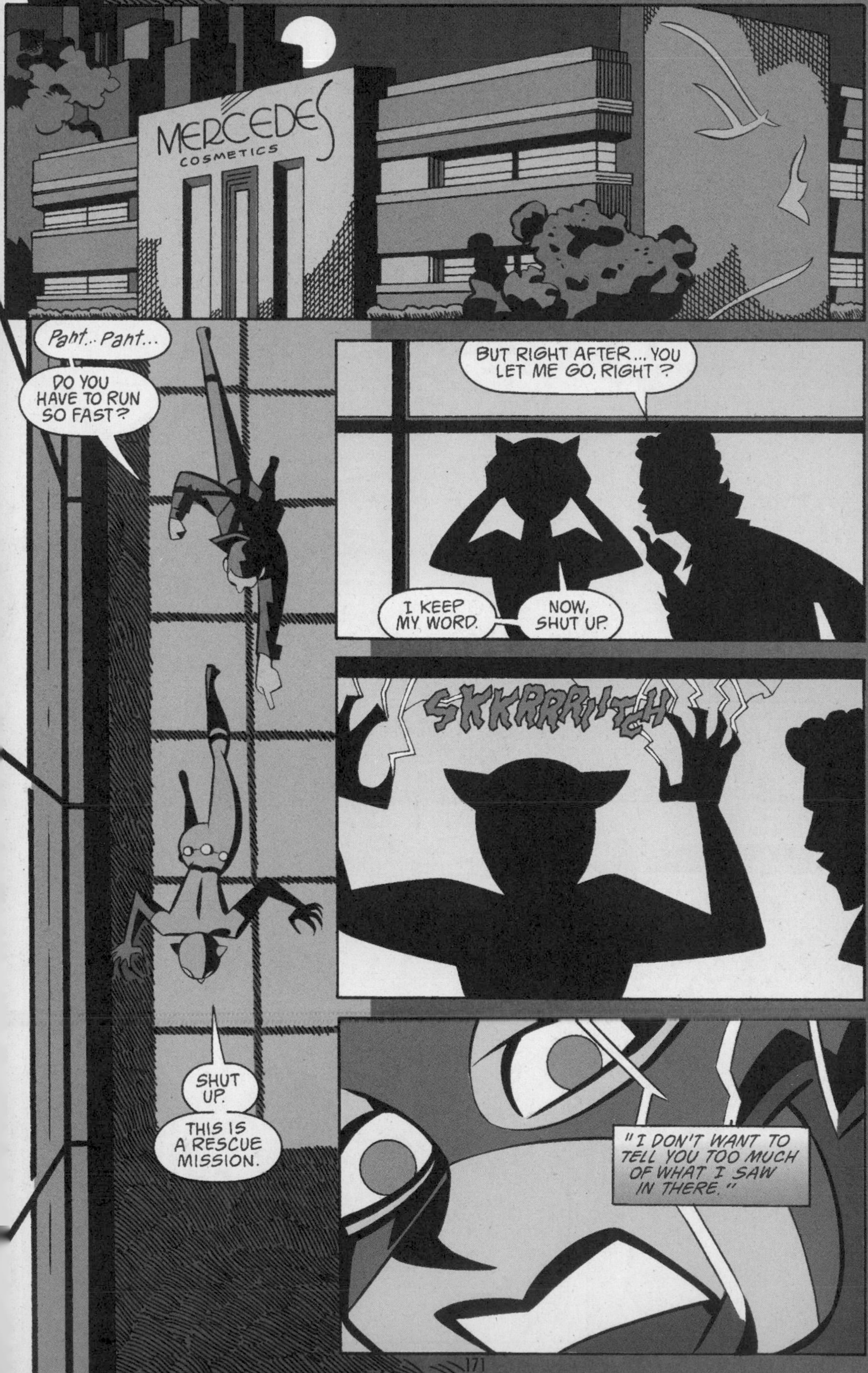
MERCEDES
COSMETICS
Pant... Pant...
DO YOU HAVE TO RUN SO FAST?
SHUT UP.
THIS IS A RESCUE MISSION.
BUT RIGHT AFTER... YOU LET ME GO, RIGHT?
I KEEP MY WORD.
NOW, SHUT UP.
SKKRRRIITCH
"I DON'T WANT TO TELL YOU TOO MUCH OF WHAT I SAW IN THERE."

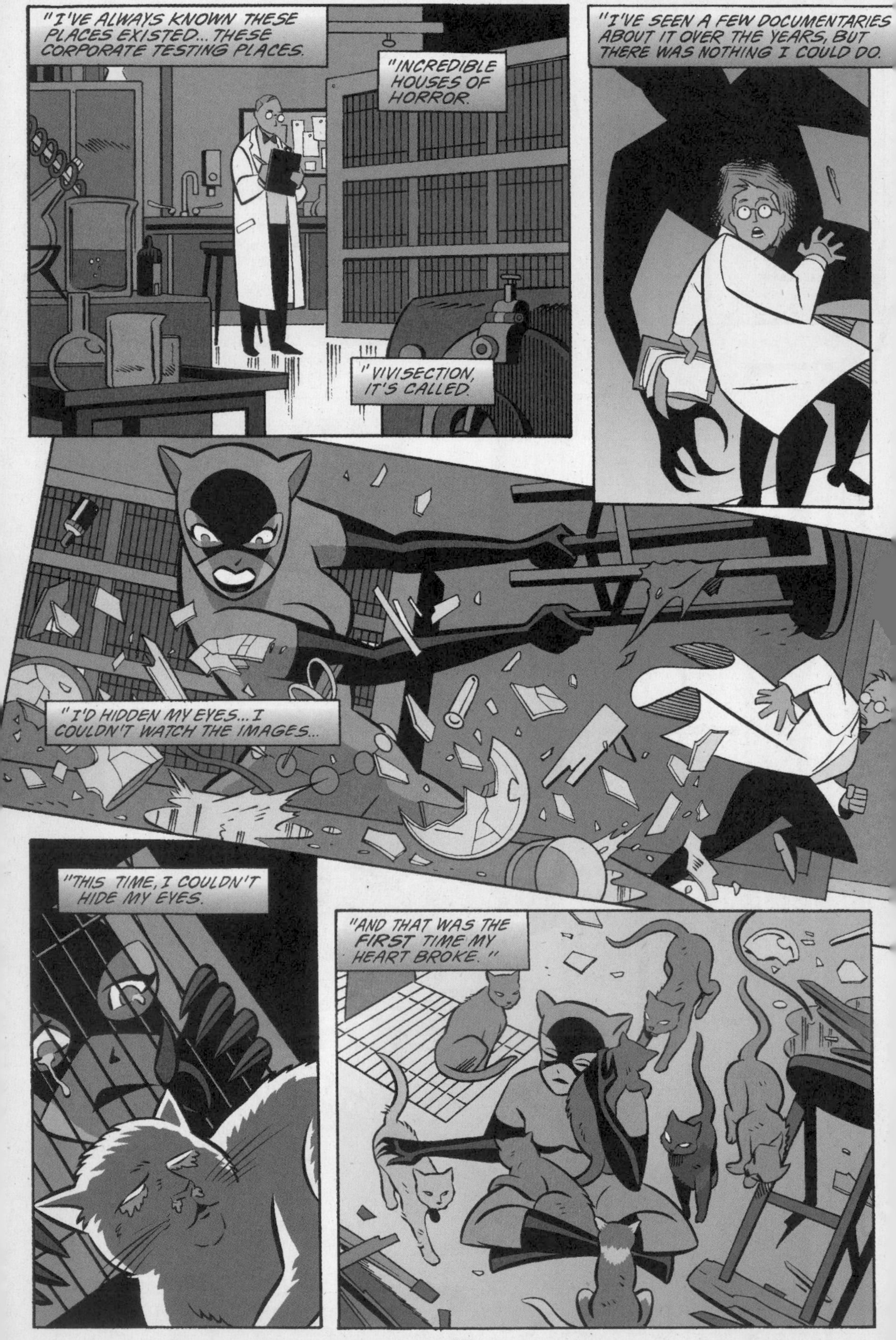
"I'VE ALWAYS KNOWN THESE PLACES EXISTED... THESE CORPORATE TESTING PLACES.
"INCREDIBLE HOUSES OF HORROR.
"VIVISECTION, IT'S CALLED.
"I'VE SEEN A FEW DOCUMENTARIES ABOUT IT OVER THE YEARS, BUT THERE WAS NOTHING I COULD DO.
"I'D HIDDEN MY EYES... I COULDN'T WATCH THE IMAGES...
"THIS TIME, I COULDN'T HIDE MY EYES.
"AND THAT WAS THE FIRST TIME MY HEART BROKE."

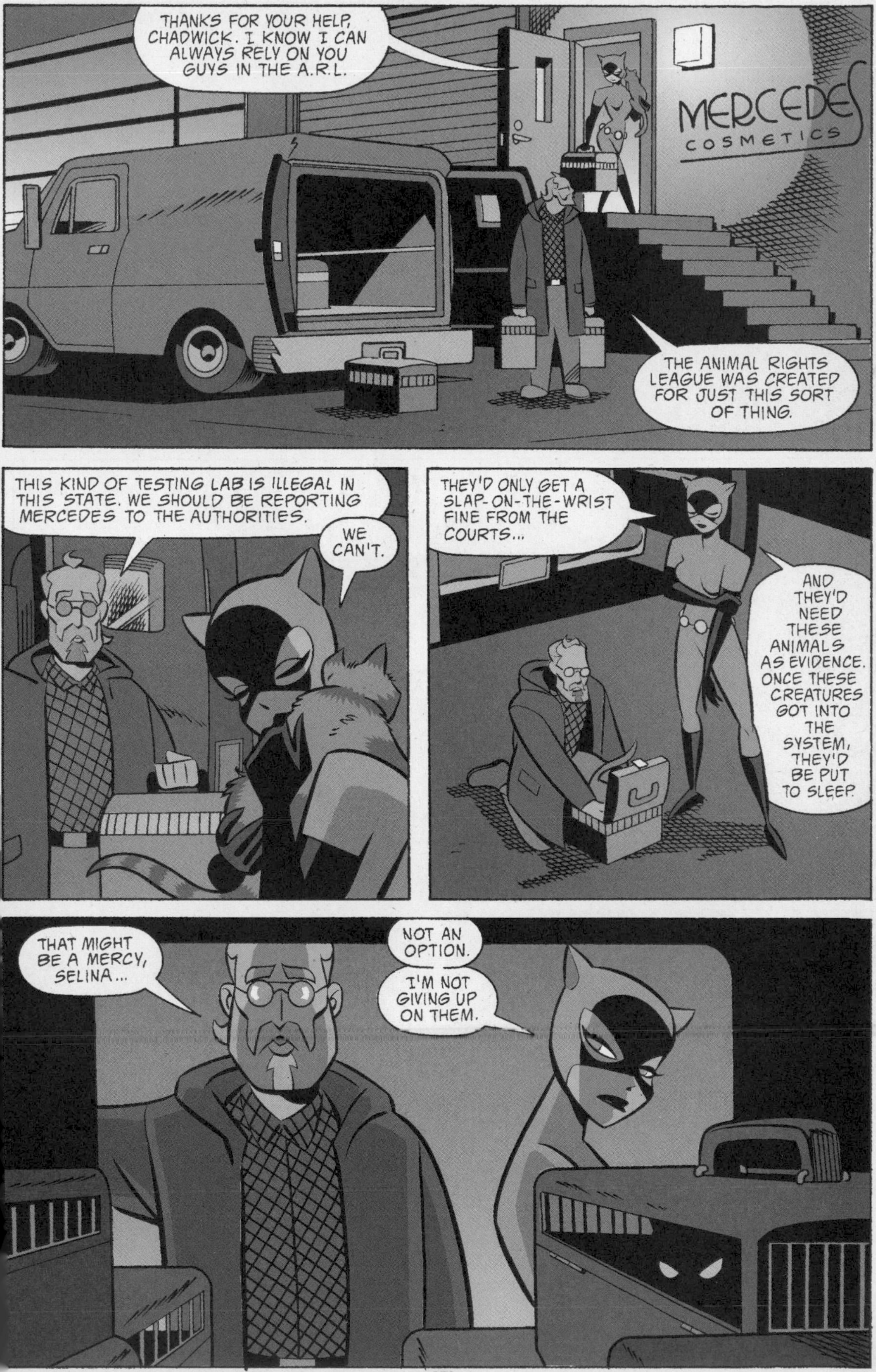
THANKS FOR YOUR HELP, CHADWICK. I KNOW I CAN ALWAYS RELY ON YOU GUYS IN THE A.R.L.
MERCEDES
COSMETICS
THE ANIMAL RIGHTS LEAGUE WAS CREATED FOR JUST THIS SORT OF THING.
THIS KIND OF TESTING LAB IS ILLEGAL IN THIS STATE. WE SHOULD BE REPORTING MERCEDES TO THE AUTHORITIES.
WE CAN'T.
THEY'D ONLY GET A SLAP-ON-THE-WRIST FINE FROM THE COURTS...
AND THEY'D NEED THESE ANIMALS AS EVIDENCE. ONCE THESE CREATURES GOT INTO THE SYSTEM, THEY'D BE PUT TO SLEEP.
THAT MIGHT BE A MERCY, SELINA...
NOT AN OPTION.
I'M NOT GIVING UP ON THEM.

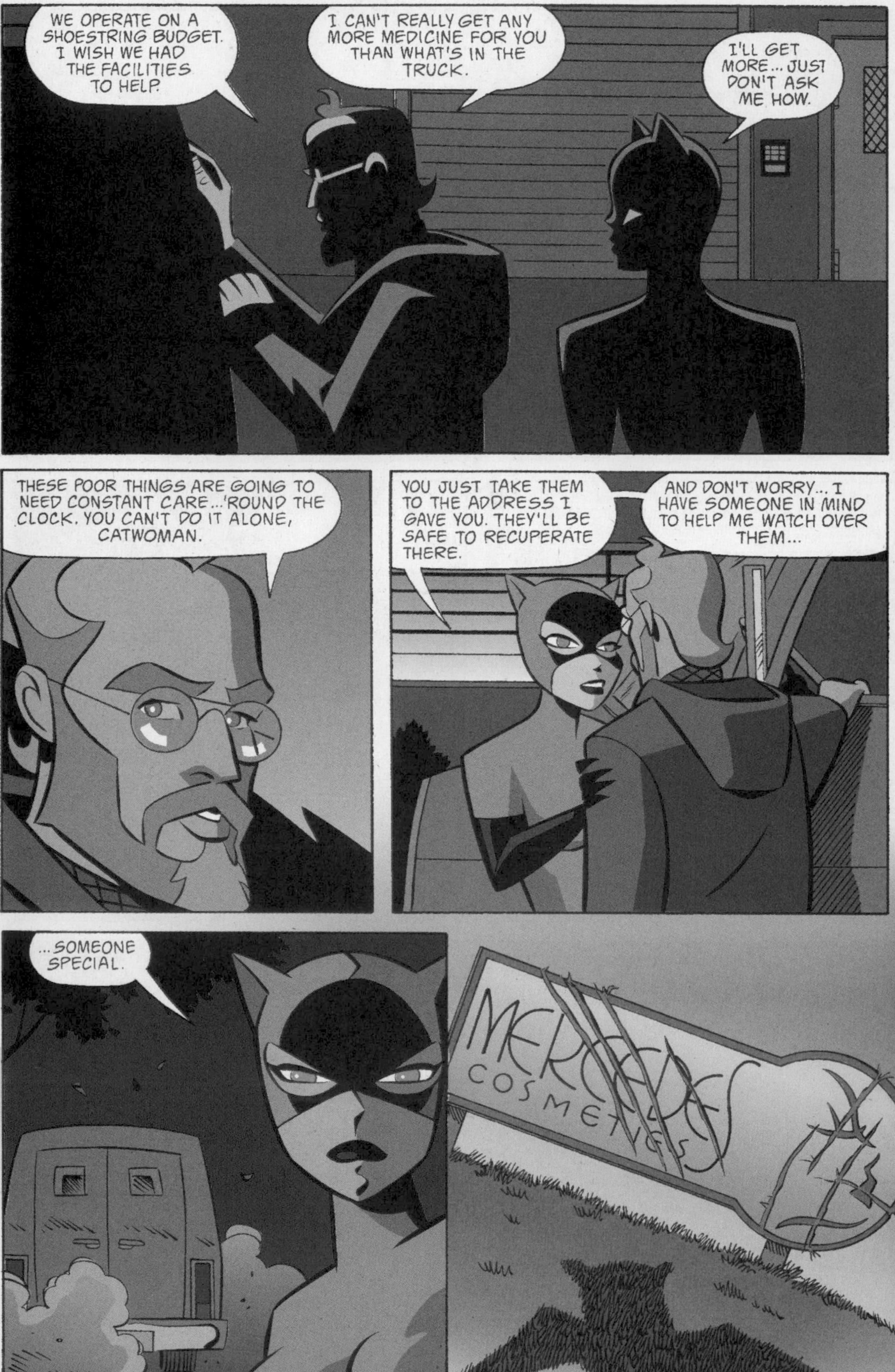
WE OPERATE ON A SHOESTRING BUDGET. I WISH WE HAD THE FACILITIES TO HELP.
I CAN'T REALLY GET ANY MORE MEDICINE FOR YOU THAN WHAT'S IN THE TRUCK.
I'LL GET MORE... JUST DON'T ASK ME HOW.
THESE POOR THINGS ARE GOING TO NEED CONSTANT CARE...'ROUND THE CLOCK. YOU CAN'T DO IT ALONE, CATWOMAN.
YOU JUST TAKE THEM TO THE ADDRESS I GAVE YOU. THEY'LL BE SAFE TO RECUPERATE THERE.
AND DON'T WORRY... I HAVE SOMEONE IN MIND TO HELP ME WATCH OVER THEM...
...SOMEONE SPECIAL.
MERCEDES COSMETICS

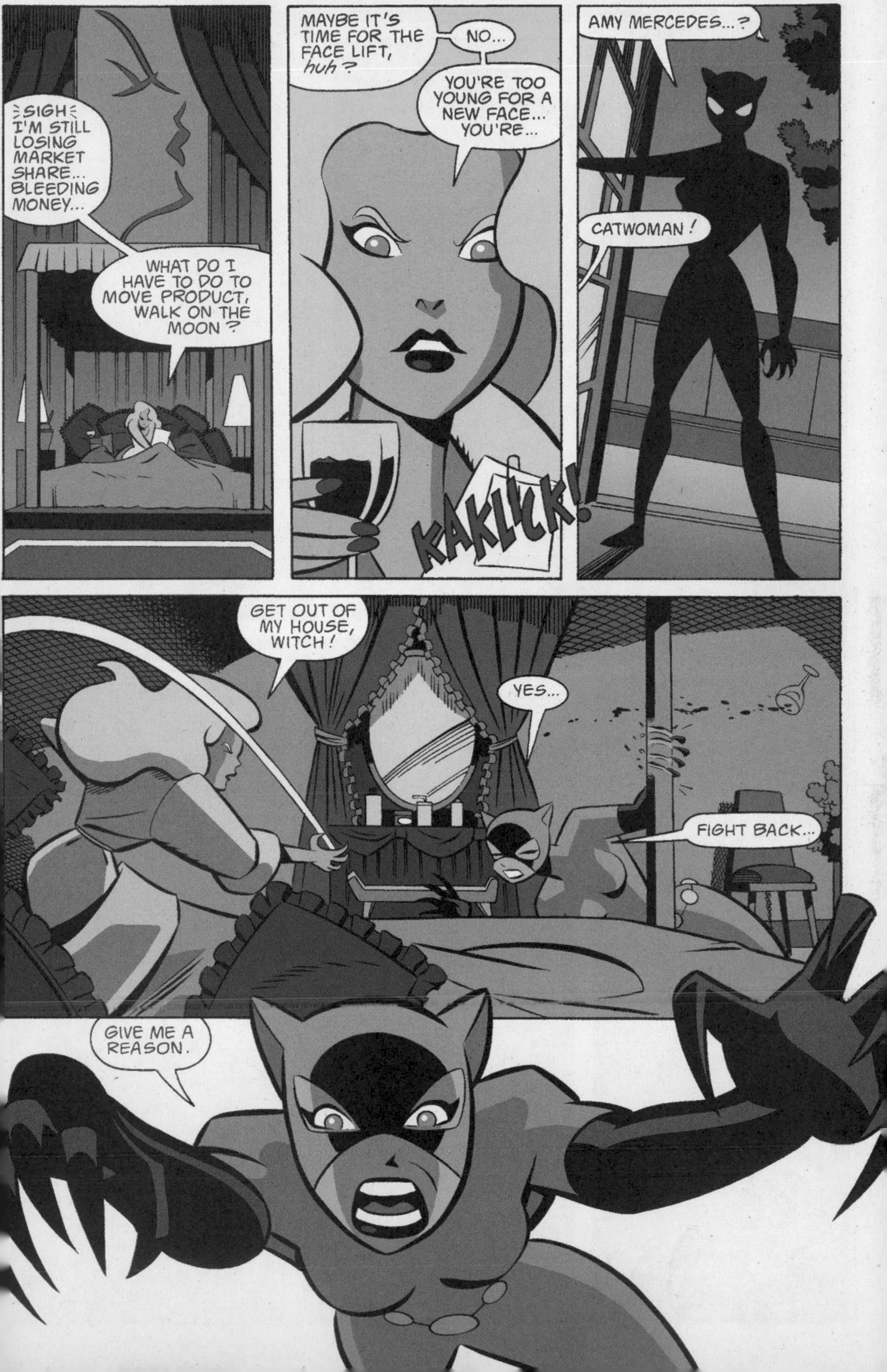

≶SIGH≷ I'M STILL LOSING MARKET SHARE... BLEEDING MONEY...
WHAT DO I HAVE TO DO TO MOVE PRODUCT, WALK ON THE MOON?
MAYBE IT'S TIME FOR THE FACE LIFT, huh?
NO...
YOU'RE TOO YOUNG FOR A NEW FACE... YOU'RE...
KAKLICK!
AMY MERCEDES...?
CATWOMAN!
GET OUT OF MY HOUSE, WITCH!
YES...
FIGHT BACK...
GIVE ME A REASON.

YOU'RE DEAD, CATWOMAN.

YOU ARE *SO* DEAD...

AND YOU ARE FAMOUS FOR BEING A *"HANDS-ON"* COMPANY PRESIDENT, MS. MERCEDES...

SO I WON'T BELIEVE YOU DON'T KNOW ANYTHING ABOUT YOUR COSMETICS TESTING FACILITIES...

...AND WHAT BUTCHERY WENT ON THERE.

THIS IS ABOUT *THAT*?

YES, THAT.

I HAVE TWENTY-FOUR SICK CATS ON MY HANDS THAT NEED CARE AND ATTENTION TO GET WELL...

THAT'S GOING TO BE YOUR JOB.

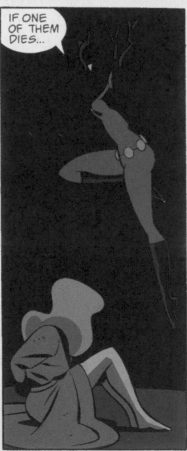

IF ONE OF THEM DIES...

...YOU'RE NEXT!

176

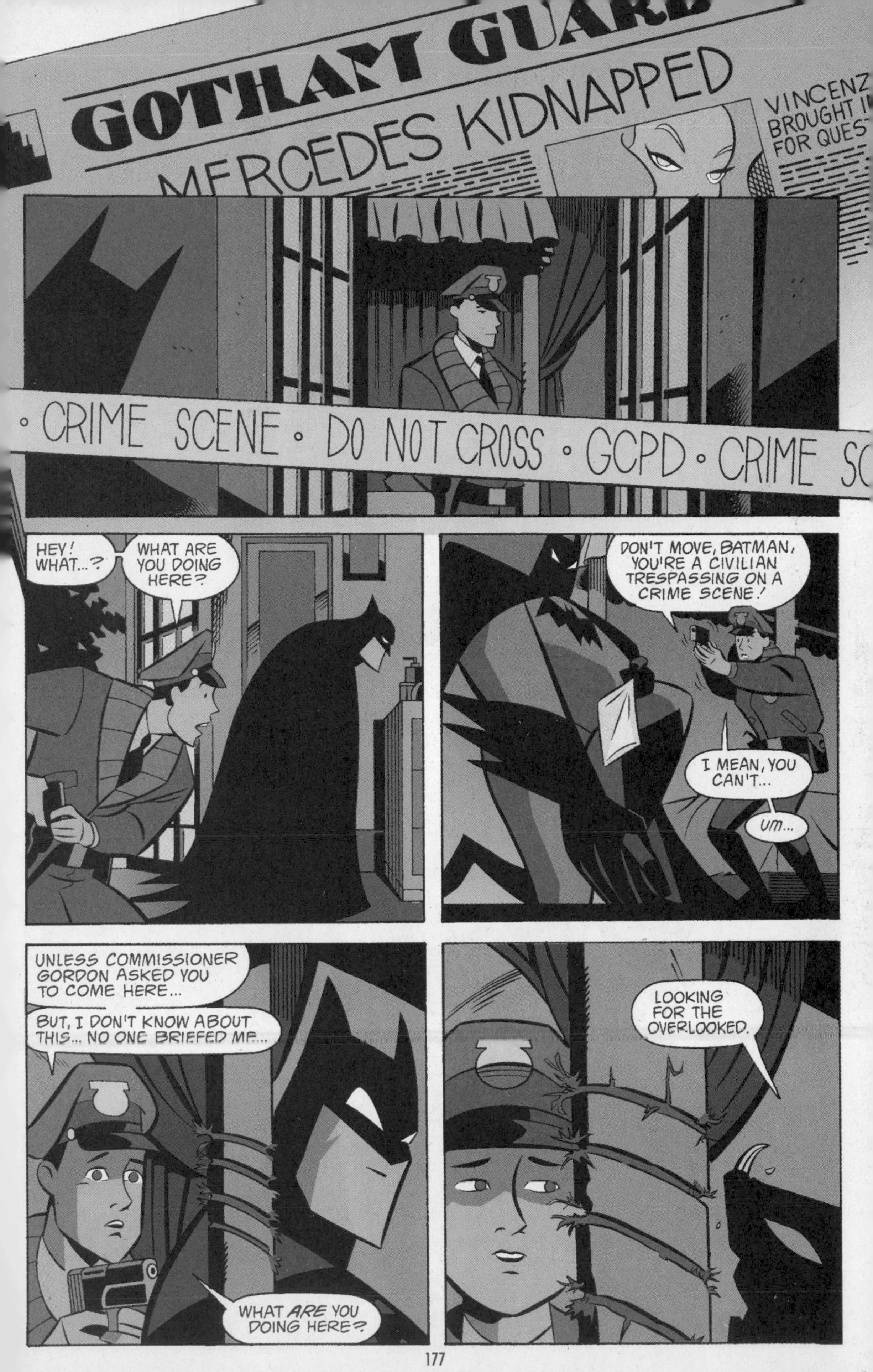

GOTHAM GUARD
MERCEDES KIDNAPPED
VINCENZ BROUGHT I FOR QUES
• CRIME SCENE • DO NOT CROSS • GCPD • CRIME SC
HEY! WHAT...?
WHAT ARE YOU DOING HERE?
DON'T MOVE, BATMAN, YOU'RE A CIVILIAN TRESPASSING ON A CRIME SCENE!
I MEAN, YOU CAN'T...
UM...
UNLESS COMMISSIONER GORDON ASKED YOU TO COME HERE...
BUT, I DON'T KNOW ABOUT THIS... NO ONE BRIEFED ME...
WHAT ARE YOU DOING HERE?
LOOKING FOR THE OVERLOOKED.

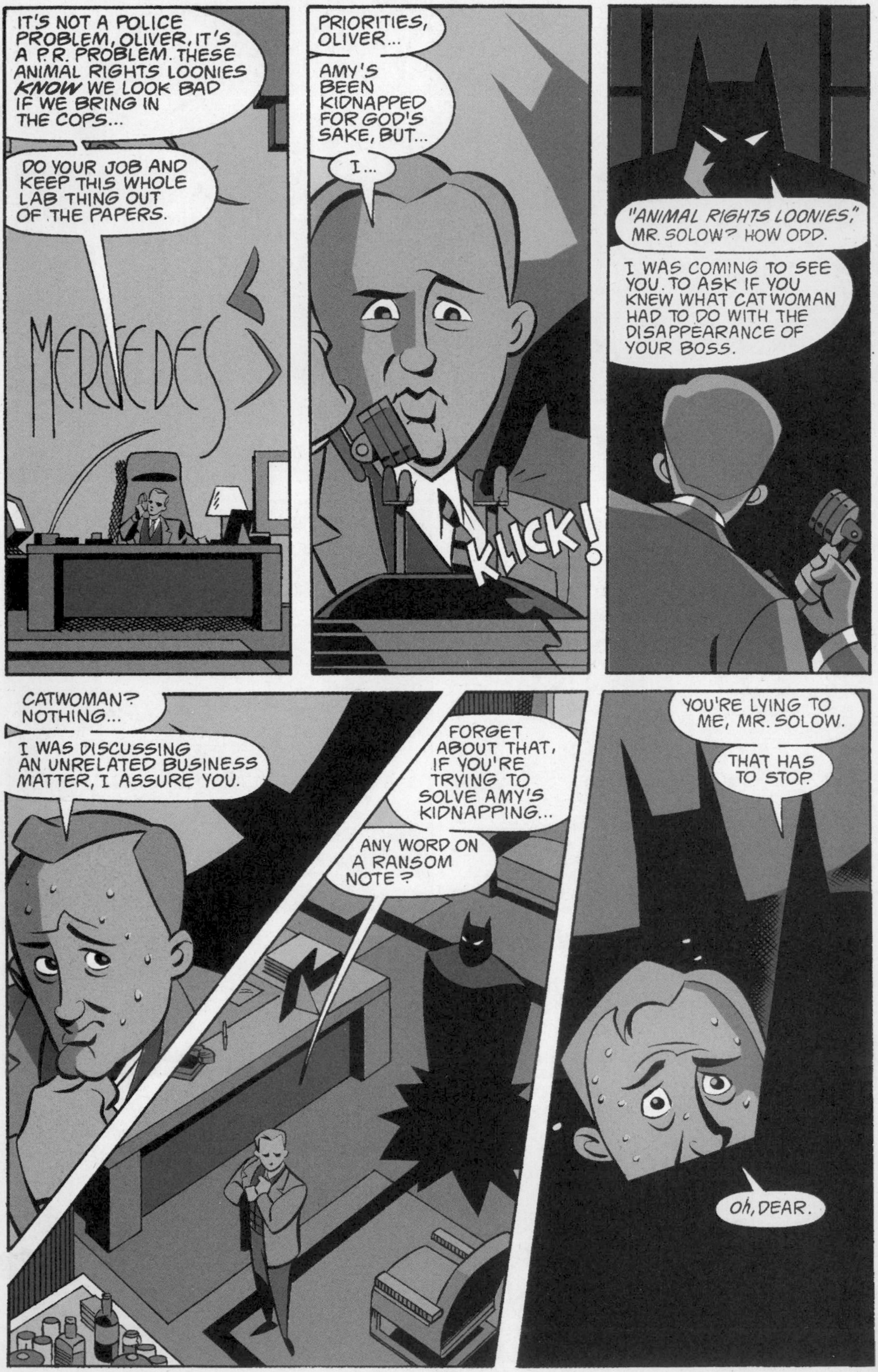
IT'S NOT A POLICE PROBLEM, OLIVER, IT'S A P.R. PROBLEM. THESE ANIMAL RIGHTS LOONIES KNOW WE LOOK BAD IF WE BRING IN THE COPS...
DO YOUR JOB AND KEEP THIS WHOLE LAB THING OUT OF THE PAPERS.
MERCEDES
PRIORITIES, OLIVER...
AMY'S BEEN KIDNAPPED FOR GOD'S SAKE, BUT...
I...
KLICK!
"ANIMAL RIGHTS LOONIES," MR. SOLOW? HOW ODD.
I WAS COMING TO SEE YOU. TO ASK IF YOU KNEW WHAT CATWOMAN HAD TO DO WITH THE DISAPPEARANCE OF YOUR BOSS.
CATWOMAN? NOTHING...
I WAS DISCUSSING AN UNRELATED BUSINESS MATTER, I ASSURE YOU.
FORGET ABOUT THAT, IF YOU'RE TRYING TO SOLVE AMY'S KIDNAPPING...
ANY WORD ON A RANSOM NOTE?
YOU'RE LYING TO ME, MR. SOLOW.
THAT HAS TO STOP.
Oh, DEAR.

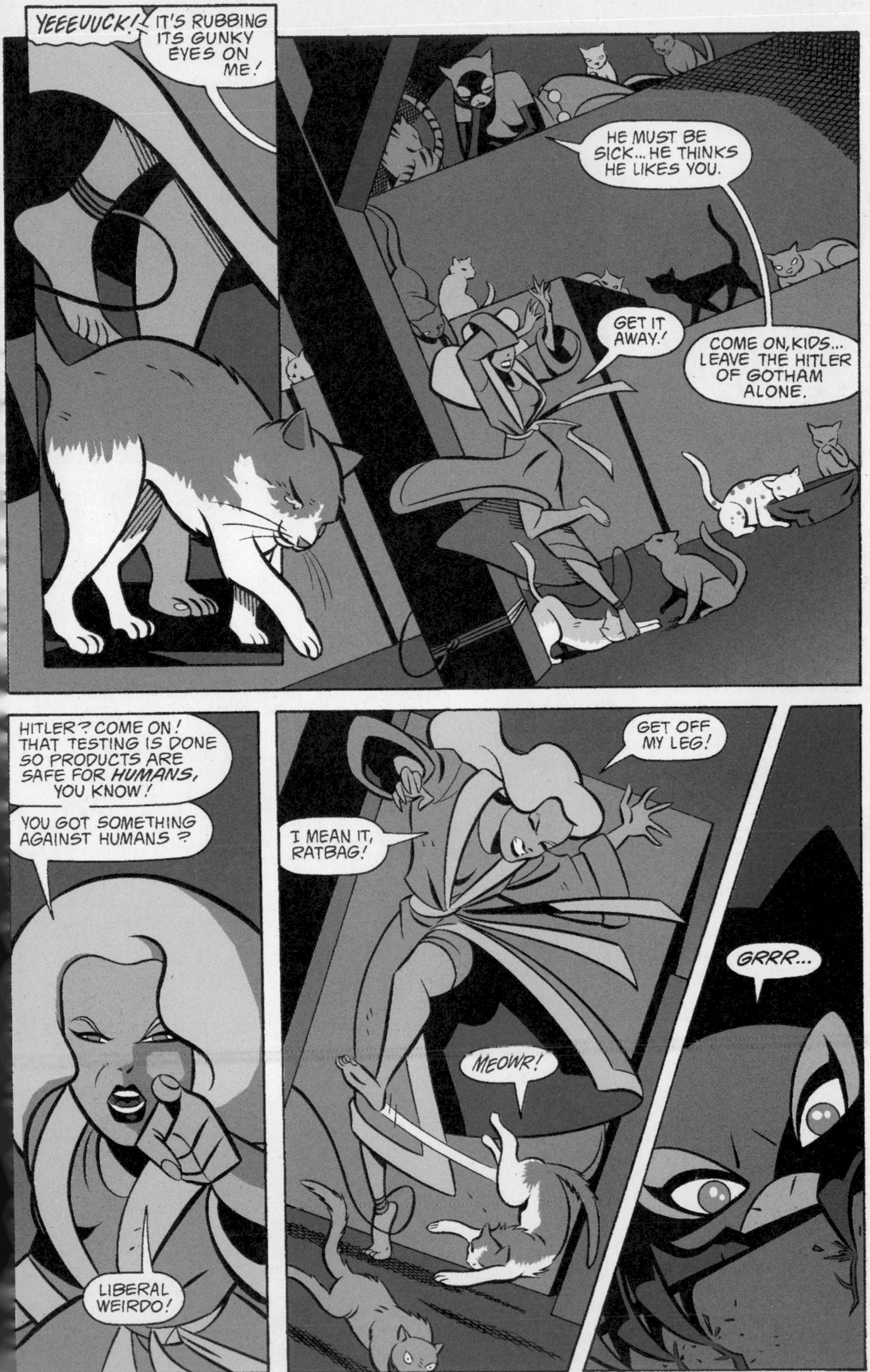
YEEEUUCK!
IT'S RUBBING ITS GUNKY EYES ON ME!
HE MUST BE SICK... HE THINKS HE LIKES YOU.
GET IT AWAY!
COME ON, KIDS... LEAVE THE HITLER OF GOTHAM ALONE.
HITLER? COME ON! THAT TESTING IS DONE SO PRODUCTS ARE SAFE FOR *HUMANS*, YOU KNOW!
YOU GOT SOMETHING AGAINST HUMANS?
LIBERAL WEIRDO!
GET OFF MY LEG!
I MEAN IT, RATBAG!
MEOWR!
GRRR...

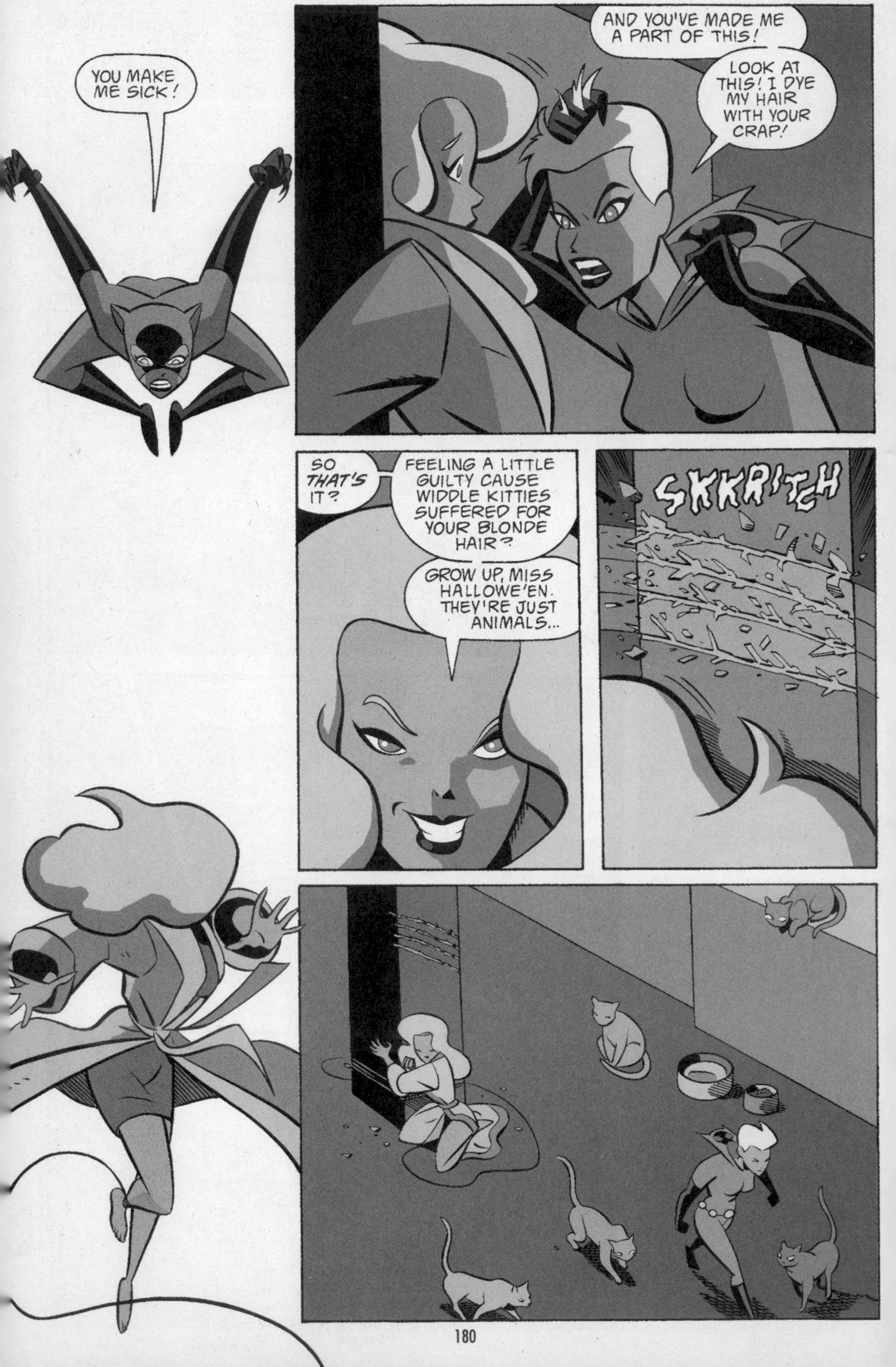
YOU MAKE ME SICK!
AND YOU'VE MADE ME A PART OF THIS!
LOOK AT THIS! I DYE MY HAIR WITH YOUR CRAP!
SO THAT'S IT?
FEELING A LITTLE GUILTY CAUSE WIDDLE KITTIES SUFFERED FOR YOUR BLONDE HAIR?
GROW UP, MISS HALLOWE'EN. THEY'RE JUST ANIMALS...
SKKRITCH

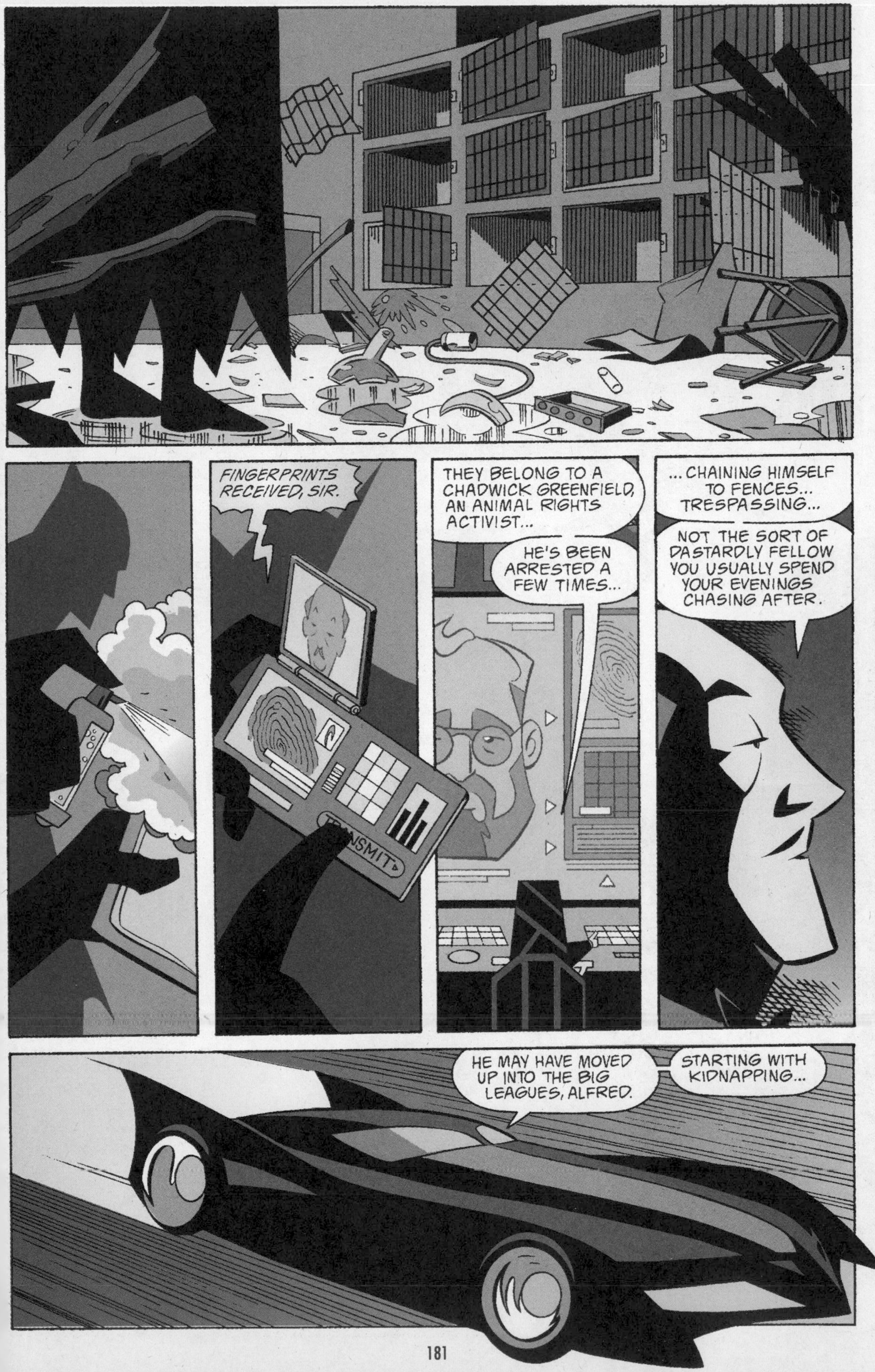
FINGERPRINTS RECEIVED, SIR.
THEY BELONG TO A CHADWICK GREENFIELD, AN ANIMAL RIGHTS ACTIVIST...
HE'S BEEN ARRESTED A FEW TIMES...
...CHAINING HIMSELF TO FENCES... TRESPASSING...
NOT THE SORT OF DASTARDLY FELLOW YOU USUALLY SPEND YOUR EVENINGS CHASING AFTER.
TRANSMIT
HE MAY HAVE MOVED UP INTO THE BIG LEAGUES, ALFRED.
STARTING WITH KIDNAPPING...

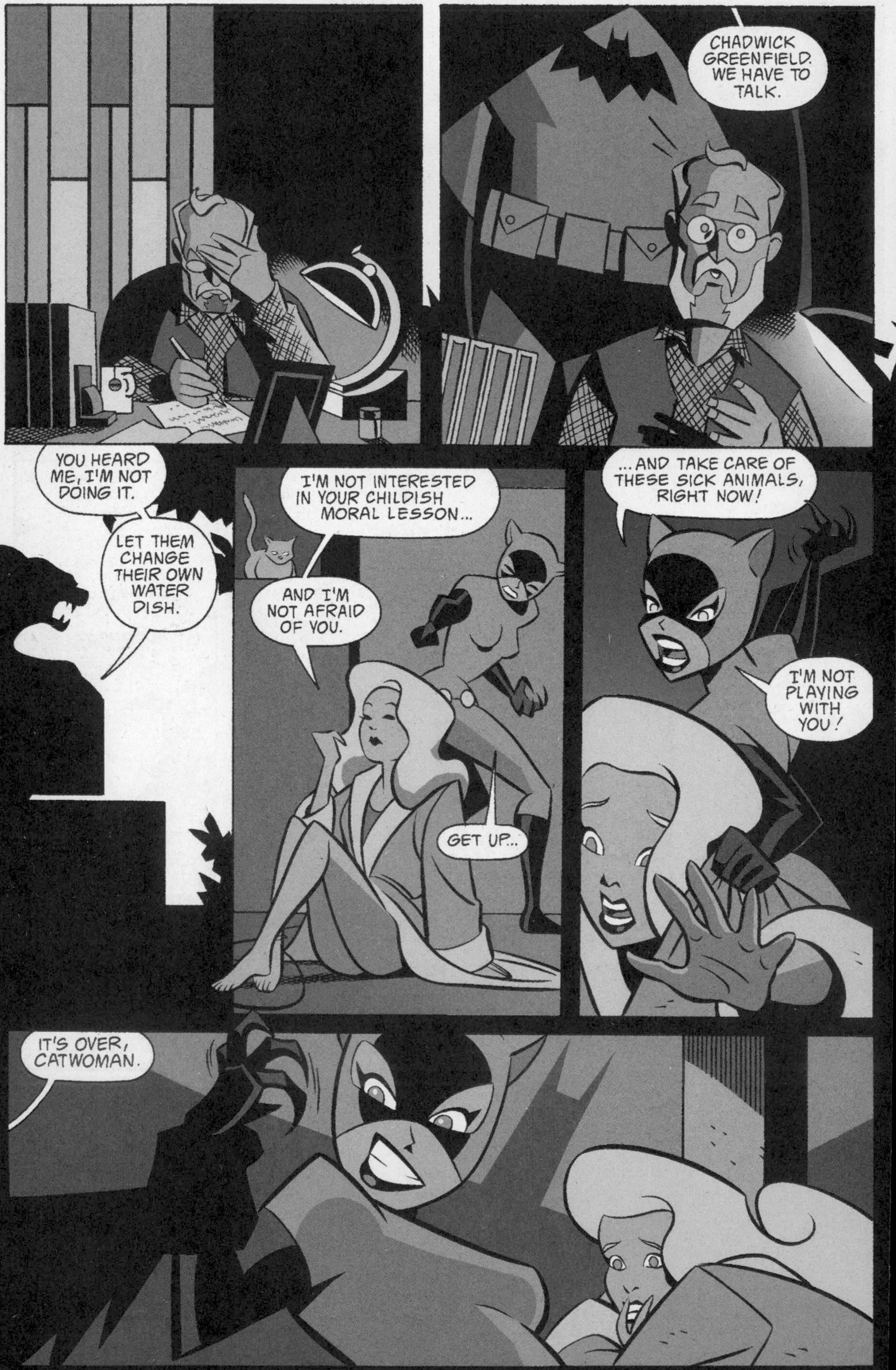
CHADWICK GREENFIELD. WE HAVE TO TALK.
YOU HEARD ME, I'M NOT DOING IT.
LET THEM CHANGE THEIR OWN WATER DISH.
I'M NOT INTERESTED IN YOUR CHILDISH MORAL LESSON...
AND I'M NOT AFRAID OF YOU.
GET UP...
...AND TAKE CARE OF THESE SICK ANIMALS, RIGHT NOW!
I'M NOT PLAYING WITH YOU!
IT'S OVER, CATWOMAN.

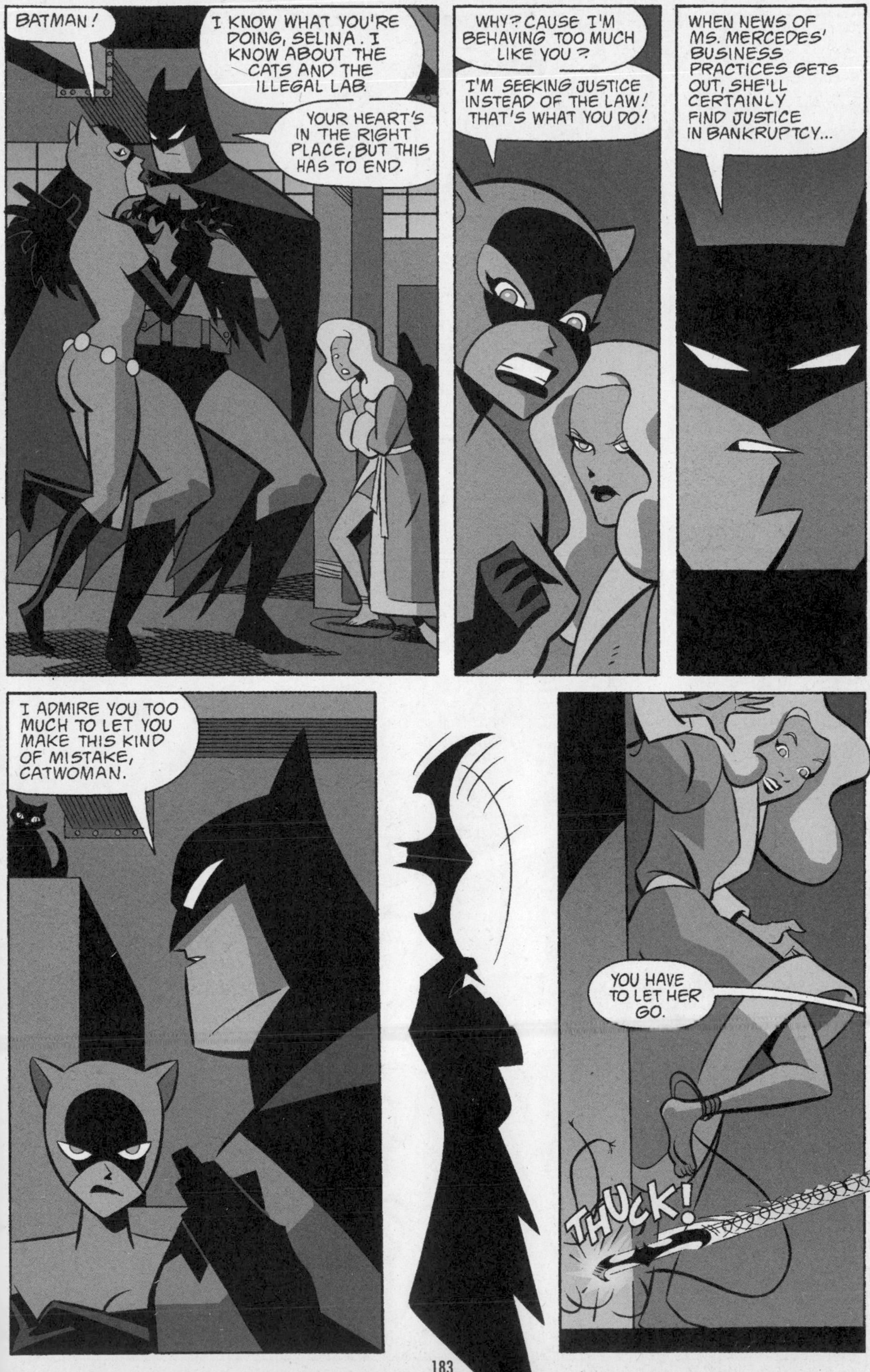
BATMAN!
I KNOW WHAT YOU'RE DOING, SELINA. I KNOW ABOUT THE CATS AND THE ILLEGAL LAB.
YOUR HEART'S IN THE RIGHT PLACE, BUT THIS HAS TO END.
WHY? CAUSE I'M BEHAVING TOO MUCH LIKE YOU?
I'M SEEKING JUSTICE INSTEAD OF THE LAW! THAT'S WHAT YOU DO!
WHEN NEWS OF MS. MERCEDES' BUSINESS PRACTICES GETS OUT, SHE'LL CERTAINLY FIND JUSTICE IN BANKRUPTCY...
I ADMIRE YOU TOO MUCH TO LET YOU MAKE THIS KIND OF MISTAKE, CATWOMAN.
YOU HAVE TO LET HER GO.
THUCK!

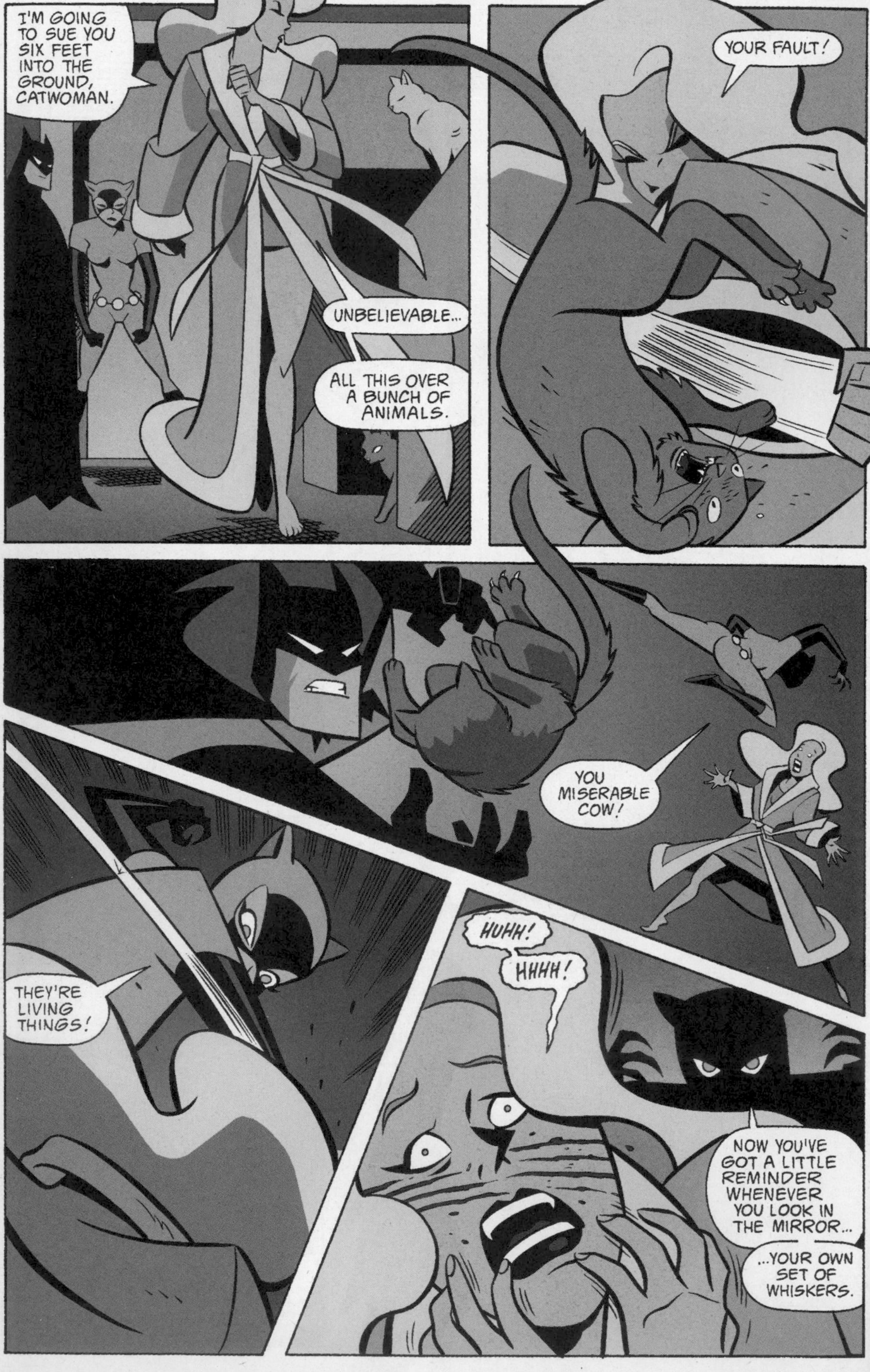
I'M GOING TO SUE YOU SIX FEET INTO THE GROUND, CATWOMAN.
UNBELIEVABLE...
ALL THIS OVER A BUNCH OF ANIMALS.
YOUR FAULT!
YOU MISERABLE COW!
THEY'RE LIVING THINGS!
HUHH!
HHHH!
NOW YOU'VE GOT A LITTLE REMINDER WHENEVER YOU LOOK IN THE MIRROR...
...YOUR OWN SET OF WHISKERS.

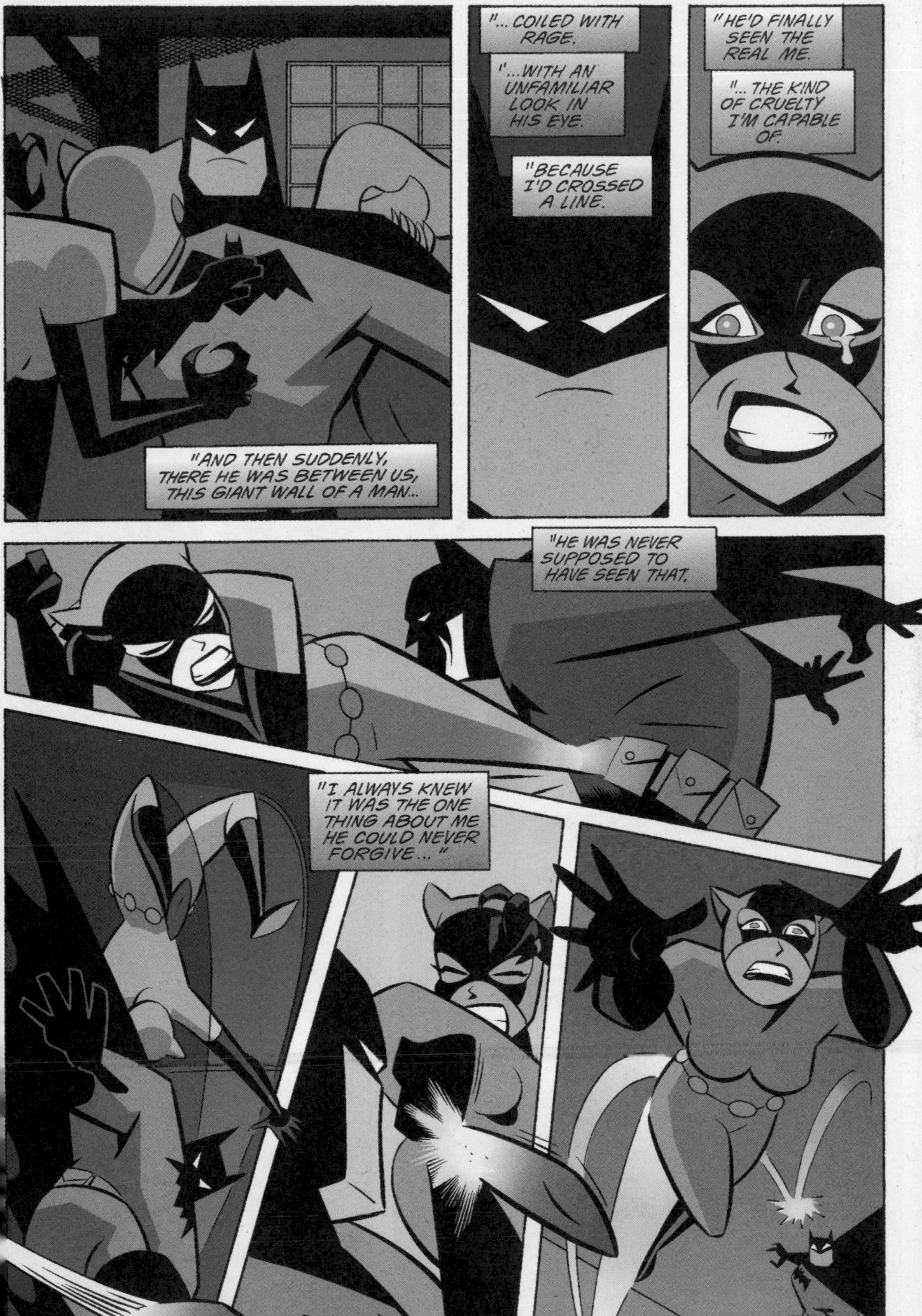
"AND THEN SUDDENLY, THERE HE WAS BETWEEN US, THIS GIANT WALL OF A MAN...
"... COILED WITH RAGE.
"...WITH AN UNFAMILIAR LOOK IN HIS EYE.
"BECAUSE I'D CROSSED A LINE.
"HE'D FINALLY SEEN THE REAL ME.
"... THE KIND OF CRUELTY I'M CAPABLE OF.
"HE WAS NEVER SUPPOSED TO HAVE SEEN THAT.
"I ALWAYS KNEW IT WAS THE ONE THING ABOUT ME HE COULD NEVER FORGIVE..."

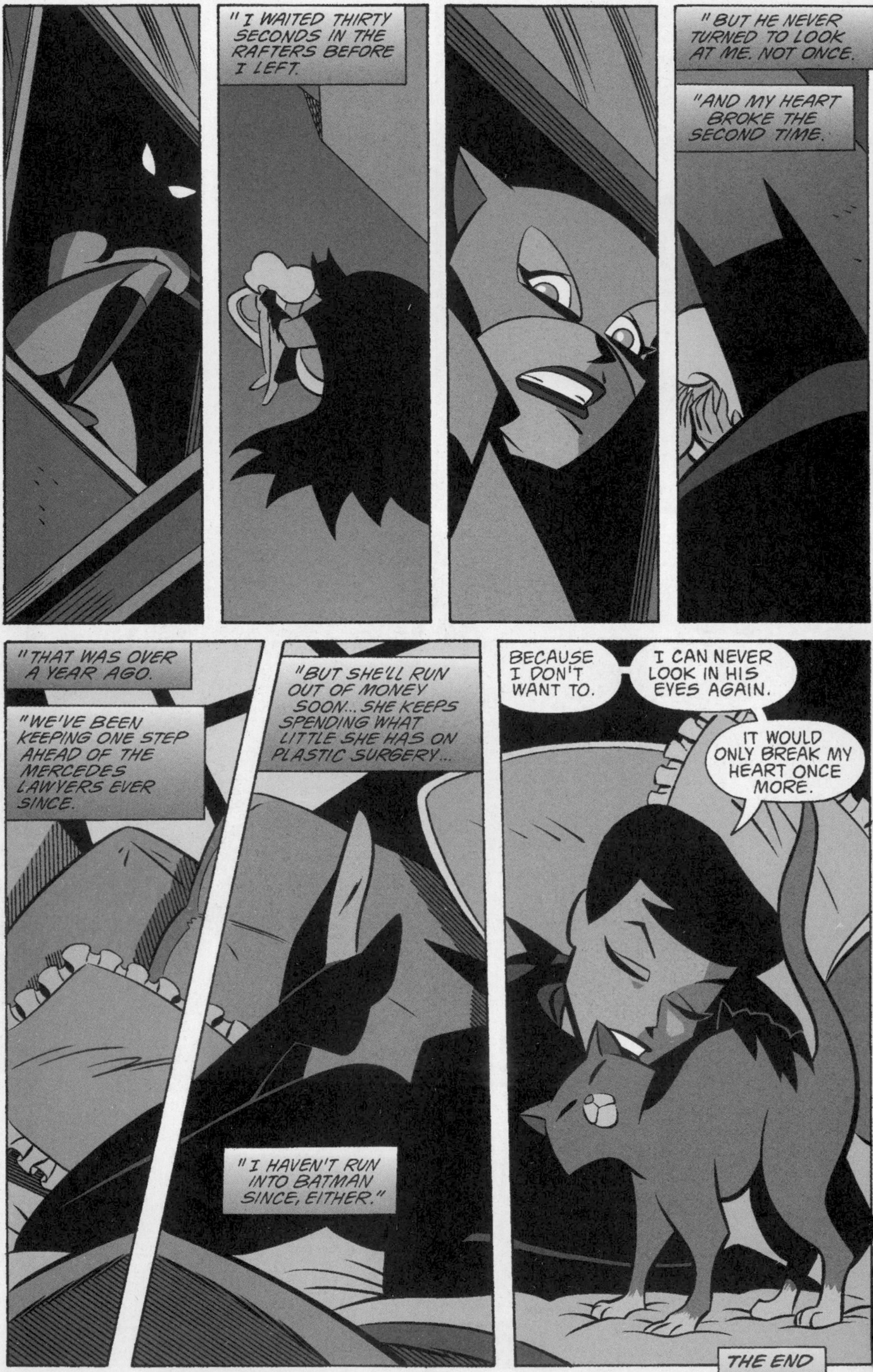
"I WAITED THIRTY SECONDS IN THE RAFTERS BEFORE I LEFT.
"BUT HE NEVER TURNED TO LOOK AT ME. NOT ONCE.
"AND MY HEART BROKE THE SECOND TIME.
"THAT WAS OVER A YEAR AGO.
"WE'VE BEEN KEEPING ONE STEP AHEAD OF THE MERCEDES LAWYERS EVER SINCE.
"BUT SHE'LL RUN OUT OF MONEY SOON... SHE KEEPS SPENDING WHAT LITTLE SHE HAS ON PLASTIC SURGERY...
"I HAVEN'T RUN INTO BATMAN SINCE, EITHER."
BECAUSE I DON'T WANT TO.
I CAN NEVER LOOK IN HIS EYES AGAIN.
IT WOULD ONLY BREAK MY HEART ONCE MORE.
THE END

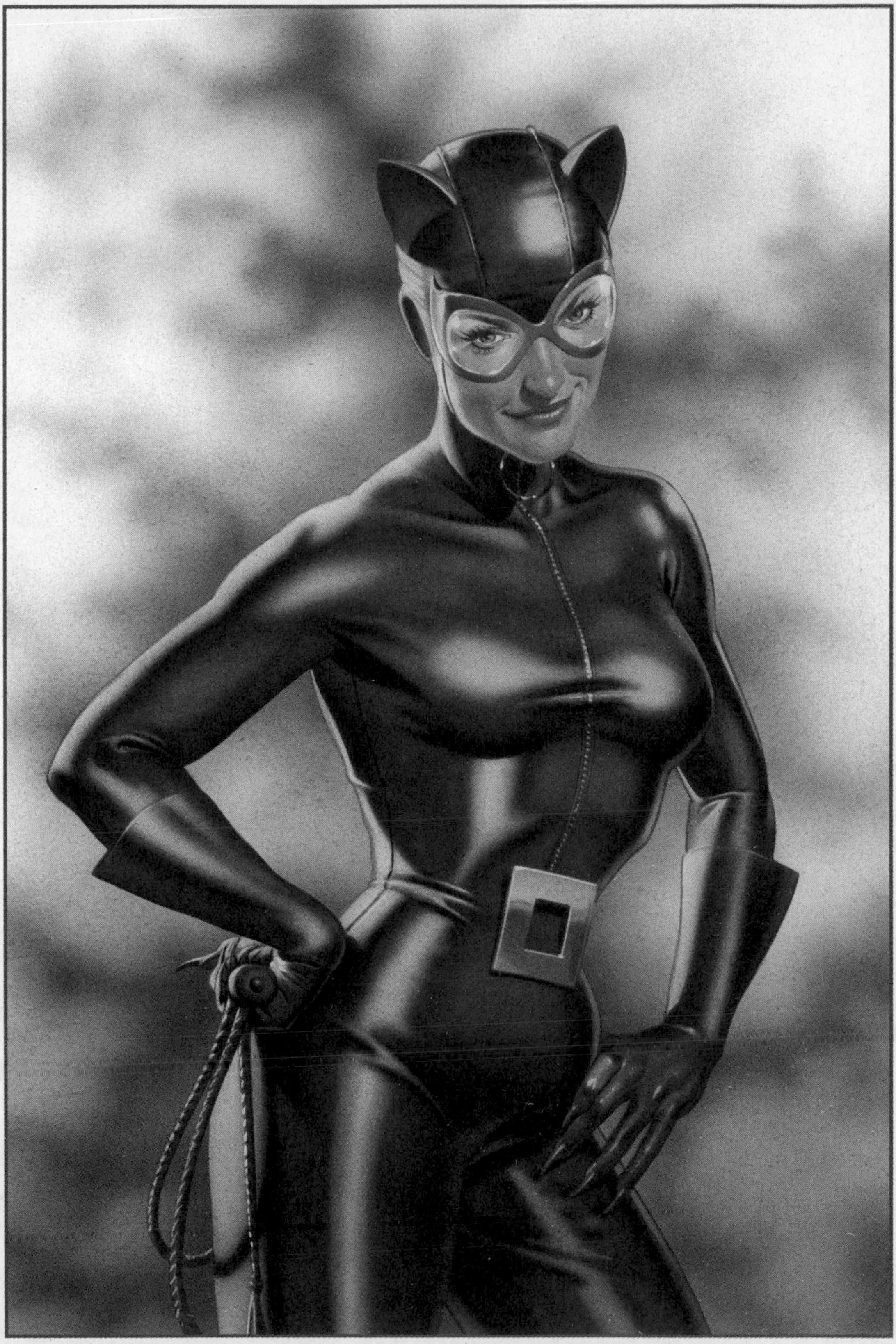

Originally painted and used in the BATMAN: GOTHAM CITY MYSTERY BOARD GAME from Mattel (2003).

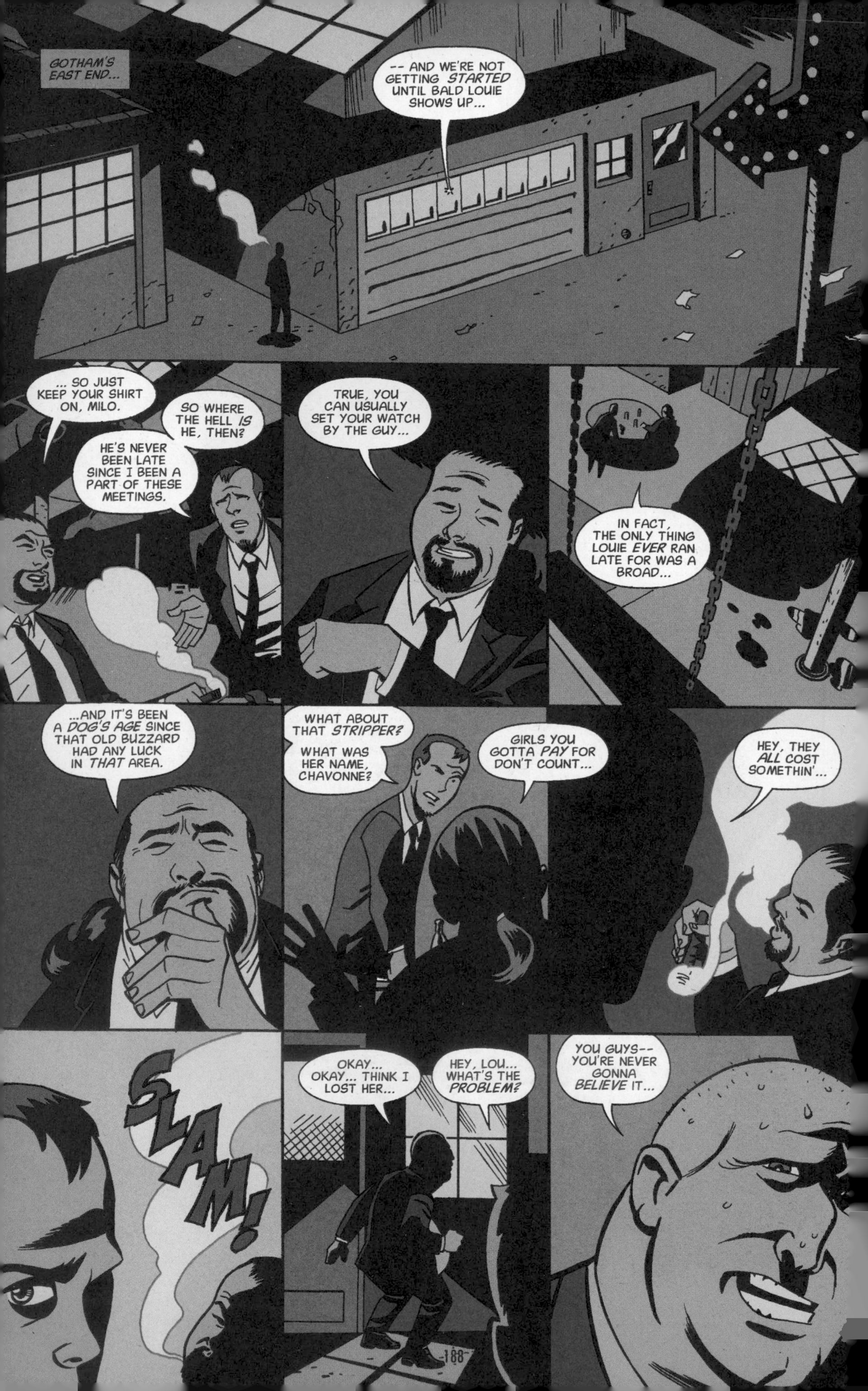
GOTHAM'S EAST END...
-- AND WE'RE NOT GETTING STARTED UNTIL BALD LOUIE SHOWS UP...
... SO JUST KEEP YOUR SHIRT ON, MILO.
SO WHERE THE HELL IS HE, THEN?
HE'S NEVER BEEN LATE SINCE I BEEN A PART OF THESE MEETINGS.
TRUE, YOU CAN USUALLY SET YOUR WATCH BY THE GUY...
IN FACT, THE ONLY THING LOUIE EVER RAN LATE FOR WAS A BROAD...
...AND IT'S BEEN A DOG'S AGE SINCE THAT OLD BUZZARD HAD ANY LUCK IN THAT AREA.
WHAT ABOUT THAT STRIPPER?
WHAT WAS HER NAME, CHAVONNE?
GIRLS YOU GOTTA PAY FOR DON'T COUNT...
HEY, THEY ALL COST SOMETHIN'...
SLAM!
OKAY... OKAY... THINK I LOST HER...
HEY, LOU... WHAT'S THE PROBLEM?
YOU GUYS-- YOU'RE NEVER GONNA BELIEVE IT...

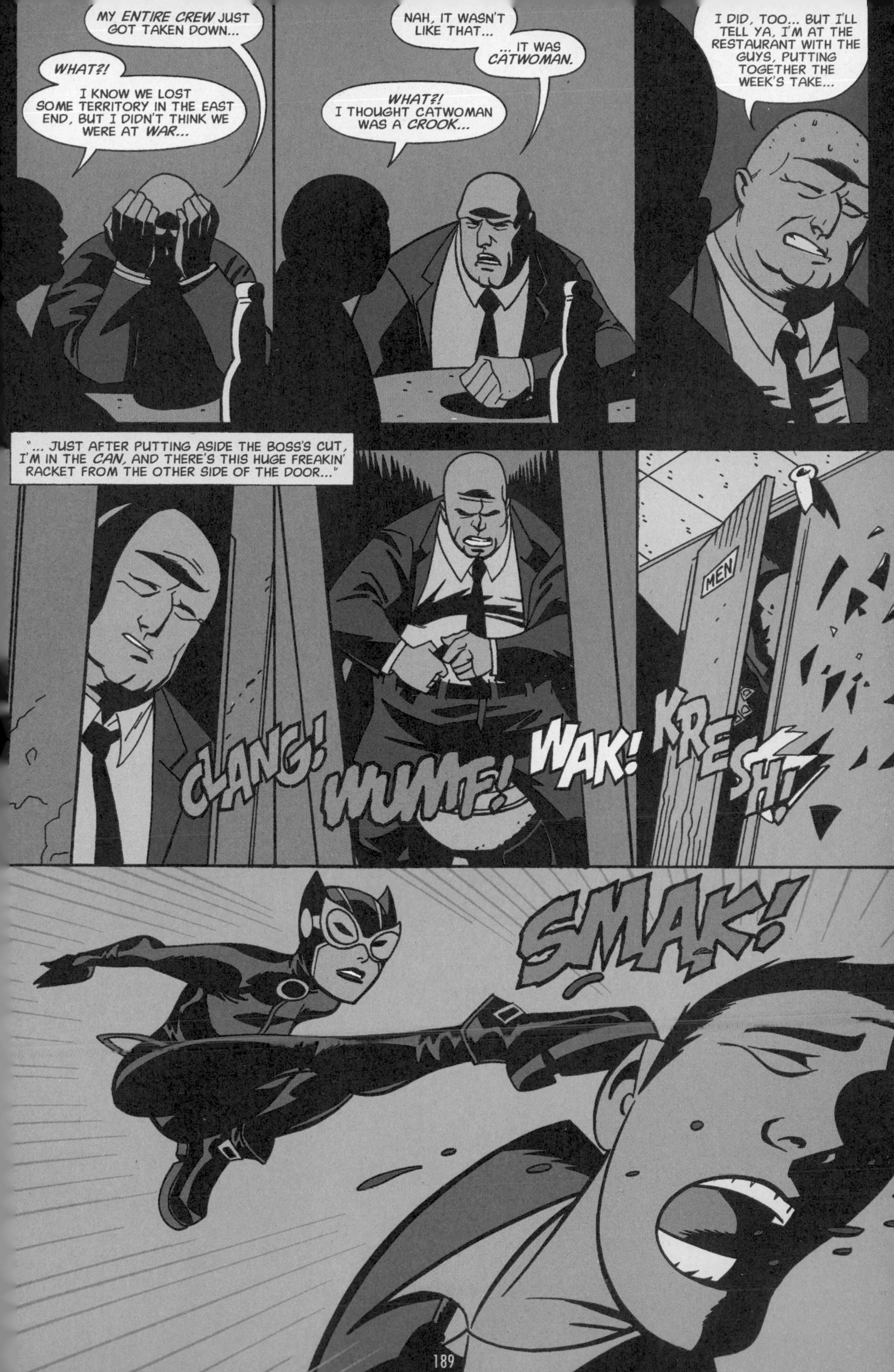
MY ENTIRE CREW JUST GOT TAKEN DOWN...
WHAT?!
I KNOW WE LOST SOME TERRITORY IN THE EAST END, BUT I DIDN'T THINK WE WERE AT WAR...
NAH, IT WASN'T LIKE THAT...
... IT WAS CATWOMAN.
WHAT?! I THOUGHT CATWOMAN WAS A CROOK...
I DID, TOO... BUT I'LL TELL YA, I'M AT THE RESTAURANT WITH THE GUYS, PUTTING TOGETHER THE WEEK'S TAKE...
"... JUST AFTER PUTTING ASIDE THE BOSS'S CUT, I'M IN THE CAN, AND THERE'S THIS HUGE FREAKIN' RACKET FROM THE OTHER SIDE OF THE DOOR..."
MEN
CLANG!
WUMF!
WAK!
KRESH!
SMAK!

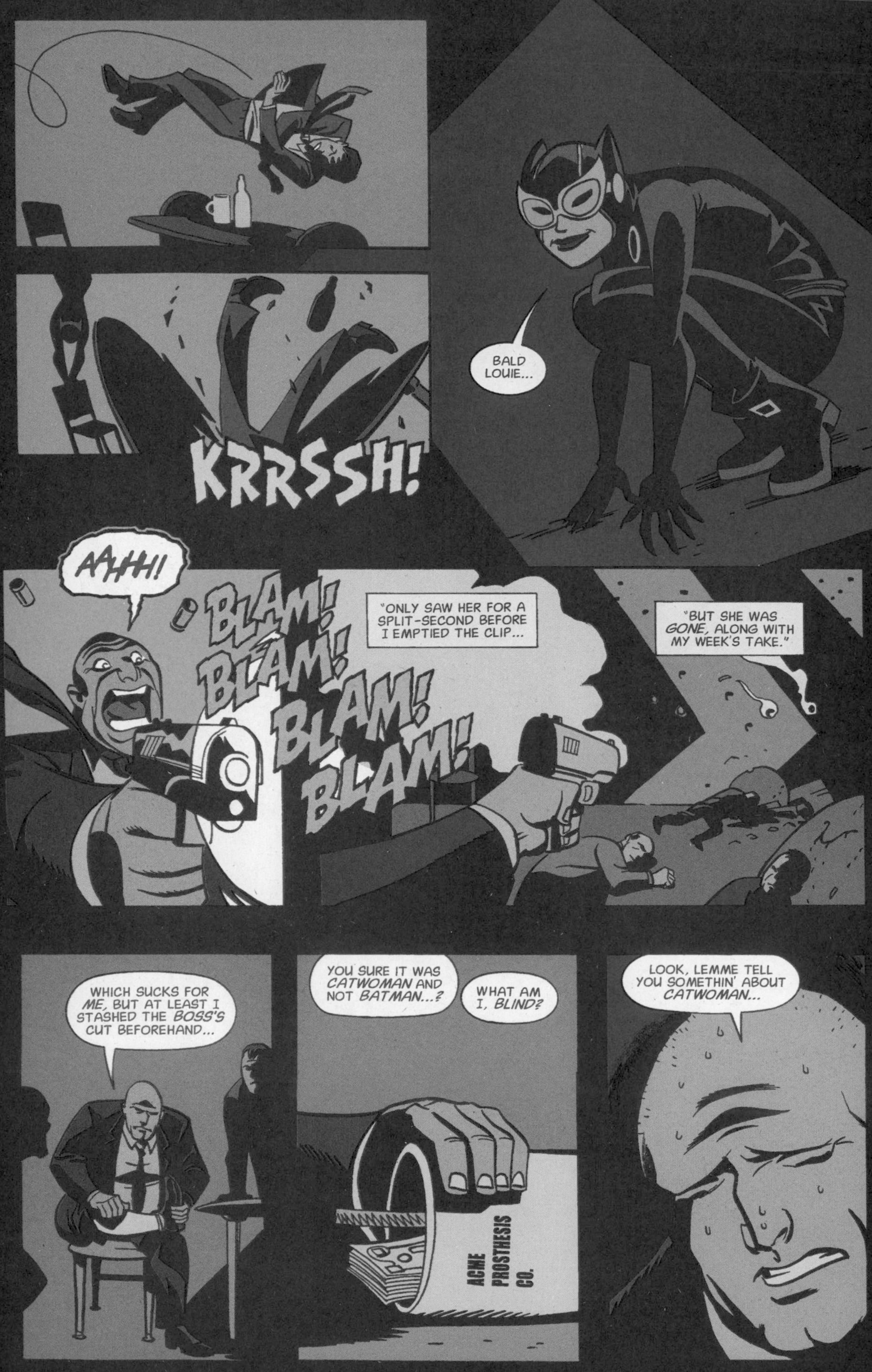

BALD LOUIE...
KRRSSH!
AAHHH!
BLAM! BLAM! BLAM! BLAM!
"ONLY SAW HER FOR A SPLIT-SECOND BEFORE I EMPTIED THE CLIP...
"BUT SHE WAS *GONE*, ALONG WITH MY WEEK'S TAKE."
WHICH SUCKS FOR *ME*, BUT AT LEAST I STASHED THE *BOSS'S* CUT BEFOREHAND...
YOU SURE IT WAS *CATWOMAN* AND NOT *BATMAN*...?
WHAT AM I, *BLIND?*
ACME PROSTHESIS CO.
LOOK, LEMME TELL YOU SOMETHIN' ABOUT *CATWOMAN*...

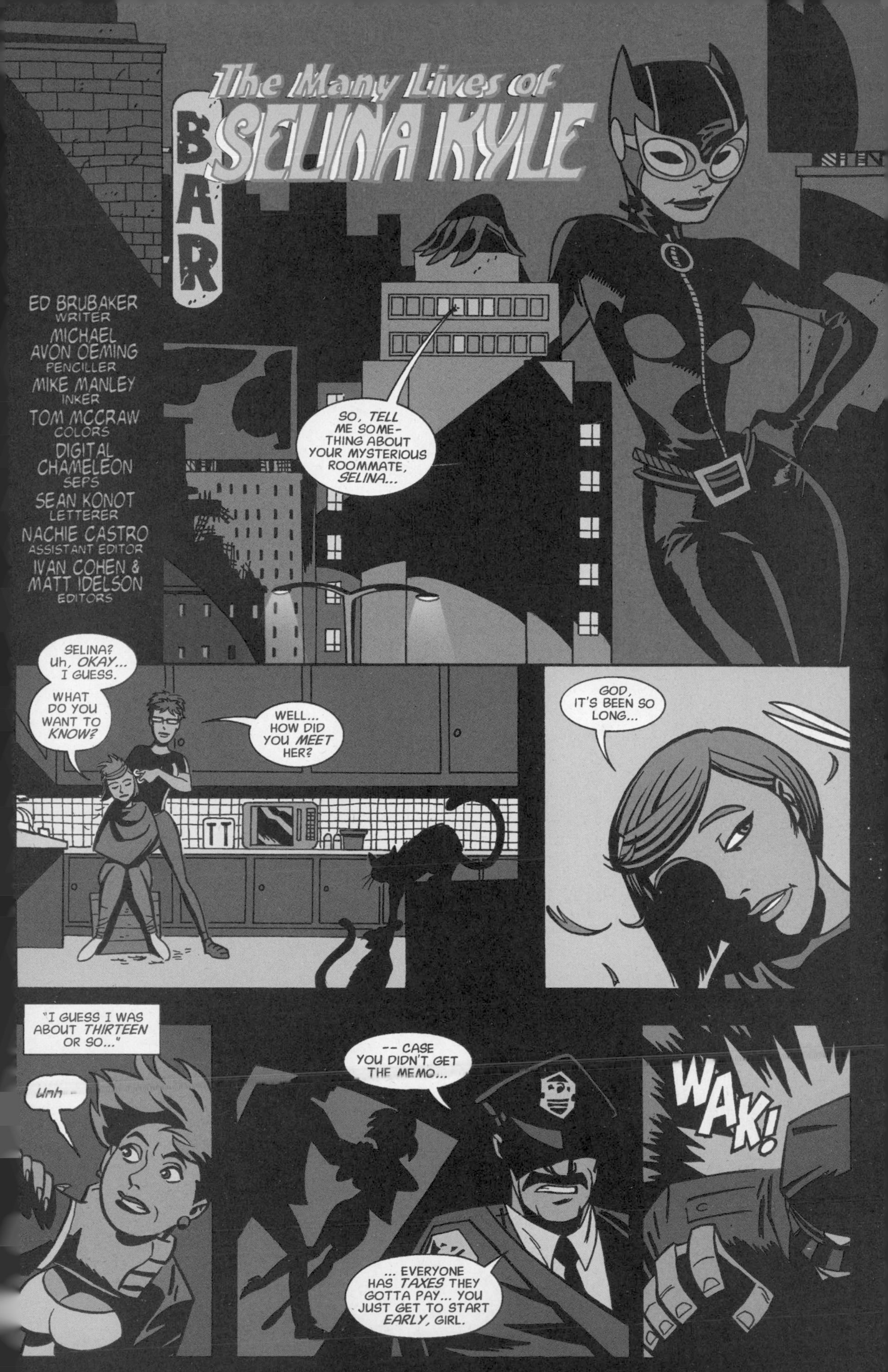

The Many Lives of SELINA KYLE
BAR
ED BRUBAKER WRITER
MICHAEL AVON OEMING PENCILLER
MIKE MANLEY INKER
TOM MCCRAW COLORS
DIGITAL CHAMELEON SEPS
SEAN KONOT LETTERER
NACHIE CASTRO ASSISTANT EDITOR
IVAN COHEN & MATT IDELSON EDITORS
SO, TELL ME SOMETHING ABOUT YOUR MYSTERIOUS ROOMMATE, SELINA...
SELINA? Uh, OKAY... I GUESS.
WHAT DO YOU WANT TO KNOW?
WELL... HOW DID YOU MEET HER?
GOD, IT'S BEEN SO LONG...
"I GUESS I WAS ABOUT THIRTEEN OR SO..."
Unh --
-- CASE YOU DIDN'T GET THE MEMO...
... EVERYONE HAS TAXES THEY GOTTA PAY... YOU JUST GET TO START EARLY, GIRL.
WAK!

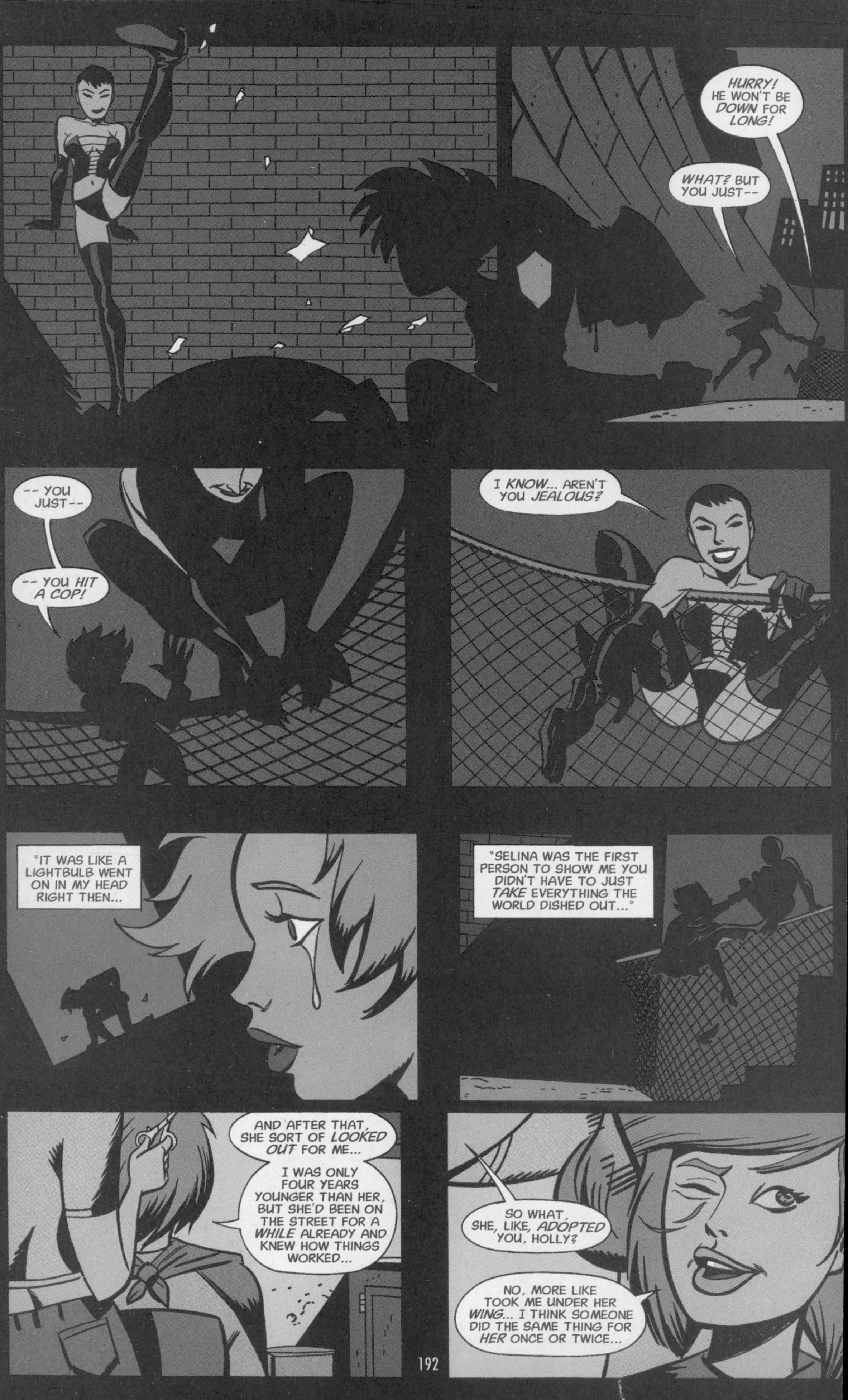
HURRY! HE WON'T BE DOWN FOR LONG!
WHAT? BUT YOU JUST--
-- YOU JUST--
-- YOU HIT A COP!
I KNOW... AREN'T YOU JEALOUS?
"IT WAS LIKE A LIGHTBULB WENT ON IN MY HEAD RIGHT THEN...
"SELINA WAS THE FIRST PERSON TO SHOW ME YOU DIDN'T HAVE TO JUST TAKE EVERYTHING THE WORLD DISHED OUT..."
AND AFTER THAT, SHE SORT OF LOOKED OUT FOR ME...
I WAS ONLY FOUR YEARS YOUNGER THAN HER, BUT SHE'D BEEN ON THE STREET FOR A WHILE ALREADY AND KNEW HOW THINGS WORKED...
SO WHAT, SHE, LIKE, ADOPTED YOU, HOLLY?
NO, MORE LIKE TOOK ME UNDER HER WING... I THINK SOMEONE DID THE SAME THING FOR HER ONCE OR TWICE...

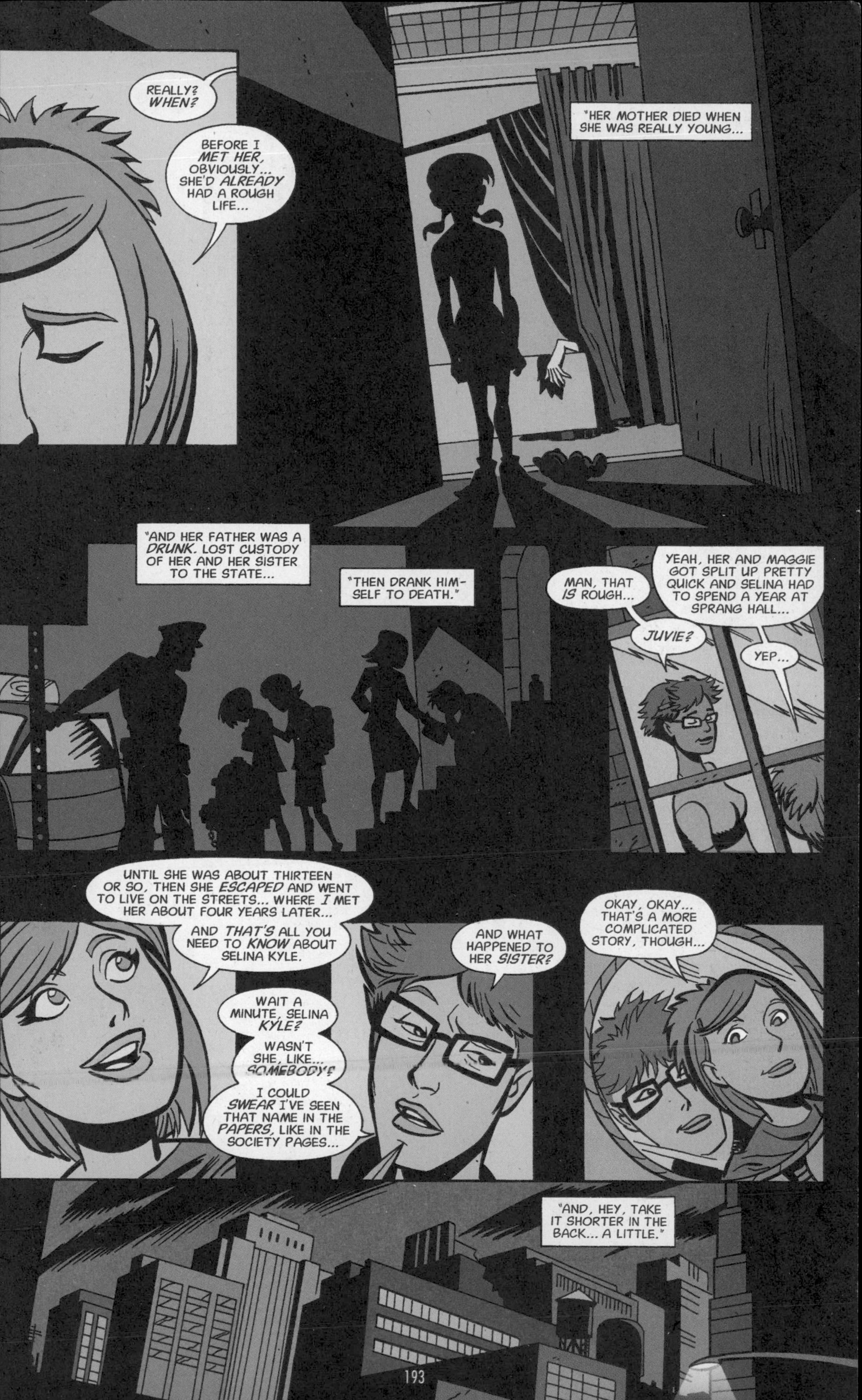
REALLY? WHEN?
BEFORE I MET HER, OBVIOUSLY... SHE'D ALREADY HAD A ROUGH LIFE...
"HER MOTHER DIED WHEN SHE WAS REALLY YOUNG...
"AND HER FATHER WAS A DRUNK. LOST CUSTODY OF HER AND HER SISTER TO THE STATE...
"THEN DRANK HIMSELF TO DEATH."
MAN, THAT IS ROUGH...
YEAH, HER AND MAGGIE GOT SPLIT UP PRETTY QUICK AND SELINA HAD TO SPEND A YEAR AT SPRANG HALL...
JUVIE?
YEP...
UNTIL SHE WAS ABOUT THIRTEEN OR SO, THEN SHE ESCAPED AND WENT TO LIVE ON THE STREETS... WHERE I MET HER ABOUT FOUR YEARS LATER...
AND THAT'S ALL YOU NEED TO KNOW ABOUT SELINA KYLE.
WAIT A MINUTE, SELINA KYLE?
WASN'T SHE, LIKE... SOMEBODY?
I COULD SWEAR I'VE SEEN THAT NAME IN THE PAPERS, LIKE IN THE SOCIETY PAGES...
AND WHAT HAPPENED TO HER SISTER?
OKAY, OKAY... THAT'S A MORE COMPLICATED STORY, THOUGH...
"AND, HEY, TAKE IT SHORTER IN THE BACK... A LITTLE."

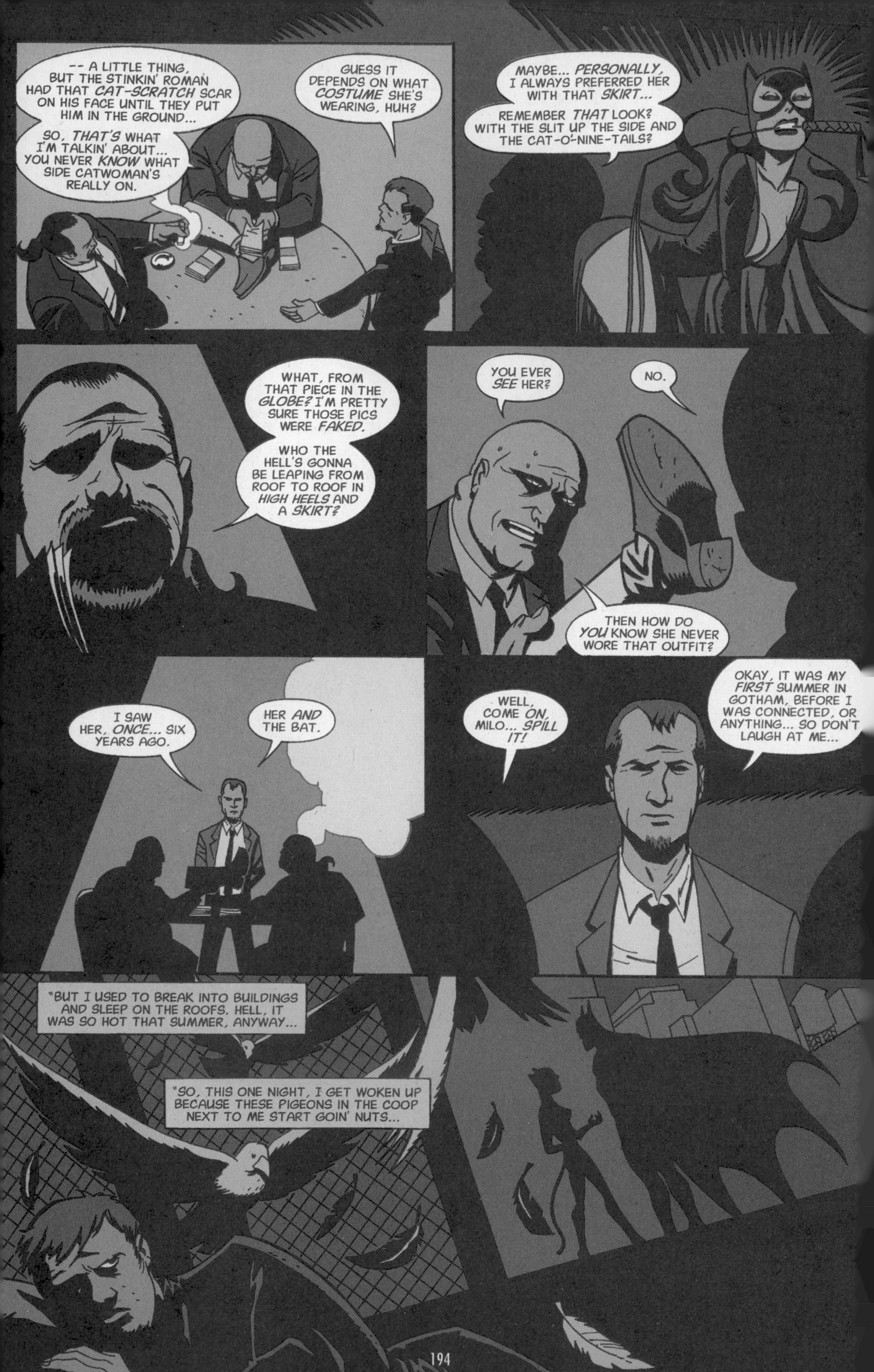
-- A LITTLE THING, BUT THE STINKIN' ROMAN HAD THAT CAT-SCRATCH SCAR ON HIS FACE UNTIL THEY PUT HIM IN THE GROUND...
SO, THAT'S WHAT I'M TALKIN' ABOUT... YOU NEVER KNOW WHAT SIDE CATWOMAN'S REALLY ON.
GUESS IT DEPENDS ON WHAT COSTUME SHE'S WEARING, HUH?
MAYBE... PERSONALLY, I ALWAYS PREFERRED HER WITH THAT SKIRT...
REMEMBER THAT LOOK? WITH THE SLIT UP THE SIDE AND THE CAT-O'-NINE-TAILS?
WHAT, FROM THAT PIECE IN THE GLOBE? I'M PRETTY SURE THOSE PICS WERE FAKED.
WHO THE HELL'S GONNA BE LEAPING FROM ROOF TO ROOF IN HIGH HEELS AND A SKIRT?
YOU EVER SEE HER?
NO.
THEN HOW DO YOU KNOW SHE NEVER WORE THAT OUTFIT?
I SAW HER, ONCE... SIX YEARS AGO.
HER AND THE BAT.
WELL, COME ON, MILO... SPILL IT!
OKAY, IT WAS MY FIRST SUMMER IN GOTHAM, BEFORE I WAS CONNECTED, OR ANYTHING... SO DON'T LAUGH AT ME...
"BUT I USED TO BREAK INTO BUILDINGS AND SLEEP ON THE ROOFS. HELL, IT WAS SO HOT THAT SUMMER, ANYWAY...
"SO, THIS ONE NIGHT, I GET WOKEN UP BECAUSE THESE PIGEONS IN THE COOP NEXT TO ME START GOIN' NUTS...

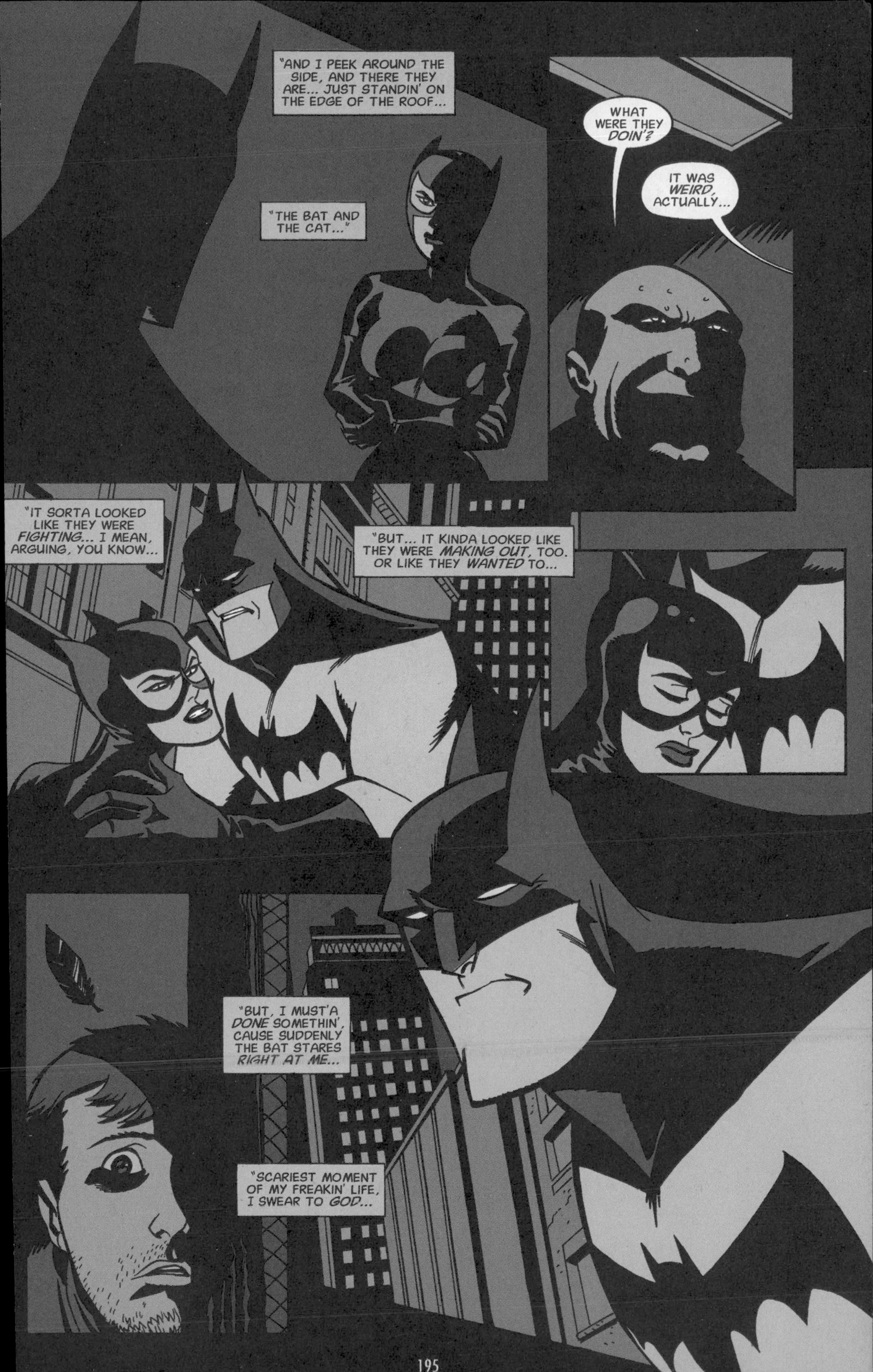
"AND I PEEK AROUND THE SIDE, AND THERE THEY ARE... JUST STANDIN' ON THE EDGE OF THE ROOF...
"THE BAT AND THE CAT..."
WHAT WERE THEY *DOIN'?*
IT WAS *WEIRD,* ACTUALLY...
"IT SORTA LOOKED LIKE THEY WERE *FIGHTING*... I MEAN, ARGUING, YOU KNOW...
"BUT... IT KINDA LOOKED LIKE THEY WERE *MAKING OUT,* TOO. OR LIKE THEY *WANTED* TO...
"BUT, I MUST'A *DONE* SOMETHIN', CAUSE SUDDENLY THE BAT STARES *RIGHT AT ME*...
"SCARIEST MOMENT OF MY FREAKIN' LIFE, I SWEAR TO *GOD*...

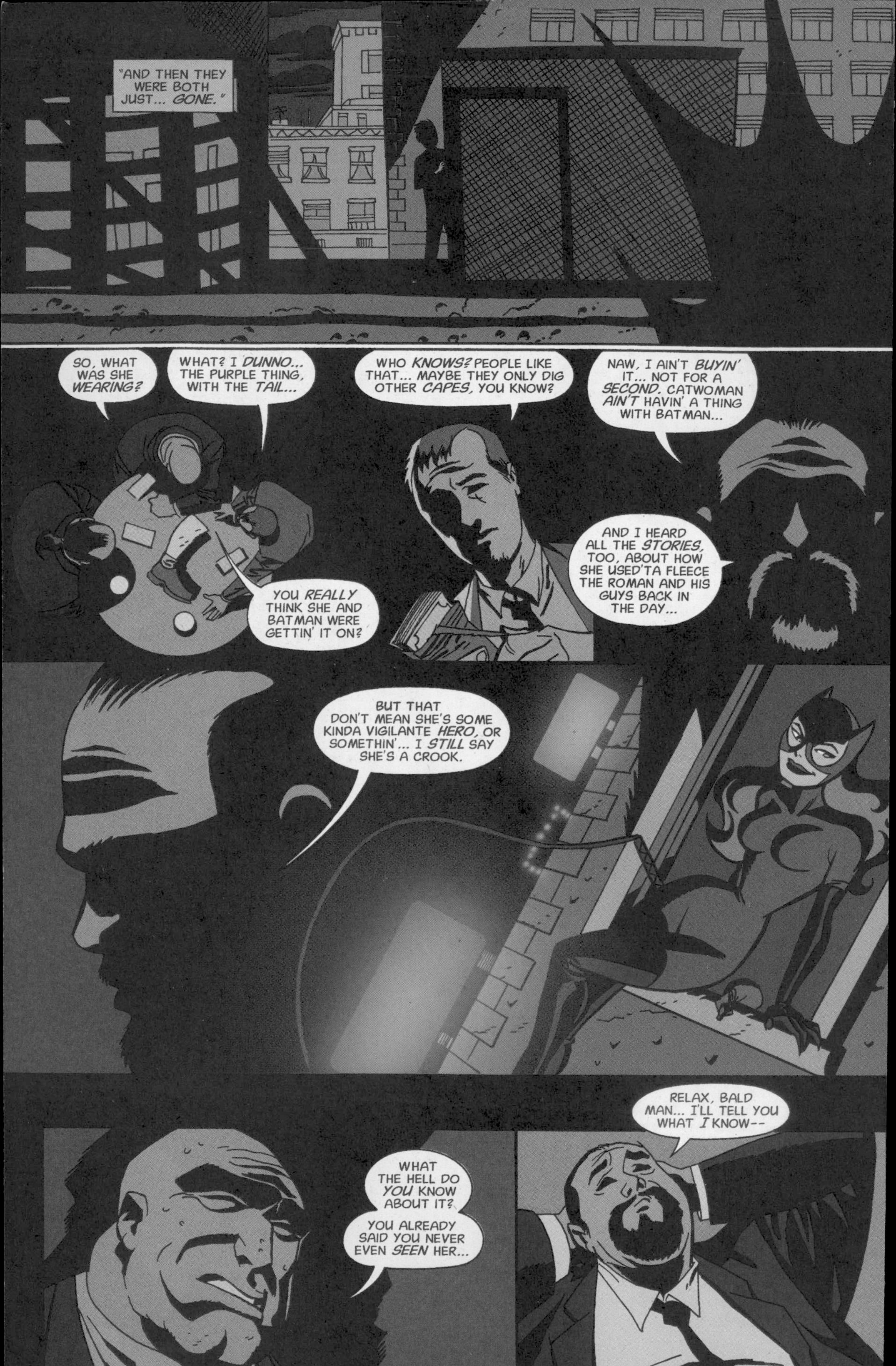
"AND THEN THEY WERE BOTH JUST... GONE."
SO, WHAT WAS SHE WEARING?
WHAT? I DUNNO... THE PURPLE THING, WITH THE TAIL...
YOU REALLY THINK SHE AND BATMAN WERE GETTIN' IT ON?
WHO KNOWS? PEOPLE LIKE THAT... MAYBE THEY ONLY DIG OTHER CAPES, YOU KNOW?
NAW, I AIN'T BUYIN' IT... NOT FOR A SECOND. CATWOMAN AIN'T HAVIN' A THING WITH BATMAN...
AND I HEARD ALL THE STORIES, TOO, ABOUT HOW SHE USED'TA FLEECE THE ROMAN AND HIS GUYS BACK IN THE DAY...
BUT THAT DON'T MEAN SHE'S SOME KINDA VIGILANTE HERO, OR SOMETHIN'... I STILL SAY SHE'S A CROOK.
WHAT THE HELL DO YOU KNOW ABOUT IT?
YOU ALREADY SAID YOU NEVER EVEN SEEN HER...
RELAX, BALD MAN... I'LL TELL YOU WHAT I KNOW--

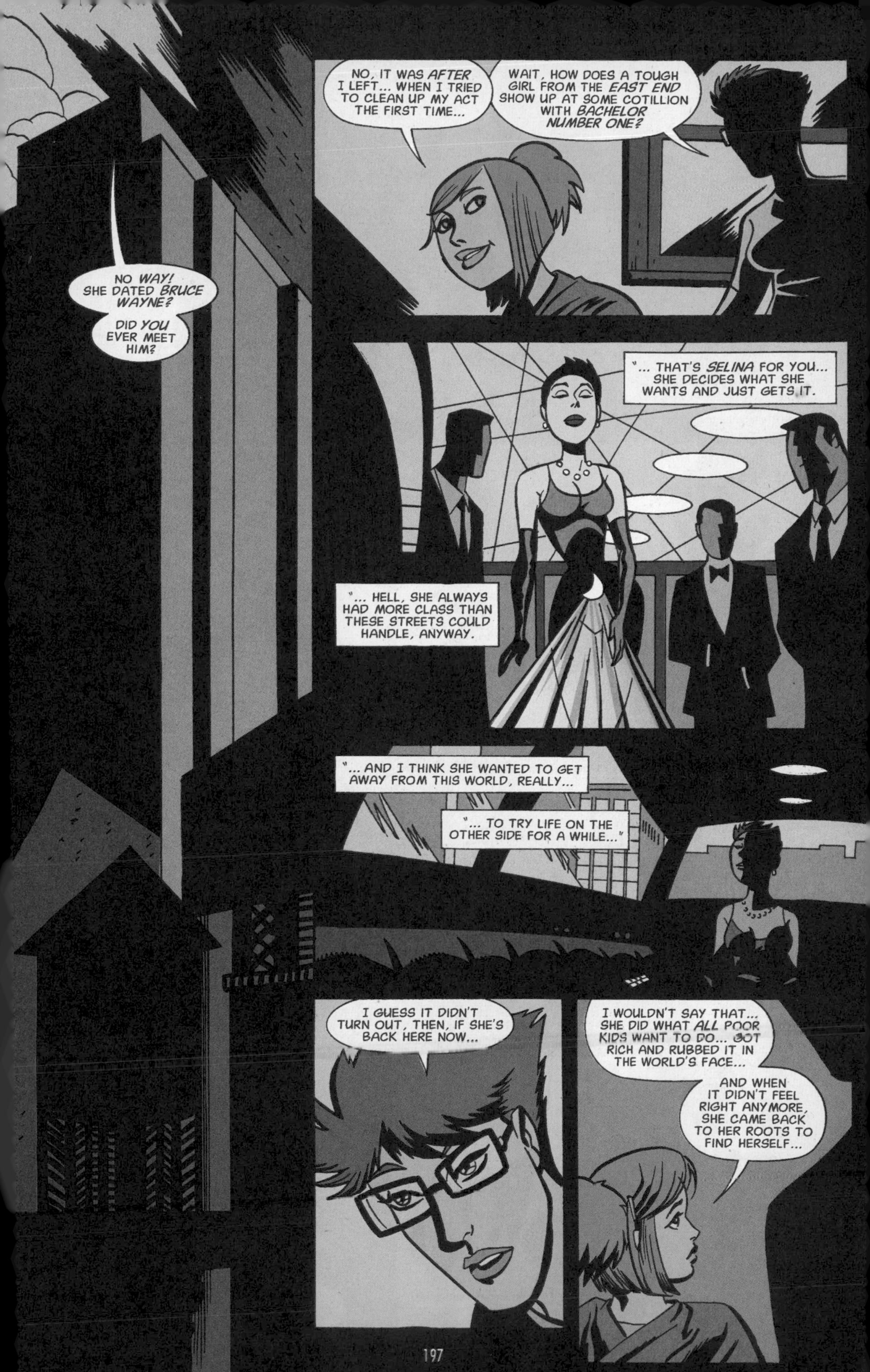
NO, IT WAS AFTER I LEFT... WHEN I TRIED TO CLEAN UP MY ACT THE FIRST TIME...
WAIT, HOW DOES A TOUGH GIRL FROM THE EAST END SHOW UP AT SOME COTILLION WITH BACHELOR NUMBER ONE?
NO WAY! SHE DATED BRUCE WAYNE?
DID YOU EVER MEET HIM?
"... THAT'S SELINA FOR YOU... SHE DECIDES WHAT SHE WANTS AND JUST GETS IT.
"... HELL, SHE ALWAYS HAD MORE CLASS THAN THESE STREETS COULD HANDLE, ANYWAY.
"... AND I THINK SHE WANTED TO GET AWAY FROM THIS WORLD, REALLY...
"... TO TRY LIFE ON THE OTHER SIDE FOR A WHILE..."
I GUESS IT DIDN'T TURN OUT, THEN, IF SHE'S BACK HERE NOW...
I WOULDN'T SAY THAT... SHE DID WHAT ALL POOR KIDS WANT TO DO... GOT RICH AND RUBBED IT IN THE WORLD'S FACE...
AND WHEN IT DIDN'T FEEL RIGHT ANYMORE, SHE CAME BACK TO HER ROOTS TO FIND HERSELF...

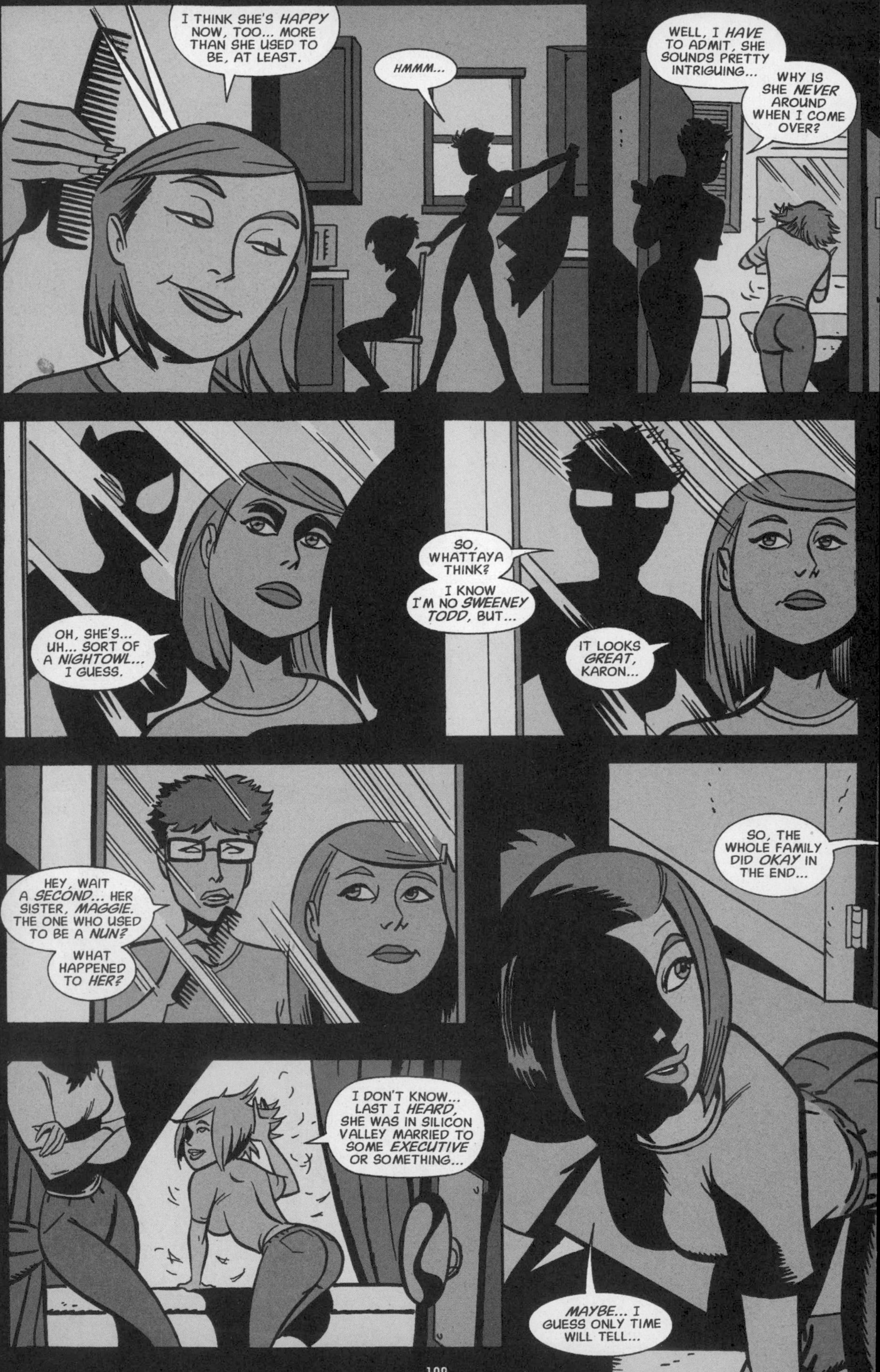

I THINK SHE'S *HAPPY* NOW, TOO... MORE THAN SHE USED TO BE, AT LEAST.
HMMM...
WELL, I *HAVE* TO ADMIT, SHE SOUNDS PRETTY INTRIGUING...
WHY IS SHE *NEVER* AROUND WHEN I COME OVER?
OH, SHE'S... UH... SORT OF A *NIGHTOWL*... I GUESS.
SO, WHATTAYA THINK?
I KNOW I'M NO *SWEENEY TODD*, BUT...
IT LOOKS *GREAT*, KARON...
HEY, WAIT A *SECOND*... HER SISTER, *MAGGIE*. THE ONE WHO USED TO BE A *NUN*?
WHAT HAPPENED TO *HER*?
I DON'T KNOW... LAST I *HEARD*, SHE WAS IN SILICON VALLEY MARRIED TO SOME *EXECUTIVE* OR SOMETHING...
SO, THE WHOLE FAMILY DID *OKAY* IN THE END...
MAYBE... I GUESS ONLY TIME WILL TELL...

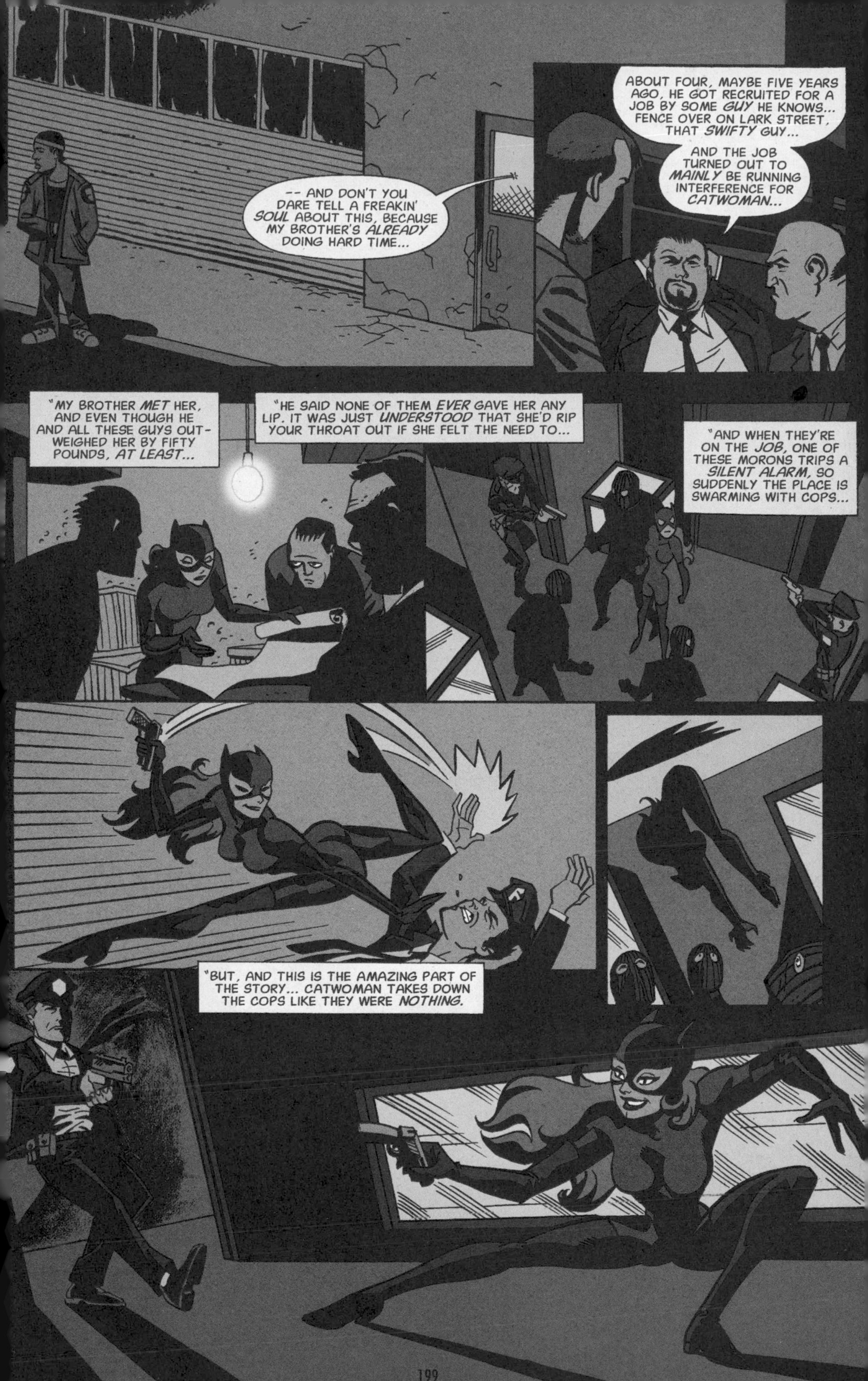
-- AND DON'T YOU DARE TELL A FREAKIN' SOUL ABOUT THIS, BECAUSE MY BROTHER'S ALREADY DOING HARD TIME...
ABOUT FOUR, MAYBE FIVE YEARS AGO, HE GOT RECRUITED FOR A JOB BY SOME GUY HE KNOWS... FENCE OVER ON LARK STREET, THAT SWIFTY GUY...
AND THE JOB TURNED OUT TO MAINLY BE RUNNING INTERFERENCE FOR CATWOMAN...
"MY BROTHER MET HER, AND EVEN THOUGH HE AND ALL THESE GUYS OUT-WEIGHED HER BY FIFTY POUNDS, AT LEAST...
"HE SAID NONE OF THEM EVER GAVE HER ANY LIP. IT WAS JUST UNDERSTOOD THAT SHE'D RIP YOUR THROAT OUT IF SHE FELT THE NEED TO...
"AND WHEN THEY'RE ON THE JOB, ONE OF THESE MORONS TRIPS A SILENT ALARM, SO SUDDENLY THE PLACE IS SWARMING WITH COPS...
"BUT, AND THIS IS THE AMAZING PART OF THE STORY... CATWOMAN TAKES DOWN THE COPS LIKE THEY WERE NOTHING.

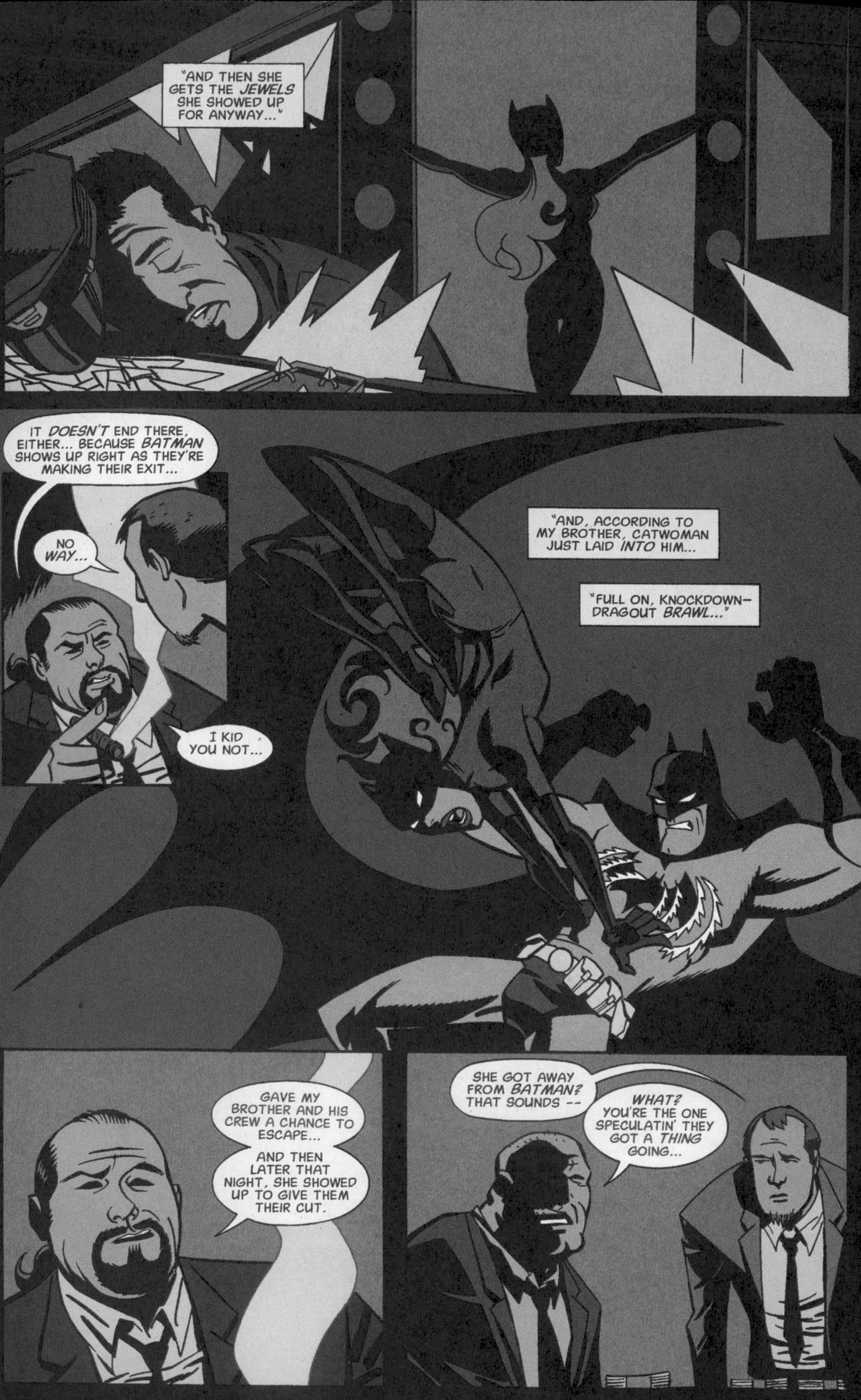
"AND THEN SHE GETS THE JEWELS SHE SHOWED UP FOR ANYWAY..."
IT DOESN'T END THERE, EITHER... BECAUSE BATMAN SHOWS UP RIGHT AS THEY'RE MAKING THEIR EXIT...
NO WAY...
I KID YOU NOT...
"AND, ACCORDING TO MY BROTHER, CATWOMAN JUST LAID INTO HIM...
"FULL ON, KNOCKDOWN-DRAGOUT BRAWL..."
GAVE MY BROTHER AND HIS CREW A CHANCE TO ESCAPE...
AND THEN LATER THAT NIGHT, SHE SHOWED UP TO GIVE THEM THEIR CUT.
SHE GOT AWAY FROM BATMAN? THAT SOUNDS --
WHAT? YOU'RE THE ONE SPECULATIN' THEY GOT A THING GOING...

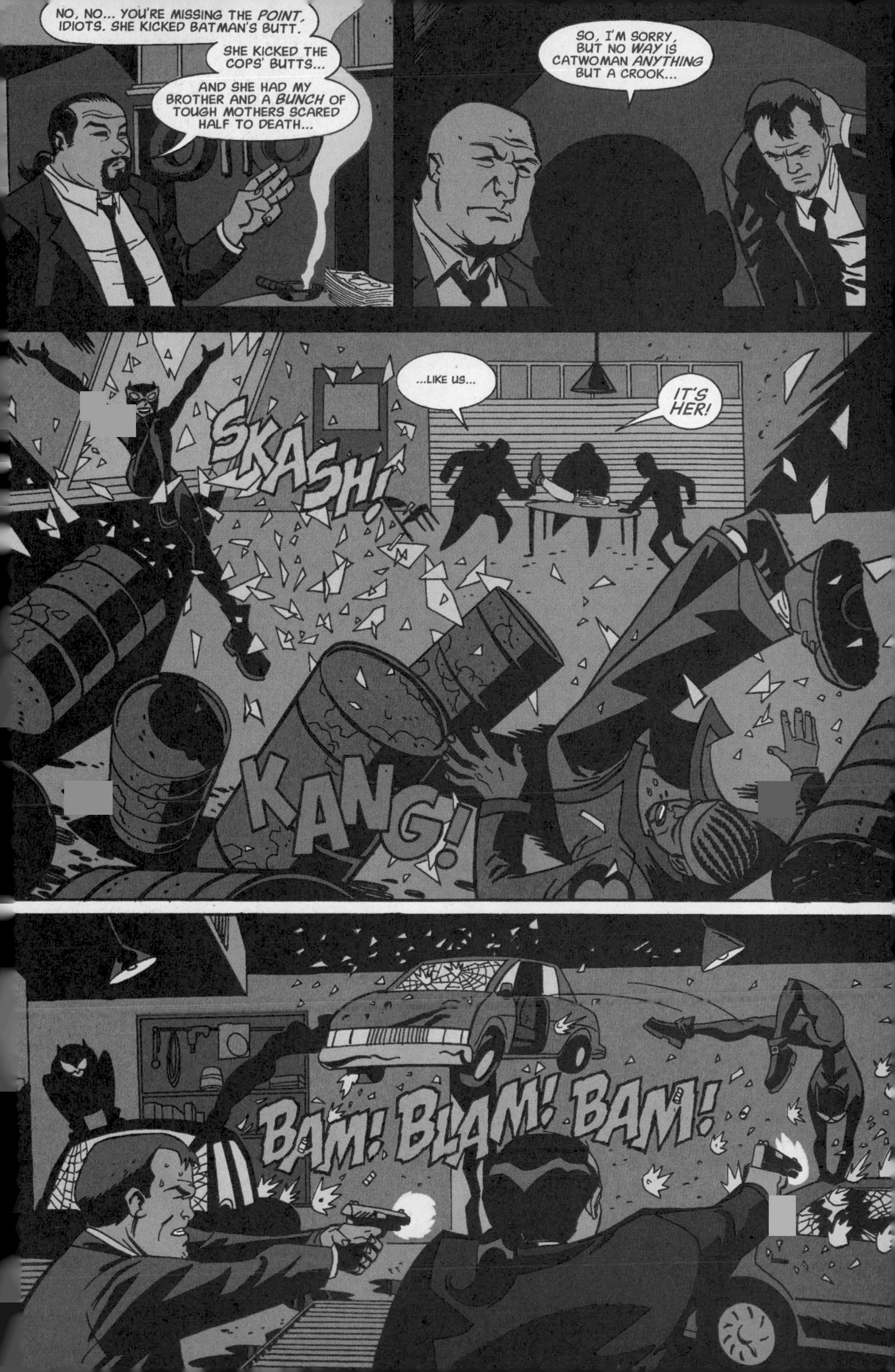

NO, NO... YOU'RE MISSING THE *POINT*, IDIOTS. SHE KICKED BATMAN'S BUTT.
SHE KICKED THE COPS' BUTTS...
AND SHE HAD MY BROTHER AND A *BUNCH* OF TOUGH MOTHERS SCARED HALF TO DEATH...
SO, I'M SORRY, BUT NO *WAY* IS CATWOMAN *ANYTHING* BUT A CROOK...
...LIKE US...
IT'S HER!
SKASH!
KANG!
BAM! BLAM! BAM!

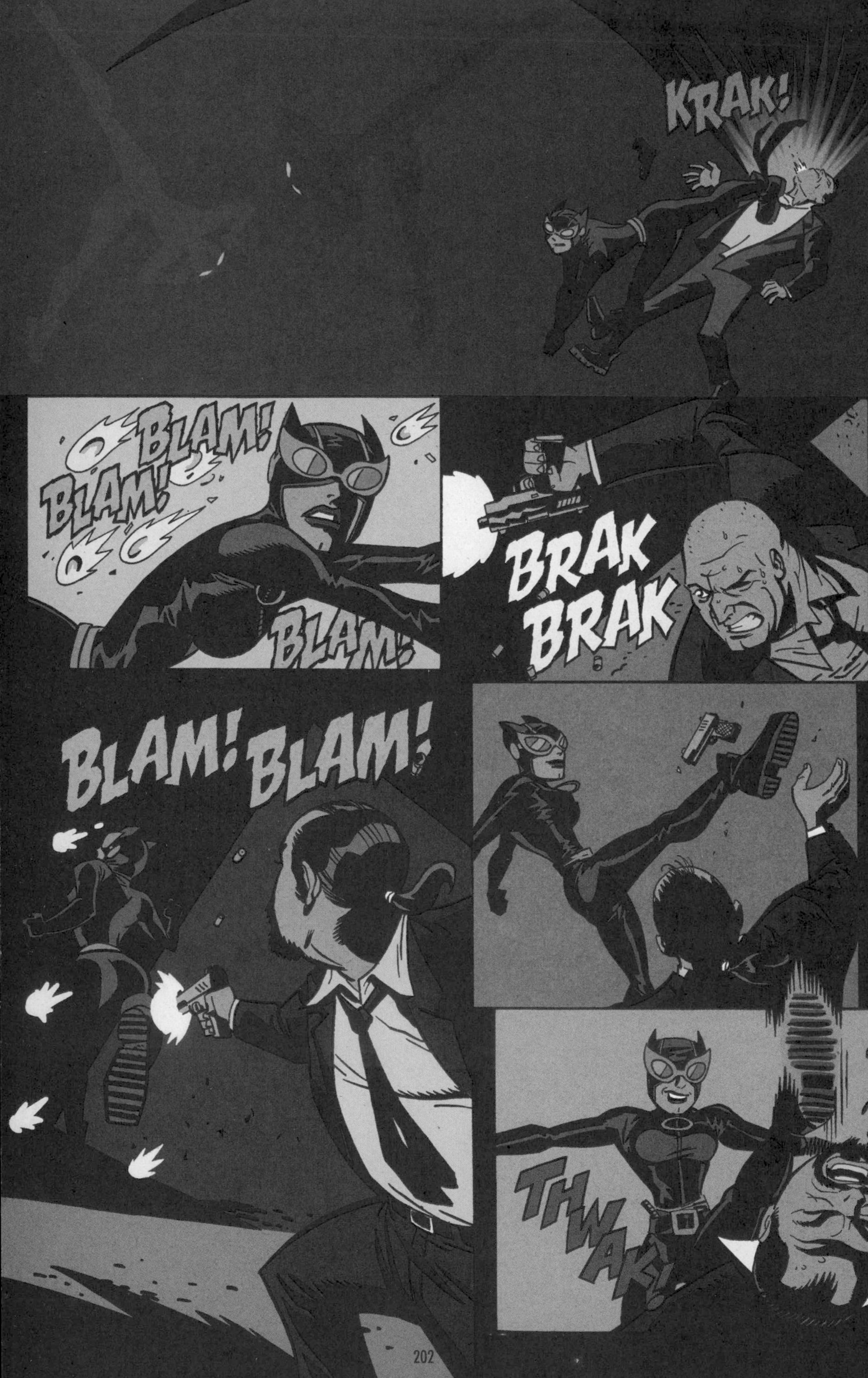
KRAK!
BLAM!
BLAM!
BLAM!
BRAK
BRAK
BLAM! BLAM!
THWAK!

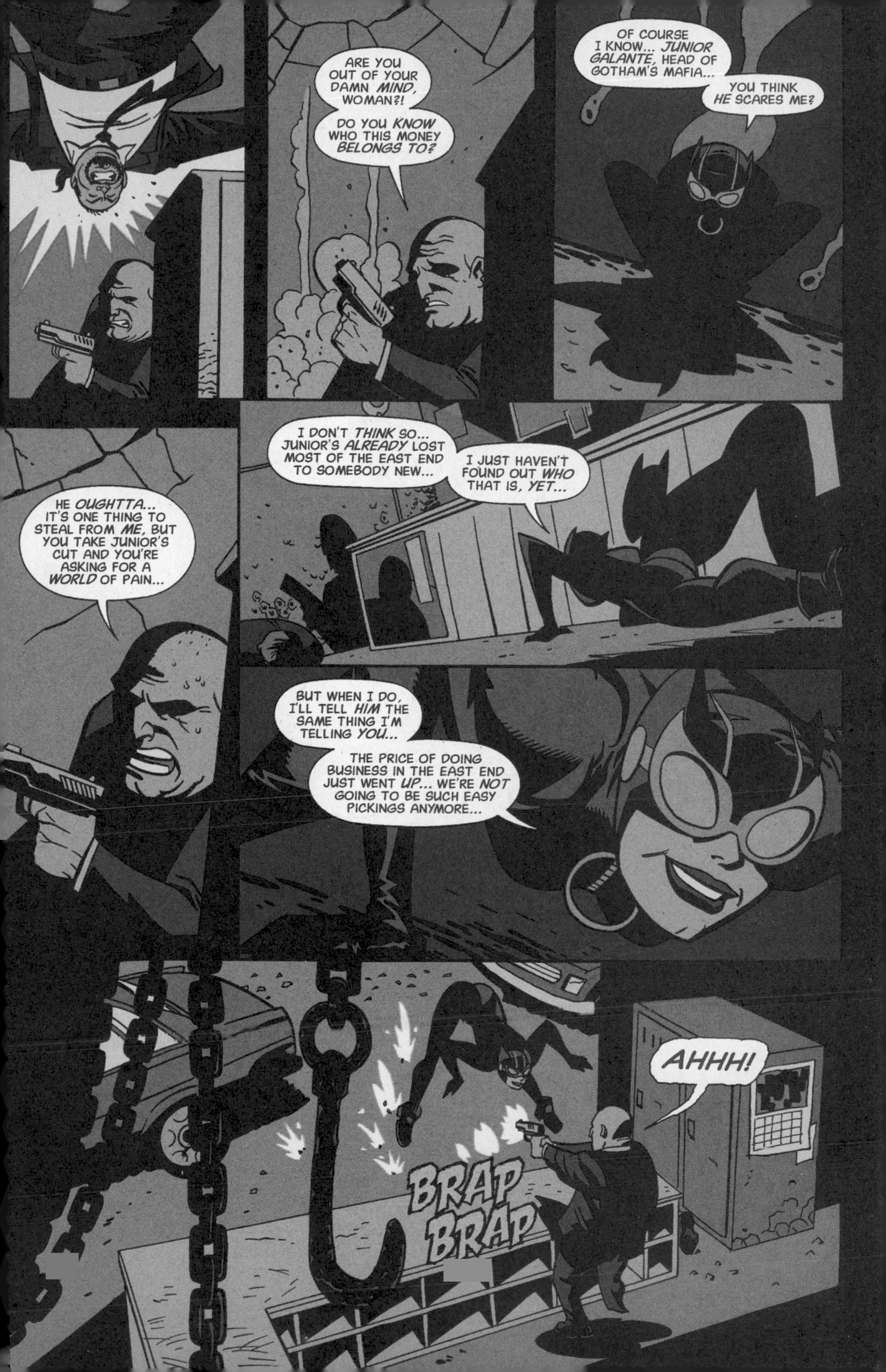
ARE YOU OUT OF YOUR DAMN *MIND*, WOMAN?!
DO YOU *KNOW* WHO THIS MONEY *BELONGS TO?*
OF COURSE I KNOW... *JUNIOR GALANTE*, HEAD OF GOTHAM'S MAFIA...
YOU THINK *HE* SCARES ME?
HE *OUGHTTA...* IT'S ONE THING TO STEAL FROM *ME*, BUT YOU TAKE JUNIOR'S CUT AND YOU'RE ASKING FOR A *WORLD* OF PAIN...
I DON'T *THINK* SO... JUNIOR'S *ALREADY* LOST MOST OF THE EAST END TO SOMEBODY NEW...
I JUST HAVEN'T FOUND OUT *WHO* THAT IS, *YET...*
BUT WHEN I DO, I'LL TELL *HIM* THE SAME THING I'M TELLING *YOU...*
THE PRICE OF DOING BUSINESS IN THE EAST END JUST WENT *UP...* WE'RE *NOT* GOING TO BE SUCH EASY PICKINGS ANYMORE...
AHHH!
BRAP
BRAP

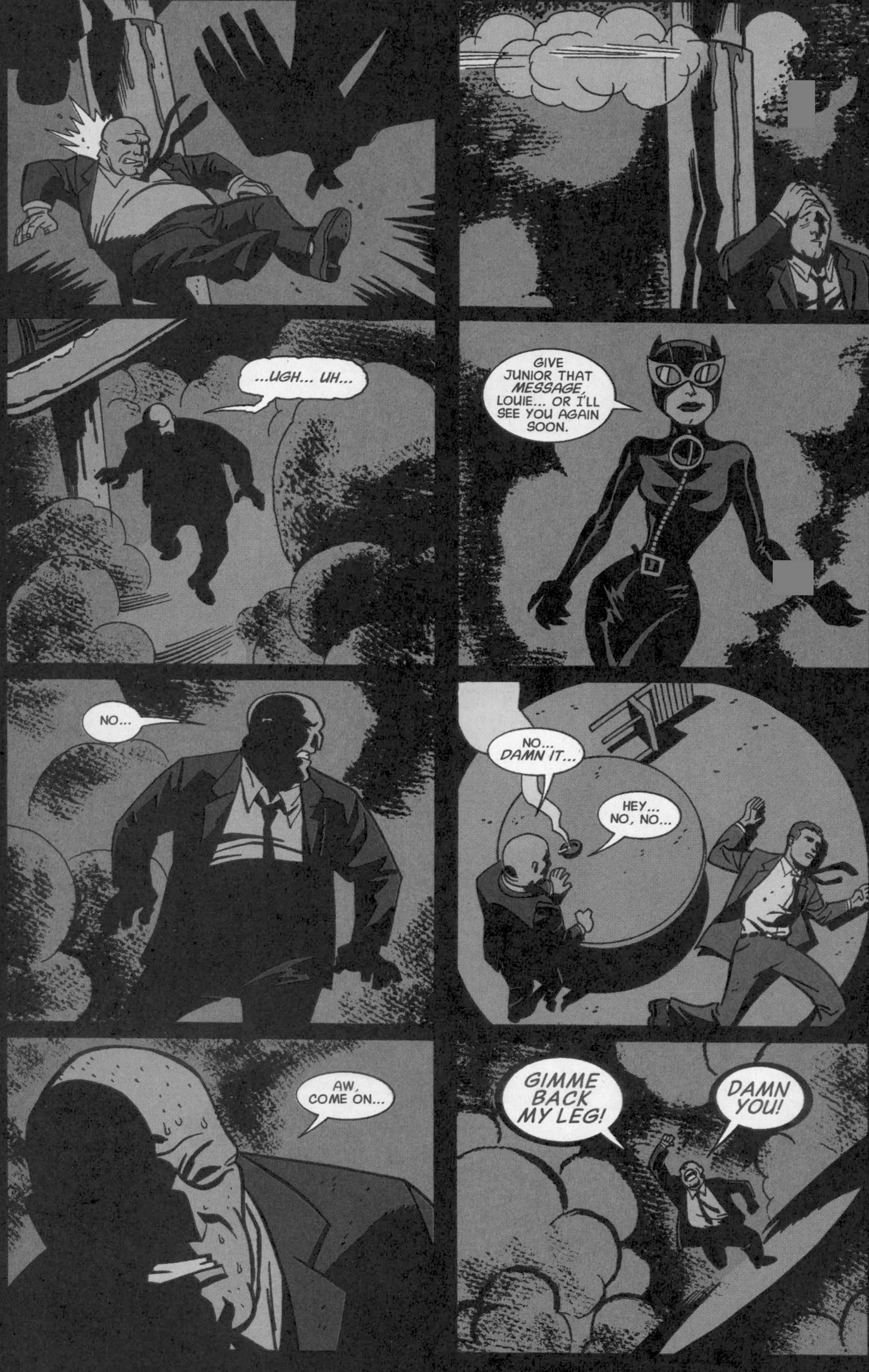
...UGH... UH...
GIVE JUNIOR THAT MESSAGE, LOUIE... OR I'LL SEE YOU AGAIN SOON.
NO...
NO... DAMN IT...
HEY... NO, NO...
AW, COME ON...
GIMME BACK MY LEG!
DAMN YOU!

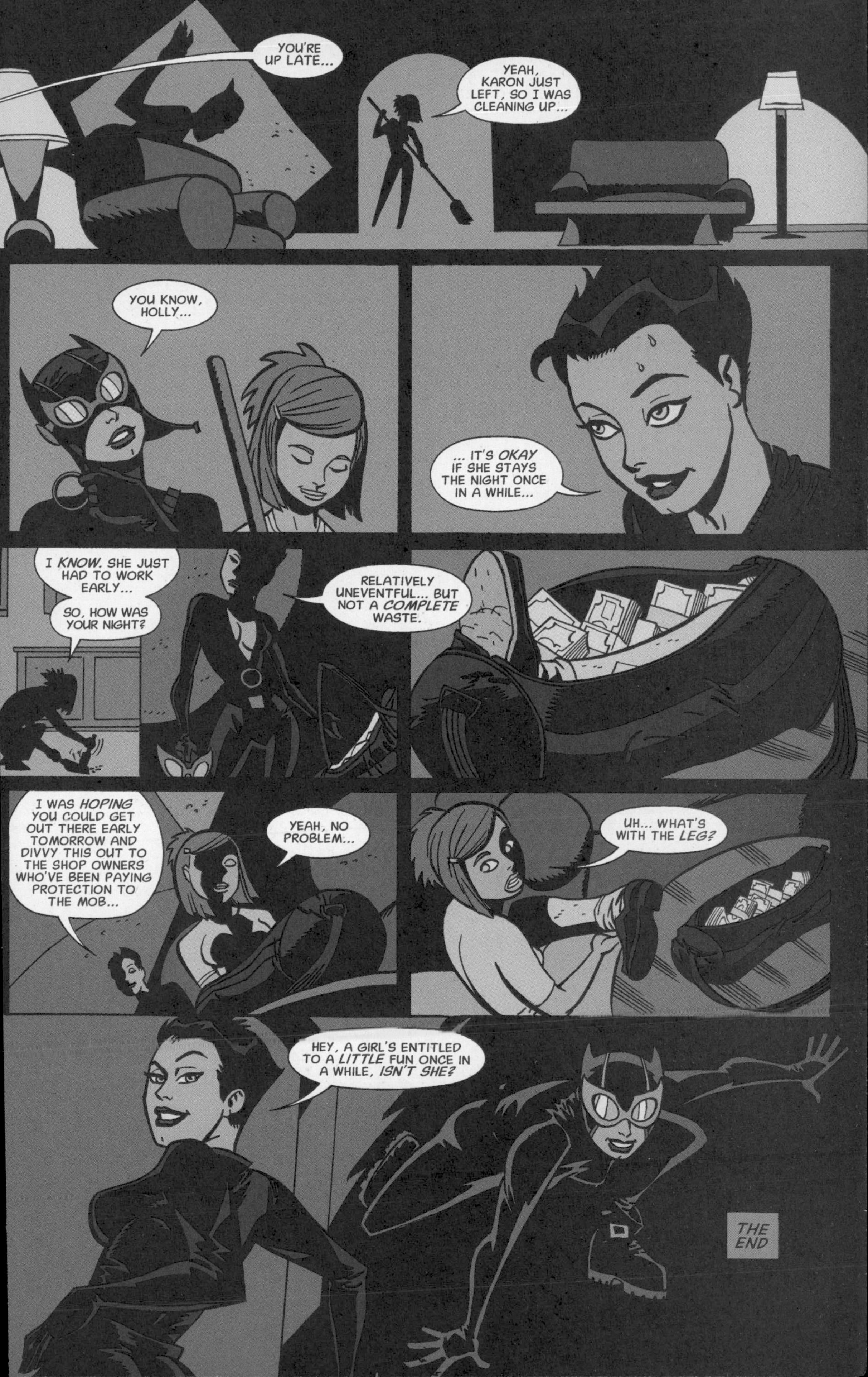

YOU'RE UP LATE...
YEAH, KARON JUST LEFT, SO I WAS CLEANING UP...
YOU KNOW, HOLLY...
... IT'S OKAY IF SHE STAYS THE NIGHT ONCE IN A WHILE...
I KNOW. SHE JUST HAD TO WORK EARLY...
SO, HOW WAS YOUR NIGHT?
RELATIVELY UNEVENTFUL... BUT NOT A COMPLETE WASTE.
I WAS HOPING YOU COULD GET OUT THERE EARLY TOMORROW AND DIVVY THIS OUT TO THE SHOP OWNERS WHO'VE BEEN PAYING PROTECTION TO THE MOB...
YEAH, NO PROBLEM...
UH... WHAT'S WITH THE LEG?
HEY, A GIRL'S ENTITLED TO A LITTLE FUN ONCE IN A WHILE, ISN'T SHE?
THE END

contributors

JIM BALENT pencilled an impressive 77-issue run of the first CATWOMAN series and has also illustrated *Purgatori* for Chaos Comics and LOBO, BATMAN and other comics for DC. His Broadsword Comics label publishes his *Tarot: Witch of the Black Rose* series.

TERRY BEATTY is well into his seventh year inking the animated-style Batman comics. His work can currently be seen in BATMAN ADVENTURES.

ED BRUBAKER is a multiple Eisner Award-nominated writer and the current scribe on the monthly CATWOMAN series. He also writes the critically acclaimed series SLEEPER and GOTHAM CENTRAL (with Greg Rucka). Previous works include BATMAN, SCENE OF THE CRIME and POINT BLANK.

RICK BURCHETT's art has been seen in nearly all the animated-style super-hero books for DC Comics. He has also been a penciller and/or inker on GREEN LANTERN, DETECTIVE COMICS, CATWOMAN, BATMAN/HUNTRESS: CRY FOR BLOOD and countless other comics.

ALAN DAVIS gained attention for his dynamic yet whimsical work on *Captain Britain* and Warrior's *Marvelman* before moving on to BATMAN AND THE OUTSIDERS and DETECTIVE COMICS. He worked for Marvel on memorable runs of *Uncanny X-Men*, *Excalibur* and *ClanDestine*. He later returned to DC for JLA: THE NAIL and its sequel, JLA: ANOTHER NAIL.

JOE DEVITO is known for painting hundreds of book covers, specializing in the science-fiction, fantasy, adventure and horror genres. His work has also been seen on magazines, comics, posters, trading cards, and sculpture.

LEO DORFMAN's comics work went mostly uncredited during his career, but he was a mainstay of Mort Weisinger's group, writing adventures of Superman, Lois Lane, Jimmy Olsen, Superboy and Supergirl as well as the WORLD'S FINEST adventures of Batman and Robin.

JAN DUURSEMA has recently been illustrating several *Star Wars* titles for Dark Horse Comics. Her previous credits include *The Incredible Hulk*, *Spider-Man* and *Wolverine* for Marvel Comics and HAWKMAN and ARION, LORD OF ATLANTIS for DC.

BILL FINGER was a legendary figure of the comics industry, having collaborated with Bob Kane on the creation of Batman. Bill went on to write Plastic Man, Green Lantern, Superman, Superboy, Blackhawk, Challengers of the Unknown, Captain America, and others. Bill Finger was still writing for DC Comics at the time of his death in 1974.

GARDNER FOX began his career as a writer in the late 1930s on Batman and went on to create such Golden Age classics as the original Flash, Hawkman, Starman, Doctor Fate, and the Justice Society of America. In the 1950s and 1960s he created and/or wrote such memorable features as the Justice League of America, Adam Strange, The Atom, Hawkman, and, of course, Batman. He retired in 1968.

JOE GIELLA first worked for DC Comics in 1951 where, in the 1960s, his style of embellishment became associated with some of the company's greatest heroes, including Batman, The Flash, and The Atom. Giella, who also pencilled and inked a run of the Batman syndicated newspaper strip during the 1960s, retired from comics in the early 1980s.

DEVIN GRAYSON has written numerous comics including BATMAN: GOTHAM KNIGHTS, CATWOMAN, THE TITANS and USER for DC Comics and *Black Widow*, *Ghost Rider* and *X-Men: Evolution* for Marvel. She is currently writing the monthly series NIGHTWING.

SID GREENE did the bulk of his work throughout the 1960s and 1970s, pencilling and/or inking a wide variety of genre stories and such features as Star Rovers, Johnny Peril, The Atom, Elongated Man, Hawkman, The Justice League of America, The Flash, Hourman, and, of course, Batman.

EDMOND HAMILTON came to comics from science-fiction pulp magazines and quickly became a major Superman writer. In addition, he wrote Tommy Tomorrow (for ACTION COMICS), WORLD'S FINEST, and LEGION OF SUPER-HEROES.

ADAM HUGHES's credits include JUSTICE LEAGUE, LEGIONNAIRES, STAR TREK: DEBT OF HONOR, GEN[13], and *Ghost*. His stunning cover work has adorned WONDER WOMAN, ROSE AND THORN, *Tomb Raider*, *Vampirella*, and much more.

BOB KANE's most famous effort, Batman, appeared in 1939 in DETECTIVE COMICS #27. Kane illustrated the Dark Knight's adventures for years, with the help of several ghosts, including Lew Sayre Schwartz and Sheldon Moldoff. He remained involved with comics until his 1968 retirement.

TOM MANDRAKE is a graduate of the Joe Kubert School of Cartoon and Graphic Art and has illustrated a number of titles for DC Comics including JLA: DESTINY, MARTIAN MANHUNTER, THE SPECTRE, FIRESTORM, SWAMP THING, and BATMAN. He is also the co-creator of the Image book *Creeps*.

MIKE MANLEY has not only worked in comics on such titles as BATMAN, THE POWER OF SHAZAM!, SUPERMAN, *Transformers*, *Barb Wire* and *Predator*, he has also done storyboard and background design work on animated TV series featuring Superman, Batman, Clerks and Spawn.

DOUG MOENCH is acclaimed for his work on *Master of Kung Fu* and *Moon Knight* at Marvel and had two long stints as the writer on BATMAN (1983-1986 and 1992-1998). Doug has contributed to Piranha Press's BIG BOOK series and written prose and animation for other companies.

IRV NOVICK began his comic-book career at the dawn of the Golden Age. He worked for DC on several war anthologies and features, including Captain Storm, and, later, on super-hero titles. During the 1960s, Novick's work was featured in BATMAN and DETECTIVE COMICS. He was later to have a long run as penciller on THE FLASH.

MICHAEL AVON OEMING began his comics career at age 14 working for Innovation Comics and has inked a number of titles for Marvel including *Daredevil* and *Avengers*. He is currently the artist on *Powers* and *Hammer of the Gods*.

CHARLES PARIS began his career inking Mort Meskin on the Johnny Quick and Vigilante features for DC in the 1940s, but he is best known for his work on Batman, a feature he inked from 1947 through 1964 over such pencillers as Jack Burnley, Fred Ray, Sheldon Moldoff, and Dick Sprang.

GEORGE PÉREZ's career spans multiple comics companies and thousands of pages of material including NEW TEEN TITANS, CRISIS ON INFINITE EARTHS, *The Avengers*, WONDER WOMAN, *Solus*, and, most recently, the epic cross-company crossover JLA/AVENGERS.

FRANK ROBBINS is an internationally recognized comics creator who, in 1944, created the long-running syndicated newspaper strip *Johnny Hazzard*. Robbins came to comic books in 1968, writing BATMAN, SUPERBOY, THE SHADOW, and THE UNKNOWN SOLDIER for DC. In addition to writing, he also drew many Batman and Unknown Soldier stories.

KURT SCHAFFENBERGER's best-loved work was for Fawcett Comics, where he illustrated *Captain Marvel* and others until the company's demise in 1953. He became the primary artist on SUPERMAN'S GIRL FRIEND LOIS LANE, illustrating dozens of Superman-related stories, WONDER WOMAN and WORLD'S FINEST before returning to Captain Marvel in 1973.

LEW SAYRE SCHWARTZ began working with Bob Kane in 1946. Schwartz started as an assistant, doing backgrounds, scenery, and filling in minor details. Eventually he graduated to doing full pencils under Kane's supervision. Schwartz's work appeared in DETECTIVE COMICS, BATMAN, and WORLD'S FINEST COMICS.

FRANK SPRINGER began his career as an assistant to George Wunder on "Terry and the Pirates." As a freelance artist, Springer has drawn a wide range of titles including BATMAN, *Transformer*, and *G.I. Joe*.

JOHN STANISCI's inking has graced the pages of numerous Spider-Man titles for Marvel Comics, as well as CATWOMAN, SUPERBOY, NIGHTWING and others for DC Comics.

BRIAN STELFREEZE is a member of Atlanta-based Gaijin Studios and has done cover work for SHADOW OF THE BAT, BIRDS OF PREY, and CODENAME: KNOCKOUT. He has also done interior work on such titles as *Domino*, GEN-ACTIVE and the upcoming MATADOR.

DAVE STEVENS's first professional work was on the *Tarzan* comic strip. He moved on to storyboard and animation work and film art before writing and illustrating his most famous creation, The Rocketeer!

CAMERON STEWART worked on several titles for Vertigo, including SWAMP THING, THE INVISIBLES and DEADENDERS, before landing the art duties on the CATWOMAN monthly series. He recently completed Vertigo's SEAGUY miniseries with Grant Morrison.

MARK STUTZMAN is best known for his rendition of the young Elvis Presley postage stamp. His illustrations continue to adorn billboards, book covers, to-go cups, Broadway and promotional posters, magazines and more. His art is frequently used on many licensed DC products.

TY TEMPLETON has drawn everything from JUSTICE LEAGUE to SUPERMAN to PLASTIC MAN. He is also known for writing and illustrating original work on books like *Stig's Inferno* and BIGG TIME. He is currently writing and drawing BATMAN ADVENTURES.

BRUCE TIMM is an award-winning comics artist and animation producer, having worked on the *Batman*, *Batman Beyond*, *Superman*, and *Teen Titans* animated series. His comics collaborations with writer Paul Dini include BATMAN ADVENTURES: DANGEROUS DAMES & DEMONS and BATMAN: HARLEY & IVY.

backlist

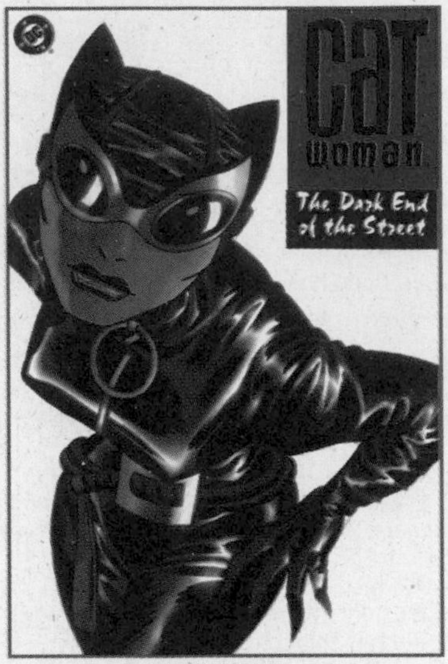

Cat
woman
The Dark End of the Street

CATWOMAN: THE DARK END OF THE STREET
Brubaker/Cooke/Allred

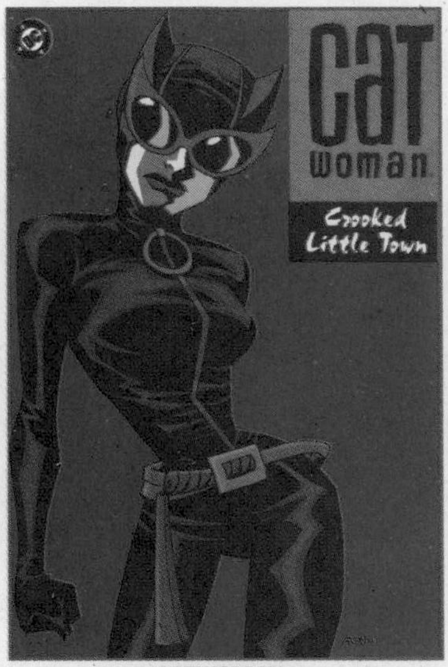

Cat
woman
Crooked Little Town

CATWOMAN: CROOKED LITTLE TOWN
Brubaker/Rader/Stewart/Burchett

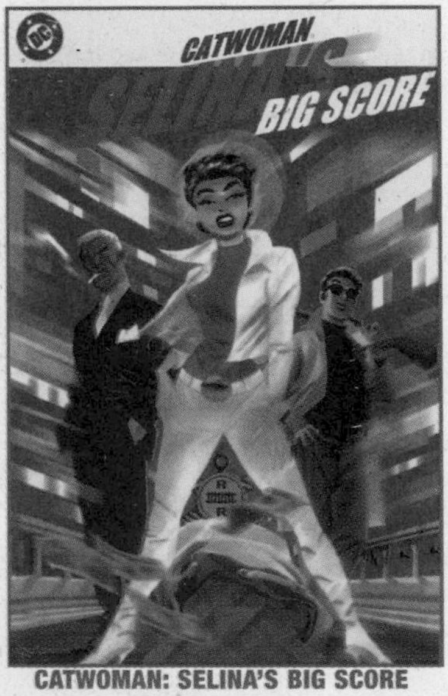

CATWOMAN
BIG SCORE

CATWOMAN: SELINA'S BIG SCORE
Cooke/various

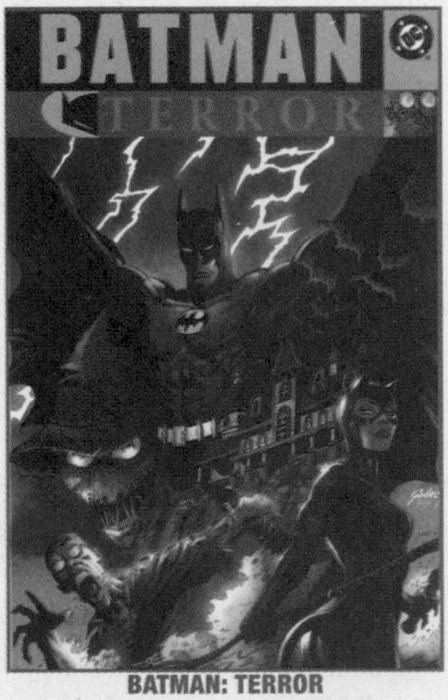

BATMAN
TERROR

BATMAN: TERROR
Moench/Gulacy/Palmiotti

Sink your claws into these dynamic collections featuring CATWOMAN!

BATMAN: CATACLYSM
various

BATMAN: CONTAGION
various

BATMAN: DARK VICTORY
Loeb/Sale

BATMAN: HUSH VOLUME 1
Loeb/Lee/Williams

BATMAN: HUSH VOLUME 2
Loeb/Lee/Williams

BATMAN: THE LONG HALLOWEEN
Loeb/Sale

BATMAN: THE MOVIES
various

BATMAN: NINE LIVES
Motter/Lark

BATMAN: YEAR ONE
Miller/Mazzucchelli

BATMAN IN THE FORTIES
various

BIRDS OF PREY
Dixon/Haley/Frank/Raffaele/various

CATWOMAN: THE CATFILE
Dixon/Balent/B. Smith

CATWOMAN: THE MOVIE AND OTHER CAT TALES
Austen/Derenick/DeKraker/various

JUST IMAGINE STAN LEE CREATING THE DC UNIVERSE VOLUME 3
Lee/various

Visit us at www.dccomics.com for more information on these and many other titles from DC Comics or call 1-888-COMIC BOOK for the comics shop nearest you, or go to your local book store.